# Pilot Mental Health Assessment and Support

The presentation of mental illness at work has different implications and consequences depending on the specific nature of the job, work context, regulatory framework and risks for the employee, organisation and society. Naturally there are certain occupational groups where human factors and/or mental illness could impair safety and mental acuity, and with potentially devastating consequences. For pilots, the medical criteria for crew licensing are stipulated by regulatory aviation authorities worldwide, and these include specific mental illness exclusions. The challenge of assessment for mental health problems is, however, complex and the responsibility for psychological screening and testing falls to a range of different specialists and groups including AMEs (authorised aviation medical examiners), GPs and physicians, airline human resources departments, psychologists, human factor specialists and pilots themselves.

Extending and developing the ideas of *Aviation Mental Health* (2006), which described a range of psychological issues and problems that may affect pilots and the consequences of these, this book presents an authoritative, comprehensive and practical guide to modern, evidence-based practice in the field of mental health assessment, treatment and care. It features contributions from experts in the field drawn from several countries, professions and representing a range of aviation-related organisations, displaying a range of different skills and methods that can be used for the clinical assessment of pilots and in relation to specific mental health problems and syndromes.

**Robert Bor**, DPhil CPsychol CSci FBPsS FRAeS UKCP Reg, is a Registered and Chartered Clinical Counselling and Health Psychologist, Registered Aviation Psychologist and Co-Director of the Centre for Aviation Psychology.

**Carina Eriksen**, MSc DipPsych CPsychol FBPsS BABCP, is an HCPC Registered and BPS Chartered Consultant Counselling Psychologist and Registered Aviation Psychologist.

**Margaret Oakes**, MA (Cantab) MSc, Dip Psych, DPsych, CPsychol, is a Counselling Psychologist and airline pilot.

**Peter Scragg**, BSc PsychD FBPsS, is a Consultant Clinical Psychologist and Principal Teaching Fellow at University College London.

# Pilot Mental Health Assessment and Support

A practitioner's guide

**Edited by**
**Robert Bor, Carina Eriksen,**
**Margaret Oakes and Peter Scragg**

Routledge
Taylor & Francis Group

LONDON AND NEW YORK

First edition published 2017
by Routledge
2 Park Square, Milton Park, Abingdon, Oxon OX14 4RN

and by Routledge
711 Third Avenue, New York, NY 10017

*Routledge is an imprint of the Taylor & Francis Group, an informa business*

*British Library Cataloguing in Publication Data*
A catalogue record for this book is available from the British Library

*Library of Congress Cataloging in Publication Data*
Names: Bor, Robert, editor.
Title: Pilot mental health assessment and support : a practitioner's guide / [edited by] Robert Bor, Carina Eriksen, Margaret Oakes and Peter Scragg.
Description: Abingdon, Oxon ; New York, NY : Routledge, 2017. | Includes bibliographical references and index.
Identifiers: LCCN 2016030855| ISBN 9781138222038 (hardback) | ISBN 9781315401942 (ebook)
Subjects: LCSH: Air pilots--Mental health. | Air pilots--Mental health services. | Aviation psychology.
Classification: LCC RC1085 .P45 2017 | DDC 155.9/65--dc23
LC record available at https://lccn.loc.gov/2016030855

ISBN: 978-1-138-22203-8 (hbk)
ISBN: 978-1-315-40194-2 (ebk)

Typeset in Bembo
by HWA Text and Data Management, London

MIX
Paper from responsible sources
FSC
www.fsc.org    FSC® C013985

Printed in the United Kingdom
by Henry Ling Limited

# Contents

# Figures

# Tables

# Contributors

**Cristina Albuquerque**, MSc CPsychol, is a Portuguese Clinical Psychologist chartered by the Portuguese Psychologists Professional Order (OPP) and is a post-graduate in Cognitive Behavioral Therapy. She is a Certified Cognitive Behavioral Psychotherapist by the Portuguese Association for Behavioral Therapy (APTC). Cristina has more than 25 years of experience in the aviation setting, working as a Clinical Psychologist in the medical department of a Portuguese airline company where she provides a wide range of psychological services: psychological assessment and counselling of aircrew and other airline workers; consultancy in the speciality of Clinical Psychology for medical licensing of pilots and air traffic controllers; critical incident stress management with aircrew and ATCs; coordination of an Employee Assistance Program for Alcohol and Drug Prevention among air-workers (1991–2010); founder and coordinator of the first group treatment programme for fearful flyers in a Portuguese airline company (2005–2009). Cristina has also been responsible for traineeship and supervision of training psychologists for several years. She is certified in Critical Incident Stress Management by the International Critical Incident Stress Foundation (ICISF) and provides training for volunteers within Emergency Response Plan (ERP) training. Cristina led the organization of Aviation Medicine Courses for general practitioners with the support of the Medical Department of the National Aviation Authority (ANAC). In 2011, Cristina created the first Portuguese centre specialising in the treatment, prevention and research of fear of flying (Voar Sem Medo) in a joint cooperation with VALK Foundation and several Portuguese aeronautical entities. She edited the first Portuguese self-help book for fearful flyers and conducts research in this field. Cristina is a Certified Aviation Psychologist accredited by the European Association for Aviation Psychology (EAAP) and is currently a board member of this association as well as associate editor of EAAP journal (*Aviation Psychology and Applied Human Factors*). Following the Germanwings incident, Cristina has included a task-group of experts from the European associations ESAM, EAAP and ECA with the aim of strengthening aeromedical assessments, taking into account the increasing relevance of psychosocial stressors, mental health aspects, and the changing working environment that pilots are exposed to.

**Robert Bor**, DPhil MA (ClinPsych) CPsychol CSci FBPsS FRAeS UKCP
Reg EuroPsy, is a UK Health and Care Professions Council Registered and
British Psychological Society (BPS) Chartered Clinical, Counselling and
Health Psychologist. He is a Certified Aviation Psychologist in Europe (EAAP)
and Co-Director of the Centre for Aviation Psychology. Rob is also a United
Kingdom Council for Psychotherapy Registered Systemic Therapist. He
is Professor and Lead Consultant Clinical Psychologist in Acute Medicine
at the Royal Free London, NHS Foundation Trust and Visiting Professor at
City, University of London, where he teaches on the MSc in Air Transport
Management. He also contributes to the MSc in Travel Health and Medicine at
the Royal Free and University College Medical School. Rob is the lead clinician
for the British Airways Pilot Peer Support Programme. He is a Fellow of the
British Psychological Society, a Fellow of the Royal Aeronautical Society and
an Associate Fellow of the Aerospace Medical Association (AsMA). He is a
Member of the American Psychological Association and Registered as a Clinical
Psychologist with the Health Professions Council of South Africa. Rob is an
Honorary Civilian Aviation Psychologist to the Royal Air Force. He is the
Chair of the BPS Aviation Psychology Task Group and Convenor of the BPS
Continuing Professional Development Course in Aviation Psychology. He has
served on the Aerospace Medical Association's Expert Working Group on Pilot
Mental Health. He regularly undertakes psychological assessments of pilots and
provides psychological counselling for aircrew. He has been an expert witness in
several aviation legal cases. He serves on the editorial board of numerous leading
international academic journals and has authored or edited 35 books and 250
papers (including *Aviation Mental Health*, and *Passenger Behaviour*) and chapters
in books. He also holds a private pilot's licence. He is on the Academic Board
of MindGym. He holds the Freedom of the City of London and is a Liveryman
of the Honourable Company of Air Pilots. He is listed on the Smithsonian
National Air and Space Museum's Wall of Honor in Washington DC. Rob is a
Winston Churchill Fellow.

**James N. Butcher**, PhD, is Emeritus Professor in the Department of Psychology
at the University of Minnesota. He was awarded honorary doctorates for his
international personality assessment research (Doctor Honoris Causa) from
the Free University of Brussels, Belgium, in 1990 and from the University
of Florence, Italy (Laurea ad Honorem in Psychology) in 2005. He received
the Bruno Klopfer Award from the Society for Personality Assessment in 2004
for longstanding contributions to personality assessment. He has maintained
an active research programme in the areas of personality assessment, abnormal
psychology, cross-cultural personality factors and computer-based personality
assessment. He has conducted extensive research on the MMPI in a broad
range of contexts. His publications include basic research works in abnormal
psychology, personality assessment, personnel screening with the MMPI-2,
including research methodology and computer applications of psychological
tests. He is a co-author of *Use of the MMPI-2 in Forensic Assessment* (Butcher,

Hass, Greene and Nelson; American Psychological Association, 2015) and has worked extensively in personnel assessment in airline pilot screening and has published a number of articles in the area.

**Ben Campion**, PMRAFNS RGN RMN DipN BSc, holds the appointment of the GBR Defence Specialist Advisor in Mental Health, working as aeromedical research officer at the RAF centre for aviation medicine. His 30 years of military experience have seen him deployed to every conflict GBR have been involved in, from the Cold War to Afghanistan, Ireland to the Balkans, Falklands to Iraq and many others, besides providing mental health support to service personnel deployed. He remains the Secretary of the NATO Military Mental Health Expert panel and Research Fellow at Kings College London's Academic Department for Defence Mental Health. His current focus is in developing both Mental Health and Aeromedical practice in the Neuroscience field, being guest speaker at a number of international congresses as well as publishing, teaching and presenting widely.

**Martin Casey**, BSc, is currently a 747 senior first officer for a major airline. He was recruited to the airline industry immediately after university having completed a degree in mathematics. He has been flying commercially for over 15 years and has accumulated over 8000 hours both in the short-haul and long-haul environment. Martin has authored chapters in aviation psychology books looking specifically at the benefits of regular physical exercise on pilot mental health. He has co-presented on pilot mental health at the European Association for Aviation Psychology conference. He is a qualified personal trainer and cycle instructor.

**Rui Correia**, MD, is a Consultant Psychiatrist and Aviation Medicine Doctor who graduated from Hospital Santa Maria in Lisbon and is certified by the Portuguese Medical Board. He graduated as an Aviation Medicine Doctor in Centre d'enseignement et de recherche de médecine aéronautique (CERMA), in Paris, in 1985. He worked as a Psychiatrist for more than 25 years mainly in the Air Force Hospital, achieving the grade of Service Director. During the same time he has worked as Flight Surgeon in operational air bases and at Aeromedical Centre of the Portuguese Air Force until 2008, leaving as Director with the rank of Colonel. He joined the Portuguese Aviation Authority in 1999, where he remains as Medical Assessor, at Medical Certification Directorate. He is invited professor to various aeronautical medicine courses, which take place in Portugal, organized by the Portuguese Air Force and certified by the Portuguese Aviation Authority. He has a special interest in the field of Addiction Disorders and is a founding member of Portuguese Association of Addiction Medicine.

**Nicklas Dahlstrom**, PhD, is Human Factors Manager at Emirates Airline and has been with the airline since 2007. In this position he has overseen

CRM training in a rapidly expanding airline and also been part of efforts to integrate Human Factors in the organisation. Nicklas also holds the position as Assistant Professor at Lund University School of Aviation in Sweden and was previously a researcher and instructor there, working mainly on projects related to safety and human factors in aviation as well as in other areas, such as maritime transportation and health care. Nicklas did his PhD with Professor Sidney Dekker as supervisor and worked with him on research projects up until he joined Emirates. His research areas in aviation have been mental workload, training and simulation, and he has written research articles and book chapters on human factors and CRM as well as delivered invited presentations, lectures and training in more than twenty different countries. Previous to his career in academia and civil aviation Nicklas was an officer and meteorologist in the Swedish Air Force, where he also underwent flight training on the SAAB 105 twin engine trainer jet aircraft. He worked in the Swedish Air Force at the Air Base F10 as well as at the Swedish Fighter Pilot School F5, where he was also an instructor for both pilots and meteorologists.

**Paul Dickens**, BA(Hons) MPhil AFBPsS CPsychol CertHSM AIBC MCMI, studied psychology and clinical psychology at the Universities of Exeter and Glasgow, and is a Chartered Clinical Psychologist and an Associate Fellow of the British Psychological Society, and holds the Certificate in Health Services Management. He is an Accredited Aviation Psychologist and a member of the European Association for Aviation Psychology. During his NHS career he practised as a clinical psychologist in learning disability services in Scotland and was Clinical Services Manager for an NHS Trust as well as being Area Head of Clinical Psychology. He also acted as a consultant to the then Scottish Office on Consultant Psychologist appointments. He left the NHS to pursue a career in organisational psychology and consulting, since when he has worked with boards, directors, chief executives, senior management and other teams in the UK, Italy, Austria, Germany, France, USA, UAE and Australia. Paul specialises in working in the defence and aerospace sector, and his clients include Airbus, BAE Systems, Eurofighter GmbH, Finmeccanica, Spirit AeroSystems, Sarfran Aircelle, Cobham, CHC Helicopters and the UK Ministry of Defence. He has specific expertise in the assessment and support of rotary-wing aircrew. He provides pro-bono psychological services to Wings for Warriors and is a trustee and non-executive director of a not-for-profit organisation providing support services to people with learning disabilities in Scotland. Paul is a regular presenter at international aviation psychology conferences and at the annual CHC Safety and Quality Summit.

**Carina Eriksen**, MSc Dip Psych DPsych CPsychol FBPsS BABCP Accredited, is a UK Health and Care Professions Council Registered and British Psychological Society (BPS) Chartered Consultant Counselling Psychologist with an extensive London-based private practice for young people, adults, couples and families. She is a Fellow of the British Psychology Society, a registered aviation psychologist and an accredited member of the British Association for Behavioural and Cognitive Psychotherapies having specialised at the Institute of Psychiatry. She has managed a team of clinical and counselling psychologists, CBT therapists and psychotherapists in the NHS for several years and she used to be an external supervisor for the Priory. She continues to supervise other psychologists in the NHS and private practice. She has extensive experience consulting in clinical and organisational settings in the UK and Europe. Along with another colleague, Carina is selecting and training British Airways pilots for a peer support programme. She is a committee member of the BPS Aviation Psychology Task Group and a trainer/presenter of the BPS Continuing Professional Development Course in Aviation Psychology. Carina and her colleagues provide a unique assessment and treatment service for people who have a fear of flying. She also offers psychological assessments and counselling to aircrew and managers. Carina has taught at several London Universities and she is a guest lecturer at the MSc in Air Transport Management at City University. She is an author and a co-author of several books and her work has been published in prestigious scientific journals. She has also contributed to various textbooks on aviation psychology, travel medicine and aviation medicine. She is actively involved in research with a specific interest in the topic of aviation mental health, fear of flying, work stress, anxiety disorders and the psychological impact of physical illness.

**Gerhard Fahnenbruck**, PhD Dipl Psych MBA, is a qualified psychologist and airline pilot. He studied psychology at the University of Bonn, the University of Vienna and the University of Hamburg. Gerard worked at a substance abuse clinic and a centre for addiction advice before returning to further studies at the University of Bonn and at the German Aerospace Research Establishment (DLR) in Hamburg. He received his professional pilot training at the Lufthansa Flight Training Centre and combined his work as a psychologist and pilot in the areas of Crew Resource Management, Human Factors and Flight Safety. He has been involved in international research projects such as the Group Interaction in High Risk Environment (GIHRE) project funded by the Daimler-Benz Foundation, where the aviation, atomic and health care industries worked together to discover commonalities and differences in team work at different high risk/high reliability organisations. Gerard worked in these areas, as well as in the banking sector, and uses his combined qualifications to work in the areas of crisis prevention, intervention and aftercare. He is a board member and the Clinical Director of Stiftung Mayday, a non-profit organization which originally focused on caring for aviation licence holders and next of kin after incidents or accidents, but nowadays also takes care of a pilot's wellbeing far beyond incident recovery.

**Maria Fonseca**, MSc CPsychol, is a Military Psychologist in the Portuguese Air Force where she has worked for 18 years. In addition to other duties and responsibilities, she is a pilot initial evaluator, Crew Resource Management instructor and Flight Safety Course instructor. These positions allow her to take part in the commission investigating military aircraft accidents and incidents, COCINV (Central Investigation Committee for aircraft accidents and incidents). She also teaches on the postgraduate course of aeronautical medicine of the Portuguese Air Force. Maria provides psycho-pedagogical support to aeronautical apprentices. She is the liaison officer of the Portuguese Civil Military Cooperation Support Unit. Maria has collaborated as an instructor of Human Performance and Limitations programme on ATPL courses. Presently, Maria is the head of the Clinical Psychology Unit Portuguese Armed Forces. She is a member of the Portuguese Association for Behavioural and Cognitive Psychotherapies as well as the Portuguese Psychologists Professional Order.

**Sean Gibbs**, BA (Hons) ATPL, who after gaining a degree in graphic design had a successful career as a graphic designer working in the UK, Australia and Canada, decided to pursue his childhood dream of becoming a pilot. His first commercial flying job was operating the Twin Otter for Loganair, a formative flying experience especially landing on Barra, the only beach airport in the world to be used for scheduled-airline services! Twenty years on and over 11,000 hours of flying experience he is now a captain for a major UK airline and has developed a keen interest in pilot welfare especially pilot mental health. Sean has recently undertaken a counselling course at City University London, and is now studying for a Diploma in Cognitive Based Therapy.

**Paul Harris**, CPsychol Reg Psychol PsSI Reg Aviation Psychol EAAP MBA MRAeS, is a Chartered Psychologist (British Psychological Society), a Registered Psychologist (Psychological Society of Ireland) and a Registered Aviation Psychologist in Europe (EAAP). He has 13 years of experience applying practical organisational psychological expertise within safety-critical transport and healthcare environments. From 2006–2010 Paul was Lead Consultant in Psychometrics at the Royal College of Surgeons in Ireland (RCSI) and its Institute of Leadership. While at the RCSI Paul advised on aspects of pedagogical policies, delivered train-the-trainer courses to senior medical consultants and lectured on Masters programmes. He has delivered critical thinking training for executive development programmes at the Irish Aviation Authority, led original healthcare research into emergency service organisations and has designed and delivered comprehensive recruitment, selection, assessment and developmental programmes for aviation clients. Since 2010 Paul served as Director and Lead Consultant for Health Psychology Ireland, a consultancy providing psychological assessment and coaching services, where he worked closely with commercial airline and military flight deck crews as well as senior flight instructors and flight training organisations. Paul is a member of the BPS Aviation Psychology Task Group, and the Royal Aeronautical Society's Human Factors in Flight Ops and Training Group, and he has been commissioned to author a book on the role of personality in aviation. Paul is on the BPS Register of Qualified Test Users for Occupational,

Ability and Personality, and registered with the European Federation of Psychologists' Associations for Work and Organisational Assessment. He is trained in psychological, structured and competency-based interview techniques and is certified to use and interpret a diverse range of advanced psychometric instruments. Paul has a focus on the role of personality in human and systems behaviour within organisations and complex, safety critical work environments.

**Kevin Herbert**, MB ChB DAv.Med, is an aviation medical examiner (AME) practising in Northamptonshire. He is President of the European Society of Aerospace Medicine (from 2012) and Chairman of the Association of Aviation Medical Examiners (from 2011). He has enjoyed a very varied career. Following qualification in 1977, and subsequent general practice training, he was in practice for 25 years in a large partnership, as managing partner for much of the time. Under his leadership the practice became a first wave Fund-holder, and later led a move to forming one of the first 17 Primary Care Trusts in the UK. As well as his leadership roles, he developed his interest in mental health, establishing a local clinical psychology service, and later appointing the first full time practice counsellor in the area. He practised hypnotherapy for many years. After leaving general practice he spent some years on the 'dark side' as an NHS Trust Chief Executive. This was primarily to ensure the completion of a community hospital in his local town, which included facilities for the Community Mental Health team. He is a lapsed private pilot and has spent the last decade pursuing his interest in aerospace medicine, promoting a move to a more preventive method of pilot fitness assessment, and emphasising the importance of the pilot/doctor relationship in such an assessment.

**Arianna Hoffmann**, BS, is a research analyst who has worked with Human Capital Management & Performance (HCMP) since 2007, where she acts as both a technical researcher and a project manager, coordinating teams of client and internal resources. She has helped to develop methodologies for pilot selection and performance tracking, including novel metric-based application screening approaches, cognitive and personality tests and structured interview processes that are currently utilised by leading aviation clients, such as FedEx and Delta. Ms. Hoffmann is also a co-author on multiple articles related to pilot hiring and performance, and she has presented her work at national and international conferences, including World Aviation Training Seminar, Asia Pacific Aviation Training Seminar, Asia Pacific Aviation Education and Training Seminar, Regional Airline Association Annual Convention, Regional Airlines Association Human Resources Seminar and Aviation, Aeronautics and Aerospace International Research Conference. Ms. Hoffmann holds a BS in chemistry from the University of North Carolina at Chapel Hill. Prior to her involvement at HCMP, she worked for several years performing medical research in labs at the Duke University Medical Center as well as working in cognitive assessment clinics at the University of North Carolina Memorial Hospital.

**Carl Hoffmann**, PhD, has been engaged for more than 30 years in helping companies around the world meet the challenges of formulating and implementing effective human resource strategies that support their business goals. From 1978 until 1999, when his company was purchased by PricewaterhouseCoopers, Dr. Hoffmann was CEO of a successful private consulting firm that focused on helping companies collect and analyse data to support strategic workforce decisions. He then joined PwC as a Partner, where he developed and led the Integrated Analytics practice for the Americas and the global Workforce Analytics practice. In 2002 when IBM acquired the PwC Management Consulting Group, Dr. Hoffmann became a Partner and Vice President of IBM's Global Business Services group. In all of these roles he designed and ran a number of large workforce transformation projects for multinational companies. Since retiring from IBM in 2007, Dr. Hoffmann has established a private consulting firm, Human Capital Management and Performance LLC (HCMP), that continues to work with corporate executives to make fact-based decisions that integrate workforce activities effectively with line operations to achieve business strategy. Dr. Hoffmann has given testimony on public policy before US House and Senate committees. He has published extensively in academic, business and public policy journals. He is lead author of a book on workforce analytics, *Calculating Success* (2011). He holds a PhD in sociology with a concentration in biostatistics from the University of North Carolina at Chapel Hill. Over the last 20 years a major focus of his research has been the study of airline pilot selection and performance at large US based international and regional airlines.

**Todd Hubbard**, EdD Lt Col USAF (ret), is the Clarence E. Page Professor on faculty in the Aviation Department of the University of Oklahoma, USA. Todd served in the United States Air Force as a pilot in the T-37, T-38, KC-135A, U-2R, and TR-1A aircraft over a nearly 21-year career. After a near-death ejection experience as a U-2R pilot, he dedicated the rest of his life to improving his knowledge about the psychology of aviators and aviation. He served the North Atlantic Treaty Organization as a Reconnaissance Staff Officer at Ramstein Air Base, Germany, in the years just after the Berlin Wall was dismantled, and flew combat missions as a U-2R Reconnaissance Squadron Commander, over two deployments to King Fahad Air Base, Kingdom of Saudi Arabia. After leaving the service, Todd worked as an Instructional Systems Designer for the Federal Aviation Administration (FAA) Academy at Mike Monroney Aeronautical Center, in Oklahoma City, Oklahoma, where he was asked to create and manage the *International Journal of Applied Aviation Studies* on behalf of the FAA as its editor. The University Aviation Association (UAA) honoured him with the Wheatley Award, for having had the most influence on aviation education in the previous 10 years. Todd has published dozens of academic papers, written or edited five books and continues to coach doctoral students through the dissertation process. He is currently the editor of the *Collegiate Aviation Review International*, chairs the Publications Committee for UAA and teaches courses in law, ethics, human factors, crew resource management and aviation mental health.

**Martin F. Hudson**, MBBS MRCP(UK) FRCP Edin, qualified from St Bartholomew's Hospital, London, in 1965. After obtaining a private pilot's licence he joined the Medical Branch of the Royal Air Force on a short service commission and gained his UK Membership of the Royal College of Physicians (MRCP UK) in 1971. From 1972–1999 he was a principal in general practice in Cheshire and became an Authorised Aviation Medical Examiner in 1977. He was awarded the Fellowship of the Royal College of Physicians of Edinburgh (FRCP Edin) in 1998 in recognition of his research and teaching in the field of hypertension. Leaving general practice in 1999 he set up an Aviation Medicine Consultancy and is an approved Aviation Medical Examiner for the European Aviation Safety Agency (EASA), UK Civil Aviation Authority (UK CAA), USA Federal Aviation Administration (FAA), Transport Canada (TC) and the Civil Aviation Safety Authority of Australia (CASA). He has been the Consultant Aviation Medicine Adviser to Thomas Cook Airlines (UK) since 2000. Dr. Hudson is a Vice-President of the UK Association of Aviation Medical Examiners having served for 12 years as its Treasurer and then its Chairman. Dr. Hudson is a Fellow of the Aerospace Medical Association (AsMA) and was the Chairman of AsMA's Air Transport Medicine Committee for four years from 2011–2015. Dr. Hudson is a committee member of the Airline Medical Directors Association (AMDA) and is also a member of the European Society of Aerospace Medicine (ESAM) Advisory Board.

**Morten Kjellesvig**, MSc ATPL, is an accident investigator and airline pilot flying the A330-340 for Scandinavian Airlines. He graduated from the MSc in Air Safety Management at City University in 2008. He is a visiting lecturer at City University, London, where he teaches on the MSc in Air Transport, Safety and Maintenance Management. He has conducted 11 accident investigations, three as Chairman in Norway. He is the Manager of Flight Operational Forum, a safety conference in Norway.

**Benjamin Lawler**, BEng(Hons), is a current airline captain with over fifteen years of experience. He has over 8000 flying hours and experience in both the long-haul and short-haul environments. Ben is an experienced Type Rating Instructor and Type Rating Examiner, and has been involved in Human Factors training for the last nine years as a Crew Resource Management Instructor (CRMI), and more recently as a CRMI Examiner. He is also involved in the design of training courses and the planning of future CRM policy within his airline.

**Sarah Mackenzie Ross**, MA MPhil DPsychol PhD, is a Consultant Clinical Neuropsychologist and Honorary Senior Lecturer on the Doctoral Programme in Clinical Psychology at University College London. Sarah has been involved in training clinical psychologists for more than twenty years and continues to teach neuropsychology at UCL and also on the post-qualification training course in clinical neuropsychology at the University of Glasgow. Her career history has included several clinical appointments within the National Health Service working as both a Clinical Neuropsychologist and a Clinical Psychologist in Adult Mental Health. She now runs her own private practice providing reports for both general healthcare and medico-legal purposes. Sarah has a longstanding research record and in the last ten years has become an internationally recognised expert in neurotoxicology. She set up the Neuropsychological Toxicology Unit at UCL in 2004 to research and promote understanding and recognition of the ways in which toxic substances affect human behaviour, cognition and emotion. The NTU was the first of its kind in the UK and between 2005 and 2009 undertook research on commercial airline pilots reporting ill health following alleged exposure to engine oil fumes. Sarah provided a report for the UK Department of Transport and gave evidence to a Government Scientific Advisory Committee (COT) and at a House of Lords Inquiry into 'Air Quality and Health'. Sarah has also given many interviews on radio and television on this subject and has appeared in a number of documentaries including *Panorama* ('Something in the Air', 2007). She has published a number of papers in scientific journals on this issue and recently put together a special edition of the high impact neuroscience journal *Cortex* on neurotoxicology, which features a paper calling for further research regarding cognitive function in airline pilots.

**Monica Martinussen**, PhD, is currently Professor of Psychology at the Arctic University of Norway, and is a licenced psychologist. She is also visiting Professor at the Norwegian Defence University College. Dr. Martinussen conducted her doctoral research in the area of pilot selection, and has been engaged in research on that topic for many years, both for the Norwegian Air Force and at the University. Her research interests include research methods and psychometrics, aviation psychology, mental health and burnout. Dr. Martinussen is a member of the Board of Directors of the European Association of Aviation Psychology. She has published over 100 articles, in addition to books and book chapters. Martinussen has, together with David Hunter, published a textbook on Aviation Psychology and Human Factors.

**Pooshan Navathe**, MBBS MD BEd MBA Dip Occ Med Dip Aviation Safety Regulation FAFOEM (RACP) FRACMA FACAsM FRAeS PhD, is an occupational physician and an aviation medicine consultant based in Australia. He is a Conjoint Associate Professor at the University of Newcastle, having formerly held Adjunct and full time Associate Professorships at the Australian National University and the University of Bangalore, and other academic positions with Auckland and Otago Universities. He is a Fellow of the Royal Aeronautical Society, a Fellow of the Aerospace Medical Association (USA) and a Member and Director of the International Academy of Aviation and Space Medicine. Pooshan has formerly worked in a senior role at the Civil Aviation Authority of New Zealand, and as the Principal Medical Officer at the Civil Aviation Safety Authority in Australia. During these tenures, he regularly undertook assessments of pilots with complex medical conditions, and has served as an expert witness in several aviation legal cases relating to medical certification of pilots. He attained a glider pilot's licence as a medical student, and even though he has flown many fixed wing and rotary wing aircraft since, he maintains that gliding is the purest form of flying. His definition of spatial disorientation was accepted by the five nations interoperability council, and he remains an authority on the subject. Pooshan is a thought leader in the realms of risk assessment and management in aviation medicine, and has developed and helped develop several paradigms for managing pilots with complex conditions. Notwithstanding his clinical workload, he is a reviewer for numerous leading international academic journals, has made nearly 150 presentations to learned academic societies worldwide, and has authored or edited over 80 chapters, guidelines and papers in a variety of areas including clinical aeromedicine, risk management and medical education.

**Shruti Navathe**, BA BSc (Hons) MIS PhD, is a forensic and organisational psychologist. She completed her PhD in forensic psychology at Victoria University of Wellington examining the world view of child sexual offenders. Shruti went on to work at the Australian National University on the impact of psychological contracts formed within the workplace. She has worked within academic and policy based settings, in roles in academia, the non-government sector as well as a consultant for government organisations. Her work on the role of values within a cognitive framework has led her to collaborate on projects that span the divide between the purely clinical and the entirely theoretical. Shruti has a broad range of research interests which include the emergence and maintenance of criminal behaviours, the nature of embodied cognition, sexual aggression, value-based reasoning, suicidal ideation and depressive realism.

**Margaret Oakes**, MA (Cantab) MSc Dip Psych DPsych CPsychol, is a Counselling Psychologist registered with the Health and Care Professions Council and Chartered with the British Psychological Society. She is also a currently active airline pilot on routes covering Europe and the Middle East for a UK airline. As a psychologist, she works and teaches in the NHS and private practice with specific interests in pilot mental health issues, trauma and the psychological implications of long-term health conditions. She has published peer-reviewed papers and contributed to a number of self-help books and textbooks. As a pilot, she has a particular interest in non-technical skills and has taught airline staff about providing psychological support to those involved in the aftermath of airline incidents. She also teaches on the MSc in Airline Transport Management at City University, London.

**Peter Scragg**, BSc PsychD FBPsS, is a Consultant Clinical Psychologist and a Chartered Psychologist with the British Psychological Society and registered with the Health Care and Professions Council. He is also an accredited Cognitive Behavioural Therapist. He has practised clinically for more than 24 years including more than 10 years of experience in the field of traumatic stress and 7 years of experience in forensic psychology (Broadmoor Hospital). In addition to his clinical work, he is a Principal Teaching Fellow at University College London. His main areas of teaching include anxiety disorders, psychological assessment and Cognitive Behavioural Therapy. His scientific publications have focused on post-traumatic stress disorder, psychological assessment and Cognitive Behavioural Therapy.

**Ries Simons**, MD, is physician and consultant in aerospace medicine. He graduated in 1973 and worked as General Practitioner in the Netherlands and as Medical Officer in Zambia and Chad. Since 1985, he is Senior Research Physician at the Netherlands Organisation for Applied Scientific Research (TNO). He has performed studies of the effects of fitness on alertness and performance of flightcrew and astronauts and on medical requirements for pilot licensing. His expertise and current research includes sleep and alertness management for safety-sensitive operations (aircrew, naval crew, maintenance crew) and military missions; medical and physiological aspects of working under extreme conditions; effects of operational and environmental factors on health and performance of aviators and astronauts; and effects of alcohol, drugs and medication on operator alertness and performance. He is presently working as senior consultant in aerospace medicine for several national authorities, European Aviation Safety Agency (EASA), aerospace medical institutes and airlines. His scientific publications include effects of fatigue, alcohol, drugs, medication and environmental factors on pilot performance and health. He is chairman of the Scientific Advisory Board of the European Society for Aerospace Medicine (ESAM).

**Gunnar Steinhardt**, Dipl-Psych., is an Aviation Psychologist and Manager of Human Factors at Cargolux Airlines International. Gunnar focuses on pilot selection and developing Pilot Support Programmes. As a psychologist he provides coaching and counselling for flight crews, works closely together with Crew Training Dept. and the Aviation Safety Dept. to support an effective integration of Human Factors Strategies into Flight Operations. With more than 20 years' experience in the field of Aviation Psychology, his career started at the German Aerospace Center (DLR) in Pilot Selection and continued with Lufthansa Cityline, leading a team of Crew Resource Mangement instructors. Thereafter Gunnar built up and developed a Human Factors Dept. at Luxair Luxembourg Airlines with the core areas of Pilot Selection, Crew Resource Management Training and Coaching and Counselling of cockpit and cabin crews. Gunnar is a member of the European Human Factors Advisory Group (EHFAG) and chairs the Operations & Licensing Focus Group to support Human Factors matters at EASA. Most recently he has been involved in the Rule Making Task (RMT) .0411 Crew Resource Management Training and RMT.0700 Aircrew Medical Fitness, implementing the recommendations made by the EASA-led Germanwings Task Force following the incident of the Germanwings Flight 9525. Besides his work in the field of aviation he is also involved in selection and training of managers and experts in health care and in the chemical industry with regard to Crisis and Emergency Management. Gunnar also served as visiting lecturer at the International University of Bad Honnef (IUBH) in the field of Aviation Management with the focus on 'Safety Management & Human Factors in Aviation'. Gunnar is a member of the European Association for Aviation Psychology and holds a private pilot licence.

# Foreword

The presentation of mental illness at work has different implications and consequences depending on the specific nature of the job, work context, regulatory framework and risks for the employee, organisation and society.

There are certain occupational groups where human factors, mental illness or sub-clinical levels of psychological distress could impair safety and mental acuity with potentially devastating consequences. Pilots are one such group. They are subject to licensing criteria including medical standards stipulated by regulatory aviation authorities worldwide, and these include specific mental illness exclusions.

The challenge of assessment for mental health problems is, however, complex and the responsibility for psychological screening and testing falls to a range of different specialists and groups including AMEs (authorised aviation medical examiners), GPs and physicians, airline human resources departments, psychologists, human factor specialists and to pilots themselves.

In our previous book, *Aviation Mental Health* (Ashgate, 2006), we described a range of psychological issues and problems that may affect pilots and some consequences of these. For airline pilots, we highlighted that the presence of certain mental health conditions and syndromes may be disqualifying with regard to crew medical licensing. An individual seeking to train as a pilot or one who is already qualified may have their medical certificate withdrawn if they have a history of, or if they develop, certain psychological disorders.

The suicide of the Germanwings first officer Andreas Lubitz on the 24 March 2015 in the French Alps whilst at the controls of the A320-200 and death of all passengers and crew, coupled with half-a-dozen other known commercial pilot suicide-murders in the preceding years, has raised questions about the screening and psychological assessment of commercial pilots. This is understandable in order to prevent pilots suffering from certain definable psychological disorders from flying, and denying medical certification to prospective pilot trainees or those at other stages in their careers who do not meet the required mental health criteria.

Some aviation regulatory authorities have highlighted certain shortcomings in the current psychological assessments of pilots and also made recommendations for how to improve these. There have been calls for routine psychological testing of pilots to enhance air safety by improving the detection of psychological issues which may have an impact on pilot performance. We would argue that there is a critical balance to be found between robust and appropriate screening and stigmatising mental health issues in aviation. Any changes need to be carefully thought through and attention given to the details of how assessments should be conducted and the way in which information gleaned in the course of such assessments is used and shared. There is a risk that some assessments may not meet the exacting standards demanded of psychologists by their own regulatory and licensing bodies. There is also the potential to inadvertently increase stigma associated with minor transient psychological distress which does not require grounding of air crew even though they may benefit from short-term psychological support while continuing to work. An increase in stigma or a perception that assessment is being imposed inappropriately among pilots could encourage some to hide treatable and manageable mental health conditions with a consequent reduction in air safety.

From the beginnings of aviation, and most especially from the Second World War onwards, there has been a keen interest in how best to select pilots. Nowadays, most pilots undergo psychological selection testing at the point of entry to pilot training and/or when applying to an airline. The tests most commonly used in pilot selection aim to ensure that pilots have the required cognitive skills, flying aptitude and other competencies to do the job. Not all airline pilots are assessed, however, for their psychological health. Tests designed to detect personality disorders and serious psychopathology are not routinely carried out and these are not always repeated at required intervals. There is also specialist neurocognitive testing, which may assist in the detection of functional impairment in an individual, though these are rarely used in population-based screening and assessments. Where psychometric tests are used – whether for selection, mental health assessments or for neurocognitive screening – the interpretation and reporting of these tests is sometimes not carried out by professionals who are clinically experienced and qualified to do so. This raises questions as to whether psychometric testing of pilots should even be mandatory and routine. A further question that warrants addressing is 'which tests are best suited to the aim of detecting mental illness?' It is questionable as to whether any single psychometric test is sufficiently sensitive for picking up rare, arguably unpredictable occurrences such as a pilot suicide. It is also important to consider whether psychometric tests alone are sufficient for detecting mental illness in the absence of a clinical interview, medical history, line training reports and simulator checks, among other sources of information on the pilot's circumstances and functioning. We argue that any mental health assessment, with potentially important – and in certain cases, devastating – implications for employment and wellbeing, should always be of a medico-legal standard.

This book, conceived in the aftermath of the Germanwings pilot suicide crash in 2015, extends and develops the ideas from the first book on 'pilot mental health' by describing in practical terms how mental health assessments can be conducted amongst pilots. We have sought to present a range of different skills and methods that can be used for the clinical assessment of pilots and in relation to specific mental health problems and syndromes. This book also addresses the important and sensitive topic of pilot support to ensure that pilots have access to and can benefit from both peer and professional support.

Our underpinning aim, when we invited each contributor to join in this project, has been to present an edited textbook which is:

• comprehensive and practical in focus;
• reflective of modern, evidence-based practice in the field of mental health assessment, treatment and care;
• authoritative, comprising insights and contributions from expert practitioners and researchers in the field drawn from several countries, professions and representing a range of aviation-related organisations;
• mindful of the need to reflect a balance between robust and useful assessments, on the one hand, and not over-burdening or stigmatising pilots, on the other; and
• liberal and compassionate with respect to pilot mental health issues, and which seeks to reduce stigma surrounding mental health in the aviation work place.

The book is divided into three parts. We start with a general introduction and overview of the field and specialism of pilot mental health assessments. In the first part (Chapters 2 to 4), we include chapters on pilot selection assessments and cover topics such as pilot ability and aptitude testing, the role of assessment in selection and personality assessments of airline pilot applicants. We also briefly describe the unusual psychosocial environment pilots experience and the potential implications for mental health assessment and screening. In the second part (Chapters 5 to 12), the focus is on the clinical assessment of pilots for mental health problems. Here, we examine the aims for and skills used in clinical interviewing; mental health conditions and exclusions for pilots; neurocognitive assessments; risk reduction and assessments; the impact of fatigue on mental health; post-traumatic incident assessments, and the inclusion of mental health screening into the time-limited annual medical checks carried out on pilots. Ethical and confidentiality issues are also addressed in this section. In the final part (Chapters 13 to 22), the focus turns to promoting mental health, wellbeing and support among pilots. Chapters in this part address issues relating to psychotropic medications and fitness to fly; human factors, mental health and flight safety; social stigma associated with mental illness among pilots; lifestyle and work-related stressors that affect pilots; behavioural dynamics on the flight deck and their relationship to mental health matters; the impact of emotions on behaviour and the development of pilot peer support programmes.

We are extremely grateful to our colleagues who have contributed to this book, all of whom are very busy practitioners, trainers, researchers, clinicians and, of course, pilots. Each readily agreed to support this project and undertook to submit chapters on highly specialist and sensitive topics, and to do so keeping to a tight deadline. The expertise gathered in this book is humbling and we hope that through the insights, experience and research findings shared here, that we have at the very least met the broad aims outlined above.

Pilot mental health has become a more prominent concern amongst aviation regulators, and also in the mind of the general public. It is important that, whatever measures are taken in order to improve the detection of mental ill health amongst pilots, an opportunity is not lost to improve the general mental wellbeing of pilots and to ensure that evidence-based and ethical methods are used for pilot screening and selection in order to protect pilots from undue bias or discrimination. We hope that this book will help to promote a positive image of mental health issues in aviation and that the expertise shared here will be translated into ethical and useful clinical practice.

RB, CE, MO and PS
*London, 2016*

# 1 Pilot mental health in the modern era

## Headlines and reality

*Robert Bor, Carina Eriksen, Margaret Oakes and Peter Scragg*

In March 2015, mental health issues among pilots became headline news when a pilot, who was later identified as having significant psychological difficulties, deliberately flew a passenger aircraft on a commercial flight into the ground killing all on board. Worldwide, the airlines and their regulators acknowledge that psychological problems within the pilot population are a potential threat to safety. Well below the severity level at which we might hypothesise about pilot suicide, psychological distress and mental health issues can cause a significant impairment to pilot performance and therefore flight safety. Psychiatric disorders are not uncommon among the general population but are frequently under recognised. Severe psychological disturbance among pilots is rare but, nonetheless, they may suffer from a range of psychological difficulties just like anyone in any other occupational group.

In this chapter, we provide an overview of current theory and practice relevant to the understanding, identification and management of mental health issues among pilots. We start with the psychological aspects of the environment in which pilots work. This is fundamental to understanding the ways in which standard clinical assessment and practice may need to be adapted for this specific occupational group. We also outline the regulatory environment in which clinical work with pilots must take place and the recommendations produced by the European regulator, European Aviation Safety Agency (EASA) in the aftermath of March 2015. We then discuss psychological assessment and its use in selecting the 'right' pilots and identifying and anticipating psychological disorders. The reader may be somewhat disappointed to learn that one cannot offer nor provide a perfect clinical tool that will predict and/or identify any and every potential psychological disorder. Psychology draws extensively on scientific methods but it is not a precise science. We recognise that pilots are subjected to the same challenges and vicissitudes in life as anyone in the general population. There are, however, some useful clinical tools, methods and skills that, when used together, can provide a robust and comprehensive psychological assessment. We present these and discuss their application to flight crew.

## Pilots' psychological environment

Pilots are in many ways a unique, and at times unusual, occupational group. Their working environment and shift patterns are psychologically and physiologically challenging (Bor and Hubbard, 2006). They also face unusual psychosocial challenges at work and home. It has been suggested that people who fly for a living may also have health concerns above and beyond those that work on the ground (Brown *et al.*, 2001; Richards *et al.*, 2006). An understanding of pilot mental health therefore requires us to consider the specific environment in which they work.

The major physiological challenges of aircrews' working environment centre on the aircraft environment, disruption to circadian rhythms, shift work, rostering anomalies and stresses, disruption to regular social support and sleeping difficulties. The immediate workplace environmental challenges are well documented elsewhere but centre on air quality, noise and restricted movement (Gradwell and Rainford, 2016). The result may be physiological stress. Depending on the type of flying undertaken, pilots can experience jet lag, multiple early starts or late finishes, limited recovery time and shifts exceeding 12 hours. Figure 1.1 shows typical schedules for a long-haul and short-haul pilot. All of these factors combine to create a significant potential for fatigue (Caldwell, 1997). Any screening or assessment process focused on pilot mental health must therefore take these physiological influences into account. At recruitment, the aim will be to identify flexible and robust individuals who will be able to handle these challenges well. When screening for possible psychological difficulties, the extent to which these physiological stressors have contributed to the presenting issue must be considered. This is apart from assessing for underlying, pre-existing or emerging mental health problems.

Fatigue is a significant factor in long-term physical and psychological well-being. Pilot fatigue has also been identified as a contributing factor in some airline incidents including a Northwest Airlines flight in October 2009 when the captain and first officer fell asleep and were unresponsive to air traffic control for ninety minutes, and the fatal Flydubai crash in Rostov-on-Don, Russia, in March 2016. The regulatory environment we describe later imposes maximum shift lengths, minimum rest periods and fatigue reporting systems. The aim is to avoid the accumulation of fatigue for those in safety critical roles; and in Europe, cabin crew and pilots are now governed by identical rules and share responsibility for fatigue management with their employer. The employer must schedule crew in accordance with the fatigue-avoiding regulations. Crew are expected to manage their time at work and away in order to be properly rested.

Imagine for a moment being one of the pilots following the schedules in Figure 1.1 living about 40 minutes from their base airport with a family including school age children. For both pilots, some of the working days will almost certainly cover weekends. On Day 1, our short-haul pilot must negotiate rush-hour traffic before completing a 12-hour shift, returning home after everyone else is asleep. Days 2 and 3 provide opportunities for a lie in but what is everyone else at home doing? The morning school run or dash to work? What interruptions might occur? If they are at home and their partner works, surely it is their turn for the school run? How much sleep is possible at home before the long night flight starting on the evening of Day 4? What are the implications for family relationships and social interactions if the pilot insists on sleeping when others are active or noisy? The point is that pilots, like most other people, have obligations and dependencies outside of work. The shift patterns in Figure 1.1 illustrate challenges related to these, which are not typical of many shift patterns.

Long-haul pilots face similar challenges trying to rest at home before a night flight on Day 1 and must then find ways of resting and maintaining contact with home in an unfamiliar hotel room to be fit for another night flight home on Day 4. On a trip that length, their social interactions are probably limited to the crew they work with – potentially rewarding, but also potentially shallow or even

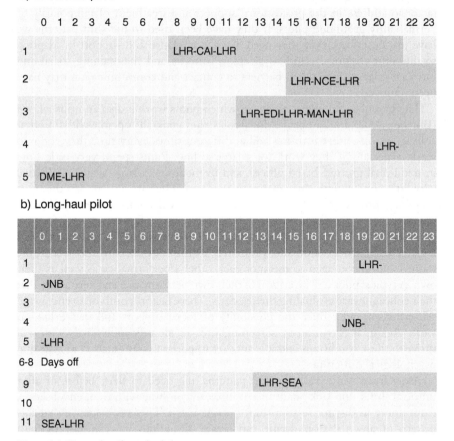

*Figure 1.1* Example pilot schedules

Columns 0–23 indicate UK time of day; rows indicate successive days, not necessarily starting on Monday; shaded blocks are flying duties

creating friction at home. By the time they return home, having battled rush-hour traffic on Day 5, they will have been awake for a minimum of 16 hours. Do they isolate themselves from the social groups they left days ago by going to sleep, or join in 'normal' routines, probably not at their best and potentially upsetting those who missed them? Days 9–11 pose similar challenges again with the addition of time differences imposing jet lag and narrow windows of opportunity for contact with home.

This brief overview and illustration is not to suggest that all pilots are unhappy or do not live fulfilling lives. They are highly motivated; their role is practically and psychologically rewarding and reasonably high status and they generally manage these challenges well. When mental health issues arise, however, the impact of their working patterns on their physiological and psychological state and the psychosocial environment we discuss below must be considered when assessing and managing the underlying clinical problem. Asking them about how they manage these challenges may be revealing. It is also an important factor to address in the professional support and treatment of temporarily or permanently grounded pilots. If they have been used to the shift patterns we have just described, they may need detailed guidance and support in adapting to different routines, standard sleeping patterns and maintaining social and intimate relationships when barriers to contact and communication may have been removed.

The psychosocial environment in which pilots work is also an unusual one (Butcher, 2002). In their professional roles, they generally operate with different colleagues, on different routes and at different times every time they come to work, especially if they work for a large airline. Pilots spend very little time in traditional ground-based offices, and in medium to large airlines will have very little contact with their management team. They are also among the most examined professions of all. Typically, a pilot will complete several days of simulator tests, a medical, a written examination and a flight under supervision every year. Failing any of these tests can result in stressful additional training and testing, disciplinary action and, ultimately, dismissal. Pilots are also specifically trained and encouraged to monitor each other's performance as well as their own. A typical pilot will be critical of their own performance and very aware that their colleagues are evaluating their actions. These factors combine to encourage self-criticism and reduce the possibility of social support and networking at work. Again, at recruitment, screening aims to identify individuals who will thrive in these conditions and it is another important consideration in assessing psychological difficulties.

Away from work, variable shift patterns, the need to sleep before or after unsocial shifts, and lack of advance notice can combine with frequent absences from home to disrupt relationships outside work. There is evidence that this pattern of absence from home can create difficulties in relationships with partners and families in a form sometimes referred to as 'intermittent spouse syndrome' (Taylor *et al.*, 1985). In brief, the working patterns of flight crew tend to impose a requirement for both partners in intimate relationships to adapt frequently and quickly to changing roles when separated and together. Of course, the exact way a couple deals with such transitions will depend on the strength of the relationship as well as each partner's ability to manage the frequent separations.

Relationship difficulties can cause stress and emotional upset (Eriksen, 2009). This can have a negative impact on performance including concentration, ability to think clearly and decision-making. There are relatively few studies demonstrating a causal link between relational problems and pilot performance, but anecdotal evidence from pilots is strong. Further investigations may be needed to assess the degree to which flight-deck duties are negatively affected by couple or family discord. Another issue to consider is whether lack of support from a spouse, friends or family could potentially reduce a pilot's ability to cope with the many stressful aspects of their jobs. Imagine, for example, the partner left at home who has had to deal with family illness or domestic flooding only to be criticised by the returning partner for some of the decisions made. Or the absent partner who generally manages family finances but finds that the family budget has been disrupted by their partner replacing an expensive broken household item while they were away. Outwardly trivial, these issues have the potential to cause arguments and diminish the enjoyment of reunions. There is a plethora of research suggesting stable relationships can have a positive impact on (pilot) mental health.

When there is a link between relational, financial or the myriad of other personal problems that can occur in anyone's life, and changes in a pilot's behaviour, it is important that pilots do not undertake further flying duties until their normal levels of functioning have been restored. This may occur when, for example, a confident and experienced captain who is usually able to make decisions becomes overly hesitant and anxious whilst operating on a flight. Jones and colleagues (1997) suggest that family issues could very well have a negative impact on pilot performance and they argue that such family issues must be addressed and resolved before allowing the pilot to resume flying. Other studies have found a link between interpersonal problems, financial difficulties and career strains to aircraft mishaps (Little *et al.*, 1990). Moreover, Raschmann and colleagues (1990) studied the psychosocial lives of pilots and observed that pilots who suffered enduring and extensive marital distress reported a reduced ability to concentrate effectively on their piloting duties and responsibilities.

Some research has demonstrated the importance of relationship support in predicting pilot performance (Levy *et al.*, 1984; Rigg and Cosgrove, 1994), but it may also be equally true that individual work competency leads to a happier domestic life. In a study on spousal support, Karlins and colleagues (1989) recognised that a stable and happy relationship with a partner could strengthen pilots' existing coping mechanisms to deal with work stress. On the other hand, disruption to personal relationships was thought to weaken a pilot's ability to manage the more stressful aspects of their jobs. This indicates that spousal relationship can buffer the effects of work stress and they may therefore play an important role in reducing the likelihood of unsafe acts in flight (Morse and

Bor, 2006). The same may be true for other kinds of supportive relationships including friends, family and colleagues. Sloan and Cooper (1986) studied the coping strategies of commercial airline pilots and found a close association between mental health problems and fatigue, lack of social support and lack of work autonomy.

Selection and mental health assessments need to consider the long-term ability of pilot recruits to manage these challenges as an important part of the assessment of pilots presenting with mental health issues.

## Regulation and training

As one would expect in a safety critical industry, aviation is highly regulated. Most countries have established national regulators who define operating standards for airlines and aircraft manufacturers and issue licences to pilots. Other smaller countries place themselves under one of the larger regulators. For an industry with its roots in the 1940s, international regulation is remarkably consistent, but any assessment of a pilot must comply with the national regulations governing their employer and their licence. Readers should consult their local aviation regulator for a copy of the regulations governing crew licensing.

In Europe, national regulators have come together under the umbrella of the European Air Safety Agency (EASA). EASA regulations define, among other issues, psychological standards for flight crew (EASA n.d.). In the USA, the Federal Aviation Administration (FAA) guide for aviation medical examiners includes specific guidance regarding psychiatric diagnoses and aerospace medical disposition. The guidance can be accessed via the FAA website (FAA, 2016). Likewise, in the United Kingdom, it is the UK Civil Aviation Authority (CAA). In Canada, it is the Canadian Aviation Regulations (CAR) (Transport Canada 2007); in the United Arab Emirates, it is the General Civil Aviation Authority (GCAA), and in Australia, the Civil Aviation Safety Authority (CASA).

The pilot's relationship with the regulator is generally fairly remote once they have completed their initial training and hold an appropriate licence: if they comply with the operating instructions issued by their airline, they will have complied with the requirements of the regulator. The airline will issue each pilot with a large set of manuals containing these operating instructions and it becomes the pilot's responsibility to be familiar with them. These bulky manuals provide a framework of standard procedures that are very effective in making it possible to operate safely with frequently changing groups of colleagues. Keeping abreast of changes and maintaining a good level of knowledge does require periodic study and can place additional demands on pilots' time and energy away from work.

Initial pilot training may be self-funded or sponsored, either from scratch or after relevant military experience. There are various routes and these do vary between national regulators. To obtain the basic licence required to fly for an airline, however, will always have involved a significant commitment in terms of time, finances and some sacrifices of social obligations in order to pass multiple written exams and practical tests. A pilot's licence becomes a very precious entity and entitlement, and medical assessments can become a threat. Throughout their career, pilots are personally responsible for maintaining valid licences and medical certificates. Without both, they cannot operate. Licences will generally be valid if the pilot has successfully completed the annual tests we described earlier and are issued directly by the regulator. Renewing medical certificates is generally done in a pilot's own time by specifically qualified aviation medical examiners (AMEs) and for some can be experienced as a peak of stress during the annual cycle of testing and training.

In order to operate a specific type of passenger aircraft, pilots must complete further training, written tests and practical exams. They must also complete training and tests related to various other career moves such as promotion to captain or taking on training roles. It is a career that imposes periodic peaks of training and testing. Our clinical experience is that some pilots who present with psychological distress or mental health issues report that their difficulties became obvious in the course of or coincided with one of these peaks. It is vitally important when completing a psychological assessment with pilots therefore, to ask them about recent training and testing experiences. It is rarely the only factor in precipitating psychological disturbance but it is often a significant one.

## Assessing mental health and identifying potential difficulties

Pilots typically encounter psychological assessment for one of three reasons: competitive job selection, annual medical assessment, or because a potential mental health or neurocognitive problem is suspected. Almost without exception, they will be very aware of the consequences of an unfavourable evaluation and some may be understandably reluctant to self-report emotional problems. This may also be due to the perceived stigma associated with having a mental health problem both within the airline community and also within society more generally. This may well distort pilot responses to both the major psychological assessment tools; interview and questionnaire measures; and make it more difficult for clinicians to identify mental health problems. Because pilots generally work with a different team of colleagues every time they fly and rarely directly interact with individual managers, observations of behaviour changes at work will also be more challenging to assess among pilots and will mostly be confined to task-oriented behaviours and general communication.

Airlines put a significant amount of effort into selecting psychologically robust pilots who are likely to thrive in their individual organisation's culture (Smallwood, 2000). Most incorporate some form of psychological testing in their selection process to assess this. Psychological testing in selection and recruitment processes may rule out a proportion of those who are psychologically unsuited to flying at that point in time. Such tests are, however, generally a poor predictor of long-term psychological well-being. While selection aims to identify pilots with 'the right stuff', pilots are human and therefore prone to all the ailments that lie dormant within one's brain chemistry as well as to life's changing fortunes.

As part of the selection process, psychological assessment aims to identify individuals who are a good fit to the person specification defined by the recruiting airline. This will include meeting medical requirements which may exceed those imposed by the regulator. It may also define psychological traits identified by an organisation as being a good fit to its own culture or operational environment. For example, 'bush pilots' and those who operate in remote or hostile environments may require different skills and specific personality traits which may differ in certain ways from those who fly executive jets or who fly for large legacy carriers. Clinicians may be involved in the definition of these criteria as well as the assessment process to determine whether the criteria have been met (Bor and Hubbard, 2006; Smallwood, 2000).

## Interviewing pilots

During an interview, clinicians can either follow a list of prescribed questions (a structured interview) or they can use a more unstructured conversational style of interview. These two styles of interview have advantages and disadvantages.

Unstructured interviews generally allow a clinician to establish rapport and to cover a wide range of topics. They allow flexibility in the interview so that the clinician can decide to go into detail for a certain topic that appears emotionally important to the interviewee. It is probably true to say that most mental health assessments take this unstructured format, although clinicians usually will impose some structure. Any such interview will, at the very least, need to cover an outline of the individual's history, their report of their emotional state, and current and historically important concerns. If the assessment has been requested because a potential problem has arisen, it will also need to cover the specific history of the problem, its implications and psychological risk factors.

The advantage of these unstructured interview assessments is that they are broad and flexible and they often facilitate the establishment of rapport. However, diagnoses developed during unstructured interviews are often unreliable (Wood *et al.*, 2002). The unreliability may stem from clinicians forgetting to cover important areas of functioning. The errors in unstructured interviews can be either random error, caused, for example, by the clinician having a bad day, or the errors can be more systematic if, for example, the clinician has a particular blind spot or prejudice. Shame, embarrassment, a tendency towards paranoia, fear of negative evaluation, and so on, can also block an interviewee in his or her revealing of problems. Clinicians may inadvertently introduce bias through errors stemming from excessive empathy and countertransference.

Some of these problems may be reduced by structured and panel interviews. The advantage of these structured interviews is standardisation, which generally improves reliability of information obtained in interviews. The disadvantage of structured interviews is that interviewees may become alienated by the fixed questions and the rigid structure. The rigid structure may also prevent or inhibit more emotionally important material from emerging in the assessment. Individuals with psychotic problems may 'hold it together' in a structured interview whereas in a more emotionally alive unstructured interview the psychotic ideas may emerge. Similarly, a person's style of interacting with others is more likely to be demonstrated in a less structured situation than a highly structured one.

A reasonable compromise is to divide a mental health assessment interview into a loosely structured first half followed by a more structured and systematic second half. For pilots, it is critical that any assessment has sufficient structure to compare their current psychological state to the regulations governing their professional licence. While this will vary geographically, it is generally necessary to rule out noticeable impairment in cognitive function, mood disturbance, significant psychological or psychiatric symptoms and any psychological risk factors.

### Questionnaire data

In mental health assessments, interview data is often complemented by questionnaire data. This can seem very attractive to the clinician wanting to deliver an objective numerical assessment of a pilot's mental state, particularly when an individual's career or livelihood are at stake. However, there is an enormous range of questionnaires used in mental health assessments that vary in their psychometric strengths and weaknesses.

Questionnaire measures range from short narrow-band assessments of one construct, for example the Patient Health Questionnaire-9 (PHQ-9; Spitzer *et al.*, 1999), General Health Questionnaire (GHQ; Goldberg and Hillier, 1979) or Beck Depression Inventory (BDI; Beck *et al.*, 1996), to instruments that contain many hundreds of questions that seek to measure a wide range of mental health problems (e.g. Minnesota Multiphasic Personality Inventory, Personality Assessment Inventory). As with interviews, there are advantages and disadvantages to the various questionnaire measures. The short narrow-band measures – which are currently much favoured in both primary care and psychological therapy services – have the big advantage of being easily completed, scored and interpreted, i.e. they make only a minimal demand on the time of the client and the time of the clinician. However, the narrowness of focus is a big limitation: if an individual completes, for example, the PHQ-9 (a nine-item measure of depression), the clinician is obviously only learning about whether the individual is reporting depressive symptoms. Furthermore, these questionnaires also only measure recent psychological functioning, and profiles reveal nothing of the cause or meaning of mood fluctuations in the first place. Clinically, they may not have much value when working in a pilot assessment context.

Some psychologists give pilots a series of narrow-band and single measures, e.g. a depression questionnaire, anxiety questionnaire, alcohol measure, interpersonal functioning measure and so on. However, this strategy results in a clumsy battery of questionnaires (often with different formats) which have been standardised on different populations. Clinicians should be aware that an astute pilot who believes he or she has been unfairly rated or diagnosed as a result of such tests alone may have grounds to contest the results of psychometric testing. Pilot mental health assessments and psychometric testing must always meet certain ethical standards as stipulated for example by the American Psychological Association or the British Psychological Society (APA, 2014 and British Psychological Society, 2016), and reports should always be of medico-legal standard.

Another potential problem with narrow-band, single-construct questionnaires (e.g. PHQ-9 and Beck Depression Inventory) is their high face validity, i.e. the questions in these questionnaires are very obvious in what they seek to measure. Furthermore, since each question in these short questionnaires is related to one construct, a pilot wishing to convey a particular impression of his or her clinical health need barely read the items. In sum these short questionnaires are useful in situations where a clinician has a fully cooperative client, who is motivated to provide an accurate report on a single issue. Their best use is often for tracking progress with treatment. They are of very limited use in situations where individuals are motivated to put their best foot forward, or the opposite.

Multi-scale inventories (often called personality inventories) include a large number of questionnaire items that measure a range of clinical constructs. The most well-known is the Minnesota Multiphasic Personality Inventory (MMPI) which was revised in 1989 to become the MMPI-2 (Butcher *et al.*, 2001). The items are objectively scored usually using a computer scoring program. Chapter 4 by Butcher discusses the use of the MMPI-2 with pilots in some detail. Here we highlight why multi-scale personality inventories like the MMPI-2 have important advantages compared to short questionnaires.

One significant advantage of the MMPI-2 and other similar multi-scale inventories over brief single-construct questionnaires such as the PHQ-9 is that imbedded in the multi-scale inventory are items that measure the degree to which a client has been careful, consistent and honest in responding to the test. These scales are known as validity scales. Although the validity scales are not infallible at detecting false reporting, they provide information on whether the client has presented him or herself in an overly virtuous manner, and/or whether he or she has exaggerated his or her problems.

Understandably, many pilots undergoing psychological evaluation are likely to be motivated to present themselves in a positive light and to down-play or even deny having psychological problems. Scores on the validity scales of multi-scale inventories can be at such a level that the results of the rest are rendered invalid. Butcher *et al.* (1997) demonstrated that in this situation pilot applicants can be informed that they were not sufficiently open on the MMPI-2 for a valid profile. They were then allowed to complete it a second time with over two-thirds of the pilot applicants providing a valid MMPI-2, and with 14 per cent revealing psychopathology that they had not reported on first administration (Butcher *et al.*, 1997).

Unlike the single-construct short questionnaires discussed above, the MMPI-2 provides information on a very wide range of emotional and mental problems. Thus the MMPI-2 goes well beyond a checklist of symptoms to provide information relevant to a comprehensive clinical formulation.

One disadvantage of the MMPI-2 is that interpreting the results requires considerable knowledge of the test, and the majority of psychologists outside the USA have not received training on the MMPI-2. The scales of the MMPI-2, while providing very useful clinical information, do not map directly onto modern diagnostic categories as set out in the *Diagnostic and Statistical Manual* (American Psychiatric Association, 2013) or ICD-10 (World Health Organization, 1992).

The Personality Assessment Inventory (PAI; Morey, 2007) is another widely used multi-scale inventory. It is 344 items long and requires less time to complete than the MMPI-2. It is a very well constructed clinical inventory that, like the MMPI-2, contains validity scales for measuring response bias. One advantage of the PAI over the MMPI-2 is that its scales map onto modern diagnostic categories and it is therefore fairly easy for a psychologist to interpret the scores of the PAI. However, unlike the MMPI-2, we are not aware of specific norms for the pilots with the PAI.

While the MMPI-2 or PAI are useful measures (and certainly likely to be more clinically useful than brief narrow-band measures), their length may evoke negative reactions in those asked to complete them. It should also be remembered that these instruments need to be administered on site, i.e. individuals being seen for assessment should never be allowed to complete questionnaire measures unsupervised.

In view of the limitations of self-report data collected either by interviewing or by questionnaire inventories, clinicians will need to review other sources of information. Corroborating information typically comes from the pilot's application form, career and work history, medical records, school records and flight-training records, among other sources. The clinician will need a thorough education in psychopathology and will need to be familiar with most common mental health problems seen in pilots, which are reviewed below.

## Common psychological disorders amongst pilots

Some of the more common psychological problems amongst pilots include adjustment disorder, mood disorder (Jones and Ireland, 2004; Steptoe and Bostock, 2011), anxiety and occupational stress (Cooper and Sloan, 1985; Girodo, 1988; Steptoe and Bostock, 2011), relationship problems (Raschmann *et al.*,1990), sexual dysfunction (Grossman *et al.*, 2004) and alcohol misuse (Harris, 2002; Krauss and Li, 2006).

Many psychological disorders are treatable and pilots can return to work but they may not always present to psychologists and psychiatrists for treatment. This may be due to a fear of jeopardising their licence and career by a visit to a mental health professional or there may be a stigma associated with psychological problems. Mental disorders that usually deny medical certification for almost every one of the major crew licensing authorities include psychosis, affective disorders (major depression), personality disorders, substance abuse or dependence, neurosis, self-destructive acts, disturbance or loss of consciousness, transient loss of control of the central nervous system, epilepsy or convulsive disorders, and a progressive disease of the nervous system.

### Adjustment disorder

Adjustment disorder is generally thought to be the most common mental disorder diagnosed in pilots. It is characterised by the development of intense emotional and behavioural symptoms in response to an identifiable stress or stressors. The most common stressors amongst pilots are relationship difficulties, career issues, occupational stress and financial difficulties (Morse and Bor, 2006). Adjustment disorders are commonly associated with functional impairment resulting from decreased concentration, depression, anxiety, inattention, insomnia, fatigue, temporary changes in social relationships and problems with decision-making. There are various subtypes depending on the predominant symptoms experienced by the pilot.

### Mood disorders

There are various types of mood disorders. The most common ones are depression and bipolar disorder. The *Diagnostic and Statistical Manual of Mental Disorders*, 5th edition (DSM-5) (American Psychiatric Association, 2013), separates mood disorders into two sections: depressive and related disorders, and bipolar and related disorders. Major depressive disorder (MDD) can be a common feature of mental illness, whatever its nature or origin. About one in ten people in the UK are thought to be affected by depression (www.nhs.uk). This number is slightly higher in the United States (Kessler *et al.*, 2003). Although it is difficult to determine the number of MDD-affected pilots because not all pilots are willing to disclose psychological illness, a recent survey commissioned by BALPA showed a higher number diagnosed with depression amongst pilots than expected (Steptoe and Bostock, 2011). The surveys indicated that 39.5 per cent of the 490 participating pilots suffered from symptoms of depression. This includes irritability, fatigue, loss of motivation, decreased concentration, lack of pleasure and sleep disturbance, loss of interest and depressed mood. Fatigue and sleep problems were thought to be the main causal factor for depression.

Depression can be treated using an antidepressant in the SSRI class, psychological therapy or a combination of both. The recommended therapy used to treat depression in the UK is cognitive behavioural therapy, mindfulness, cognitive therapy, behavioural therapy and counselling (NICE, 2016). The use of SSRIs to treat depression in pilots used to result in immediate grounding. In 2010, the Federal Aviation Administration (FAA) changed the guidelines to allow pilots to fly under certain conditions and certain types of antidepressants. However, this is done on a case-by-case basis and therefore not all pilots taking antidepressants are able to continue to fly. Some other regulatory authorities have also introduced schemes whereby pilots diagnosed with depression may be permitted to resume flying once stable on medication, provided that this is monitored, although there is normally a period when flying is again temporarily suspended when tapering off medications to ensure that there are no untoward effects.

### Anxiety disorders

Anxiety is another common form of psychological illness in the UK and the rest of the world. It is estimated that 1 in 5 people suffer from anxiety at some stage in their lives. There are many types of anxiety disorders including a generalised anxiety disorder (GAD) (Tyrer and Baldwin, 2006; Mearers and Freeston, 2012), obsessive compulsive disorder (OCD) (Abramovitz *et al.*, 2009; Veale and Wilson, 2009b), panic disorder and agoraphobia (Grant *et al.*, 2006; Silove and Manicavasagar, 2009), specific phobias (Parsons and Rizzo, 2008), health anxiety (Kessler *et al.*, 2003; Veale and Wilson, 2009a), social anxiety (Doehrmann *et al.*, 2013; Oakes, *et al.*, 2012), fear of flying (Bor *et al.*, 2009; Forman *et al.*, 2006), post-traumatic stress disorder (PTSD) (Hathaway *et al.*, 2010) and acute stress (Jamieson *et al.*, 2013).

Whilst it is beyond this chapter to give a detailed outline of each specific disorder, all of these types of anxiety disorders have apprehension and impaired function in common. The presentation of anxiety disorders involves a complex interplay of biological, genetic and stress factors. Although each type of anxiety may carry its own set of physical, cognitive and emotional impairments, there are some general symptoms including: increased worry, catastrophic interpretations of the feared event(s) or stimuli, racing mind, irritability, restlessness, increased heart palpitations, hyperventilation, sweating, tingling sensations, nausea, dizziness, chest pains and avoidance of the feared event(s) or stimuli. A study investigating anxiety and depression amongst pilots in the UK and Europe found that 39.8 per cent of the participating pilots had possible anxiety disorders (Steptoe and Bostock, 2011). Pilots who suffer from anxiety are most likely to experience physical symptoms. They may even present to a physician thinking that they are suffering from physical ill health.

### Alcohol and substance dependency

Alcohol and substance dependency is generally thought of as a condition in which a person is dependent on a substance including alcohol, other sedatives and hypnotics such as opioids, or central nervous stimulants such as cocaine or amphetamines to name a few. Dependency is evidenced by increased tolerance to a substance, withdrawal symptoms, impaired control of use, and continued use despite damage to physical health, career, finance and social relationships. Experts often make a distinction between substance dependency and substance abuse. Unlike substance dependency, substance abusers have some ability to set limits to their drinking. However, their abuse is still self-destructive, dangerous to themselves and others. Alcohol and drug misuse may be a co-factor in other psychiatric disorders, including adjustment disorders, anxiety disorders and mood disorders. A dependency may begin with the use of alcohol and/or drugs to 'self-medicate' against emotional upsets over a relationship break-up, financial difficulties or problems at work. In the long term, there is a risk of dependency as well as physical and mental impairment.

The FAA standards state that substance dependency and substance abuse are disqualifying and require an FAA decision before a medical certificate can be issued. Pilots with a diagnosis of substance abuse or substance dependency must submit clinical evidence, satisfactory to the Federal Air Surgeon, of recovery. This includes a total abstinence from the substance(s) for not less than two years.

The most common form of substance abuse amongst pilots may be alcohol usage. Alcohol usage affects the central nervous system and can impair reaction times, balance, coordination, reasoning and speech, and produce long-term effects such as dementia and relationship problems both at work and at home. The dangers associated with alcohol use by pilots is far-reaching and remains a public concern. The federal regulation prohibits any individual from acting or attempting to act as flight crew within eight hours of having alcohol or while having a blood-alcohol concentration (BAC) of 40mg or greater. Krauss and Li (2009) studied the frequency of reported incidents of alcohol abuse amongst pilots in US-based newspapers and found an significant increase of alcohol violation by pilots since 2001.

The National Transportation Safety Board (NTSB) conducted a study on drug-use trends (prescribed and over-the-counter) in aviation and the subsequent risk of pilot impairment (NTSB, 2014) and found that the overall risk of drug-related pilot impairment is increasing due to the growing use of potentially impairing drugs. Furthermore, they noted an increasing number of pilots flying without a medical certificate whilst using prescribed or over-the-counter drugs without periodic assessment with an aviation medical examiner.

### Organic mental disorders

Not all mental disorders may be related to psychiatric or psychological problems. Some disorders may produce dementia syndromes or produce cognitive defects that would be disqualifying for flying. These include Alzheimer's disease, Huntingdon's disease and Wilson's disease. Other conditions that may cause cognitive changes are metabolic disorders (thyroid disturbance, vitamin deficiencies and anoxia), chronic inflammatory conditions, head trauma and central nervous system infections to name a few. Toxic conditions may also be relevant to the airline environment including exposure to industrial agents, solvents and pollutants. These disorders are considered disqualifying by the FAA.

### Pilot suicide

Although there may be various ways to define suicide, it is generally agreed that a suicide is an act of intentionally ending one's life. The UK Department of Health published a report on suicide rates within the general population in the UK in February 2015 (Department of Health, 2015). There were 4727 suicides recorded in 2013. This corresponds to a total rate of 17.8 to 100,000 population. The majority of suicides occur in adult males, accounting for over three quarters (78 per cent) of all suicides in 2013. It is estimated that 1272 suicides were by people in contact with mental health services the year prior to committing suicide. The first ever comprehensive report on suicide across the world by the World Health Organization (2014) suggests that one person in the world dies by suicide every 40 seconds. The report concludes that suicide rates vary enormously from one country to another depending on the cultural, social, religious and economic environment in which people live and sometimes want to stop living.

Suicide by pilot refers to an aviation disaster in which pilots deliberately crash or attempt to crash an aircraft as a way to kill themselves (pilot suicide) and very occasionally passengers on board or people on the ground (pilot murder-suicide). In a systematic review of aircraft-assisted pilot suicides in the United States 2003–2012, the authors concluded that pilot suicides account for less than one percent of all aircraft fatalities (Lewis *et al.*, 2014) and the vast majority did not involve commercial flight operations. There have been six documented pilot murder-suicides involving commercial flights since 1982.

An aircraft crash is only classified as suicide when there is compelling evidence that the pilot was doing so and this will be established through a 'psychological post-mortem'. This may include a suicidal note, previous attempts, threats of suicide, or a history of mental illness. Not all incidents stem directly and exclusively from pilot mental illness. Other factors include occupational stress and conflict, relationship jeopardy, family bereavement, legal issues, financial problems, and diagnosis of illness (Kenedi *et al.*, 2016).

Cullen (1998) documented three cases of aviation-related suicide in the United Kingdom from 1970–1996. In a comparative analysis of suicide by aircraft, Bills and colleagues (2005) report 36 pilots committed, and one attempted, suicide by aircrafts. Of the 37 cases, all pilots were men and private pilots, with 36 resulting in pilot fatality and one resulting in a death to a passenger. Pre-existing domestic and social problems were noted as a contributing factor in 46 per cent of cases, followed by legal problems (41 per cent) and psychiatric conditions (38 per cent). This indicates that far smaller percentage of aviation-related suicides reported a history of psychiatric conditions in comparison to the 90 per cent of suicide victims believed to suffer from a psychiatric disorder at the time of their death.

*Psychological treatment for mental health problems*

There are various psychological and psychiatric treatments for pilot mental health problems. Whilst counselling and psychotherapy is less likely to disqualify the pilot from flying, the recovery may be slow and not all forms of treatment are equally effective. Psychotropic medications, on the other hand, may lead to a more rapid recovery but will generally disqualify the pilot from flying during and for at least six weeks after treatment. Depending on the severity and nature of the mental health issue, either one or both types may be needed for successful recovery.

Pilots may not always present to psychologists and psychiatrists for treatment. This may be due to a fear of jeopardising their licence and career by a visit or there may be a stigma associated with psychological problems. Stigma and fear can amplify some symptoms and create additional stress that would be avoidable. Furthermore, the pressure of loss of licence may lead some pilots to seek help outside of the aviation specialist field. This could lead to incorrect or misguided treatment, especially if there is no communication between the external professionals and an AME specialist.

Pilot peer support programmes have been mooted as an important step forwards to assist pilots with common and manageable mental health problems to obtain emotional support and to sign-post them to more specialist services should their condition warrant this. The effectiveness of such programmes is yet to be determined but it seems that pilots themselves welcome these services which must be a vital first step in an industry where pilots fear stigma and breaches of confidentiality. It is also central to reducing mental health stigma more generally within the airline industry.

## Looking ahead

This chapter has so far demonstrated that thorough and robust psychological assessment of mental health issues among pilots is possible, even if this is at times imprecise. The nearest to a gold standard we can highlight at the time of writing is to combine psychometric measures with the clinical interview with an appropriately qualified specialist and an understanding of the pilot's professional role and working environment, and to relate this to the pilot's personal, family, medical and work history.

Early identification of disruptive health threats can help pilots to deal with emerging issues before they affect psychological well-being. Occupational stress is increasingly recognised as a factor in health and safety. Following an incident that took place on 27 March 2012, where a pilot of a major commercial airline experienced a serious disturbance in his mental health, the Aerospace Medical Association formed an ad hoc working group on pilot mental health. The group recommended greater attention to be given to mental health issues by aeromedical examiners, especially to the more common and detectable mental health conditions and life stressors that can affect pilots and flight performance.

This could be achieved by increased education and global recognition of the importance of mental health in aviation safety (Aerospace Medical Association, 2012; 2016).

Sadly, the attention given to pilot metal health escalated again in the aftermath of the Germanwings incident in 2015. The BEA report of the incident (2016) clearly identified a deliberate act of destruction by one of the pilots and attributed this to mental health issues. They were unable to identify the specifics of the pilot's psychological history of assessment and treatment due to German privacy laws. EASA quickly formed a European taskforce and as we write are in the process of publishing and implementing a number of recommendations. Those most relevant to the assessment and treatment of mental health issues include:

- psychological evaluation for all pilots before they commence employment and as a formal part of the recurrent medical renewal – airlines will be required to ensure this has been satisfactory before offering employment;
- increasingly robust oversight and education for AMEs in psychological assessment and screening;
- implementation of pilot peer support networks;
- formal structures for sharing medical information about pilots that find an appropriate balance between sharing safety-critical information and protecting patient confidentiality.

Currently, these ideas are very much in their infancy, and as you will see from chapters later in this book, there is a significant amount of knowledge available to support those engaging in pilot assessment and screening and there are some fledgling peer support programmes in existence.

This book brings together theory and practice in the major elements of the assessment and screening of pilot mental health. As such, it provides a basis for the education and professional development of those involved in these processes and their oversight. We said at the beginning that we could not offer a single robust clinical tool capable of accurately predicting future psychological disturbance. The combination of tools presented in this book do, however, provide the foundation of best practice consistent with international regulation and recommendations.

## References

Abramowitz, J., Taylor, S., & McKay, D. (2009) Obsessive-compulsive disorder. *The Lancet*, 374, 9688, 491–499.

Aerospace Medical Association (2012) Pilot mental health: expert working group recommendations. *Aviation, Space & Environmental Medicine*, 83, 1184–5.

Aerospace Medical Association (2016) Co-author of: Pilot mental health: expert working group recommendations – Revised 2015. *Aerospace Medicine and Human Performance*, 87(5), 505–507.

American Psychiatric Association (2013) *Diagnostic and statistical manual of mental disorders* (5th edition). Arlington, VA: American Psychiatric Association.

APA (American Psychological Association) (2014) *Standards for educational and psychological testing*. Washington, D.C.: American Psychological Association.

BEA (Bureau d'Enquetes et d'Analyses pour la securite l'aviation civile) (2016) *Final report of the March 2015 accident of Airbus A320, D-AIPX*. https://www.bea.aero/uploads/tx_elydbrapports/BEA2015-0125.en-LR.pdf

Beck, A.T., Steer, R.A., & Brown, G.K. (1996) *Beck depression inventory, Second edition, manual*. San Antonia, TX: The Psychological Corporation.

Bills, C.B., Grabowski, J.G., & Li, G. (2005) Suicide by aircraft: a comparative analysis. *Aviation, Space and Environmental Medicine*, 76, 715–719.

Bor, R., & Hubbard, T. (eds) (2006) *Aviation mental health*. Aldershot: Ashgate.

Bor, R., Eriksen, C., & Oakes, M. (2009) *Overcome your fear of flying*. London: Sheldon Press.

British Psychological Society (2016) *Code of good practice for psychological testing*. Leicester: British Psychological Society.

Brown, T., Rushton, L., Schucher, L., Stevens, J., & Warren., F. (2001) *A consultation on the possible effects on health, comfort and safety of aircraft cabin environments*. Leicester: Institute for Environment and Health.

Butcher, J.N. (2002) Assessing pilots with 'the wrong stuff', a call for research on emotional health factors in commercial aviators. *International Journal of Selection and Assessment*, 10(1–2), 168–184.

Butcher, J.N., Moffit, R.C., Rouse, S.V., & Holden, R.R. (1997) Reducing MMPI-2 defensiveness: the effect of specialized instructions on retest validity in a job applicant sample. *Journal of Personality Assessment*, 62(2), 385–401.

Butcher, J.N., Dahlstrom, W.G., Graham, J.R., Tellegen, A., & Kaemmer, B. (2001)*The Minnesota multiphasic personality inventory-2 (MMPI-2): manual for administration and scoring*. Minneapolis, MN: University of Minnesota Press.

Caldwell, J. (1997) Fatigue in the aviation environment: an overview of the cause and affect as well as recommended countermeasures. *Aviation, Space & Environmental Medicine*, 68, 932–938.

Caldwell, J.A. (2012) Crew schedules, sleep deprivation and aviation performance. *Current Directions in Psychological Science*, 21(2), 85–90.

Cooper, C., & Sloan, S. (1985) Occupational and psychological stress among commercial airline pilots. *Journal of Occupational Medicine*, 27, 570–576.

Cullen, S.A. (1998) Aviation suicide: a review of general aviation accidents in the UK, 1970–96. *Aviation, Space and Environmental Medicine*, 69(7), 696–698.

Department of Health (2015) *Statistical update on suicide*. London: Office for National Statistics.

Doehrmann, O., Ghosh, S.S., Polli, F.E., Reynolds, G.O., Horn, F., *et al.* (2013) Predicting treatment response in social anxiety disorder from functional magnetic resonance imaging. *Journal of the American Medical Association, Psychiatry*, 70(1), 87–97.

EASA (n.d.) Air Crew. https://www.easa.europa.eu/easa-and-you/aircrew-and-medical/aircrew

Eriksen, C. (2009) *Managing work and relationships at 35,000 feet*. London: Karnac.

FAA (2016) Guide for aviation medical examiners. http://www.faa.gov/about/office_org/headquarters_offices/avs/offices/aam/ame/guide/media/guide.pdf

Forman, F., Bor, R., & Van Gerwen, L. (2006) Flight or fright? Psychological approaches to the treatment of fear of flying. In R. Bor & T. Hubbard (eds), *Aviation mental health*. Aldershot: Ashgate.

Girodo, M. (1988) The psychological health and stress of pilots in a labor dispute. *Aviation, Space and Environmental Medicine*, 59(6), 505–510.

Goldberg, D., & Hillier, V. (1979) A scaled version of the General Health Questionnaire. *Psychological Medicine* 9(1), 139–145.

Gradwell, D.P. & Rainford, D.J. (eds) (2016) *Ernsting's aviation and space medicine* (5th edition). Boca Raton, FL: CRC Press.

Grant, B., Hasin, D., Stinson, F., Dawson, D., Goldstein, R., Smith, S., Huang, B., & Saha, T. (2006) The epidemiology of DSM-IV panic disorder and agoraphobia in the United States: results from the National Epidemiologic Survey on Alcohol and Related Conditions. *Journal of Clinical Psychiatry*, 67(3), 363–374.

Grossman, A., Barenboim, E., Azaria, B., Sherer, Y., & Goldstein, L. (2004) Oral drug therapy for erectile dysfunction: an overview and aeromedical implications. *Aviation, Space and Environmental Medicine*, 75(11), 997–1000.

Harris, D. (2002). Drinking and flying: causes, effects and the development of effective countermeasures. *Human Factors in Aerospace Safety*, 2(4), 297–317.

Hathaway, A., Boals, A., & Banks, J. (2010) PTSD symptoms and dominant emotional response to a traumatic event: an examination of DSM-IV criteria. *Anxiety, Stress, & Coping*, 23, 119–126.

Jamieson, J., Mendes, W., & Nock, M. (2013) Improving acute stress responses: the power of reappraisal. *Current Directions in Psychological Science*, 22(1), 51–56.

Jones, D., & Ireland, R. (2004) Aeromedical regulations of aviators using selective seretonin reuptake inhibitors for depressive disorder. *Aviation, Space and Environmental Medicine*, 75(5), 461–470.

Jones, D., Katchen, M., Patterson, J., & Rea, M. (1997) Aerospace psychiatry. In R. De Hart (ed), *Fundamentals of aerospace medicine*. Baltimore, MD: Williams & Wilkins.

Karlins, M., Koss, F., & McCully, L. (1989) The spousal factor in pilot stress. *Aviation, Space & Environmental Medicine*, 60, 1112–1115.

Kenedi, C., Friedman, H., Watson, D., & Preitner, C. (2016) Suicide and murder-suicide involving aircraft. *Aerospace Medicine and Human Performance*, 87(4), 388–396.

Kessler, R., Berglund, P., Demler, O., Jin, R., Koretz, D., & Merikangas, K. (2003) The epidemiology of major depressive disorder: results from the National Comorbidity Survey Replication (NCS-R). *Journal of the American Medical Association*, 289, 3095–3105.

Krauss, C., & Li, G. (2006) Pilot alcohol violations reported in U.S. newspapers 1990–2006. *Aviation, Space & Environmental Medicine*, 77, 1288–1290.

Levy, D., Faulkner, G., & Dixon, R. (1984) Work and family interactions: the dual career family of the flight attendant. *Journal of Social Relations*, 11, 67–88.

Lewis, R., Forster E., Whinnery, J., & Webster, N. (2014) *Aircraft assisted pilot suicides in the United States 2003–2012*. Oklahoma City, OK: Civil Aerospace Medical Institute, Federal Aviation Administration.

Little, L., Gaffney, I., Rosen, K., & Bender, M. (1990) Corporate instability is related to airline pilots stress symptoms. *Aviation, Space & Environmental Medicine*, 61, 977–982.

Mearers, K., & Freeston, M. (2012) *Overcoming Worry*. London: Robinson.

Morey, L.C. (2007) *Personality Assessment Inventory (PAI) professional manual* (2nd edition). Odessa, FL: Psychological Assessment Resources.

Morse, J., & Bor, R. (2006) Psychiatric disorders and syndromes among pilots. In R. Bor & T. Hubbard (eds), *Aviation mental health*. Aldershot: Ashgate.

NICE (2016) Depression. https://www.nice.org.uk/guidance/conditions-and-diseases/mental-health-and-behavioural-conditions/depression?unlid=688302217201611905717

NTSB (National Transportation Safety Board) (2014), *Drug use trends in aviation: assessing the risk of pilot impairment*. Safety Study NTSB/SS-14/01. Washington, DC: NTSB.

Oakes, M., Bor, R., & Eriksen, C. (2012) *Coping successfully with shyness and social anxiety.* London: Sheldon Press.

Parsons, T.D., & Rizzo, A.A. (2008) Affective outcomes of virtual reality exposure therapy for anxiety and specific phobias: a meta-analysis. *Journal of Behavior Therapy and Experimental Psychiatry,* 39, 250–261.

Raschmann, J., Patterson, J., & Schofield, G. (1990) A retrospective study of marital discord in pilots. The USAFSAM experience. *Aviation, Space & Environmental Medicine,* 61, 1145–1148.

Richards, P., Cleland, J., & Zuckerman, J. (2006) Psychological factors relating to physical health issues: how physical factors in aviation affect psychological functioning. In R. Bor and T. Hubbard (eds), *Aviation mental health.* Aldershot: Ashgate.

Rigg, R., & Cosgrove, M. (1994) Aircrew wives and the intermittent husband syndrome. *Aviation, Space and Environmental Medicine,* 65, 654–660.

Silove, D., & Manicavasagar, V. (2009) *Overcoming panic and agoraphobia.* London: Robinson.

Sloan, S., & Cooper, C. (1986) *Pilots Under Stress.* London: Routledge & Kegan Paul.

Smallwood, T. (2000) *The airline training pilot.* Aldershot: Ashgate.

Spitzer, R.L., Kroenke, K., & Williams, J.B. (1999) Validation and utility of a self-report version of PRIME-MD: the PHQ primary care study. Primary Care Evaluation of Mental Disorders. Patient Health Questionnaire. *Journal of the American Medical Association,* 282, 1737–1744.

Steptoe, A., & Bostock, S. (2011) *A survey of fatigue and wellbeing among commercial airline pilots.* Unpublished survey commissioned by BALPA. University of London Psychology Group.

Taylor, R., Morrice, K., Clark, D., & McCann, K. (1985) The psycho-social consequences of intermittent husband absence: an epidemiological study. *Social Science and Medicine,* 20(9), 877–885.

Transport Canada (2007) Personnel licensing and training. https://www.tc.gc.ca/eng/ civilaviation/regserv/cars/part4-standards-t42402-1412.htm

Tyrer, P., & Baldwin, D. (2006) Generalised anxiety disorder. *Lancet,* 368(9553), 2156–2166.

Veale, D., & Wilson, R. (2009a) *Overcoming health anxiety.* London: Robinson.

Veale, D., & Wilson, R. (2009b) *Overcoming obsessive compulsive disorder.* London: Robinson.

Wood, J.M., Garb, H.N., Lilienfeld, S.O., & Nezworski, M. (2002) Clinical assessment. *Annual Review of Psychology,* 53, 519–543.

World Health Organisation (1992) *International classification of diseases: classification scheme for mental and behavioural disorders* (10th edition). Geneva: WHO.

World Health Organization (2014) *Preventing suicide: a global imperative.* Geneva: WHO.

# Part I
# Pilot selection assessments

# 2 Pilot selection

## An overview of aptitude and ability assessment

*Monica Martinussen*

## Introduction

Few psychological tests have been left untried when it comes to pilot selection, and few occupational groups have been so extensively studied as pilots (Carretta & Ree, 2003; Hilton & Dolgin, 1991; Hunter & Burke, 1995; Martinussen, 2010; Paullin *et al.*, 2006). There are probably several reasons for this, one of which is the military importance pilots have played since WWI. Furthermore, successful selection is associated with reduced training costs and improved operational readiness (Hunter, 1989). In the case of civil aviation, training costs may also be a factor in addition to increased safety and passenger satisfaction. From a more long-term perspective, other organizational outcomes such as engaged and satisfied workers, effective leadership and reduced turnover are desired outcomes of a successful selection and training process (Sackett & Lievens, 2008).

The selection process usually involves a step-wise procedure, whereby the assessment of a large number of abilities and characteristics is evaluated using different types of methods such as tests, interviews, simulator performance and an assessment center. Aptitude for flying has been defined by Carretta and Ree (2003) as encompassing both 'innate and acquired capabilities' and, in principle, may include cognitive abilities, psychomotor skills and knowledge, as well as personal and social skills. This chapter will focus on ability assessments for pilot candidates. The use of non-cognitive skills in the selection process, including personality traits, will be addressed in Chapter 8, and the important distinction between select-in versus select-out processes, based on mental health problems, is outlined in later chapters.

For the most part, military selection involves so-called *ab-initio* pilots (without any prior experience); whereas commercial airlines often prefer to hire experienced pilots but may also select *ab-initio* pilots, providing the initial training themselves (e.g., Lufthansa and KLM). In both types of selection, the less expensive methods are usually implemented first with the larger applicant group, while the more expensive and time-consuming methods are used later in the process when fewer applicants remain to be tested. Figure 2.1 presents an example of how an *ab-initio* selection process is conducted, illustrating the different stages or steps involved.

The first step usually includes different types of formal requirements related to such things as educational level and health, in addition to a background screening. Those who qualify past the first step are invited to the initial testing, which often includes simple measures of general mental ability, in addition to tests measuring more specific cognitive abilities such as spatial ability, mathematical and mechanical reasoning, and language skills. Usually, for those who pass this first phase, more advanced and time-consuming tests/ methods are then administered. These are frequently computer-based and may assess, for instance, psychomotor ability and multi-tasking in addition to more specific cognitive abilities. The candidates may also complete tests of aviation knowledge and personality measures as part of the selection process. The last step often involves some form of interview that may be more or less structured. In addition to impressions formed during the interview, information collected at earlier stages in the selection process may form the basis for a final decision about whether or not the candidate should be accepted. In many cases only between 5 and 10 percent of the applicants for *ab-initio* pilot selection are finally accepted and able to start basic flight training (Martinussen & Torjussen, 2004).

When selecting pilots who have already completed basic training, the airlines may initially place more weight on type of experience, certificates, references and flying hours, but may also supplement such requirements with the results of psychological testing, simulator performance and interviews. Not all commercial airlines will use psychological tests as part of their selection process when hiring pilots, and some may rely more on previous experience and impressions formed during the interview. The final decision whether or not to accept a candidate is usually based on different types of information including test results and perceived organizational fit, motivation and potential.

The various methods mentioned above have different predictive validities (how well they predict pilot performance), and they also vary in relation to cost and time efficiency. The utility of any selection process depends on many factors including the predictive validity of the methods used (see, e.g., Schmidt & Hunter, 1998), the selection ratio (proportion of the applicant group that will be selected) and the base rate (quality of the applicants). Based on these parameters

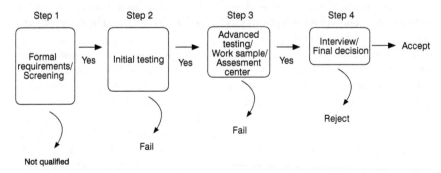

*Figure 2.1* Selection system

it is possible to calculate the added value of using a selection system in terms of increase in correct decisions or increase in performance. It is also possible to calculate the financial gain, in which case the costs of the selection system and the value of a good pilot versus a candidate that, for example, fails training, need to be considered. Examples of such calculations have been described by Goeters and Maschke (2002) for commercial aviation and by Hunter and Burke (1995) for military aviation.

## How to measure?

A large number of abilities and skills may be relevant when selecting pilots, all of which may also be measured by several methods; e.g., paper-and-pencil tests, computer-based assessments and work sample tests. Regardless of the construct measured or the assessment method used, it is important to ensure high-quality assessments as specified by various professional guidelines; for instance, those from the European Federation of Psychologists' Association (EFPA, 2013) or those cited in the Standards for Educational and Psychological Testing, developed by the American Educational Research Association and the American Psychological Association (2014). These standards emphasize the importance of using reliable and valid measures, appropriate norms in addition to considering aspects such as fairness and applicant reactions to testing for selection purposes. The International Air Transport Association (IATA, 2010) has also published guidance materials for pilot aptitude testing based on a worldwide survey of 66 organizations.

### Estimating reliability

Reliability refers to the extent to which a test measures consistently with little measurement error, and is a necessary but insufficient condition for validity. Within Classical Test Theory it is defined as the correlation ($r$) between two parallel tests (Magnusson, 1967). A correlation coefficient is an index that varies between $-1.0$ and $+1.0$, whereby the number indicates the strength of the association, and the sign ($+/-$) of the direction of the association. A correlation of 0 means that there is no association between the variables, while a correlation of $-1.0$ or $1.0$ indicates a perfect association between variables in which all points form a straight line. Test reliability may be estimated in several ways, for example by computing the test-retest reliability or by estimating the internal consistency (e.g., Cronbach's alpha). Test-retest reliability indicates stability over time and is frequently used for tests conducted under time constraints. Other forms of reliability provide information about the internal consistency (split-half and Cronbach's alpha) or consistency across versions (parallel form). The calculated correlations should be as high as possible, preferably .70 or .80; however, lower values may sometimes be accepted. More modern test theory, including IRT (Item Response Theory), may use other approaches for estimating reliability (see, e.g., Thompson, 2003). A more general definition of test reliability is the ratio of *true variance* over *observed variance*. The observed variance includes true variance as well as random or occasionally systematic error. Many factors may influence test reliability, some of which include standardized ways of administering and scoring the test, the number of items, and other aspects related to the applicant such as motivation or fatigue.

## Test validity

There are different types and aspects of test validity that may be examined in empirical studies. Construct validity signifies the extent to which it is possible to document that a test actually measures the intended construct; e.g., perceptual speed or memory. A validation study to assess the construct validity of a test may include an analysis of the factor structure of the test to see if it matches the underlying theory or model. Another approach may be to examine the correlations with other measures of the same construct. Another type of test validity is predictive validity, meaning the extent to which a test may be used to predict future performance, such as pilot performance or pilot training success rate. This is particularly important when using a test or method for personnel selection. Predictive validity, which is typically reported as a correlation coefficient ($r$), is often examined by comparing test results with subsequent criteria of work or training performance. When interpreting such test results, one may use the rules of thumb outlined by Cohen (1988), whereby a small correlation is .10, medium .30 and large .50. However, the context and methodological factors that may influence the size of the correlation, such as poor reliability or range restriction, should also be considered (Hunter & Schmidt, 2003). It is important that the validation study consists of a sufficient sample size to ensure adequate statistical power. For estimating the combined predictive validity of many tests or predictors, multiple regression analysis or logistic regression is frequently used depending on the type of criterion used (continuous or dichotomous).

## Norms

In order to compare an applicant's test performance with that of other applicants, the raw score is frequently converted into something that may be easier to use and communicate; e.g., T-scores ($M = 50$, $SD = 10$) or Stanine scores ($M = 5.0$, $SD \approx 2.0$). The raw score itself has little meaning unless it is compared to something, e.g., developmental level or a well-known comparison group. In order to do so, it is important to have a norm group that is relevant to the use of the test. For pilot selection, norms should be based on the applicant group whenever possible. Relating the applicant's score to norms based on the general population or norms from other countries may not be correct, thus providing a biased picture of the applicant's performance.

# Methodological problems in validation studies

Hunter and Schmidt (2003) have described a number of factors or circumstances that may affect the size of the observed correlation or validity coefficient. Three such statistical sources of error are lack of criterion reliability, restriction of range, and the use of a dichotomous criterion (e.g., pass/fail) rather than a continuous measure. The lower the score reliability is, the lower the observed correlation will be. It is possible to correct for this artifact if the reliability of the criterion is known (Hunter & Schmidt, 2003). The test or predictor reliability will also influence the observed validity coefficient; however, predictor reliability is not normally corrected in selection research, as the primary interest is to examine the predictive validity of the test with its actual flaws and shortcomings. The second factor that affects the size of the correlation is reduced test score variation (restriction of range) on one or both variables as a result of the selection process. This type of problem involves missing data, whereby the control group has been eliminated on the basis of test results or other predictors. If only the best half of the applicant group has been selected, then it will only be possible to collect criterion data for this half of the group. The calculated correlation will be much lower for this group than if we had studied the entire applicant group, including those who were not selected. The effect on the observed correlation can be dramatic, given that a very small percentage of the applicant group is usually accepted when it comes to pilot selection.

The correction for range restriction is based on information about the test score standard deviation in the whole group compared to that of the selected group or information about the proportion of applicants selected (Hunter & Schmidt, 2003). When the selection is based on several tests, or tests used in combination with other types of information, the situation becomes more complicated, requiring the application of more advanced models for range restriction correction (Lawley, 1943; Johnson & Ree, 1994; Sackett & Yang, 2000).

The third statistical artifact is the application of a dichotomous criterion (e.g., pass/fail in training) when the performance (flying skills) may be viewed as a continuous variable. This artifact also leads to a lower correlation between test and criterion than if we had measured performance on a continuous scale. This statistical artifact can be corrected if the distribution between the pass/fail ratio is known. The further away from a 50/50 distribution of pass/fail, the greater the correction.

Validation studies may differ in terms of these three statistical errors or biases which, in turn, will reduce the size of the observed correlation. It is possible to correct for one or more of them, provided the necessary information is available in the primary studies. Therefore, results from validation studies are often reported in terms of both corrected and uncorrected correlations.

## Job analysis

The first phase in designing a selection system is frequently a job analysis in order to determine what skills, abilities and personal qualifications are important for optimal job performance. A job analysis may be conducted in several ways involving various techniques that may be used for this purpose (see, e.g., Wilson, 2007). It often involves the use of highly experienced and skilled workers, who may be observed or interviewed to obtain information about work content and the abilities or skills needed to successfully perform the tasks of the job. The results of a job analysis can be used both to select predictors and to determine criteria for work performance that may be used in a validation study. One example of a job analysis method is the Critical Incident Technique, developed by Flanagan to map the job performance of fighter pilots during WWII (Flanagan, 1954). The main purpose of this method is to identify behavioral examples of good and poor performance on critical tasks. Experts must agree on what these critical tasks are in addition to the characteristics of good and poor work performance. The work proceeds by sorting task descriptions in order to create categories. There may be many tasks that require teamwork and many that require the ability to perform calculations. Another technique is the Job Analysis Survey (Fleischman, 1975), in which employees are asked to rate the extent to which different abilities, personality traits and skills are relevant to job performance. There are a total of seven main areas that respondents are asked to consider in addition to sub-categories. For example, cognitive ability includes a total of 21 sub-categories such as spatial orientation, time-sharing and attention; whereas psychomotor abilities consists of 10 sub-categories. Fleischman's job analysis method has been used in several studies of pilots including one of commercial pilots ($N = 141$) for Lufthansa (Goeters *et al.*, 2004), in which a few new scales were added to the original system. Many of the cognitive abilities on the list were described as relevant or highly relevant; e.g., time-sharing, spatial orientation, selective attention, perceptual speed, number facility (quick and accurate calculation), memorization and visualization. In terms of psychomotor abilities factors, such as rate control, control precision, response orientation, multi-limb coordination and reaction time were rated as relevant or very relevant. None of the physical abilities were rated as relevant or very relevant, but some of the sensory abilities and skills, like reading plans and map-reading, were rated as relevant or very relevant to the work of an airline pilot (Goeters *et al.*, 2004). Many of the interactive and social skills were also given a high rating.

For military pilots, a revised version of the Fleischman method was used in a NATO study (Carretta *et al.*, 1993) where pilots from several countries were asked to assess 12 critical tasks specific to the job of fighter pilot. They were then asked to specify and rank the abilities and skills that were important when conducting these tasks. The most important abilities chosen were situational awareness, memorization, achievement motivation, reasoning and perceptual speed. Least important were written expression and comprehension, in addition to leadership (Carretta *et al.*, 1993). The study of NATO pilots was included in a review by Damos (2011), the purpose of which was to determine Knowledge, Skills, Abilities and Other traits (KSAOs) needed for successful performance as a military pilot. The review was based on nine studies, seven of which were conducted using Fleishman's method (Fleishman & Reilly, 2001). The categories for some of the studies included in the review had been modified and new abilities and skills had been added to the original taxonomy. Moreover, definitions had been changed and composite abilities were created (e.g., situational awareness). One problem with this approach, as noted by Damos (2011), was the lack of consistency in defining abilities across studies, which made it difficult to integrate and compare the nine located studies. Spatial orientation and perceptual speed were given a high rating by subject-matter experts in many of the studies included in the review (Damos, 2011). Numerical ability, mechanical aptitude, multi-tasking, multi-limb coordination, selective attention and situational awareness were also mentioned in some of the studies; however, sometimes given differing definitions and mixed support (Damos, 2011).

Many of the cognitive and psychomotor abilities listed in the job analyses are measured in the test batteries normally used for pilot selection (Hunter & Burke, 1995); however, one has to wonder if these abilities will be important for tomorrow's pilots as well. It is naturally difficult to predict what the future will bring, but DLR (The German Aerospace Center) completed a project in 2009, where they indeed tried to picture the aviator in 2030 (Eißfeldt *et al.*, 2009). Both pilots and Air Traffic Controllers (ATCOs) were used as experts who participated in workshops trying to predict future Air Traffic Management (ATM) scenarios in addition to performing simulations of simple tasks. Job analyses were used to determine changes in the abilities and skills required to perform the job well. Many cognitive abilities were rated as important or more important for pilots of the future. Some changes were noted; for instance, an increase in the importance of deductive reasoning and a decrease in the importance of number facility (calculations). Furthermore, visual color discrimination was expected to be more important in addition to increased resilience (social/personal skills).

The results from a job analysis may be used to select specific tests to be administered during the selection process and may also be applied when determining appropriate criteria for work performance which, in turn, may be used in a validation study. Many would argue, therefore, that a job analysis is an important and necessary first step in the selection process. However, meta-analyses have demonstrated that cognitive ability tests more or less predict job performance regardless of the occupation (Schmidt & Hunter, 1998), perhaps suggesting that a very detailed job analysis may not be required for pilot selection. On the other hand, job analyses of pilots and air traffic controllers have demonstrated the importance of a number of highly specialized cognitive skills, for which a test of general intelligence may not provide an adequate measure.

# Predictors and criteria of work performance

## Predictors

The methods used to select applicants are identified as predictors, while measures of work performance are labeled as criteria. As indicated in previous job analyses, cognitive and psychomotor abilities are highly relevant to successful performance. The best way to measure such abilities is through standardized tests. Although some tests that are designed for completely different purposes may measure cognitive abilities in general, they may not necessarily be suitable for pilot selection. Many of the tests used in the selection of pilots have been developed specifically for this profession. Test development has reflected, to some extent, contemporary theories of intelligence within the psychometric tradition (Kline, 1991). Early test development was inspired by Charles Spearman (1904), who focused on general mental ability (*g*), whereby every test measured both *g* along with some specific ability; e.g., spatial or numerical ability. Thurstone's theory (1938) on seven primary abilities, in which focus was placed on measuring a variety of aptitudes, has inspired many of the test batteries developed since WWII. More contemporary theories of intelligence outline a hierarchy of abilities with a common *g*-factor in addition to eight broader factors (e.g., fluid and crystallized intelligence), followed by more specific factors at the third level or stratum (Carroll, 1993). This implies that a test of spatial ability, for example, will also measure the *g*-factor in addition to more specific factors.

## Criteria of work performance

Work performance, as assessed by flight instructor evaluation or academic grades from basic flight training, may be used as criteria when validating the selection process. Regardless of the type of criterion, it is important that it is measured in a reliable way and that it measures the intended outcome; e.g., pilot performance (construct validity). One may also argue that it is important for the criterion to represent something relevant to the organization; e.g., in military *ab-initio* selection it is important that candidates pass initial flight training, as candidates who fail training constitute a considerable expense. It is easy to argue that this criterion is important to the organization, even if it does not represent the ultimate and more long-term goal of predicting work performance as a fighter pilot. In validation studies, an overall criterion of work performance is frequently used. For many jobs, one can argue that this is not adequate and that it would be more reasonable to apply multiple criteria to describe actual job performance (see, e.g., Sackett & Lievens, 2008). With multiple criteria, the validation effort becomes more complicated, leaving room for the possibility that different predictors may not predict all criteria equally well.

In many cases, instructors or superiors are used to assess performance, and it is important that such ratings are reliable. One way to assess reliability would be to allow two instructors to evaluate the same candidates and then study the degree of agreement between them. There are a number of known errors or cognitive biases in such personal evaluations; for example, if an individual is good at one task or activity, it is automatically assumed that he or she performs other tasks equally well (the halo effect). It may also be difficult to ensure that observers will use the entire scale; i.e., all performance may be assessed as average, or there may be little variation between different items rated for each applicant. In order to achieve consistent inter-rater reliability, it is important to train the observers, and to specify what constitutes good and poor work performance, preferably with a well-defined rating scale.

## Evidence-based practice in selection

In medicine and clinical psychology the principle of evidence-based practice is widely accepted (Sackett *et al.*, 1996; Levant, 2005). This means that the choice of treatment should be based on the best available research evidence and clinical expertise, including a critical evaluation of the evidence, and should also take into consideration the client's or patient's characteristics, culture and preferences. High-quality studies may not always be available for all types of problems or client groups, and sometimes decisions about the treatment will have to be based on other types of knowledge, including studies with poorer methodological quality, theory or clinical experience.

If we apply these principles to pilot selection, an evidence-based practice should be based on the best available research evidence and expertise in personnel selection, in addition to considering both the applicant and the needs of the organization selecting the pilots (see Figure 2.2).

Ideally, when choosing a selection system and the predictors to be used, decisions should be based on research evidence documenting the predictive validity of the tests or methods used. This could be based on results from a local

*Figure 2.2* Evidence-based practice

validation study with a sufficiently large sample, carefully selected predictors and criteria based on a job analysis. However, this may not always be possible as organizations may not have the resources or sample sizes available to conduct a high-quality validation study. Another option would be to rely on validation studies from other countries and companies or systematic reviews and meta-analyses of validation studies. A meta-analysis is a quantitative way of summarizing findings from a large number of studies. Typically, a validation study will report the results in terms of correlation coefficients. Correlation coefficients may be combined using meta-analytical techniques, the main result of which is a mean weighted correlation coefficient. In addition, meta-analyses may be used to study variation between studies in order to determine if the findings may be generalized across different types of countries and organizations. This requires a sufficient number of validation studies in order to accurately examine the effect of so-called moderators or variables that may influence the size of the correlation coefficient. There are different types of meta-analysis traditions, but the methods most commonly used to summarize validation coefficients are based on the work of Hunter and Schmidt (2003). The available evidence should be evaluated, in terms of findings (effect sizes), the quality of the evidence and the relevance to the current selection situation. More modern approaches to validity generalization outline how evidence from local validation studies may be combined with meta-analytic findings when estimating validity (Murphy, 2003).

Furthermore, selection expertise involves comprehensive knowledge of how to administer tests and interpret the results in addition to a full understanding of their limitations. The selection procedure should also consider fairness and cultural appropriateness as well as the rights and reactions of the applicant and, finally, the needs of the organization selecting pilots or students for pilot training.

## How well do the different methods work?

When it comes to pilots, a large number of validation studies have been conducted since WWI. Several literature reviews have been conducted (see, for example, Carretta & Ree, 2003; Hunter, 1989; Paullin *et al.*, 2006) in addition to two large-scale meta-analyses (Hunter & Burke, 1994; Martinussen, 1996). Two other meta-analyses were conducted with more limited scopes of summarizing personality trait findings (Campbell *et al.*, 2010), and comparing single and multiple task measures (Damos, 1993). Despite procedural differences in the two larger meta-analyses conducted, and the fact that they were based on slightly different samples, these two meta-analyses resulted in very similar findings. The meta-analysis from 1996 was based on 50 studies and a total of 66 independent samples (Martinussen, 1996). The studies were conducted in 11 different nations with approximately 50 percent from the US. The median sample size was 196 and the median year of publication was 1973 (range 1919–1993). Most of the subjects were military pilots and 67 per cent reported results from fixed-wing flying. An overview of the average correlations for the different test and predictor categories is presented in Table 2.1.

*Table 2.1* Meta-analysis results for tests used for predicting a global criterion of pilot performance (based on Martinussen, 1996)

| Tests/predictors | N | K | Mean r uncorrected | Mean r corrected | 90% CV |
|---|---|---|---|---|---|
| General intelligence tests | 15,403 | 26 | .13 | .16 | .03 |
| Cognitive ability tests (e.g., mechanical or spatial abilities) | 17,900 | 35 | .22 | .24 | .07 |
| Psychomotor/information process | 8,522 | 29 | .20 | .24 | .10 |
| Combined index (several sub-tests) | 5,362 | 14 | .31 | .37 | .19 |
| Aviation information | 3,736 | 16 | .22 | .24 | .14 |
| Academic grades | 4,267 | 9 | .15 | .15 | .11 |
| Training experience (flying) | 5,806 | 10 | .25 | .30 | .07 |
| Personality measures | 6,304 | 21 | .13 | .14 | .00 |
| Biographical inventory | 11,347 | 13 | .21 | .23 | .00 |

*Note.* N = total sample size, K = number of correlations, Mean r corrected = mean weighted correlation corrected for dichotomization, 90% CV = lower 90% credibility value.

The uncorrected mean correlations varied between .13 and .31. The only correction possible was for dichotomization (pass/fail in training), which some studies had used as a criterion; however, correction for criterion reliability or restriction of range was not done due to missing information in the primary studies. All categories of cognitive ability and psychomotor tests predicted pilot performance, and the lower end of the respective credibility intervals did not include zero. This would suggest that the tests predicted pilot performance even if there was significant variation between studies. More specific cognitive ability tests (e.g., spatial ability, mechanical comprehension or attention) had a higher mean validity than tests measuring general mental ability or intelligence. The best predictive validity contained the category of combined indexes, with a predictor that combined both cognitive and psychomotor abilities (mean $r_u = .31$, mean $r_c = .37$). Other types of predictors include previous training experience and information about aviation, with mean correlations between .25 (mean $r_c = .30$) and .22 (mean $r_c = .24$). Personality measures had a relatively low mean validity coefficient of .13 (mean $r_c = 14$), and the lower end of the credibility interval included zero, indicating that these measures may fail to predict pilot performance in some situations. It is also important to note that these validation coefficients represent conservative estimates of the true validity, as they are not corrected for the most important statistical artifacts.

The meta-analysis by Hunter and Burke (1994) was based on a total of 68 studies published between 1940 and 1990, including a total sample of 437,258 participants. Those who are interested in the predictive validity for specific abilities should consult the original article by Hunter and Burke (1994), as it contained more sub-categories for cognitive and psychomotor tests than the analysis by Martinussen (1996). For all test categories in the Hunter and Burke analysis (1994) there was some true variation between studies; and for the categories of general intelligence, verbal skills, fine motor ability, age, education and personality, the credibility interval included zero, implying that the predictive validity in some situations was zero. This means that, for the other categories, the predictive validity was greater than zero even though there was some true variance between studies. The two meta-analyses were consistent in their findings that tests measuring more specific cognitive or psychomotor abilities had higher predictive validity than tests measuring general mental ability.

The meta-analysis by Damos (1993) compared multiple task performance to single task performance based on 14 and 12 different studies, respectively. Both types of measures were predictive of flight performance with mean uncorrected validities of .23 (multiple task performance) and .18 (single task). The types of test (single and multiple task performance) included in the meta-analysis correspond to the category of psychomotor/information processing in the Martinussen meta-analysis (1996), which was based on 29 studies and had a mean uncorrected validity of .20. The findings from Damos (1993) and Martinussen (1996) were based on different samples and conducted with different meta-analysis methods; nonetheless, they resulted in highly similar findings.

One limitation with three of the four meta-analyses conducted so far is that they are more than 20 years old. Consequently, they probably include very few computer-based tests as many of the primary studies are also quite old. Furthermore, these meta-analyses are heavily biased towards military pilot selection and training criteria as very few validation studies based on commercial pilot selection have been published. In other words, a new and updated meta-analysis is long overdue. Some more recent validation studies conducted have examined computer-based assessment. A study of the computer-based assessment system for the Norwegian Air Force (Martinussen & Torjussen, 2004) included a total of 13 tests administered in step three of the selection process (see Figure 2.1). The combined test score (unit-weighted) was significantly correlated with pass/fail in training ($N = 108$), and the predictive validity was .26. The correlations between individual tests and pass/fail varied from .01 to .22, some significantly (.02–.31 corrected for multi-variate range restriction). Carretta and colleagues have conducted several validation studies for predicting military pilot performance (Carretta, 2000; Carretta, 2011; Carretta *et al.*, 2014). The selection for the US Air Force is based on a weighted composite (Pilot Candidate Selection Method [PCSM] score) which includes the results of the Air Force Officer Qualifying Test (AFOQT), the Test of Basic Aviation Skills (TBAS) and prior flying experience (Carretta, 2011). The TBAS is a computer-administered test battery with a total of eight cognitive and perceptual-motor tests designed for pilot selection. A validation study ($N = 883$) examined the predictive validity of both the different parts of the selection system and combinations of predictors against pass/fail in training. The TBAS was .22 correlated with pass/fail ($r_c$ = .42, fully corrected for range restriction and dichotomization). A recent study by DLR (German Aerospace Center) of approximately 400 applicants indicated that the correlations between individual tests and pass/fail in training varied from .01–.12 (uncorrected), some significantly, and that the multiple *R* was .14 (uncorrected) for all eight tests (Zierke, 2014). The test battery included tests measuring concentration, memory, quantitative ability and spatial orientation. The computer-based tests are used as part of a more comprehensive selection system (Zierke, 2014).

## Fairness, cultural issues and applicant reactions

Pilots are often recruited from countries and cultures outside the normal place of operation and recruitment (Damos *et al.*, 2015). This raises many issues including the topic of fairness, which is frequently understood as the extent to which the tests have the same predictive validity for both the majority and the minority within a selection group (Rothstein & McDaniel, 1992). In many cases tests that are used have been developed and validated in one cultural context and then administered in a language that is foreign to the candidate. This may leave some candidates at a disadvantage, and there is the added risk that the tests may measure not only the intended ability but also the language proficiency to some degree. There are a few studies that have examined the hypothesis of differential validity for pilot selection tests. Results comparing the predictive validity of two test batteries, AFOQT and TBAS, for candidates born in the US versus those born outside the US indicated that the cognitive ability tests also predicted performance for candidates born outside the US; furthermore, the correlation coefficients were generally somewhat higher among the minority than among the majority (Damos *et al.*, 2015). Another study of US Air Force applicants found no gender difference in the test's predictive validity in relation to flight performance (Carretta, 1997). One problem with examining fairness and differential validity is that the sample sizes for the minority group are usually very small, making analyses and comparisons between groups difficult. The fact that there are few findings that indicate differential validity for pilot selection tests so far does not mean that the problem should be ignored, and the issue is still debated within the realm of personnel selection (Berry *et al.*, 2011). For more information, international guidelines for translating and using tests in other countries/cultures should be consulted (EFPA, 2013).

### *Applicant reactions*

Another aspect of examining the predictive validity of a test is to consider the selection process from the applicant's perspective. How does the individual perceive the selection methods, and what kind of impression does he or she get from the organization on the basis of the selection process? There are several studies that examine what the applicants or volunteers (often students) think about different methods, such as ability tests, personality tests or interviews. Two studies of pilot applicants examined what the candidates thought about the selection process. One study was based on pilot selection for Lufthansa (Maschke, 2004), while the second study consisted of pilot selection for the Norwegian Air Force (Lang-Ree & Martinussen, 2006). In both cases the applicants were satisfied with the selection process, and the procedures were considered to be fair. The applicants were also asked to rate different tests and methods used, and the computerized tests received the highest ratings.

## Summary and conclusion

This chapter has dealt with important principles in the selection of pilots and has advocated the use of an evidence-based approach to selection. Development of a selection system should start with a job analysis where the abilities and personal characteristics required to accomplish the job should be specified. Subsequently, methods that are suitable for precisely measuring those capabilities or characteristics should be chosen. There is considerable evidence, from both meta-analyses (Hunter & Burke, 1994; Martinussen, 1996) and individual studies, that it is indeed possible to predict pilot performance based on tests measuring a variety of cognitive and psychomotor abilities. The importance of cognitive and psychomotor abilities has also been supported in job analyses. The majority of studies, however, are conducted on military samples using training criteria. More studies are needed to examine the validity of selection methods in commercial aviation, using more long-term criteria for pilot performance.

## References

American Educational Research Association, American Psychological Association, & National Council on Measurement in Education (2014). *Standards for educational and psychological testing.* Washington, DC: American Educational Research Association.

Berry, C.M., Clark, M.A., & McClure, T.K. (2011). Racial/ethnic differences in the criterion-related validity of cognitive ability tests: A qualitative and quantitative review. *Journal of Applied Psychology*, 96(5), 881–906.

Campbell, J.S., Castaneda, M., & Pulos, S. (2010). Meta-analysis of personality assessments as predictors of military aviation training success. *The International Journal of Aviation Psychology*, 20(1), 92–109.

Carretta, T.R. (1997). Male-female performance on U.S. Air Force pilot selection tests. *Aviation, Space and Environmental Medicine*, 68, 818–823.

Carretta, T.R. (2000). US Air Force pilot selection and training methods. *Aviation, Space and Environmental Medicine*, 71, 950–956.

Carretta, T.R. (2011). Pilot candidate selection method: Still an effective candidate predictor for US Air Force pilot training performance. *Aviation Psychology and Applied Human Factors*, 1(1), 3–8.

Carretta, T.R., & Ree, M.J. (2003). Pilot selection methods. In P.S. Tsang & M.A. Vidulich (eds), *Principles and practice of aviation psychology* (pp. 357–396). Hillsdale, NJ: Lawrence Erlbaum Associates.

Carretta, T.R., Rodgers, M.N., & Hansen, I. (1993). *The identification of ability requirements and selection instruments for fighter pilot training.* Euro-NATO Aircrew Human Factor Working Group. Technical report No. 2. Retrieved from http://www.dtic.mil/dtic/tr/fulltext/u2/a266340.pdf (3 January 2016).

Carretta, T.R., Teachout, M.S., Ree, M.J., Barto, E.L., King, R.E., & Michaels, C.F. (2014). Consistency of the relations of cognitive ability and personality traits to pilot training performance. *The International Journal of Aviation Psychology*, 24(4), 247–264.

Carroll, J.B. (1993). *Human cognitive abilities: A survey of factor-analytic studies.* New York: Cambridge University Press.

Cohen, J. (1988). *Statistical power analysis for the behavioral sciences* (2nd edn). Hillsdale, NJ: Lawrence Erlbaum Associates.

Damos, D. (1993). Using meta-analysis to compare the predictive validity of single- and multiple-task measures to flight performance. *Human Factors*, 35(4), 615–628.

Damos, D. (2011). *KSAOs for military pilot selection: A review of the literature.* Report number AFCAPS-FR-2011-0003. Randolf AFB, TX: Air Force Personnel Center Strategic Research and Assessment.

Damos, D.L., Rose, M.R., Martinussen, M., & Lorenz, J.L. (2015). Panel on cross-cultural selection. *Proceedings of the 18th International Symposium on Aviation Psychology* (pp. 476–481). Dayton, OH: Wright State University.

EFPA (European Federation of Psychologists' Association) (2013). *EFPA Review model for the description and evaluation of psychological tests: Test review form and notes for reviewers*, v 4.2.6. Retrieved from http://www.efpa.eu/professional-development (4 March 2015).

Eißfeldt, H., Grasshoff, D., Hasse, C., Hoermann, H-J., Kissing, D.S., Stern, C., Wenzel, J., & Zierke, O. (2009). *Aviator 2030. Ability requirements in future ATM systems II: Simulations and experiments.* Hamburg: Deutsches Zentrum für Luft- und Raumfahrt e. V. Institut für Luft- und Raumfahrtmedizin, Luft- und Raumfahrtpsychologie. Retrieved from http://www.dlr.de/me/Portaldata/25/Resources/dokumente/Aviator_2030_Report_FB_2009-28.pdf (3 January 2016).

Flanagan, J.C. (1954). The critical incident technique. *Psychological Bulletin*, 51, 327–358.

Fleischman, E.A. (1975). Toward a taxonomy of human performance. *American Psychologist*, 30, 1127–1149.

Fleishman, E.A., & Reilly, M.E. (2001). *Handbook of human abilities.* Potomac, MD: Management Research Institute, Inc.

Goeters, K.M., & Maschke, P. (2002). Cost-benefit analysis: Is the psychological selection of pilots worth the money? Paper presented at the 25th conference of EAAP, Warsaw, Poland, 16–20 September.

Goeters, K.M., Maschke, P., & Eißfeldt, H. (2004). Ability requirements in core aviation professions: Job analysis of airline pilots and air traffic controllers. In K.M. Goeters (ed.), *Aviation psychology: Practice and Research* (pp. 99–119). Aldershot: Ashgate.

Hilton, T.F., & Dolgin, D.L. (1991). Pilot selection in the military of the free world. In R. Gal & A.D. Mangelsdorff (eds), *Handbook of military psychology* (pp. 81–101). New York: John Wiley.

Hunter, D.R. (1989). Aviator selection. In M.F. Wiskoff & G.F. Rampton (eds), *Military personnel measurement: Testing, assignment, evaluation* (pp. 129–167). New York: Praeger.

Hunter, D.R., & Burke, E.F. (1994). Predicting aircraft pilot-training success: A meta-analysis of published research. *International Journal of Aviation Psychology*, 4, 297–313.

Hunter, D.R., & Burke, E.F. (1995). *Handbook of pilot selection.* Aldershot: Avebury Aviation.

Hunter, J.E., & Schmidt, F.L. (2003). *Methods of meta-analysis: Correcting error and bias in research findings*. Beverly Hills, CA: Sage.

IATA (International Air Transport Association) (2010). *Guidance material and best practices for pilot aptitude testing*. Montreal: International Air Transport Association. Retrieved from https://www.iata.org/publications/Documents/pilot-aptitude-testing-guide.pdf (1 January 2016).

Johnson, J.T., & Ree, M.J. (1994). Rangej: A Pascal program to compute the multivariate correction for range restriction. *Educational and Psychological Measurement*, 54, 693–695.

Kline, P. (1991). *Intelligence: The psychometric view*. New York: Routledge.

Lang-Ree, O.C., & Martinussen, M. (2006). Applicant reactions and attitudes towards the selection procedure in the Norwegian Air Force. *Human Factors and Aerospace Safety*, 6, 345–358.

Lawley, D.N. (1943). A note on Karl Pearson's selection formulae: *Proceedings of the Royal Society of Edinburgh*, 62 (section A, part 1), 28–30.

Levant, R.F. (2005). *Report of the 2005 Presidential Task Force on evidence-based practice*. American Psychological Association. Retrieved from http://www.apa.org/practice/resources/evidence/evidence-based-report.pdf (24 August 2016).

Magnusson, D. (1967). *Test theory*. Reading, MA: Addison-Wesley Publishing.

Martinussen, M. (1996). Psychological measures as predictors of pilot performance: A meta-analysis. *International Journal of Aviation Psychology*, 6(1), 1–20.

Martinussen, M. (2010). Personnel selection. In M. Martinussen & D.R. Hunter, *Aviation psychology and human factors* (pp. 73–98). New York: Taylor and Francis.

Martinussen, M., & Torjussen, T.M. (2004). Initial validation of a computer-based assessment battery for pilot selection in the Norwegian Air Force. *Human Factors and Aerospace Safety*, 4, 233–244.

Maschke, P. (2004). The acceptance of ab-initio pilot selection methods. *Human Factors and Aerospace Safety*, 4, 225–232.

Murphy, K.R. (ed.). (2003). *Validity generalization. A critical review*. Mahwah, NJ: Erlbaum.

Paullin, C., Katz, L., Bruskiewicz, K.T., Houston, J., & Damos, D. (2006). *Review of aviator selection*. Technical report 1183. Minneapolis, MN: United States Army Research Institute for the Behavioral and Social Sciences.

Rothstein, H.R., & McDaniel, M.A. (1992). Differential validity by sex in employment settings. *Journal of Business and Psychology*, 7, 45–62.

Sackett, P.R., & Lievens, F. (2008). Personnel selection. *Annual Review of Psychology*, 59(1), 419–450.

Sackett, P.R., & Yang, H. (2000). Correction for range restriction: An expanded typology. *Journal of Applied Psychology*, 85(1), 112–118.

Sackett, D.L., Rosenberg, W.M., Gray, J.A., Haynes, R.B., & Richardson, W.S. (1996). Evidence based medicine: what it is and what it isn't. *British Medical Journal*, 312(7023), 71–72.

Schmidt, F.L., & Hunter, J.E. (1998). The validity and utility of selection methods in personnel psychology: Practical and theoretical implications of 85 years of research findings. *Psychological Bulletin*, 124, 262–274.

Spearman, C. (1904). 'General intelligence', objectively determined and measured. *American Journal of Psychology*, 15, 201–293.

Thompson, B. (ed.) (2003). *Score reliability. Contemporary thinking on reliability issues*. Thousand Oaks, CA: Sage Publications Inc.

Thurstone, L.L. (1938). *Primary mental abilities*. Psychometric Monographs 1, Chicago, IL: University of Chicago Press.

Wilson, M. (2007). A history of job analysis. In L. Koppes, *Historical perspectives in industrial and organizational psychology* (pp. 219–241). Mahwah, NJ: Lawrence Erlbaum Associates.

Zierke, O. (2014). Predictive validity of knowledge tests. *Aviation Psychology and Applied Human Factors*, 4(2), 98–105.

# 3 The role of assessment in pilot selection

*Carl Hoffmann and Arianna Hoffmann*

## Introduction

The recent tragic crash of Germanwings Flight 9525, an apparent suicide of the copilot, Andreas Lubitz, that also took the lives of 149 innocent people, has captured the attention of the flying public, commercial airlines and regulatory agencies. How could a pilot with apparent psychological problems be hired by a commercial airline and be trusted with the lives of hundreds of passengers each day? The impact of this tragedy was amplified by other recent crashes. Perhaps the most mysterious was Malaysia Airlines Flight 370 on 4 March 2014. At the time of this writing there remains speculation about what role, if any, the pilots played in the disappearance and crash of the aircraft hundreds of miles away from its planned flight path, causing the deaths of 239 passengers and crew.

Pilot suicide in commercial flight is horrifying. The dramatic betrayal of trust and loss of innocent lives in such circumstances is an appalling prospect. Fortunately, it is also a rare event. The fact is there have until now been few commercial aviation crashes that are documented as acts of suicide, perhaps seven or eight since 1976. Though historically rare, if the causes are not understood and measures put in place to prevent them, we can expect more of these tragedies to occur as air travel increases and the number of airline pilots grows over the next decades.

While the two crashes noted above may have involved the intent of one of the pilots to do harm to himself and the passengers, there are other recent tragedies that raise awareness of the need to monitor the selection, training and management of pilots, as well as their psychological makeup.

- 28 December 2014: Why did the pilots of AirAsia Flight 8501 wait so long to divert away from a line of severe weather and why were they unable to deal with an apparent aerodynamic stall, killing 162 people?
- 6 July 2013: Why did the pilots of Asiana Airlines Flight 214 not recognize that their approach to the runway at San Francisco International Airport was far too low and slow and not take action until it was too late, resulting in the death of three passengers and injuring 187 people, with a potential loss of life of 307 people?

- 1 June 2009: Why were pilots of Air France Flight 447 unable to recognize the problems they were having with the instruments and take proper action to first avoid and then recover from a high altitude stall, killing 228 people?
- 12 February 2009: Why did the pilots of Colgan Air Flight 3407 lose vigilance over the aircraft systems and then respond to a loss of control by taking action that was the exact opposite of what was required to recover the aircraft, killing 50 people, including a resident of a house at the crash site?

These accidents involving pilot error are by far more common than the handful that involve suicide. Identifying reliable, effective ways of measuring the underlying knowledge, skills, abilities that contribute to avoiding pilot error, as well as psychological traits and vulnerabilities, is essential as the number of accidents resulting from human error far exceeds those involving suicide or psychopathology. By some measures there have been 200 or more of these accidents since 1950. By one estimate, pilot error accounts for approximately 70 percent of all accidents (Wiegmann & Shappell, 2003). These more recent accidents have once again caused government agencies and commercial airlines around the world to ask, "What can be done to prevent these accidents from happening?" Clearly this question covers a wide array of topics and fields within psychology. Airlines have taken these events very seriously and are reviewing their entire process of selecting, training, evaluating and managing their pilots. This chapter deals very broadly with the importance of a well-designed selection process for commercial airline pilots.

We have been involved over the last 25 years in consulting with three major international airlines and four regional airlines based in the US. Pilot candidates for these airlines have already gone through commercial flight training and certification and have had some experience as professional pilots, including military and civilian flight backgrounds. Working in collaboration with our corporate clients we have developed hiring models that have been used to assess over 10,000 major airline candidates and 3,500 regional candidates. While much of the work that forms the basis of what follows is proprietary, we will illustrate the development processes required to build a robust hiring model based on that experience.

- First, we describe the role of a modern airline pilot. Pilots must routinely perform a very detailed and demanding job, while avoiding or resolving circumstances that lead to accidents and crashes. In addition to concern with promoting flight safety, organizations can realize other significant benefits from an effective hiring system.
- Clearly, hiring and training the best pilots depends on establishing an accurate and thorough understanding of the knowledge, skills, abilities, and personality traits (KSAPs) that determine performance on the job in a particular airline organization. Identifying these KSAPs requires a careful analysis that specifies and catalogs the many tasks that pilots must

accomplish in doing their job. We will describe both these processes and give examples from our experience with clients.

- Once the process of establishing the activity framework and the resulting KSAP framework is described, we address the next steps in building an effective selection model:
  - identifying effective assessment tools to assess KSAPs;
  - choosing the performance criteria to measure successful outcomes;
  - constructing an analysis framework to examine the predictive validity of the selection measures;
  - enhancing the power of the selection process in the future;
  - establishing a methodology for continuing improvement.

## The role of a modern pilot

Safety in commercial aviation is achieved through defining the activities pilots need to perform the job well, and then finding the pilots who are capable of and enthusiastic about performing those duties over a long career. Analyzing the activities associated with the role of pilot appears at first glance to be easy. On an operational basis it is very structured. Aircraft manufacturers design the aircraft and the systems anticipating how the pilot will operate that aircraft. Regulatory agencies are responsible for broadly setting the guidelines for safe flight operations. They also establish the infrastructure: flight paths, approaches to airports and the air traffic control systems that are designed to ensure safety. Finally, years of experience and study by the airlines have reinforced a set of activities that support safe and efficient operation of the aircraft.

That standardization is reflected in how airlines divide up the work performed for each flight into phases, each with its own distinct set of activities: pre-flight, gate, push back, taxi, takeoff, climb, cruise, descent, approach, landing, taxi in, gate and shutdown. Each phase of flight has a set of activities to ensure safety. For instance, during pre-flight, there is a process of understanding the demands of that flight. If it is the first flight of the day, this may also include a discussion about the entire set of flights the crew may be assigned for that day: the number of takeoffs and landings, the characteristics of the aircraft as they relate to the specific demands of the airports, the weather they will encounter as well as an assessment of the crew members' experience, personality and readiness to fly. While at the gate, pilots check the aircraft and systems for problems, deal with mechanics if there are problems, ensure the passengers, baggage, fuel and supplies are loaded, program the flight management system and finally work with their crew and flight attendants on what to expect during the flight and whether their passengers have any special needs. Similar sets of activities can be defined at each phase of flight.

Each phase has checklists to ensure that the pilots have reviewed and accomplished the needed tasks. Each phase requires substantial gathering of information and analysis, communication and decision-making. Workloads on approach and landing are very intense, especially when in a heavily used airport, where planes are sequenced in for landing with little separation, and approach paths require constant course adjustments while maintaining proper configuration of the aircraft, airspeed and rates of descent. Visibility and weather conditions – snow, wind, thunderstorms – make the workload even more intense.

In order to support the execution of this complicated set of tasks, there are two primary divisions of labor in a modern cockpit. First, the traditional hierarchy of captain and first officer defines the ultimate authority structure and decision-making. The other dichotomy in the cockpit divides the roles of *pilot flying* and *pilot monitoring*. The *pilot flying* role encompasses activities associated with controlling the aircraft, managing the workload and tracking the progress of the flight. Those associated with *pilot monitoring* are activities associated with communications, vigilance, and analysis and verification of the tasks performed by the pilot flying. Clarity in those roles is critical to safe operations.

What we have just described are "normal operations." Failure of systems, fire or damage to the aircraft or the emergency needs of passengers and crew require special and often instant reaction from pilots. While abnormal events are rare, airlines go to a great deal of effort to define procedures to help pilots take action in dealing with these threats to safety.

There are two other factors that must be considered in establishing the requirements of the pilot position. One is the isolation of the pilot's role, the other the need to adapt to change over the professional lifetime of the pilot. Pilots often lead a very isolated work life. Many pilots live far away from their base of operation, have to commute long distances, seldom fly with the same crewmembers and can have limited contact with gate agents, flight attendants, ground crews and mechanics. Their contact with the company is often limited to emails, websites and training. This limited personal contact with coworkers and managers can jeopardize their sense of community and the sense of belonging to a team with shared purpose, values and responsibilities.

From the time of hire, each pilot will undergo changes in their capabilities and their desire to perform this demanding job. These changes are both internal and external. Internal changes include the acquisition of experience, judgment, changes in their attitudes toward their work, and motivation to prepare for and perform their job, shifts in their emotional make up and potential decrease in cognitive ability associated with age. External factors that affect the pilot's ability and willingness to do their job arise from changes in their families, their communities, the complexity of the operating environment and the aircraft they fly.

## Benefits of an effective selection process

A well-designed and executed pilot selection program that is in harmony with the training program and the management and culture of the cockpit can predict the long-term performance of new-hire pilots, saving money, and potentially saving lives.

## Safety

As we will show, there is a great deal of effort and cost associated with designing, running and maintaining an effective pilot recruitment and selection process. Hiring pilots who will fly their aircraft safely is, of course, the primary goal of the selection process. Recognizing and hiring pilots with the capability to deal with dangerous and unexpected, albeit rare, events is a huge benefit to companies. Screening out pilots who may have psychological problems that would cause them to ignore safety or actively engage in activities that endanger themselves and others is undeniably critical to safe operations. Problems that inhibit the pilot from actively engaging in the planning, preparation and necessary vigilance may be based in cognitive dysfunction, psychopathology or traits that may be within the normal personality spectrum.

## Training efficiency

Airlines are a business and, like all businesses, they seek to be efficient in how they operate. Companies spend a great deal of money on training to ensure that pilots meet the standards of the airline. Pilots undergo repeated and rigorous technical and procedural training throughout their careers. They must consume a great deal of information in a short period of time and demonstrate their proficiency repeatedly. Hiring the right pilots, capable of learning quickly, and applying that knowledge to their work can save millions of dollars in training costs over the long span of their employment.

## Productivity

Finding a highly qualified pilot who is willing and able to meet the operational needs of the airline helps to ensure that the pilot will enjoy the job. The happier that pilot is with his or her work, the more productive, engaged and focused that pilot will be. An important benefit of a rigorous selection program is higher pilot productivity and less effort required to manage the behavior of pilots who become disaffected with their work. If pilots enjoy their work and are engaged in it, they will do their jobs well and be safer pilots. So, we come full circle back to safety.

## Building an effective selection process

### Conducting a pilot job analysis

The field of industrial and organizational psychology (I.O. Psychology) has developed a variety of ways of accomplishing effective job analysis (see Gael, 1988). The process has two major steps. First, each of the essential activities associated with the job must be identified, defined, and cataloged with an understanding of the time demands and intensity of those activities and their importance to accomplishing the pilot's job at a particular airline. Second, once those activities have been identified they need to be linked to the knowledge, skills, abilities and personality traits required to perform that work. We stress the need to understand the structure of the job at each airline, for while *what* needs to be accomplished is fairly standard, *how* that work is accomplished varies from airline to airline.

### Capturing the pilot activities

A variety of methods is required to best identify the activities pilots perform. First, individual pilots who are recognized suject matter experts (SMEs) within the airline are interviewed face-to-face to establish what they do to successfully accomplish their work. Much of this effort is focused on cataloging the daily activities associated with flying operations, but attention is also paid to activities away from flying that are in support of safe flight. These include activities associated with training, keeping current on changes to regulations and procedures, and maintaining physical, mental and emotional fitness for duty. Special attention should be given to the conditions and environment in which pilots perform their job: the scheduling, weather, rhythm of operation, and integration with other airline personnel. The demands placed by these environmental factors help to determine the personality and cognitive structures that must be considered.

The initial list of job activities is then validated in focus groups of captains and first officers across the variety of aircraft the company flies. This helps standardize the language and clarify variations in the missions and operational demands of each aircraft type. After thorough focus group processing and documentation, the classification of job activities by position and aircraft type is presented to management pilots for review. This step helps confirm not only what the company requires but also whether the practice of the crew force is consistent with the philosophy and approach of management.

The airline's philosophy of how the cockpit is managed is also critical to knowing what capabilities should be stressed in hiring pilots. This information is also obtained through interviews with individual SME pilots, pilot focus groups and surveys, and discussions with airline management. Some airlines take what one might call an "equipment operator" approach to the execution of the activities of flying. They stress procedures and detailed definitions of how each activity is to be performed, defining multiple circumstances and what action to take in each circumstance. Other airlines feel they cannot anticipate all conditions the pilot will encounter and stress the principles of aircraft operation and the importance of decision-making and taking effective action within a safety envelope. The latter group puts the responsibility of performance on the pilot; the former puts the responsibility of performance on the definition and completeness of the procedures. An airline that looks to hire new and inexperienced pilots may have to rely on the detailed description of each activity and procedure, while an airline that targets experienced pilots can rely more on the established capabilities and judgment of seasoned pilots. There is a long-term impact of each philosophy. Our experience is that the approach that puts primary responsibility on the pilot invites the pilot to be actively engaged in operations because they own the consequences of their decisions. A detailed operational approach has the potential to separate the pilot from engagement and responsibility because the results may be seen as a consequence of adhering to defined procedures. The capabilities that are required and the personalities that thrive in each environment are very different.

While the detailed work of defining pilot activities is best done in small groups using SMEs, surveys can also be used to reach the general population of pilots to confirm those practices in the broader population. It is critical to safety that the company understands the attitudes and behaviors of pilots who are committed to their craft. Surveys can capture differences in how pilots prioritize these activities, and how they execute the division of tasks based on their roles of pilot flying and pilot monitoring. Surveys are also useful in understanding what motivates pilots and keeps them engaged in their job. Finally, systematically collecting information from a broad range of pilots in the company can help create an understanding of how pilots deal with the less attractive conditions of the job: the schedules that disrupt their sleep and personal lives, the demands of repeated takeoffs and landings, the tight time constraints, and pressures of working in a highly integrated organization. Pursuing a thorough analysis of the aspects of work required by the airline operation is key to defining not only the technical knowledge and cognitive skills, but also the personality traits required to do the pilot job well.

### Linking job activities to required capabilities

The next step is to link the pilot activities to the capabilities required to accomplish those activities. This can be done very effectively in focus groups, by asking experienced and highly proficient pilots (SMEs) in the organization what they have to know and what skills, abilities and personality traits they need to accomplish those tasks effectively. It should be noted that the language that the pilots use reflects their own professional vernacular and may not be that of a researcher in I.O. psychology. Pilots will use terms that are not well-defined such as team player, leader, sense of humor, or "a good traveling companion" to describe characteristics they value in their fellow pilots. Thus, time needs to be spent working with pilots to understand their precise meaning and then connect those concepts to the way they have been operationalized in the scientific literature. The lists of capabilities assembled from these sessions and the needed translations from pilot vernacular should then be compared to other findings in the scholarly literature. Are the capabilities demanded of the job consistent with other studies of the requirements of the job, and where they are different is that difference consistent with the company's philosophy of operation?

*Developing a framework of pilot activities*

Generally speaking, the catalog of job activities that is generated will contain 200 to 300 discrete tasks spread over each phase of flight. It is difficult to manage pilots based on a list of 300 distinct activities. An essential part of the job analysis process is to aggregate these tasks into a taxonomy that reflects both the task areas and the management philosophy of the cockpit. Different management philosophies result in different stresses on which pilot activities are most central and how they are to be accomplished. These differences result in important variations in the final taxonomies across organizations.

Below we offer one illustration of an activity framework that was developed with a client and follow it with the associated knowledge, skills, abilities and traits that were identified as required for the execution of those activities. These frameworks are offered as examples of the products of a careful job analysis process. In order to achieve the *benefits* of job analysis, it is essential that such frameworks be developed as described above within the organization that will use them.

*A pilot activity framework*

- *Planning and preparation.* Planning activities are vital for successful team performance and management of the flight. Pilots need to come to work rested, focused and prepared to carry out their work. Pilots need to review the flight plan, weight, fuel requirements, and weather along the route, as well as airport requirements and other data to anticipate what challenges may arise and how they can prepare for them.
- *Adherence to regulations, procedures and clearances.* Regulations and procedures exist to ensure that the aircraft is operated safely in all conditions and locations. Not only should pilots comply with regulatory requirements, in addition to their company's operating procedures, they should also understand the underlying reasons for those regulations and procedures.
- *Aircraft Control Activities.* Skill in direct control of the aircraft is vital to safety, especially when automation may be compromised. Instead of being an isolated activity, safe control of the aircraft is the result of all the activities listed here especially the appropriate use of automation, since much of the activity of controlling the aircraft in flight is automated in making heading, speed and altitude adjustments.
- *Flight management activities.* Appropriate flight management is vital to establishing the conditions for effective vigilance and analysis through interaction with aircraft systems, as well as adherence to regulations, procedures, and clearance. This involves anticipating and managing the varying workloads in each phase of flight.
- *Navigation and interaction with aircraft systems.* Pilots use a variety of tools to navigate: visual information, charts, radio signals, and electronic data to establish and maintain course and clearances and determine the appropriate

corrections and adjustments as required. This includes programing and updating the flight management systems and accomplishing preflight systems checks and aircraft maintenance logs.

- *Vigilance, analysis, and situational awareness.* These activities include monitoring information from visual scans, communications, instruments, weather and other aircraft to build a dynamic four-dimensional model of the conditions of the aircraft and the environment in which the aircraft is operating. Accomplishing this set of activities also includes projecting those dynamic conditions forward in time to anticipate future actions needed for the safe completion of the flight.
- *Teamwork.* One pilot cannot accomplish all of the tasks required for safe flight alone. This requires establishing and confirming the division of labor in the cockpit, the individual roles of the crew and their responsibilities. Part of teamwork involves assessing fellow crewmembers and addressing the requirements of the flight and needs of the crew. Crewmembers must work at creating an atmosphere of open and effective communication and collaboration within the cockpit and all sources of support during flight, including the flight attendants, ground support, schedulers, operations center staff, and air traffic controllers. This will facilitate management of the workload and sharing of vital information during the execution of the flight.
- *Decision-making and leadership.* This process covers a broad range of routine decisions, such as the number and sequence of engines to start, push back, and taking the runway as well as less routine decisions, such as adjusting course due to weather, choosing alternative airports, to go around on approach, when to hand fly the aircraft and dealing with abnormal situations. These activities include evaluating situational information along with input from the crew, communicating the risks and benefits of alternative courses of action, and finally coordinating and executing the best decision.
- *Effective communication.* Clear communication is the foundation for the successful coordination and completion of the entire set of activities a pilot must perform. Good cockpit communication includes clear, timely and concise statements of inflight observations and their implications, as well as requests for action. Shared information should be followed up by confirmation on the part of the recipient of what has been stated, how it was understood, and any requests for clarifications. The context of the situation, role of the pilot and tone are important parts of effective communication.
- *Maintaining fitness for duty.* This is the basis of safe operations and professional competence. Being fit for duty requires pilots taking responsibility for their health and fitness to fly, awareness of alerts, changes in regulations, company policies and updates associated with aircraft and training.

It is remarkable how large a proportion of a pilot's focus and time are spent in executive function: planning, collecting and analyzing information, managing systems and workloads, decision-making, developing team roles, communicating, and leading. These are not the ways we tend to think of the work of pilots as they are focused on the procedures of flying the plane.

*A framework of pilot capabilities*

Based on the framework of pilot activities described above, the following knowledge, skills, and abilities and personality traits were determined to be required:

- *Knowledge.* Pilots clearly need to know the principles of aviation and have the ability to solve problems using those principles. They must be able to apply this knowledge to both routine and abnormal situations where the problem and solution may not be obvious. The critical knowledge breaks down into three main subject areas: aerodynamics, navigation, and engineering and aircraft systems.
  - *Aerodynamics.* This covers the physics of flight – what forces allow a plane to become and stay airborne and how the atmosphere, the speed, the weight of the aircraft and its distribution, momentum and attitude affect those forces.
  - *Navigation.* This includes understanding heading, course, track, bearing and relationships among them, the effect of altitude and wind on course and schedule. Perhaps most critical is the ability to navigate safely around airports and the descent to approach and landing.
  - *Engineering and aircraft systems.* This includes a wide array of diverse knowledge. This area covers understanding the principles of turbine engines, fuel, hydraulics, landing gear, control and electrical systems. While the pilot of a modern aircraft does not need to be an expert in each field, they do need to understand the operating principles of each field, diagnose problems when they arise, and interact with mechanics with enough confidence to know that those problems have been properly addressed.
- *Skills and abilities.* We will not make distinctions here between skills and abilities, and we will also use terms in the pilot's lexicon. There are many more than stated below, but these are among the most important.
  - *Spatial and situational awareness*, or the ability to build a four-dimensional model of a dynamic environment and project the aircraft's movement through it as other objects in that environment change position relative to the aircraft's movement (Endsley, 1995; Damos, 1993).
  - *Multitasking/timesharing*, or the ability to keep track of several inputs while processing their meaning and acting on several different tasks. The intensity of input and the need for focus and action is especially high during approach and landing (Yakimovich *et al.*, 1995).
  - *Analysis and decision making*, or the ability to process information from a variety of sources, evaluate the risks and benefits of action, and take a

course of action in a timely manner (O'Hare & Wiggins, 1993; Stokes *et al.*, 1992).

○   *Leadership,* or the ability to understand operational needs, assess coworkers, set expectations, build a focused and collaborative environment, observe performance and guide improvements in others by mentoring and setting an example (Chidester *et al.*, 1990).

○   *Stick and rudder skills,* or the ability to control the aircraft within safe tolerances during normal and abnormal operations (Fleischman, 1956; Street & Dolgin, 1994).

○   *Communication skills,* or the ability to communicate precisely and effectively.

•   *Personality traits.* Various components of the Five Factor Model of personality have been shown to play a role in being a successful pilot (Barrick & Mount, 1991; Street & Helton, 1993; Fitzgibbons *et al.*, 2004). From our own research we see particular factors stressed at different airlines and different points in the pilot's career:

○   *Conscientiousness:* being dependable, careful, thorough, responsible and organized to achieve a goal is very important.

○   *Openness:* being imaginative, curious, and broad-minded is a desirable attribute to a point but this should not get in the way of closure and decision-making.

○   *Neuroticism:* expressing anxiety, depression, anger, being insecure or overly sensitive to criticism can interfere with being focused on the immediate problems and taking appropriate action.

○   *Agreeableness:* particularly being courteous, flexible, cooperative, forgiving and tolerant.

○   *Extroversion:* sociability, gregariousness and assertiveness is an important part of willingness to communicate.

In addition to the above, our research has shown that a passion for flying is a critical asset. As we noted earlier there are stresses and unattractive aspects of this work. A pilot must derive joy from the act of doing their work well and taking pride in it, or some of the negative aspects of the work can detract from the engagement in the work and satisfaction in doing that job well. A bored pilot, detached from the routine activities of flight operations, is a dangerous pilot.

## Next steps in building an effective selection model

As we have described above, a clear operational picture of the job of pilot at a given organization is accomplished by defining the tasks that pilots must accomplish and the capabilities they must have to perform those tasks well. The next steps in building a reliable and valid selection process are as follows:

1   identify effective tools to measure the applicants' critical capabilities during the selection process;

2 choose performance criteria to assess pilot performance in training and on the job;
3 construct an analysis framework to determine what measures are predictive of performance;
4 enhance the power of the selection process by adding additional data points;
5 establish a methodology for continuing improvement.

Each of these steps must be carefully customized to fit the needs of the particular airline in question. In much the same way that we exemplified the process of developing KSAPs by describing our experience with a representative client, the following process is again intended to be illustrative. The power of the analytical framework is in customizing selection models to the specific needs of the airline, in order to find the right fit for a particular pilot job.

### Identifying effective assessment tools

Selection tests provide the bedrock for gauging a candidate's knowledge base, skill set, and abilities. Based on the job analysis and associated KSAPs identified for an airline client, we reviewed a range of published assessment instruments. Our search for appropriate tools required mapping test content and the published research to each of the separate KSAPs. From this work, we selected a battery of tests of aptitude and ability that was likely to have utility in a commercial airline setting. In the trial phase of designing the new hiring process we employed the extensive set of measures listed in Table 3.1 to determine which measures added the most value to the process. We included measures of verbal, numeric, spatial and situational awareness, mechanical, psychomotor and cognitive ability, as well as assessments of critical thinking, and normal personality.

After selecting from commercially available tests relevant to the KSAPs, we found a critical area to be unrepresented – understanding of the principles of aviation. Most of the published research on the use of tests in pilot hiring is concerned with *ab-initio* pilots who arrive with little or no practical flight experience or academic instruction in aviation. That literature focuses on measuring aptitude and potential to become a pilot. In the US there has been a sufficient supply of experienced pilots for major airlines. In fact as of this writing, virtually all passenger airlines are required by law to hire experienced pilots. This experienced labor force has allowed many major and regional airlines to have very short training footprints. In the words of one airline instructor, "I really don't have time to teach the principles of aviation and problem-solving. I am focused on certifying that the pilot, at the end of training, can operate the aircraft safely." Therefore, companies rely on new pilots arriving with a bank of knowledge and experience that puts them in position to quickly learn how to operate a particular type of aircraft and understand the company's particular approach to aircraft systems management, procedures and maneuvers. However, airlines also need the pilot to come equipped with the ability to anticipate the consequences of their actions and diagnose and solve problems as they arise.

We searched for a test that measured the ability of the pilot to apply the principles of aerodynamics, engineering and systems, and navigation to solve problems regularly confronted in flying for an airline. In the mid-1990s because there was no such test, we developed a proprietary Job Knowledge Test for one of our clients consistent with our job analysis of their pilot role. The Job Knowledge Test was developed to assess the extent to which a pilot candidate possesses the requisite knowledge that allows them to analyze and solve problems, as well as engage effectively with other professionals (mechanics, schedulers, operation center personnel and air traffic control) in flight support roles. It was also thought that this test of applied knowledge would be less subject to cultural bias than general aptitude tests. We worked with SME pilots at the airline using syllabi from the US Navy, Air Force and leading aviation programs at three US universities in developing the test. Over time, to ensure that the material remains contemporaneous with present aviation instruction,

*Table 3.1* Tests administered in trial phase

| *Aptitude and ability* | *Test focus* |
| --- | --- |
| Differential Aptitude Test | Verbal and numeric ability |
| Bennett Mechanical Comprehension Test | Aptitude for learning mechanical skills |
| Minnesota Paper Form Board Test | Spatial visualization |
| United States Navy's Psychomotor/Dichotic Listening Test (PMT/DLT) | Multi-tasking: dexterity and reaction times |
| Tabular Speed Test | Perceptual speed |
| Raven's Advanced Progressive Matrices | Non-verbal measures of abstract reasoning |
| Watson Glazer Test of Critical Thinking | Critical thinking |
| CogScreen Aero Medical Edition | Cognitive abilities |
| Simulator Exercises | Airmanship |
| *Personality* | |
| NEO PI-R | Normal adult personality |
| Minnesota Multiphasic Personality Inventory 2 | Adult psychopathology |
| *Job knowledge and problem solving* | |
| Delta's Job Knowledge Test | Problem-solving in aerodynamics, navigation, and engineering |

the test items have been reviewed by aviation sciences faculty at leading four-year aviation universities.

While there was research to suggest that each of the tests listed in Table 3.1 might be useful to measure a component of the targeted KSAPs, we knew that administering so many tests to applicants would be impractical for the long term. These tests required a full two-day testing protocol. It was understood from the outset that administering all of these tests was neither logistically nor economically feasible as a continuing process. Our focus was on using the initial experience with a rich battery of tests to evaluate which measures in combination would yield the most utility in predicting performance after hire.

## The structured interview

In addition to testing, another important measure of an applicant's capabilities and cultural fit is a highly structured face-to-face interview. In developing the interview with our client airline, considerations were given to the composition of the interview team, the need for thorough interview training, careful standardization of evaluation criteria, and the importance of establishing inter-rater reliability. In our experience, successful interview teams should have representation from human resources, as well as flight operations. Retired pilots can be a valuable addition to the team, but the inclusion of active pilots is indispensable. They fully understand the current operational requirements and culture of the airline and know that they may very well end up sitting in a cockpit seat next to the new hire. These pilots also have a closer connection to the industry the applicant is coming from, with an appreciation of the career path displayed by that applicant. Careful initial and recurrent training of the interview team is crucial to reinforce appropriate processes and standards of evaluation.

The interview team was provided with topics and associated questions that had been developed and refined by pilot focus groups, along with clear measureable rating anchors that ensured objective scoring of applicant responses. This scenario allowed effective examination of the applicant's background and preparation to be a professional pilot, as well as opportunity to assess the judgment, decision-making, leadership, passion for flying and teamwork capabilities that were required by the management philosophy of the cockpit.

## Assessing psychopathology

Computerized tests and structured interviews can be very good at measuring the capabilities of a pilot but they cannot assess the mental or emotional health of the applicant. This requires the use of a standardized mental health screening tool combined with a clinical psychological interview of the candidate. For the airline in this example, we chose the Minnesota Multiphasic Personality Inventory-2 (MMPI-2). It has been well researched for the pilot population and also has been produced in many languages and studied in many countries

(Butcher, 1994; Butcher & Williams, 2009). In conformance with US law, after the initial hiring offer, all new hires were administered the MMPI-2 and were interviewed by a clinical psychologist to screen for potential psychopathology.

Clinical psychologists who are experienced with the MMPI and also have substantial knowledge of airline operations are key to using this inventory effectively. Pilots as a population tend to be more confident and present themselves more favorably than the normal population. Because of this, the norms were adjusted to this population and strategies developed to deal with a group that may have elevated scores on the validation scales (Butcher, 1994). The clinical interview was designed to probe the specifics of the individual's MMPI inventory. Special care needs to be taken in interpreting the findings of the MMPI and the clinical interview. A process should be put into place to handle cases in which possible issues surface regarding psychopathology. (See Borum *et al.*, 2003, for more information on similar evaluations used to assess fitness for duty.) The psychologist should not be in a position to operate in isolation in making a final decision about rescinding the initial job offer.

## Choosing the performance criteria

In order to evaluate whether chosen selection measures are delivering the pilots that individual airlines require, it is necessary to identify available outcome variables that can be used as indicators of successful job performance. These should include performance measures that are collected routinely in an established, standardized way. Data collected during initial training and initial operating experience (IOE) constitute the most apparent and widely used outcome data. Since training is meant to prepare the pilot for the challenges he or she will face when they reach the line, problems in training can be a reasonable surrogate for on-the-job performance. It is important to take the time to fully understand the data that are available. Have syllabi or grading scales changed over time? Is there sufficient comparability between fleets and modules? Are students paired in a simulator graded together or individually? What level of granularity is available and reliable in recorded grades?

Available indicators of on-the-job performance may include productivity, as well as indications of disciplinary action. Other outcome measures should also be considered, for instance using observations of the pilot's behavior in the cockpit (Hoffmann *et al.*, 1998) and flight data recordings (Yakimovitch *et al.*, 1995). Other operational data may exist, but it is often protected from access by collective bargaining agreements. Once the constellation of outcome measures has been defined and obtained, it is time to proceed with undertaking statistical analysis of how well the assessment tools actually predict performance after hire.

## Constructing the analysis framework

A series of studies over an extended period of time was undertaken to select the combination of tests that best predicted performance in multiple areas:

training, productivity, performance in the cockpit and differentiation between experienced and recreational pilots (see Hoffmann *et al.*, 1998; Hoffmann *et al.*, 2011). The complexity of the analysis required many months of work after the data were assembled. These findings have been replicated over the years with this client. We do not have space here to relate the statistical and methodological issues that were addressed in these studies, but will give a quick overview of the results.

All the tests listed in Table 3.1 with the exception of the MMPI-2 were included in multiple analyses, including factor analysis, cluster analysis, various forms of the general linear model and logistic regression. Regression allows for partitioning the explanatory power and overlap of each test and their associated components. From the regression analyses we arrived at three assessment tools that were most important in predicting the targeted outcomes. These three tests are the CogScreen Aeromedical Edition (Kay, 1995), the NEO PI-R (Costa & McCrae, 1992), and the proprietary Job Knowledge Test (JKT). Combining the scores from components of these three instruments using regression modeling produces a very robust measure of a pilot's subsequent success in training, level of productivity, and performance on the job. Additional tests of ability and aptitude added little or no significant predictive power to our equations.

We believe that the reason these three assessment tools are effective selection measures on their own is due to their tailored fit with assessing requirements for good pilots. The JKT is not only a test of knowledge, but also a test of aptitude. The CogScreen overlaps with many of the tests of ability and aptitude, while at the same time measuring multi-tasking or timesharing. The degree of precision that CogScreen offers in measuring speed, accuracy, throughput and process measures add to the reliability of the measures. Finally, the NEO PI-R measures many of the dimensions required to be a good pilot, e.g., conscientiousness, openness, personal resilience etc.

The regression equations produced from this analysis allowed us to build a compensatory model for selection that is intuitively satisfying. Very few pilots are superior on all aspects of job knowledge, personality and cognitive ability. Successful pilots draw on different combinations of capabilities in the realms of job knowledge, cognition, and personality traits to meet the performance standards of their airline. Multiple component scores were drawn from each of the three assessment instruments. There is no set pass/fail based on an individual test or sub-test. The regression equations combined the significant variables into an equation that produces a single cut score. The compensatory model has several advantages. It creates a more diverse group of pilots with different strengths which can lead to more effective teamwork and crew interaction. It also allows the airline to hire a larger pool of pilots than it could if strict pass/fail scores were applied to the individual tests.

We have also found that pilots at different stages of their careers draw on a different mix of personality, cognitive ability and job knowledge (Hoffmann, 2013). Those early in their careers draw on their ability to learn quickly and absorb the lessons of their instructors and captains, while those later in their careers rely more on executive function – analysis, leadership, and decision-making. Regression modeling of the scores on the components of these three assessment tools allowed us to adjust the importance of different attributes of to the unique needs of each company's job requirements, based on empirically observed performance.

We also determined that, although very popular in pilot selection, the use of simulator exercises was not required. This is consistent with other findings (see Taylor *et al.*, 2000). The qualities measured in the simulator were more effectively gauged by the combination of the three computer-based tests. Typically simulator assessment scores were not as focused, precise or reliable as the combined test scores in our regression model. A simulator might provide some value if it were able to expose the candidate to novel circumstances and assess their ability to learn, adapt, marshal resources and maintain function under pressure. In reality, selection simulators are rarely able to achieve this.

## Enhancing the power of the selection process

The selection model we just described is only one part of building a complete selection process. Once a process has been developed and validated, the addition of more data points and continuing analysis can only serve to improve it. Data points can come in the form of independent variables, i.e., collecting more information about the applicant pre-hire, or dependent variables, i.e., collecting additional performance data post-hire.

### *Application and background screening*

A well-structured application review that scores each stage of the pilot's development can add to the selection process. This is a low-cost way of determining what an applicant's education, training, and experience bring to the table in order to invite in candidates who are more likely to succeed in the costly in-person assessment of capability. Education, flight training and work experience provide not only a set of facts about the areas of study, the quality of the institutions, and the types of aircraft flown, but also a portrait of how the applicant has handled their development and career and their dedication to the profession. An essential part of the application review is the development of a standardized quantitative scoring of each stage of the candidate's development; education, training, experience, and growth as a professional pilot, as well as their meticulousness and diligence in preparing the application. All of these things can be translated into variables that can be used within the analysis framework and evaluated for their ability to predict performance in the selection process and after hire. If particular background characteristics are found to be valid and reliable measures of later performance, they can then be incorporated into the screening and selection process.

We have found that application and background screening, along with information collected from the structured interview, also can be an important enhancement of the clinical psychological assessment. Even highly qualified applicants may have subtle indications of problems in education, training and employment, or a lack of progression and advancement at work. The scores on these components combined with the evaluation of the interviewers, who have the ability to explore the candidate's background in depth, can add significant information to the psychological evaluation. This is what Raymond King (2014) has referred to as evidence of "occupational impairment" which may be extremely helpful in evaluating the results of psychological screening by instruments like the MMPI-2 along with interviews conducted by clinical psychologists.

## *Probationary assessments*

The observations of pilot candidates during selection may take only a day or two, depending on the process. During that short period of time, candidates can present themselves very favorably. The probation period offers the ability to observe the pilot's attitude over an extended period of time. This is a useful window through which to observe the pilot's understanding and use of aircraft systems, and execution of procedures and maneuvers both in training and in line operations. In addition, airlines are using this time to assess the behaviors of their pilots based on how they approach their work. Does the pilot come to training or the scheduled flight prepared and focused on the tasks at hand? Are they supportive of their fellow trainees and crew? Do they handle criticism well?

All of the characteristics assessed in probationary evaluations can be incorporated into the analysis framework to determine whether or not the selection process is adequately predicting these behavioral characteristics after hire. If negative attitude and/or behaviors exist in a significant proportion of new hires, the airline can adjust their selection model to preventing hiring of these individuals in the future.

This approach is beneficial because, while technical proficiency is the foundation of safety, in many cases it is the attitude and behavior of pilots that lead to management problems and safety issues. Airlines are also coming to appreciate the need to understand how to select for superior performance, rather than just focusing on eliminating poor performers. Superior skills in leadership, judgment, and decisions making can be the catalyst in the cockpit to help solve problems in abnormal situations.

Initial performance in training can be used to establish the validity of the selection process and set the early cut scores for each component of the selection process, but it is the continued good performance in the execution of the job that is the ultimate goal of airlines. This requires continuous monitoring and collection of information on the pilot's performance throughout the probationary period and continuing over their career.

## Establishing a methodology for continuing improvement

As we discussed, on-the-job assessments during probation and throughout the course of pilot careers provide important feedback for the selection process. An example of the predictive power of a selection model is summarized in the results of a long-term study (see Hoffmann *et al.*, 2011). Using the regression equations designed to predict performance immediately after hire, we divided 330 candidates hired in 1996 into five equally sized groups based on the scores they received on the computer-based tests. We then looked at the performance of these pilots over a 12-year period. Pilots that were in the bottom 20 percent of the group had, on average, six times greater likelihood of a problem in training than those in the top 40 percent. Just as interesting, those who did well on the selection model were also less likely to miss work for which they were scheduled. Even though the initial analysis had been performed based on immediate training outcomes, the predictive validity persisted throughout a very large portion of the pilots' careers, including training for transition to different aircraft, upgrade to the captain's position, and regularly scheduled recurrent training.

Table 3.2 also illustrates an approach for determining the pass/fail cut scores based on analysis of the test's predictive power for applicant success in training. Those who scored in the lowest quintile cost more money to train. The lowest quintile also had on average twenty more lost productivity days than the next lowest quintile. Setting the cut score to eliminate the lowest quintile from being hired in the future would produce savings well in excess of developing and maintaining the selection process.

Continuously evaluating the power of the selection measures to predict performance allows the company to explore important questions that will improve the selection process and, consequently, the crew force. Were there indications in the selection process that could have helped avoid problems that some pilots may be displaying after hire? Are there additional measures that could be collected in the selection process that would allow the airline to anticipate or avoid these problems? Is the pool of qualified applicants diminishing so it may be necessary to change the approach in training by adding time or content?

*Table 3.2* Actual training outcomes by predicted performance group

| Predicted performance category | Average training problems per pilot, 1996–2008 | Average lost productivity hours, 1996–2008 |
| --- | --- | --- |
| 1 Highest performers (N=66) | .12 | 195 |
| 2 (N=66) | .11 | 232 |
| 3 (N=66) | .23 | 227 |
| 4 (N=66) | .45 | 223 |
| 5 Lowest performers (N=66) | .73 | 243 |

## Ab-initio *hiring*

There is substantial overlap between the selection considerations for hiring both experienced pilots and *ab-initio* pilots. It can be argued that two of the three components we evaluate in computer-based testing – cognitive skills and personality measures – are both relatively well-established by early adulthood and relatively stable over the candidate's lifetime. While it is not possible to test for job knowledge before teaching the content of the job, it is possible to test for the apparent precursor – the aptitude and ability to learn and apply science, technology, engineering and math.

There are challenges to hiring *ab-initio* pilots that are not present in hiring experienced pilots. The path a person follows as he or she progresses through education, training and employment demonstrates how the candidate has excelled and where they may have encountered problems. First and foremost, the fact that an applicant has gone through flight training and acquired enough hours of flying to apply for a professional pilot job means that the candidate has invested substantial time and endured low pay and hard work to acquire the needed experience and skill. This is a strong indication of commitment to a craft that will continue to demand a great deal of focus and dedication. This early experience and related challenges are all in the future for *ab-initio* candidates. In addition, attrition from the profession is a significant factor. Candidates who are established professional pilots have already demonstrated the grit, desire and determination to overcome challenges inherent in the job. Especially as the reduction in the supply of pilots becomes a bigger consideration in the US and worldwide, it is worthwhile to carefully consider other ways to measure characteristics in *ab-initio* candidates that are observable to a large degree in established pilots.

## Conclusion

Pilot selection is only one pillar in support of safety in flight. It plays the important role of gatekeeper, focused on providing the airline with the most capable professionals required by the company. Most pilots will be with large mainline companies for 25 to 35 years. Even regional carriers have seen a significant proportion of their pilots stay for over 10 years. Selection must take into consideration not only the current demands of the pilot position, but also the ability of the pilot to constantly adapt to the inevitably changing demands of the position as aircraft, technology and industry evolve over time.

Furthermore, each individual pilot selected at a point in time will be different from that same person who matures for the next twenty to forty years. Over that period many things will change. They may get married, divorced, have children. Their parents will grow old, have medical problems and die. They may confront both physical and mental health problems. They may have a change in attitude towards flying or toward the priority that the craft has in their lives. The job of the pilot is an isolated and potentially alienating position. Any of these stresses can produce temporary or sustained psychological issues that can affect judgment and stability. Increasingly, commercial airlines are recognizing the need to rethink processes to address fitness for duty. Safe flight requires formal support systems; these systems have to help identify pilots dealing with problems that may affect their work and intervene where necessary in a supportive fashion. The majority of this book is devoted to this subject.

## References

Barrick, M.R. & Mount, M.K. (1991). The Big Five personality dimensions and job performance: A meta-analysis. *Personnel Psychology*, 44, 1–26.

Borum, R., Super, J., & Rand, M. (2003). Forensic assessment for high-risk occupations. In A.M. Goldstein (ed.), *Handbook of psychology, Vol. II*, 133–147, New York: John Wiley & Sons.

Butcher, J.N. (1994). Psychological assessment of airline pilot applicants with the MMPI–2. *Journal of Personality Assessment*, 62, 31–44.

Butcher, J.N. & Williams, C.L. (2009). Personality assessment with the MMPI-2: historical roots, international adaptations, and current challenges. *Applied Psychology Health and Well-being*, 1, 105–135.

Chidester, T.R., Kanki, B.G., Foushee, H.C., Dickinson, C.L., & Bowles, S.V. (1990). *Personality factors in flight operations: Vol. 1. Leader characteristics and crew performance in a full-mission air transport simulation*. NASA TM-102259, Moffett Field, CA: NASA Ames Research Center.

Costa, P.T. & McCrae, R.R. (1992). *NEO PI-R professional manual*. Odessa, FL: Psychological Assessment Resources.

Damos, D.L. (1993). Using meta analysis to compare predictive validity of single and multiple-task measures to flight performance. *Human Factors*, 35, 615–628.

Endsley, M.R. (1995). Measurement of situational awareness in dynamic systems. *Human Factors*, 37(1), 65–84.

Fitzgibbons, A., Davis, D., & Schutte, P.C. (2004). *Pilot personality profile using the NEO-PI-R*. NASA/TM-2004-213237, Hanover, MD: NASA Center for Aerospace Information.

Fleischman, E.A. (1956). Psychomotor selection tests: Research and application in the United States Air Force. *Personnel Psychology*, 9, 449–467.

Gael, S. (1988). *The job analysis handbook for business, industry and government*. Volume I and II, New York: John Wiley.

Hoffmann, A.K. (2013). Performance driven pilot selection: Building a feedback loop from selection through training. Paper presented at the Regional Airline Association Annual Convention, 2–5 May, Montreal, Canada.

Hoffmann, C.C., Hoffmann, K.P., & Kay, G.G. (1998). The role that cognitive ability plays in CRM. Paper presented at NATO Conference, Edinburgh, April 20–22.

Hoffmann, C.C., Spetz, S.H., & Hoffmann, A.K. (2011). Long-term study of pilot selection at Delta Air Lines. *Proceedings of the Sixteenth International Symposium on Aviation Psychology*, 6–9 May, Dayton, Ohio.

Kay, G.G. (1995). *Cog Screen: Professional manual*. Odessa, FL: Psychological Assessment Resources.

King, R. (2014). Personality (and psychopathology) assessment in the selection of pilots. *The International Journal of Aviation Psychology*, 24(1), 61–73.

O'Hare, D. & Wiggins, M. (1993). Expertise in aeronautical decision making: A cognitive skill analysis. In R.S. Jensen & D. Neumeister (eds), *Proceedings of the Seventh International Symposium on Aviation Psychology*, Columbus, OH: Ohio State University.

Stokes, A.F., Kemper, K.L., & Marsh, R. (1992). *Time-stressed flight decision-making: A study of expert and novice aviators*. Tech Rept ARL-93-1/INEL-93-1, Savoy, IL: University of Illinois, Aviation Research Laboratory.

Street, D. & Helton, K. (1993). The 'right stuff': Personality tests and the five factor model in landing craft air cushion crew training. In *Proceedings of the Human Factors and Ergonomics Society 37th Annual Meeting*, 11–15 April, Seattle, WA, pp 920–924.

Street, D.R. & Dolgin, D.L. (1994). *Computer-based psychomotor tests in optimal track assignment of student naval aviators*. (NAMRL-1391). Pensacola, FL: Naval Aerospace Medical Research Laboratory.

Taylor, J., O'Hara, R., Mumenthaler, M., & Yesavage, J. (2000). Relationship of CogScreen-AE to flight simulator performance and pilot age. *Aviation, Space, and Environmental Medicine*, 71, 373–380.

Wiegmann, D. & Shappell, S. (2003). *A human error approach to aviation accident analysis: The human factors analysis and classification system*. Aldershot: Ashgate.

Yakimovich, N.V., Strongin, G.L., Govorushenko, V.V., Schroeder, D., & Kay, G.G. (1995). Flight performance and CogScreen test battery performance in Russian pilots. Paper presented at the Annual Meeting of the Aerospace Medical Association, 6–12 May 1994, San Antonio, Texas.

# 4 Personality assessment of airline pilot applicants

*James N. Butcher*

Psychopathology in the workplace can have a profound impact on public safety particularly when it involves malicious behavior in high-risk occupations such as airline pilots, police officers, air traffic controllers, or fire department personnel. Notable recent events in the airline industry, in which psychologically maladjusted individuals have intentionally acted against others in harmful and unanticipated ways, are important examples. In 1999, investigators determined that the co-pilot of an Egypt Air plane deliberately crashed into the Atlantic shortly after takeoff from New York's John F. Kennedy International Airport. All 217 people on board died. In 2015, a co-pilot from Germanwings (Lufthansa) Airline flight maliciously took control of the airplane and crashed it into a mountain in France killing all 150 passengers and crew on board.

Although the majority of airline pilots and pilot applicants are very well-adjusted and highly motivated to pursue an aviation career, some pilots or potential pilots are not well-suited for the job or possess personality characteristics that can place airline passengers at risk. The current status of assuring airline pilot mental health adjustment is, however, in flux. Following the recent pilot aggression against the public, government agencies in several countries and airline employment programs at commercial airlines are reevaluating pilot assessment programs in order to more closely evaluate mental health problems. Pilot assessment evaluation systems are likely to undergo some tightening of requirements to assure that these past events can be avoided in the future. However, there are also forces that resist change as well, for example, organizational programming costs and pilot unions' resistance to change suggest that major improvements may be difficult to implement. At this point, not all US airlines conduct psychological evaluations of pilot applicants. In fact, the majority of airlines do not perform pre-employment psychological screening of pilots. Moreover, airlines do not typically perform periodic evaluations to screen for mental health problems (except the medical exams that are required every six months which devote little attention to mental health factors) even though, over time, some people with no history of mental illness develop psychological problems as a result of life change and stressful life circumstances.

Air carriers that conduct pre-employment pilot assessment include the use of personality-based measures that are conducted in employment screening assessments (usually after the person has been determined to be qualified for the job and made a preliminary offer). Other employment assessment situations may involve the psychological evaluation of existing employees, for example fitness-for-duty evaluations for employees who have experienced work-related problems with a psychological element, or evaluations to aid employees to obtain counseling for a mental health problem such as substance abuse (e.g. in an employee assistance program).

In order for a person to be acceptable and to make a valuable contribution to airlines, psychological adjustment factors may be considered important for the personnel psychologist to address in assessing clients for these responsible positions of public trust. The psychological assessment team may choose to incorporate personality measures to obtain information about the applicant's level of adjustment or whether there are any emotional problems that could place the public at risk. Examples of these psychological adjustment factors include emotional stability, judgment and public responsibility, ability to deal with situations that induce extreme stress, capability of dealing effectively on an interpersonal level for jobs that require teamwork among flight crews, and the presence of severe personality disorders that may result in rule violations or careless and impulsive behavior patterns.

In making personnel decisions on the basis of psychological test measures, two general strategies exist: *inclusion* versus *exclusion* decision criteria strategies. Under inclusion strategies, an applicant would be considered eligible for the desired position if his or her test scores occur in a given range that suggested positive qualities needed for the job, such as having a high score on an IQ test that would qualify them for a position that requires a particular level of intelligence. Or, a position on a particular job that requires effective social skills might require an inclusion score on a personality measure that validly predicts sociability.

Using *exclusion* rules, on the other hand, an applicant would be eliminated from the acceptable applicant pool if test scores are in a range that are considered to be associated with negative characteristics such as personality problems, emotional instability, or possible substance abuse problems. In personnel screening in which mental health status is considered a key factor in the assessment procedure, the exclusion criteria rules are followed. If the individual is determined to likely be experiencing behavioral or mental health problems they are excluded from employment and their preliminary offer rescinded.

One important point to consider in using psychological tests in personnel decisions is whether the measured variables (e.g. test scores) are valid and reliable with a substantial empirical research basis. Another point to consider is the important information available on the applicant's background or work record. For example, if the psychological evaluation raises concerns regarding an applicant's impulsivity or poor judgment, these hypotheses should be confirmed or verified in the applicant's record or background; for example, have there been instances of arrests, job loss through questionable behavior, driving problems (e.g. DUI) and so forth.

One major US airline follows a careful examination program that involves going a step further in the evaluation process in order to assure that the potential for hiring problematic pilots is low while there is fairness to the applicant in the process—the applicant's evaluation is thorough and decisions "not to hire" are soundly based through the following procedures:

- Phase 1 of the process involves airline personnel staff assuring that the applicant meets all the work and background requirements for the job, including flight experience, information, reference verification, human resources interviews assuring that the applicant is qualified to meet the work requirements. If these requirements are met the applicant is sent to the next phase.
- Phase 2 of the process involves a medical and psychological examination. The psychological examination is conducted by a qualified clinical psychologist who administers an interview and a Minnesota Multiphasic Personality Inventory (MMPI-2). If the applicant does not show any physical health or mental health issues in this phase then they are hired. If questions are raised in the MMPI-2 or interview process the applicant is sent to the next phase of the process.
- Phase 3 involves a thorough review of the applicant's records, background, and psychological test results by a team that includes: a clinical psychologist, an equal opportunity department member, a senior airline pilot, and an attorney. Any mental health or behavioral problems are given close consideration and, if necessary, additional information is sought if further problem verification is needed.

## Airline pilot applicant screening with the Minnesota Multiphasic Personality Inventory (MMPI)

Hathaway and McKinley (1940) developed the original MMPI as a means of evaluating mental health symptoms and behavioral problems in clinical patients. The instrument was found to be valuable in assessing clients in other settings as well. During World War II the MMPI came to be widely used in military settings to evaluate people with psychological problems and for screening potential pilots in the Army Air Force to assure that people with psychological problems were not placed in responsible flight positions.

Extensive research has been conducted on the use of the MMPI and MMPI-2 in evaluating applicants in personnel settings (Butcher, 2016) to assure that the scales on the test were appropriate, reliable, and valid in predicting behavior pertinent to screening applicants in high-risk occupations such as police personnel, firefighters, religious leaders, nuclear power plant employees, or airline pilots. The first published validity study of the MMPI in personnel selection was conducted by Abramson during World War II, shortly after the MMPI was published.

Abramson (1945) established the value of the MMPI in pilot selection. A few years later, the combined use of several MMPI scales to make predictions as to adjustment in US Navy aviation cadets was studied (Melton, 1955).

After the MMPI was revised and validated in 1989, the MMPI-2 performance of airline pilot applicants was described and analyzed with a large sample of pilot applicants (Butcher, 1994). A measure for detecting invalidating response conditions in personnel assessment, the Superlative Self Expression Scale or *S*, was developed using a sample of pilot applicants to address the tendency of some applicants to claim extreme virtue through presenting oneself in a superlative manner (Butcher & Han, 1995). The development and subsequent validation of the test-retest method (to be discussed below) was completed. The procedure uses special instructions for administering the MMPI-2 in order to reduce test defensiveness and obtain a higher percentage of valid protocols in personnel screening (Butcher *et al.*,1997; Butcher *et al.*, 2009; Cigrang & Staal, 2001).

### The MMPI-2-RF in personnel selection

In order to clarify for readers who are unfamiliar with the MMPI-2, the important distinction between the MMPI-2 and a new measure that is derived from a portion of the items referred to as the MMPI-2-RF is needed. There are clear problems with the MMPI-2-RF in personnel assessment that users need to be aware of to distinguish the MMPI-2-RF from the well-researched and extensively validated MMPI-2. The MMPI-2-RF is a shortened test (only 60 percent of the full MMPI-2 item pool) that has little relationship with its namesake, the MMPI-2. Two-thirds of the 50 scales on the MMPI-2-RF are new measures introduced for the first time by the test developers and publisher (Ben-Porath & Tellegen, 2008; Tellegen & Ben-Porath, 2008); the original MMPI clinical scales are not included in the MMPI-2-RF.

The MMPI-2-RF is composed of its core measures, the Restructured Clinical Scales (Tellegen *et al.*, 2003), along with a number of new content-based measures. The RC scale authors published the RC scales in an effort they thought might psychometrically improve the MMPI-2 clinical scales. Two well-described problems with the MMPI-2-RF scales are that these measures are not as sensitive to psychopathology as the original clinical scales. That is, they do not predict mental health problems as well as the original clinical scales (see discussion by Butcher *et al.*, 2015). Another reason that the MMPI-2-RF does not address problematic behavior in personnel settings is that many of the test items relevant to work-related behavior were deleted from the item pool and do not appear on the MMPI-2-RF (Work Functioning items that were deleted from the MMPI-2 item pool to make the MMPI-2-RF a shorter inventory were: 15, 19, 54, 136, 174, 211, 402, 409, 428, 440, 457, 460, 503, 517, 531, 535, 541, 559, 560, 561, 566).

Another important reason to avoid using the MMPI-2-RF in personnel screening is that the problems and controversies with the test could result in difficulties for the assessment psychologist using the MMPI-2-RF if a rejected client takes his or her case to court and challenges the personnel decision. The MMPI-2-RF has been heavily criticized by MMPI-2 experts. Six recent MMPI-2 textbooks have recommended against using the MMPI-2-RF in evaluations rather than the MMPI-2 because it is a new test with a limited research base. For example, Graham (2012, p. 415) pointed out:

> In settings where the goal of assessment is a comprehensive understanding of test takers, this author would choose the MMPI-2 because it is his opinion that interpretations based on the MMPI-2 can yield a more in-depth analysis of personality and psychopathology.

The more recent MMPI-2/MMPI-2-RF textbook by Friedman and colleagues (2015) pointed out:

> Despite the MMPI-2 designation for both the standard MMPI-2 and MMPI-2-RF versions, the RF form should be considered to be an essentially new instrument, as distinct from a mere revision or updating of the MMPI-2, as was the case in its transition from the original MMPI … In short, the MMPI-2-RF is a new and, to this point, largely untested psychometric instrument, and does not yet have the wealth of empirical support and interpretive data enjoyed by the MMPI-2.
>
> (Friedman *et al.*, p. 593)

The United States Federal Aviation Administration, based upon research conducted, recommended against using the MMPI-2-RF in pilot and air traffic controller screening. They recommend that the MMPI-2 be used as the standard (FAA, 2013, n.p.):

> Personality domain, to include the Minnesota Multiphasic Personality Inventory-2. (The MMPI-2-RF is not an approved substitute. All scales, subscales, content, and supplementary scales must be scored and provided. Computer scoring is required. Abbreviated administrations are not acceptable.)

## The MMPI-2 clinical and supplemental scales in pilot screening

Extensive information on interpretation of MMPI-2 scales is available for the widely used personality inventory. Readers interested in obtaining a more detailed description of the scales and interpretive background for MMPI-2 would find the following resources helpful: Butcher, 2011; Graham, 2012; Friedman *et al.*, 2015.

### The MMPI-2 validity scales

There are a number of measures on the MMPI-2 that are designed to provide the examiner with information as to how cooperative the client was in responding to the test items:

- *? (Cannot Say):* The total number of unanswered items. A defensive protocol is suggested if the raw score is 30 or more unanswered items.
- *TRIN (True Response Inconsistency):* TRIN is made up of pairs of items to which a combination of true or false responses is inconsistent. Extreme scores (80 or higher) reflect a tendency to answer inconsistently false (i.e., "nay saying") or inconsistently true (i.e., "yea saying"). A constant of 9 is added to the score to avoid negative numbers. Raw scores are converted to linear T scores based on the normative sample.
- *VRIN (Variable Response Inconsistency):* VRIN is made up of pairs of items for which one or two of four possible configurations (true-false, false-true, true-true, false-false) represent inconsistent responses. The scale is scored by summing the number of inconsistent responses. Extreme *VRIN* elevations of 80 or higher indicate an invalid response style. The *VRIN* scale is an effective measure of random responding.
- *Percentage of true responses:* An extremely high true percentage (95 percent or higher) reflects a highly distorted response pattern that invalidates the profile.
- *Percentage of false responses:* An extremely high false percentage (95 percent or higher) reflects a highly distorted response pattern that invalidates the profile.
- *F (Infrequency):* The *F* or Infrequency scale was developed by determining which of the MMPI items are rarely endorsed by the general population. Items that were endorsed by less than 10 percent of the population were considered to be Infrequently endorsed items, *F*. Items on the *F* scale occur within the first 370 items in the booklet. High scores (T above 90) suggest some extreme responding that may be due to reading difficulties, confusion, inconsistent responding, exaggeration, or possibly serious psychopathology. A T score of 100 on *F* suggests invalid responding.
- *F(B) (Infrequency):* The *F(B)* or Back Infrequency scale was developed by determining which of the MMPI items are rarely endorsed by the general population occurring toward the end of the MMPI-2 booklet. Extreme scores on the *F(B)* scale indicate that the scales that have items occurring at the rear of the item booklet, such as the content scales, may be affected by symptom exaggeration.
- *F(p) (Psychiatric infrequency scale):* The *F(p)* scale provides an estimate of infrequent responding in a psychiatric setting. This scale assesses the extent to which a person has responded to infrequently endorsed items compared with patients who are being evaluated in a psychiatric setting. High scores indicate that the client has endorsed more extreme symptoms that even hospitalized psychiatric patients rarely acknowledge.

- *L (Lie):* A measure of a rather unsophisticated or self-consciously "virtuous" test-taking attitude. Elevated scores (above 65 T) suggest that the individual is presenting him or herself in an overly positive light, attempting to create an unrealistically favorable view of his or her adjustment.
- *K (Defensiveness):* Measures an individual's unwillingness to disclose personal information or to discuss his or her problems. High scores (T greater than 65) reflect possible reluctance to disclose personal information.
- *S ( Superlative self-presentation scale):* The *S* scale was developed to measure test defensiveness. The research population studied was airline pilot applicants. People who endorse high scores on *S* endorse few minor faults or problems. High scores on *S* are associated with low symptom acknowledgment and fewer negative personality characteristics. High scorers endorse extreme "self control."

## The clinical scales

- *Scale 1 Hs (Hypochondriasis):* Applicants taking the MMPI-2 who score high on *Hs* tend to present numerous vague physical problems and may be unhappy, self-centered, whiny, complaining, and attention-demanding. They also report feeling dissatisfied with life and cynical toward others.
- *Scale 2 D (Depression):* People who score high on the *D* scale report feeling depressed, having low self-esteem, and feelings of inadequacy. Scale elevations reflect low mood, great discomfort and a need for change or symptomatic relief. High scorers tend to be pessimistic and unhappy, feel useless, and are indecisive and socially withdrawn.
- *Scale 3 Hy (Hysteria):* High scorers tend to rely on psychological defense mechanisms such as denial and repression to deal with stress. They tend to be dependent and naive. They show little insight into problems. High levels of stress may be accompanied by the development of physical symptoms. The *Hy* scale is sometimes elevated above a T score of 65 for job applicants who are presenting a highly virtuous and overly positive presentation of their mental health adjustment.
- *Scale 4 Pd (Psychopathic Deviate):* Elevations on the *Pd* scale measure acting-out behaviors—anti social attitudes, rebelliousness, disrupted family relations, lying, impulsiveness, school or legal difficulties. Alcohol or drug problems may be present.
- *Scale 5 Mf (Masculinity-Femininity):* High-scoring males are described as having an unusual pattern of stereotypically feminine interests. Because the direction of scoring is reversed, high-scoring females are seen as having stereotypically masculine or "macho" interests.
- *Scale 6 Pa (Paranoia):* Elevations on this scale are often associated with being suspicious, aloof, shrewd, guarded, worrying, and overly sensitive. High scorers tend to be hostile and argumentative. They are often found to have problems in relationships.

- *Scale 7 Pt (Psychasthenia):* High scorers on this anxiety measure tend to be quite anxious, and report being tense, overly preoccupied with details, obsessional, and rigid. High scorers tend to have low self-confidence.
- *Scale 8 Sc (Schizophrenia):* High scorers may have an unconventional or schizoid lifestyle. They can be withdrawn, shy, and moody, and they may feel inadequate, tense, and confused. They may have unusual or strange thoughts, poor judgment, and erratic moods. Career problems and low personal achievement are quite possible.
- *Scale 9 Ma (Mania):* High scorers may be impulsive and overly energetic. Acting-out behaviors and life problems occur among high-scoring clients.
- *Scale 0 Si (Social introversion-extroversion):* High scorers tend to be introverted, shy, withdrawn, socially reserved, submissive, over controlled, lethargic, conventional, tense, inflexible, and guilt-prone. Low scorers tend to be extroverted, outgoing, gregarious, expressive, and talkative.

### *Important supplemental scales in pilot assessment*

- *MAC-R (MacAndrew alcoholism scale):* High scores indicate that the individual has endorsed content relevant to assessing alcohol or drug use and related problems (MacAndrew, 1965).
- *AAS (Addiction acknowledgment scale):* Individuals who score high on AAS are acknowledging problems with alcohol or drugs. High scores suggest the tendency for the individual to develop alcohol or drug use problems (Weed *et al.*, 1992).
- *APS (Addiction proneness scale):* High scorers who are prone to developing problems with alcohol and other drugs tend to be risk-takers. High scores are associated with similarity of membership in samples of substance-abusing patients (Weed *et al.*,1992).

## Information from the MMPI-2 of use in airline pilot selection

A summary of personality factors that are addressed by MMPI-2 scales that can be of value in conducting personnel screening evaluations of airline pilot applicants is provided as follows:

- The MMPI-2 validity measures, *L, K,* and *S,* provide information about the applicant's cooperativeness with the evaluation. Moreover, their defensive approach to dealing with conflicts and relationships can be reflected in these measures. The applicant with score elevations such as high *K* and *S* tends to be defensive, rigid, and evasive in dealing with others; can be ineffective in dealing with conflict; or tends to be self-defensive under pressure.
- The possibility of low stress tolerance or low emotional control can be reflected in several measures. The person may panic under stress; may make inappropriate decisions under pressure; or may react to stress with

negative behaviors such as alcohol abuse, and show physical symptoms (as shown by high scores such as high *Hy*, *Pt*, *D*, Addiction proneness scale [*APS*], and MacAndrew alcoholism scale-revised [*MAC-R*]).

- Several MMPI-2 measures can provide information about an applicant's low acceptance of feedback and supervision. The applicant may tend to externalize blame; become defensive when criticized. He or she may not accept authority as shown by score elevations such as high *Pa*, *Pd*, *Ma*, and *CYN*.

- Low impulse control and failure to think ahead in making decisions before acting; an applicant may make rash decisions as reflected in score elevations such as high *Pd*, *Ma*, *ASP* or Antisocial personality.

- The presence of negative attitudes can be reflected in several MMPI-2 measures. The applicant may demonstrate low positive social skills; hold an overly cynical view of others; or may show low trust by elevations on the *Si*, *CYN*, and *Pa*.

- Potentially low dependability and unreliability can be appraised through some MMPI-2 scales. The applicant may show characteristics of personality problems, procrastination, or careless behavior. Characteristics such as impulsivity, that could create difficulties on the job, are reflected in scale elevations on *Pd*, *Ma*, *Sc*, *ASP*, and *CYN*).

- Several MMPI-2 measures address issues of low work initiative or low achievement motivation. The person may need careful supervision; is low in energy; and may show disabling psychopathology, as shown by score elevations such as high *Sc*, *D,* and *WRK* or Work interference.

- The MMPI-2 contains measures that suggest that the applicant may fail to conform to rules and regulations. May show low respect for authority; may not follow recommended testing procedures as shown by elevations on scales such as high *Pd*, *Ma*, and *ASP*.

- Personality characteristics or behavioral problems such as low anger control, interpersonal relationship problems or having a tendency toward reactive aggression is reflected in scale score elevations such as high *ANG* or Anger, *ASP*, *DISC*, *Pd*, and *Ma*.

- Behavioral characteristics of low adaptability to environmental demands and low flexibility of dealing with life changes can be evaluated in several MMPI-2 measures. The person may show a low capacity to change behavior to meet new demands; or have difficulty accepting new job demands; or may not be able to work on more than one task at a time can be reflected in high scale elevations such as *Pt*, *Si,* and *WRK*.

- Successful aircraft operations are dependent upon teamwork among the flight crewmembers. Possible problems with teamwork, working with others, or showing a low capacity to develop and maintain good working relationships can be appraised by score elevations such as *Pd*, *Sc*, *ANG*, and *ASP*.

## Use of the test-retest method in pilot selection

Many men and women who seek positions as airline pilots tend to present themselves in their interviews and in psychological evaluations as extremely well-adjusted, morally strong, and void of any mental health problems. When taking psychological tests prior to employment, pilot applicants who have personality problems and other mental health symptoms can respond in a way to "mask" those problems. Consequently, test protocols might be invalidated or considered to have minimal information because the applicant has presented an overly "rosy" picture of his or her adjustment.

In the pilot assessment process with the MMPI-2, if an applicant produces an overly defensive and invalid pattern such as an extremely high L score (L equal or greater than 65; or K equal or greater than 70) then the examiner is unable to draw personality-based conclusions about their psychological adjustment from the clinical or content scales. Thus, no personality information is available in the protocol and in most cases the person is not offered employment. However, some applicants may not be psychologically maladjusted but simply making the mistake of presenting themselves in an overly virtuous manner—not uncommon in airline pilot assessments. In order to reduce the number of applicants who invalidate their MMPI-2 on the basis of overly virtuous responding, a procedure was developed in which the applicant who invalidates the protocol is given an opportunity to retake the MMPI-2 with the request for them to be less defensive in their responding in the retest. Here are the instructions that are provided in the re-administration:

### Test-retest instructions

Because of test defensiveness, your first test results were not valid and, thus, cannot be used as part of your evaluation.

When people take the Minnesota Multiphasic Personality Inventory-2 (MMPI-2) in employment settings, they sometimes respond to the questions in a manner that will create a favorable self-impression, emphasizing their strengths and de-emphasizing what they perceive to be their weaknesses.

The MMPI-2 contains several measures that were constructed to allow the interpreter to evaluate test-taking attitudes, and test protocols that are invalid, unfortunately cannot be used as part of the evaluation.

We hope that you will consent to retake the MMPI-2. If you do so, please answer all the items unless they really do not apply to you, and be as accurate as possible about yourself in terms of your responses to the test questions.

A number of studies have been reported showing that when the retest method is employed, the applicant tends to be more forthcoming on the second testing (Butcher *et al.*, 2009; Butcher *et al.*, 1997; Butcher *et al.*, 2000; Cigrang & Staal, 2001; Fink & Butcher, 1972; Walfish, 2007, 2011). Butcher *et al.* (1997) reported that when defensive pilots were told that they had invalidated the test because they were too defensive and were allowed to retake the test, they tended to provide a more frank and open appraisal in the readministration. Over two-thirds of the applicants produced a valid protocol the second time, and over 14 percent of those being retested showed scale elevations on the MMPI-2 clinical scales suggesting psychopathology that they had not shown in the initial evaluation.

Butcher and colleagues (2009), employing test results on candidates for the fast-track security assessment program of the Department of Energy, reported similar findings with respect to the percentage of applicants who responded more openly on the second administration following the retest procedure. On initial administration, 21 percent presented as defensive invalid, and 79 percent produced initial valid profiles. Upon readministration using the modified instructions, the initial defensive invalid group ($N=297$) produced valid profiles in 84 percent of the applicants that initially produced defensive invalid profiles. Of the retest group, only 15 percent ($N=47$) remained defensive/invalid.

## Case illustration: MMPI-2 in employment screening

### Applicant's background

Edwin S. was a 36-year-old pilot applicant who currently flies C-130 transport planes for the Air National Guard. He was born and raised in a rural city in Georgia where he attended high school. His father was a manager of a grocery store and his mother was a florist. Mr. S. had two older sisters. During high school he was active in sports and played baseball for his high school team. After he graduated from high school, he completed his BA degree in aviation at Purdue University. Upon graduation from college, he entered the U.S. Air Force and completed flight school, after which he flew C-130s for eight years. During his time in the Air Force he attained the rank of captain. When he was discharged from the Air Force he continued flying C-130s in the Air National Guard.

Mr. S. has been married for seven years and is currently separated. He and his wife have one child, three years old, and his wife has custody of their daughter. Mr. S. has experienced a number of driving problems over the past eight years; he received six speeding tickets over the past five years and a careless driving charge after he changed lanes and drove on the right side of the highway to get around traffic five years earlier. When he was 17 he had his driving license suspended for six months for an open bottle offense after he was stopped for a traffic violation and the arresting officer found several empty beer cans and an open bottle of rum on his back seat. He was given a breathalyzer test to determine his blood alcohol level, but was not found to be above the legal limit and did not receive a DUI.

## Interview Information

Mr. S. was appropriately dressed in business attire for the interview. He was initially uncomfortable in the interview process, however, he became more talkative as the interview proceeded except when specific, more personal history questions were asked. He appeared to be somewhat vague in many of his responses and tended to gloss over issues related to his driving problems and his departure from the Air Force. For example, he reported that he had been somewhat disappointed that he was not given a higher command and additional

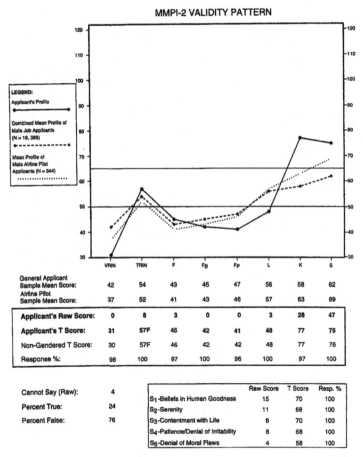

| | VRIN | TRIN | F | F$_B$ | F$_P$ | L | K | S |
|---|---|---|---|---|---|---|---|---|
| General Applicant Sample Mean Score: | 42 | 54 | 43 | 45 | 47 | 56 | 58 | 62 |
| Airline Pilot Sample Mean Score: | 37 | 52 | 41 | 43 | 46 | 57 | 63 | 69 |
| **Applicant's Raw Score:** | 0 | 8 | 3 | 0 | 0 | 3 | 28 | 47 |
| **Applicant's T Score:** | 31 | 57F | 45 | 42 | 41 | 48 | 77 | 75 |
| Non-Gendered T Score: | 30 | 57F | 46 | 42 | 42 | 48 | 77 | 76 |
| Response %: | 98 | 100 | 97 | 100 | 96 | 100 | 97 | 100 |

| Cannot Say (Raw): | 4 |
|---|---|
| Percent True: | 24 |
| Percent False: | 76 |

| | Raw Score | T Score | Resp. % |
|---|---|---|---|
| S$_1$-Beliefs in Human Goodness | 15 | 70 | 100 |
| S$_2$-Serenity | 11 | 68 | 100 |
| S$_3$-Contentment with Life | 8 | 70 | 100 |
| S$_4$-Patience/Denial of Irritability | 8 | 68 | 100 |
| S$_5$-Denial of Moral Flaws | 4 | 58 | 100 |

*Figure 4.1* Validity scale profile in the initial administration of the MMPI-2 to Edwin S.

Excerpted from *The Minnesota Report™: Revised Personnel System, 3rd Edition* by James N. Butcher. Copyright © 1989, 1991, 1994, 1995, 2001, 2003 by the Regents of the University of Minnesota. Portions excerpted from *MMPI®-2 (Minnesota Multiphasic Personality Inventory®-2) Manual for Administration, Scoring, and Interpretation, Revised Edition* by Butcher *et al.* Copyright © 2001 by the Regents of the University of Minnesota. Reproduced by permission of the University of Minnesota Press. All rights reserved. "MMPI®" and "Minnesota Multiphasic Personality Inventory®" are registered trademarks, and "MMPI-2", "Minnesota Multiphasic Personality Inventory-2" and "The Minnesota Report" are trademarks of the University of Minnesota.

duty assignments. His military performance reviews showed some past crew-related problems. At one point, he was suspended from flight status for a period of time during an investigation into a disagreement he had with another pilot.

In addition to the assessment interview that was conducted with Mr. S. he was also administered the MMPI-2. His initial MMPI-2 was invalid as a result of defensiveness (see Figure 4.1). He agreed to re-take the MMPI-2 and was provided the test-retest administration instructions. His performance in the second administration was more cooperative and forthcoming and he produced a valid and interpretable MMPI-2 performance (see Figure 4.2).

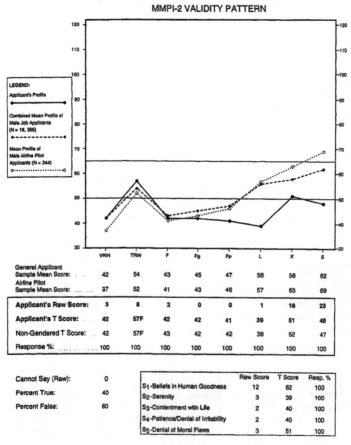

*Figure 4.2* Validity scale profile in the readministration of the MMPI-2 to Edwin S.

Excerpted from *The Minnesota Report™: Revised Personnel System, 3rd Edition* by James N. Butcher. Copyright © 1989, 1991, 1994, 1995, 2001, 2003 by the Regents of the University of Minnesota. Portions excerpted from *MMPI®-2 (Minnesota Multiphasic Personality Inventory®-2) Manual for Administration, Scoring, and Interpretation, Revised Edition* by Butcher *et al.* Copyright © 2001 by the Regents of the University of Minnesota. Reproduced by permission of the University of Minnesota Press. All rights reserved. "MMPI®" and "Minnesota Multiphasic Personality Inventory®" are registered trademarks, and "MMPI-2", "Minnesota Multiphasic Personality Inventory-2" and "The Minnesota Report" are trademarks of the University of Minnesota.

### Interpretation of Mr. S's MMPI-2 clinical and supplemental profiles

#### Profile validity

Mr. S's second MMPI-2 was valid and interpretable (see Figure 4.3). His approach to the test items was open and cooperative. His normal range validity scales may be viewed as a positive indication of his involvement with the evaluation.

#### Mental health symptoms

Mr. S's elevation on the MMPI-2 *Pa* and *Pd* scales indicate a number of likely personality problems that could interfere with his work functioning. The high-point *Pa* scale indicates that he is likely overly sensitive, mistrustful, and easily

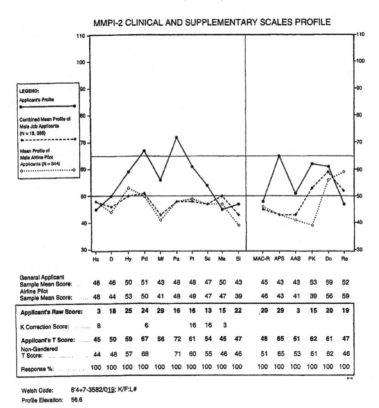

**MMPI-2 CLINICAL AND SUPPLEMENTARY SCALES PROFILE**

| | Hs | D | Hy | Pd | Mf | Pa | Pt | Sc | Ma | Si | MAC-R | APS | AAS | PK | Do | Re |
|---|---|---|---|---|---|---|---|---|---|---|---|---|---|---|---|---|
| General Applicant Sample Mean Score: | 48 | 46 | 50 | 51 | 43 | 48 | 48 | 47 | 50 | 43 | 45 | 43 | 43 | 53 | 59 | 52 |
| Airline Pilot Sample Mean Score: | 48 | 44 | 53 | 50 | 41 | 48 | 49 | 47 | 47 | 39 | 46 | 43 | 41 | 39 | 56 | 59 |
| Applicant's Raw Score: | 3 | 18 | 25 | 24 | 29 | 16 | 16 | 13 | 15 | 22 | 20 | 29 | 3 | 15 | 20 | 19 |
| K Correction Score: | 8 | | 6 | | | | 16 | 16 | 3 | | | | | | | |
| Applicant's T Score: | 45 | 50 | 59 | 67 | 56 | 72 | 61 | 54 | 45 | 47 | 48 | 65 | 51 | 62 | 61 | 47 |
| Non-Gendered T Score: | 44 | 48 | 57 | 68 | | 71 | 60 | 55 | 46 | 46 | 51 | 65 | 53 | 61 | 62 | 46 |
| Response %: | 100 | 100 | 100 | 100 | 100 | 100 | 100 | 100 | 100 | 100 | 100 | 100 | 100 | 100 | 100 | 100 |

Welsh Code: 6'4+7-3582/019: K/F:L#
Profile Elevation: 56.6

*Figure 4.3* MMPI-2 clinical and supplementary scale profile for Edwin S.

hurt by others. He approaches difficult life circumstances in somewhat rigid and self-righteous ways. He tends to remain aloof and detached, and he is cautious around other people, fearing they will take advantage of him. He is somewhat touchy and may be argumentative at times. He tends to blame other people for his own failings. His elevation on the *Pd* scale indicates that he is also prone to acting-out behaviors—antisocial attitudes, rebelliousness, disrupted family relations, and impulsive behavior. He appears to have had a great deal of conflict with authority in the past and is quite resentful of societal and parental standards of conduct. He reported having some antisocial beliefs and attitudes. At times, he may seem naïve in relationships. His denial of negative impulses and his unusual espousal of high moral standards probably influence his attitudes toward others.

*Interpersonal relations*

Mr. S's MMPI-2 scores suggest that he is somewhat rigid and aloof and does not fully trust anyone. He may be difficult to deal with owing to his rigid, opinionated, and rather argumentative style. The relatively high elevation of the scales in his clinical profile shows high profile definition. If he is retested at a later date, his peak scores are likely to retain their relative salience. His highpoint score on *Pa* is likely to show moderate test-retest stability. Thus, the applicant's personality pattern is not likely to change significantly over time. He may appear somewhat intractable and is typically rigid, detached, and somewhat suspicious. He may have periods in which hostility, increased mistrust, and anger are salient features of his personal relationships.

*Possible employment problems*

His psychological adjustment problems are likely to result in difficulties for him. His capacity to work closely with others in a crew environment requires further evaluation. He may have some problems with supervision because he is not very open to suggestions from others. The applicant's rigid and mistrustful behavior may produce stress in work relationships. He may appear docile and cooperative with superiors but aggressive and demanding toward subordinates. He may be hostile to other employees.

Some individuals with this applicant's elevation on the MMPI-2 substance abuse indicators encounter lifestyle problems. His past behavior and habits should be evaluated through careful background or reference checks.

*Recommendation*

Mr. S. was not recommended for employment with the airline. His performance on the MMPI-2, suggesting likely long-term personality problems that could impact work relationships including suspicion and mistrust of authority, anger control, and difficulties in interpersonal relationships were considered problematic for participating in the cooperative environment of commercial aviation. The MMPI-2 profile pattern appears to be consistent with his past behavioral problems. His difficulties in working with others and his problematic impulsive behavior as noted by the MMPI-2 were confirmed in the background information and interview. His work history that apparently interfered with his military career, the background information and driving offenses along with past substance abuse problems were considered potential adjustment difficulties.

## Summary

Psychopathology in the workplace can have a great impact on public safety, particularly when it involves malicious, aggressive behavior that has occurred in trusted occupations such as airline pilots. Recent air disasters that killed hundreds of passengers were caused by psychologically maladjusted flight crew-members whose psychological disturbance was not detected by authorities prior to the incidents. Many US and international airlines do not conduct psychological evaluations of pilot applicants prior to employment or perform periodic evaluations to screen for mental health problems that develop over time, even though some people with no history of mental illness develop psychological problems.

Some air carriers that conduct pre-employment pilot assessment evaluations include the use of personality-based measures that are conducted in employment screening assessments (usually after the person has been determined to be qualified for the job and made a preliminary offer). One of the most frequently used clinical personality instruments used in pre-employment screening is the MMPI-2. The clinical scales of the MMPI-2 have a long history of application in pilot screening and have a substantial research base supporting their interpretation.

This chapter addresses the application of the MMPI-2 in pilot screening and describes the scales that provide important information assessment that psychologists find pertinent to making employment decisions. A procedure that was developed to reduce the invalid defensive protocol, the test-retest method, was described and illustrated. A case study was provided to illustrate the information from the MMPI-2 that can be of value in pilot assessment.

## References

Abramson, H.A. (1945). The Minnesota personality test in relation to selection of specialized military personnel. *Psychosomatic Medicine*, 7, 178–184.

Ben-Porath, Y.S., & Tellegen, A. (2008). *MMPI-2-RF manual for administration, scoring, and interpretation*. Minneapolis, MN: University of Minnesota Press.

Butcher, J.N. (1994). Psychological assessment of airline pilot applicants with the MMPI-2. *Journal of Personality Assessment*, 62, 31–44.

Butcher, J.N. (2002). Assessing pilots with 'the wrong stuff': A call for research on emotional health factors in commercial aviators. *International Journal of Selection and Assessment*, 10(1), 1–17.

Butcher, J.N. (2011). *A beginner's guide to the MMPI-2* (3rd edition). Washington, DC: The American Psychological Association.

Butcher, J.N. (2012). 25 historical highlights: significant contributions for use of the MMPI/MMPI-2 in personnel applications Retrieved from http://www.umn.edu/mmpi

Butcher, J.N. (2016). MMPI-2 Reference Files. *MMPI-2, MMPI-A, and Minnesota Reports: Research and Clinical Applications*. Retrieved http://mmpi.umn.edu/index.php (accessed 9 September 2016).

Butcher, J.N., & Han, K. (1995). Development of an MMPI-2 scale to assess the presentation of self in a superlative manner: The S Scale. In: J.N. Butcher and C.D. Spielberger (eds) *Advances in personality assessment Vol. 10.* (pp. 25–50). Hillsdale NJ: Lawrence Erlbaum Associates Inc.

Butcher, J.N., Atlis, M., & Fang, L. (2000). The effects of altered instructions on the MMPI-2 profiles of college students who are not motivated to distort their responses. *Journal of Personality Assessment*, 74(3), 492–501.

Butcher, J.N., Gucker, D.K., & Hellervik, L.W. (2009). Clinical personality assessment in the employment context. In: J. N. Butcher (ed.) *Oxford handbook of personality assessment.* (pp. 582–598). New York: Oxford University Press.

Butcher, J.N., Hass, G.A., Greene, R.L., & Nelson, L.D. (2015). *Using the MMPI-2 in forensic assessment.* Washington, D.C.: American Psychological Association.

Butcher, J.N., Morfitt, R., Rouse, S.V., & Holden, R.R. (1997). Reducing MMPI-2 defensiveness: The effect of specialized instructions on retest validity in a job applicant sample. *Journal of Personality Assessment*, 68(2), 385–401.

Cigrang, J.A., & Staal, M.A. (2001). Readministration of the MMPI-2 following defensive invalidation in a military job applicant sample. *Journal of Personality Assessment*, 76, 472–481.

FAA (2013). *Guide for aviation medical examiners: Decision considerations, disease protocols, psychiatric and psychological evaluations.* Washington DC: Federal Aviation Administration. http://www.faa.gov/about/office_org/headquarters_offices/avs/offices/aam/ame/guide/dec_cons/disease_prot/ppevals/ (accessed 9 September 2016).

Fink, A.M., & Butcher, J.N. (1972). Reducing objections to personality inventories with special instructions. *Educational and Psychological Measurement*, 32, 631–639.

Friedman, A.F., Bolinsky, P.K., Levak, R., & Nichols, D.S. (2015). *Psychological assessment with the MMPI-2/RF* (3rd edn). New York: Routledge.

Graham, J.R. (2012). *MMPI-2: Assessing personality and psychopathology* (5th edition). New York: Oxford University Press.

Hathaway, S.R., & McKinley, J.C. (1940). A multiphasic personality schedule (Minnesota): I. Construction of the schedule. *Journal of Psychology*, 10 , 249–254.

MacAndrew, C. (1965). The differentiation of male alcoholic outpatients from nonalcoholic psychiatric outpatients by means of the MMPI. *Quarterly Journal of Studies on Alcohol*, 26, 238–246.

Melton, R.S. (1955). Studies in the evaluation of the personality characteristics of successful naval aviators. *Journal of Aviation Medicine*, 25, 600–604.

Tellegen, A., & Ben-Porath, Y.S. (2008). *MMPI-2-RF technical manual.* Minneapolis, MN: University of Minnesota Press.

Tellegen, A., Ben-Porath, Y.S., McNulty, J.L., Arbisi, P.A., Graham, J R., & Kaemmer, B. (2003). *The MMPI–2 L scales: Development, validation, and interpretation.* Minneapolis, MN: University of Minnesota Press.

Walfish, S. (2007). Reducing Minnesota Multiphasic Personality Inventory defensiveness: Effect of specialized instructions on retest validity in a sample of preoperative bariatric patients. *Surgery for Obesity and Related Diseases*, 3, 184–188.

Walfish, S. (2011). Reducing MMPI-defensiveness in professionals presenting for evaluation. *Journal of Addictive Diseases*, 30(1), 75–80.

Weed, N.C., Butcher, J.N., McKenna, T., & Ben-Porath, Y.S. (1992). New measures for assessing alcohol and drug abuse with the MMPI-2: The APS and AAS. *Journal of Personality Assessment*, 58(2), 389–404.

# Part II
# Pilot clinical assessments

# 5  Between the joystick and the seat

## Getting inside pilots' minds using clinical interviewing

*Paul Dickens*

We've looked into the problems you've been having with your motor vehicle sir, and we've discovered that the problems lie somewhere between the steering wheel and the seat

(Automotive service director, Edinburgh)

This book looks at a number of issues concerning pilot mental health, and in particular the prevalence, assessment and impact of such issues on effective and safe operation of aircraft. In this chapter I will explore how insights into the psychological functioning of pilots can be gained using the process of clinical interviewing. The background for this and its place in an array of assessment techniques are already covered, so this chapter will focus purely on the process and techniques of a key element in assessing pilot mental health – the clinical interview. There does not seem to be much coverage of this topic elsewhere, either clinical interviewing as such, or its application to aviation. Robert Bor has written of its place in a comprehensive assessment of pilot mental health (Bor, 2006), and Ray King goes into detail on the process and techniques for clinical interviewing in his book on aerospace clinical psychology (King, 1999). Much of what follows is based on my own experience of interviewing direct-entry captains and first officers for a major international commercial helicopter operator, although the techniques described are equally applicable to *ab-initio* assessments and obviously to those for the fixed wing population. In covering clinical interviewing I will also discuss the outcome from the process, looking at formulation and reporting, as clinical interviewing is a means to an end – exploring the mental health of pilots – and that end needs to influence the process and techniques employed, as well as being key topics in themselves. As a result there are three sections to this chapter:

*   the process of clinical interviewing
*   techniques
*   formulation and reporting.

Before covering these three areas, it is worth defining what clinical interviewing is, and how it differs from recruitment or appraisal interviewing.

## Clinical interviewing defined

In their comprehensive book on clinical interviewing, Sommers-Flanagan and Sommers-Flanagan (2009) review various definitions before suggesting one that covers an essentially process-driven view of the topic.

> From our perspective, a good definition of clinical interviewing includes the following factors:
> 1   A positive and respectful professional relationship between interviewer and client is established.
> 2   The interviewer and client work collaboratively (more or less, depending on the situation) to establish and achieve mutually agreeable client goals.
> 3   In the context of a professional relationship, interviewer and client interact, both verbally and nonverbally, as the interviewer applies active-listening skills and psychological techniques to evaluate, understand and achieve goals.
> 4   The quality and quantity of interactions between interviewer and client are influenced by many factors, including interviewer and client culture, personality style, attitudes and goals.
>                         (Sommers-Flanagan and Sommers-Flanagan, 2009, p18)

Key points in that definition are, first, the importance of the clinical interview being an interactive process, not a one-way inquisition of interviewee by interviewer, with a collaborative process shaped by both parties in real time. Second, there is an agreement about the outcome of the interview and why the process is being used. Third, there is recognition of the techniques that shape the process, especially the key element of active listening. Last, the definition takes account of factors that can influence both process and outcome, particularly on the part of the interviewer.

Of course in the context of pilot mental health screening there is scope for a more precise definition of clinical interviewing that takes into account not only the points raised above, but also the unique nature of both aviation and particularly of pilots as an occupational group. In an aviation application, the goal of clinical interviewing is quite specific. Rather than being about understanding and improving the psychological well-being of the client, it is about exploring and gaining vital understanding of a pilot's mental state, which is a crucial safety issue. The aviation culture within which clinical interviewing is applied is one of regulation and regular health checks (see for example FAA, 2015), so there is a higher degree of expectancy and tolerance of interviewing processes that goes beyond the normal range of vocational and recruiting interviews. Pilots experience such in-depth examination from the *ab-initio* stage, through to airline selection procedures and on to regular physical and mental health monitoring for license retention. This has an impact on the nature of the professional relationship between interviewer and interviewee – the interview is often mandated by the employer and takes place mainly in the recruitment context or in an appraisal context where mental health issues are suspected, which in turn changes the motivation and participation level of the person being interviewed. Pilots also tend to show fairly specific personality characteristics that have an impact on the clinical interviewing process used in aviation. My own research (Dickens, 2014) on rotary-wing pilots using the Big-5 personality factors shows them to be more agreeable, more conscientious and less anxious than the general population, findings that support those in the wider pilot population (King, 2014).

Before leaving the subject of definition it is worth outlining the potential content of a clinical interview, rather than the process as discussed above. The FAA (2015) set out a set of minimum standards for a clinical interview as part of a thorough psychological evaluation:

> A thorough clinical interview includes a detailed history regarding psychosocial or developmental problems, academic and employment performance, legal issues, substance use/abuse (including treatment and quality of recovery), aviation background and experience, medical conditions, and all medication use, and behavioral observations during the interview.
>
> (FAA, 2015, p2)

This is probably more comprehensive than most clinical interviews, and in the recruitment context some of that will be covered in any recruiter interviews and structured competency-based interviews. For the purpose of this chapter the clinical interview is aimed at covering a deeper understanding of mental state gained by a conversation about developmental history, description of everyday functioning, any previous psychological morbidity, and current ways of coping especially in potentially stressful situations. Specific processes and techniques to uncover that information will be covered in the rest of this chapter.

## The clinical interview process

The clinical interview process has three clear stages:

- building rapport
- gathering information
- closure and summary.

To this could be added a fourth stage – formulation and reporting – but I will treat this as a separate entity and discuss it in depth later.

## Building rapport

Given that pilots come in to the clinical interview process with a lot of career-defining outcomes hanging on the process (such as successful recruitment, or return to duties after an incident), they often have heightened situational anxiety. This may not be immediately evident, given that pilots as a group tend to show lower levels of anxiety than the general population (King, 2014) and, if from a military background, have learnt coping mechanisms to minimize the impact of emotions on behavior. As a result the process of building rapport at the start of the interview functions not only as an introduction and structure-setting activity, but also as a means to putting the person at ease in the potentially stressful situation. Building rapport is also the start of the information-gathering aim of the interview, as how a pilot behaves gives clues about their mental state – for example how anxious they are, their attitude to being assessed etc. The interviewer therefore needs to be alert to verbal and non-verbal behavior from the moment the pilot arrives for the interview. There is an evidential basis for using many cues as the basis for Big 5 personality factor judgments (Gosling, 2008), and physical appearance and manner of dress may well be one set of cues to be corroborated later in the interview. The rapport-building activity also is a chance to build mutuality, and establish your expertise as an essential part of the interaction (Cialdini, 2008), which in turn aids in reassuring the pilot that you know what you are doing! Ray King (King, 1999) advocates the need for clinicians working in aviation to understand and be familiar with aviation concepts and terminology, as this is necessary not only to understand the context of information gained, but also to display empathy and understanding of the aviation context. The rapport-building part of the interview should take about the first ten minutes of the time allotted. Sommers-Flanagan and Sommers-Flanagan (2009) discuss the whole issue in depth, linking it to Rogerian thinking about developing empathy, warmth and genuineness as key elements to successful clinical interactions.

## Gathering information

Once sufficient rapport has been established, the information-gathering process part of the interview can begin. The general techniques used by the interviewer to aid this part of the process will be described later, but the most usual guideline for this stage is to start general and become more specific, rather like a filter funnel. A very open question is most useful to start off – I generally use "Tell me about yourself" as a stimulus question, which in my experience elicits personal information that can then be further questioned in more detail. It is also interesting to me how the pilot makes their opening response – for example, do they start off from their childhood, or do they start straight in on aviation-related experiences – as this might give clues as to how they view themselves, and how they respond to unstructured situations. It is also interesting to note if the interviewee seems as if they have prepared what they are going to say at this stage. In my clinical experience the word goes out very effectively on the pilot grapevine about what is likely to be required of them during the interview process – if in any doubt have a look at www.pprune.org, the "Professional Pilots Rumour Network" where there are often discussions of interview requirements for various airlines' recruitment processes.

Once the flow of information has started, the task of the interviewer is to:

- enable the pilot to maintain the flow of information using verbal and non-verbal cues;
- provide a structure that keeps the interview on track whilst allowing for freedom of expression;
- continually evaluate what is being heard, and formulate more detailed questions to explore specific aspects of the pilot's psychological framework;
- maintain rapport;
- start the process of formulation by making inferences about what is being heard.

This stage is where clinical interviewing becomes more of an art than a science – it can rely a lot on intuition, experience and hypothesis-testing. The phrase "flying by the seat of your pants" is accurate! As a result the emphasis is likely to be on available techniques for effective interviewing and information gathering as we will explore later in this chapter. Typically during this stage the interviewer needs to use these techniques to gain the deepest possible understanding of the pilot in the allotted time, and needs to have a notional structure in his or her mind for doing that without the interview seeming formulaic or too process-driven but being more like a natural conversation between two people. This structure is essentially following a time-line of the person's life, with the general open questions being followed up by more specific probing questions on areas of interest or concern in the pilot's psychological framework.

### Closure and summary

It is worth discussing at this stage how long the clinical interview should last. It is more than likely that this will be determined by other constraints – for example the schedule for the full assessment process if this is a recruitment situation, or the time availability of the interviewer. A typical effective clinical interview will last between one and two hours. Of course there will always be a situation where the interview is shorter than that, particularly if the interviewee is taciturn or if enough information has been gathered quickly, or longer than that, if there is a need to pursue a particularly important line of information, or if the pilot is happy to talk at length about themselves (as is often the case!). What is key, however, is for the interviewer to manage the time and the process of closure so that a satisfactory and fulfilling ending is reached, however long the session lasts, and without a sense of "watching the clock". Closure also means offering a quick summary of the conversation, again at a general level, without pre-empting post-interview reflection and formulation. I am often asked what my thoughts are and whether the pilot is a "pass or fail". I do not answer this question directly and usually explain that I need time to review the information gathered before coming to any conclusion.

I find that an additional open question can be used to signal the end of the interview, along with a preparatory statement, offering the opportunity to add more information about themself. Sommers-Flanagan and Sommers-Flanagan (2009) discuss how interviewees often behave, feel and think at the end of an interview in a way that reveals even more of their potential psychopathology. This often drives the "doorknob statement" familiar to many clinicians – the key revelation or question that is made as the interviewee gets up to leave the room or as they walk out of the door:

> By the way Doctor, I've been feeling very down since my father died last year....

> I've got this friend who's having problems getting into the cockpit since his recent poor sim check ride.

Whether to open up this discussion at this closure stage of the interview or not is difficult if the interviewer is under time constraints, but it might be indicative of something that requires further analysis. As a result I pre-empt this by asking an open question that both signals termination but also offers the possibility for further revelation on the part of the pilot. Typically this is:

> Well we've covered a lot of ground, you've been very open about yourself and I think I have enough information to work on, but is there anything that you think I need to know about you that I haven't asked you about?

For most pilots the answer is negative or sometimes facetious (e.g. "I play off a handicap of 5"), but occasionally a piece of information is revealed that is important and not been evident before and which needs discussion and exploration even if it means extending the interview.

In a recruitment situation legislation usually requires that a clear statement about what will be done with the information needs to be given, and about what the interviewee has the right to access. This is usually the opportunity to view the subsequent report, and the possibility to discuss with the interviewer, but in most jurisdictions that is on active request rather than routine disclosure. Whatever the situation I always outline the conditions under which the data will be reported, accessed and maintained by me in line with current legislation and good clinical practice, and I always give reassurances of confidentiality.

# Techniques used in clinical interviewing

Throughout the preceding sections I've mentioned a number of techniques that facilitate clinical interviewing – such as asking open questions – which are also sometimes part of the process – for example building rapport. In this section some specific techniques will be discussed that can be used judiciously during the interview to provide structure, initiate and maintain the flow of the conversation and also to enable the interviewee to disclose things about their psychological makeup in a comfortable and secure environment. Clinical interviewers need an attitude of professional and respectful curiosity, which allows the interview to be a guided conversation rather than an inquisition or a checklist-completion exercise. There are guidelines available for content (see FAA, 2015, quoted above). The Present State Inventory (Wing *et al.*, 1973) provides a framework for the evaluation of psychopathology although it is more focused on diagnosis of specific psychological states rather than general formulation about a person's mental health and well-being. What follows is not intended as an exhaustive list of interviewer competencies, but is more a set of useful activities and processes that achieve those ends.

## *Observation*

An essential part of the clinical interview is the observation of non-verbal behavior and attributes as well as using listening skills to evaluate the information gained and to guide the course of the interview process. As we've seen earlier when describing the rapport-building process, information gathering starts the minute the pilot appears for interview, or even before that – for example do they arrive in plenty of time or are they there at the last minute? The former might indicate someone high on conscientiousness, being organized and reliable, whilst the latter might indicate a degree of disorganization linked to low score on the same Big 5 personality factor. Another pre-interview observation might be how they interact with other people – for example receptionists. In my usual interview location the experienced receptionist is often the source of initial information – she is very quick to pick up on arrogant, overbearing or rude pilots and let me know! From Gosling's work (Gosling, 2008) we know that these initial impressions are often a reliable indicator of Big 5 personality factors – in the case of the receptionist she is most likely picking up cues about the pilot's relative degree of the factor of agreeableness and their personal warmth. Pre-interview observations might also include their non-verbal behavior – is the pilot overtly showing signs of anxiety or are they appropriately relaxed, and physical appearance – how are they dressed? Lastly how they introduce themselves can be revealing – there are different clues about psychological make-up to be gained from "Hi I'm Will" or from "Good morning I am Squadron Leader Wales"! Overall demeanor and attitude to the interviewer is all part of the clinical information that might have a bearing on the final formulation.

During the interview the observation process will continue involving non-verbal behavior and the non-verbal aspects of speech (Argyle, 1988), and interpretation of the clues observed. In particular, non-verbal cues often guide the move from general questions to more specific probing, such as when discussion of a particular topic instigates obvious signs of distress or discomfort on the part of the pilot. This non-verbal behavior may be directly challenged – "you seem anxious when discussing that situation – can you expand or clarify that?" – and might need sensitive handling if there is obvious distress being shown.

### Questioning skills

Asking questions is at the core of clinical interviewing, and involves both the process (the type of question being asked) and the content (what information is required in the answer). However using too many questions in a clinical interview will turn an information-gathering conversation into an inquisition, as Benjamin (1987) points out. Questions are the starting point and way of encouraging pilots to speak openly about themselves, whilst also having a probing function when further information is required. Sommers-Flanagan and Sommers-Flanagan (2009) emphasize the importance of preparing questions before the clinical interview, and of preparing the interviewee to answer, flagging up to them the role of questions in the interview process.

There are a number of types of question that can be used to elicit information, and each has a potential type of response. A key component of the art of clinical interviewing is deciding which type to use when!

### Open questions

Open questions generally facilitate people talking as they cannot be answered with a simple yes or no. Typically they begin with *how, what, where, when, who* and *why*, with the first two stimulus words being the most effective as they can only be answered by dialogue, whereas the others are only partially open as they may be answered by simple statements. *Why* as a question opening needs care as it can be perceived as critical and elicit a defensive answer. Open questions have a key role in opening up the conversations (see above for an example I use) and in encouraging someone to speak about themselves if they are reticent or guarded about talking about themselves (not something you come across often in pilots!). Some examples of open questions in this context are:

How did you feel when you were first turned down for flight school?

What sort of experiences did you have when you were deployed to Iraq?

Where did you grow up?

When did you first feel unhappy about working in the North Sea?

Who was your biggest role-model when you were doing your CPL?

Why did you decide to leave the Air Force?

## Closed questions

This type of question can be answered with a yes or no response, and as such they have a value in closing down a conversation or redirecting it if it is going into irrelevant areas. They also have a role in providing confirmation or denial of a hypothesis on the part of the interviewer. They usually begin with the words *do, did, does, is, was* or *are,* and they also have a role in moving the interview towards closure as a signal of the end of the session. Some examples are:

Do you generally feel relaxed as pilot flying?

Have you completed a CRM course this year?

## Swing questions

These questions can be either answered with a simple yes or no, but are designed to elicit a more extended discussion of feelings and thoughts. They tend to invite a response rather than demand one and possibly are the most open types of question as they leave the nature and extent of the response to the interviewee. The key factor in this decision is the level of rapport between interviewer and interviewee – if this is high then they will elicit an extensive answer, if it is low they will function as closed questions – so the use of such questions needs careful attention to the dynamic of the situation. Typically they begin with *can, could, would* or *will* as in these contextual examples:

Could you talk some more about when you first started to notice you were getting anxious on final approaches?

Will you tell me some more about the strained relationship you had with Captain X?

## Indirect questions

Indirect questions are implied questions and indicate that the interviewer is curious about something that the interviewee has said and also when the dynamic of the situation indicates that it might not be useful to pressure the interviewee to reply. They need careful use as they can appear manipulative, and seem to be leading towards a particular answer or the confirmation of an interviewer's hypothesis. For example:

I wonder how you feel about being transferred to the new base?

You must have felt angry after being blamed for that runway incursion?

## Projective questions

In a clinical interview this type of question helps people explore and articulate thoughts and feelings that might be unconscious or unclear concerning hypothetical situations. In doing so they provide information about values, attitudes, emotions and behavior, and link directly to critical incident analysis (see below) as an information-gathering component of aviation clinical interviews. Typically they begin with *what if* as in:

What if you could go back and change how you behaved during that disagreement with the Flight Ops Manager, what would you do differently?

## Active listening

As we saw above, the role of questioning in the clinical interview is to enable and facilitate the interviewee to speak openly and be comfortable about sensitive and personal issues, and to allow the interviewer to gain sufficient in-depth information to draw conclusions about the interviewee's mental state and psychological framework. Active listening skills are essential to understand the information given, gain insight into the pilot's mental composition, and at a practical level maintain the flow of the conversation. Essentially active listening is an example of attending behavior (Ivey and Ivey, 1999) and there are both verbal and non-verbal components to it. These authors identify four main components of attending behavior: eye contact, general body language, vocal qualities and verbal tracking. The former two are well-known and described elsewhere (see Argyle, 1988) whilst the second two are less evident. Vocal qualities refer to the non-verbal aspects of speech such as intonation, pitch, rate and fluency – essentially not what you say, but how you say it – and these are often indicative of underlying emotional responses both of the interviewer and the interviewee. Verbal tracking is the competence of the interviewer in keeping "in the zone" with the person being interviewed, staying focused on their speech and not being distracted either by something the interviewee has said, or by the interviewer's personal thoughts and feelings. A common distraction is the interviewer thinking about what smart question to ask next rather than focusing on what the interviewee is saying – as the saying goes "most people don't listen, they just wait their turn to speak"!

Active listening also involves giving cues back to the interviewee that the interviewer is listening and tracking what they are saying. Taking notes on what is being said is a behavior that indicates the interviewer is taking note (literally!) although it needs to be balanced with giving visual attention to the interviewee. Non-verbal cues such as nodding or verbalizations such as "uh-huh" need to be similarly used with care as they may appear artificial and can interrupt the flow of conversation. Cultural, gender and individual differences will also influence the way in which listening is signaled to the interviewee – for example in some cultures eye contact duration is lower than in others as it signals dominance. More effective as an active listening tool is the use of summarization and paraphrasing, which is essentially a brief review of topics covered during the interview. It can also be used as a punctuation point to signal a change in topic or a method of closure if the interviewee is becoming too detailed or too focused on one aspect of the interview. Care is needed however in not over-interpreting the listener's remarks during this process, or adding a meaning or direction that is not that of the interviewee. Typically a summary begins with "So what I've heard you saying is…" or similar. It is often followed by a question to check for understanding such as "Have I got that right?" or may be followed by a request for clarification – "That's what I heard you say – can you just clarify one of the things you said earlier?"

Active listening also involves using silence, which Sommers-Flanagan and Sommers-Flanagan (2009) describe as the most non-directive of all listening responses. Allowing silence provides the opportunity for the interviewer to collect their thoughts about what they've heard and for the interviewee to reflect and maybe add additional information in response to a question. It can be uncomfortable, however, for both parties and can interfere with the flow of the conversation and be daunting to the interviewee.

## Critical incident technique

I referred above to the use of projective questioning and mentioned the critical incident technique (CIT) as a tool that might form part of a clinical interview especially with pilots, who may well be used to this as part of a post-incident debriefing process. CIT was devised by Flanagan (1954) for use as a part of research into effective and ineffective aviation performance and in particular pilot errors. Used as part of the clinical interview it allows rich insight into pilot's behavior in significant situations, and gives information not only on how they handled the specific incident but also their learning from it and their attitude and behavior while describing it.

A general question begins the process, with the selection of the incident left open to the interviewee:

> "I'd like you to tell me about a significant incident that has happened to you whilst flying."

There are four areas covered:

- the cause, description and outcome of the incident;
- the action and behavior taken by the pilot during the incident;
- the pilot's feelings during and after the incident;
- the learning outcomes gained.

Occasionally a pilot may not be able to readily identify a critical incident and may need prompting – sometimes I indicate that the incident might not have been one with negative consequences. The pilot may also need to be reassured of the confidentiality of the interview situation as there may be fears of repercussions. Given the regulated and controlled nature of aviation and the existence of just culture environments and safety regimes, this is not usually an issue. What is more likely however is the triggering of strong emotions from the original situation which can sometimes be overwhelming for the interviewee and need sensitive and empathic handling by the interviewer. Such a response is also an issue worth probing in itself, as it might be linked to a diagnosis of PTSD.

### Using a strengths-based approach

Strengths-based approaches have become more popular following the rise of the positive psychology movement – see Lewis (2011) for a good summary of this approach to individual and organizational understanding. In the context of clinical interviewing, a strengths-based approach to enquiry is often useful on two levels – the content and the process. On the content level, what a pilot mentions in response to a question about their strengths is of interest, particularly in how it corroborates or refutes what has been said by them previously in answer to more specific questions or in response to psychometric testing. On the process level, how easy they find the task is important – for example it offers insight into how self-aware they are, how reticent or otherwise they are about talking about themselves, and lastly how positive they feel about themselves which is indicative of levels of self-esteem. To counter some cynicism that pilots may show, especially if they have been through a number of screening interviews before, and to avoid the repetition of a pre-learnt compendium of core competencies, I use a question that does not mention strengths but asks:

"What do you value about yourself?"

This usually elicits information, but very occasionally a pilot finds it difficult to articulate or respond, so I expand on that by asking what they value about themselves as a person, or quite explicitly what do they see as their strongest attributes. The focus is always on them as a person, not as a pilot, so if the response begins to sound like a list of technical skills I refocus them on themselves. I often detail the information gathered verbatim in the report I write (see below) as it is usually of great interest in the way it has been expressed by the pilot.

## Use of psychometric tests

This has been covered elsewhere in this book, and there is a large and detailed body of research into the use of psychometric tests in pilot assessment and screening (King, 2014). Test results can also be used as an adjunct to the clinical interview as they can provide a template to guide the course of the interview and the discussion. A brief mental health screening inventory such as the GHQ series of tests (Goldberg and Williams, 1988) covers the presence of basic psychiatric symptomology and offers scope for more detailed questioning of any positive responses during interview. Similarly a personality inventory gives insight into personal characteristics and response styles, and allows questioning of these. The use of a measure of the "Big 5" personality factors such as the NEO-PI-R (Costa and McCrae, 1992) has shown that scores of the five factors can be linked to pilot performance in a number of situations such as training outcomes in military flight training (King, *et al.,* 2012) and performance in safety-related incidents (King *et al.*, 2001). Exploration of an individual's scores on such a test is a rich source of information that can also corroborate the clinical impression gained during interview.

## Formulation and reporting

Having gathered a rich vein of information about the interviewee by using some or all of the above techniques, the final part of the clinical interviewing process concerns making sense of that information, and – usually – writing a cogent report that summarizes it. The key skill required from the clinical interviewer at this stage is that of formulation. A recent set of guidelines available from the British Psychological Society's Division of Clinical Psychology provides the best overview of this skill available (British Psychological Society Division of Clinical Psychology, 2011). Although the document is aimed at the use of formulation in a diagnostic or therapeutic context, it defines formulation as:

> Psychological formulation is the summation and integration of knowledge that is acquired through (an) assessment process that may involve psychological, biological and systemic factors and procedures. The formulation will draw on psychological theory and research to provide a framework for describing a client's problem or needs, how it developed and is being maintained.
>
> (British Psychological Society Division of Clinical Psychology, 2011, p6)

It is clear that the core of this definition still applies – the integration of information gained and applying a psychological knowledge, experience and expertise to produce an overview of a person's psychological make up – in the aviation context. Formulation is both an output – the written report – and a process – the integration activity. In keeping with the description of clinical interviewing in the aviation context that is given above, it is also an integration of both the factual information and the personal response of the interviewer combining scientific principles with intuition and reflection. Essentially it is about producing a hypothesis about a pilot's psychological profile based not only on a knowledge of the evidence from research, and from the interview process, but also on a reflective process involving using cues from the interview (for example non-verbal behavior) and from experience and intuition. An effective formulation following an aviation-related clinical interview therefore includes:

- basic biographical information;
- a summary of information gained during the interview as a result of direct questioning;
- additional information gained by observation, use of critical incident techniques and any relevant psychometric test information;
- an integration of the above information with knowledge of the aviation context, the evidence base on what makes an effective pilot and the organization context within which the assessment is being undertaken.

Following such a structure predicts the format of the report that results from the formulation. In my own practice I follow a "funnel" model starting with the most general information first – such as biographical data – then gradually reporting on any key issues in more depth and backing up my thoughts by reference to the data gathered in interview (often reported verbatim) and by drawing on the evidence base on pilot personality and effectiveness. Typically such a report runs to about three pages of A4, with an introductory paragraph setting out the reason for the interview, and then a body of text structured as suggested above.

Before concluding this section on formulation and reporting, the issue of ethics and confidentiality needs to be discussed. By its nature, clinical interviewing reveals personal and sensitive information about the individual pilot, which needs to be handled within a professional and legislative framework of ethics and confidentiality. The information gathered belongs first and foremost to the person being interviewed, and in most jurisdictions they have a right to access and challenge that information if need be. This may at times be at odds with the organizational intention of the interview, and the clinician has at all times to protect the right of the person's privacy even in the face of organizational pressures. As a matter of course I offer the person access to my written report, but usually on request, and always remind them that I need a time of reflection before writing the report so no instant judgments are provided even if asked for (e.g. "Have I passed, Doctor?"). European legislation often requires the person's consent for any personal information to be shared with the organization, and I ask this at the end of the interview.

A more challenging scenario for the interviewer is when a revelation on the part of the pilot has a direct bearing on safety to fly, or one which indicates overt mental illness or criminality. Reporting this may well breach confidentiality – the recent Germanwings Flight 9525 incident highlights a situation where this was potentially necessary. In response to that incident an EASA task force set out guidance for handling such sensitive information (EASA, 2015), stating:

> The implementation of data protection rules should balance the need to protect patient confidentiality with the need to protect public safety.
>
> (EASA, 2015, p14)

Clearly such reporting may well end the pilot's career, and cause distress to the interviewer, but the overall safety of the public, passengers and aircraft is paramount, and not least that of the pilot themselves.

## Conclusion

This chapter has looked at clinical interviewing as a mainstay of the process of assessing pilot mental health, and has drawn on the clinical literature for the structure, processes and outcomes required for a thorough evaluation to be made of pilots in either a recruitment situation or as part of an investigation following an incident. It has stressed the importance of both the content and the process in any clinical interview, and of using all the information available to reach an informed hypothesis or conclusion. An important part of the clinical interview is what is done with the data, and we have looked at formulation as a skill and as a key part of the evaluation of the data gathered. As stated at the start of this chapter, clinical interviewing is both a science and an art, and the evaluation of the data involves knowledge of the evidence base on pilot mental health, allied to a willingness to reflect and use intuition coupled with experience on the part of the interviewer. It has a key part to play in the process of getting inside a pilot's head.

## References

Argyle, M. (1988) *Bodily communication* (2nd edn). London: Routledge.

Benjamin, A. (1987) *The helping interview with case illustrations.* Boston, MA: Houghton Mifflin.

Bor, R. (2006) Psychological factors in cockpit crew selection. In R. Bor and T. Hubbard (eds) *Aviation mental health.* Aldershot: Ashgate.

British Psychological Society, Division of Clinical Psychology (2011) *Good practice guidelines on the use of psychological formulation.* Leicester: British Psychological Society.

Cialdini, R.B. (2008) *Influence: The psychology of persuasion* (revised edition). Glasgow: HarperCollins.

Costa, P.T. and McCrae, R.R. (1992) *Revised NEO Personality Inventory (NEO-PI-R) and NEO Five Factor Inventory (NEO-FFI) professional manual.* Odessa, FL: Psychological Assessment Resources.

Dickens, P. (2014) Big 5 personality profiles of rotary-wing aircrew. In A. Droog (ed.) *Proceedings of the 31st Conference of the European Association for Aviation Psychology* (pp 149–158). Valletta, Malta: European Association for Aviation Psychology.

EASA (2015) *Task force on measures following the accident of Germanwings Flight 9252: Final report.* Cologne: European Aviation Safety Agency (EASA).

FAA (2015) *Specifications for psychiatric and psychological evaluations*. Paper retrieved from: http://www.faa.gov/about/office_org/headquarters_offices/avs/offices/aam/ame/guide/dec_cons/disease_prot/ssri/

Flanagan, J.C. (1954) The critical incident technique. *Psychological Bulletin*, 51(4), 327–358.

Goldberg, D. and Williams, P. (1988) *A users guide to the General Health Questionnaire*. Windsor: NFER-Nelson.

Gosling, S.D. (2008) *Snoop: What your stuff says about you*. New York: Basic Books.

Ivey, A.E. and Ivey M.B. (1999) Toward a developmental diagnostic and statistical manual: The vitality of a contextual framework. *Journal of Counseling and Development*, 77(4), 484–490.

King, R.E. (1999) *Aerospace clinical psychology*. Aldershot: Ashgate.

King, R.E. (2014) Personality (and psychopathology) assessments in the selection of pilots. *International Journal of Aviation Psychology*, 24(1), 61–73.

King, R.E., Retzlaff, P. and Orme, D.R. (2001) *A comparison of US Air Force pilot psychological baseline information to safety outcomes*. Final Technical Report AFSC-TR-2001-0001. Kirtland AFB, NM: US Air Force Safety Center.

King, R.E., Retzlaff, P., Barto, E., Ree, M.J. and Teachout, M.S. (2012) *Pilot personality and training outcomes*. Final Technical Report AFRL-SA-WP-TR-2011-0008. Dayton, OH: Wright-Patterson AFB, Air Force Research Laboratory, School of Aerospace Medicine.

Lewis, S. (2011) *Positive psychology at work: How positive leadership and appreciative inquiry create inspiring organizations*. Chichester: Wiley-Blackwell.

Sommers-Flanagan, J. and Sommers-Flanagan, R. (2009) *Clinical interviewing* (4th edn). Hoboken, NJ: John Wiley and Sons Inc.

Wing, J.K., Cooper, J.E. and Sartorius, N. (1973) *Present state examination* (9th edn). Cambridge: Cambridge University Press.

# 6 The practicalities of clinical history-taking and mental state assessments of pilots

*Robert Bor, Carina Eriksen, Peter Scragg and Margaret Oakes*

Most other chapters in this book address topics relating to pilot mental health assessment and screening from a theoretical, conceptual or empirical base. This chapter departs from these underpinnings and orientations, and instead offers a practical perspective to pilot assessments, with an emphasis on the clinical interview and mental state assessment. As the book evolved and developed, and during the course of many liaison and consultation meetings with fellow colleagues in aviation medicine, clinical and aviation psychology, human resources managers in airlines and with aviation regulators, it became increasingly clear to us that some guidance on how to develop the clinical interview with pilots in the course of assessments was sought. This chapter endeavours to offer this.

The contents of this chapter and guidance offered should not be seen as prescriptive, nor complete. As every clinician is aware, patient assessments often proceed in different ways although a physical examination, the results of an array of tests and procedures, coupled with history-taking and a mental state examination are usually the basis for most assessments. How and when these are completed, in what order and the specific format followed may vary depending on the nature of the clinical problem, the history or story of the patient's evolving problem, resources available to the clinician, findings from initial tests and the skills and preferences of the clinician. Assessment and diagnosis may draw on or approximate scientific methods, but art and personal style still have an important role to play in clinical assessments.

Our interest in learning more about the clinical interview and mental state assessments derives in part from our clinical training, experience working in healthcare and in medico-legal settings, and teaching medical and psychology students communications skills, but mostly from our recognition that as psychologists, communication with patients is at the heart of our practice and the dialogue that evolves between patient and clinician determines each next stage when working with the patient. There is a Socratic underpinning although not exclusively so. The dialogues between patient and clinician are mostly a form of improvisation as we do not follow a laid out or pre-determined script, but we do generate ideas about clinical problems that then become hypotheses that we then test out through further enquiry. The clinical interview should seem seamless, reasonably (but probably not wholly) relaxed and natural, and patient-centred, though it should seek to address and answer a number of specific questions about the physical and mental functioning of the pilot. For most pilots, the annual or six-monthly medical examination will pass off without any requirement for further assessments. For some, medical or psychiatric questions will arise that may require further investigation by relevant specialists in their fields.

In our experience, for most pilots the clinical interview can be quite daunting as they may not feel in control of the situation and there may be some suspicion or fear about the nature and purpose of some questions, and their reticence to engage fully, as might a patient seeking psychological or psychiatric care, and this is understandable. They may also worry that they could inadvertently 'give something away' to the clinician – however small or insignificant it may seem – and which could have implications for their career, making their guardedness even more understandable. Some pilots may dismiss, deny or understate personal health issues or concerns that they fear could arouse the interest of their medical examiner. This is unfortunate as the overwhelming majority of clinicians are 'on the side of the pilot' and wish nothing but to put the pilot's interests, welfare and career above all else, even if safety considerations are at the very top of this.

The recent focus, following the Germanwings pilot suicide crash, on pilot mental health, safety and well-being among airline regulators, airline managers and aeromedical medical examiners has altered the nature and format of the medical assessment. The inclusion of more robust mental health screening makes this a specific and directed activity. Whereas many of the standard medical criteria for fitness can be checked through tests and physical examinations, and be 'ticked off' as the examiner deals with each in turn, mental health cannot be accurately or robustly checked and recorded through such a straightforward exercise. The answer to an enquiry of the pilot 'Is there anything affecting your psychological health?' is seldom likely to reveal an accurate reflection of their mental state due to their downplaying of this aspect of the assessment and also they may lack insight into the wider and deeper meaning of this enquiry. The examiner has to look up and observe the pilot; eye-ball him or her; note responses to questions and how they are responded to; and check their developing opinion and assessment of the pilot with the pilot him- or herself in the first instance. This is described in more detail in the remainder of the chapter.

## The clinical interview

With the exciting technological advances being made in clinical medicine, it is easy to be swept along by the science of medicine and to forget the ancient aim of the physician: 'To cure sometimes, relieve often, comfort always'. In the context of the aeromedical assessment, it is still necessary to conduct this with the pilot's interests at heart as the examiner has, as always, a duty of care to the pilot – patient, whilst keeping in mind a responsibility for pilot and operational safety.

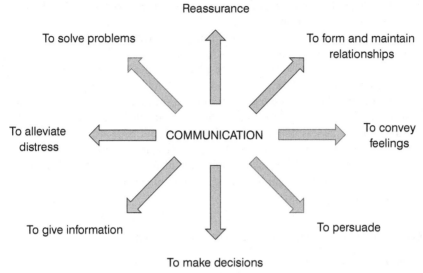

*Figure 6.1* Pilot interactions

### What is good communication?

It is appropriate here to mention a study carried out some years ago by Dr Peter Maguire in Manchester (Maguire and Pitceathly, 2002). Patients who had been interviewed by medical students were asked for their opinion of the students' interviewing abilities. Patients preferred interviews where the clinician:

- was warm and sympathetic;
- was easy to talk to;
- introduced themselves;
- appeared self-confident;
- listened to the patient and responded to their verbal cues;
- asked questions that were easily understood and were precise;
- did not repeat themselves.

### Why is good communication important?

The short answer is 'better care for our patients'. There is considerable evidence to show that clinicians who communicate well with patients are more likely to:

1   Make an accurate, comprehensive diagnosis. Good communication skills enable one to collect information about a patient's problems that is comprehensive, relevant and accurate. It has been shown that doctors who have received training in communication skills are more likely to diagnose psychiatric morbidity in their patients than those who have not been trained.

2   Detect emotional distress in patients and respond appropriately.

3   Have patients who are satisfied with the care they have received and are less anxious about their problems.
4   Have patients who agree with and follow the advice given.

Most aeromedical assessments take place in a health care setting (e.g. GP practice, aeromedical centre, occupational health unit etc.) and both privacy and confidentiality (within limits) are essential to facilitate good communication. Lighting and temperature are important to ensure the setting is comfortable. Always start the assessment when both you and the pilot are seated, never go straight into a physical examination. This is where the purpose of the assessment is conveyed and the pilot is given some idea of how it will proceed and how much time is available. The following section summarises the guidelines for conducting the assessment.

## Guidelines for conducting a clinical interview

### Beginning the interview

- Greet the patient by name ('Good morning Captain Richardson') and shake hands, if it seems appropriate.
- Ask the patient to sit down.
- Introduce yourself ('I am Dr Stephen Gibbs, an aeromedical examiner').
- Explain the purpose of the interview ('I would like to carry out a full medical assessment as required by the aviation authority').
- Say how much time is available.
- Explain the need to take notes and complete forms and ask if this is acceptable.

### The main part of the interview

- Maintain a positive atmosphere, warm manner and good eye contact.
- Use open questions at the beginning.
- Listen carefully.
- Be alert and responsive to verbal and non-verbal cues.
- Facilitate the patient both verbally ('Tell me more') and non-verbally (using posture and head nods).
- Use specific (closed) questions when appropriate.
- Clarify what the patient has told you.
- Encourage the patient to be relevant.

### Ending the interview

- Summarise what the patient has told you and ask if your summary is accurate.
- Ask if the patient would like to add anything.
- Thank the patient.

*The unfolding assessment interview*
…the interview is potentially the most powerful, sensitive instrument at the command of the physician.

(Engel and William, 1973)

In these days of high-technology medicine, this statement, made by George Engel in 1973, may surprise some. But the medical interview is still powerful and is likely to remain so. What is it that happens between doctor and patient that can make the interview such a powerful instrument?

Pilots may occasionally bring to the doctor their problems, usually in the form of symptoms or complaints, but more especially their anxieties about their being diagnosed with a problem. They also have expectations about how the doctor will deal with them as a pilot. The interview between pilot and doctor is the cornerstone of the problem-solving process. The doctor's role is to gain as accurate a picture as possible of the pilot's health problems. This information must then be processed in such a way that will enable the doctor, ideally in collaboration with the pilot, to develop a plan for managing a problem, if indeed one is found.

1　Establish a rapport with the pilot using the skills outlined above. This will enable the pilot to tell his or her story, including underlying concerns, as completely as possible.
2　Use a framework for taking a medical history, as discussed later in this chapter.
3　Process the information acquired, supplemented by the results of the examination and appropriate investigations. This stage involves the knowledge of clinical aerospace medicine and decision-making processes that develop with experience. These will be discussed later in this chapter.
4　Explain to the pilot what may be wrong, if any problems are found, and how he or she might be helped. To do this successfully demands good communication skills and involving the pilot in his or her management.
5　Close the assessment by summarising what the pilot has told you and thank the pilot for his or her time.

## Gathering information: taking a medical history

A nineteenth-century French physician, René Laennec, advised: 'listen to the patient. They are giving you the diagnosis'. His remark stresses the importance of a patient's history in making a diagnosis, and this has been confirmed in subsequent studies.

Often we are required to medically assess a pilot – an expression that implies that the process flows in one direction, from pilot to doctor. But we have seen that what the doctor does (e.g. body language, manner of questioning and listening) influences how pilots divulge their problems. It has been said that doctors should learn to receive, not take, a medical history. Remember that you will obtain a more accurate and relevant history of the pilot's problems if you develop good communication skills.

There is a different nuance when assessing a pilot medically as he or she probably would not be undergoing a medical assessment unless it was a regulatory requirement. The pilot may assume that he or she is (a) physically well and healthy, (b) free of obvious clinical symptoms, or (c) if there are any, that these would be minor and non-disqualifying , at the very least. Whilst the pilot may be co-operative, and engaging they may fear that their medical could spell the end of their flying days. This fear is understandable and the aeromedical examiner has a clear duty to try to put the pilot at ease and convey a measure of empathy with them. Common courtesies, such as using the pilot's name, not rushing the assessment, covering the pilot and drawing a curtain around the examination couch are obvious starting points. Be prepared to spend time with the pilot if you wish to learn something about their psychological functioning and mental state. Whatever first impressions you have of the pilot, there may be considerably more to their situation that is only evident as you engage more with them. It is arguably an axiom of the clinical interview; the longer it takes, and the more time is spent with the pilot, the more can be observed, heard and learned from them. These hints are obviously already well known to most experienced aeromedical examiners.

The remainder of the chapter focuses on communication with the pilot that is likely to reveal something about their psychological functioning.

The clinical interview is most effective when: good rapport is established with the pilot; active listening is in evidence; mainly open questions are asked; verbal and non-verbal cues are picked up and responded to; and a summary of what has been seen and heard is also used to check for accuracy. Questions facilitate the interview and assessment, provided not too many are asked potentially disrupting the pilot's story flow or responses. Questions that are too long, complicated or confusing have the same negative effect. Questions framed in such a way that they may bias answers given are also a sign of poor interviewing skills on the part of the clinician.

The clinical interview specifically affords the clinician the opportunity to:

- gain a broader picture of the pilot, any problems, the context of the pilot and/or problem and the history;
- identify any triggers, causes or co-factors in the onset, maintenance or resolution of any clinical problems;
- examine vulnerability in an individual and also identify and explore resilience;
- identify individual risk factors;
- assess patient understanding and insight;
- sometimes 'observe' the problem;
- assess cognitions and higher level mental functioning.

### Open and closed questions

Asking open questions enables you to obtain a great deal of information and also allows the pilot to tell their own story. Open questions should be used as much as possible, particularly at the start of the interview, e.g. 'Would you please tell me how you have been feeling over the past few months?' asking specific (i.e. closed) questions will give the pilot little choice in the way in which they answer, and usually will elicit a 'yes' or 'no' answer, e.g. 'Have you been feeling unwell in the last day or so?'

An open style of questioning is preferable because:

- more relevant information can be obtained in a given time;
- the pilot will feel more relaxed in the interview;
- the pilot can express all the concerns and anxieties about their problems, these may be missed if closed questions are asked.

However, using open questions does have some disadvantages:

- the interview may take longer and be difficult to control;
- some of the information may not be relevant;
- recording answers may be more difficult.

### Probing questions

It is usually necessary during the interview to use probing questions that help a pilot to think more clearly about an answer he or she has given. Probing questions may be used to:

- Clarify: What do you mean by that?
- Justify: What makes you think that?
- Check accuracy: You definitely had no further symptoms after that illness?

### Questions to be avoided

The questions asked during an interview should be easily understood and asked in a way that does not influence the pilot's response. Complex questions and leading questions should be avoided.

Complex questions that encompass several questions in one are likely to confuse both the pilot and the interviewer. For example, how would you respond to the question 'Have you ever felt depressed and even thought of ending your life?' The chances are that only one part of the question would be answered.

Leading questions encourage the person responding to give the answer that the interviewer expects or wants. In the context of interviewing pilots, leading questions may be useful as an opening ploy, but on the whole they are to be avoided for reasons that will become obvious. There are three types of leading question:

1   *Conversational:* can be used to open or stimulate conversation; they can encourage rapport, e.g. 'Aren't we having awful weather this year?'
2   *Simple:* these influence the pilot to agree with the interviewer's viewpoint and should not be used, e.g. 'You don't sleep well do you?'
3   *Subtle:* these use the wording of the question to influence the respondent. They should be avoided, but it is easy to use them without realising.

A good example of how the wording of a question can influence the answer was shown in a study of the frequency of headaches in a group of individuals (Lloyd and Bor, 2009). When the respondents were asked 'Do you get headaches frequently and, if so, how often?' the average response was 2.2 headaches per week. When the question was slightly changed to 'Do you get headaches occasionally and, if so, how often?' the average response was 0.7 headaches per week.

What would help us to listen in such a way that information is registered and passed on accurately? Possible ways include:

•   taking notes and completing forms;
•   asking the pilot to repeat or clarify points that are not clear;
•   checking that the information received is accurate by repeating or summarising it.

Listening involves not only receiving information, but also, and more importantly, being 'in tune' with the speaker and responding appropriately. This is *active* or *effective* listening. It is not easy, and demands effort and concentration. When interviewing a pilot it is important to demonstrate that you are paying attention and trying to understand what the person is saying and feeling. The key features of active listening are:

•   gathering and retaining the information accurately;
•   understanding the implications for the pilot of what is being said;
•   responding to verbal and non-verbal cues;
•   demonstrating you are paying attention and trying to understand.

### Picking up cues

Pilots, like most patients, may be unable or unwilling to articulate their real concerns and feelings. However, they are likely to reveal something of these during the course of the interview, and it is important that their verbal and non-verbal cues are picked up.

*Verbal cues*

Listen carefully to the way the pilot describes their problems for signs of their underlying concerns. They may reveal these only if you respond appropriately to their verbal cues.

*Non-verbal cues*

We reveal a lot of information about ourselves and our feelings in our body language – the way we dress, our posture, gestures and facial expressions. When you interview a pilot, you can obviously learn a good deal by watching the pilot enter the room (appearance, posture and gait). It is also important to be sensitive to the pilot's body language during the interview.

Here are some examples of non-verbal cues:

- *Eye contact:* difficulty in maintaining eye contact may indicate that the pilot feels depressed or embarrassed about what is being discussed. The lack of eye contact could be a sign that you have not secured the pilot's cooperation or that s/he is uninterested in the conversation. Conversely, excessive eye contact may indicate anger and aggression.
- *Posture:* the confident pilot will sit upright; the pilot who feels depressed may sit slouched with head bent forward.
- *Gestures:* for example, an angry pilot may sit with clenched fists whereas an anxious pilot may wring the hands or tap the feet continuously.
- *Facial expressions:* sadness, anger and happiness.
- *The way the voice is used:* tone, timing, emphasis on certain words and vocalisation other than with words (this is sometimes called paralinguistics).

More information on observing the interviewee is discussed in the section on the mental state below.

### Content versus process-oriented questions

The clinical interview yields the most useful and pertinent information for the clinician when process-related questions or interventions are most used. Content-based questions mostly reveal facts or information. An example may be: 'What is your date of birth?' or 'When last did you have an endoscopy?' Process-oriented questions may be similar, but their effect is to challenge the interviewee to reveal more about something and also helps to shed light on their thought patterns, unscripted responses to a story or challenge, and current mental state. Rather than draw on a clinical example, here are a series of security-oriented process-based questions that are sometimes asked of passengers when selected for a secondary screening by a security official. Note that these questions can be asked a) slowly or more rapidly, b) repeatedly, and c) with different affect by the interviewer, revealing different thoughts and behaviours in the passenger.

- Where have you just come from?
- Did you come directly from there?
- Did you stop anywhere on the way?
- Who was with you when you packed your bag?
- What is your home address?
- How long have you lived there?
- Why are you travelling today?
- Do you have kids?
- How old are they and what are their names?

A clinical interview should, of course, not resemble a security interview, but you can see from the kinds of questions and how they could be asked that the interviewee cannot easily anticipate the questions and probably cannot readily script answers. The effect is to feel challenged and someone who has nothing to hide will not be unduly perturbed by this. There are usually no right or wrong answers to these questions, but there is (or should be) an internal coherence to the answers given. The pilot is challenged to think, reflect and elaborate. Both verbal and non-verbal communication can be analysed and it is possible to repeat and check responses during the assessment.

Now read aloud the above questions again. Try doing so very slowly and showing great consideration and courtesy to the interviewee and smile at the same time. Now do so yet again, with 'rapid-fire' questions, also smiling (slightly incongruously) but conveying that you mean serious business. Imagine the effect on the recipient in each case. This should hopefully convey the difference questions that focus on content, and those that are more challenging, penetrating and arguably a bit more unsettling for the interviewee. This method or approach can be used in the clinical interview or when assessing a person's mental state. You are the 'tool' of the investigation and your tone, affect, speed of delivery of questions, extent of eye contact, physical proximity to the patient etc. will all influence their behaviour and/ or responses. If you remain unconvinced, next time you enter a lift and there is but one other passenger in it, stand close to them (utter no words) and watch what happens, where they look and how they cope with the stress of the situation.

Examples of process-oriented questions in the aeromedical assessment of a pilot are:

- What most affects your mood/concentration?
- If your partner/friend was here, how might they describe you? How is this relationship?
- What feedback did you receive after your last sector? How come? What did you make of this?
- What has been most challenging for you personally in the past six months?
- What emotional problems do pilots generally experience? How have you been affected by any of these?

- What keeps you awake at night?
- Why do you think I am asking you these questions?

The order of questions can (and should) be changed between pilots' assessments so as to avoid a response style or predictability – both of which decrease the efficacy of the questioning. The questions help to build up a picture of the pilot leading to more specific hypothesis testing. The mental health aspect of the clinical interview should be raised early on in the assessment. It can also be broken into two or more parts, such as near the start, and then followed up again after the physical examination has been completed. Pursuing certain topics in some depth can also help to overcome response bias in questionnaires. The interview approach can be repeated and undertaken by another colleague. It reveals much about a person's neutral stability.

## Types of questions

Finally, in the context of the clinical interview, there are different types of questions that can be used. Each can open a different line of enquiry with the pilot and can lead to different explorations of issues.

1   *Linear or closed questions*: These questions typically lead to 'yes' or 'no' answers. They constitute the backbone of most questionnaires and content-based questions. For example: 'Are you currently taking any prescribed medication?'
2   *Circular questions*: Circular questions link ideas, beliefs and relationships in a way that helps people to view problems from different perspectives. A circular question taken from a stance of 'unknowing' might be: 'What did you think about your GP's idea that you should have some counselling?' Other examples of circular questions are: 'What do you think your wife/ partner might say if I asked them the same question about your alcohol consumption?' and 'How do you think your airline might view this problem and, from their perspective, what concerns do you think this raises?'
3   *Questions prompting differentiation and temporal perspectives*: Questions that show or reveal a difference between the present, the past and the future help people consider different perspectives to a dilemma or problem. For example: 'How do you think you would manage things if your licence was suspended for a period of time?'
4   *Hypothetical and future-oriented questions*: This type of question includes the words 'if', 'when', 'what if', 'how might'. Their use helps to explore the perceptions of others, address difficulties and prepare for the future by linking ideas that may not have otherwise been considered. Such questions address future concerns while the reality of these situations is some distance away and possibly therefore not as threatening. For example: 'If in six months from now, looking back, you had the option for early retirement but had waited for a while longer to see what would

become of this condition, what might you be thinking and feeling if it had worsened?'

5   *Behaviour-based questions:* These type of questions seek examples. They are often the follow-up questions to an open questions. For example, the open question could be 'What do you least like about being a pilot?' Depending on the pilot's answer the behaviour-based question could ask 'So tell me about the last time you had to handle XYZ?' Thus, these questions seek concrete past event information.

## Broad goals for the pilot clinical interview

1   Engagement of the pilot, i.e. development of rapport.
2   Collection of valid data/information – this will require attention to multiple sources of information, e.g. interview data (what is reported by pilot and behaviour in interview), psychometric results, review of medical records, occupational records, and possibly interview of significant others or colleagues.
3   Diagnosis and formulation, if appropriate.
4   Treatment plan if problems identified.
5   Diagnosis/formulation and treatment plan compared to regulator standards and reporting requirements.
6   Instillation of appropriate levels of hope if problem is a treatable problem.
7   Agreed route for co-operating with employer and regulator, and managing confidentiality.

## Areas to cover in interview

1   Welcome pilot by name and introduce yourself.
2   Structure the interview: explain the length of the interview, limits of confidentiality and the topics likely to be covered in the interview.
3   Help the pilot explain why he/she has been referred, i.e. use open questions to initiate pilot into telling his or her story.
4   If the pilot acknowledges a problem, then take a brief chronology of the complaints, e.g. 'when (and who) first noticed'; 'how did the pilot and others react?'; 'what situation was the pilot in when the problem started?'; 'how has the pilot attempted to cope?'
5   Evaluate the level of impairment: examine how the pilot's relationships with colleagues, family and other significant people changed; examine if biological functions have changed (sleep, sexual activity, eating and maintenance of body weight).
6   Double check for increase in alcohol use as a coping strategy and any use of medication or drugs. Check suicidal ideation/intent by asking directly.
7   Check for significant changes in routines, lifestyle, hobbies, etc., as well as any legal or financial issues, recent, current or pending.
8   Check for sleep patterns, fatigue as well as work and personal stress.

9   Examine thinking: what does the pilot think will happen at times when he/ she is experiencing the problem.
10  How does the pilot make sense of the problem(s)?
11  Listen carefully for signs of abnormal beliefs.
12  History: professional including training records; recent or impending promotions; checks or courses; incidents at work; employer actions such as performance management or disciplinary procedures; as well as family and personal history. Check if other colleagues are aware of how they are coping or not coping. Explore previous coping strategies, e.g. shift patterns, social disruption, maintaining relationships.
13  Personal history: childhood, school, difficulties attaining goals at school, who he/she turned to for help when troubled as child, adolescence, occupational history (including how he/she became interested in flying), relationship history (children, quarrels).
14  Mental state examination.

## The practicalities of mental state assessments

The Federal Aviation Administration requires physicals for pilots once a year, and every six months for older pilots. However, the FAA does not require psychological checks but an approved aviation medical specialist can order further investigation if he or she thinks this is needed. Following the Germanwings incident in March 2015, the psychological assessment of pilots is likely to change and may even become a regular feature of pilots' annual check-up with an approved aviation specialist (Chan, 2015). The purpose of a mental state examination is to assess whether a pilot is suffering from psychological problems and if such problems are having a negative impact on the pilot's level of functioning, ability to carry out flying duties and if there are any risk of harm to self or to others (Jacobs, *et al.*, 2003). It is often used by psychiatrists, psychologists, therapists and other medical professionals to capture evidence of individual psychological symptoms with the aim of helping clients overcome their problems.

The assessment allows the clinician to develop an insight into the pilot's inner world. It is perhaps akin to a snapshot or a photographic representation of a person's innermost thought, feelings, urges, impulses, perceptions and interpretations. It is important that the clinician seeks to do justice by the pilot using further questioning and seeking to understand the idiosyncratic features of his or her presentation. The information collected helps the clinician to make a diagnosis and formulation. This is then shared with the pilot and together with the clinician the two parties can begin to discuss a suitable treatment plan (Lewis, 2011). The mental state examination is not a standalone assessment but often used in combination with biographical and historical information of psychological well-being to obtain a comprehensive cross-sectional insight into a person's state of mind.

There are various ways to collect data on pilot mental health and these are often used in combination at various stages of the assessment. This includes focused questions about current symptoms, Socratic questions to elicit information on a person's thoughts and feelings and unstructured observations. The clinician may also collect biographical and social data as well as relevant medical information from the pilot's medical doctor or other professionals if necessary. Psychological tests may also be used to aid the assessment. This includes questionnaires such as the Minnesota Multiphasic Personality Inventory (MMPI-2) or the Personality Assessment Inventory PAI (for further information see Chapters 1 and 4, this volume). These lengthy tests are probably too time-consuming for screening but they can be very useful as part of a comprehensive clinical psychological evaluation. As has been mentioned elsewhere in the book, pilots may not always wish to self-disclose due to fear of jeopardising their licence, shame or stigma (Bor and Hubbard, 2006). Tests such as the MMPI-2 provide information on defensiveness or the degree to which the individual has been open and honest.

There is a huge selection of psychological tests available for professionals to use throughout the assessment. The exact test selected will depend on the individual presentation of the pilot in question. If the pilot, for example, displays symptoms of depression, a short diagnostic questionnaire that targets depressions such as the Becks Depression Inventory (BDI) or the Patient Health Questionnaire (PHQ-9) may be used. However, it should be noted that these short questionnaires are transparent and obvious in content, and unlike the MMPI-2 provide no check for openness or honesty of responses.

If, on the other hand, there are suspected learning difficulties, which may be rare amongst pilots but not impossible, a battery of specialised questionnaires could be administered to collect further information on the type and intensity of the learning difficulty. It is worth mentioning that most psychological tests can only be administered by professionals with additional training in the use of psychometric questionnaire. There are various levels of training and the more specialised area such as personality inventories (e.g. MMPI-2) or diagnostic psychometric tests for learning difficulties (see Chapter 7) will typically require more advanced training.

Although there is no exact way or order of doing a mental state assessment, most clinicians tend to structure the client interview in a way that allows a range of different domains to be covered including a person's appearance, attitude, behaviour, mood and affect, speech, thought process, thought content, perceptions, cognition, insight and judgment (DSM-5, The American Psychiatric Association, 2013). A good mental state assessment allows a professional to use information from each domain to develop a coherent picture of a pilot's mental state. This is a little bit like the work of a scientist, information from each domain acts as cues as to what areas of the assessment need further questioning and what type of psychological questionnaires to use (Trzepacz and Baker, 1993).

Typically the clinician takes notes using a pen and paper to systematically record the interviewee's statements and visual observations throughout the process. Once the clinician has introduced him or herself to the pilot, the interview often starts with a brief outline of the assessment process. This may include a brief outline of the purpose of the interview, the expected duration of the interview, where and how the data will be stored, who will see the data, and the process of future treatments if needed as well as encouraging questions to be asked whenever necessary. Cultural differences may be a factor for consideration when conducting interviews, especially if the assessment is conducted in a cross-cultural context. This may be important when assessing pilots as many airlines recruit an international workforce due to operational requirements around the world. It is important that the uniqueness of the individual pilot including language, educational and financial background is taken into consideration throughout the assessment.

### Typical domains to be covered in a mental state examination

#### Appearance

How does the person look (thin, well-groomed or scruffy, pale or flushed)? For example, appearing too thin or underweight may signal a depressive disorder, excessive stress/anxiety or anorexia. Is there a noticeable odour? A smell of alcohol may indicate alcoholism whereas a stale sweat odour may indicate lack of self-care (which can be a symptom of several psychological problems including excessive stress, depression or more severe psychiatric disorders). The appearance alone is not sufficient for the clinician to develop an understanding of the pilot's presentation. This single source of information may equally well be caused by something else. The alcohol odour, for example, may be driven by anxiety where a person consumes a glass of wine 'to quell nerves' before the interview.

#### Attitude/rapport

How does the person approach the interview process? Do they come across as engaged, collaborative and willing to part take in the assessment? Are they, for example, able to answer questions asked by the professional? Do they appear forthcoming with information or do they need a lot of probing. Do they ask questions? A person who appears forthcoming with information may feel more at ease with being questioned or talking about themselves and they may be keen to obtain help for their problems. A person who is less forthcoming with information may be reluctant to take part in the process perhaps because they did not choose to do so themselves (the examination may have been booked by a partner or ordered by an airline manager for example). On the other hand, shyness, lack of confidence and social anxiety may also lead people to be less forthcoming with information during interviews. The quality of an interview may be enhanced by reflecting on the interview process where the clinician takes into account the other person's ability to establish rapport. This could be done by encouraging a collaborative approach between the clinician and the pilot which can enhance the quality of the information gathered. Asking periodically questions that elicit feedback may enhance collaboration, for example, 'How are you finding my questions this morning?' or 'Do you feel that I am understanding your situation correctly?' This may be especially relevant when compared to the more traditional doctor–patient relationship where the doctor was seen as the one being in power and making decisions and thereby perhaps discouraging the patient to ask questions or even challenge the doctor's diagnosis if necessary.

## Mood and affect

Mood is often described using the person's own words such as sad, angry, neutral, anxious or apathetic. This could be done by asking 'How are you feeling?' 'When are you most likely to feel this way (time of the day, particular days of the week?', 'What do you think may be causing you to feel this way?'. Focused questions may be used to encourage further information about the intensity of mood. For example, pilots may be asked to rate their mood on a scale from 1(low) to 10 (high) and/or the typical duration of the specific mood (minutes, hours, days). Affect refers to the observed non-verbal behaviour conveyed by a person when labelling their emotions. For example, a pilot who is showing a flat and non-reactive emotion when describing a traumatic experience could be described as showing incongruent affect, which might suggest depression or even a post-traumatic stress disorder. A pilot who shows a range of heightened or over-dramatic emotions during the assessment may, for example, be signalling symptoms of a manic episode or a histrionic personality.

## Behaviour

Observing a person's behaviour during the assessment can often give an indication of how a person is feeling. Lack of eye contact may for example indicate shyness, shame, learning difficulties or social anxiety to name a few possible reasons. Tics (excessive movements that are often associated with obsessive thoughts or compulsive behaviours) such as frequent pulling of the hair, repetitive tapping with hands or feet may indicate an obsessional compulsive disorder or obsessive compulsive personality disorder. Restlessness such as an inability to sit still, exaggerated fidgeting or pacing up and down the interview room may indicate depression, anxiety, attention deficiency disorder or side effects of a medication.

## Thought process

It is difficult to directly observe people's thought processes as these can really only be described by people themselves or inferred by their speech. Thus, we can infer from a person's speech the degree to which his or her thoughts are organised. However, as much as we would probably like to be able to read other people's minds, we have to rely on people to share their inner thoughts with us. A pilot who describes a rapid catastrophic circular thinking process (or a racing mind) may suffer from excessive worry and anxiety. A tendency to become fixated or repeatedly experiencing obsessive and repetitive thoughts may signal an obsessive compulsive disorder, whereas a slow and almost 'vacant' thought process may be symptomatic of depression. A fast-paced burst of millions of ideas over a relatively long period of time could be indicative of a manic episode or symptoms of the hyperactive component in an attention deficiency disorder.

*Thought content*

The content of thought helps to assess a person's preoccupation, obsessions, fears and overvalued ideas. This is best done by initiating an open-ended conversation allowing a person to elaborate on their thoughts, the extent to which they believe their thoughts belong to themselves or to a third party/ independent person separate from self. It is also possible to assess the intensity and frequency of the emotion associated with the thoughts by using more structured questions such as 'How does it make you feel when you experience this particular thought?' It is worth noting that some people may find it difficult to access their thoughts because a large part of our thinking may be automatic and therefore not within our conscious minds. Emotions or even situations can then be used as cues to help people identify the content of their thoughts and help automatic unconscious thoughts be brought into our conscious awareness. Negative or critical thoughts may indicate a problem with depression whereas overvalued ideas of being overweight may be symptomatic of anorexia or bulimia. A preoccupation which has an undue repetitive occupation in a pilot's mind may include thoughts of self-harm; suicide or fearful beliefs may be indicative of cognitive distortions, personality disorders, anxiety or depression; whereas delusional thoughts may signal features of a psychotic disorder. There are many different types of delusional disorders including depressive psychosis, paranoid delusions and mood incongruent delusional content which are more typically an indication of schizophrenia. A delusion is defined as a false belief or thought which is not reflective of a person's educational, cultural or social background. Although psychiatric disorders such as schizophrenia, delusional thinking or personality disorders may be rare amongst pilots, it is important that the assessment is broad enough to capture a full range of psychological and psychiatric disorders.

*Cognition*

This section covers the entire system of a person's ability to think including alertness, orientation, memory, concentration, attention, visuospatial functioning, language functions and executive functioning. One of the easier aspects of cognition to observe is alertness which includes a person's awareness of, and responsiveness to the environment. Do they appear drowsy, alert or confused? Orientation can be assessed by asking questions such as what day, time and month it is or where a person lives, their name or their date of birth. Assessing a pilot's attention or concentration may require more structured questions such as describing what they can see in the room for 20 seconds or spelling a word backwards. Short-term memory is typically assessed by recalling numbers or set of words after short intervals whereas long-term memory may be examined by asking questions about the past to assess information retrieval. Visuospatial functioning is best assessed by asking the pilot to draw an object or a diagram and observe how they cope with the task. It is worth noting that mild impairment of concentration and attention is often a common indicator of depression, anxiety, insomnia. Other more specialised medical and/or psychological tests may be needed to assess the severity and type of cognitive difficulty (Trzepacz and Baker, 1993).

*Perception*

This domain is mainly concerned with sensory experiences which can be registered via the five sensory channels including auditory, visual, touch, taste and smell. Hallucinations (when a person experiences an object or situation as real in the absence of an external actuality of such object/situation), pseudo hallucinations (when a person experiences for example voices in their head but is aware that these voices belong to themselves), and illusions (when people experience a distortion of a sensory experience such as seeing an object and for a second thinking that they saw a different object). Most people will also have experienced a distorted sense of time (déjà vu), which is another sensory abnormality. It is not uncommon for pilots who suffer from intense anxiety or depression to experience a distortion of the sense of self (depersonalisation) or a distorted sense of reality (derealisation). Hallucinations can occur in any of the five senses. Auditory hallucinations, for example, can be a symptom of psychosis whereas visual hallucinations could be indicative of organic conditions such as drug withdrawal or epilepsy.

## Insight and judgment

How much understanding does a person have of his or her own well-being? Do they think they have problems or are they not aware of their difficulties/in denial? This could be evaluated by using open-ended questions to elicit views and accounts of the problem and treatment options. Is the person able to make decisions that are reasonable and responsible? Impaired judgment may often be associated with disorders affecting the frontal lobe of the brain. For example, it would be reasonable to assume that an alcoholic would not be able to make reasonable and responsible decisions whilst under the influence of alcohol. This may have implications for the pilot's own safety and also that of others if there are dependencies.

# Conclusion

Having described the mental state examination in some detail it is important to remember that it is a component of the interview not the entire evaluation. If problems are detected then a detailed examination of the history of the problem will be essential for differential diagnosis and development of a clinical formulation (Morrison, 2014). A detailed personal and family history will be essential for developing a sound clinical formulation. While we have presented the ideas above as the basis for a single clinical interview/evaluation there may be occasions where it is necessary to see the pilot for a number of interviews to gain a reliable picture of the pilot's functioning.

# References

American Psychiatric Association. (2013). *Diagnostic and statistical manual of mental disorders.* 5th edition. Arlington, VA: American Psychiatric Publishing.

Bor, R. & Hubbard, T. (2006). *Aviation mental health: Psychological implications for air travel.* Aldershot: Ashgate.

Chan, M. (2015). FAA does not require psychological tests for pilots, experts say: Critics call for change after Germanwings co-pilot, Andreas Lubitz 'deliberately' crashes plane. *New York Times,* 26 March http://www.nydailynews.com/news/national/faa-not-require-psychological-tests-pilots-experts-article-1.2163359. retrieved 23 April 2016.

Engel, G. L. and William L. M. (1973). *Interviewing the patient.* London: Saunders.

Jacobs, D., Baldessarini, R., Conwell, Y. *et al.* (2003). *Assessment and treatment of patients with suicidal behaviors.* The American Psychiatric Association Practice Guidelines. *PsychiatryOnline.* http://psychiatryonline.org/pb/assets/raw/sitewide/practice_guidelines/guidelines/suicide.pdf

Lewis, Y. (2011). Assessing a client's mental state. In: R. Bor. & M. Watts, *The trainee handbook: A guide for counselling and psychotherapy trainees.* 3rd edition. London: Sage Publications.

Lloyd, M. and Bor, R. (2009). *Communication skills for medicine.* Edinburgh: Churchill Livingstone.

Maguire, P. and Pitceathly, C. (2002). Key communications skills and how to acquire them. *British Medical Journal,* 325, 697.

Morrison, J. (2014). *Diagnosis made easier: The principles and techniques for mental health clinicians.* 2nd edition. New York: Guilford Press.

Trzepacz, P. & Baker, R. (1993). *The psychiatric mental state examination.* Oxford: Oxford University Press.

# 7 Assessing cognitive function in airline pilots

## The importance of neuropsychological assessment

*Sarah Mackenzie Ross*

Professional airline pilots who fly passengers and cargo around the world are ultimately responsible for the safety of everyone on board the aircraft. They are an occupational group where intact cognitive function is essential because human error in the cockpit can have catastrophic consequences. Aircrew selection procedures include aptitude testing and computerised cognitive assessment to ensure high functioning, mentally capable pilots are selected for the job. However cognitive function may become compromised at any time during service by a number of factors including job-specific issues such as sleep disruption, fatigue and stress coupled with the fact that the incidence of various medical and neurological conditions which impair cognitive function increases with age (Hirtz *et al.*, 2007). Therefore, it is important that appropriate and sensitive procedures are in place to identify pilots whose mental state may be deteriorating. In the UK, cognitive function is not routinely assessed following initial personnel selection, the assumption being that any cognitive problems that develop during a pilot's career will be disclosed by the pilot during regular health checks and/or detected by aviation medical examiners (AMEs) or during line and simulator checks. The first part of this chapter will consider the validity of this assumption and how sensitive these procedures are likely to be at detecting cognitive impairment.

## Medical evaluations

Commercial airline pilots must possess a valid class 1 medical certificate to be eligible to fly, and attend medical evaluations every year until the age of forty and then every six months until the age of 65, to ensure they remain fit to fly and retain their certification. The medical standards that have to be met are laid down by aviation authorities and specify which medical and psychological conditions will invalidate certification (e.g. heart disease, neurological illness, psychosis). In the UK, AMEs evaluate the health of pilots by interviewing them about their past medical history, current state of health, medications taken and by undertaking a physical examination to elicit any physical signs that may indicate a medical condition that may otherwise go undetected. Further investigations and clinical tests may also be requested where indicated or at periodic intervals depending on age, such as blood and urine testing, visual and hearing tests, lung function and electrocardiogram (heart function) tests (Civil Aviation Authority, n.d.). This information is then used to determine a pilot's fitness to fly.

However, there are a number of reasons why sole reliance on AMEs to detect cognitive and emotional problems in aircrew is unwise. First, AMEs are dependent on pilots to disclose any concerns about psychological functioning during interview, but pilots may be reluctant to do so for fear of being grounded or losing their licence to fly (Bor *et al.*, 2002). Second, certain disorders are difficult to detect early in development and it is unlikely an AME would be able to detect mild degrees of cognitive impairment during routine medical evaluations. The use of brief cognitive screening tools, commonly used in clinical medicine such as the Mini Mental State Examination (MMSE) or asking pilots if they can learn and recall a name and address during interview, are unlikely to improve detection rates as these methods often fail to detect mild to moderate cognitive impairment in the general population, never mind high functioning individuals like pilots (Kulas & Naugle, 2003; Mitchell, 2009; Hoops *et al.*, 2009). Third, AMEs come from a range of different medical backgrounds, but are not mental health practitioners and may not have received training in the detection of cognitive and emotional disorders.

## Simulator tests

In the UK, a pilot's fitness to fly is checked regularly via line checks, simulator training and proficiency checks. The traditional process of training and evaluation requires pilots to undergo a licence proficiency check (LPC) and an operator proficiency check (OPC) in a simulator once a year and these checks are alternated so that the pilot is examined in the simulator every six months. The LPC is used to determine whether a pilot's skills are up to licensing standards, whereas the OPC evaluates a pilot's knowledge and use of airline specific procedures and how they manage cabin crew and passengers in an emergency. Both proficiency checks require pilots to demonstrate in a simulator, their knowledge of normal aircraft operating procedures (e.g. pre-flight inspections, taxiing, take-off and landing) and incorporate management of some sort of critical incident (e.g. engine failure on take-off, single engine approach, go-round and landing).

Simulator checks may not be the most reliable method of detecting cognitive impairment for the following reasons: they follow a set format such that pilots can predict some of the tasks they will be asked to do in the test. Some of the skills being evaluated are highly developed and 'overlearned' which means they have been practised beyond the point of mastery. Overlearned skills tend to be maintained under stress and may be retained during the early stages of cognitive decline, unlike cognitive abilities such as novel reasoning, problem-solving and decision-making. If a pilot has problems with executive functions such as problem-solving, strategy selection and flexibility of thinking, these are more likely to become apparent when the pilot is asked to manage a critical incident in the simulator test, unless the scenario chosen is one that has been frequently rehearsed (e.g. engine failure on take-off), in which case cognitive difficulties may be missed. An instructor/examiner decides whether a pilot has passed or failed the simulator test, but examiners' ratings may be influenced by the instructor's feeling towards the examinee and different interpretations of the grading system. Also, a pass only indicates that a pilot has met minimal acceptable standards and does not necessarily detect subtle changes in performance over time. Finally, examiners are not trained to detect cognitive impairment or mental health issues in pilots.

In 2006, an alternative training and qualification programme (ATQP) was introduced across Europe which allows operators to propose and provide more operator-specific recurrent training and evaluation for aircrew; but UK operators have to obtain approval from the CAA before implementing ATQP. Operators must demonstrate that their standards are higher than core requirements, that this will lead to increased safety and that they have appropriate experience to run such a programme. ATQP allows operators to replace some of the simulator-based OPC checks with on-the-job assessments and allows them to extend the interval between LPCs (Civil Aviation Authority, 2013). Operators who implement ATQP can introduce more varied scenarios in their simulator tests to assess pilots' problem-solving abilities and operators can make use of more detailed grading systems when evaluating performance in the cockpit. This should increase the likelihood that cognitive problems will be detected, but not every airline has the ability to invest in the requirements of the programme or has the expertise to implement it yet.

Even though the process by which pilots' cognitive functioning is evaluated at present is not perfect, it is important to note that rigorous personnel selection, extensive flight training, regular medical evaluations, simulator testing and the attention to safety demonstrated by the airline industry make flying the safest mode of transport. No other form of transportation is subject to so much scrutiny and monitoring and incorporates so many safety procedures to minimise error. Indeed other professions, such as medicine, have adopted some of the safety procedures used in aviation (checklists and procedural manuals) to reduce human error during surgical procedures (Clay-Williams & Colligan, 2015).

Although air accidents are infrequent, when they do happen they can be catastrophic and are usually widely reported in the media, heightening public anxiety, and they inevitably lead to questions about whether they could have been prevented and if human error was to blame. A series of tragic events in 2014 including the disappearance of Malaysia Airlines Flight MH370, and a number of crashes (AirAsia Flight QZ8501, Air Algerie AH5017, TransAsia GE222 and more recently Germanwings Flight 9525, in March 2015) remind us not to become complacent about air safety. We must regularly review procedures, identify gaps and make suggestions for further improvement to ensure flying remains as safe as possible.

The remainder of this chapter considers the circumstances in which it might be necessary to go beyond routine medical evaluation and simulator testing to determine whether a pilot shows evidence of cognitive impairment. This chapter will review common causes of cognitive impairment in pilots and describe the process of neuropsychological assessment and how it differs from computerised cognitive testing methods which have become popular in countries such as the USA. The advantages and limitations of cognitive testing will be discussed and recommendations for the future will be highlighted.

## Causes of cognitive impairment in pilots: the work environment

As mentioned previously, cognitive function may become compromised at any time during service by a number of factors including job-specific issues. Although pilots must be free of certain medical conditions (e.g. heart disease) stipulated by regulatory authorities such as the UK Civil Aviation Authority (CAA), it is not unusual for aircrew to complain of a range of non-specific symptoms which appear to relate to their working environment, as they are exacerbated by longer flight durations (Nagda & Koontz, 2003; McNeely *et al.*, 2014), for example ear, nose, throat and skin irritation, breathing difficulties, intestinal complaints and bloating, musculoskeletal problems, earache, sleep disorder and neurological symptoms such as headaches, light-headedness, numbness or tingling in extremities and cognitive impairment (i.e. memory loss). Potential causes in the working environment include cabin pressure, low humidity, temperature, noise, vibration, ozone, hypoxia and poor air quality. Cabin air can also become contaminated by various chemicals such as volatile organic compounds (e.g. limonene), ozone-initiated reaction products of limonene, such as formaldehyde (Wolkoff *et al.*, 2016); and some aircrew have expressed concern about the potential impact on health and cognition of exposure to neurotoxic substances contained in engine oil fumes which can sometimes enter the bleed air supply when seals become worn and faulty (Harrison & Mackenzie Ross, 2016).

Getting an adequate amount of sleep is essential for cognitive performance and emotional well-being, yet sleep deprivation (SD) is common in modern society and can be a major problem in certain occupational groups such as aircrew. Shift work, long hours of duty and trips across different time zones disrupt circadian rhythm and lead to fatigue and exacerbation of jet lag. Sleep deprivation can be total or involve the partial chronic restriction of sleep which is more common in everyday life. It has often been assumed that SD only affects long-haul pilots, but recent studies have found short-haul pilots also suffer sleep loss and report severe fatigue, particularly those who work for low-cost airlines, as commercial pressure results in pilots being asked to work close to the legal maximum flying hours and at unsociable hours of the day (Jackson & Earl, 2006). Both total and partial SD adversely affects cognitive function by impairing attentional processes and vigilance, working memory, visuo-motor performance, decision-making, processing speed and accuracy, in other words cognitive skills required in the cockpit. A New Zealand study found higher reporting of emotional disturbance and cognitive impairment amongst pilots reporting high levels of fatigue compared to both medium- and low-fatigue groups (Petrie & Dawson, 1997). Sleep is considered important for body restitution and the consolidation of new memories. Sleep loss can lead to high blood pressure, impaired immune function, metabolic changes, disturbed mood and a decline in cognitive performance particularly when engaged in routine, monotonous tasks requiring vigilance and reaction speed. Although cognitive processing usually recovers following sleep restitution, evidence suggests it takes longer following partial SD than acute SD (Alhola & Polo-Kantola, 2007; Kilgore, 2010) so short-haul pilots working for low-cost airlines may be at greater risk of cognitive impairment than previously thought and longer periods of leave may be required for short-haul pilots to recover. It is also important to note that pilots who are chronically fatigued may attempt to manage their condition with a combination of stimulants and sedatives (e.g. caffeine and energy drinks, over-the-counter sleep aids such as sedating antihistamines, melatonin and herbal products) which may impact on cognitive function, particularly when combined with alcohol. It is therefore imperative that the aviation industry makes efforts to reduce sleep deprivation in aircrew and/or allow sufficient recovery time; and that AMEs regularly assess how much sleep a pilot is getting.

## Causes of cognitive impairment in pilots: neurological injury /disease

The incidence of many neurological disorders in adulthood increases with age and although pilots retire early between 55 and 65 years of age, they may nevertheless develop a neurological illness or sustain a neurological injury (e.g. head injury) during their flying career. Some conditions can onset at any age for example; migraine affects around 6 per cent of men and 18 per cent women and usually onsets somewhere between puberty and the age of 30 years; multiple sclerosis tends to affect people between the age of 20 and 50 with an average age of onset of 34 years; traumatic brain injuries (often the result of vehicle crashes, sports injuries or assaults) are particularly common in young men aged 15–29 years of age, but can occur at any time and may increase an individual's risk of suffering an epileptic seizure in the future. Epilepsy can thus follow a head injury but may also be caused by systemic or metabolic disruption, or as a consequence of substance abuse and even sleep deprivation. A number of viral infections can affect brain function such as the human immunodeficiency virus (HIV). United Kingdom statistics indicate that 103,000 people are living with HIV in the UK (NAT, n.d.) and over 60 per cent of them are aged between 35–54 years so it is likely that a proportion of these people are employed in the airline industry. Studies suggest around a fifth of HIV-infected individuals develop cognitive dysfunction (Robertson *et al.*, 2007). Finally, some airline pilots may be at increased risk of exposure to other viruses that can attack the brain, such as Japanese encephalitis and meningitis, if they travel to/spend time in certain locations (rural areas of southeast Asia, the Pacific islands and the Far East).

Other neurological disorders are more likely to onset later in life, after the age of 60 years, such as Alzheimer's disease (AD), Parkinson's disease (PD), amyotrophic lateral sclerosis (ALS) and stroke, but it is important to note that two per cent of Alzheimer cases onset before the age of 60 years (42,325 people were thought to be living with young-onset dementia in the UK in 2013 [Prince *et al.*, 2014]) and one in four strokes occur in people under the age of 65 years. In the past the most common cause of pilot disqualification was cardiac disease, but recent epidemiological surveys of airline and regulatory body records suggest neurological problems such as vascular events are also a major cause of unfit notifications and incapacitation (Evans & Radcliffe, 2012; Arva & Wagstaff, 2004). Psychological problems have also been reported to be a major cause of in-flight incapacitation and loss of licence (Bor *et al.*, 2002; Evans & Radcliffe, 2012), the most common problems being anxiety disorders, depression and alcohol abuse, all of which can impair cognitive function.

## When should a pilot be referred to a specialist for further evaluation?

It is important that AMEs or any other professional involved in evaluating pilots' mental health refer pilots for further evaluation if they have concerns about their mental status or the clinical picture warrants this, for example, if (1) an AME detects something in a pilot's medical history that may impact on cognitive function such as a recent head injury, HIV diagnosis or change in prescription medicine; (2) if a pilot appears to be suffering from chronic sleep deprivation, is under stress or has recently experienced stressful life events; (3) or if a pilot exhibits or reports symptoms of cognitive impairment during an evaluation.

As mentioned previously, pilots may be reluctant to spontaneously disclose concerns about psychological functioning for fear of the consequences, but the likelihood of eliciting any problems may be increased by asking explicit questions (see Table 7.1 for suggestions), but please note, affirmative answers to these questions do not necessarily indicate pathology as memory lapses are common in everyday life. Rather these questions are useful prompts for triggering conversations about cognitive function in everyday life.

Between 2006 and 2011, several studies were undertaken at University College London, of commercial airline pilots who believed exposure to engine oil fumes on board aircraft had affected their health and cognitive function. These studies identified a highly specific pattern of cognitive impairment. Formal cognitive testing found general intellectual ability, language and perceptual ability to be intact, but pilots reported alarming cognitive failures at work such as being unable to retain or confusing numerical information from air traffic control; and their performance on tests of psychomotor speed, attention and visual sequencing was weak (Mackenzie Ross *et al.*, 2006; Mackenzie Ross, 2008; Mackenzie Ross *et al.*, 2011). The issue of whether exposure to contaminated air was responsible for these difficulties remains unclear as objective evidence of exposure was lacking, but these studies highlighted the fact that pilots can develop cognitive impairment during their flying career which may not be detected since many of the pilots evaluated at UCL were still flying.

For safety reasons it is important to identify pilots who are cognitively impaired, and a particularly effective method of doing so is neuropsychological assessment. This is a highly sensitive method of identifying the presence of central nervous system dysfunction, before structural abnormalities are observable on brain imaging. Indeed, a Norwegian study which looked at the reasons for medical disqualification amongst commercial pilots over a 20-year

*Table 7.1* Examples of general and specific questions that could be used to elicit cognitive difficulties

*General questions*

Have you had any difficulty concentrating recently?
Do you read something and then have to re-read it several times because you find you have not been concentrating?
Do you struggle to follow TV programmes or the storylines in books and magazine articles?
Do you start a task then get distracted and forget to return to it?
Have you noticed any problems with your memory recently?
Do you frequently forget where you have put things?
Do you have to go back and check whether you have done something?
Do you leave appliances on or doors unlocked?
Do you forget where you have placed things?
Do you forget what people have told you?
Do you repeat to others things you have just told them?
Do you get lost in places you have been to many times before?
Do you have difficulty picking up new skills?
Do you forget appointments?
Do you forget to pass on messages to people?
Do you have difficulty making decisions
Do you get lost more often?
Do you have difficulty finding your way around?
Do you feel mentally slowed down?
How would you describe your mood? Happy, sad, worried?

*Specific questions*

Have you had any difficulty recalling instructions from air traffic control?
Do you struggle to do things in the correct order/sequence?
Do you forget which items have been completed & need to refer to checklists?
Do you have difficulty doing more than one task at a time or switching between tasks?
Have you forgotten whether you have completed certain tasks on the flight deck, e.g. whether the undercarriage has been lowered?
Are you struggling to keep pace at work?
Do you forget the names of colleagues you are working with?
Do you forget information given to you by colleagues?
Do you have difficulty navigating?

period found the disqualification rate for neurological conditions had increased over time, with many cases being detected by neuropsychological testing (Arva & Wagstaff, 2004).

## What is clinical neuropsychology?

Neuropsychologists study the relationship between brain structures, brain systems and psychological functions such as cognition, emotion and behaviour. Clinical neuropsychology is the application of neuropsychological knowledge to the assessment, diagnosis and rehabilitation of individuals who have suffered brain damage following injury or illness. In the UK, clinical neuropsychologists are fully qualified clinical psychologists who have chosen to specialise in neuropsychology and acquired specialist knowledge of functional neuroanatomy, brain development, neurological disorders and the psychological and behavioural manifestations of neurological disorders.

## What does a neuropsychological assessment involve?

The clinical neuropsychologist measures deficits in intelligence, memory, language, perception, personality, emotion and behaviour using a battery of psychometric tests which take several hours to administer. In addition to observing the patient's behaviour during testing and considering test results, clinical neuropsychologists review relevant medical records and the opinions of experts from related disciplines such as neurology and psychiatry. They conduct a thorough clinical interview to determine the nature and history of any complaints, explore developmental, psychosocial, medical and psychiatric background, review educational and occupational history, and evaluate mental health and coping, including alcohol and recreational drug use and prescribed medication. Clinical neuropsychologists also interview relatives, carers and other informants (see Table 7.2). The results are used to determine the most likely cause of a person's difficulties (i.e. assist in diagnosis and localisation of cerebral pathology), determine current level of functioning, monitor the progress of treatment or identify goals for rehabilitation. One of the most common reasons patients are referred for a neuropsychological assessment is to determine whether they show evidence of cognitive impairment and if so, whether this reflects neurological injury or psychiatric disorder (Lezak *et al.*, 2004).

The battery of psychometric tests administered may vary depending on the referral question, but a broad range of cognitive functions are usually evaluated

*Table 7.2* Overall content of a neuropsychological assessment

| |
| --- |
| Clinical interview and history taking |
| Interview carers and informants |
| Review medical, school and/or occupational records |
| Evaluate mental health |
| Psychometric testing |

*Table 7.3* Psychometric test battery and examples of commonly used tests

| |
|---|
| *Premorbid IQ* |
| Test of Premorbid Functioning (TOPF: Wechsler, 2011) |
| *Current IQ* |
| Wechsler Adult Intelligence Scale-IV (WAIS-IV: Wechsler, 2008) |
| *Attention* |
| Digit Span subtest from the WAIS-IV<br>Paced Auditory Serial Addition Test (PASAT: Gronwall, 1977)<br>Test of Everyday Attention (TEA: Robertson *et al.*, 1994) |
| *Memory* |
| Wechsler Memory Scale-IV (WMS-IV: Wechsler, 2008)<br>BIRT memory and information processing battery (BMIPB: *Oddy et al.*, 2007) |
| *Language* |
| Verbal fluency (COWA: Spreen & Strauss, 1998)<br>Object naming (GNT: McKenna & Warrington, 1983) |
| *Perception* |
| Visual object and space perception battery (VOSP: Warrington & James, 1991) |
| *Processing speed* |
| Symbol search and coding subtests from the WAIS-IV<br>Trail Making A & B (Spreen & Strauss, 1998) |
| *Executive function* |
| Colour Word Reading Interference Test (STROOP: Trenerry, 1988)<br>Delis-Kaplan Executive Function System (DKEFS: Delis *et al.*, 2001)<br>Behavioural Assessment of the Dysexecutive Syndrome  (BADS: Wilson *et al.*, 1996) |
| *Symptom validity/effort tests* |
| Test of Memory and Malingering (TOMM: Tombaugh, 1996)<br>Word Memory Test (WMT; Green, 2005) |
| *Mood questionnaires* |
| Generalised Anxiety Disorder Scale (GAD-7: Torbay and South Devon NHS Trust)<br>Patient Health Questionnaire (PHQ-9: Torbay and South Devon NHS Trust)<br>Hospital Anxiety and Depression Scale (HAD: Zigmund & Snaith, 1983)<br>Beck Depression Inventory (BDI-II: Beck, 1996)<br>Beck Anxiety Inventory (BAI: Beck, 1990) |

including premorbid functioning, current level of intellectual functioning, attention, memory, language, perception, processing speed and executive function. It is also extremely important that tests of effort or symptom validity are included to enable the clinician to determine whether test results are valid and provide an accurate reflection of a patient's current level of functioning (Bush *et al.*, 2005). Table 7. 3 provides examples of commonly used tests.

## Interpretation

The clinical neuropsychologist integrates findings from formal testing, clinical interviews and other sources to determine whether a patient shows evidence of cognitive impairment and if so, what the likely cause might be. There are many reasons an individual may obtain low scores on cognitive tests. Test scores alone are non-specific and need to be interpreted in the context of other information. First, a person's results need to be compared to an appropriate reference group of the same age, gender, level of education, social class and cultural background as these factors can affect test performance. Second, a range of other factors can affect performance on psychometric tests and need to be considered as they may limit the conclusions that can be drawn such as linguistic factors, poor comprehension, low motivation, malingering, pain, fatigue, anxiety and depression. The neuropsychologist will then decide whether symptoms and the profile of performance on psychometric tests makes medical sense, is consistent with what has been observed in clinical populations; and rules out alternative diagnoses (Lezak *et al.*, 2004). Therefore, it is imperative that the results of a neuropsychological assessment are interpreted by a clinical neuropsychologist in order to be of any benefit to the patient.

## How does a clinical neuropsychological assessment differ from the computerised cognitive testing used in the selection of pilots?

Cognitive function testing has been used to select capable pilots in both military and commercial aviation for decades. The tests are designed to ensure pilots have the necessary skills for the job, and some of the skills tested during the recruitment process are also examined in a neuropsychological assessment such as memory, spatial awareness, verbal and numerical reasoning, attention and processing speed, multi-tasking and decision-making. The key difference between cognitive testing used in the selection of pilots and a neuropsychological assessment is in terms of aim and purpose. The former is used to select high-functioning individuals to work in aviation whereas a neuropsychological assessment is used to assess brain function/dysfunction and is not designed to predict performance in the cockpit. Another important difference concerns the number and type of tests administered and the way in which psychometric tests are administered and interpreted.

When it comes to pilot selection, different flight training organisations and airlines use different test providers but in most cases tests are administered and scored by a computer and assess functions relevant to aviation. In the USA, Dr Gary Kay developed a computerised test called CogScreen with the dual aim of predicting an individual's performance in the cockpit and screening pilots for subtle changes in cognitive functioning which could impair performance (Kay, 1995). It is not a test of flying knowledge and skill, but rather the cognitive functions thought to be necessary for the performance of aviation duties such as information processing speed, attention, memory, visual perceptual functions, sequencing and problem-solving. CogScreen consists of a series of computerised cognitive tasks, each presented with instructions and a practice segment. It has been found to be sensitive to mild brain dysfunction and to predict an individual's performance in the simulator (Taylor *et al.*, 2000). It has the advantage of being relatively inexpensive, quick to administer (around 50 minutes), computer administration and scoring make it possible to screen large numbers of people simultaneously. It has multiple forms allowing it to be administered several times to the same pilot enabling progress over time to be monitored and results correlate with pilot performance in the cockpit. However, some of its advantages are also disadvantages. In being computer administered and scored, there is no way of evaluating behaviour during testing or identifying factors that may impair performance such as anxiety, fatigue, poor effort, cultural or linguistic factors that could impact on the comprehension of instructions, etc. A limited number of cognitive functions are assessed and although they assess skills relevant to flying, CogScreen lacks sensitivity to other forms of cognitive impairment which could be indicative of an underlying neurological condition. Indeed a sample CogScreen report available online (Sample Report. Retrieved from http://www.cogscreen.com/sampleaeromedicalreport.pdf) specifies that (1) 'no decisions should be based solely' on CogScreen results and that material from other sources should be sought before making decisions about an individual, and (2) not all brain disorders produce cognitive deficits that will be detected by CogScreen, and (3) 'scores falling in the impaired range do not necessarily reflect brain dysfunction'. Finally, feedback is limited to ratings of task speed, accuracy, the amount of work accomplished plus a statistical estimate of the probability of brain dysfunction.

Although results of computerised cognitive assessment are useful for large-scale research and screening, provide a baseline against which to monitor performance over time and can highlight the need for further evaluation, it does not equate to a thorough cognitive assessment and should not be relied upon for diagnosing acquired brain injury/disease or when making major decisions such as whether a pilot is fit to fly. When there is doubt about a pilot's cognitive function, competency and ability to fly, a referral should be made for neuropsychological assessment to assist differential diagnosis and define the pilot's functional strengths and weaknesses.

The advantages and disadvantages of neuropsychological assessment include the following. On the plus side, a neuropsychological assessment is also relatively inexpensive, portable, reliable and capable of detecting signs of cognitive impairment/brain dysfunction even in the absence of other neurological signs. Despite major advances in neuroimaging, not all forms of brain damage are detectable using structural CT and MRI scans such as the early stages of dementia, concussion following mild head injury, transient ischaemic attacks, epilepsy, some infectious, toxic and metabolic conditions and hypoxia (Kulas & Naugle, 2003; Lezak *et al.*, 2004; Harvey, 2012). Even when structural lesions are detected on brain scans, it can be difficult to predict the functional sequelae, for example, some patients with brain lesions observable on imaging have normal cognitive function. The only way to determine the extent of retained and impaired cognitive abilities is via neuropsychological assessment.

In contrast to screening measures like CogScreen, a neuropsychological assessment covers a broad range of cognitive domains, enabling clinicians to engage in a process of differential diagnosis. It leads to the identification of problems in everyday life, even in the absence of a clear diagnosis, and can be used to monitor cognitive function over time (i.e. serial assessment). Neuropsychological assessment identifies areas for intervention and can be used to evaluate the effectiveness of treatment programmes, both medical (surgery, radiotherapy, pharmacological interventions, occupational therapy, etc.) and psychological. Psychometric tests are administered by a person (although some may be computerised) and the psychologist will consider all factors that may impair performance and all aspects of a person's life that may be relevant, including the working environment, relationships and social networks. They communicate diagnoses in a sensitive way with sufficient time allowed for discussion and follow-up and offer support and individually tailored cognitive rehabilitation, as a diagnosis is of limited value unless it leads to support and intervention.

The disadvantages of neuropsychological assessment include the fact that it takes much longer than brief screening measures like CogScreen. Testing is administered and interpreted by clinicians limiting the number of individuals who can be assessed simultaneously and there may be a shortage of clinical neuropsychologists and long waiting-lists in certain parts of the UK. Neuropsychological test results alone are relatively non-specific and it is not always possible to arrive at a definitive diagnosis. It is of limited value for certain individuals (e.g. individuals with sensory or motor impairments, those whose first language is not English) because of test design or because normative data is only available for English-speaking populations. Normative data may not be available for high-functioning individuals like pilots and the criteria used to detect changes in patients in general may be of limited value in aviators (King *et al.*, 2011); and finally, the neuropsychological tests used in clinical practice were not designed to predict performance in the cockpit.

## Conclusions and recommendations

The assessment and monitoring of cognitive function of pilots is essential for safety reasons. Although pilots undergo cognitive testing at the point of selection/ recruitment or when they change employer, routine assessment of cognitive function does not form part of the ongoing medical evaluation of pilots in the UK. This is concerning because a pilot's cognitive function may become compromised at any time during their career as a result of job-specific issues such as sleep disruption and the fact that the incidence of various medical and neurological conditions which impair cognitive function increases with age. At present, the responsibility for identifying and reporting cognitive and emotional problems lies with the airline pilot, who may conceal any difficulties for fear of losing their licence and AMEs who may not be trained or have sufficient time to detect psychological problems during routine health checks.

It is therefore important that AMEs and other members of the aviation community (i.e. those involved in the training and evaluation of pilots and those who work alongside them such as flight and cabin crew) are educated with regard to the causes of cognitive impairment in pilots, potential warning signs and screening techniques that can be used to elicit symptoms of cognitive impairment. They also need to know when and to whom to refer a pilot for specialist evaluation. The latter should be undertaken by a neurologist and clinical neuropsychologist and not by means of computerised testing, unless the results of the latter will be interpreted by a clinical neuropsychologist. It would also be useful to provide clear guidance with regard to conditions that will result in loss of licence and those that may result in suspension until a programme of treatment has been completed (e.g. cognitive impairment secondary to fatigue or substance abuse), as this may reduce anxiety amongst pilots about the consequences of reporting cognitive difficulties, making it more likely problems will be reported.

## Acknowledgements

I would like to thank former Senior First Officer Adriana Osborne and Captain Sam Quigley, type rated instructor and examiner for providing technical knowledge and helpful comments regarding the content of this chapter.

## References

Alhola, P., & Polo-Kantola, P. (2007). Sleep deprivation: Impact on cognitive performance. *Neuropsychiatric Diseases and Treatment*, 3(5), 553–567.

Arva, P., & Wagstaff, A.S. (2004). Medical disqualification of 275 commercial pilots: Changing patterns over 20 years. *Aviation, Space, and Environmental Medicine*, 75(9), 791–794.

Beck, A.T., & Steer, R.A. (1990). *Manual for the Beck Anxiety Inventory*. San Antonio, TX: Psychological Corporation.

Beck, A.T., Steer, R.A., & Brown, G.K. (1996). *Manual for the Beck Depression Inventory-II*. San Antonio, TX: Psychological Corporation.

Bor, R., Field, G., & Scragg, P. (2002). The mental health of pilots: An overview. *Counselling Psychology Quarterly*, 15(3), 239–256.

Bush, S., Ruff, R.M., Troster, A.I., Barth, J.T., Koffler, S.P., Pliskin, N.H., Reynolds, C.R., & Silver, C.H. (2005). NAN position paper. Symptom validity assessment: Practice issues and medical necessity. NAN Policy & Planning Committee. *Archives of Clinical Neuropsychology*, 20, 419–426.

Civil Aviation Authority (2013). *Standards Document 80_Version 1. Alternative Training and Qualification Programme (ATQP) Industry Guidance*. Safety and Airspace Regulation Group Licensing and Training Standards. Retrieved on 25 May 2016 from www.caa.co.uk/standardsdocuments

Civil Aviation Authority (n.d.). Medical standards, https://www.caa.co.uk/Aeromedical-Examiners/Medical-standards/

Clay-Williams, R., & Colligan, L. (2015). Back to basics: Checklists in aviation and healthcare. *British Medical Journal Quality and Safety*, 24(7), 428–431.

Delis, D.C., Kaplan, E., & Kramer, J.H. (2001). *Delis-Kaplan Executive Function System*. San Antonio, TX: The Psychological Corporation.

Evans, S., & Radcliffe, S.A. (2012). The annual incapacitation rate of commercial pilots. *Aviation, Space, and Environmental Medicine*, 83, 42–49.

Green, P. (2003, revised 2005). *Word Memory Test for Windows: User's manual and program*. Edmonton: Green's Publishing.

Gronwall, D.M.A. (1977). Paced auditory serial addition task: A measure of recovery from concussion. *Perceptual and Motor Skills*, 44, 367–373.

Harrison, V., & Mackenzie Ross, S.J. (2016). An emerging concern: Toxic fumes in airlplane cabins. *Cortex*, 74, 297–302.

Harvey, P.D. (2012). Clinical applications of neuropsychological assessment. *Dialogues in Clinical Neuroscience*, 14(1), 91–99.

Hirtz, D., Thurman, D.J., Gwinn-Hardy, K., Mohamed, M., Chadhuri, A.R., & Zalutsky, R. (2007). How common are the "common" neurologic disorders? *Neurology*, 68, 326–337.

Hoops, S., Nazem, S., Siderowf, A.D., Duda, J.E., Xie, S.X., Stern, M.B., & Weintraub, D. (2009). Validity of the MoCA and MMSE in the detection of MCI and dementia in Parkinson disease. *Neurology*, 73(21), 1738–1745.

Jackson, C.A., & Earl, L. (2006). Prevalence of fatigue among commercial pilots. *Occupational Medicine*, 56, 263–268.

Kay, G.G. (1995). COGSCREEN: Professional Manual. Odessa, FL: Psychological Assessment Resources.

Kilgore, W.D. (2010). Effects of sleep deprivation on cognition. *Progress in Brain Research*, 185, 105–129.

King, R., Barto, E., Ree, M.J., Teachout, M.S., Retzlaff, P. (2011). *Compilation of pilot cognitive ability norms*. Wright-Patterson ABF, OH: Air Force Research Laboratory.

Kulas, J.F., & Naugle, R.I. (2003). Indications for neuropsychological assessment. *Cleveland Clinic Journal of Medicine*, 70(9), 785–789.

Lezak, M.D, Howieson, D.B.,. & Loring, D.W. (2004). *Neuropsychological assessment* (4th edition). New York: Oxford University Press.

Mackenzie Ross, S.J. (2008). Cognitive function following exposure to contaminated air on commercial aircraft: A case series of 27 pilots seen for clinical purposes. *Journal of Nutritional and Environmental Medicine*, 17(2), 111–126.

Mackenzie Ross, S.J., Harper, A., & Burdon, J. (2006). Ill health following exposure to contaminated aircraft air: Psychosomatic disorder or neurological injury? *Journal of Occupational Health and Safety – Australia and New Zealand*, 22(6), 521–528.

Mackenzie Ross, S.J., Harrison, V., Madeley, L., Davis, K., Abraham-Smith, K., Hughes, T., & Mason, O. (2011). Cognitive function following reported exposure to contaminated air on commercial aircraft: Methodological considerations for future researchers. *Journal of Biological Physics and Chemistry*, 11, 180–191.

McKenna, P., and Warrington, E.K. (1983). *The Graded Naming Test: manual*. Windsor: NFER-Nelson.

McNeely, E., Gale, S., Tager, I., Kincl, L., Bradley, J., Coull, B., & Hecker, S. (2014). The self-reported health of U.S. flight attendants compared to the general population. *Environmental Health*, 13:13, DOI: 10.1186/1476-069X-13-13.

Mitchell, A.J. (2009). A meta-analysis of the accuracy of the mini-mental state examination in the detection of dementia and mild cognitive impairment. *Journal of Psychiatric research*, 43(4), 411–431.

Nagda, N.L., & Koontz, M.D. (2003). Review of studies on flight attendant health and comfort in airliner cabins. *Aviation, Space, and Environmental Medicine*, 74(2), 101–109.

NAT (National AIDS Trust) (n.d.). Latest UK HIV statistics. http://www.nat.org.uk/HIV-in-the-UK/HIV-Statistics/Latest-UK-statistics.aspx

Oddy, M., Coughlan, A., & Crawford, J. (2007). BIRT Memory & Information Processing Battery. Horsham, UK: Brain Injury Research Trust.

Petrie, K.J., & Dawson, A.G. (1997). Symptoms of fatigue and coping strategies in international pilots. *International Journal of Aviation Psychology*, 7(3), 251–258.

Prince, M., Knapp, M., Guerchet, M., McCrone, P., Prina, M., Comas-Herrera, A., Wittenberg, R., Adelaja, B., Hu, B., King, D., Rehill, A., & Salimkumar, D. (2014). Dementia UK: Second Edition – Overview. Alzheimer's Society.

Robertson, I., Nimmo-Smith, I., Ward, T., & Ridgeway, V. (1994). *Test of everyday attention*. Bury St Edmunds, UK: Thames Valley Test Company.

Robertson, K.R., Smurzynski, M., Parsons, T.D., Wu, K., Bosch, R.J., Wu, J., McArthur, J.C., Collier, A.C., Evans, S.R., & Ellis, R.J. (2007). The prevalence and incidence of neurocognitive impairment in the HAART era. *AIDS*, 21(14), 1915–1921.

Spreen, O., & Strauss, E. (1998). *A compendium of neuropsychological tests*. New York: Oxford University Press.

Taylor, J.L., O'Hara, R., Mumenthaler, M.S., & Yesavage, J.A. (2000). Relationship of CogScreen-AE to flight simulator performance and pilot age. *Aviation, Space, and Environmental Medicine*, 71(4), 373–380.

Tombaugh, T.N. (1996). Test of memory malingering. North Tonawanda, NY: Multi Health Systems.

Torbay and South Devon NHS Trust. GAD7 and PHQ 9. Retrieved on 23 May 2016 from http://www.torbayandsouthdevon.nhs.uk/uploads/score-sheet-gad-7-anxiety-and-phq-9-depression.pdf

Trenerry, M.R., Crosson, B., DeBoe. J., & Leber, W.R. (1988). *STROOP neuropsychological screening test manual*. Odessa, FL: Psychological Assessment Resources.

Warrington, E.K., & James, M. (1991). *Visual Object and Space Perception Battery*. Bury St Edmunds, UK: Thames Valley Test Company.

Wechsler, D. (2008). *Manual for the Wechsler Adult Intelligence Scale-IV (UK)*. San Antonio, TX: Pearson.

Wechsler, D. (2011). *Test of Premorbid Functioning – UK edition*. London, UK: Pearson.

Wilson, B.A., Emslie, H., Evans, J.J., Alderman, N., & Burgess, P.W. (1996). *Behavioural assessment of the dysexecutive syndrome*. Bury St Edmunds, UK: Thames Valley Test Company.

Wolkoff, P., Crump, D.R., & Harrison, P.T.C. (2016). Pollutant exposures and health symptoms in aircrew and office workers: Is there a link? *Environnent International*, 87, 74–84.

Zigmond, A.S., & Snaith, R.P. (1983). The Hospital Anxiety and Depression Scale. *Acta Psychiatrica Scandinavica*, 67(6), 361–370.

# 8 Assessment of personality

*Paul Harris*

## Introduction

The present paradigm around selection and assessment of pilots in commercial aviation has been arrived at over many decades, albeit perhaps in a relatively ad hoc manner. It has been reasonably effective in understanding, and predicting, many aspects of pilot aptitude and ability. However, predicting safe and effective behaviour based on pilots' personality data has proved more elusive. Furthermore there currently exists an understandable inclination in aviation organisations to favour personality 'testing' and screening in or screening out individuals on the basis of their personality profiles. An additional and somewhat noisy factor is the large commercial industry of psychometrics with thousands of variations of personality questionnaires available, each proclaiming to accurately and reliably measure or 'test' personality. It has been estimated that this industry is worth somewhere between $2 billion and $4 billion per year (*The Economist*, 2013).

Over the last number of years I have become increasingly interested in the limitations of this approach to personality assessment, and, by implication, the conventional utility of the resulting profiles. Given the focus of this book, might there now be timely opportunities to rethink what is typically understood by personality assessment of pilots, to shift the paradigm in service of a more useful set of outcomes for pilots and the organisations in which they work? With that in mind, in this chapter it is proposed to examine and challenge aspects of the predictive validity, methodology and utility of current models of personality assessment, and to suggest novel ways to increase the quality and practical utility of the resulting data.

### What is meant by personality?

For the purpose of this brief introduction it is helpful to outline a working definition of what is meant by personality. According to the definition proposed by the American Psychological Association, personality refers to 'individual differences in characteristic patterns of thinking, feeling and behaving'. The relatively persistent nature of thoughts, feelings and behaviours has been demonstrated in well-established trait theories of personality. Furthermore, the underlying components of these traits and patterns are reasonably well understood, and lend themselves to quantitative assessments. The Five Factor Model (FFM) of personality (McCrae & Costa, 1987) consolidates this view. Over several decades of comprehensive, peer-reviewed research (see for example McCrae & Costa, 1997; McCrae, 2002; Schmitt *et al.*, 2007), this model has evolved to become the most established, evidence-based and widely used taxonomy of personality. Moreover, in recent years the FFM has been further supported by research that shows evidence for interesting extensions of the FFM and distinct biological substrates for the factors (DeYoung *et al.*, 2007), the psychological functions underlying each of the factors (Denissen & Penke, 2008; DeYoung & Gray, 2009; DeYoung, 2010), and that four of the five factors are related to the size of different areas of the brain (DeYoung *et al.*, 2010). While no theory or model can ever be considered complete, and the FFM is not without its critics (e.g. Block, 1995; McAdams, 1992), it has yet to be robustly falsified. It is arguably the most useful model we have at present to allow us to objectively describe and understand the widest range and deepest nuance of human personality.

One of the most important considerations when discussing personality is the dynamic and reciprocal interaction of people, their environment, and their behaviour. Isolating personality away from the dynamics of the situations in which it manifests is, at best, an academic exercise that fails completely to reflect the practical reality. To do so is as futile as the 'nature versus nurture' debates of the past. Everything is connected. That is simply the natural state of things. Why should it be any other way?

Based on these working concepts of personality this chapter will address three main areas:

- the highly dynamic nature of personality;
- the quality of data generated by personality questionnaires;
- the organisational utility of a personality profile.

I will also comment on several smaller facets that are worthy of discussion.

It is my belief that a broader understanding of these three areas can act as a catalyst for new and germane thinking about how aviation organisations and, in particular, their pilots, can understand and work with personality assessment. This will be timely given the rapidly changing work context in which today's early career pilots find themselves, and the projected increases in demand for their services (Airbus, 2015; Boeing, 2015; PwC, 2015).

### The dynamic nature of personality

Established trait theories of personality, such as the FFM, sit well with a thesis of social constructivism, whereby individuals and groups participate in the construction of their perceived social reality. It is also understood that some people are more consistent in their thoughts, feelings and behaviours (i.e. their manifest personality) than others (Snyder & Tanke, 1976). Additionally, the influence of certain traits on behaviour tends to be stronger or weaker depending on the situation (Ross & Nisbett, 2011; Sherman *et al.*, 2010). An everyday example of this is how the expectation of a looming and important exam might affect two students with different amounts of the conscientiousness trait (composed of several components, including, for example, personal organisation and self-discipline) in different ways. Likewise, in those same two students, different amounts of the trait of conscientiousness can affect how they will perceive and respond to being invited to a wild weekend party two days before the exam.

There is a profound interaction between our personalities, the wide variety of situations in which we find ourselves, and the people we interact with in those situations. The way in which we adapt ourselves to new situations plays a key role in these interactions. If this were not the case, then we would find it very difficult to apply newly formed, or forming, constructs of what we learn about the world and those around us, to more specific situations. These adaptive interactions allow us to learn how 'to be' in those situations.

By way of another example, consider the behaviours of two people heading to an airport to take the same flight. Their common behavioural goal is simply to get to the same destination. Now assume one of them has a fear of flying strong enough to cause in him a degree of anxiety about the journey, but not so strong as to cause him to seek an alternative mode of transport. Let's also consider that this person is naturally a very anxious character, i.e. is prone to frequent worrying. The other person for the purposes of this example is not afraid of flying and has a naturally low level of anxiety. So we can easily imagine differences in how each individual might think, feel and behave in the following situations:

- arriving at the airport;
- standing in the security line;
- boarding the aircraft;
- seeing the doors sealed shut on completion of boarding;
- during the safety announcements;
- as the aeroplane starts its taxi to the runway.

Now, let's make a further assumption, that the person without the fear of flying and high levels of anxiety is, in fact, the captain of the flight, who flies this route many times each week. It should therefore be clear that people *in* similar situations could have very different ways of perceiving, reacting and adapting *to* those situations.

Additional examples come quickly to mind; imagine your likely thoughts, feelings and behaviour in any of the following scenarios:

- 15 minutes prior to giving an important presentation at a major conference;
- 15 minutes prior to sitting in the audience to watch someone else give that presentation;
- attending a church for the wedding of friend;

- attending a church for the funeral of a friend;
- arriving at the pub of a quiet weekday evening for a glass of wine with two close friends;
- arriving late at the same pub on a weekend night to meet a very large group of friends, all of whom have consumed enough alcohol to fully disinhibit their extraverted selves!

It is clear that the situation in which we find ourselves (and with which people) influences how we think, feel and behave. Conversely, our personalities have a strong influence over the choice of situations in which we will involve ourselves. In the above scenarios, some may imagine themselves enjoying the last more than the second last, or vice versa, depending on the make up of their own unique personality.

At a more general level, consider again the trait of conscientiousness. The characteristic components of this trait typically include orderliness, achievement striving, self-discipline, competence, deliberation and dutifulness. People who have high levels of conscientiousness can oftentimes possess low levels of another trait known as neuroticism, also described as the inverse of emotional stability. It is typically the case that a person with a high level of conscientiousness is likely to generate more positive work and life opportunities, at an earlier stage, than someone with a low level of the same trait. Highly conscientious people can create environments that are notably more stable, with less materially for them to worry about (anxiety being a key component of the trait of neuroticism). Thus high conscientiousness could be thought to interrelate directly with neuroticism, acting as a governing agent on the trait, and keeping it at a low level. In this way not only does the situation act on personality, and vice versa, but also personality fundamentally interacts with itself.

So far this may sound like common sense – our success as a species has clearly been a function of our ability to effectively adapt to many different situations. However, perhaps less commonly known research suggests that aspects of our personalities are subject to degrees of change within a number of days (Judge et al., 2014). Such research does not imply extreme or pathological mood-swings, but simply the importance of noticing the granularity of available data demonstrating that how we feel on a given day can affect how we behave the following day. Considering then the infinite variety of highly complex variables comprising our interactions between colleagues at work, commuters in transit, families at home, friends and so forth, we can better appreciate the largely automatic and extraordinary adaptive biological, neurological and psychological mechanisms we simply take for granted.

It is a widely held notion that one aspect of being an expert or a professional, particularly in a safety-critical role such as a pilot, is the ability to fully compartmentalise one's personal life when on the job, to 'leave it at home' so to speak. It is questionable how realistic a goal this can ever really be, and, as already stated: everything is connected. It is reasonable to suggest that, in all circumstances, some quantity of our concerns, worries, fears, hopes and beliefs are implicated in reciprocal interaction with our thoughts, feelings and behaviours. In relation to our ability to compartmentalise (or any other ability for that matter), research has consistently demonstrated that how competent we think we are is subject to persistent cognitive bias (Alicke & Govorun, 2005). For instance, when asked, 'how good a driver are you?' The majority of people reading that question will likely be thinking something along the lines of 'above average', despite the fact that, statistically, this cannot hold. Research has consistently shown that people, males more so than females, tend to over-estimate their abilities, especially where there is perceived expertise involved (Bench *et al.*, 2015; Dunning *et al.*, 2003; Lundeberg, 1994). Notwithstanding a professional's valiant attempts to compartmentalise, frequently he (less often she) will simply be unwittingly overconfident about his actual ability to do this. He will discount, or dismiss outright, evidence to the contrary, because to acknowledge it will create a degree of psychological discomfort typically at the very time when he is expected to behave as a professional.

*Quality of personality assessment data*

Generally speaking, a pilot might complete a personality assessment at several stages of his or her career. The prevalence of this will depend on the airline organisation. This might happen, for example, (i) during Airline Transport Pilot Licence (ATPL) training (though for many flight training organisations this is not typically the case); (ii) during recruitment to an airline either as an officer or a direct entry captain; (iii) as an experienced first officer undergoing initial assessments to progress to command upgrade training.

When such personality assessments are conducted, they are most often completed using the format of self-report questionnaires, i.e. the pilot responds to a series of questions about typical ways in which he or she might think, feel or behave in different situations. The questionnaire in use should always be based upon an underlying and established psychological construct of personality, for example, the FFM discussed above. This model includes an analysis of personality across five broad factors: extraversion, agreeableness, openness, conscientiousness and neuroticism. Each of these five factors is composed of a number of underlying facets. These facets form the basis of the questions in the questionnaire, which are arrived at using systematic analysis and extensive validation in various populations.

It is important to emphasise that there is neither an objectively correct nor incorrect answer to these questions; only an answer that the respondent feels is most representative of his or her self. The particular pattern of answering across many questions is statistically compared with a relevant norm or comparison group of other people who have completed the questionnaire. In other words, if an individual's answers form a particular pattern, then their personality can be considered to be similar to others who have answered with a similar pattern. Of course, in aggregate, broad patterns are discernible. For example, historically, a common pattern in a pilot's personality was described as a "stable extravert".

However, even where for a number of people the aggregate pattern is the same, the specific, discrete answers that underlie such aggregate descriptions will yield considerable individual variance. This variance will ultimately conspire to describe the subtle yet important differences between people. By way of a perhaps extreme analogy, in aggregate, all pilots have broadly similar hands, thumbs, and fingers, yet it is clear that each individual's fingerprints are unique.

The results from such a questionnaire provide a profile that can be interpreted by an appropriately qualified and experienced psychologist[1]. Some might suggest that, from this personality profile, a pilot's behaviour can be accurately predicted in certain circumstances. Having been deeply involved in this area for a number of years I have found myself increasingly questioning such a predictive approach. One must consider, for example, what is the evidence base for predictive validity of this data in the actual day-to-day tasks of a pilot? Moreover, how can a static profile of a pilot's personality at a particular stage in his or her career (i.e. when completing the questionnaire) faithfully represent the on-going dynamic of that pilot's personality over time? Which answers to the specific business needs of the airline does it provide? Moreover, to what extent does such a profile, based on self-reported data, gathered in such circumstances, allow an airline to predict safe and effective behaviour of that pilot throughout and within his or her career?

Two realities are important to consider in relation to the parameters within which the personality assessment of pilots currently takes place:

1   Any personality assessment or 'test' is in fact self-reported, and the particular questionnaire chosen will be of variable quality with respect to its underlying scientific basis and, therefore, its operational validity – more on this later.
2   Such a self-reported questionnaire by definition can only reflect a static snapshot of aspects of the pilot's personality. While a profile may indicate a general range within which aspects of personality can fluctuate – in reality, this represents statistical measurement error rather than deep insight – it cannot accurately reflect the particular dynamic and interactive nature of the personality of that individual across time and differing situations.

This questionnaire data will likely have some impact on important, potentially career-defining decisions made by management about a pilot. So a question then arises: given the above parameters, what is the quality of the data generated from the personality assessment? I suggest there are at least three influences that can affect the quality of these data:

a.   the state of mind of the pilot completing the questionnaire;
b.   the questionnaire itself, i.e. the psychometric instrument used;
c.   the administration of the questionnaire;

THE PILOT

For the pilot completing the questionnaire, it is important to acknowledge that there is typically much at stake for that individual depending on the outcome of the overall decision process. It is reasonable to assume, given the nature of pilots' training, that they can perceive a tight coupling between the outcome of the overall assessment decision, and the more technical and knowledge-based aspects of their job. However, most will only have a limited understanding of personality, so a pilot's perceived connection between the overall assessment outcome and a personality assessment will likely be looser, more opaque, and less robust. Therefore, it is realistic to believe that pilots – who can often be data hungry, objectively thinking people – might view a personality questionnaire (or 'test') with some scepticism, possibly cynicism and perhaps trepidation. This can lead some pilots to behave in such a way as to minimise their *perceived* risk of giving the 'wrong' answers. Thus they may be tempted to manipulate their responses in an effort to give the impression of someone who is safe, or conservative, or 'average' in all areas.

Pilots typically undertake their training at significant personal financial cost. They are likely on a steep learning curve, which demands a high degree of self-study and rapid technical proficiency in many areas. They will want to demonstrate the ability to keep calm under pressure and to show clear-headed critical decision-making, often in circumstances where there is incomplete data or uncertainty. In all cases, the pilots' objectives will be to minimise risks to ensure the conservative and safe operation of a flight. Moreover, many young, early career pilots are in significant debt on completion of their training, when seeking their first paying job at an airline. It is understandable that they will do everything they can to satisfy what they perceive as the criteria to land the job.

It is quite often the case that pilots might view this part of their assessment as another obstacle to get past. As a result they can try to develop strategies to 'game' the questionnaire, so as to give an impression of a relatively stable and benign personality. Such a personality, they could reasonably think, is unlikely to have a deleterious effect on their selection process. Even where an airline involves an additional follow-up interview with a psychologist, many candidates may see this as simply a matter of answering questions in a relatively conservative manner so as not to raise any flags. In other words, the very attempt to garner personality information from the candidate, can lead him or her to behave in a way that will obfuscate the process, or to provide data that is not fully representative of the way the candidate behaves, thinks, or feels. Is it any wonder then that they might be inclined to adopt a risk-minimising strategy when seated in front of a personality questionnaire, a psychologist or, for that matter, an aero medical examiner?

It might then sensibly be asked, what can be done to mitigate this risk of poor quality data into the questionnaire? Several personality questionnaire publishers claim to have clever algorithms in place embedded in their questionnaires, to cross-validate answers and, therefore, to detect deception. However there are several issues with such an approach. It is predicated on 'bad data' having already been entered, and, therefore, it is post hoc and not preventive. Further, the degree to which an active 'deception' can be assumed is unclear, unless a certain nominal threshold has been exceeded, for example, by a pilot answering without any regard whatsoever to the questions; this is a most unlikely scenario. Moreover, in the face of any such concerns large or small, there is simply no agreement on what remedial action can be taken to meaningfully correct such a profile. A preventive approach may prove far more useful long term. For example, before a pilot gives his or her consent to complete a personality questionnaire, the organisation should strive to ensure that the pilot is:

a.   As *relaxed* about the process as is practicable – nerves might be expected, and can be minimised in a number of ways. For example, providing timely and comprehensive pre-assessment information, including sample assessment questions. However negativity or cynicism about completing such a questionnaire must be countered as much as possible, otherwise the exercise is largely futile.

b.   As *informed* about the purpose of the questionnaire as is reasonable. Whatever questions the pilot has (and there are no stupid ones, only stupid answers), should be addressed calmly and thoroughly by the competent and experienced person administering the instrument. This can include providing information around its scientific credibility, why it is helpful to know about personality, how it works, and so forth.

c.   As *engaged* as possible in the process – good data comes from full and enthusiastic engagement when completing the questionnaire. It should always be recognised that pilots are the de facto experts about their own personalities, and the organisation is requesting their help in understanding these personalities.

If these simple steps are not carried out to a high standard, then 'bad data in' can be expected. Any subsequent interpretation of these data can be considered akin to building a house on unstable foundations.

## THE QUESTIONNAIRE

Moving to the personality questionnaire itself, two approaches are typically seen in airlines: (i) to outsource the entire area of psychometrics to a psychologist or other third-party service provider, or (ii) to leverage the human resources (HR) function to administer a product from a psychometric publisher. Outsourcing to a third party, such as a firm or individual psychologist providing consultancy services, might be considered costly, until, perhaps, it is compared with the cost of placing the wrong person on the flight deck. However, this approach offers a number of benefits, for example, by providing concise, interpreted data, from an appropriately qualified and experienced psychologist, with whom a conversation can be had if there are queries or areas of concern.

Leveraging HR to administer the psychometrics can appear to be more cost-effective, but it also can be prone to a deficit of in-house expertise when it comes to critically understanding the evidence base for a given personality questionnaire, and interpreting the results in context. This can lead to reliance upon automated or computer-generated reports from the publisher of the questionnaire. Such reports are usually lengthy and comprehensive, as they need to completely describe personality as envisaged by their own particular brand/model. Additionally, in many situations the report is the final deliverable, and there is no opportunity for a qualified discussion of specific areas that may be of concern. Furthermore, such reports usually have a more quantitative rather than qualitative summary by providing a number/score on the aspects of the personality being looked at. This can often lead to a 'test outcome' mentality whereby there are minimum scores, below which someone is considered to have failed the 'test'. It is fair comment that, in a minority of extreme cases, such an outcome might indicate potential pathology to be further explored. However, in the majority of cases, personality, at least in the way it is being discussed here, is not easily amenable to such a test-oriented mind-set. Therefore any conflation of personality data with typical pass/fail testing is unhelpful at best. Additionally, as a final comment here, it is important to recognise an aspect of what can perhaps be understood as a specific case of the efficiency–thoroughness trade-off (Hollnagel, 2010). An HR department's diligence in choosing the optimal suite of assessment and selection protocols and instruments is a function of the organisation's need for pilots within a fixed budget and timeframe. In times where demand is very high, it is reasonable to assume there may be a degree of trade-off between what is optimally desired versus what is practicable, both in terms of rigour of assessment and quality of candidates' attributes deemed acceptable. This could also be understood as a type of organisational 'satisficing' (Simon & Barnard, 1947; Simon, 1956).

Earlier I mentioned I would return to the issue of the variable quality of personality questionnaires. This is because commercially available personality questionnaires have different levels of scientific provenance, evidence base, and theoretical foundation. The bottom line here is a simple argument: no safety critical organisation should tolerate or accept into use any personality instruments that are not fit for purpose, scientifically reviewed, proven, reliable and valid. If the organisation does not already have an in-house appropriately qualified and experienced psychologist to lead them through the commercial quagmire of offerings in this space, then they should obtain the services of one. To assume the quality of an instrument simply on the basis of the words and brochures of a publisher's marketing department is, at best, lazy. A poorly chosen instrument in a selection and assessment process can form part of a decision to accept pilots who turn out to be less than the expected quality, or to reject pilots who would in fact have been of the quality hoped for.

THE ADMINISTRATION

The method of administration of the questionnaire can exert an important influence on the quality of obtained data. For instance, a qualified invigilator can administer such a questionnaire to one or many candidates, in a controlled setting, using paper and pen or a computer interface. Alternatively, and because personality questionnaires are not like typical tests, there is the option to administer the instrument remotely via the internet, in an unsupervised manner, thus allowing it to be completed at a time and location of the pilot's choosing. Both approaches offer advantages and disadvantages some of which I summarise in Table 8.1.

In addition to the three areas outlined above, each of which will influence the quality of the data generated, arguably the most important element to consider is the way in which the results are interpreted. Effective interpretation of this data is predicated on the candidate having provided good data in the first place. Clearly, if the data going in has been dishonestly or superficially given (in an attempt to 'game' the questionnaire), then any effort of interpretation is largely futile. Worse for the candidate, if selected on the basis of a 'gamed' personality profile, he or she can wind up accepting a position in an organisation for which his or her actual personality may be unsuited. This may represent a risk factor to be subsequently managed in relation to, for example, workplace interactions. However, because personality questionnaires are largely unsupervised, and

*Table 8.1* Advantages and disadvantages of different methods of administering personality questionnaires

| Administration | On site, in person, supervised | Remote, via internet, unsupervised |
| --- | --- | --- |
| Advantages: | Controlled environment with appropriate optics of an assessment. Pilots can ask questions/get clarifications/have concerns allayed by a qualified invigilator/assessment administrator. More opportunity to relax, inform and engage the candidates. | Less resource intensive/lower cost per candidate. Pilots have choice and privacy as to time and location of assessment. |
| Disadvantages: | Requires pilot to go to assessment centre, fewer options for time/place of completion. More resource intensive/ higher cost per candidate. | Uncontrolled environment. Limited opportunity to relax, inform and engage the candidates. Subject to technical failures due to diversity of end user hardware/ software platforms and internet connectivity. Difficult to validate identity of the individual sitting the questionnaire. |

typically do not contain answers that can be correct or incorrect, it can be difficult to identify with certainty when someone has been less than candid with their responses. Where practicable, I am of the view that the personality questionnaire should be augmented by an interview with an appropriately qualified and experienced psychologist. During this interview, the results of the personality assessment can be explored with the pilot, including discussion around any areas of concern or ambiguity. A skilful psychologist, through a semi-structured interview, can, in this way, ascertain the veracity or otherwise of the results, and weight such information accordingly in their interpretation. While this step is often overlooked, it is most inadvisable to simply take at face value the automatically generated personality results. It could be that a genuine error has occurred during completion of the instrument, for example, an online glitch, or the candidate may have become distracted, or may not have fully understood the question.

### Organisational utility of a personality profile

When decisions have been made in relation to the pilot being assessed, it is useful to ask what now happens to the personality profile, and what utility did it provide? Typically it can be assumed that, following the assessments, the profile forms part of a file for that pilot, which is stored securely along with the rest of their results in a folder within the HR department. So it could be argued that the sum total utility of that personality profile was to inform the assessment and selection decision-making process. However, in what specific way did it inform the decision-making process? I was once approached by a commercial aviation organisation to come up with a suite of robust mental health and personality assessments to guarantee them that any pilot who passed these assessments would not represent an unacceptable level of risk to the airline. In general, it seemed to me that this betrayed a naïve understanding of the nature of risk. Aviation has always been an activity filled with inherent jeopardies, and risk is not something that can be totally eliminated. Moreover, even the most stringent selection processes can only hope to identify risks to be effectively managed. The on-going management of that risk lasts throughout the pilot's career. That career may span many decades, throughout which a young pilot will likely have significant life changes; they may get married, have children, lose loved ones, get divorced, experience physical and mental health issues of different degrees of severity, or be involved in critical incidents.

The personality of a pilot as it manifests in the twenties, when they might join an airline, can undergo significant changes during the intervening decades as the pilot progresses through their career and life. One aspect of personality questionnaire data that can be easily overlooked is that, unlike more concrete ability tests such as cognitive or psychomotor tests, personality questionnaires are typically produced with the caveat of having a relatively short shelf life, typically between 12 and 18 months. This is testament to the accepted notion that aspects of one's personality can change over time (e.g. Helson *et al.*, 2002).

It is reasonable to assume that the 'snapshot' recorded at one stage, drawn from data that were subject to various potentially invalidating influences (as discussed above), is not necessarily an accurate representation of the pilot's personality at a later career stage.

However, take, for example, a situation of repeated reports about a pilot in relation to Crew Resource Management (CRM). This pilot's personality profile might be revisited in an attempt to understand the pilot's behaviour, but of course, the personality data behind the profile may be past its shelf life. In such a circumstance, the organisation may be inclined to 're-test' the pilot and get a new snapshot. Given what we know are likely influences on the pilot when completing the questionnaire in such a circumstance, for example, if the pilot feels he or she is the subject of an investigation into his or her behaviour, a question must be asked: how much more, or less, accurate can we assume this next snapshot to be? Moreover, how can it inform the organisation as to the likelihood of the pilot repeating the behaviour? Any claims by publishers that their personality instruments can accurately predict an individual pilot's exact behaviour at any given time in the future are, frankly, unrealistic.

To be clear, I do not mean to dismiss any utility of the personality data of pilots, quite the opposite; my intention is to question how the data can be made even more useful to an airline organisation. I propose a few ways to help overcome many of the shortcomings.

If the organisation is using personality assessments as part of their selection process, then it is paramount that the observations in the earlier section 'Quality of personality assessment data' are fully appreciated and accounted for. The onus is on the aviation organisation to ensure this is done as much as is practicable. Assuming this is done, it can be said that a well-designed process was in place, and some limited utility was gained from the personality data, specifically, to assist in the decision-making process around the recruitment of pilots.

But is this really the only utility we can expect? Consider the large quantity of well-proven research studies into personality and individual differences from psychology and, increasingly, from neuroscience. Allied with this is a rapidly decreasing cost base for highly adaptive, interactive and responsive technology. I believe we can raise our expectations significantly, and open our thinking to entirely new ways of using personality data. For example, new thinking here could take the form of information used to augment specific training modules for pilots and instructors, or applications to help prevent deterioration of existing, good mental health of pilots. But to derive these and other benefits requires a paradigm shift in what it is to assess personality and this, in turn, implicates significant changes in the mind-sets of airline organisations and pilots alike.

For example, typically, in many airlines and other organisations, the collection of assessment and selection data is managed as one of the many functions of the HR department. Frequently, HR departments play a critical role in present-day organisations, particularly in areas relating to recruitment, safety and welfare, employee relations, compensation and benefits, compliance, and training and development. In the context of an airline's pilot recruitment programme, personality profiles as we have been discussing them, are usually part of wider assessment and selection data that typically reside within an HR department, and often are only accessible by appropriately qualified personnel. It is the case that a minority of airlines' HR departments occasionally are able to provide an opportunity for the individual candidate pilot to receive comprehensive feedback on his or her tests, including a specific discussion around the personality data. However this is not the norm for the industry and, in the current paradigm of recruitment and selection, most pilots are assessed in numbers large enough to preclude such individual feedback being a practicable option for the airline.

In my opinion, there are some initial changes that will need to happen prior to any larger scale benefits becoming reality.

- Once the selection decision has been made, and HR has copies of the personality profile for their files, remove HR as default gatekeepers (perceived or real) of the pilot's personality data.

I do not mean to lessen the role of HR in this regard. I mean remove it. Entirely. The reality is that leaving a pilot's static 'snapshot' personality profile, sitting locked in a drawer in a HR department and decaying towards its expiry date, prevents any further utility being extracted from that it. Many other relevant personnel in an airline organisation could potentially benefit from an increased understanding of that pilot's personality including, for example, cabin crew, Type Rating Instructor/Type Rating Examiner (TRI/TRE), CRM instructors, co-pilots and so forth. But none of this can ever happen until another condition is fully satisfied:

- Hand over full and complete ownership and control of the personality profile to the pilot.

The most important beneficiary of increased understanding of a pilot's personality is, in fact, the pilot. Qualified and experienced pilots have in common a shared knowledge of each other's training, and are therefore able to assume in each other the basic competencies that such training instils. This means they are able to recognise in each other certain characteristics. For example, they can be expected to be data hungry, objective, competent, technically oriented, goal-directed, confident decision-makers and highly trained and skilled operators. I make an assumption here that most pilots would respond with 'yes' to the question of 'would you like some more data that can help you maintain and possibly improve your performance on the flight deck in relation to optimum safe and effective behaviour?' Personality data, assessed, gathered, updated and explained in the right way, will offer this opportunity.

It is highly likely that technological advances in psychometric instruments (i.e. instruments specifically designed to measure aspects of human cognition, personality, emotion and so forth) will enable individuals to review their personality profile on an on-demand and private basis. This will be facilitated by using ubiquitous, highly portable and reliable, internet-connected technology. Imagine a scenario where pilots, upon entry to an airline, are equipped with:

1   initial access to qualified resources with which they can fully explore and understand aspects of their own personality and how it can influence their behaviours on the flight deck and elsewhere;
2   the ability and tools to, at any time, update their own personality profiles with current data as is relevant to their stage of career or life, simply, conveniently, and privately.

To illustrate this a little more, consider the current state of affairs in relation to the utility of pilots' personality profiles in airlines after a selection decision has been made. The profile might be revisited following an incident or an accident, in an attempt to discover what went wrong. However, given the likely expired shelf life, and the cobwebs that may have gathered on such data over time, this can only be a lagging indicator at best, and is probably not very useful from a preventive standpoint. Instead, consider an alternative scenario, but firstly let us assume that the conditions discussed previously in relation to excellent instruments used, and 'good data in', are satisfied. Then:

1   The pilots become fully engaged to give the most forthright and honest self-report information into the process. They are assured that, following the selection process and regardless of outcome, they will have full access to their own personality data. If they are selected, specific sessions to help them understand and integrate the full dynamic of how their personality influences their behaviour will be provided. Such sessions would also form part of their recurrent CRM training.
2   They could have access to a private and confidential telephone or internet-enabled channel of communication, at arm's length from the airline, in order to discuss or further understand any aspect of their personality. This can be considered similar to a reference system they can use to gain deeper understanding and, therefore, more utility from their personality in their work.
3   They can update their personality profile at any time, by privately inputting updated data into the instrument. This enables them to have access to interpretive information based on the most current dataset, and to avoid it 'going stale'.
4   They can choose to share their current profile with specific trusted and nominated colleagues. This then opens the door to, for example, their instructor or co-pilot or any member of their team, on board or on the ground, being made aware of that individual's personality dynamic. Can we not assume that an instructor or type-rating examiner would like to know, in advance of putting the pilot in a simulator scenario, in which situations that pilot's personality might benefit or hinder their performance?[2]

Furthermore, imagine a pilot with significantly fuller awareness of how his or her specific personality influences behaviour and interacts with the situations he or she is in. Some might, for example, wish to enhance, or attenuate certain traits in line with how they understand them to be helpful or a hindrance. Old thinking might suggest that we cannot change our personalities. But this is only true in an aggregate sense, and, as discussed above, our personalities are in fact malleable within certain parameters, and frequently this happens automatically. Whilst it is obvious that we cannot change into entirely different people, there is evidence to suggest we can change aspects of our personalities in line with specific desired outcomes (Hennecke *et al.*, 2014). Therefore why not look to equip pilots with the ability to monitor and update their data, and implement specific strategies to change aspects of their personality to enhance their safe and effective behaviours?

Taking this idea a few steps further, within a short number of years it should be possible to have one's personality profile represented in the form of a (virtual) living, breathing, fully interactive and dynamic entity. It will then be possible to simulate this profile in specific situations in order to preview in advance likely areas about which to be mindful when actually in those situations. This may sound like I am now making an argument for a predictive model. If such a prediction, or more likely projection, is being made by the pilot him- or herself, in the service of maintaining optimal safe and effective behaviour, then I think this is highly desirable. More than prediction, this is in fact about leveraging a tool to extend our capacity to imagine other realities. I would argue that no industry understands the implementation and benefits of advanced simulation better than aviation does.

Other opportunities can be identified, for example, in the context of Alternative Training and Qualification Programme (ATQP) and European Air Safety Agency (EASA) guidelines which will specify that personality awareness, attitudes and behaviours, self-assessment and self-critique are to be required aspects of recurrent CRM training. Why should it not be possible to include the relevant personality data of a particular pilot as part of the tailoring of their flight simulator training session? Perhaps an obvious question arises here around confidentiality of personality data, as it does in many circumstances. However I believe there are always sensible ways to accommodate such concerns without jettisoning the benefits. In the above example, for instance, it could be that the training instructor is not given access to the personality data of the pilot, but is assisted by an independent, trusted third party, to recommend adjustments to the design of a simulator session in ways that are particular to the personality of that pilot. Given the likely developments in machine intelligence, it may well be possible that, in time, such manipulations of training scenarios could be partially or fully automated. A benefit for the instructor is that it will be possible to customise the sim session for that particular pilot, and the corresponding benefit for pilots is that they can get the most personalised utility and learning from the session. This approach may be more accepted into a training scenario rather than a checking one.

No doubt more specific discussions and debates need to happen around the practicalities and cost–benefit analyses of implementing these and other ideas. My intention with this chapter is not to be prescriptive, but to start a conversation amongst people who can remain open-minded enough to realise that things can be changed. Such changes can bring desirable benefits for all involved in airline operations, and, by extension, in any safety critical organisational endeavour.

In the context of aviation safety, the received wisdom up to recently was that safety could be considered as the absence of accidents and incidents. Furthermore, things went wrong because of identifiable issues with systems and constituent components, the most variable of which was the human. Therefore, risk assessment aimed to identify the inherent probability of such failures and 'human errors'. However, Erik Hollnagel and like-minded colleagues have shown that such a focus on why things go wrong failed to account for why, in the majority of occasions, things go right. In respect of human performance, the infinite nuances of human variability allow for minute and wide-ranging adjustments to highly complex interconnected systems, such as those that comprise the aviation industry today. The argument Hollnagel makes is for an augmentation of the 'minority of occasions when things go wrong' approach – termed Safety I – with an approach that looks at 'the majority of occasions when things go right' – termed Safety II (Hollnagel *et al.*, 2013). This approach has received much acceptance and significant support in safety critical contexts, including healthcare and aviation.

The objective of focusing on personality data to help explain when things go wrong is, by definition, limited. Moreover, this approach can naturally lead pilots to be sceptical and worried about the consequences of self-reporting personality data, irrespective of how it is used. Such a system as it exists does not acknowledge the opportunities to use personality data to understand how and why most things go right, and, by implication, to understand what to maintain and what to improve. To paraphrase Hollnagel, I propose we move from Personality I to Personality II so to speak, and begin to acknowledge there is much more we can do to assist pilots in maintaining existing and everyday safe and effective behaviours. If we adopt a starting perspective that looks for something wrong in a system, we will inevitably be led to discover it. In the context of aviation mental health however, why should this be the only starting point? Why wait until pathology either is identified, or worse, is not identified? Alongside the existing approaches, could we not also adopt a non-pathological and preventive approach with personality assessment? This can be used to assist pilots in maintaining everyday safe behaviours and decision-making, and resilient mental health. Doing so will also likely help to offset the probability of material deterioration in mental health status.

## Conclusion

In this chapter I have presented a working concept of what is understood by personality, based on the most widely accepted and proven taxonomy that currently exists, the Five Factor Model. In particular, attention is drawn to the highly dynamic nature of personality and how it is interactive with, and influenced by, the situations in which we find ourselves. I have suggested that the typical ways in which personality of pilots is assessed within, for example, airline organisations, may help the organisation to have a sense of the personality of that pilot *at that time* but in a rather limited way. It is proposed that one goal of an airline is to maintain and enhance optimal safe and effective behaviour of its pilots. If this is accepted, then the data around personality can offer a great deal more utility than is currently available for the pilot, and therefore for the organisation.

To reap these benefits will require a paradigm shift in the way personality is assessed, managed and understood within the aviation industry. I described a future state of affairs where, following the nominal use of personality data as part of a selection and assessment context, each pilot is actively encouraged and incentivised to voluntarily take full ownership of his or her complete personality assessment data, in confidence and with assured privacy. From this point, pilots can be facilitated to monitor and update their personality data, and to understand how it influences their behaviour in a dynamic way when interacting with others in any given situation. Based on such understanding, pilots will be better informed and motivated to manage their thoughts, feelings and behaviour in an optimal way for safe and effective operations. This of course can be greatly mediated by technological advances and ubiquitous devices, which will become part and parcel of personality assessments of the near future. Pilots could use this enhanced and on-going understanding of their personality dynamics to monitor and more effectively manage their thoughts, behaviours and feelings across the different stages of their career, for example, the transition from first officer through to command training.

Finally, I proposed that, instead of mainly focusing on pathological personality indicators in an attempt to predict and screen out what might be wrong with a pilot's ('snapshot') personality, we spend more time focusing on the frequent, typical and everyday performance of pilots. Here we can find a far richer and larger dataset (than that of pathology) with which it will be possible to identify, manage and promote those aspects of personality-driven behaviour, at the level of the individual, which are shown to be most safe and effective. This approach can play a significant role in helping to prevent deterioration in mental health states, and thereby help to minimise the chances of personality and behaviour drifting, oftentimes imperceptibly, into a range that could be considered clinical.

## Notes

1  I am of the view that such a psychologist should be appropriately recognised by a national authority. In the UK for example, they should be Chartered by the British Psychological Society (BPS), reflecting a demonstrated gold standard of psychological knowledge, expertise and ethical practice, teaching and research. Additionally this person should be current on the BPS Register of Qualified Test Users for any personality assessments they are proposing to use or interpret. In

the context of aviation, he or she should also be a Registered Aviation Psychologist with the European Association for Aviation Psychology (EAAP), reflecting their experience of practising in an aviation psychology context.

2  Of course it must also be taken into account that pilots will likely want to make their sim check as straightforward as possible, and will therefore prefer simple, non-challenging scenarios.

# References

Airbus. (2015). *Flying By Numbers: Global Market Forecast.* Blagnac: Airbus.

Alicke, M.D., & Govorun, O. (2005). The better-than-average effect. In M.D. Alicke, D.A. Dunning, & J.I. Krueger (eds), *The Self in Social Judgment* (pp. 85–106). New York: Psychology Press.

Bench, S.W., Lench, H.C., Liew, J., Miner, K., & Flores, S.A. (2015). Gender gaps in overestimation of math performance. *Sex Roles, 72*(11–12), 536–546.

Block, J. (1995). A contrarian view of the five-factor approach to personality description. *Psychological Bulletin,* 117(2), 187–215.

Boeing. (2015). *Current Market Outlook 2015–2034.* Seattle, WA: Boeing.

Denissen, J.J.A., & Penke, L. (2008). Motivational individual reaction norms underlying the five-factor model of personality: first steps towards a theory-based conceptual framework. *Journal of Research in Personality,* 42(5), 1285–1302.

DeYoung, C.G. (2010). Toward a theory of the big five. *Psychological Inquiry,* 21(1), 26–33.

DeYoung, C.G., & Gray, J.R. (2009). Personality neuroscience: explaining individual differences in affect, behaviour and cognition. In P.J. Corr, & G. Matthews (eds), *The Cambridge Handbook of Personality Psychology* (pp. 323–346). Cambridge University Press.

DeYoung, C.G., Quilty, L.C., & Peterson, J.B. (2007). Between facets and domains: 10 aspects of the big five. *Journal of Personality and Social Psychology,* 93(5), 880–896.

DeYoung, C.G., Hirsh, J.B., Shane, M.S., Papademetris, X., Rajeevan, N., & Gray, J.R. (2010). Testing predictions from personality neuroscience: brain structure and the big five. *Psychological Science,* 21(6), 820–828.

Dunning, D., Johnson, K., Ehrlinger, J., & Kruger, J. (2003). Why people fail to recognize their own incompetence. *Current Directions in Psychological Science,* 12(3), 83–87.

*The Economist.* (2013). Personality testing at work: emotional breakdown – can leaders be identified by psychometrics? 6 April. Retrieved 10 April 2016, from http://www.economist.com/news/business/21575817-can-leaders-be-identified-psychometrics-emotional-breakdown

Helson, R., Jones, C., & Kwan, V.S.Y. (2002). Personality change over 40 years of adulthood: hierarchical linear modeling analyses of two longitudinal samples. *Journal of Personality and Social Psychology,* 83(3), 752–766.

Hennecke, M., Bleidorn, W., Denissen, J.J.A., & Wood, D. (2014). A three-part framework for self-regulated personality development across adulthood. *European Journal of Personality,* 28(3), 289–299.

Hollnagel, E. (2010). *The ETTO Principle: Efficiency-thoroughness Trade-off: Why Things That Go Right Sometimes Go Wrong.* Roca Baton: CRC Press

Hollnagel, E., Leonhardt, J., Licu, T., & Shorrock, S. (2013). *From Safety-I to Safety-II: A White Paper.* Brussels: European Organisation for the Safety of Air Navigation (EUROCONTROL).

Judge, T.A., Simon, L.S., Hurst, C., & Kelley, K. (2014). What I experienced yesterday is who I am today: relationship of work motivations and behaviors to within-individual variation in the five-factor model of personality. *Journal of Applied Psychology*, 99(2), 199–221.

Lundeberg, M.A. (1994). Highly confident but wrong: gender differences and similarities in confidence judgments. *Journal of Educational Psychology*, 86(1), 114–121.

McAdams, D.P. (1992). The five-factor model in personality: a critical appraisal. *Journal of Personality*, 60(2), 329–361.

McCrae, R.R. (2002). Cross-cultural research on the five-factor model of personality cross-cultural research on the five-factor model of personality. *Online Readings in Psychology and Culture*, 4(4), 1–12.

McCrae, R.R., & Costa, P.T. (1987). Validation of the five-factor model of personality across instruments and observers. *Journal of Personality and Social Psychology*, 52(1), 81–90.

McCrae, R.R., & Costa, P.T. (1997). Personality trait structure as a human universal. *American Psychologist*, 52(5), 509–516.

PwC. (2015). *Tailwinds: 2015 Airline Industry Trends*. New York: PwC.

Ross, L., & Nisbett, R.E. (2011). *The Person and the Situation: Perspectives of Social Psychology*. London, UK: Pinter & Martin Publishers.

Schmitt, D.P., Allik, J., McCrae, R.R., & Benet-Martinez, V. (2007). The geographic distribution of big five personality traits: patterns and profiles of human self-description across 56 nations. *Journal of Cross-Cultural Psychology*, 38(2), 173–212.

Sherman, R.A., Nave, C.S., & Funder, D.C. (2010). Situational similarity and personality predict behavioral consistency. *Journal of Personality and Social Psychology*, 99(2), 330–343.

Simon, H.A. (1956). Rational choice and the structure of the environment. *Psychological Review*, 63(2), 129–138.

Simon, H.A., & Barnard, C.I. (1947). *Administrative Behavior: A Study of Decision-making Processes in Administrative Organization*. New York: Macmillan.

Snyder, M., & Tanke, E.D. (1976). Behavior and attitude: some people are more consistent than others. *Journal of Personality*, 44(3), 501–517.

# 9 The role and scope of psychological testing in risk reduction

*Pooshan Navathe and Shruti Navathe*

The Chicago Convention, in 1945, identified a set of articles of agreement to facilitate aviation across the globe. Article 32 of the convention requires the pilot of every aircraft and the other members of the operating crew of every aircraft engaged in international navigation to be provided with certificates of competency and licences issued or rendered valid by the state in which the aircraft is registered. This licencing includes medical fitness.

The International Civil Aviation Organization (ICAO), being the apex body that regulates international aviation, has mandated periodic pilot medical examinations, and assessments, as follows (ICAO, 2011):

> 1.2.4.1 an applicant for a licence shall, when applicable, hold a Medical Assessment issued in accordance with the provisions of Chapter 6.

and

> 1.2.4.3 the period of validity of a Medical Assessment shall begin on the day the medical examination is performed. The duration of the period of validity shall be in accordance with the provisions of 1.2.5.2.

ICAO also sets the scope of the examinations as follows (ICAO, 2011):

*6.2.2 Physical and mental requirements*

An applicant for any class of Medical Assessment shall be required to be free from:

a.  Any abnormality, congenital or acquired; or
b.  Any active, latent, acute or chronic disability; or
c.  Any wound, injury or squeal from operation; or
d.  Any effect or side-effect of any prescribed or non-prescribed therapeutic, diagnostic or preventive medication taken;

such as would entail a degree of functional incapacity that is likely to interfere with the safe operation of an aircraft or with the safe performance of duties.

With specific reference to the area of mental health, ICAO requires the following for Class 1 medical certificates (professional pilots) (ICAO, 2011):

6.3.2.1 the applicant shall not suffer from any disease or disability which could render that applicant likely to become suddenly unable either to operate an aircraft safely or to perform assigned duties safely.

6.3.2.2 The applicant shall have no established medical history or clinical diagnosis of:

a.   an organic mental disorder;
b.   a mental or behavioural disorder due to use of psychoactive substances; this includes dependence syndrome induced by alcohol or other psychoactive substances;
c.   schizophrenia or a schizotypal or delusional disorder;
d.   a mood (affective) disorder;
e.   a neurotic, stress-related or somatoform disorder;
f.   a behavioural syndrome associated with physiological disturbances or physical factors;
g.   a disorder of adult personality or behaviour, particularly if manifested by repeated overt acts;
h.   mental retardation;
i.   a disorder of psychological development;
j.   a behavioural or emotional disorder, with onset in childhood or adolescence; or
k.   a mental disorder not otherwise specified;
l.   such as might render the applicant unable to safely exercise the privileges of the licence applied for or held.

Identical provisions apply to Class 2 medical certificates (recreational pilots).

Various jurisdictions have implemented medical examination and assessment regimes for pilots to help identify problems that could impact aviation safety throughout the working lives of pilots (and that includes the functional flying lives of recreational pilots).

The advent and progress of liberal thinking over the last century and particularly in the postwar period has resulted in an increasing emphasis on individual freedoms and is reflected in the universal approach to reducing regulation. This has seen an increasing shift to individual responsibility as an alternative to – rather than in addition to – state-enforced regulation. This change has been reflected in the increasing devolution of authority to the pilots themselves in the recreational aviation arena. Regulations now allow varying levels of self-declaration-type regimes to allow a minimal level of oversight by the national regulator, thereby allowing the pilots to essentially manage their own medical risks, as in the National Private Pilots Licence (NPPL), Recreational Pilots Licence (RPL), etc. Importantly, most of these schemes allow for this low-level oversight to apply only where there are no serious medical conditions – if there are any medical conditions the risk assessment is then taken over and centrally managed. This has significance because it means that all those people who have medical conditions – whether professional or recreational – are required to go through a structured medical certification process.

Watson (2005) has defined aeromedical decision making as an evidence-based risk management process, and Navathe and colleagues (2014) have provided a prescription that may be used to make evidence-based aeromedical decisions. This paradigm works for those situations where there is an overt medical condition. However, if there is an asymptomatic individual, then the paradigm is not triggered. Good medicine requires positive testing to attempt to discover these overt conditions, and some of these form parts of the routine medical examination. Examples of routine examinations are urine tests, chest X-rays etc. Many regulators have chosen to add additional tests such as spirometry, cardiac investigations such as ECGs, stress tests, and so on. The level and extent of testing required is usually based on the risk offered – based on likelihood criteria, e.g. age, ethnicity, family history, or based on consequence criteria – the class of medical certificate, the type of flying intended, etc.

It is logical, and indeed required by most jurisdictions, that a medical examiner should exclude or manage serious psychiatric medical conditions. That is relatively easy to do if the pilot is honest (we operate in an honesty-based system, so that is largely a given), and has insight into the condition. Insight affects reporting of its ongoing presence and its severity, both of which are based on a self-assessment, and therefore subjected to a variable level of bias. It follows that we should attempt to objectively identify any mental health condition that might adversely affect aviation safety.

Safety risk management is defined as the identification, analysis and elimination (and/or mitigation to an acceptable or tolerable level) of the hazards, as well as the subsequent risks, that threaten the viability of an organization (ICAO, 2013).

Mental health conditions have many presentations, but looking at the hazards that arise out of mental health conditions (taken as a whole), the following hazards can be identified as having an impact on aviation safety:

1    reduced cognition;
2    impulsive behaviours;
3    suicidal behaviour;
4    reduced executive functioning;
5    any of the above being caused, precipitated, or accentuated by treatment for a medical condition (including a mental health condition).

### Reduced cognition

Cognition is a complex set of mental processes which involve a large number of discrete sub-processes. These include memory (long-term and short-term), the transformation and reduction of sensory data into recognizable information, and of 'filling in' missing information based on our past experience. It also includes the ability to pay attention to changes in the incoming perceptual signals. Following on from these relatively low-order functions, cognition also deals with the integration of the information received and processes into judgements and decisions about the best responses in any given situation.

Cognitive functioning in particular domains can and has been studied and tested. A great deal of the focus in recent years has been on how judgements are made by individuals. Looking at situated cognition, expertise and heuristics provides an overlapping picture of how an individual may make decisions, especially under conditions of uncertainty and stress (Fiske & Taylor, 1991). When examining social cognition a key aspect is understanding the cognitive constructs associated with that behaviour (Hollon & Kriss, 1984). Specifically there needs to be an emphasis on the subjective experience of an individual's worldview – their own actions as well as the actions of others. To this end Sherman and colleagues (1989) argue that three main questions must be answered in order to clearly understand cognition: a) how the content is stored and structured in memory, b) how organization of this knowledge affects ongoing processing of social information and the responses and c) how existing knowledge structures can be changed.

Social cognition is concerned with how each of us uniquely experiences and makes sense of our social world (Fiske & Taylor, 1991). Cognition is understood in social psychology as being a complex process by which information is organized, stored and retrieved by an individual as per their needs. Cognitive structures refer to the configuration of cognition; cognitive processes refer to the on-line mechanisms involved in understanding events and cognitive products to statements reported (Gannon *et al.*, 2005). Over the years, specific aspects of cognition have been studied, and the only thing about which there is widespread agreement is that the structures, processes and products of cognition are complex.

Broadly speaking, knowledge structures (that include cognitive content) are structured through associative links to form networks of easily accessible information. These take the form of well-developed schema through which new information is then processed. With unlimited resources, these schemas would be rigorously updated and examined in a rational manner. However, in practice most individuals act as 'cognitive misers' who rely on existing schema to understand new information and discard information that does not fit. Schema can also be primed through the use of context and activated more readily in specific situations, making them cognitively efficient, but not necessarily accurate.

Managing or disrupting schema requires consistent presentation of disconfirming evidence. These must challenge the fundamental aspects of the schema to have any effect as small pieces of disconfirming evidence can be subsumed in the overall schema by being either dismissed or subtyped as a particular and unusual outlier case. Monitoring and changing information processing to rely less on pre-existing knowledge requires monitoring as well operating upon one's own cognition. The suppression and substitution of cognitive heuristics only occurs when sufficient resources are available, leading to a rebound effect where individuals are easily able to access cognitive content they seek to supress and lack the resources to substitute with others that would be more reasoned.

Beck (1963) conceptualized intrusive, disruptive and often unrealistically negative cognitions of those suffering from depression as a cognitive distortion. At the most basic level, this kind of cognition is characterized by some kind of departure from rationality. In the case of depression, for example, a pervasive and untrue negative worldview is suggested as being part of the problem, though there is some question as to whether this is an unrealistic view based on more recent research on the optimism bias shown in healthy subjects (Ingram, 2012).

When predicting actions and judgements, an explanatory theory has to account for the onset, development as well as the maintenance of the behaviour under study (Gannon *et al.*, 2005). Typically this has meant that events are analysed in terms of the effects of proximate as well as distal factors.

Proximal factors are usually defined as those factors that emerged from the functioning of underlying vulnerabilities. These often act as triggers for events and can be affective states, dynamic contextual variables and lifestyle factors. Proximal factors can often act to disinhibit the ability of individuals to regulate their internal states; this inability can lead to an increased likelihood of offending behaviour. Proximal factors (disinhibition) would address the 'how' offending occurred and point to micro-explanations of the behaviour under study (Navathe *et al.*, 2008).

Distal factors refer to vulnerabilities that emerge as a result of developmental history and genetic inheritance and can be seen as predispositions and thus proximally removed from the event itself. Distal factors address the 'why' point to macro-level explanations – such as a personality variable, e.g. impulsivity.

It is important to note the interactions between proximal states and distal traits that lead to particular actions and to be constantly aware that there is a far from direct link between cognition and action (Blasi, 1980; Williams & Ericsson, 2007).

This complex interplay of variables can have a negative impact on flying, where sensory perceptions are received from a variety of intra- and extra-cockpit sources, and where the total time for decision-making is extremely short – thereby time compressing the entire cognitive processes. The large number of human-factor accidents is indicative of the criticality of cognition even in normal functioning individuals.

### Impulsive behaviour

Children behave impulsively, and as they grow and recognize the impacts of their actions (whether physical, social or emotional), they commence to manage their impulses. However, a proportion of adults have difficulty in managing their impulsivity, and some of them have the problem to an extent of it present as a recognizable syndrome such as ADHD, pyromania, kleptomania etc. (Webster & Jackson, 1997). There is also a proportion of people who while not having impulsivity to the extent of it being recognizable as a syndrome, nevertheless have traits of impulsivity that present occasionally in a set of unusual circumstances.

There is an ongoing interest in determining which parts of an individual's behaviour are fixed dispositions – whether as a result of biological, social or psychological factors, and which are mutable. Typically those characteristics that are linked to early development (such as attachment styles) and have a global influence on behaviour are referred to as trait variables. Those characteristics that are more mutable, or dependent on context, situation or need to emerge are referred to as state variables.

Personality traits are seen as stable over time and difficult to change, hence the need to run psychometric tests to ensure that undesirable characteristics are weeded out through organizational recruitment processes. While there is debate as to how and how much personality variables determine behaviour, there is sufficient evidence to suggest that there are some personality traits (psychopathy) that can be experimentally tested. Affect and cognition have more proximal effects on behaviour. In fact evidence suggests that there is a complex, mediated relationship between affect and cognition that varies based on distal socio-economic factors (Augoustinos & Walker, 1995). Emotional regulation and impulsivity are therefore a matter of providing situation context and triggering behaviour, whereas a tendency towards high-risk situations and impulsivity speak to ingrained habits that are largely independent of the proximal trigger.

Impulsivity when studied as a trait is seen as a negative trait that leads to reckless or, at least, less-reasoned behaviours. As a result a great deal of work done on impulsivity focuses on its pathology and ways of managing and limiting its effects. Impulse control has been studied within the context of managing clinical disorders such as OCD, anxiety, depression, as well as the forensic context for reducing recidivism in sexual offending, aggression etc.

The main risk to aviation stems from the risk of making impulsive (and irrational) decisions without thinking through the options that may be available in a given situation. If pilots have a mental health condition such as depression, anxiety, bipolar disorder, OCD or ADHD, their decision-making could be affected by impulsivity. In experienced pilots, decisions are sometimes made in time-critical situations by 'satisficing' (satisfy plus suffice – a decision-making cognitive heuristic that involves searching through available alternatives until an acceptability threshold is met) (Simon, 1956), and this might appear impulsive unless a careful analysis is carried out.

*The interplay between cognition, impulsivity and action*

While the preceding paragraphs have attempted to separate cognition and impulsivity, it is important to reiterate that the relationship between cognition and action is one that is far from straightforward. There is a wealth of evidence to suggest that how we think has an effect on how we act – but there are perhaps as many exceptions as there are rules. As a result, predicting behaviour as a result of cognition is, at best, playing with the likelihood of the behaviour being displayed or the action being undertaken. This is perhaps why there is more of an emphasis on managing the state variables that affect impulse control than the trait variables that pre-dispose one towards disinhibition.

## Suicidal behaviour

When understanding suicide, it is important to examine the differences between the action and the underlying variables such as a) cognitive processes and patterns, b) comorbidity – especially with other psychiatric illnesses and c) the translation of cognition into action. In the literature around suicide, this takes the form of distinguishing between suicidal ideation, characterized as the consideration of the idea of completing the act; suicide planning, characterized as the solidifying of the intent through the creation of a more concrete plan to complete; and suicide attempts, characterized by carrying out an attempt to complete the act. These distinctions while intuitively appealing are not entirely unproblematic. For instance some researchers have argued that ideation is a common and natural part of the human existential examination (Goldney & Spence, 1987), while others have pointed out the need to differentiate between idle and serious ideation (Beck *et al.*, 1979) – which can often only be done within an existing relationship with a clinician (rather than accurately tested).

The measurement of prevalence of suicidal ideation varies greatly across populations. Suicidal ideation can vary between 5 and 50 per cent of subjects, leading some researchers to question the value of relying on it as a marker (Goldney, 2005; Hawton & Heeringen, 2000). What is consistent across populations is the marked increase in suicidal ideation and attempts in adolescence, an increase that continues into adulthood. Measures of suicidal ideation are embedded into standardized surveys, which further calls into question the validity of using them as markers of whether or not a subject is suicidal. The issue of whether a particular individual is suicidal can be a clinical judgement based on a range of information gathered (psychometric instruments, presentation at interview, comorbidity etc.).

Prediction of suicidal behaviour has typically relied on the results of epidemiological studies and proximal (12 months) attempts to commit suicide. The literature from epidemiological studies provides insight into the overall percentages for adults who seriously considered suicide (9.2 per cent), those who show evidence of planning (3.1 per cent) and those who have made at least one attempt in their lifetime to commit suicide (2.7 per cent). When looking at prevalence within the past 12 months these numbers fall to 2 per cent for ideation, 0.6 per cent for planning and 0.3 per cent for attempts (Goldney & Spence, 1987). Overall only a small number of those who have suicidal ideation or intent follow up that with attempting suicide.

One can argue that anyone who has suicidal ideation presents an aeromedical risk, because of the significant performance decrement that arises from what Edwin Shneidman describes as constriction, a cognitive state with a rigid and narrow pattern of thinking resembling tunnel vision and narrowing of focus – resulting in a temporary inability to engage in effective problem-solving behaviour (Shneidman, 1998).

A much more dramatic and severe risk is that of suicide by aircraft. Unfortunately, as the BEA report (2015) reveals, suicide by aircraft does happen occasionally. From a constrained aeromedical perspective, suicidal behaviour is not a risk unless it involves the use of an aircraft in its causation. However, it is virtually impossible to predict whether a suicidal pilot will use an aircraft for suicide, and most preventive regimes would try to intervene by trying to exclude those pilots who are a high risk of suicide.

There remains significant variation across jurisdictions about certification following attempted suicides. The debate about the risks of suicidality and about measures of detecting them have resurfaced after the recent Germanwings incident.

### Executive functioning

The term 'executive functions' is an umbrella term comprising a wide range of cognitive processes and behavioural competencies, which have been described as organizational or regulatory. They are also described as cold or hot, depending upon whether or not there is significant emotional arousal as a result. The cold or organizational components of executive functioning are logical or mechanistic (Grafman & Litvan, 1999) and include problem-solving, cognitive flexibility, planning, sequencing, verbal reasoning, the ability to sustain attention and resist interference, utilization of feedback, multitasking, and the ability to deal with novelty (Chan *et al.*, 2008). The hot or regulatory components involve those functions involving more emotional arousal as can be caused by such as the experience of reward and punishment, and regulation of social behaviour (Bechara *et al.*, 1999; Bechara *et al.*, 1996; Grafman & Litvan, 1999).

Executive functions are believed to be a function of the frontal lobe, and any impairment can severely limit an individual's capability to function effectively. It is no surprise that good executive function is a prerequisite for flying, as the organizational (cold) skills are vital in the procedural/organizational aspects of flight (the list of functions reads like a prerequisite for flying), and the regulatory (hot) skills are crucial in maintaining flight-deck relationships, and in maintaining decision-making capability in moments of stress while in flight.

## Medication

Medications used in mental health are, by definition, psychoactive medications, and are designed to alter mental processes. Most of these have discernible impacts on cognition, but some of these may wear off or reduce after a period of administration. The impact and duration of the medications are variable and depend upon individual susceptibility, other medications used, the duration of use of the medications, dosage etc. To add to this uncertainty is also the difficulty in identifying whether there is a decrement in cognition (a question of assessment), and to try to apportion the decrement to the medication and to the underlying medical condition (often there is no reliable cognitive assessment done before the medications are commenced).

## Identifying these conditions – the context

Before looking at the options that we have for identifying these conditions, it becomes important to identify the level of effort that we need to put in place to discover these conditions. A recent review of the Germanwings incident (BEA, 2015) said:

> The safety assumption stating that 'the pilot will self-declare his unfitness' failed in this event.
>
> This raises the question of the relevance of this assumption when the illness affects the person's psyche. The assumption is based on evaluation and decision-making capacity, which are directly affected by the illness itself. The self-declaration principle is therefore weakened when it applies to people consuming psychoactive substances or suffering from psychotic episodes.
>
> The robustness of self-declaration is also questionable when the negative consequences for the pilot seem higher for him/her than the potential impact of a lack of declaration. Pilots are selected for their high motivation, their passion for flying, and their need for achievement. Therefore losing their right to fly might be difficult to accept for pilots, not only in financial terms, but also in terms of self-esteem, social recognition and job motivation. Moreover, the potential impact in terms of safety may be underestimated by pilots, who may overestimate their ability to compensate their decrease in fitness.

This impression formed by the BEA report is supported by a study carried out in the USA. In this study, fatal accidents were investigated and those cases where a toxicological exam revealed the presence of a psychoactive substance (medication) were investigated further. The FAA medical certification was studied (Sen et al., 2007) and it was found that 59 of the 61 pilots who had SSRI residues had medical records in the FAA's Certification Database. Seven of the pilots reported psychological conditions and three of those seven reported the use of SSRIs. No medication or medical condition was declared by 52 pilots (88 per cent of the 61 tested).

In another toxicological study of 4,143 pilots (Canfield *et al.*, 2006), medications for mental health, cardiovascular condition and neurological conditions were found in 387 pilots. Of these, 14 out of 223 reported a psychological condition, 69 out of 149 reported cardiovascular conditions and 1 out of 15 reported a neurological condition to the FAA.

US Airline Pilots Association data for the period 1977–2001 reveal that of 1,200 pilots with depression, 60 per cent continued to fly without treatment, 15 per cent failed to report to FAA, and only 25 per cent wanted to declare they took pills and stop flying.

The evidence appears to indicate that a proportion of pilots do not declare their medical conditions, and therefore active investigation of their condition needs to be considered. There have been suggestions that since the volume of pilots is so large, it is impossible to carry out a detailed investigation, and so only those pilots with a declared history should be examined and followed up. This is flawed logic, as it is well-recognized anecdotally and from the studies mentioned, that a large number of pilots with mental illness remain 'underground'.

Much is made of the 'if the climate exists for declaration, pilots will declare' mantra, and that argument has been used to drive change in the USA. However, looking at Australian statistics (Australian Bureau of Statistics, 2009), of the 16 million Australians aged 16–85 years, almost half (45 per cent or 7.3 million) had a lifetime mental disorder, i.e. a mental disorder at some point in their life. One in five (20 per cent or 3.2 million) Australians had a 12-month mental disorder. There were also 4.1 million people who had experienced a lifetime mental disorder but did not have symptoms in the 12 months prior to the survey interview. Since the medical examinations for professional pilots are conducted every 12 months (as an average), one would expect a significant percentage (about 20 per cent) to declare depression. The numbers declared to the Civil Aviation Safety Authority in Australia are significantly lower. Either professional aviation is an environment that is protective and reduces depression-related mental health problems, or someone is being economical with the information provided. This is especially interesting as the Australian Civil Aviation system is tolerant and accepting of depression (indeed arguably it is the most accepting in the world), and provided the pilot is in remission, allows pilots who have variable levels of treated depression to return to flying (while being monitored).

Understanding whether a pilot with a mental health condition is being honest but lacks insight, as against another who may have insight but is dishonestly representing the situation in a manner so as to get secondary gain, is an important differentiation which has implications in the regulator's decision-making approach. However, this differentiation is only possible where the regulator has access to enough information so that assessments can be carried out and judgements made.

### Is there a way to identify those mental health conditions that could impact aviation safety?

The best way to identify medical conditions is through a good history. Sandler (1980) showed that for a large number of conditions the history is crucial, with examination and routine investigations showing little added benefit in the diagnostic process. Indeed, most doctors have heard the aphorism, 'A careful history will lead to the diagnosis 80 per cent of the time'. In the area of mental health, where there are limited physical examinations (except to exclude comorbidities), history is a predominant discriminator. Therefore unless the person (pilot) has overt signs that are clearly detectable in an interview, working without a history, or with a history that is believed to be unreliable, makes the diagnosis extremely difficult – indeed one can argue that we move from the realms of diagnosis into those of detection.

Detection is based on multiple discrete and often unlinked pieces of information being provided to a person (or a team) with the ability to make judgements about the relative value of each information piece, and in making predictions about the future based on a synthesis of the information received. The worldwide occurrence of terrorist incidents even where multiple jurisdictions have large resources invested in detection raises questions about the validity of this method, but it is potentially the best option that is available.

When dealing with pilots, we are dealing with a much smaller group, and one that is identified as such. So obtaining information about their behaviours, their performance at work, in education etc., is (at least theoretically) possible. This can be carried out by identifying the sources of information (professional, and personal) and requiring information to be provided to the decision-maker. In addition to information from treating medical professionals and psychologists, there is also much information that serves as a surrogate for mental illness. A paper on ADHD (Fitzgerald *et al.*, 2011) provides a good starting point about the kind and sources of information that can be of use. They require the following:

- Copies of medical records from date of diagnosis to the present;
- Copies of records from government health authorities detailing consultations and prescription of medications;
- An up-to-date assessment by the treating paediatrician or psychiatrist if available detailing:
  - History of condition,
  - Precise confirmation of the diagnosis with reference to DSM-IV criteria,
  - Comorbidities, including drug and alcohol use,
  - Requirement and response to treatment,
  - Current clinical status with respect to DSM-IV criteria, and
  - Current functional status, with reference to collateral information if available from school, family, workplace etc.;

- Copies of any special investigations performed such as quantitative EEG or neuropsychological testing.
- Completion by the paediatrician/psychiatrist and the chief flying instructor of a questionnaire regarding symptoms in the context of and noting the implications to both the normal day-to-day life and the conduct of aviation;
- Copies of academic records and employment history;
- Copies of traffic infringements and criminal records.

(Fitzgerald *et al.*, 2011, p. 553, order changed)

The list above is required for pilots with a diagnosis of ADHD, but if we are dealing with undeclared or undiagnosed conditions, the surrogates that would be useful are the last three in the list, and also reports from colleagues, team mates (sports and work), spouses or ex-spouses, and other personal contacts.

There are a large number of cognitive tests that are available to attempt to identify a variation in cognition in individuals. These include tests of intelligence, inductive reasoning, memory, cognitive development, spatial orientation etc. There are also tests that deal with cognition in aviation such as CogScreen. Many tests such as the Wisconsin card-sorting test or the first edge palm test are useful to assess executive functioning. There are also tests of personality, such as 16 PF, MMPI etc., many of which incorporate validity scales that enable us to judge the veracity of what is being declared by the person doing the test.

The difficulties in the use of these tests are twofold. The tests are time-consuming, and while some of them can be administered online, many of them require face-to-face attendance, thereby costing the pilots by way of lost income, as well as for the time spent by the psychologists doing the assessments. The other issue is one of validity. There are ongoing arguments as to whether some of these tests are ecologically valid – whether real world functioning is matched by scores on tests. Even allowing for high-quality assessments (and the authors' experience indicates a variable standard in the selection, conduct and analytical quality of assessments conducted), the question that arises is 'so what?' Has the pilot always had a particular issue, has coped with it all along, and is still coping? Or is it is an indication of decompensation? Some tests have a premorbid predictor, but they are only usable in identified specific issues such as head injury. One of the authors has seen several cognitive assessments of pilots in the context of medical certification. Since it is well-known that pilots are as a group in a higher quartile cognitively, how do we manage a pilot who has 'average' results following an episode of medical decompensation? This is very difficult, given that very few employers require a pre-placement cognitive examination (though some may require aptitude testing). In airline pilots, it is possible to compare premorbid simulator assessments with repeat assessments done after the event. These too are difficult because they can be subjective, and are increasingly assessments of the pilot and co-pilot as a team.

The statistical sensitivity and specificity of studies of suicide prevention/ prediction are not encouraging. An oft-quoted study by Pokorny (1992) found that for 67 patients who had committed suicide, 35 could have been predicted by the presence of risk factors such as schizophrenia, depression, prior attempts and overt markers at clinical examinations. As Goldney and Spence (1987) have pointed out, while superficially encouraging, the 55 per cent sensitivity and 74 per cent specificity of the predictive power is only possible when retrospectively examining cases where suicides have occurred – and the risk of a false positive is high, leading to a very low negative predictive value. Another concern is that given the low base rates of suicide in the general population, any predictive test requires realistically unachievable sensitivity and specificity (Murphy, 1983). Overall, where the outcome lies in the future and is therefore unknown, the prediction of suicide as an outcome based on traditionally accepted risk factors is problematic both for its inability to correctly predict the commission of suicide as well as for its high rates for incorrectly identifying those who are never going to commit suicide (Glenn & Nock, 2014; Goldney, 2005). The 20 factors that have been used in the studies above include six questions on depression and on other topics. Since the link between depression and suicidality is also difficult to predict, the question is whether we can implement a regime requiring all pilots to do a test which at best (even with open and honest responses) is able to predict suicidality only slightly better than the toss of a coin (55 per cent).

Over the last two decades since Pokorny's seminal work, many attempts have been made to identify factors that could help to predict suicides in the short term. Some researchers have suggested that questions can help to assist in prediction (Glenn & Nock, 2014). Current so-called 'third-generation' paradigms for suicide prediction include electronic monitoring, but even so, accept that the goal of predicting suicide remains aspirational (Claassen *et al.*, 2014). Attempts have been made to cluster suicide factors, and to make the link with impulsivity (Baca-Garcia *et al.*, 2001), anxiety (Bentley *et al.*, 2016), and borderline personality pathology (Nakar *et al.*, 2016) without much success. Some workers (Cho *et al.*, 2016, p. 711) suggest 'the possible mechanisms by which risk factors result in a completed suicide in the absence of a mental disorder should be explored', thereby widening the factors to be considered beyond those listed by Schwartz-Lifshitz and her colleagues in their excellent review (Schwartz-Lifshitz *et al.*, 2012). Goldney puts the issue of suicide prediction and prevention in perspective when he says

> It is important to emphasize that clinicians are well aware of subtle nuances of patient presentation that may herald suicidal behaviour. The task remains to quantify such phenomena in order to provide more accurate prediction … There are no simple answers. We must address our efforts to alleviate the despair and hopelessness which is the basis for most suicides.
>
> (Goldney, 1992, p. 50)

While the psychological issues are difficult to identify, the one exception to this is the testing for the presence of medications that can alter any of the other hazardous conditions. Medications can be detected easily and efficiently by the use of high pressure liquid chromatography (HPLC). The tests are inexpensive (as compared to neuropsychological testing), and valid. Once a panel is set (the medications that are being looked for), the tests are completely dependable and reliable. The question that remains is that such testing can only be justified on the basis of dishonesty in reporting, and there is no fig leaf (as can be used for mental health conditions – insight, memory affected by the illness etc.). Therefore the objections to such testing go back to the libertarian arguments of rights and freedom.

The preceding discussion identifies some significant difficulties in identifying the conditions that can affect aviation safety. Two questions arise:

1   Is there a justification to carry out such testing or investigation?
2   Is it legally permissible or possible to carry out such testing or information collection?

It is accepted that such a separation of the two issues is artificial as one will, and does, impact the other. However, to the extent that is possible, they are studied as two independent issues.

## Is there a justification to carry out such testing or investigation?

Recent years have seen the tightening of health budgets and of the creation of a new specialization – that of health economics. This specialty has developed metrics that help to make decisions about the utility of interventions in healthcare, e.g. the numbers needed to treat (NNT) metric. This metric identifies how many patients would need to be treated to save one life (or some similar outcome measure).

The advent of newer and more expensive investigations have created a plethora of new methods for assessing the best investigation for each condition. Some examples are:

*   cost-minimization, which looks only at costs and assumes equal effectiveness of the intervention;
*   cost–benefit analysis, which values cost and health in monetary units;
*   cost-effectiveness analysis, which looks for objective measure of effectiveness;
*   cost–utility analysis, which looks at subjective measure of effectiveness.

Cost-effectiveness analysis is the best of the above measures to assess whether the extra monetary cost (in a standardized currency) of the intervention (e.g. the psychological testing) is able to identify a specific outcome measure, for example a mental health condition. A decision needs to be made about what is an appropriate outcome measure. It could be argued with some merit that unless the process identifies a serious medical condition that is sufficiently serious to merit disqualification, the outcome is not germane to aviation safety. The reverse of that argument is that if a condition is identified, and it is non-serious, it is then possible to intervene to prevent it from becoming serious, which improves aircrew retention and thereby safety (as aircrew retention equals more experience equals better safety).

It is the authors' view that these methodologies are likely to be useful mainly to assess the value of those interventions that have been accepted for (or are in the pipeline for) introduction due to political reasons.

How, then, should decisions be made about what testing can or should be carried out for pilots? This is the nub of the question, and the answer depends upon the person who is charged with answering that question. When we look at the range of the stakeholders in this space, it ranges from the community, the regulator (who, often by statute, is there to protect the community), the government (including organs of government whose role is monitor levels of safety, safety regulation, and the relationship between the two), the pilots and their employers.

The community has an expectation that all aviation must be completely safe all the time, and all pilots are at the highest level of performance and have *no* risks of any medical incapacitation, whether subtle or sudden. This expectation is not only not managed, it is encouraged by frequent utterances by our politicians who constantly refer to their primary purpose being 'the safety of the people of [insert country]'. The increasing presence of terrorism means that the community is able to see that the governments are able to bring in changes to legislation, infrastructure and human resources to manage that threat. It is hardly surprising, then, that there remains an expectation that regulators will be tasked by their governments to do 'whatever it takes' to eliminate the risks of medical risks in their pilots. At one level, this expectation is unattainable because the aspects of chance and human variation mean that the risk cannot be eliminated – but that is acceptable to the community once they can be satisfied that all that can be done is being done.

The problem is in the other aspect, that of doing 'whatever it takes'. Regulators must operate in the real world and therefore they must consider the impact of any changes to regulation that they may envisage. Indeed, in most jurisdictions, a regulatory impact statement is required to be tabled along with any change in regulation, and this includes a financial impact statement. Therefore, any such change does ultimately go through a level of cost analysis – and the community, which has been led to believe that safety is all, is increasingly intolerant of the very fact of a cost analysis, knowing that it can and will temper safety interventions. Governments are therefore only able to justify not intervening if they can show that the intervention is not linked to a safety outcome.

Another vexed question is 'who pays?' If the individual pays, licencing costs increase, and this is vigorously opposed by the pilots. If the employers are asked to pay, that means that the cost of doing business increases, costs are passed on to customers and the employers become increasingly less competitive in that most global of all marketplaces – the aviation industry. If the government is to fund all these changes, then there needs to be a budget allocation, and again, there needs to be a needs analysis and a cost-effectiveness analysis to support a financial outlay. Whether or not any intervention is considered necessary, and if so which options or what combination of options will be considered, is a matter of political priority.

The authors propose a generic decision-making framework to assist those who have to make a decision about whether or not testing should be done for a specific condition. The framework is based on aeromedical experience, risk management, and public policy considerations.

The framework considers the following factors:

- The extent of the prevalence of the condition or conditions in the community. This information is available in medical prevalence statistics.
- The risk of the condition compromising aviation safety. This is based on the signs and symptoms of the condition, its impacts on judgement and cognition, and the potential impacts on an individual in command of an aircraft. The knowledge of accidents or incidents which can be attributed to these conditions are not a prerequisite, but can help bolster the risk assessment.

Based on these two factors, a decision can be made as to whether or not it is justifiable to look for that condition in pilots. At that point, the following factors are considered:

- the likelihood that history of the condition is likely to be reliable – this encompasses occupational motivations, insight, stigma etc., and evidence will usually be based on anecdote;
- the presence of a good screening test;
- the presence of a good confirmatory test.

Based on these factors, if all three apply, then a process can be designed that looks for information outside the history/routine-examination boundary. The extent of resource will depend on the risk afforded by the individual circumstances of the pilot. Three sets of considerations will apply:

1   individual factors – social and personal circumstances, openness and honesty displayed;
2   occupational factors – type of employment/authorization (fare-paying passengers etc.);
3   medical factors – natural history of the illness, progression in the individual, insight family history, past history.

This framework allows a generic decision to be made based on jurisdictional priorities, and allows for an individualized programme of assessment for the particular pilot based on an assessment of the risk levels that he or she presents

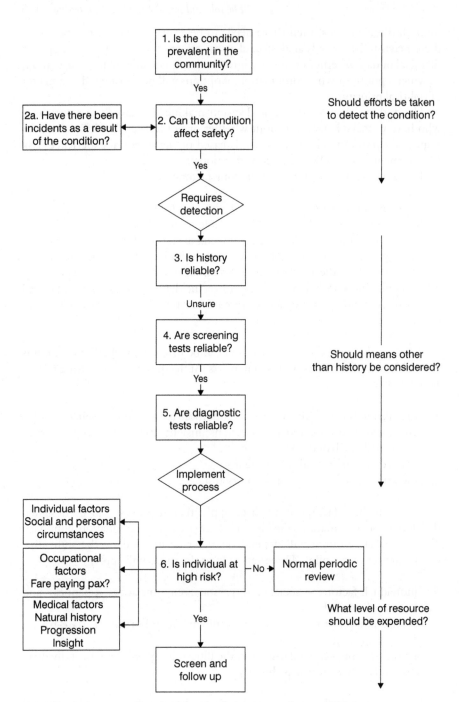

*Figure 9.1* Decision-making framework of when to test for a condition

to the safety of aviation (see worked example below). This framework is diagrammatically represented in Figure 9.1.

If we apply the framework to depression as an example of a condition that has the potential to affect cognition, impulsivity, executive function and suicidality, we get the following outcomes:

1   The condition has a high rate of prevalence in the community.
2   The condition can cause safety compromise.
    ○   There have been incidents as a result of the condition (this is not required to justify testing, but having incidents adds to the risk assessed).
3   History of illness is not particularly reliable due to occupational non-disclosure, and problems with insight, stigma etc.
4   Screening tests are not particularly reliable (many tests are based on reporting), 360 reporting may be patchy, and cognitive tests are difficult to interpret.

The outcome is that testing in this manner should not be done. However, the next step in the process is:

5   Diagnostic tests (interview with psychiatrist) are a reliable test.

This is a situation where the screening test is unreliable but the confirmatory test is reliable. This situation is one that is not infrequently encountered in medical practice. Most health economists would not recommend any publicly funded testing at this point. However, it is also true that patients with financial means do occasionally choose to enhance their understanding of personal risk by carrying out the next test – at their own financial cost. The extension of this argument raises the question of whether a jurisdiction should go to that extreme and carry out confirmatory testing on all pilots. The resource required is huge (and arguably much is wasted), and the return on investment is very, very low. As such, while such testing is a theoretical possibility, in practice it has no place in policy. Moreover, while a clinical interview is a reliable test, it is valid when it is conducted within a therapeutic relationship. The validity of a forensic clinical interview is subject to different variables and is likely to be affected by the level of openness and honesty that is promoted by the rapport developed (which is probably lower than within a therapeutic relationship).

If the screening tests are reliable (or become so in the future), then a decision needs to be made as to the extent of effort that needs to be taken to 'prove' the presence or its absence. A similar dichotomy exists in law – proving something 'on the balance of probability' (civil legal matters) versus 'beyond a reasonable doubt' in a criminal matter. The legal test affects the depth of the evidence necessary and thereby the resource required. In the setting of mental health in aviation, depending upon whether the individual is identified as being high risk or not, the policy test can be identified.

6    If the individual is at high risk (airline etc. *or* personal factors, e.g. family history, past history etc.) then the screen is applied. If not, then the normal periodic screen will remain in place.

One question that arises when we do a worked example through the framework is whether there should be a somewhat improved process that is incorporated into the normal periodic screen. Such an improvement would enhance the sensitivity of the routine periodic examination (for mental health conditions).

What this discussion demonstrates is that the current state of testing is not dependable enough to justify testing for mental-health-related hazards. However, as science progresses, with the development of more valid, sensitive and specific tests, it will be necessary to return to the framework periodically to assess whether that decision should change.

## Is it legally permissible or possible to carry out such testing or information collection?

Most privacy legislation worldwide identifies medical information as sensitive and has a high bar for the release of such information. In most jurisdictions, there is an exclusion that enables information to be released (to the appropriate authority – this is unwritten but understood) in the event of an "'imminent' threat to public safety, or an individual". The difficulty with this is that if an individual has a condition that reduces aviation safety, this risk is not always imminent. One of the authors has faced a situation where a pilot was frankly psychotic and was intending to fly the next day. In that situation, it was easy for the treating psychiatrist to argue imminent danger, and the information was disclosed to the appropriate authority and the pilot grounded. More commonly, the situation is one where the pilot is stressed and is being treated for depression. In this situation it is difficult to argue imminent danger, and many medical professionals will not breach confidentiality and place their personal careers at risk.

There are many ways to approach this situation. The Australian legislation allows the information-handling requirements imposed by some Australian Privacy Principles to be overruled if a 'permitted general situation' exists. The permitted general situation is the lessening or preventing a serious threat to the life, health or safety of any individual, or to public health or safety. The test of lessening a serious threat to public safety is a much lower test than that of imminent danger, and many professionals will be willing to disclose such information, though they do not *have* to do so. (In Australia there is an additional protection written into the Civil Aviation regulation that is specifically protective for releasing information to the national regulator about pilots.)

New Zealand requires all doctors to declare any condition in respect of a pilot (if they know he or she is a pilot), where they have a reasonable belief that the medical condition can have implications for aviation safety. No consent is required from the patient, though most often as a courtesy, they are advised. Similar provisions are enshrined in legislation in Norway, Canada and Israel.

We have seen that testing carried out in isolation has many limitations. The only way that some tests might be able to be of value is if they are accompanied by multiple information sets that enable the decision-maker to better translate the uncertainty into a recognizable trend. As a generalization, such information is predominantly held by health professionals who are (with the significant exception of the National Health Service in the UK) under no obligation to share information with a central database or with anybody else (and may not even know that such a risk exists). There is in medicine a deeply embedded culture of privacy and confidentiality of patient information, and it's something that most professionals do not adhere to just because it's legally required, but because they all strongly believe in it. Absent clear legal provisions and a culture change, doctors and other health professionals are so deeply indoctrinated into protecting their patients' private medical information, that merely permitting them to breach confidentiality subject to their judgement is unlikely to have significant impacts on disclosure to the national regulators.

For now, therefore, in most jurisdictions, it is very difficult to carry out meaningful testing of aviators.

## Conclusion

The basis for any medical examination must be based in a risk-assessment framework, and the conduct of psychological testing to identify at-risk individuals has merit. However, the practical difficulties of the low validity, and doubtful specificity of the testing processes make the outcomes of such a testing process either over-predictive of abnormalities that are at the boundaries of normal experience, or to be such as to miss many cases which could have significant issues. There remain other important problems – time, cost and privacy legislation considerations.

To make such a process useful and meaningful, jurisdictions will require the political will to bring about a degree of social change, the willingness to change legislation, policy and process, and the ability to fund the cost of these interventions. While these determinations are undoubtedly risk-management decisions with an impact on aviation safety, they will be made by the political masters of those jurisdictions, and the role of the medical professionals in these decisions is limited to providing appropriate and adequate information.

## References

Augoustinos, M., & Walker, I. (1995). *Social cognition: An integrated introduction*. New Delhi, India: SAGE Publications.

Australian Bureau of Statistics. (2009). Mental health. *Australian social trends* Canberra: Australian Bureau of Statistics. Retrieved from http://www.ausstats.abs.gov.au/

ausstats/subscriber.nsf/LookupAttach/4102.0Publication25.03.094/$File/41020_
Mentalhealth.pdf

Baca-Garcia, E., Diaz-Sastre, C., Basurte, E., Prieto, R., Ceverino, A., & Leon, J. de. (2001). A prospective study of the paradoxical relationship between impulsivity and lethality of suicide attempts. *The Journal of Clinical Psychiatry*, 62(7), 560–564.

BEA (Bureau d'Enquêtes et d'Analyses pour la securite de l'aviation civile) (2015). *Final report: accident on 24 March 2015 at Prads-Haute-Bléone (Alpes-de-Haute-Provence, France) to the Airbus A320-211 registered D-AIPX operated by Germanwings.* Paris: BEA. Retrieved from https://www.bea.aero/uploads/tx_elyextendttnews/BEA2015-0125. en-LR_03.pdf

Bechara, A., Damasio, H., Damasio, A.R., & Lee, G.P. (1999). Different contributions of the human amygdala and ventromedial prefrontal cortex to decision-making. *The Journal of Neuroscience*, 19(13), 5473–5481.

Bechara, A., Tranel, D., Damasio, H., & Damasio, A.R. (1996). Failure to respond autonomically to anticipated future outcomes following damage to prefrontal cortex. *Cerebral Cortex*, 6(2), 215–225.

Beck, A.T. (1963). Thinking and depression: I. idiosyncratic content and cognitive distortions. *Archives of General Psychiatry*, 9(4), 324–333.

Beck, A.T., Kovacs, M., & Weissman, A. (1979). Assessment of suicidal intention: The Scale for Suicide Ideation. *Journal of Consulting and Clinical Psychology*, 47(2), 343–352.

Bentley, K.H., Franklin, J.C., Ribeiro, J.D., Kleiman, E.M., Fox, K.R., & Nock, M.K. (2016). Anxiety and its disorders as risk factors for suicidal thoughts and behaviors: A meta-analytic review. *Clinical Psychology Review*, 43, 30–46.

Blasi, A. (1980). Bridging moral cognition and moral action: A critical review of the literature. *Psychological Bulletin*, 88(1), 1–45.

Canfield, D.V., Salazar, G.J., Lewis, R.J., & Whinnery, J.E. (2006). Pilot medical history and medications found in post mortem specimens from aviation accidents. *Aviation, Space, and Environmental Medicine*, 77(11), 1171–1173.

Chan, R., Shum, D., Toulopoulou, T., & Chen, E. (2008). Assessment of executive functions: Review of instruments and identification of critical issues. *Archives of Clinical Neuropsychology*, 23(2), 201–216.

Cho, S.-E., Na, K.-S., Cho, S.-J., Im, J.-S., & Kang, S.-G. (2016). Geographical and temporal variations in the prevalence of mental disorders in suicide: Systematic review and meta-analysis. *Journal of Affective Disorders*, 190, 704–713.

Claassen, C.A., Harvilchuck-Laurenson, J.D., & Fawcett, J. (2014). Prognostic models to detect and monitor the near-term risk of suicide: state of the science. *American Journal of Preventive Medicine*, 47(3 Suppl 2), S181–185.

Fiske, S.T., & Taylor, S.E. (1991). *Social Cognition*. McGraw-Hill.

Fitzgerald, D.J.P., Navathe, P.D., & Drane, A.M. (2011). Aeromedical decision making in attention-deficit/hyperactivity disorder. *Aviation, Space, and Environmental Medicine*, 82(5), 550–554.

Gannon, T.A., Polaschek, D.L.L., & Ward, T. (2005). Social cognition and sex offenders. In: M. McMurran & J. McGuire (eds), *Social problem solving and offending: evidence, evaluation and evolution* (pp. 223–247). New York, NY: John Wiley & Sons.

Glenn, C.R., & Nock, M.K. (2014). Improving the short-term prediction of suicidal behavior. *American Journal of Preventive Medicine*, 47(3 Suppl 2), S176–180.

Goldney, R.D. (1992). The prediction of suicide. In: S. McKillop (ed), *Preventing youth suicide,* Canberra: Australian Institute of Criminology. Retrieved from http://citeseerx. ist.psu.edu/viewdoc/download?doi=10.1.1.553.5278&rep=rep1&type=pdf

Goldney, R.D. (2005). Suicide prevention: A pragmatic review of recent studies. *Crisis*, 26(3), 128–140.

Goldney, R.D., & Spence, N.D. (1987). Is suicide predictable? *Australian and New Zealand Journal of Psychiatry*, 21(1), 3–4.

Grafman, J., & Litvan, I. (1999). Importance of deficits in executive functions. *The Lancet*, 354(9194), 1921–1923.

Hawton, K., & Heeringen, K. van. (2000). *The international handbook of suicide and attempted suicide*. West Sussex, UK: John Wiley & Sons.

Hollon, S.D., & Kriss, M.R. (1984). Cognitive factors in clinical research and practice. *Clinical Psychology Review*, 4(1), 35–76.

ICAO (International Civil Aviation Organization) (2011). Personnel licensing: International standards and recommended practices. In: *Convention on International Civil Aviation* (11th edition). Montreal: ICAO.

ICOA (International Civil Aviation Organization) (2013). *Safety management manual (SMM)* (3rd edition). Montreal: ICAO.

Ingram, R.E. (2012). *Contemporary psychological approaches to depression: Theory, research, and treatment*. New York, NY: Springer Science & Business Media.

Murphy, G.E. (1983). On suicide prediction and prevention. *Archives of General Psychiatry*, 40(3), 343–344.

Nakar, O., Brunner, R., Schilling, O., Chanen, A., Fischer, G., Parzer, P., et al. (2016). Developmental trajectories of self-injurious behavior, suicidal behavior and substance misuse and their association with adolescent borderline personality pathology. *Journal of Affective Disorders*, 197, 231–238.

Navathe, P., Drane, M., & Preitner, C. (2014). Aeromedical decision making: From principles to practice. *Aviation, Space, and Environmental Medicine*, 85(5), 576–580.

Navathe, S., Ward, T., & Gannon, T. (2008). Cognitive distortions in child sex offenders: an overview theory, research, and practice. *Journal of Forensic Nursing*, 4(3), 111–122.

Pokorny, A.D. (1992). Prediction of suicide in psychiatric patients: Report of a prospective study. In: R.W. Maris, A.L. Berman, J.T. Maltsberger, & R.I. Yufit (eds), *Assessment and prediction of suicide* (pp. 105–129). New York: Guilford Press.

Sandler, G. (1980). The importance of the history in the medical clinic and the cost of unnecessary tests. *American Heart Journal*, 100(6 Pt 1), 928–931.

Schwartz-Lifshitz, M., Zalsman, G., Giner, L., & Oquendo, M.A. (2012). Can we really prevent suicide? *Current Psychiatry Reports*, 14(6), 624–633.

Sen, A., Akin, A., Canfield, D.V., & Chaturvedi, A.K. (2007). Medical histories of 61 aviation accident pilots with postmortem SSRI antidepressant residues. *Aviation, Space, and Environmental Medicine*, 78(11), 1055–1059.

Sherman, S.J., Judd, C.M., & Park, B. (1989). Social cognition. *Annual Review of Psychology*, 40(1), 281–326.

Shneidman, E.S. (1998). *The suicidal mind*. Oxford: Oxford University Press.

Simon, H.A. (1956). Rational choice and the structure of the environment. *Psychological Review*, 63(2), 129–138.

Watson, D.B. (2005). Aeromedical decision-making: An evidence-based risk management paradigm. *Aviation, Space, and Environmental Medicine*, 76(1), 58–62.

Webster, C.D., & Jackson, M.A. (1997). *Impulsivity: Theory, assessment, and treatment*. New York: Guilford Press.

Williams, A.M., & Ericsson, K.A. (2007). Introduction to the theme issue: Perception, cognition, action, and skilled performance. *Journal of Motor Behavior*, 39(5), 338–340.

# 10 Assessment for fatigue among pilots

*Ries Simons*

> My mind clicks on and off. I try letting one eyelid close at a time while I prop the other with my will. But the effect is too much, sleep is winning, my whole body argues dully that nothing, nothing life can attain is quite so desirable as sleep. My mind is losing resolution and control.
>
> (Charles Lindbergh about his 33½ hours Transatlantic Solo Flight, May 1927)

## Introduction

Fatigue is considered a major cause of impairment of pilot performance, and pilot fatigue is a recognised threat to aviation safety and is considered a continuing problem facing crews flying aircraft of all sizes (e.g. Goode, 2003; Eriksen *et al.*, 2006). In one third of all reports to the UK Confidential Human Factors Incident Reporting Programme (CHIRP), reporting pilots attribute incidents, errors or problems to fatigue. NASA's Aviation Safety Reporting System indicates that 21 per cent of reported aviation incidents are fatigue related (CAA UK, 2005). The US National Transport Safety Board (NTSB) reported that twenty percent of the 182 major NTSB investigations completed between 2001 and 2012 identified fatigue as a probable cause, contributing factor, or a finding in air, sea, road, or rail transport accidents. Since, in commercial aviation operations, about 70 per cent of fatal accidents are considered to be related to human error, it can be assumed that the risk of fatigue of the operating crew contributes about 15–20 per cent to the overall accident rate (ECA, 2015). Fatigue manifests in the aviation context not only when pilots fall asleep in the cockpit, but perhaps more importantly, when their cognitive performance is impaired and they are insufficiently alert during take-off and landing. There is no simple formula for evaluating the contribution of aircrew fatigue to a safety event. Reported fatigue-related events have included procedural errors, unstable approaches, lining up with the wrong runway, and landing without clearances.

Fatigue is a complex phenomenon, involving a number of psychosocial and behavioural processes. As a result, various definitions have been proposed.

Fatigue is defined in terms of subjective feelings, performance decrement, and in terms of physiological changes. Fatigue is often used as a synonym for drowsiness, sleepiness and tiredness (Åkerstedt, 2000). Rogers *et al.* (1999) characterised mental fatigue as a syndrome whose symptoms include, amongst other elements, subjective tiredness and a slowing of normal cognitive function, while others define fatigue as the increasing difficulty to perform physical or mental activities (Baker *et al.*, 2003). Perelli (1980) states that fatigue is best defined as a subjective feeling, and provided that the intensity of the fatigue stressor is severe enough, the subjective report of fatigue should be expected to be associated with a wide range of performance decrements. In laboratory research, results of a range of performance tasks show various levels of correlation with subjective scores of fatigue. A practical definition of pilot fatigue, which is presently generally accepted in the aviation community, is formulated by the International Civil Aviation Organisation (ICAO-IATA-IFALPA, 2011), which defined pilot fatigue as

> a physiological state of reduced mental or physical performance capability resulting from sleep loss or extended wakefulness, circadian phase, or workload that can impair a crewmember's alertness and ability to safely operate an aircraft or perform safety related duties.

In the present time of economic pressures and strong competition of airlines, job stresses of pilots are increasing. More demanding rosters lead to an increase of fatigue and sleep loss, while increasing density of air traffic and delays lead to an increase of workload. This unfavourable situation may be compromised by high social, financial, and family demands. In such context, it can be anticipated that fatigue risks and psychological stresses will increase and that mental health problems may arise when coping mechanisms are unsuccessful. In this respect, the group of young pilots who are atypically employed may need special consideration. Because they have financial debts and are sometimes paid by the flight hour, they tend to disregard the symptoms of severe fatigue or mental problems and do not report unfit for duty, while they should.

It should be emphasised that, when a pilot reports to be 'fatigued', one should always ask this pilot to describe in more detail what she/he means with 'fatigue', what the symptoms are and what the – subjectively perceived – causes are. It should be considered that 'fatigue' can be caused by operational demands and social problems, but it can also be caused by mental health problems, such as depression, or physical illness, or a mixture of these factors.

## Pilot fatigue

In the aviation environment, three types of fatigue are distinguished: transient, cumulative, and circadian. Transient fatigue is acute fatigue brought on by extreme sleep restriction or extended hours awake within one or two days. Cumulative fatigue is fatigue brought on by repeated sleep restriction or extended hours awake across a series of days. Circadian fatigue refers to the reduced performance during night-time hours, particularly during an individual's window of circadian low (WOCL between 2:00 a.m. and 6:00 a.m.). Everyone carries some level of fatigue during their working hours which impacts on alertness. However, at the point where this interferes with operational processes and acceptable crew performance, it becomes a risk that must be addressed in a safety management system. Therefore, the management of pilot fatigue is a major concern in the aviation industry.

### Symptoms of pilot fatigue

Very high levels of fatigue may cause pilots to fall asleep, or have micro-sleeps in the cockpit (Rosekind *et al.*, 1992), and impair cognitive performance and alertness even during take-off and landing. According to polls carried out by the European Cockpit Association in Austria, Sweden, Germany, and Denmark, four out of five pilots have to cope with fatigue while in the cockpit (ECA, 2012). Sixty-five per cent of Dutch and French pilots report problems with 'heavy eyelids' during flights. Between 43 per cent and 54 per cent of pilots surveyed in the UK, Denmark, Norway, and Sweden reported falling asleep involuntarily in the cockpit while flying, while a third of the pilots in the UK are said to have woken up to find their colleague sleeping as well. A considerable number of pilots in Sweden (71 per cent), Norway (79 per cent) and Denmark (80–90 per cent) acknowledge to have made mistakes due to fatigue, while in Germany this was four out of five pilots (ECA, 2012). Although these subjective data may be biased by coincident actions of pilot unions against the proposal for Flight and Duty Time Regulations by the European Aviation Safety Agency (EASA), they indicate that at least a considerable number of airline pilots experience undesirable levels of fatigue and fatigue symptoms during their work in the cockpit. While all above symptoms are related to subjective feelings of sleepiness and impaired performance, impairment of some important cognitive functions may go unnoticed. These common cognitive symptoms of high levels of fatigue include (Petrie & Dawson, 1997; Co *et al.*, 1999; Caldwell & Gilreath, 2002):

- reduction in speed and accuracy of performance;
- lapses of attention and vigilance;
- delayed reactions;
- impaired logical reasoning and decision-making, including a reduced ability to assess risk or appreciate consequences of actions;
- reduced situational awareness;
- low motivation to perform optional activities.

In an operational context of adverse flight conditions, these symptoms may cause aircrew to:

- choose wrong priorities, pre-occupation with one task, often a minor issue;
- be unaware of a dangerous situation;
- ignore alarm signals;
- neglect normal checks and procedures;
- choose risky options;
- be unaware of impaired task performance;
- become irritated; bad team work.

### Fatigue: contributing factors

A variety of factors contribute to whether an individual experiences fatigue as well as the severity of that fatigue. The major factors affecting fatigue include:

- *Time on task.* The longer a person has continuously been doing a job without a break, the more likely he or she is to be fatigued and alertness is impaired (Table 10.1).
- *Circadian factors.* Fatigue is, in part, a function of the phase of the circadian cycle. During night flights circadian sleep pressure is maximal and fatigue and sleepiness are most severe during the Window of Circadian Low (WOCL), which is commonly defined as the time period between 2:00 a.m. and 6:00 a.m. Table 10.1 shows that in a daylight flight departing at 10:00 a.m. alertness is impaired to a blood alcohol level (BAC) of 0.42‰ after 15.2 hrs of duty. In a night flight starting at 18:00 this level is reached after 10.3 hrs (Spencer *et al.*, 1998).
- *Amount of pre-duty sleep.* If a pilot has had significantly less than seven hours of sleep in the past 24 hours, he or she is more likely to be fatigued during the flight (Valk & Simons, 1998). Scientific research and experimentation have consistently demonstrated that adequate sleep sustains performance. There are considerable inter-individual differences in how much sleep one needs. Allegedly, Albert Einstein needed at least 10 hours of sleep, while Thomas Edison only needed four hours. For most people, seven to eight hours of sleep in each 24-hour period is optimal to sustain their performance. Sleep during the WOCL provides the most recuperative value. Within limits, shortened periods of night-time sleep may be nearly as beneficial as a consolidated sleep period when augmented by additional sleep periods, such as naps before evening departures, during flights with augmented flight crews, and during layovers.
- *Time since awake.* A pilot who has been continually awake for a long period of time since his or her last major sleep period is more likely to be fatigued.
- *Cumulative sleep debt.* For the average person, cumulative sleep debt is the difference between the amount of sleep a person has received over the past several days, and the amount of sleep he or she would have received with seven to eight hours of sleep each night.
  - *Workload.* A high workload as well as a very low workload may contribute to fatigue. Traffic density is very high in the European airspace, causing

high levels of workload on short-haul routes. Long-haul cruise flights are often monotonous which may facilitate sleepiness, lower the level of arousal and thus affect vigilance.

○   *Medication, hangover.* Sedative medications, such as antihistamines and benzodiazepines, and/or residual effects of alcohol may contribute to subjective fatigue, lowered alertness, and increased sleepiness.

○   *Cabin environmental conditions.* The ambient pressure in the aircraft cabin may be as low as 0.75 atmosphere. The consequent increment of the partial oxygen pressure causes the oxygen saturation of the blood to decrease by 5–8 per cent. Although there is no convincing evidence that this would affect cognitive function, this phenomenon may contribute to the feeling of weariness and subjective fatigue. This feeling might be further intensified by the low relative humidity prevailing in the cockpit. In addition, high ambient temperature, noise, and turbulence may contribute to fatigue in sensitive individuals.

○   *Disorders,* such as obstructive sleep apnoea (OSA), chronic diseases, and an unhealthy lifestyle may lead to sleep deprivation and unfitness and a higher in-flight fatigue risk.

○   *Psychological factors and life stress.* Life stress is defined as physical and psychological symptoms caused by difficult life circumstances, such as work-related problems, financial worries, health concerns, bereavement issues, relationship/family difficulties, separation from family, and social demands. These factors may also disrupt sleep, which in turn may lead to higher fatigue levels.

○   *Individual variation.* Individuals respond to fatigue factors differently and may become fatigued at different times, and to different degrees of severity, under the same circumstances.

*Table 10.1* Alertness vs blood alcohol level

|  | Alertness score | | | | | | |
| --- | --- | --- | --- | --- | --- | --- | --- |
|  | 80 | 70 | 60 | 50 | 40 | 30 | 20 |
| Hours before level reached during FDP starting at 10:00 | 6.1 | 8.4 | 10.7 | 12.9 | 15.2 | 17.5 | 19.7 |
| Hours before level reached during FDP starting at 18:00 | 1.2 | 3.5 | 5.7 | 8 | 10.3 | 12.6 | 14.9 |
| Equivalent level BAC (‰) | 0.00 | 0.03 | 0.14 | 0.27 | 0.42 | 0.62 | 0.85 |

Notes: Alertness scores (Visual Analogue Scale) and equivalent blood-alcohol levels (BAC promille ‰) related to flight duty hours and start of flight duty. Highest alertness scores 100. In a daylight flight departing at 10:00, alertness is impaired to a BAC level of 0.42‰ after 15.2 hrs of duty. In a night flight starting at 18:00, this level is reached after 10.3 hrs (Spencer *et al.*, 1998)

### Operational factors contributing to fatigue

Due to economic pressure, requiring maximal aircraft and aircrew utilisation, aircrew are increasingly confronted with irregular duties, long flight duty periods (FDPs), early starts, late arrivals, night flying, and circadian disruption. This may lead to impaired sleep and cumulative sleep debt, lowered alertness, and fatigue, which may affect flight safety and health.

Causes of fatigue are often compound as is, for instance, illustrated by the problems associated with early starts. Most pilots who have to report for duty around 04:30 in the early morning go to bed in the early evening around 21:00 in order to obtain sufficient sleep. However, their biological clock is not set for sleeping at that time. In most cases, they only succeed in falling asleep around midnight for a three hour sleep to awake at 03:00. While a pre-duty sleep of three hours is considered to be insufficient, these pilots have to take off when the level of their circadian sleep pressure is still high (WOCL). There is evidence that the combination of insufficient sleep and departing during the WOCL may lead to impaired alertness during the entire flight (Simons & Valk, 1998).

## Fatigue and sleep

Sleep reduction may lead to lowered alertness and impaired performance (Carskadon & Dement, 1981; Horne & Wilkinson, 1985; Valk *et al.*, 2003), while flying requires optimal cognition and alertness. Reduction of sleep length and quality, due to operational demands, is an important cause of fatigue in aircrew. Sleep is a vital physiological body function and sufficient sleep is the major countermeasure against fatigue, lowered alertness, and in-flight sleepiness. It is therefore important for flight crew to utilise the scheduled rest periods to obtain the best possible sleep. The literature provides sufficient evidence that duration and quality of pre-trip sleep are important determinants of pilot performance and alertness (e.g. Carskadon & Dement, 1981; Carskadon & Dement, 1982; Rosekind *et al.*, 1992; Pascoe *et al.* 1994; Valk & Simons, 1998). Because fatigue problems of aircrew are interrelated with sleep problems and circadian disruption, it is useful to briefly discuss some basics of sleep science and circadian physiology in the context of this chapter.

### Sleep

Sleep is composed of two distinct states: non-rapid eye movement, or NREM, and rapid eye movement, or REM, sleep. During NREM sleep, physiological and mental activities slow (e.g., heart rate and breathing rate slow). NREM sleep is divided into four stages, with the deepest sleep occurring during stages 3 and 4. Deep sleep, also called slow-wave sleep (SWS), is considered to have important recuperative and growth-inducing properties involved in maintaining general health. If awakened during deep sleep, an individual may take some time to wake up and then continue to feel groggy, sleepy, and perhaps disoriented for 10 to 15 minutes. This phenomenon is called sleep inertia. REM sleep is associated with an extremely active brain that is dreaming, and with bursts of rapid eye movements; during REM sleep, the major motor muscles of the body are immobile. If awakened during REM sleep, individuals can often provide detailed reports of their dreams. REM sleep is considered to be important for mental recuperation and mental capacities, such as memory, learning, cognitive performance and mental health.

Over the course of a typical night, NREM and REM sleep occur in cycles. Stage 1 or drowsy sleep usually occurs during the transition from waking to sleep. Stage 2 sleep normally occupies 50 per cent of the sleep period. The time taken to reach the first episode of stage 2 is termed 'sleep onset latency'. Deep sleep (stages 3 and 4) predominates in the early part of the sleep period and is influenced by the duration of prior wakefulness. Episodes of REM sleep occur at intervals. The normal sequence of sleep stages during the night is: waking, stage 1, stage 2, stage 3, stage 4, stage 3, stage 2, REM sleep, followed by the next cycle starting with stage 2, etc. Each sleep cycle lasts around 90–100 minutes. As the night proceeds, the content of the sleep cycles alters, with less SWS sleep and more REM sleep in later cycles. The last part of a normal night's sleep generally consists mainly of sleep stages 1 and 2.

### Recuperative sleep

It is generally believed that for optimal recuperation of physical and psychological functions both NREM and REM sleep are important. To be recuperative, the duration of sleep should be sufficiently long to allow for NREM and REM. Sleep duration is the principal determinant of the recuperative value of sleep (Dinges *et al.*, 1997; Wilkinson *et al.*, 1966).

In aircrew, quality and duration of pre-flight sleep may be impaired by operational demands and circadian disruptions. Several studies of the sleep of aircrew during layovers after time zone transitions found impaired sleep. In particular, the second and third night during layovers showed poorer sleep quality (e.g. Simons *et al.* 1994; Petrilli *et al.* 2006; Gander *et al.*, 2014).

Impaired pre-flight sleep and circadian disruption may result in lowered alertness and performance levels during the flight. In-flight alertness and performance levels may further be lowered by long work periods, night flying, and monotony during cruise flight. Table 10.1, based on an alertness model derived from a large database of experimental data, clearly shows that alertness decreases as flight duty times become longer (Spencer *et al.* 1998). Therefore, augmentation of the crew and implementation of in-flight sleep periods may be necessary to maintain sufficient alertness and performance levels during a long-haul flight. Moreover, Table 10.1 shows that in-flight alertness levels are highly influenced by the time of day that a flight duty period starts. This is particularly important for scheduling of rest periods on ultra-long range flights.

## *Circadian aspects*

The human sleep–wake cycle is regulated by the circadian timing system, which is controlled by endogenous factors, as well as external '*zeitgebers*', which are social or environmental cues such as light and dark cycles, which is the most important *zeitgeber*, mealtimes and other factors that influence our internal time-keeping systems. The normal human circadian cycle is shaped around daytime waking and restorative sleep during the night. Irregular patterns of work, especially those that include night work, can lead to significant circadian disruption. To maintain round the clock operations, aircrew often have to sleep during the day when their circadian clock dictates wakefulness, and to fly during the night when their clock dictates sleep. Daytime sleep is more difficult to obtain, and is known to be of a lower quality than sleep obtained during the night (Åkerstedt, 1998). During night flights, circadian sleep pressure is maximal during the WOCL between the hours of 2:00 a.m. and 6:00 a.m., and fatigue and sleepiness are most severe.

Short-haul aircrew are often faced with irregular work schedules, early morning departures, and late arrivals, resulting in impaired sleep and in-flight sleepiness (e.g. Simons & Valk, 1998; Spencer & Robertson, 2002; Bourgeois-Bougrine *et al.*, 2003; Powell *et al.*, 2007).

Long-haul operations are characterised by rapidly alternating time-zone transitions and night flying (e.g. Graeber, 1986; Lowden & Åkerstedt, 1998; Robertson & Spencer, 2003; Petrilli *et al.*, 2006). Crossing three or more time zones may cause jet lag symptoms of which the most prominent symptoms are impaired sleep during the local night, and sleepiness and impaired cognitive functioning during the local day. Complete adaptation to the new time zone will take around three to five days when travelling westward and a bit longer when travelling eastward. For long-haul aircrew, layovers are often too long to keep sleep and activity patterns anchored to home time, and too short for complete circadian adaptation to the local environment. Their circadian body clock does not have enough time to adapt to any of the destination time zones. Rapidly alternating time-zone transitions together with night flying lead to a unique combination of shifted time and shifted work, this results in compound circadian disruptions. Consequences, such as impaired sleep, lowered alertness, and fatigue, may affect flight safety and health (e.g. Samel & Wegmann, 1993; Petrie *et al.*, 2004; Eriksen *et al.*, 2006; Jackson & Earl, 2006).

## Assessment of pilot fatigue

Data regarding the causes and consequences of fatigue are essential to be able to develop, construct, and evaluate flight and duty time regulations, feed fatigue management systems, and develop countermeasures to reduce fatigue. In that context, data on subjective fatigue, cognitive performance, quantity and quality of sleep, and sleepiness are collected together with data on operational circumstances, such as trip schedule, crew roster, and rest periods. Such data are used for detection, reporting, and investigation of fatigue risk and can be used to feed scientific information sources on fatigue.

A number of assessment tools with respect to fatigue have been developed. However, there is no objective tool to measure fatigue, because in essence fatigue is a complex subjective feeling. As noted above, fatigue is defined in terms of subjective feelings, performance decrement, and in terms of physiological changes. A wide variety of fatigue measures are used in scientific research, but essentially most measures address subjective feelings, performance, and physiological characteristics. There is no single measurement that is the 'gold standard', because fatigue-related impairment affects many skills and has multiple causes. Fatigue measurements can be based on pilots' recall or current perception of fatigue (subjective measures) or on objective measurements, such as performance tests and different types of physical monitoring. Each type of measure has strengths and weaknesses. To decide which types of data to collect, the most important consideration should be the aim of the investigation and the problem definition of the study. Subjective and objective assessments of pilot fatigue aim to identify the causes of fatigue, tiredness, sleepiness, and performance impairment and to judge the fitness to fly or work of the affected person.

A prerequisite for assessment methods to be used in the context of rulemaking or fatigue risk management is that 1) the measures should be scientifically validated and have been shown to be sensitive; 2) the measures should not interfere with the operational duties of the pilots; and 3) they have been used in different types of flight operations, so data can be compared. In the context of this chapter, only methods that satisfy the above criteria will be discussed.

### Pilots' recall of fatigue risks during flight

Individual pilots can give vital information on fatigue risks where and when they occur in an operation. Many operators have developed their own fatigue reporting forms that can be used in the context of their safety management system (SMS) and/or fatigue risk management system (FRMS). A series of fatigue reports on a particular route can be a trigger for further investigation by the operator's safety management.

Fatigue report forms (either paper-based or electronic) should include information on recent sleep and duty history (minimum last three days), time of day of the fatigue event, and measures of different aspects of fatigue-related impairment (for example, validated alertness or sleepiness scales). It should also provide space for written commentary so that the persons reporting can explain the context of the event and give their view of why it happened. An example of a fatigue report form can be found in the ICAO-IATA-IFALPA *FRMS Implementation Guide for Operators*, Appendix B (ICAO-IATA-IFALPA, 2011).

### Retrospective Surveys

Retrospective surveys are a relatively inexpensive way to obtain information from larger groups of pilots on experience of fatigue on duty; amount and quality of sleep at home and on trips; and views on the causes and consequences of fatigue on duty. However, time and costs are involved in developing and distributing the survey questionnaire, entering the information into databases and analysing it. The main limitation of retrospective surveys is that the information collected is subjective, which may limit the reliability, because for crewmembers, it may be difficult to accurately recall details of past events, feelings, or sleep patterns. It should also be considered that pilots might adapt their responses for personal or industrial reasons (e.g. industrial conflict concerning duty times). However, extreme ratings are obvious when compared with group averages. Despite limitations, retrospective surveys can be a useful source of information in the context of fatigue management. Wherever possible, validated scales and standard questions should be used for gathering information on common topics such as sleep problems.

For example, the Epworth Sleepiness Scale is a validated tool for measuring sleepiness and its effects on daily life (Johns, 1994). It is widely used to evaluate whether an individual is experiencing excessive sleepiness. The questionnaire asks the subject to rate his or her probability of falling asleep on a scale of increasing probability from 0 to 3 for eight different situations that most people engage in during their daily lives (e.g. sitting and reading, watching TV, etc.). The scores for the eight questions are added together to obtain a single number. A number in the 0–9 range is considered to be normal while the higher the number in the 10–24 range, the more severe the sleepiness problem is.

## Measurement of pilot fatigue during flight operations

During flight operations, fatigue can be measured either subjectively by having crewmembers rate how they feel, or objectively by measuring crewmembers' performance.

### Subjective fatigue and sleepiness ratings

The following should be considered when choosing rating scales for monitoring crewmember fatigue and sleepiness during flight operations:

- The rating scale should be quick and easy to complete.
- It should be designed to be completed at multiple time points, e.g., pre-flight, across a flight, at top of descent, and post-flight.
- It should be validated to be sensitive to the effects of sleep loss and the circadian body clock cycle under controlled experimental conditions.

- The results should show sufficiently high correlation with the results of objective measures such as vigilance and performance tasks.
- The results of the scale should be available of different aviation environments in order to compare fatigue levels.

Three scales that are widely used in industrial and aviation environments and that meet the above criteria will be discussed here: the Samn-Perelli Crew Status Check, which rates subjective fatigue, the Stanford Sleepiness Scale, and the Karolinska Sleepiness Scale, which both measure subjective sleepiness.

The seven-point Samn-Perelli Crew Status Check (SP7, Table 10.2) asks people to rate their level of fatigue 'right now', and is a simplified version of the Samn-Perelli Checklist (Samn & Perelli, 1982). The SP7 has been used in previous aircrew studies (e.g. Spencer & Robertson, 2002; Samel *et al.*, 1997; Spencer & Robertson, 2004; Powell *et al.*, 2011). This rating scale is easy to use and the results are easy to interpret. It can be used to collect subjective data on fatigue of large groups of pilots at several stages of flight. A useful development by Powell *et al.* (2011) is to program the scale as an input page into the flight management system of the aircraft, asking pilots to input their alertness levels according to the seven-point Samn-Perelli fatigue scale. This automated method of collecting subjective fatigue ratings appears relatively simple to implement and may yield large quantities of data in a non-intrusive way. This method enables airlines to collect data related to critical phases of flight (e.g. top of descent) from all their pilots during all flights. Such data can be used for identifying problem flights and for examining trends across the operation, which is important information in the context of an airline's fatigue risk management system (FRMS) (Powell *et al.*, 2011).

An example of in-flight SP7 ratings is shown in Figure 10.1, where 36 pilots rated their fatigue levels on a personal digital assistant (PDA) at wake up, pre-flight, before and after in-flight rest, five minutes before top of descent (TOD), and post duty. When interpreting the scores (using Table 10.2), it can be seen that pilots were more fatigued after the onboard rest and that the fatigue level remained at the 'after rest' levels towards TOD (Simons *et al.*, 2009). Based on these results, the airline decided to improve the onboard rest facility.

The Stanford Sleepiness Scale (SSS) is a well-validated method to assess subjective sleepiness (Hoddes *et al.*, 1973). This subjective rating scale has proven to be sensitive in detecting any significant increase in sleepiness or fatigue. SSS measures are highly correlated with performance and threshold of information processing speed during periods of intense fatigue (Perelli, 1980). The SSS consists of seven ranked statements describing various degrees of alertness/sleepiness from '1—feeling active and vital; alert; wide awake' to '7—almost in reveries; sleep onset soon; lost struggle to remain awake'. Subjects are asked to choose the one statement that best describes their present state of sleepiness. The statements contained within the SSS are a mixture of adjectives describing sleep propensity, energy/fatigue and cognitive performance. Thus, as Johns (1994) has pointed out, the SSS does not measure sleep propensity directly;

limiting its validity as a measure of sleep propensity, but perhaps increasing it as a more global measure of 'sleepiness'.

The Karolinska Sleepiness Scale (KSS, Table 10.3) is a measure of sleepiness and has been validated with respect to decrements in performance and objective measures of sleepiness (Åkerstedt & Gillberg, 1990; Gillberg *et al.*, 1994). The KSS is a modification of the SSS. To allow for a more detailed gradation in scores, two extra scores were added to the SSS so that sleepiness scores range from 1 to 9. Because the two extra scores bearded no description, the KSS rating

*Table 10.2* SP7 Fatigue Scale

| Rate | Verbal descriptions |
| --- | --- |
| 1 | Fully alert, wide awake |
| 2 | Very lively, responsive but not at peak |
| 3 | Okay, somewhat fresh |
| 4 | A little tired, less than fresh |
| 5 | Moderately tired, let down |
| 6 | Extremely tired, very difficult to concentrate |
| 7 | Completely exhausted, unable to function effectively |

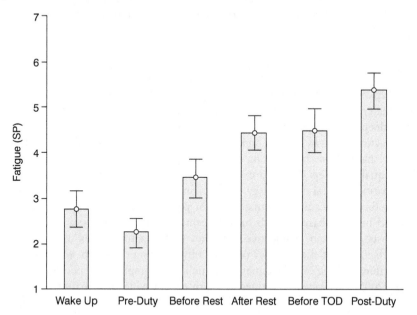

*Figure 10.1* Means and 95% confidence intervals of mean scores on the seven-point SP Fatigue Scale

Note: Scores of 36 pilots at wake up pre-flight, before and after in-flight rest, five minutes before top of descent and post duty (Simons *et al.*, 2009)

*Table 10.3* KSS 9 sleepiness scale

| Rating | Verbal descriptions |
| --- | --- |
| 1 | Extremely alert |
| 2 | Very alert |
| 3 | Alert |
| 4 | Rather alert |
| 5 | Neither alert nor sleepy |
| 6 | Some signs of sleepiness |
| 7 | Sleepy, but no effort to keep alert |
| 8 | Sleepy, some effort to keep alert |
| 9 | Very sleepy, great effort to keep alert, fighting sleep |

scale was modified by Reyner & Horne (1998) by adding descriptions to the two extra scores, which facilitates the interpretation and analysis of the scale. The KSS has been extensively used in studies of shift workers, driver fatigue, and aircrew (Harma *et al.*, 2002; Gillberg, 1998; Reyner & Horne, 1998; Spencer & Robertson, 2004; Simons *et al.*, 2009). The KSS, as modified by Reyner & Horne (1998), is currently the method of choice of most researchers of subjective sleepiness in an aviation environment.

### Subjective sleep measures: sleep and activity logs

In sleep research, subjects keep a sleep diary to record their bedtime, sleep onset latency, wake up time, get up time, number of awakenings, and estimated total sleep time together with operational data, such as duty times. Diaries are practical in field studies and may identify gross changes in the sleep and activity pattern, such as a long sleep latency, early awakening, and impaired sleep quality. Sleep diaries are cheap compared to objective forms of sleep monitoring. Digital diaries (e.g. on a personal digital assistant, iPad, or iPhone) are preferred, because information from paper diaries needs to be manually entered into databases, which may take much time, and analysis of diary data has costs associated. Subjective estimates of the actual times of sleep onset and offset, and of the number of awakenings during the sleep, are sometimes unreliable, making objective methods, such as actigraphy, indispensable (Signal *et al.*, 2005). However, the questionnaire can provide information about the perception of the sleep in terms of how refreshing or recuperative it has been, and this cannot yet be inferred from objective assessment methods. Analysis of the TNO Sleep and Alertness database showed that subjective estimation of the time spent in bed correlated strongly with actigraphy data on sleep duration ($r=.90$ $p<.001$). It also showed that the diary data are a useful check for the reliability and interpretation of objective methods, such as actigraphy. Diaries and actigraphy are frequently used as complementary methods in field studies (e.g. Valk *et al.*, 2003; Signal *et al.*, 2005; Simons *et al.*, 2011). Diaries alone are a cheap way to gather information on the average amount of sleep obtained by groups of crewmembers.

As part of a sleep diary, a sleep quality rating scale can be used. The Groningen Sleep Quality Scale (GSQS) is an example of such rating scale (Leppämäki *et al.*, 2003). The GSQS was developed and validated by the University of Groningen (Mulder-Hajonides van der Meulen *et al.*, 1980). It has been extensively used in studies on the sleep quality of maritime pilots, bus drivers, aircrew, and patients with depressive illness. The result of the GSQS is a score from 0 to 14, where 0 signifies the optimum and 14 the poorest quality. The score enables to determine gradations of the quality of sleep. Subjects have to complete the GSQS 15 minutes after waking up. The GSQS is well-validated and brings a large database including results of diverse populations. This database greatly enables interpretation of results. The GSQS has been used in a variety of studies on sleep disturbances among airline and helicopter pilots (Valk & Simons, 1998; Simons & Valk, 1998; Valk *et al.*, 2003; Simons *et al.*, 2011).

### Objective sleep and sleepiness measures

*Polysomnography (PSG)*

PSG is the accepted gold standard for objectively monitoring sleep and is currently the only method that gives reliable information on the internal structure of sleep and on sleep quality. However, the relationship of PSG data with subjectively experienced sleep quality is ambiguous. PSG involves sticking removable electrodes to the scalp and face and connecting them to a recording device, to measure three different types of electrical activity: 1) brainwaves (electro-encephalogram or EEG); 2) eye movements (electro-oculogram or EOG); and 3) muscle tone (electro-myogram or EMG) (see Figure 10.2). In addition to monitoring sleep, polysomnography can be used to monitor waking alertness, based on the dominant frequencies in the brainwaves, and patterns of involuntary slow rolling eye movements that accompany sleep onset. When it is important to be certain about the amount and type of sleep that crewmembers are obtaining, polysomnographic monitoring is the most trusted method. However, PSG is mainly used in laboratory settings and difficult to use in larger field studies and assessments over longer time periods, due its cost, the technical expertise required, the degree of compliance required by the subjects, and the inconvenience. For in-flight recordings, such as shown in Figure 10.2, the electrical contacts need to be checked periodically to assure sufficient impedance of the electrodes and to make sure that the signals are still clean. Therefore, EEG methods involve the presence of a technician or researcher on the flight deck, which is costly and may interfere with the study results (e.g. pilot's interactions with the accompanying researcher may mitigate sleepiness). Another drawback of PSG is that the

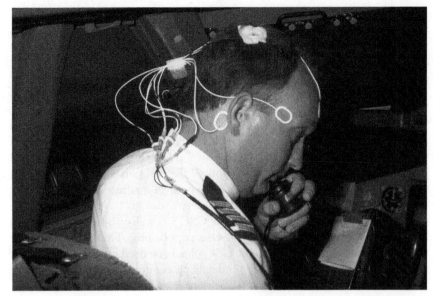

*Figure 10.2* In-flight recording of electro-encephalogram and electro-oculogram

currently accepted standard for analysing polysomnography is to have a trained sleep scoring technician work through the entire recording to decide for each 30 second epochs whether the crewmember was awake, or in which stage of sleep he/she spent most of these 30 seconds. For quality assurance, it is usual to have a second trained technician score at least some of the records to check the reliability of scoring between the two technicians. This is time-consuming and relatively expensive. A number of groups are working on automated scoring systems for polysomnography, but as yet none of these are widely accepted by the sleep research and sleep medicine communities. There have been a number of studies of flight crew sleep that have used polysomnography and these have provided useful information on states of extreme sleepiness (micro-sleeps) and the sleep stages pilots had during their onboard rest (e.g. Rosekind *et al.*, 1992; Simons *et al.*, 1994; Signal *et al.*, 2005).

*Actigraphy*

As is shown in Figure 10.3, an actigraph is a small device, similar to a wristwatch, worn on the wrist that contains an accelerometer to measure movement along the X, Y, and Z axes and a memory chip to store 'activity counts' at regular time intervals (e.g. one minute epochs). Depending on the amount of memory available, they can be worn for weeks to months before the data are to be downloaded to a computer for analysis. There are several manufacturers of actigraph devices, and each type comes with custom software that scans through the activity record and decides (based on a validated algorithm), whether the person was asleep or awake in each recorded epoch. Some devices have light

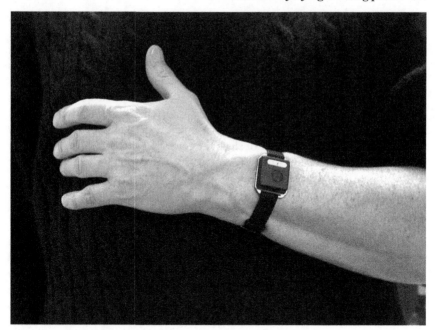

*Figure 10.3* Wrist-worn actigraph for ambulant sleep monitoring

sensors and some also have a regular watch face so that the wearer does not need to wear a normal watch as well, to keep track of time.

Actigraphs are small and unobtrusive to wear, and actigraphy is cheap compared to polysomnography. Not all actigraphs on the market have been validated by comparing their algorithms for estimating sleep quantity and quality with polysomnography, and some have not yet been demonstrated to be robust and reliable for sleep monitoring during flight operations. Battery life can be a problem in some devices. At present, the accepted standard for analysing actigraphy records is to use a sleep diary to identify when a crewmember was trying to sleep (as opposed to just sitting still or not wearing the actigraph). The sections of the record where the crewmember was trying to sleep are then analysed for sleep duration and quality (activity during sleep, fragmentation of sleep). It is generally claimed that estimates of sleep and nap times made from the actigraph agree closely with estimates made from PSG. However, the sleep latency measured by actigraphy depends on the investigator's definition of exactly when sleep starts. The main limitation of actigraphy is that it monitors activity (not sleep) and it cannot distinguish between someone being asleep versus being awake but not moving.

Some investigators report actigraphy data simply as activity counts. However, different devices, different data collection strategies, and different scoring algorithms produce very different counts for the same activity (Gorny & Spiro, 2001). These differences have made direct comparisons between the various studies difficult and contentious. Although relative changes in activity can be valuable, more direct comparisons following computer processing of the data (such as sleep/wake scoring) are more meaningful (Ancoli-Israel *et al.*, 2003). Inspection of the record indicates the times of sleep and naps and assessment of these times has often been the main aim of the study. This applies to pilots working at night or having undertaken time-zone transitions.

Actigraphy is useful for obtaining objective records of the sleep/wake patterns of crewmembers across multiple days. This is currently the most practical and reliable way to look at whether pilots accumulate a sleep debt across their duty roster, compared to the amount of sleep they average when off duty. Actigraphy can also provide useful information on recovery sleep after a trip (e.g. Spencer & Robertson, 1999; Carvalho Bos *et al.*, 2003; Signal *et al.*, 2005).

### Assessment of sleepiness

For clinical evaluations of increased sleep propensity (e.g. daytime sleepiness in patients with obstructive sleep apnoea), sleepiness can be objectively assessed using the Multiple Sleep Latency Test (MSLT; e.g. Carskadon *et al.*, 1986; Arand *et al.*, 2005). This is one of the first and still most widely used measures of objective sleep propensity. The MSLT consists of four to five nap opportunities (sessions) at two hour intervals across the day, beginning an hour and a half to three hours after waking up. Each session includes 20–30 minutes of electrophysiological and electro-oculogram recordings. Subjects are asked to lie in a quiet darkened room and are encouraged to fall asleep. A mean sleep latency of 10–15 minutes is generally considered indicative of a normal to mild level of daytime sleepiness; 5–10 minutes indicative of moderate sleepiness; and less than 5 min indicative of severe or 'pathological' sleepiness (Thorpy, 1992). The Maintenance of Wakefulness Test (MWT; Mitler *et al.*, 1982) is considered as a more sensitive and valid measure of sleep propensity than the MSLT, specifically the ability to maintain wakefulness when called upon to do so, as opposed to allowing oneself to fall asleep. Subjects are asked at two-hour intervals to sit upright in bed in a quiet, darkened room and instructed to 'remain awake' for 20, 30 and 40 minutes. The time to onset of sleep is determined by means of electrophysiological criteria.

Both the MSLT and MWT need electro-encephalography to measure the onset of sleep, which is impractical and costly in field studies.

Electro-oculographic recording (EOG) of slow rolling eye movements (SREMs) is another objective method to objectively assess sleepiness. Eye movements can be recorded by using two electrodes placed on the outer canthi (ROC/A1 and LOC/A2). The criteria for SREMs are movements with an amplitude of more than 100 microV and a duration of more than 1 sec. We have applied this method in the form of the 'Stare at the Dot'-test (Åkerstedt & Gillberg, 1990) to measure sleepiness in pilots: subjects had to stare for three minutes at a dot at a distance of one metre at eye level (Simons *et al.*, 1994). Although it provides a robust and easy-to-interpret signal, it is not practical for measurement of in-flight sleepiness due to the same logistic and cost aspects that apply to in-flight EEG measurements.

For field studies, the most practical objective, but indirect, method to measure the effects of fatigue is to measure the level of alertness or vigilance by means of the Psychomotor Vigilance Task (PVT; Dinges & Powell, 1985; Balkin *et al.*, 2004), or the Vigilance and Tracking task (VigTrack; Valk *et al.*, 2004). Both methods are described in the next section.

### Objective performance measures

The complex combinations of skills needed by pilots to safely fly an aircraft can be assessed during simulated flight. Such flight simulator studies may have face validity for pilots, but have several disadvantages. Type-specific flight simulators are expensive and the test subjects have to be fully proficient to fly the simulator. Therefore, one either need to train the test subjects to fly the simulator, or one has to use pilots with a type rating for the specific simulator. Both possibilities are very expensive. Moreover, it is often difficult to define face-valid outcome variables.

A range of more simple objective performance tests are used in laboratory studies, but they usually measure very specific aspects of performance (e.g. vigilance, reaction time, short-term memory, logical reasoning, etc.). Although these tasks lack face validity in the context of a pilot's flying task, these simple performance tests are considered 'probes' or indicators of a crewmember's capacity to carry out his or her duties (e.g. whether the pilot sufficiently vigilant). Such tests can be performed in a laboratory as well as in-flight and are generally inexpensive, easy to apply, and easy to learn. Moreover, outcome variables can be clearly defined and results are easy to interpret. One should consider the following when choosing performance tests for monitoring crewmember fatigue and sleepiness during flight operations:

- How long does the test last? When crewmembers have to perform a task several times during a flight, vigilance tasks longer than 5–10 minutes tend to decrease the motivation of the crew.
- Can it be completed at multiple time points during the flight, without interfering with the pilot's duty requirements? For example, it would be unsafe to ask crewmembers to perform a test during the approach and landing. Therefore, most researchers ask the crew to take the test just before top of descent (TOD), which is before the start of the approach/ landing phase of flight.
  - Has it been validated? For example, has it been shown to be sensitive to the effects of sleep loss and the circadian sleep pressure under controlled experimental conditions?
  - What is the predictive value for more complex flying tasks?
  - Has it been used in other aviation operations, and are the data available to compare fatigue levels?

## Vigilance tasks

Vigilance tasks incorporate a low level of workload and have an arousal-decreasing effect. Therefore, they are very sensitive for the effects of sleepiness and lowered alertness. They are easy to use at multiple time points in in-flight studies (e.g. after wake up, pre-flight, before and after in-flight rest, at top of descent (just before the start of the approach for landing) and after the flight. Although these in-flight tasks take only 5 to 10 minutes to perform, crewmembers are required to be out of the operational control loop for that time; and of a two-man crew, only one pilot can do the test while the other is pilot-flying. Crewmembers are instructed to perform the task at operationally quiet time periods during the flight. Although we are interested in the level of alertness during a safety-critical phase of flight, such as landing, we ask the pilots to perform a five-minute vigilance task 10–15 minutes before top of descent (TOD), which is the flight stage after which the approach for landing is commenced. In that way, we know the level of the pilot's alertness just before he/she is engaged in the landing procedure, but not the level of alertness during the landing. A disadvantage of in-flight testing is that pilots may be distracted by operational events and this may increase the variability of performance. Pilots are, therefore, instructed to stop the test session when they are clearly aware that they are or have been distracted and start all over again later. Of course, all in-flight testing is stopped in case of operational demands needing the attention of both pilots.

### Psychomotor vigilance task (PVT)

A performance test that meets most of the above criteria is the Psychomotor Vigilance Task or PVT (Dinges & Powell, 1985; Balkin *et al.*, 2004). In the most widely used version of the PVT, the test lasts for 10 minutes and is carried out on a purpose-built hand-held device. Some studies (Balkin *et al.*, 2004) and large aviation field studies have been using a five-minute version of the PVT programmed on a personal data assistant (PDA) device. There is evidence that the PVT is sensitive to the effects of sleep deprivation (Dinges *et al.*, 1994) and alcohol (Powell *et al.*, 2001). The PVT has also been used to demonstrate the effect of circadian disturbance on sleep and performance of astronauts during space shuttle flights (Dijk *et al.*, 2001).

The psychomotor vigilance task (PVT) is a sustained-attention, reaction-timed task that measures the speed with which subjects respond to a visual stimulus. The PVT is a simple task where the subject presses a button as soon as a light appears. The light will turn on randomly every few seconds for 5–10 minutes. The main outcome variable of this task is the number of lapses of attention, i.e. how many times the button is not pressed when the light appears. Also, the reaction time can be recorded. The purpose of the PVT is to measure sustained attention, and give a numerical measure of sleepiness by counting the number of lapses in attention of the tested subject. Recently a new sensitive PVT outcome metric has been developed for determining neurobehavioural deficits from sleep loss (Basner *et al.*, 2015). The PVT does not require practice trials, except to make sure that crewmembers know how to operate the testing device. Various versions of the PVT (e.g. 5 and 10 minute versions, different stimuli, such as light, bulls-eye symbol, etc.) have been deployed in several field studies in aviation and space environments (e.g. Van den Berg *et al.*, 2015; Gander *et al.*, 2013; Basner *et al.*, 2014; Abe *et al.*, 2014; Petrilli *et al.*, 2006).

### Pilot Alertness Test

The Pilot Alertness Test was developed by Air New Zealand (Powell *et al.*, 2010). It is a sustained choice reaction time task in which a stimulus in the form of a circle is presented at pseudo-random intervals in one of four corners of the device screen. The response is to press the appropriate one of four buttons below the screen as quickly as possible; the reaction time is displayed and recorded. This test includes 100 stimulus presentations, taking around eight minutes to complete. The task is performed on a Palm Pilot on which also questionnaires and operational data can be completed. Up until now, data collected using the Pilot Alertness Test has been mainly limited to aircrew of Air New Zealand.

### Vigilance and Tracking Task (VigTrack)

The VigTrack task is a dual-task measuring vigilance performance under the continuous load of a compensatory tracking task (Valk *et al.*, 1997). The task has been successfully applied in field studies concerning effects of fatigue and sleepiness in pilots (Simons & Valk, 1998; Valk & Simons, 1998; Simons *et al.*, 2011). The sensitivity of the VigTrack for sedative effects of antihistamines or alcohol on performance has been established (Valk *et al.*, 1997; Valk *et al.*, 2004; Valk & Simons, 2009). The VigTrack is sensitive to show performance-deteriorating effects on vigilance, arousal, and effects of sleep deprivation by significant impairment of perceptuo-motor skills and signal detection. For in-flight measurements a five-minute version of the task is programmed on a PDA together with several subjective rating scales and questions about the flight operations and rosters. During the tracking task, pilots have to steer a blue disc, using a stylo, and try to position it underneath a red disc, located in the middle of the screen. The blue disc is programmed to continuously move away from its position, depending on the force input from the stylo. While performing this tracking task, participants have to perform a vigilance task. In the middle of the red disk a black square rotates. When at random intervals, a hexagon is presented instead of the square, participants have to respond as quickly as possible by pressing the 'fire button' on the PDA. For in-flight testing the duration of the test is set to five minutes (longer versions are available). Outcome variables are: root mean square (RMS) tracking error, percentage of missed targets, reaction time, and number of false reactions.

As already mentioned, the vigilance and tracking task (VigTrack) is sensitive for the effects of sleep loss, sedative medication, and alcohol. When pilots had 4–6 hours, or 6–7 hours pre-flight sleep instead of seven hours or more, the tracking component of the VigTrack performance was still significantly impaired at TOD by 33 per cent (4–6 hours sleep) and 15 per cent (6–7 hours sleep) (Valk *et al.,* 2003). Using alcohol up to a blood alcohol level of 0.05 per cent (= 0.5‰ = limit in Dutch road safety law) increased the number of missed targets in the vigilance task by 39 per cent and the tracking performance was impaired by 20 per cent.

## Complex task performance

Vigilance tasks do not measure skills such as situation awareness and decision-making. More complex tasks to measure these types of skills usually require many practice trials before they can be considered fully learnt and ready to be used for measuring changes due to fatigue. Therefore, and because these tasks often need more complex equipment, they are not commonly used in in-flight studies of cockpit crew and the use is mainly limited to laboratory situations. Many complex tasks are available. One of the few complex tasks that were used in an in-flight study (Simons *et al.*, 1994) is the Multi Attribute Task Battery (MAT) developed by NASA/Langley Research Center (Comstock & Arnegard, 1992). The MAT represents a task battery that incorporates tasks analogous to activities that aircraft crewmembers perform in-flight, while providing a high degree of experimenter control and performance data on each sub-task. Features include a system monitoring task, a tracking task, and a resource management task, which have to be performed simultaneously during 10 minutes. The MAT Battery has frequently been employed in studies of effects of sleep loss or medication on pilot performance (Valk *et al.*, 1997; Valk *et al.*, 2004), where it appeared that complex information processing, as tasked with the MAT battery, was not as sensitive for the effects of sleep loss or sedative effects of drugs as the vigilance and tracking task (VigTrack). This phenomenon might be explained by the fact that these vigilance tasks incorporate a low level of workload and have an arousal-decreasing effect. In combination with the negative effects of sleep loss or sedative compounds, alertness function and sustained attention are affected resulting in impaired performance. In contrast, complex tasks are more challenging and are characterised by a high level of workload. This increases the level of arousal, which may mask possible negative effects.

## Monitoring the circadian body clock cycle

The circadian body clock cycle is an important contributing factor to crewmember fatigue, but it is difficult to monitor during flight operations. Reliable data of the circadian cycle would be useful to improve the predictive power of bio-mathematical models for fatigue hazard identification, and might provide tools to tailor personal mitigation strategies for crewmembers (e.g. morning-types versus evening-types). In the laboratory, the cycle of the body clock is usually monitored by measuring the daily rhythm in core body temperature and/or the daily rhythm in levels of the hormone melatonin, which is secreted by the pineal gland at night. During the 1980s, a number of research teams monitored the circadian body clocks of crewmembers by tracking the rhythm of core body temperature (Gander *et al.,* 1998). This can be done with thermometers, which is logistically difficult in-flight, and by using temperature pills that are swallowed and transmit temperature measurements as they transit through the digestive system. The circadian rhythm of core body temperature has been established in resting subjects under well-controlled conditions. However, in working individuals, core temperature is affected by the level of physical activity and stress which may mask the actual circadian clock-driven component of the temperature rhythm. Therefore, core body temperature is not commonly used in studies of aircrew.

The second rhythm that is monitored to track the cycle of the circadian body clock is the level of the hormone melatonin. The secretion of melatonin peaks in the middle of the night and gradually falls during the second half of the night. Melatonin can be measured in blood or saliva samples taken at regular intervals, and its metabolites can be measured in urine samples. The collection and frozen storage of the samples during flight operations are difficult. The most complicating factor is, however, that the production of melatonin is inhibited by light and permitted by darkness. For this reason melatonin has been called the 'hormone of darkness'. Even low light levels can diminish melatonin production to some extent. If aircrew is exposed to daylight or even room light (e.g. 200 lux) during their 'biological night', melatonin secretion will stop or decrease. This makes it impossible to track the normal circadian cycle of melatonin across trips. The scarce data that have been collected of aircrew show considerable variability between individuals on the same trip patterns.

## Bio-mathematical models

A scientifically validated bio-mathematical model that has been programmed for use as a computer-based simulation tool can be used to support the identification of the fatigue hazard associated with proposed schedules. Bio-mathematical models are aimed at predicting the average fatigue hazard for groups of people, based on sleep/wake or duty history and the daily cycles in alertness and performance driven by the circadian body clock. In designing rotations or rosters, bio-mathematical models can be used to compare the various available solutions that will meet operational needs, to predict which is likely to produce the least fatigue hazard.

Model predictions should not be used in isolation to make decisions about trip and roster/schedule design, but need to be considered along with operational experience (ICAO-IATA-IFALPA, 2011). Model predictions should also be validated by monitoring actual fatigue levels where the fatigue hazard is expected to be high, or where there is a high level of uncertainty about the extent of the fatigue hazard (for example on a new type of trip that is very different from existing operations) (ICAO-IATA-IFALPA, 2011).

All bio-mathematical models contain assumptions and have limitations that need to be taken into account. Some models are (partly) based on data from scientific field studies and it should be taken into account that most of these scientific studies have used subjective ratings of fatigue and/or sleepiness. Although these methods are well validated and provide a reliable measure of subjectively perceived fatigue and/or sleepiness, they may be sensitive to 'expectation' bias; viz. one expects to become more fatigued as duty length and/or workload (number of sectors flown) increase.

Currently available models predict group averages and do not take into account the impact of workload or personal and work-related stressors that may affect flight crew fatigue levels. They predict the average level of crewmember fatigue that might be expected across an operation. Only few available models take into account the effects of countermeasures that may be in use (e.g. improved rest facilities, crew augmentation, etc.). It is particularly important to recognise that current bio-mathematical models do not predict the safety risk that fatigued crewmembers represent in a particular operation, i.e., they are not a substitute for risk assessment (ICAO-IATA-IFALPA, 2011).

A two process model of sleep regulation (Borbély, 1982; Daan *et al.*, 1984) is at the core of many models addressing the regulation of fatigue and performance. These models capture two key biological processes: a homeostatic process balancing wakefulness and sleep, and a circadian process tracking time of day. These two processes interact to determine fatigue, thereby modulating attention and cognitive functioning over time. Other factors that contribute to fatigue, such as anxiety, illness, workload, and distractions, are typically not included in bio-mathematical models of fatigue.

A range of bio-mathematical models have been commercialised and are marketed as tools for predicting fatigue hazards related to scheduling. Some examples are SAFE (System for Aircrew Fatigue Evaluation – Belyavin & Spencer, 2004); SAFTE/FAST (Sleep, Activity, Fatigue, and Task Effectiveness – Hursh *et al.*, 2004); CAS (Circadian Alertness Simulator – Moore-Ede *et al.*, 2004); FAID (Fatigue Audit InterDyne – Roach *et al.*, 2004); TPM (Three Process Model of Alertness – Ingre *et al.*, 2014) and the Boeing Alertness Model (BAM) which is built on the TPM and extended with advanced sleep prediction, task load, and crew augmentation.

Each model has its advantages and disadvantages, of which a detailed discussion is beyond the scope of this chapter (see Mallis *et al.*, 2004, for an overview). Which model is best fit for specific airline operations, depends on the specific character and needs of the airline.

## The contribution of fatigue to safety events

As has been mentioned in the introduction, there is no simple formula for evaluating the contribution of pilot fatigue to a safety event. For the purposes of fatigue risk management, the aim is to identify how the effects of fatigue could have been mitigated, in order to reduce the likelihood of similar occurrences in the future. Basic information can be collected for all fatigue reports and safety events, with more in-depth analyses reserved for events where it is more likely that fatigue was an important factor and/or where the outcomes were more severe. To establish that fatigue was a contributing factor in an event, it has to be shown that the pilot or crew was in a fatigued state and took particular actions or decisions that were causal for the safety event. It should also be considered that those actions or decisions are consistent with the type of behaviour expected of a fatigued crewmember. In that context, the Canadian Transportation Safety Board produced guidelines for fatigue analysis in which they suggest four initial questions to decide whether or not fatigue was a contributing factor to an event (TSB Canada, 1997):

1  At what time of day did the occurrence take place?
2  Was the crewmember's normal circadian rhythm disrupted?
3  How many hours had the crewmember been awake at the time of the occurrence?
4  Does the 72-hour sleep history suggest a sleep debt?

If the answer to any one of these questions indicates a problem, then fatigue should be investigated in greater depth.

In most cases, accidents are caused by a complex interaction of operational, environmental, and human factors. Therefore, it is often difficult to exactly specify the contribution of fatigue to an accident, which is shown by the following example (National Transportation Safety Board, 2008, p. viii).

> On February 18, 2007, about 15:06 eastern standard time, Delta Connection Flight 6448, an Embraer ERJ-170, N862RW, operated by Shuttle America, Inc., was landing on runway 28 at Cleveland Hopkins International Airport, Cleveland, Ohio, during snow conditions when it overran the end of the runway, contacted an instrument landing system (ILS) antenna, and struck an airport perimeter fence. The airplane's nose gear collapsed during the overrun. Of the 2 flight crewmembers, 2 flight attendants, and 71 passengers on board, 3 passengers received minor injuries. The airplane received substantial damage from the impact forces.

The National Transportation Safety Board (2008) determined that the probable cause of this accident was the failure of the flight crew to execute a missed approach when visual cues for the runway were not distinct and identifiable. Contributing to the accident were (1) the crew's decision to descend to the ILS decision height instead of the localiser (glideslope out) minimum descent altitude; (2) the first officer's long landing on a short contaminated runway and the crew's failure to use reverse thrust and braking to their maximum effectiveness; (3) the captain's fatigue, which affected his ability to effectively plan for and monitor the approach and landing; and (4) Shuttle America's failure to administer an attendance policy that permitted flight crewmembers to call in as fatigued without fear of reprisals.

The captain had slept only one out of the past 32 hours, and he did not advise his company of his fatigued state, nor did he attempt to take himself off of the trip because he had been notified by his company that he had used an excessive number of sick calls and that if he used more he could be subjected to discipline, including termination. He had asked the first officer to be the flying pilot for the flight. The first officer reported that he would have preferred not to be the flying pilot because he had just completed a 3-day, 6-leg trip sequence but that he agreed to be the flying pilot because of the captain's references to fatigue and lack of sleep the night before. (The first officer did not verbalise this preference to the captain before the flight.)

(National Transportation Safety Board, 2008, pp. 8–12)

The probable cause was something along the lines of the captain's faulty decision to continue this approach. But contributing to the probable cause was the captain's fatigue, which affected his ability to effectively plan for and monitor the approach and landing, and also the company's failure to administer an attendance policy that permitted crew members to call in as fatigued without fear of reprisals.

## Management of fatigue risks

Because it is generally recognised that pilot fatigue is a threat to aviation safety and health of pilots, mitigating and reducing fatigue risks is a major task for the aviation industry. The traditional regulatory approach to managing crewmember fatigue has been to prescribe limits on maximum daily, monthly, and yearly flight and duty hours, and require minimum breaks within and between duty periods (Flight Time Limitations, FTL regulations). The approach reflects understanding that long unbroken periods of work could produce fatigue (known as 'time-on-task' fatigue), and that sufficient time is needed to recover from work demands and to attend to non-work aspects of life. Nowadays, the limitations of this approach are recognised and attention is also paid to other causes of fatigue in addition to time-on-task: the importance of adequate sleep for restoring and maintaining all aspects of waking function; and the daily cycle of the circadian biological clock that drives the ability to perform mental and physical work, and the ability to fall asleep and stay asleep. These insights have led to new ways to manage fatigue risks of which a fatigue risk management system (FRMS), as developed and recommended by ICAO, IATA, and IFALPA, offers a very promising method to ensure that aircrew is sufficiently alert so they can operate to a safe level of performance. ICAO defines an FRMS as

A data-driven means of continuously monitoring and managing fatigue-related safety risks, based upon scientific principles and knowledge as well as operational experience that aims to ensure relevant personnel are performing at adequate levels of alertness.

(ICAO-IATA-IFALPA, 2011)

For management of fatigue risks of pilots at company level, an FRMS in addition to basic Flight and Duty Time Limitations prescribed by the authorities may offer the best possibility to keep fatigue levels of most pilots within safe limits. The aim of the FRMS approach is to reduce the fatigue risks for all pilots working for the airline in question or flying the specific routes and rosters concerned. According to the ICAO-IATA-IFALPA guidelines, implementation of an FRMS needs the formation of a fatigue risk management team in which management, schedulers, crewmembers, and other specialists (as required) work together. The first task of such a team is to identify potential fatigue hazards; then assess fatiguing rotations, rosters, and practices; next estimate the risks associated with the identifiable hazards; and then mitigate risk (adapt rosters/ rotations, use countermeasures) in conjunction with stakeholders. Thereafter the reduction of risk has to be monitored and evaluated.

The fatigue risk management team should also provide procedures and training concerning fatigue risk awareness, sleep hygiene, personal countermeasures, and a healthy lifestyle. Personal countermeasures include pursuing at least seven to eight hours pre-flight sleep, utilising available time for pre-flight or in-flight power naps, sensible use of caffeine, and personal strategies to cope with time zone crossing.

In addition to the FRMS approach, managers, colleague pilots, instructors, and aeromedical doctors should be alert to identify individual cases of pilots who have difficulty coping with job stresses, life stresses, and/or health problems. As such problems may lead to severe fatigue, sleep problems, and mental health issues, these pilots need personal care and support to keep them healthy and safely flying. In that context, it should be considered what the cause of the problems is and whether specialist expertise (psychologist, psychiatrist) and/or peer support is needed.

# References

Abe T, Mollicone D, Basner M, & Dinges DF. (2014). Sleepiness and safety: where biology needs technology. *Sleep and Biological Rhythms*, 12(2):74–84.

Åkerstedt T. (1998). Shift work and disturbed sleep/wakefulness. *Sleep Medicine Reviews*, 2(2):117–28.

Åkerstedt T. (2000). Consensus statement: fatigue and accidents in transport operations. *Journal of Sleep Research*, 9:395.

Åkerstedt T, & Gillberg M. (1990). Subjective and objective sleepiness in the active individual. *International Journal of Neuroscience*, 52:29–37.

Ancoli-Israel S, Cole R, Alessi C, Chambers M, Moorcroft M, & Pollak CP. (2003). The role of actigraphy in the study of sleep and circadian rhythms. *Sleep*, 26(3): 342–92.

Arand D, Bonnet M, Hurwitz T, Mitler M, Rosa R, & Sangal RB. (2005). The clinical use of the MSLT and MWT. *Sleep*, 28(1):123–44.

Baker A, Heiler K, & Ferguson SA (2003). The impact of roster changes on absenteeism and incident frequency in an Australian coal mine. *Occupational and Environmental Medicine*, 60:43–9.

Balkin TJ, Bliese PD, Belenky G, *et al.* (2004). Comparative utility of instruments for monitoring sleepiness-related performance decrements in the operational environment. *Journal of Sleep Research,* 13:219–27.

Basner M, Dinges DF, Mollicone DJ, *et al.* (2014). Psychological and behavioral changes during confinement in a 520–day simulated interplanetary mission to mars. *PLoS One,* 9(3):e93298.

Basner M, Mcguire S, Goel N, Rao H, & Dinges DF. (2015). A new likelihood ratio metric for the psychomotor vigilance test and its sensitivity to sleep loss. *Journal of Sleep Research,* 24(6):702–13.

Belyavin AJ, & Spencer MB. (2004). Modeling performance and alertness: the QinetiQ approach. *Aviation, Space and Environmental Medicine,* 75(3 Suppl):A93–103.

Borbély AA. (1982). A two process model of sleep regulation. *Human Neurobiology,* 1:195–204.

Bourgeois-Bougrine S, Cabon P, Mollard R, Coblentz A, & Speyer JJ (2003). Fatigue in aircrew from short-haul flights in civil aviation: the effects of work schedules. *Human Factors and Aerospace Safety,* 3(2):177–87.

CAA UK. (2005). *Aircrew fatigue: a review of research undertaken on behalf of the UK Civil Aviation Authority.* CAA Paper 2005/04. Norwich: The Stationery Office.

Caldwell JA, & Gilreath SR. (2002). A survey of aircrew fatigue in a sample of U.S. Army aviation personnel. *Aviation, Space and Environmental Medicine,* 73:472–80.

Carskadon MA, & Dement WC. (1981). Cumulative effects of sleep restriction on daytime sleepiness. *Psychophysiology,* 18:107–13.

Carskadon MA, & Dement WC. (1982). Nocturnal determinants of daytime sleepiness. *Sleep,* 5:S73–81.

Carskadon MA, Dement WC, Mitler MM, Roth T, Westbrook PR, & Keenan S. (1986). Guidelines for the multiple sleep latency test (MSLT): a standard measure of sleepiness. *Sleep,* 9(4):519–24.

Carvalho Bos S, Waterhouse J, Edwards B, Simons R, & Reilly T. (2003). The use of actimetry to assess changes to the rest-activity cycle. *Chronobiology International,* 20(6):1039–59.

Co EL, Gregory KB, Johnson JM, & Rosekind MR. (1999). *Crew factors in flight operations XI: a survey of fatigue factors in regional airline operations.* Report no NASA/TM-1999–208799. Moffett Field, CA: NASA-AMES Research Center.

Comstock JR, & Arnegard RJ. (1992). *The multi-attribute task battery for human operator workload and strategic behavior research.* NASA Technical Memorandum 104174. Retrieved 22 December 2015 from http://matb.larc.nasa.gov/files/2014/03/Comstock-Arnegard-Original-TM.pdf

Daan S, Beersma DGM, & Borbély AA. (1984). Timing of human sleep: recovery process gated by a circadian pacemaker. *American Journal of Physiology,* 246:R161–78.

Dijk DJ, Neri DF, Wyatt JK, *et al.* (2001). Sleep, performance, circadian rhythms, and light-dark cycles during two space shuttle flights. *American Journal of Physiology Regulatory, Integrative and Comparative Physiology,* 281(5):R1657–64.

Dinges DF, & Powell JP. (1985). Microcomputer analysis of performance on a portable, simple visual RT task during sustained operation. *Behavior Research Methods, Instruments, and Computing,* 17:652–5.

Dinges DF, Douglas SD, Zaugg L, *et al.* (1994). Leukocytosis and natural killer cell function parallel neurobehavioral fatigue induced by 64 hours of sleep deprivation. *Journal of Clinical Investigation,* 93:1930–9.

Dinges DF, Pack F, Williams K, *et al.* (1997). Cumulative sleepiness, mood disturbance, and psychomotor vigilance performance decrements during a week of sleep restricted to 4–5 hours per night. *Sleep*, 20(4):267–7.

ECA (European Cockpit Association). (2012). 4 of 5 pilots suffer from fatigue while flying. Retrieved 30 November 2015 from https://www.eurocockpit.be/sites/default/files/ftl_en_dive_12_1108.pdf

ECA (European Cockpit Association). (2015). *Fatigue in accidents.* Retrieved 15 November 2015 from: https://www.eurocockpit.be/pages/fatigue-in-accidents

Eriksen CA, Åkerstedt T, & Nilsson JP. (2006). Fatigue in trans-Atlantic airline operations: diaries and actigraphy for two- vs. three-pilot crews. *Aviation, Space, and Environmental Medicine*, 77:605–12.

Gander PH, Mulrine HM, Van den Berg MJ, *et al.* (2014). Pilot fatigue: relationships with departure and arrival times, flight duration, and direction. *Aviation, Space, and Environmental Medicine*, 85:833–40.

Gander PH, Signal TL, van den Berg MJ, *et al.* (2013). In-flight sleep, pilot fatigue and Psychomotor Vigilance Task performance on ultra-long range versus long range flights. *Journal of Sleep Research*, 22(6):697–706.

Gander PH, Gregory KB, Miller DL, Rosekind MR, Connell LJ, & Graeber RC. (1998). Flight crew fatigue V: long-haul air transport operations. *Aviation, Space, and Environmental Medicine,* 69:B37–48.

Gillberg M. (1998). Subjective alertness and sleep quality in connection with permanent 12-hour day and night shifts. *Scandinavian Journal of Work & Environmental Health* 24 (Suppl 3):76–80.

Gillberg M, Kecklund G, & Åkerstedt T. (1994). Relations between performance and subjective ratings of sleepiness during a night awake. *Sleep* 17(3):236–41.

Goode JH. (2003). Are pilots at risk of accidents due to fatigue? *Journal of Safety Research*, 34:309–13.

Gorny SW, & Spiro JR. (2001). Comparing different methodologies used in wrist actigraphy. *Sleep Review*, Summer:40–2.

Graeber RC. (1986). Sleep and wakefulness in international aircrews. *Aviation Space and Environmental Medicine*, 57:B1–64.

Harma M, Sallinen M, Ranta R, Mutanen P, & Muller K. (2002). The effect of an irregular shift system on sleepiness at work in train drivers and railway traffic controllers. *Journal of Sleep Research* 11(2):141–51.

Hoddes E, Zarcone V, Smythe H, Philips R, & Dement WC. (1973). Quantification of sleepiness: a new approach. *Psychophysiology*, 10:431–6.

Horne JA, & Wilkinson RT. (1985). Chronic sleep reduction: daytime vigilance performance and EEG measures of sleepiness with particular reference to practise effects. *Psychophysiology*, 22:69–78.

Hursh SR, Redmond DP, Johnson ML, *et al.* (2004). Fatigue models for applied research in warfighting. *Aviation, Space, and Environmental Medicine*, 75(3,Suppl.):A44–53.

ICAO-IATA-IFALPA. (2011). *Fatigue Risk Management System (FRMS) Implementation guide for operators.* Retrieved 28 November 2015 from http://www.icao.int/safety/fatiguemanagement/frms%20tools/frms%20implementation%20guide%20for%20operators%20july%202011.pdf

Ingre M, Van Leeuwen W, Klemets T, *et al.* (2014). Validating and extending the three process model of alertness in airline operations. *PLoS ONE* 9(10):e108679.

Jackson CA, & Earl L. (2006). Prevalence of fatigue among commercial pilots. *Occupational Medicine (London),* 56(4):263–8.

Johns MW. (1994). Sleepiness in different situations measured by the Epworth Sleepiness Scale. *Sleep,* 17:703–10

Leppämäki S, Meesters Y, Haukka J, Lönnqvist J, & Partonen T. (2003). Effect of simulated dawn on quality of sleep – a community-based trial. *BMC Psychiatry,* 3:14. http://www.biomedcentral.com/1471-244X/3/14

Lowden A, & Åkerstedt T. (1998). Sleep and wake patterns in aircrew on a 2-day layover on westward long distance flights. *Aviation, Space and Environmental Medicine,* 69(6): 596–602.

Mallis MM, Mejdal S, Nguyen TT, & Dinges DF. (2004). Summary of the key features of seven biomathematical models of human fatigue and performance. *Aviation, Space, and Environmental Medicine,* 75:A4–14.

Mitler MM, Gujavarty KS, & Browman CP. (1982). Maitenance of wakefulness test: a polysomnographic technique for evaluating treatment efficacy in patients with excessive somnolence. *Electorencephalography & Clinical Neurophysiology,* 53:658–61.

Moore-Ede M, Heitmann A, Croke D, et al. (2004). Circadian alertness simulator for fatigue risk assessment in transportation: application to reduce frequency and severity of truck accidents. *Aviation, Space, and Environmental Medicine* 2004, 75(3,Suppl.):A107–18.

Mulder-Hajonides van der Meulen WREH, Wijnberg JR, Hollander JJ, De Diana IPF, & van den Hoofdakker RH. (1980). Measurement of subjective sleep quality. *European Sleep Research Society* (abstr.), 5:98.

National Transportation Safety Board. (2008). *Runway overrun during landing, Shuttle America, Inc., doing business as Delta connection flight 6448, Embraer ERJ-170, N862RW, Cleveland, Ohio, February 18, 2007.* Aircraft Accident Report NTSB/AAR-08/01. Washington, DC: NTSB.

Pascoe PA, Johnson MK, Montgomery JM, Robertson KA, & Spencer MB. (1994). *Sleep in rest facilities onboard aircraft: questionnaire studies.* IAM Report no 778. Farnborough: RAF Institute of Aviation Medicine.

Perelli LP. (1980). *Fatigue stressors in simulated long-duration flight.* Technical Report 80–49. Brooks AFB, TX: USAF School of Aerospace Medicine.

Petrie KJ, & Dawson AG. (1997). Symptoms of fatigue and coping strategies in international pilots. *International Journal of Aviation Psychology,* 7:251–8.

Petrie KJ, Powell D, & Broadbent E. (2004). Fatigue self-management strategies and reported fatigue in international pilots. *Ergonomics,* 47(5):461–8.

Petrilli RM, Roach GD, Dawson D, & Lamond N. (2006). The sleep, subjective fatigue, and sustained attention of commercial airline pilots during an international pattern. *Chronobiology International,* 23(6):1357–62.

Powell DM, Spencer MB, Holland D, Broadbent E, & Petrie KJ. (2007). Pilot fatigue in short-haul operations: effects of number of sectors, duty length and time of day. *Aviation, Space, and Environmental Medicine,* 78:698–701.

Powell DMC, Spencer MB, & Petrie KJ. (2010). Fatigue in airline pilots after an additional day's layover period. *Aviation, Space, and Environmental Medicine,* 81:1013–7.

Powell DMC, Spencer MB, & Petrie KJ. (2011). Automated collection of fatigue ratings at the top of descent: a practical commercial airline tool. *Aviation, Space, and Environmental Medicine,* 82:1037–41.

Powell NB, Schechtman KB, Riley RW, Li K, Troell R, & Guilleminault C. (2001). The road to danger: the comparative risks of driving while sleepy. *Laryngoscope,* 111:887–93.

Reyner LA, & Horne JA. (1998). Evaluation of 'in-car' countermeasures to sleepiness: cold air and radio. *Sleep,* 21(1):46–50.

Roach GD, Fletcher A, & Dawson D. (2004). A model to predict work-related fatigue based on hours of work. *Aviation, Space, and Environmental Medicine*, 75(3, Suppl.):A61–9.

Robertson KA, & Spencer MB. (2003). *Aircrew alertness on night operations: an interim report.* QinetiQ Report No. QINETIQ/KI/CHS/CR021911/1.0. London: QinetiQ.

Rogers AS, Spencer MB, & Stone BM (1999). *Validation and development of a method for assessing the risks arising from mental fatigue.* HSE Contract Research Report 254/1999. London: HSE.

Rosekind MR, Graeber RC, Dinges DF, Connell LJ, Rountree M, & Gillen KA. (1992). *Crew factors in flight operations: IX. Effects of cockpit rest on crew performance and alertness in long-haul operations.* NASA Technical Memorandum Report No. 103884. Moffett Field, CA: NASA Ames Research Center.

Samel, A., & Wegmann, H.M. (1993). Extended range operations – a review of recent developments. *Recent advances in long range and long endurance operation of aircraft* (pp. 16/1–16/10). Neuilly-sur-Seine: NATO-AGARD.

Samel A, Wegmann HM, Vejvoda M, Drescher J, Gundel A, *et al.* (1997). Two-crew operations: stress and fatigue during long-haul night flights. *Aviation, Space, and Environmental Medicine*, 68:679–87.

Samn SW, & Perelli LP. (1982). *Estimating aircrew fatigue: a technique with implications to airlift operations.* Technical Report No. SAM-TR-82–21. Brooks AFB, TX: USAF School of Aerospace Medicine.

Signal TL, Gale J, & Gander PH. (2005). Sleep measurement in flight crew: comparing actigraphic and subjective estimates of sleep with polysomnography. *Aviation Space and Environmental Medicine*, 76(11):1058–63.

Simons M, & Valk PJL. (1998). *Early starts: effects on sleep, alertness, and vigilance.* AGARD-CP-599, Neuilly-sur-Seine: NATO-AGARD.

Simons M, Valk PJL, de Ree JJD, Veldhuijzen van Zanten OBA, & D'Huyvetter K. (1994). *Quantity and quality of onboard and layover sleep: effects on crew performance and alertness.* Report RD-31-94. Soesterberg: Netherlands Aerospace Medical Centre.

Simons R, Wilschut E, & Valk P. (2009). Extended flight duty periods: method to assess alertness-related flight safety. Paper presented at 2009 International Conference on Fatigue Management in Transportation Operations: A Framework for Progress. March 24–26, Boston, MA. Retrieved 28 December 2015 from http://depts.washington.edu/uwconf/fmto/FatigueManagementAbstracts.pdf

Simons R, Wilschut ES, & Valk PJL. (2011). Sleep and alertness in North Sea helicopter pilots. *Aviation Space Environmental Medicine*, 82(7):704–10.

Spencer MB, & Robertson KA. (1999). *The Haj operation: alertness of aircrew on return flight between Indonesia and Saudi Arabia.* DERA Report No. DERA/CHS/PPD/CR980207/1.0, Farnborough: DERA.

Spencer MB, & Robertson KA. (2002). *Aircrew alertness during short-haul operations, including the impact of early starts.* QinetiQ Report No. QINETIQ/CHS/PPD/CRO10406/1.0, Farnborough: QinetiQ.

Spencer MB, & Robertson KA. (2004). *Aircrew alertness on the Singapore–Los Angeles route: final report.* QinetiQ Report No. QINETIQ/KI/CHS/CR050022/1.0, Farnborough: QinetiQ.

Spencer MB, Wilson AL, & Bunting AJ. (1998). *The CHS Alertness Model and the prediction of performance.* DERA Report No. DERA/CHS/PPD/CR980191. Farnborough: DERA.

Thorpy MJ. (1992). The clinical use of the multiple sleep latency test, *Sleep* 15:268–76.

Transportation Safety Board of Canada. (1997). *A guide for investigating for fatigue*. Gatineau, Quebec: Transportation Safety Board of Canada.

Valk PJL, & Simons M. (1998). *Pros and cons of strategic napping on long haul flights*. AGARD-CP-599 (pp. 5–1/5–5), Neuilly-sur-Seine: NATO-AGARD.

Valk PJL, & Simons M. (2009). Effects of Loratadine/Montelukast on vigilance and alertness task performance in a simulated cabin environment. *Advances in Therapy*, 26(1):89–98.

Valk PJ, Simons M, Struyvenberg PA, Kruit H, & Van Berge Henegouwen MT. (1997). Effects of a single dose of Loratadine on flying ability under conditions of simulated cabin pressure. *American Journal of Rhinology*, 11:27–33.

Valk PJL, Simons M, Goei JH, & van Hijum SM. (2003). Evaluation of the fit-to-fly checklist on long haul and short haul flights. *Proceedings 15th EASS – FSF & ERA Conference "Change: A safety Challenge"*, March, Geneva, Switzerland (pp. 9–16). Alexandria, VA:. Flight Safety Foundation.

Valk PJL, vanRoon DB, Simons RM, & Rikken G. (2004). Desloratadine shows no effect on performance during 6h at 8000 ft simulated cabin altitude. *Aviation, Space, and Environmental Medicine*, 75(5):433–8.

Van den Berg MJ, Signal TL, Mulrine HM, Smith AA, Gander PH, & Serfontein W. (2015). Monitoring and managing cabin crew sleep and fatigue during an ultra-long range trip. *Aerospace Medicine & Human Performance*, 86(8):705–13.

Wilkinson RT, Edwards RS, & Haines E. (1966). Performance following a night of reduced sleep. *Psychonomic Science*, 5(12):471–2.

# 11 Assessment following incidents, accidents and trauma

*Morten Kjellesvig*

This chapter is based on the author's own experience after having investigated 11 accidents and interviewed many crewmembers after the accident. The assessment of the human factor (HF) issue is very difficult and after accidents and incidents pilots, mechanics and ATC controllers can become greatly disturbed, or sometimes the opposite is the case where they are apparently not affected at all.

An investigator has to be alert to the state of mind the pilot, mechanics and ATC controllers are in and conduct the interview accordingly. After an accident there are also many technical investigations that have to be done. This chapter will cover the aspects of an interview and the assessments following incidents, accidents and trauma.

The interview of pilots is probably the best way to understand what happened. The importance of an interview can vary (Wood & Sweginnis 2006) based on the incident or accident. After an accident there is plenty of evidence for the investigators, however identifying which facts are significant can be hard to identify. With a properly performed interview a lot of clues can be explored and all the pieces of evidence will fall in place.

As mentioned, the interview is very important and when there are survivors or witnesses they can be of great help. Witnesses are very keen to help, they have seen or witnessed something and they will share what they remember to the best of their ability. However, psychologists estimate (Wood & Sweginnis 2006) that as interviewers we are only able to recover about 30 per cent of what a witness knows. In accordance with ICAO Annex 13, it is not the purpose of this activity to apportion blame or liability. The performance, style, and atmosphere you create as an interviewer is important. The following factors should be taken into account when interviewing witnesses to an accident or incident:

- *Be well prepared:* know a little about the witness, where the witness was when the accident happened and be prepared with topics you want to have the answers for.
- *Set the tone:* it is very important to allow for the witness to feel welcome. When starting an interview mention something about the background

for the investigation, have some food or drinks available and bring paper to make sketches on or even models of the aircraft. Once the tone is set, ask the witness to tell his story, without interruption, his words of what happened. Once you start asking questions you limit the witness to the questions you have been clever enough to figure out, not what the witness actually experienced. By letting the witness speak freely he will explore what he remembers, not what you could figure out. Tact and diplomacy is very important because if you step in the wrong direction you block the communication. As an example for one case, an investigation was mounted after a crew experienced an engine failure after V1 (decision speed) and elected to abort their takeoff. They stopped safely on the runway and taxied in. When investigating such an incident it is important to know your objectives, for example: what happened; why did it happen and what can be done to prevent this from happening again? The main task is to find out why did the engine fail and interviewing the pilots will be important in order to know what happened. When the first question asked was "why did you abort above V1" all communication with the pilots was blocked and they elected to leave the interview. Instead of asking the more open and curious question such as "tell me what happened from when you taxied out", the interviewer showed a negative and adversarial approach towards the pilots. While the investigation needed to deal with the aborted takeoff (because the abort was not in accordance with standard operating procedure), this should not be the first question. Instead it is very important to build trust between the investigators and the crew if good information is to be elicited from all involved.

- *Take notes:* you need to remember what the witness said and by taking notes you have a personal version of what has been said. After the witness is finished go through your notes (paraphrasing) and confirm with the witness that you understood correctly what he said. On the one hand, recording an interview can give investigators a more reliable account of an interview. It also allows the interviewer to give all their attention to the witness during the interview. On the other hand, communication is a lot more than the words spoken, an important element of it is the body language which can't be recorded unless you use a video recorder. A potentially serious disadvantage to either video or audio recording is that the witness may be much more careful with what he or she says when knowing that the interview is being recorded. Whether or not a recoding is made, it is important to build trust in order for the witness to be willing and able to share all information.

- *Time factor:* It is important to have sufficient time for the interview and to not rush into it. Once the interviewee starts to tell his or her story, it is best not to interrupt even for a small question. Once the witness has started speaking his or her mind they will create a story as close to his or her reality of the occurrence as the mind can create. Asking a question will just interrupt the mind's logic and the story will most likely be not as precise. It is important to wait with the questions to the end.

- *Question types:* There are four typical question types: closed, open-ended, leading and loaded.
  - Closed questions require only a single word or short answer. *Is that your final answer?*
  - Open-ended questions require more than one word for the answer and challenges the witness a bit more. "Tell us what happened after…"
  - Leading questions anticipate an answer in the question. "Was the aircraft banking steeply to the right?"
  - Loaded questions are when the question type contains a controversial statement or an assumption. "Was there any black smoke coming from the engine?"
- It is important to have the objective for why you would ask the question and a common question an investigator should ask is: "Do I need to ask this question now?" The fact that a witness very often is not able to remember everything, you might consider dropping a question that would put the witness in an unfavorable position if not knowing the answer.

Knowing the different elements of HF is a must when you analyze an incident or accident from an HF perspective. Many professionals describe different failure modes and typical behavior. James Reason in his book *Managing the Risks of Organizational Accidents* describes hazards, defenses and losses. The hazard or threat has many and various defenses and when the defenses are penetrated the losses occur. In order to build defenses one has to understand the threat and the consequences, and Reason (1999) describes the elements of an active failure and a latent condition.

> Since people design, manufacture, operate, maintain and manage complex technological systems it is hardly surprising that human decisions and actions are implicated in all organizational accidents.
>
> (Reason 1999)

Those at the sharp end – pilots, controllers and maintenance crew – are very often the last defense and if this defense fails, the label "pilot error" often comes into play.

Most people react differently to the same situation and it is hard to predict how one will react. In general, the state of the witness depends on how serious the accident or incident was. Some may be traumatized, some may feel guilty, some might by be frightened or in shock and some not very much affected at all. If one looks at the ways pilots have been trained they were basically told that if you follow the rules and regulations then you will not have an accident. So if something happens you will take the blame and the first interview is always very important.

The captain has at the accident site three priorities: his passengers, his crew and himself. The two first are easy to understand but the third is just as important. Having an accident impacts the body with the release of stress hormones. When an individual realizes that things are going badly wrong the adrenalin rises to a very high level and stays there for some time. When the individual is being interviewed some hours after the accident the adrenalin will have often dropped to a level below baseline standard and he or she is now very vulnerable. Having been "told" if you follow the book you will not crash, the individual is likely to conclude, "it has to be my fault". Talking in such a state of mind is not very advisable and the author has experienced this himself. Landing an F-16 at very high weight in reduced visibility, the drag chute and brakes were used to stop the aircraft. However the drag chute split and the brakes got hot and tire pressure depleted. Writing the report afterwards the author wrote that the drag chute was deployed at too high speed, even though it was not. Three days after the incident the investigator called and said, "Come over here and look at the drag chute." It was torn apart and the material was very brittle, and would tear when pulling it slightly. The drag chute had been used 107 times more than its service life and that could explain why it was torn apart. The reason the author wrote in the report that the drag chute was dropped at a too high speed was that he was feeling guilty and could not see any other reason for what happened. Thus in investigating human factor it is very important to be aware of what condition the crew member is in and bear in mind that the task is not to apportion blame or liability (ICAO Annex 13).

Captain Robert Piché managed to land his Airbus 330 on the 24 August 2001 safely in the Azores after it lost all power due to fuel exhaustion. One can imagine what must have gone through his mind as he glided his A330 to a safe landing. At Flight Operational Forum in 2016 he told his story and said he was available for the investigation team after the accident, and he flew two months after the incident and is still an active airline captain. He indicated that he should probably have waited two years. As a rule of thumb, the Royal Norwegian Air Force (RNoAF) has the objective of getting crewmembers into the cockpit again as soon as possible after an accident. But in some cases it is wise to keep the crew on the ground in order for them to be available to the investigators.

"Care of the Flyer" is an important program in the Royal Norwegian Air Force and the aim is to take care of the crew during a crisis or after an accident. It is flight safety through health promotion and disease prevention (RNoAF BFL 315–16) and it regulates the flight surgeon's tasks and responsibilities at airbase on aircrew physical and mental health. One important issue here is that in order to fulfill this duty there is a need to be in an environment where you meet the same people regularly and can observe any changes.

In an airline, any organization or a military squadron, an important issue is to know your staff. In a large airline with many pilots that is not always possible; and if you fly with a crew member today, maybe the next time will be a year away. It is therefore not so easy to see changes in people. Many airlines do not even have an ordinary "manager to employee" talk. If an employee shows up for work, does his or her job properly then they could go through their whole career without even having a single formal conversation with management. However, without knowing your staff, how can you see any changes?

According to Vivianne Fonne at Flight Operational Forum in 2016, "Mental health is a natural topic in all yearly medicals"; and when a pilot is doing his or her yearly check the medical examination takes just a few minutes, but the dialogue the physician starts is to reveal whether the pilot is balanced and in good shape for flying. Nevertheless this is a difficult task and if the pilot is suicidal then most likely s/he will be able to hide it. Detecting the telltale signs of suicidality is very often a lot easier after the person has committed suicide, when all the small bits of data links fit together. However, after an incident such as suicide there is often a lot of reasoning in hindsight. Indeed it is very hard to prospectively detect who has a mental illness that will lead to serious harm.

One of the advantages of interviewing a pilot shortly after an accident is that the memory is still clear. The mental impact (if any) will often be more visible a bit longer after the accident. During the interview the investigators have a focus on the mental issue and will be able to advise both managers and medical personnel if they think help is needed. Shortly after an accident most people need someone to talk to, someone they trust and can share their inner thoughts with. This can be a very important step in order to get back to flying quickly, but there is never an exact answer to how it should be done; it has to be done individually and in the time frame that is required by the pilot who is affected.

Aviation safety is very much a people problem (Woods 2003) since most accidents are related to how the equipment is used, rather than failure of the equipment itself. This means that human factors are very involved, and investigating and understanding the human factor is vital to any accident investigation. Investigating people, interviewing pilots is a demanding task and in order to get the most out of an affected person one has to practice interviewing.

## References

ICAO (2010) Convention on International Civil Aviation, Annex 13, Montreal: ICAO.

Reason, J. (1999) *Managing the Risks of Organizational Accidents*, Farnham: Ashgate.

Royal Norwegian Air Force (1980) Bestemmelse for Luftforsvaret, BFL 315-16.

Wood, R. (2003) *Aviation Safety Programs: A Management Hanbook*, Englewood, CO: Jeppesen Sanderson.

Wood, R. and Sweginnis, R. (2006) *Aircraft Accident Investigation*, second edition, Casper: WY: Endeavor Books.

# 12 The practicalities of fitting mental health screening into the time-limited annual medical check and the problems of confidentiality

*Martin Hudson and Kevin Herbert*

## Introduction

Throughout the world, all pilots are subject to regular medical checks in order to assess their continuing fitness to fly. The rules that govern such medical checks vary from country to country and are based upon Standards and Recommended Practices (SARPS) published and periodically updated by ICAO, the International Civil Aviation Organisation, which is an agency of the United Nations (ICAO, 2012).

These medical checks are undertaken by a doctor with specialist training in aerospace medicine, known as an aviation medical examiner (AME), designated aviation medical examiner (DAME) or a medical assessor. The latter category would normally work in an aviation authority medical section. The level of training required increases with the type of pilot being examined.

The highest level required for examining commercial pilots is generally known as a Class 1 examiner. In this chapter, for the purposes of simplicity, these doctors will be referred to as AMEs. Many AMEs will also possess a higher qualification in occupational medicine, and some will be specialists in other fields, for example general practice, anaesthetics or ophthalmology.

Many AMEs have an interest in aviation and hold private pilots' licences, and a select few are also commercial pilots. In addition to examining pilots, AMEs may also examine air traffic controllers (ATCOs) and cabin crew members.

AMEs may work as independent practitioners, as part of a group at an aeromedical centre, or be employed by an airline medical department.

In this chapter we will consider the key role undertaken by an AME in making an assessment of fitness, in particular the challenge of mental health or psychological problems.

## Incapacitation risk and 'the 1% rule'

It is clear that sudden medical incapacitation presents a risk to flight safety. The historic basis of the pilot medical assessment is on medical screening with the aim of managing the risk of incapacitation. It is impossible to remove risk altogether, as any human being, whatever the level of perceived or measured health, carries a risk of an acute medical problem: for example acute onset of myocardial infarction or renal colic. The acceptable level of risk of sudden cardiac incapacitation was calculated some years ago and is summarised as 'the 1% rule' (Tunstall-Pedoe, 1988).

The 1% rule in aviation medicine has its origins going back to the 1970s when it was proposed as a method of assessing the risk of human incapacitation based upon the premise used to assess the risk of aircraft mechanical failure. This was defined as needing to be no greater than 1 in 10 million flying hours, and described as being 'extremely remote'.

The UK CAA convened a number of workshops in the 1980s, and set out to apply the methodology to the risk of incapacitation from cardiovascular disease. The principle adopted was that human incapacitation should be the cause of a fatal accident no more than once in 1000 million flying hours.

The calculation that followed can be regarded as a mathematical construct, based on a number of significant assumptions, for example,

- the average flight lasting one hour;
- the critical phases of flight are take-off and landing, which represent 10 per cent of the flight;
- two pilot operations and in 99 per cent of cases the effective taking over of control from the incapacitated pilot;
- significant 'rounding up' of numbers, e.g. 8760 hours in a year becomes 10,000.

The 1% rule has been adopted with varying levels of enthusiasm by aviation authorities around the world. The validity of the rule remains controversial and is a topic of debate nearly four decades on. It is still regarded as a useful benchmark.

The process of making a decision of a pilot's fitness to fly against such a benchmark is significantly clearer when robust morbidity and mortality data for the condition being considered are available, such as in cardiovascular disease, and in the more common types of cancer. However this is more of a challenge in mental illness where the data for morbidity and mortality is less well defined.

As the rate of cardiovascular illness, morbidity and mortality has declined over the past three decades (Scarborough et al., 2011) other causes of incapacitation have become relatively more common. Mental health and psychological problems, including substance misuse, and the use of 'performance enhancing' medications are of concern. In parallel with this there is an increasing awareness that if aerospace medicine is to continue to make a significant contribution to flight safety in the second century of human flight, and beyond, then a wider assessment of a pilot's health and well-being needs to be made.

Thus AMEs should not neglect the risks of sudden incapacitation, but look for risks of more subtle incapacitation leading to poor performance, and decision-making. This approach is summarised in the European Society of Aerospace Medicine (ESAM) 'Fly Safe – Fly Well' project. This ability to look for more subtle psychological problems as well as the routine physical assessment is undoubtedly a challenge.

## National aviation authority regulations

Before looking at the ways in which the wider medical and psychological assessment of pilots could be achieved, it is helpful to look at what now happens during the medical assessment.

Most countries have a set of rules regarding fitness to fly, which are usually part of national law. These rules are administered by a national regulator. In the European Union, these rules are part of European law, and are overseen by the European Agency for Aviation Safety (EASA, 2011).

In turn each member state appoints a regulatory authority to implement these rules; in the case of the UK it is the Civil Aviation Authority. Superficially, the task appears to be simple. To make an assessment based upon a clear set of rules is a comfortable and defensible position, but in reality it is far from being simple.

Each human being shares one thing in common. Each is unique! 'One rule fits all' is a difficult concept. Aviation is a global activity, and yet the rules vary significantly from country to country. Even in Europe, the scope for different interpretation of the rules, through a mechanism known as 'alternative means of compliance', undermines the consistent application of the rules.

The rules for physical illness are often clearer and more measurable than for mental and psychological illness because of the clarity of measurable parameters such as 'the resting blood pressure shall be less than 160/95'.

It is difficult, perhaps impossible, to have such clear parameters for mental illness. Where measurement tools exist to help with mental health assessment, the majority have not been validated in the pilot population.

Medical technology, diagnosis and intervention are advancing at a rate previously unknown in human evolution. It is a major challenge to keep the rules up-to-date in this environment.

## The role of the aviation medical examiner (AME)

The role of an AME is, therefore, perhaps more complicated than it appears. The AME is fulfilling a number of roles when making assessments and is attempting to apply a set of generic, often incomplete, rules to the individual being examined. This is performed under the scrutiny of the regulator, who has the shared aim of aviation safety. At the same time, AMEs are acting as doctors, not in a treating capacity, but as an amalgam of regulator, physician and assessor. In reality, and where it works best, they are advocates of health and wellbeing, fellow human beings, educators and supporters.

A pilot medical examination is based upon the standard clinical interview and clinical examination followed by some investigations, such as a resting electrocardiogram and audiogram. However the predictive value of such tests is not proven. The relevance of some of the tests which are part of the examination, for example the use of a resting electrocardiograph in pilots under 40 is of dubious predictive value validity. Often tests are done, because they can be done!

## Completing the application form: consent and confidentiality

The current EASA medical questionnaire contains two questions related to mental health:

1   Have you ever attempted suicide?
2   Have you ever suffered from any psychiatric or psychological disorder?

It is very hard to imagine any human beings who could answer honestly that they have never suffered from some anxiety (for example at exam time, or when their medical or simulator check is due). Where the threshold of such psychological illness is set, depends upon the cultural norm for acceptance of some degree of psychological (human) fallibility; this will determine whether an honest answer is given.

Whatever format the medical examination takes, and this will vary in different countries, there are several key factors which underpin the effectiveness of the process. These are honesty and trust, both of which are dependent upon confidentiality. Medical confidentiality is the basis of any good doctor/pilot relationship.

The understanding of the word 'confidential', generally defined as the act of keeping a secret, is often confused with 'confidentiality'. The difference is subtle in the English language, and there is a risk of loss of that subtlety when translated into other languages. As a result, confidentiality is often misinterpreted as secrecy, whereas it is more generally accepted as referring to a set of rules which define the circumstances under which the AME can share medical information with another individual. The result is a common understanding of the word confidential, but a widely varying interpretation of the concept of confidentiality, especially in a medical context.

As a general principle medical information should only be shared, with the consent of the pilot, after a clear explanation of the reasons why such sharing of information is beneficial. Such consent should be in written form, fully informed, and witnessed by signature of the AME. It is usually obtained at the time of the medical appointment. This can be problematic, for although potentially significant medical problems can be detected at the time of the medical, when the consent is explicit, will the pilot be prepared to notify the AME of medical problems between periodic medical examinations? The consent in this situation is implied, but the AME may need to remind the pilot about the signed consent, and clarify with whom the information will be shared. It is generally the case that further information will be required from the treating doctor or specialist, and the request for such reports, particularly for insurance purposes, may be subject to other specific legislation, which will vary in different countries.

There are other circumstances where information can be shared, if necessary by breaching confidentiality – but this varies enormously from one jurisdiction to another. At one end of the spectrum, such breach would never be permitted, but more generally it is permitted in two specific circumstances:

1   where it is required by law;
2   where such disclosure is in the interest of public safety.

In the UK these circumstances are set out in detail in the General Medical Council publication, 'Confidentiality' (GMC, 2009) and more generally in 'Good Medical Practice' (GMC, 2013). See also Regulation (EC) No. 216/2008 of the European Parliament and of the Council laying down technical requirements and administrative procedures related to civil aviation aircrew.

Even though such a clear and well-defined duty exists, in the event that a doctor breaches confidentiality, without consent, because it is in the interest of public safety, this does not imply any legal indemnity for the doctor. There may still be a risk of litigation if a pilot disagrees that the risk to safety was not sufficient to justify the breach of confidentiality. It has been proposed that the doctor should be protected by some form of automatic legal indemnity in such situations. This may cause more problems than it solves, and is the subject of ongoing discussion.

The whole subject of confidentiality is an important part of the building of a relationship of trust between AME and pilot. On the one hand the pilot should understand the overriding duties of the doctor (AME) who is conducting the examination in a specific jurisdiction, and on the other hand for the AME to be open and honest about what these duties are. There is also a risk that pilots who do not wish to disclose a medical condition to the licensing authority, may opt to have their medical examination in a country where there is a stronger requirement to maintain secrecy and not to share such information. There is also the risk that a pilot will simply withhold information from the AME. This is an unsafe situation, but the AME does not have access to any better test of honesty than the rest of society! It is for this reason that a culture of disclosure should be fostered, in an environment based on mutual trust. It is worth noting that in the case of a consultation between the typical AME and typical pilot, (both male and of a 'certain age') they both share a strikingly similar psychological profile, one specific feature of which is a reticence to discuss their problems (Fonne, 2015).

It could be concluded from this situation, that the AME is walking a tightrope; on one side there is the need to maintain confidentiality, and on the other the doctor's duty to breach that confidentiality when there may be a risk to public safety. However in day-to-day practice, this is not the case. Whilst a medical condition could pose a risk to safety, it will also always pose a risk to the pilot's own health. However strong the desire to fly is, the vast majority of pilots also wish to stay well and return to their families at the end of the day. When the expectations of both pilot and AME can be aligned towards the maintenance of a lifelong safe and fulfilling flying career, it results in an optimal outcome for both parties, and for the safety of the flying public.

## Establishment of mutual trust between the pilot and the AME

Why is this relationship of mutual trust essential? Most of the information that the AME will learn about the pilot will be from history taking rather than by the examination or other tests. It is important that an atmosphere of disclosure exists. There needs to be two thresholds: one low and one high. The threshold for disclosure by the pilot of sometimes embarrassing, often worrying, and potentially career-threatening information, needs to be low. The threshold for breaching confidentiality by the AME must be high. Consider what is going through the mind of a pilot who is experiencing symptoms, or who more commonly has already sought medical help and has been given a diagnosis of a potentially disqualifying (or even life-threatening) condition. It must take a degree of courage to discuss such problems with an AME.

This is what we are asking of the pilot. It is often easier when a pilot has a diagnosis of a physical nature, as there is likely to be clear guidance regarding necessary investigations and treatment options. When the problem is a mental health one, or of a 'psychosocial' nature, the situation is considerably less clear. The tools available for an AME to assist in such an assessment are often poor or even non-existent. It is important to have good communications between the AME, the pilot's general medical attendant and specialist, in arriving at a decision of fitness to fly.

It is relatively rare for pilots to present with florid acute mental illness such as schizophrenia or bipolar disorder. On the other hand, conditions at the less severe end of the spectrum of mental illness are quite common. Fatigue, which can be a significant factor in mental illness, is a particularly common problem disclosed by pilots. If left unmanaged it can present serious risks for flight safety.

Stigma is a serious impediment to a pilot's acceptance of a risk of mental illness, and remains a significant impediment in the public at large. This is despite the compelling evidence regarding the incidence of some form of mental illness during a normal lifetime (Alonso *et al.*, 2004). The psychological profile of a typical pilot tends to gravitate against the acceptance of susceptibility to such problems.

It is only in recent years that more enlightened regulatory authorities have permitted pilots to return to flying duties who have been suffering from a depressive illness, but are in the recovery phase even if continuing to take specific antidepressant medication. This is in stark contrast to the past, where such an illness meant many months of grounding, with likely adverse effects on well-being. The more worrying prospect was of pilots failing to disclose their symptoms and continuing to fly. Possibly even worse is the risk of self-diagnosis and treatment using information obtained from the Internet and the 'global pharmacy' which is readily available on the World Wide Web! It is hard to decide which is the worse option.

There is a need to extend the enlightenment that has allowed pilots on antidepressant medication to continue to fly. This philosophy needs to be extended to all pilots, the regulators, the law makers and aeromedical specialists. They should all play a part in helping to raise awareness of the reality of mental illness, and thereby reduce its stigma.

It is superficially attractive to believe that a set of well-constructed clinical questionnaires will unlock this conundrum. It will not. Pilots are smart people and are highly motivated. They possess perhaps a unique motivator compared with other professions, which is the simple but strong desire to fly. This should not be underestimated.

## The practicalities of the assessment

All pilots must undergo routine medical examinations to assess medical fitness so that they can operate their aircraft safely. The general public, who nowadays are frequent travellers by air, are very reassured by this pilot health check process.

This assessment includes not only commercial pilots but also recreational pilots. Pilots have become accustomed, along with line checks and simulator checks of their flying competence, to accept the medical examination as a normal part of the job. This acceptance does not remove the fact that many find the process stressful.

This process can have a tendency to become routine and a 'box ticking' exercise but at the same time can be stressful for the pilot whose very livelihood rests on being passed as fit by the medical examiner. Thus the AME can be seen as a threat to the pilot, and the annual medical examination a process to be completed as quickly as possible. Despite the very small pick-up rate for the detection of physical illness at the routine examination, the pilot is nevertheless fearful of the outcome and may minimise any health problems to ensure continuation of medical fitness.

There is therefore a tendency for the pilot/AME relationship to be strained and little opportunity presents itself to allow a more professional doctor/patient relationship to develop. Pilots may decide to move from one AME to another in an attempt to find an examiner who is regarded as more likely to find the pilot fit without too detailed an assessment. In recent years there has been an initiative, spearheaded by ICAO (2011) and supported by the ESAM 'Fly Safe – Fly well' programme, to promote the annual examination as not only being able to detect clinical illness but also to promote good general health. Through discussion with the pilot the AME can advise about lifestyle factors such as diet, exercise, alcohol consumption and smoking habits. This initiative, which initially was a recommended practice, is likely to become a standard in the near future.

## Psychological assessment

There is however one aspect of this medical assessment which so far has not been considered and that is the psychological state of the pilot. No part of the examination specifically addresses this issue. As the career for many airline pilots has become more stressful, due to a variety of factors, psychological illness is becoming more prevalent. Recent high profile major aviation accidents such as the GermanWings tragedy and the disappearance of the Malaysian aircraft MH 370, has highlighted the possibility that these accidents were the result of severely disturbed mental behaviour in a pilot. With the former accident, the final BEA report (BEA, 2015) concludes that the pilot was suffering from a mental disorder, most likely to be a depressive illness with psychotic symptoms, for which inpatient treatment had been recommended. It is noted that a personality disorder could not be ruled out. Tragically the pilot's non-disclosure to his AME or to his employer was compounded by the strict interpretation of the medical secrecy laws in the pilot's country of origin. For the Malaysian accident the cause remains speculative as no evidence has been found to prove what was the reason for the loss of the aircraft.

There has been much discussion about the need for a more detailed psychological assessment as part of the routine annual physical examination. How this could be achieved in the time-limited annual physical examination is a major question. Should this be a formal process where each pilot completes a series of psychological tests at each examination?

There are several reasons why a formal process is not recommended. Which tests should be used and what tests have proved to be clinically reliable? Most of the standard tests are freely available on the Internet and pilots would soon learn which answers would give them the best chance to pass! The tests would become another 'box-ticking exercise' completed for the sake of passing the examination and would not achieve any useful purpose. If this assessment is not to be a formal process what else could be done? The answer is to use the medical examination to talk to the pilot, listen to the pilot and carefully observe the pilot's demeanour.

## The annual medical examination

Diagnosis is a three-part process: history taking, clinical examination and investigations; however these do not have the same emphasis and the proportion of time that should be spent on each part is not equal as Figure 12.1 shows.

Thus by far the most important part of the examination is the taking of a comprehensive history covering not only standard medical questions, but should include a whole raft of psychosocial questions.

This requires skill and tact, but is the basis for a thorough and effective medical examination. The physical examination, though important, and which must be completed, has less importance. Any necessary investigations such as blood tests, urine examination, ECG, audiograms are also required and give essential information but do not and should not carry the same emphasis as a good and thoroughly professional medical interview. The skilled AME will also be carefully observing the pilot's reaction to questions, and the way the questions are answered. This process begins as soon as the pilot enters the consulting room.

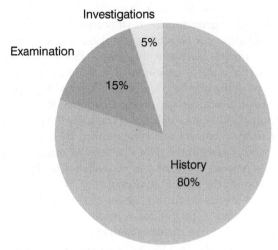

*Figure 12.1* Time allocation during a typical medical examination

## Developing the AME/pilot relationship

In any medical consultation the need for trust and understanding between the 'patient' (pilot) and the doctor (AME) is the foundation which will lead to a satisfactory and clinically productive outcome. This relationship takes time to develop and it may be several consultations before the feeling of trust and confidence is established. The initial consultation is the foundation on which this mutual trust and respect is built so it is important that the AME has developed a consultation process which is straightforward, welcoming and thorough. Pilots should not regard the AME as a threat to their careers but as a highly professional yet friendly doctor who is there to make the process of the annual medical examination as pleasant and as thorough a process as possible. If problems are found these should be dealt with professionally and expeditiously with the main aim to enable pilots if possible to continue to enjoy their careers. Thus the following criteria should be established.

1   *Information and appointment booking arrangements:* The AME should provide accurate, relevant and user-friendly information which enables the pilot to make an appointment with ease and with a feeling of confidence. The basis for this is an informative and well-structured website which is easy to find and to follow. The website should give clear instructions how to make an appointment whether this is by telephone call or an online booking system. There should be a clear description of the location of the doctor's premises with maps and a post code for satellite navigation users. Such a system will give the enquiring pilot confidence and reassurance that he or she is dealing with a professional yet friendly AME service. If the initial contact is by telephone this process should be friendly and welcoming.

2   *Practice premises and administrative arrangements:* The initial impression gained by the pilot about the AME's premises, staff, administrative requirements, the consultation room and the manner and decorum of the AME will do much to enable that initial consultation, which must be established on the very best foundation, to be a success. Pleasant waiting room and reception facilities also help to create a good atmosphere which will reassure the pilot. The consultation must not be rushed. Thus adequate time needs to be allotted to the consultation, and a minimum of one hour for each consultation is recommended. The consultation should start at the appointed time.

## The initial consultation

The initial consultation needs to establish the identity of the pilot so a current photo ID and sight of the pilot's current medical certificate is necessary.

Discreet enquiries can be made why the pilot has selected that particular AME. With the development of the EASA system it is possible for pilots to move from AME to AME either in the same country or even to travel abroad for their examination. The choice of a particular AME could be a simple matter of a convenient location or a change of job and base. On the other hand the pilot may have had an unsatisfactory assessment at the previous medical examination, if so what was the reason? Is the pilot 'AME shopping' and hoping to find an examiner with a more casual approach so the examination can be passed more easily? Or could the reason be financial and the pilot is looking for the cheapest cost for the medical examination? These situations present difficulties for the AME and the questioning needs to be subtle yet thorough to establish the facts.

The pilot should also be asked if he/she holds any other national aviation medical certificate such as FAA, CASA etc. and if a medical certificate has ever been denied or suspended by any aviation authority. This is important as the pilot may decide to obtain a medical certificate from another authority and choose not to disclose a previous refusal to issue a medical certificate.

To assist this identification process in Europe, EASA is proposing to create a comprehensive database which will include the name and date of birth of all pilots as well as unique identifying numbers. The entry will show the date and location of the last medical examination and if the pilot holds a current valid medical certificate. Any limitations will be noted but the nature of the limitation will not be divulged. There will be no medical information held on the database. The database will be secure and the AME will require a log-in password to access the system.

Fortunately in the vast majority of cases this identification process will be entirely straightforward but the AME cannot assume this to be the case and thorough checks are necessary.

The initial medical examination should be friendly yet thorough and complete and so result in the issuing of the new medical certificate. This will help to establish a mutual feeling of trust and professionalism which is the foundation for a good doctor/patient relationship. The pilot will be reassured and confident and should return not only on an annual/six-monthly basis to that particular AME but also make contact with the AME for advice in between medical examinations if the pilot experiences any medical issues during that time. These issues may include personal problems at work or family troubles which are causing stress and which could lead to impaired work performance, clinical anxiety or depression.

## Completing the application form

This is the foundation for the consultation and needs to be thorough. The pilot should be reminded that this form, as well as providing the necessary medical information, is a legal document and that accuracy, completeness and honesty is of paramount importance. It should be stressed to the pilot that incomplete or inaccurate information, whether through casual or deliberate omission, is a very serious offence with major repercussions not only to the pilot's career but also from a legal point of view. Some pilots regard the completion of the application form as a somewhat tedious process and have a tendency to 'tickitis' by ticking all the boxes without reading the questions! Deliberate non-disclosure can and does occur and is a serious offence. Pilots need to be reminded about this and it is important for the AME to ensure that all relevant information is included. The AME must make sure that every question on the form is completed. It is surprising how often with further questioning pilots recall some medical event which they had omitted to declare. The observant doctor will, for instance, notice a body scar which when pointed out reminds the pilot of a previous surgical procedure which may never before have been disclosed!

## The medical interview

This is the most important part of the consultation and needs time and discreet questioning. This is the essence of a 'psychological' assessment of the pilot which is not done in any formal way and is not a 'tick-box' exercise.

The AME needs to question the pilot about a variety of issues and this questioning can be achieved not only during the initial part of the consultation but as a continuous process throughout the examination.

The following questions should be included:

- *The job:* type of flying – employer details – length of service in current employment – full-time or part-time – total flying hours – hours flown since last medical – type of flying – roster pattern: long-haul, medium-haul or short-haul – number of sectors flown in a duty period – is this fair and reasonable? – fatigue – job satisfaction? Attitude towards flying. Is it just a job, or as is more often the case, a vocation? Are there aspirations for future career development, e.g. a training role, or long-haul flying? Is the employer sympathetic to an individual's personal or work problems? Does the company offer any form of peer support?

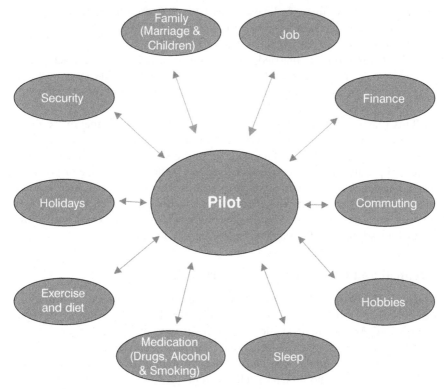

*Figure 12.2* The component parts of a thorough pilot medical interview

- As mentioned earlier, pilots usually have very strong motivation to continue flying, sometimes to the extent of blurring recall of medical issues.
- *Finance:* concerns about money – debts – overtime – second job?
- *Commuting:* home location – distance to work – the commuting time – ease of commuting – mode of travel – return journey home
- *Hobbies:* what other interests or hobbies does the pilot enjoy? What does the pilot do in his/her spare time?
- *Sleep:* quality and amount of sleep – jet lag – quality of sleeping at or away from home – rest arrangements prior to duty pattern – medication to aid sleep?
- *Medication:* prescribed medication – over-the-counter medication, or medication acquired via the Internet or down route. The range of medication which can be purchased without medical consultation varies widely across the globe.
- *Drugs/alcohol/smoking habits:* alcohol type and amount – time elapsed after alcohol consumption and reporting for duty – smoking habits – social drugs – legal highs – driving licence offences? (The use of performance-enhancing drugs is an increasing problem amongst younger pilots.)
- *Exercise and diet:* exercise activities, type and frequency, diet, airline food

- *Holidays*: How many holidays in past year? Where do the family go on holiday? Do the children join with the family on holiday?
- *Security:* airport security checks, fear of terrorism?
- *Family arrangements:* married, co-habiting or single – is the relationship a same sex or heterosexual one – ages of children – child care – school/college/university – family life – health issues – partner employment?

This may seem a daunting list of questions but the information received from these discreet enquiries is essential in order to build up a picture of the pilot's work and family life. The answers to these questions will give clues to potential problems which could lead to stress. If there is evidence of potential problems which are revealed by these questions then an in-depth interview can and should be performed which can reveal psychological problems. This may require the services of an aviation psychologist who can proceed with more formal questioning and possibly the use of psychological tests.

## Medical and psychological support for the pilot

It may be necessary to set up a plan with the pilot, his employer and medical advisers to establish if there is a significant level of stress, anxiety or even depression? Arrangements could then be made with the employer for time off with full employer support ensuring that complete confidentiality is maintained. The use of an 'in-house' *peer support* system is invaluable and all airlines or employers of pilots should have such a system.

If during the medical interview it is apparent that the pilot may be depressed, anxious or have a drug or alcohol problem then a more formal psychological evaluation can be arranged using local psychiatric or psychological support.

It is best if this support is given by a specialist with aviation medical training and experience. At this stage more formal psychometric tests such as a Hamilton Depression Scale, Epworth Sleep test or a CAGE questionnaire are appropriate and can be performed by the AME or by an aviation-trained psychologist. On recovery the AME should review the pilot during a follow-up consultation and reassess if a return to work is possible and if necessary with a modified work pattern. This decision may require confirmation from the aviation authority.

With practice and experience these various points can be covered during the examination process without interrupting the natural flow of the conversation. Many of the questions will be discussed at the beginning of the medical interview but others can be fitted in at various times during the examination. For instance exercise can be discussed while weighing the pilot. The setting up for the ECG is a convenient time to enquire about family and personal life issues. The old fashioned 'gut reaction' which experienced doctors develop can have value and should not be ignored.

*The established AME/Pilot relationship*

As the AME/pilot relationship develops over a number of annual medical examinations the AME will build up a picture of the pilot and already know the answers for many of these questions, but it is useful to be able to check with the pilot if all is still well. It is useful to have an aide-memoire in the pilot's medical record such as the names of the children, noting a new arrival in the family or a particular holiday location enjoyed in the previous year. This information, when 'remembered' at a subsequent examination, helps to cement the AME/pilot relationship.

Enquiring about these activities will help the AME/pilot relationship and show to the pilot that the AME is genuinely concerned about these matters. It is also important that the AME/pilot relationship does not become too close or 'cosy' as important matters may not be disclosed or may be glossed over as being too sensitive or embarrassing.

The AME should stress to the pilot the need to maintain contact with the AME throughout the period between medical examinations and to report without delay any medical issues that occur between medical examinations. The AME should always remind the pilot of the guidance about a decrease in medical fitness which is clearly stated on the front of the medical certificate.

## Liaison with other doctors or healthcare professionals

If during the taking of the history or as a result of the physical examination there is a need to obtain more information it will be necessary to liaise with a doctor or healthcare worker who has been seeing the pilot prior to the medical examination. This can present problems of breach of confidentiality not only for the AME but also for the healthcare worker who is being asked to provide more information. After the pilot has completed the application form the pilot's signature is required to confirm that what has been declared on the form is complete and accurate and that no relevant information has been omitted either by deliberate deception or through inadvertent memory lapse.

## Legal aspects of the application form

It is important that the AME emphasises this fact and informs the pilot that the completion of the form has legal and insurance implications. Before the pilot signs the form, the declaration in Box 12.1 should be read.

This declaration does not specifically state that the AME may approach other doctors or health care workers to seek more information but this is implied in the declaration. However the AME should discuss with the pilot the need to obtain more information and that this information will be sought usually by correspondence. The AME should make a contemporaneous record on the pilot's AME records that this matter has been discussed and agreed, and it is

*Box 12.1*

Declaration: I hereby declare that I have carefully considered the statements made above and that to the best of my belief they are complete and correct and that I have not withheld any relevant information or made any misleading statement. I understand that if I have made any false or misleading statement in connection with this application, or fail to release the supporting medical information, the Licensing Authority may refuse to grant me a medical certificate or may withdraw any medical certificate granted, without prejudice to any other action applicable under national law.

CONSENT TO RELEASE OF MEDICAL INFORMATION: Please read the statement below in relation to disclosure of information. The CAA takes the security of your personal information very seriously. Information is only disclosed to persons who are subject to a duty of confidentiality and where there are sufficient security measures in place to protect personal data. If you do not consent to the disclosure of information as described below, you may make representations to medicalweb@caa.co.uk.

In submitting this application, I am consenting to the disclosure to third parties of all information which I have provided to the CAA and that relates to me. I understand that information would only be disclosed to third parties by the CAA for regulatory purposes. This may include providing information to other medical professionals.

Administrative workers and/or IT workers who are assisting the CAA with its regulatory functions may also be given access to personal information in the course of their professional duties. My attention has been drawn to the CAA Medical Department's Fair Processing Notice which is published on the CAA's website.

Date:

Signature of applicant: ...........................
Signature of AME (Witness): ............................

wise to ask the pilot to sign a consent form, a copy of which can be sent to the doctor or health care worker from whom information is being sought.

There is no reason why pilots cannot contact their own general practitioner, consultant or other healthcare worker to request copies of medical reports, and this is frequently done. In this instance the pilots are fully cooperative and consent is implied so is not formally required.

## General practitioner/consultant liaison with the AME

There can sometimes be a problem when an airline human resources department or the airline's medical adviser request information about the fitness of pilots and the reasons for sickness absence. These requests are reasonable and are often required as part of the contractual duties of the employee but it is imperative that full consent is obtained from pilots before any response is made. This consent should be in writing and a copy of the consent forms should be included with the AME's referral letter asking for medical information from the employee's GP, consultant or other healthcare worker. Once the AME has received replies, pilots have the right to see any medical report or letter which the AME intends to send to the airline before it is released. Though pilots can request that the report be amended, the AME is not obliged to alter the report though it should be made clear to the airline where the employee disagrees with the AME's findings. Pilots can include their own statements outlining where they disagree with the report. In practice this rarely happens.

This whole process does not need to be confrontational or in any way threatening to pilots because by agreeing to this procedure, pilots are enabling the AME to complete the medical assessment and, wherever possible, to issue a medical certificate and thus permit a return to flying.

It is important to stress that the role of the AME does not begin and end with the annual medical examination. For most pilots there will only be a requirement to see the AME annually as no medical problems have occurred in the intervening 12 months. However pilots are obliged to 'seek without undue delay, aeromedical advice whenever they experience a decrease in their medical fitness'. There is a statement to this effect on the front of every medical certificate. The AME should remind pilots of their obligations in this respect. This is best done when issuing the medical certificate, ensuring it is signed by both the pilot and the AME.

## Maintaining contact between medical examinations

If a pilot contacts the AME in between medical examinations to report an illness, accident, operation or other decrease in physical or mental fitness the AME should find out more details and record this information in the pilot's medical file. Medical reports from GPs, consultants or other healthcare workers should be requested. The same rules for consent as previously mentioned apply and should be followed implicitly. At this stage the AME will issue to the pilot a letter confirming that the pilot has been made temporarily 'unfit' and should inform the relevant aviation authority. Later, when the pilot and his/her medical advisers consider that full physical and mental fitness has returned, the AME should arrange to see the pilot to assess if the temporary suspension of the medical certificate can be lifted. This will require obtaining further written reports from the pilot's consultant, GP or other healthcare worker. If the AME deems that the pilot is fully fit, a 'fit' letter is issued following further consultation (often by a telephone call) with the relevant national aviation authority.

## European Society of Aerospace Medicine Report

Recently the European Society of Aerospace Medicine (ESAM) in conjunction with the European Cockpit Association (ECA) and the European Association for Aviation Psychology (EAAP) have produced an excellent report on the subject of psychological assessments of airline pilots together with a most useful leaflet which hopefully will be widely seen by pilots and by AMEs (ESAM, 2015).

This includes an endorsement of the Aerospace Medical Association's (AsMA) Pilot Mental Health Working Group Recommendations (ASMA, 2015).

The leaflet lists several points which the AME should know before starting a medical examination.

These points are:

- Is the pilot at ease about the medical examination?
- Has the AME established the identity of the pilot as well as his/her state of licence issue (SOLI), and seen a copy of the last medical certificate?
- Does the AME know if the pilot is attending by choice or because of an employer's request?
- The AME should be clear what type of medical the pilot requires and what tests are needed? Is the AME aware of any conflict of interest?

The advice continues to stress that the pilot should fully understand the reason behind all the questions, the physical examination and the investigations being performed. The pilot should also have trust and confidence in the AME's judgment.

The AME should also know about the pilot's employer and whether or not the pilot has access to an effective peer support programme.

The AME should also understand how the employer would respond to the pilot being made temporarily unfit and what level of support there would be for the pilot.

## Summary and conclusions

We have sought to demonstrate in this chapter that the process of assessing the physical and mental well-being of an aviator is based upon a thorough clinical history taking, as well as an appropriate physical examination, including clinical tests.

The AME can incorporate various predefined questions into the interview process, without interfering with the 'flow' of the process. AME training should include the process of follow-up questioning when the standard questions reveal matters of concern, and the AME should be able to access appropriate support, both for themselves in the decision making process, and for the pilot when further investigations are indicated.

The interaction between AME and pilot should be based on trust, and in the context of their occupational and social circumstances. The ultimate aim is to encourage disclosure, both during and between periodic medical examinations.

From this, it can be concluded that the effectiveness of the process is highly dependent upon the training, clinical skills and personality of the doctor. For some, this may be seen as a risky, and a difficult to validate process, and there is no doubt some truth in this. There is a need for appropriate and ongoing training for the AME, and for research into validated questions to be incorporated into a structured clinical interview.

It must not be forgotten that the primary reason for the medical assessment of a pilot is to assess fitness to fly, and thereby contribute to flight safety. At its best the interaction between pilot and AME is conducted in an atmosphere of mutual trust, with a shared goal of ensuring a full, fulfilling, and safe flying career.

## References

Alonso, J., Angermeyer, M.C., Bernest, S. *et al.* (2004) Prevalence of mental disorders in Europe: results from European Study of the Epidemiology of Mental Disorders. (ESE Med) project. *Acta Psychiatrica Scandinavica* Supp 109(420): 21–27.

ASMA (2015) Aerospace Medical Association (AsMA) Pilot Mental Health Expert Working Group *Aerospace Medicine and Human Performance* 86(12): 1013. Accessed at https://www.asma.org/asma/media/AsMA/pdf-policy/2015/Mental-Health-Screening-in-Aviators.pdf

BEA (2015) Accessed at https://www.bea.aero/en/investigation-reports/notified-events/detail/event/accident-to-the-airbus-a320-211-registered-d-aipx-flight-gwi18g-on-24-march-2015/ (8 September 2016).

EASA (2011) Part-Med/AMC/GM- EASA: Acceptable Means of Compliance and Guidance Material to Commission Regulation (EU) No 1178/2011 of 3 November 2011.

ESAM (European Society of Aerospace Medicine) (2015) *The Pilot/AME Relationship*. Accessed at www.esam.aero (8 September 2016).

Fonne, V. (2015) *Psychology and pilots: A dark art for the enlightened?* ESAM meeting at the Aerospace Medical Association Conference, May 2015. Orlando, FL.

GMC (2009) Confidentiality. Accessed at http://www.gmc-uk.org/guidance/ethical_guidance/confidentiality.asp

GMC (2013) Good practice. Accessed at www.gmc-uk.org/guidance/good_medical_practice.asp

ICAO (2011) *Manual of civil aviation medicine*. Montreal: ICAO. Accessed at: http://www.icao.int/publications/documents/8984_cons_en.pdf (8 September 2016).

Scarborough, P., Wickramasinghe, K., Bhatnagar, P. and Rayner, M. (2011) *Trends in coronary heart disease 1961–2011*. London: British Heart Foundation.

Tunstall-Pedoe, H. (1988) Acceptable cardiovascular risk in aircrew: Introduction. *European Heart Journal* 9 (Suppl.G): 9–1.

# Part III
# Mental health, well-being and support for pilots

# 13  The use of psychotropic medications and fitness to fly

*Rui Correia*

Most of the medications used in psychiatry have clinical or side effects that are not compatible with the requirements of flight personnel and the standards of flight safety. Professional activity for flight crew comprises a unique working environment which places physiological strains such as hypoxia, acceleration, jet lag and others. In addition to physical effects these can result in psychological changes which themselves become more significant than they might be for other occupations, due to the flight requirement of good psychomotor and cognitive skills (Richards & Zuckerman, 2006). To pilot an aircraft requires the utilization of a complex set of physical and cognitive skills. Interference with any aspect of these skills and their coordination may have serious personal and public safety consequences. The assessment of mental fitness shall therefore be made with due regard to the privileges of the license and to the conditions in which the applicants will have to carry out their duties (ICAO, 2016: Chapter 9).

The impact of psychiatric disorders on pilot performance must not be underestimated. The early diagnosis and treatment of psychiatric disorders among pilots is critical to maintain aviation safety, and to reducing the effect of this disorder on the pilot's health and quality of life. Pilots with an identified psychiatric disorder must be grounded until full recovered, and in some cases, a period of observation will be required prior to any consideration of a request to return to flying duties (Bor & Hubbard, 2006).

Since the beginning of history of modern psychopharmacology in the 1940s, many advances were obtained on the understanding of the mechanism of action of psychotropic drugs. In 1949 Cade described the treatment of mania with lithium, the first mood stabilizer. Some years later, in 1952, Delay and Deniker discovered the antipsychotic action of chlorpromazine, the first drug with efficacy in schizophrenia treatment.

There are different types of centrally acting medications that are used according to the pathology diagnosed or with the symptoms that the patient presents; we can analyze them by groups of 'psychopharms'.

Psychopharms are drugs that can be prescribed for people with psychiatric disorders or with psychopathology affecting significantly their mental status. They are chemical agents acting on the central nervous system (CNS), changing some mental processes: behavioral, perceptive, cognitive and affective. Usually they act by modifying neurotransmission and modulating the concentration of different neurotransmitters in synapsis and neurons. Many important psychopharmacological drugs target ion channels or enzymes that are important regulators of synaptic neurotransmission. These actions cause alterations in the brain which are linked to the therapeutic effects of various psychotropic drugs.

The European Aviation Safety Agency (EASA) published a set of rules (EASA, 2011), contained in acceptable means of compliance (AMC) and Guidance Material to Part-MED[1], that are very useful in respect to medical conditions that are – or are not – compatible with the issuance of a medical certificate. Regarding the type of flight and aircraft used, medical certificates can be Class I, Class II or LAPL. Class I applies to professional pilots usually flying as commercial pilots; Class II applies to non-professional pilots usually with leisure flights. Finally, LAPL applies to light aircraft pilot licenses.

Air traffic controllers have their own medical certification (Class III certificate) which is determined by the particular needs of the job and in accordance with European legislation, taking in account the specific functions and high levels of air safety needed in air traffic control.

The medical requirements for professional pilots to have a Class I medical certificate are published in different chapters of the EU Implementing Rules and AMC – acceptable means of compliance – and one of them refers to psychiatric requirements. Most of the disorders imply a permanent inaptitude, others are disqualifying during the acute phase; in other cases is the medication disqualifying by itself.

In accordance with Acceptable Means of Compliance and Guidance Material to Commission Regulation (EU) No1178/2011of 3 November 2011, the main categories of psychiatric disorders for denial of medical certification for Class I pilots are:

- psychotic disorder;
- organic mental disorder;
- psychotropic substances (use or abuse);
- schizophrenia, schizotypal or delusional disorder;
- mood disorder;
- neurotic, stress-related or somatoform disorder;
- personality or behavioral disorder;
- disorders due to alcohol or other substance use;
- deliberate self-harm.

However it is important to distinguish between psychiatric symptoms and psychiatric syndromes or disorders. Mild anxiety symptoms, such as intrusive worrying thoughts, irritability, insomnia, physical and autonomic symptoms, are part of the common human experience from time to time, in response to stressful events, where they may be described as adjustment disorder. But they may also reflect the presence of a more clinically significant anxiety disorder –

like generalized anxiety disorder, specific phobia, panic disorder with or without agoraphobia, social phobia or PTSD (post-traumatic stress disorder) (Reid, 2016).

There are two important systems of classification for psychiatric disorders currently used in most countries: the World Health Organization (WHO) ICD-10 (WHO, 2016b) and the American Psychiatric Association (APA) DSM-5 (APA, 2013). The most recent versions are ICD-10, the tenth revision of *International Statistical Classification of Diseases*; and DSM-5 updated in 2013 is the fifth edition of the *Diagnostic and Statistical Manual of Mental Disorders*. In order to ease their use, DSM-5 and ICD-10 have corresponding categories of diagnosis, despite some differences of terminology in each manual. The aim of these classification systems has been to foster a common language for psychiatry and clinical psychology, to operationalize definitions and to provide a lexicon of psychiatric syndromes independent of an etiological theory. However, all classifications of mental disorder are temporary and incomplete, and psychiatric diagnosis still remains at descriptive syndrome level, describing symptoms clusters.

The most serious disorders – psychoses in all the different subtypes (such as schizophrenia, bipolar disorder, organic mental disorder or delusional disorder) – lead to permanent unfitness to fly, and antipsychotic drugs (neuroleptics) are out of the question for use by aviators. The great challenge for medical certification are the mood disorders – mainly depression – in all is different clinical presentations. The rules clearly state that "an established mood disorder is disqualifying." But they also say that:

> after full recovery and after full consideration of an individual case a fit assessment may be considered, depending on the characteristics and gravity of the mood disorder, if a stable maintenance psychotropic medication is confirmed, a fit assessment should require a multi-pilot limitation.
>
> (EASA, 2011, p. 22)

Thus, the controlled use of antidepressants – especially those with fewer side effects and with more clinical data about its use – are candidates for prescription in pilots.

There is also a chapter of psychology with psychological requirements where it is stated that:

> where there is suspicion or established evidence that an applicant has a psychological disorder, should be referred for psychological opinion and advice. After the evaluation the psychologist should submit a written report to AME (AeroMedical Examiner), AeMC (Aeromedical Center) or licensing authority as appropriate, detailing his opinion and recommendation.
>
> (EASA, 2011, pp. 22–23)

A well-conducted process of selection is very important to exclude *ab-initio* candidates that do not fulfill the "profile" to be an aviator. Hence, it is necessary to exclude people with psychiatric disorders, principally those with more severe psychopathology and worse prognosis. Indeed there are only a few syndromes (i.e. dysthymias) compatible with flight duties and medical certification, because they impact minimally on the performance and behavior of the pilot.

Another important aspect of selection of *ab-initio* candidates is examination of their motivation to fly and understanding whether their desire to fly is genuine or circumstantial. Flying has intrinsic rewards like the acquisition and performance of high-level skills, the social exclusiveness of the flying world, the high esteem in which pilots are held, and the high level of physical health expected. The task itself – flying – has high levels of satisfaction in the successful performance of high-level sensorimotor skills and also emotional rewards. Mastery and control are powerful reinforcers of behavior and it is not unusual to hear pilots stating that s/he always wanted to fly. Indeed, many experienced aviators describe their enjoyment of their sense of control in the air. There is also a sense of escape from more mundane concerns, a distancing from other and perhaps not so easily controllable issues. It is, for most, a highly enjoyable activity and one that many of them relinquish reluctantly. But motivation to fly is a dynamic drive, subject to change in the face of developmental and environmental factors. Factors motivating a young pilot may change throughout their career as they age. All these factors may result in the appearance of anxiety (usually non-clinical), a re-evaluation of the aviator's aims, a change in motivation to avoidance and a decision to leave flying. Sometimes an unresolved or unadmitted motivational issue is likely to confound attempts at treatment of any anxiety disorder that may develop, and it is important to evaluate the motivation to fly.

## Psychopharmacology and the regulations

### Antipsychotic drugs

This type of drugs also known as neuroleptics are not accepted because the disorders for which they are prescribed are disqualifying. Disorders like schizophrenia in all its subtypes, bipolar disorder and all the different types of dementia are not compatible with medical certification for pilots. EASA standards do not allow any kind of neuroleptics, even if they are prescribed for certain symptoms like insomnia, psychomotor agitation, severe anxiety or tics. Clinical action and side effects of neuroleptics with sedation, psychomotor retardation and decreased arousal drastically affect performance.

### Central nervous system stimulants

Stimulant medicines are prescribed for conditions such as narcolepsy, with daytime sleepiness or sleep apnea associated with significant daytime drowsiness despite CPAP (continuous positive airway pressure) treatment.

The most common drug prescribed is Modafinil, a powerful CNS stimulant with significant side effects like agitation, insomnia, increasing impulsiveness and anxiety. The medical conditions for which Modafinil is prescribed are disqualifying, and others, stimulants of the CNS are still forbidden (Civil Aviation Authority, 2015).

### Anti-epileptics and medications for neuropathic pain

Epilepsy is disqualifying and so these drugs are incompatible with medical certification. For severe migraine prophylaxis the use of Valproate is not allowed because of severe side effects like sedation. For different types of neuropathic pain, the use of Gabapentin, Pregabalin or Carbamazepine is not acceptable because of the risk of unacceptable side effects.

### Smoking cessation medication

Smoking is a well-known risk factor for many diseases, especially for cardiovascular and cerebrovascular acute incidents like heart attack or stroke. Pilots and all the flight personnel are strongly advised to adopt healthy behaviors that help to keep fitness to fly. For those with nicotine dependency, medical practitioners can prescribe nicotine replacement therapy which is acceptable for medical certification.

Other drugs used for smoking cessation are Varenicline or Bupropion, but both are not compatible with fitness to fly. Varenicline is a selective nicotine receptor partial agonist but it has common side effects such as drowsiness, dizziness and insomnia. Less frequently it can cause atrial fibrillation, palpitations, panic attacks, mood lability, visual disturbance, anxiety, depression, irrational behavior, psychosis and suicidal ideation. Bupropion is also used for smoking cessation although its mode of action is still controversial. Pilots receiving Bupropion are unfit to fly due to side effects like anxiety, impaired concentration, dizziness, visual disturbance or mental confusion.

### Hypnotics

Flight operations, especially long-haul flights, may lead to sleep disturbances. Disruption of circadian rhythms is very frequent when crossing time zones and so it is difficult to fall sleep after some flights. The use of hypnotics can be useful in these situations allowing pilots to wake up in good shape and without somnolence and, if necessary, ready to fly again. However, pilots should not receive hypnotic medications that have a long half-life. The prescribing physician should select a hypnotic medication with a short action such as Temazepam. Temazepam has been used for many years in military and civil aircrew for the short-term treatment of insomnia associated with circadian rhythm disturbance. Historically it was used by aircrew of the Royal Air Force during the Falklands War in 1982 in long-haul operations with military aircraft. Since Temazepam is short-acting, hangover effects are uncommon. It should be taken no less than eight hours before the next flight to avoid the risk of minor side effects that can interfere with duties. Temazepam should not be used continuously for more than one week because the risk of dependence is considerable. Another short-time acting hypnotic, Zaleplon, is also acceptable. Medical certification is subject to the same considerations as Temazepam.

All the other hypnotics, including Zolpidem, Zopiclone, Flurazepam, Lorazepam, Brotizolam and others are disqualifying for medical certification. The same policy applies for "over-the-counter" preparations such as promethazine or diphenhydramine.

Melatonin is a hormone produced nocturnally by the pineal gland and serves as a circadian time cue promoting sleep. Melatonin production declines with age and the prevalence of sleep disorders increases, particularly insomnia. However, there is no evidence that melatonin is effective in treating secondary sleep disorders accompanying sleep restriction, such as jet lag. In addition, melatonin preparations are not always pure and may contain herbs such as valerian or camomile, together with amino acids, calcium or magnesium. The lack of evidence on the effectiveness of melatonin tablets together with the quality-control issues means that the use of melatonin is not accepted for EASA in terms of medical certification.

### Anxiolytics

Anxiolytics are prescribed for anxiety disorders and most of them are benzodiazepines (BZDs). They act by enhancing GABA (gamma-aminobutyric acid) actions at the cerebral amygdala and prefrontal cortex. GABA is the principal inhibitory neurotransmitter in the brain and normally plays an important regulatory role in reducing the activity of many neurons. Unfortunately, they all have, in different degrees, some actions that don't allow them for use by flight personnel. Those effects are muscle relaxation, sedation, sleep induction affecting alertness, and risk of dependence when used for a long time. In conclusion benzodiazepines are not useful for pilots and must be avoided except in acute situations and used for short periods – no longer than four weeks – it being necessary during their use to stop aerial activity. The use of Clonazepam – a short half-life benzodiazepine – to treat tics (Tourette's syndrome) is also disqualifying. Medical certification is incompatible with anxiolytic medication in general terms and with benzodiazepines especially.

### Antidepressants

Depression is a very common psychiatric disorder within the general population, but in a large majority of cases has a good prognosis and can be overcome after some months of appropriate treatment. The United Nations World Health Organization (WHO) estimates that it affects more than 350 million people worldwide and represents the leading cause of disability and a major contributor to the overall global burden of disease (WHO, 2016a). Each year about one million people take their own lives; suicide is the worse consequence of depression especially if left untreated. Major symptoms for diagnostic of depression are depressed mood, loss of interest or pleasure (anhedonia), feelings of guilt or low self-esteem, disturbed sleep (more frequently insomnia), poor appetite, lack of energy, disturbed appetite and poor concentration. The negative effects of depression in psychomotor and cognitive functions – reasoning, memory and concentration – are well-known and sometimes designed as cognitive toxicity. These symptoms can lead to substantial impairments in an individual's ability to take care of their everyday responsibilities. WHO experts estimate that 60 to 80 percent of people with depression can be effectively treated with antidepressant medications and "brief, structured forms of psychotherapy." However, some antidepressant medications have side effects that are not acceptable for pilots and must be avoided in all cases. Older antidepressants usually classified as tricyclic have important side effects like sedation, weight gain, dry mouth, blurred vision, urine retention and constipation. Other possible side effects are orthostatic hypotension and dizziness. Amitriptyline has a half-life of 18 to 24 hours, and active metabolites with longer half-life and sedation occurs at all dose levels. As a result of side effects and long half-life, EASA rules do not allow medical certification with tricyclic medications.

The most used and better-studied antidepressants are SSRIs – serotonin selective reuptake inhibitors. All the antidepressants of this class share a single major pharmacological feature: selective and potent inhibition of serotonin reuptake, also known as inhibition of the serotonin transporter (SERT). SSRIs cause their therapeutic actions by increasing serotonin at synapses where reuptake is blocked and serotonin release is disinhibited. Increasing serotonin in desirable pathways and at targeted receptors subtypes leads to well-known therapeutic actions of these drugs (Stahl, 2008). One of the first SSRIs introduced was Prozac, with the active ingredient fluoxetine. After Prozac, many others appeared on the market and are widely prescribed. However, only three SSRI are allowed by the EASA – sertraline, citalopram and escitalopram.

The usual daily doses for sertraline are between 50–100 mg, citalopram 10–40 mg and escitalopram 10–20 mg, depending on clinical symptoms and severity of depression. When treatment starts in an acute phase of depression the pilot should be grounded and, if necessary, an assessment by a specialist in psychiatry evaluating the degree of illness (usually expressed as slight, moderate or severe), in addition the existence – or not – of side effects that can impair psychomotor or cognitive functions must be assessed. Clinical rating scales such as the Hamilton Depression Scale may be used to track how the disorder responds to treatment. After three or four months of disability with the pilot grounded it is appropriate to wait a minimum of four weeks following resolution of symptoms before his or her suitability to fly is considered. When the pilot returns to flying, it is appropriate to apply a multi-crew limitation.

This specific limitation – OML (*valid only as or with qualified co-pilot*) – is applicable to Class I certificates only. For Class II certificates and LAPL, OSL is used"valid only with safety pilot and in aircraft with dual controls". The duration of certificate limitations varies as appropriate, taking care of clinical evaluations made by specialists – psychiatrists – with regular reports to the AME or AeMC and if necessary with psychological or neuropsychological support. During the maintenance phase of medication with lower doses of antidepressants – the authorized SSRIs – and with clinical stabilization of depression with minimal symptoms, it is possible to remove the limitations.

Other SSRIs are not useful for flight personnel because they have significant side effects such as sedation or psychomotor retardation which occurs in medicines such as Paroxetine and Fluvoxamine.

SNRIs – serotonin norepinephrine reuptake inhibitors are widely prescribed to patients with depressive disorders. This class of antidepressants block the reuptake of both serotonin and norepinephrine neurotransmitters and are very effective in mood disorders. These agents combine the robust SERT inhibition of the SSRIs with various degrees of inhibition of the norepinephrine transporter (or NET). NET inhibition increases norepinephrine and also dopamine in prefrontal cortex. That is why SNRIs have "two and a half" mechanisms: boosting serotonin throughout the brain, boosting norepinephrine throughout the brain, and boosting dopamine in prefrontal cortex (Stahl, 2008). However for medical certification they are not allowed, probably because they are more recent than SSRIs and for that reason there are fewer studies about their effects. Hence, while duloxetine or venlafaxine are both quite effective treatments, they need to be avoided in pilots.

The policy of Federal Aviation Administration (FAA) concerning depression and the use of antidepressant drugs is different in several aspects (FAA, 2016). In fact, depressive disorders and medications are medically disqualifying for pilots. However, the Federal Air Surgeon has established a policy for authorizations for special issuance of medical certificates for pilots treated with selective serotonin reuptake inhibitors (SSRI) medications who meet specific criteria. An applicant may be considered for an FAA authorization of a special issuance (SI) of a medical certificate if they meet certain conditions.

1    The applicant has one of the following diagnoses:
   ○    major depressive disorder (mild to moderate) either single or recurrent episode;
   ○    dysthymic disorder;
   ○    adjustment disorder with depressed mood;
   ○    any non-depression-related condition for which the SSRIs are used.
2    For a minimum of six continuous months prior, the applicant has been clinically stable as well as on a stable dose of medication without any aeromedical significant side effects and/or increase in symptoms. If the applicant has been on the medication under six months, the examiner must advise that six months of continuous use is required before SI (special issuance) consideration.
3    The SSRI used is one of the following (single use only):
   ○    fluoxetine
   ○    sertraline

○   citalopram

○   escitalopram.

If the applicant is on an SSRI that is not listed above, the examiner must advise that the medication is not acceptable for SI consideration.

4   The applicant does not have symptoms or clinical history of:

○   psychosis

○   suicidal ideation

○   electroconvulsive therapy

○   treatment with multiple SSRIs concurrently

○   multi-agent drug protocol use (prior use of other psychiatric drugs in conjunction with SSRIs).

If the applicant meets all of the above criteria and wishes to continue use of the SSRI, they must be advised that further evaluation by a human intervention motivation study (HIMS) AME is necessary.

The HIMS AME will also conduct the follow-up evaluation after initial issuance.

Comparing the drugs for depression treatment accepted for medical certification by EASA and the FAA, they are almost the same except that fluoxetine is accepted by FAA but not by EASA.

Depression or SSRI medication may produce cognitive deficits that would make an airman unsafe to perform pilot duties. In such a situation a neuropsychological evaluation must be conducted by a licensed clinical psychologist who is either board-certified or "board eligible" in clinical psychology. This means that the psychologist has the education, training and clinical practice experience that would qualify him or her by the American Board of Professional Neuropsychology. If the pilot is certified by FAA, medical examiners should make records available to the neuropsychologist prior to the evaluation, including:

•   copies of all records regarding prior psychiatric or substances-related hospitalizations, observations or treatment not previously submitted to the FAA;

•   a complete copy of his agency medical records – a pilot should request a copy of agency records to be sent directly to the psychiatrist or psychologist by the Aerospace Medical Certification Division (AMCD) in Oklahoma City.

After these procedures what must the neuropsychological evaluation report include?

•   A review of all available records – periods of observation, treatments, psychiatric hospitalizations and so on. Records must be in sufficient detail to permit a clear evaluation of the nature and extent of any previous mental disorders.

- A thorough clinical interview to include a detailed history regarding psychosocial or developmental problems, academic and employment performance, legal issues, substance use or abuse including treatment and recovery. After that it is important to evaluate aviation background and experience, previous or current medical conditions, and all medication use as well as behavioral observations during the interview and testing.
- A mental status examination paying attention to the existence – or not – of relevant psychopathology.
- Interpretation of testing that can include MMPI (Minnesota Multiphasic Personality Inventory), projective tests, performance tests or cognitive tests evaluating intelligence, memory, attention, processing speed or problem solving.

All tests administered must be the most current edition of the tests and, at the discretion of the examiner, additional tests may be clinically necessary to assure a complete assessment.

Even though there are not many data concerning this issue, I consider two studies that may have a bearing on future rules of prescribing anti-depressants.

### Australian study

An Australian study (Ross *et al.*, 2007) about antidepressant use and safety in civil aviation reports 10 years of data. There is increasing evidence that the supervised and appropriate use of antidepressant medication by pilots or air traffic controllers does not increase the risk of aviation incidents or accidents. The authors of the study estimated that about 4.5 percent of the adult population uses antidepressant medications, but only 1 percent of aviation certificate holders could be identified as having taken antidepressants while certificated. The authors suggested that the lower rate among pilots and air traffic controllers may reflect under-reporting of antidepressant use, rather than different levels of medication among pilots and controllers. Australian aeromedical authorities have allowed the supervised use of antidepressants since 1987. According to the study and the analysis of 10 years of aviation safety data from Australia, there was no statistical difference between the number of accidents and incidents involving crew taking antidepressant medication and those not doing so. This robust study reviewed the cases of 962 pilots and controllers, half of whom were treated with prescribed antidepressants and half of whom were not. The authors found no evidence of adverse safety outcomes arising from permitting individuals to operate as commercial or private aircrew or air traffic controllers while using antidepressants, provided specific criteria are met and maintained.

The Civil Aviation Safety Authority of Australia (CASA) defines the criteria for assessing and supervising medication use among pilots and controllers. These require pilots and controllers using medication to be under the care of a medical practitioner with experience treating depression. They must be stable on a established and appropriate dose of medication for at least four weeks before resuming flight or control duties and have minimal side effects, no drug interactions and no allergies to antidepressant medications. Other CASA requirements call for those taking antidepressants to undergo a clinical review at least once a month and to submit a progress report to CASA every six months for at least the first year of treatment. In addition, CASA requires an absence of other significant psychiatric problems and no use of other psychoactive medications, along with the control of all symptoms of depression like an absence of suicidal thoughts, rage or irritability, and presence of "normal" sleep pattern.

CASA's decision to allow pilots and controllers taking antidepressants to maintain their medical certification came soon after the introduction of a class of antidepressants, SSRIs, that marked important improvement compared with previous drugs like "old" monoamine oxidase inhibitors (MAOIs) or tricyclics. In fact SSRIs have an efficacy equivalent to that of older medications but they have significantly fewer side effects and are much better tolerated.

CASA guidelines today specify that the authority may "on a case-by-case basis" certify applicants who are prescribed the SSRIs sertraline or citalopram. There is also an antidepressant belonging to a different class of SNRIs authorized in pilots or controllers – venlafaxine.

Differences were not found in accident or incident history based on the type of antidepressant being taken. Data indicated that a slightly higher number of events occurred among pilots and controllers immediately before the start of antidepressant medication. Although the increase was considered statistically insignificant, the authors suggested that the data might indicate that the earlier use of antidepressants might actually improve flight safety for individuals who subsequently go on to use them. If so, early identification and treatment of this group may improve aviation safety while allowing continued flying or controlling duties. The authors suggested that if there is an excess of accidents in aircrew who would benefit from antidepressants but were not using them at the time of the accident, this might provide an argument for wider use of antidepressants than is currently the case in Australia, and has profound implications in those jurisdictions where antidepressants use is prohibited by certificate holders.

### Canadian study

This study is conducted by Transport Canada (TC) (Transport Canada, 2004) and it was cited by Linda Werfelman (2008) in her article "Antidepressants in aviation". Civil aviation authorities in a few countries, in addition to Australia, have already taken steps to allow some pilots to fly while taking antidepressants.

In Canada, for example, a long-term study is being conducted involving several pilots taking specific types of antidepressants to evaluate their performance while using the medications. The Canadian authority – Transport Canada (TC) – is continuing to review related medical literature. TC permits pilots taking antidepressant medication to fly only as part of a two-member crew (Transport Canada, 2004). A representative of TC (Dr. Hugh O'Neill) said that they are proceeding very cautiously with this study while looking for "some consensus of opinion throughout the world."

There is a study, published in 2007 by Sen and colleagues ("Medical histories of 61 aviation accident pilots with postmortem SSRI antidepressant residues"), which examined the medical histories of 61 pilots involved in fatal incidents with postmortem SSRI antidepressant residues. The aeromedical history of the pilots was retrieved from the Federal Aviation Administration Aerospace Medicine Database; additional pilot medical information and the cause or main factor of the accidents were obtained from the National Transportation Safety Board's (NTSB) Aviation Accident Database.

There were 59 pilots who had medical records in FAA's Certification Database. Disqualifying psychological conditions were self-reported in the past examinations of only seven pilots (12 percent) of the 59 pilots, and the use of an SSRI was reported by three of the seven pilots. In later examinations, six of the seven indicated that they were free from the conditions and not taking SSRIs: thus they were reissued with medical certificates. Such conditions and/or drug use were not self-reported in the aeromedical records of the remaining 52 (88 percent) pilots. Nevertheless, the NTSB investigators revealed 12 (20 percent) of the 61 pilots had a history of a psychological condition and/or an SSRI use as suggested by their personal medical records. During civil aviation accident investigations, postmortem samples from aviators submitted to the FAA's Civil Aerospace Medical Institute (CAMI) are routinely analyzed for the presence of fire gases, alcohol and drugs. The drugs include a wide range of prescription, non-prescription, and controlled drugs – for example analgesics, antidepressant, antihistamines, barbiturates, benzodiazepines and others. Findings of such analyses are maintained in the CAMI Toxicology Database. In a study (Akin & Chaturvedi, 2003), the prevalence of SSRI's in civil aviation pilot fatalities found four different SSRIs – citalopram, fluoxetine, paroxetine and sertraline. These four SSRIs were found to be present in 61 of 4184 pilot fatalities of US civil aviation accidents that occurred during 1990–2001. Of these 61 accidents 56 were of the general aviation category, 2 were of the air taxi and commuter category, 2 were of the agricultural category and 1 was of the ultralight category. The use of an SSRI was found to be a contributing factor by the NTSB in 9 of the 61 accidents. Overall, current findings suggest that in the majority of the fatal accidents involving SSRIs, pilots were certificated and they were primarily private pilots. However, there were a number of pilots who chose to fly without medical certificates and flying licenses. In the group of 61, there were experienced and inexperienced aviators, ranging from young to older age groups. Although the presence of SSRIs in the aviators was analytically demonstrated, their use was not reported in the last aeromedical examinations. Additionally, most of the airmen had not self-reported their psychological conditions and medications while they were continuing a regular SSRI treatment. The number of SSRI-related accidents was low, however the interactive effects of other drugs, ethanol, and altitude hypoxia in producing adverse effects in the pilots cannot be ruled out.

The findings suggest that SSRIs were used by aviators but were not reported in their last aeromedical examinations. The findings from the study should be useful in investigating SSRIs and other substance-involved accidents and in making decisions concerning the use of these antidepressants in aviation.

## Worldwide research and studies

Worldwide, the opinions of some aeromedical specialists and psychiatrists with aerospace medicine backgrounds are changing. The danger posed by untreated pilots with depression is real. Identification and diagnosis is complicated by the understandable fears of losing medical certification, the stigmatization related to mental disorders in general and particularly depression. The studies discussed here suggest that the danger, and potentially reluctance to report can be minimized by judicious and controlled use of antidepressants.

We would argue that the evidence shows that it is better to have a policy that allows pilots using medication to continue to operate with appropriate supervision and precautions than one which grounds pilots when they have to take any kind of antidepressant. This rigidity of previous attitudes may have resulted in pilots flying when depressed and untreated or failing to declare mental health conditions in the process of renewing medical certification. A significant risk under this type of regime is that pilots may take antidepressants prescribed by non-aviation specialists. The result may be unacceptable side effects in the aviation environment and a significant risk to flight safety.

Despite the increasing tendency to believe that some use of antidepressant medication by pilots would be acceptable, debate continues about precisely what medications are acceptable. There is also active debate about what problems or disorders among pilots and controllers should be treated by these medications, which sometimes are prescribed not for depression but for anxiety disorders. The logic of introducing such medications – namely antidepressants of the SSRI or SNRI class – without compromising safety is not yet fully harmonized, although there are already points of agreement. Following this way of thinking, in closely managed cases of depressive disorders, special issuances or waivers for the clinical use of well-studied antidepressants with minimal side effects are justified.

There is another psychological issue related to depression: the prevention of seasonal affective disorder (SAD). SAD is a seasonal pattern of recurrent major depressive episodes that most commonly occurs during autumn or winter with remission in spring. The prevalence of SAD in the United States ranges from 1.5 percent to 9 percent, depending on latitude. The predictable seasonal aspect of SAD provides a promising opportunity for prevention. We focus on Agomelatine and melatonin as preventive interventions (Kaminski-Hartenthaler, 2015).

Agomelatine is a new antidepressant drug with different action mechanisms to SSRIs or SNRIs. Agomelatine leads to blocking of 5HT2C receptors in the brain and causes release of both norepinephrine and dopamine, which is why these agents can be called norepinephrine dopamine disinhibitors or NDDIs (Stahl, 2008).

Melatonin is a hormone produced nocturnally by the pineal gland and serves as a circadian time cue promoting sleep.

No available methodologically sound evidence indicates that melatonin or Agomelatine may or may not be effective interventions for SAD. Lack of evidence clearly shows the need for well-conducted, controlled studies on this topic. A well-conducted randomized controlled trial of melatonin or Agomelatine for prevention of SAD would assess the comparative benefits and risks of these interventions against others currently used to treat the disorder. Furthermore, there are insufficient clinical data in using Agomelatine in flight personnel and its consumption is not recommended in such cases.

## Conclusions

Psychiatric requirements for medical certification must consider the implications of the full range of mental health disorders. The psychotic disorders have a special gravity; psychopathology includes psychotic symptoms such as different types of hallucinations – aural or visual – and delusional thoughts, sometimes with paranoia. They have a poor prognosis and are usually associated with chronic evolution and progressive mental deterioration. Psychoses such as schizophrenia or bipolar disorder are not compatible with medical certification for pilots or air traffic controllers and the use of antipsychotic medication is out of the question.

On the other hand, anxiety disorders can be controlled most of the time without serious consequences for the performance of the aircrew and are compatible with medical certification under supervision after the acute phase.

Mood disorders, particularly depression, are challenging in terms of medical certification. In severe cases, depression is a fearsome disease with serious effects in performance with disturbance of thoughts and behavior that can lead to dramatic consequences such as suicidal ideation and acting out. The positive is that well-conducted treatment often results in recovery with the possibility of renewed medical recertification after the acute phase and with sustained clinical stabilization. The prescription of recent antidepressants with good efficacy and few side effects can be accepted in accordance with rigorous protocols and periodic evaluations ensuring that flight safety will not be affected. Antidepressant drugs classified as SSRIs are the best choice, mainly those with fewer sedative clinical effects.

There is currently a wide consensus about thier use in Europe (EASA), United States of America (FAA) and Australia (CASA) with small differences concerning the drugs approved. EASA accepts the use in pilots of three SSRIs – sertraline, citalopram and escitalopram – and the FAA also accepts fluoxetine. The Australian authority, CASA, follows the same rules with some slight nuances that include acceptance of the SNRI drug venlafaxine. This more flexible policy makes it possible to return flight personnel to work more quickly and without raising concerns about flight safety, avoiding cases of untreated pilots flying while depressed without the permission of licensing authorities.

Aviators need to be aware of their responsibility to seek advice from authoritative sources whenever the initiation of drug therapy is necessary. Furthermore, they must reflect very carefully before taking any agent that might have active pharmacological properties, no matter how innocuous the substance may appear. With appropriate precautions and advice, however, it is gratifying to acknowledge that many advances of modern medicine are now available for inclusion in the healthcare of pilots without compromise to their active flying careers. The judicious use of antidepressants, especially the approved SSRIs by medical certification authorities, is a good example of the progress done in this still controversial field of medication and air crew.

## Note

1 Commission Regulation (EU) No 1178/2011 of 3 November 2011 laying down technical requirements and administrative procedures related to civil aviation aircrew pursuant to Regulation (EC) No 216/2008 of the European Parliament and of the Council.

## References

Akin, Ahmet & Chaturvedi, Arkin K. (2003). Selective serotonin reuptake inhibitors in pilot fatalities of civil aviation accidents, 1990–2001. *Aviation, Space and Environmental Medicine*, 74(11):1169–1176(8).

APA (2013). *Diagnostic and statistical manual of mental disorders (DSM-5)* (fifth edition). Arlington, VA: APA.

Bor, R. & Hubbard, T. (2006). *Aviation mental health: Psychological implications for air transportation*. London: Routledge.

Cade, J.F.J. (1949). Lithium salts in the treatment of psychotic excitement. *Medical Journal of Australia*, 2(36): 349–352.

Civil Aviation Safety Authority (n.d.). Designated aviation medical examiner's handbook. http://services.casa.gov.au/avmed/dames/handbook/default.asp

Delay, J. & Deniker, P. (1952). Utilisation en thérapeutique d'une phénothiazine d'action centrale selective. *Annales Médico-psychologiques*, 1952a, 110: 112–17.

EASA (2011). Acceptable Means of Compliance and Guidance Material to Part-Med. Annex to ED Decision 2011/015/R.

European Commission (2015). Commission Regulation (EU) No 1178/2011 (2015): Consolidated version of Regulation 1178/2011 as amended by 290/2012, 70/2014, 245/2014 and 445/2015, of 8 April 2015.

FAA (2016). Guide for aviation medical examiners. http://www.faa.gov/about/office_org/headquarters_offices/avs/offices/aam/ame/guide/

ICAO (2012) *Manual of civil aviation medicine* (third edition). Doc 8984 AN/895, Quebec: International Civil Aviation Organization.

Kaminski-Hartenthaler, A., Nussbaumer, B., Forneris, C.A., Morgan, L.C., Gaynes, B.N., Sonis, J.H. & Gartlehner, G. (2015). Melatonin and agomelatine for preventing seasonal affective disorder. *Cochrane Library*, 11, article CD011271.

National Transportation Safety Board (n.d.). National Transportation Safety Board http://www.ntsb.gov/Pages/default.aspx

Reid, Geoffrey E. (2016). Aviation psychiatry. In David Gradwell & David J. Rainford (eds) *Ernsting's Aviation and Space Medicine* (fourth edition). Boca Raton, FL: CRC Press.

Richards, P. & Zuckerman, J. (2006). Psychological factors relating to physical health issues: How physical factors in aviation and travel affect psychological functioning. In R. Bor & T. Hubbard (eds) *Aviation mental health – psychological implications for air transportation*. Ashgate Publishing Limited: 27–39.

Ross, J., Griffiths, K., Dear, K., Emonson, D. & Lambeth, L. (2007). Antidepressant use and safety in civil aviation: A case-control study of 10 years of Australian data. *Aviation, Space and Environmental Medicine,* 78(8): 749–55.

Sen, A., Akin, A., Canfield, D. V. & Chaturvedi, A.K. (2007). Medical histories of 61 aviation accident pilots with postmortem SSRI antidepressant residues. *Aviation, Space and Environmental Medicine,* 78(11): 1055–9.

Stahl, S.M. (2008). *Stahl's essential psychopharmacology* (third edition). New York: Cambridge University Press.

Transport Canada (2004). Handbook for civil aviation medical examiners. Transport Canada Online https://www.tc.gc.ca/eng/civilaviation/publications/tp13312-2-menu-2331.htm

Werfelman, L. (2008). Antidepressants in aviation. *Aero Safety World.* February: 24–7.

WHO (World Health Organization) (2016a). Fact sheet depression management. http://www.who.int/mediacentre/factsheets/fs369/en/

WHO (World Health Organization) (2016b). *International statistical classification of diseases (ICD-10)* (tenth revision). Geneva: WHO. http://www.who.int/classifications/icd/en/

# 14 Human factors and factor of the human

## Pilot performance and pilot mental health

*Nicklas Dahlstrom*

Human factors (HF) is a cross-disciplinary field of science that is strongly associated with safety, especially in regards to the role of human performance in ensuring safe actions and outcomes. Although 'cross-disciplinary' in this context represents the admirable aim to use all available knowledge to enhance safety, even the field of human factors has to outline the limitations of itself as a field of science. Such limitations may be constructive in defining human factors as an academic field, but may in practice also have the effect of excluding important influences on human performance which fall outside of these limitations. Recent aviation accidents and incidents related to mental health issues have revealed what seems to be an exclusion of the field of mental health in human factors and thus in the understanding of pilot performance. The resulting rift has roots that need to be understood and bridged to ensure and enhance the current level of safety in the aviation industry.

This chapter is written from the perspective of a human factors practitioner, who develops and delivers human factors training, performance coaching and operational advice to pilots of an airline with 4000 pilots from over one hundred countries and an operation that has one of the most extensive route networks in the industry. The chapter will reflect and explore the limited understanding of mental health issues in human factors, with the aim to contribute to an understanding of the origins and current character of this situation. In addition, some ways forward to increase understanding, communication and cooperation between the fields are proposed.

## Human factors and pilot performance

In safety critical industries such as aviation, but also in maritime and rail transportation as well as in nuclear and chemical industry, the main focus of human factors is on how to optimise safe and efficient human performance in the socio-technical systems that these industries represent. Another field where human factors is increasing in importance is that of medicine and health care. The UK Health and Safety Executive (2015) has proposed the following definition of human factors:

Human factors refer to environmental, organisational and job factors, and human and individual characteristics which influence behaviour at work in a way which can affect health and safety. ... In other words, human factors is concerned with what people are being asked to do (the task and its characteristics), who is doing it (the individual and their competence) and where they are working (the organisation and its attributes), all of which are influenced by the wider societal concern, both local and national.

To this definition could be added a more explicit statement on the role of technology and design, which have had important roles in accidents as well as in solutions that prevent accidents. In fact, it is from resolving human performance challenges with engineering solution that the origins of human factors can be traced, from resolving hypoxia with oxygen masks in the pioneering days of aviation, to the development of more intuitive flight controls via shape coding during in the 1940s (Chapanis *et al.*, 1949) and improved displays (Fitts & Jones, 1947). This is why human factors often have been strongly associated with engineering and still are today in the form of cockpit design, flight deck automation as well as via engineering approaches to human behaviour and learning such as standard operational procedures (SOPs) and training needs analysis (TNA). Batteau has encapsulated the dominance of the engineering paradigm:

Human flight is an experience of perfection: in flight, polished skills and highly engineered devices enable aviators and their acolytes to transcend normal human limitations. The devices are significant: it is the marriage of man (yes, man) and machine, or more accurately the subservience of man to machine, that enables this transcendence. Those who submit are allowed to enter the sacred spaces of flight: the control tower, the flight deck, the sky. In these sacred spaces "human factors" are almost an afterthought, a grudging acknowledgment or faintly heretical statement that there might be a concern for adaptation between this excellent machinery and the imperfect humans who depend on it.

(Batteau, 2001, p. 202)

Although the origins and current content of human factors can be attributed as much to psychology as to engineering, recognition of the close but uneven relationship that emerged between them in aviation is important. Engineering was always the stronger partner, leading the way while psychology mainly tried to compensate the consequences of the situations that engineering put pilots in regarding physical environment, display of information, methods of controlling the aircraft and later in relation to automation. Also, checklists and procedures can be seen as a 'mechanisation' of the work that once was the domain of the bold and brave 'artists' of the skies. In fact, in the 1940s the term 'human engineering' represented much of the activities that today can be looked back at as the 'adolescence of engineering psychology' (Roscoe, 1997).

This uneven relation is also manifested currently by the attempts to observe and measure pilot performance by counting 'errors', as exercised with the concept of 'line operational safety audit' (LOSA). Pilot behaviour in every possible operational situation is also expected to be captured with clear and well-defined 'behavioural markers', such as those provided by the NOTECHS framework. These, and previous examples, could all be described as belonging to the field of psychology, albeit an applied form of psychology that always has been intertwined with engineering. However, in all the examples above, the underlying assumptions about the behaviour of pilots and their interactions with the world around them represent the perspectives and paradigms of engineering.

In airlines today the 'systemic', or perhaps 'industrialised', engineering view of pilots and their colleagues as components in a large machine is obvious. A pilot's work (and life) is planned in a rostering system for which pilots can bid, but the roster is then worked out in computer system where the wishes of the pilot is only one of many variables amongst others, such as routes, flight-time limitations, vacations etc. Pilots are recruited using standardised selection processes via computerised tests and with limited human input. Training is regulated and standardised in terms of the time for training, the content of it and in the assessment of the outcome. The uniformed operator of an aircraft is to a large extent as much a component of the 'system' of an airline as one of the technical components on the aircraft.

Human factors have managed to put critical aspects of the human side of the work of a pilot at the centre of flight operations and training, such as workload management, decision-making, communication and cooperation. The critical role of human factors for flight safety is today well-accepted in the industry (although it has been a long road to get there). As such, it has been a successful endeavour of introducing and applying a cross-disciplinary field, where physiology, psychology and other fields together have provided useful input to the design and operation of aircraft with the aim of improving safety and efficiency. Still, the roots of human factors in engineering are important to understand why there may even today be discontinuities or even divisions in aviation between how to address issues of pilot performance and pilot mental health.

## Human factors: pilot mental health

Pilots have always been suspicious of doctors, and even more so of psychologists, since these professionals have had the authority to, temporarily or permanently, prevent a pilot from flying. Underlying this suspicion is probably an asymmetry of knowledge (pilots not knowing medicine, doctors not knowing aviation) as well as the asymmetry of power (the doctor's decision may be final and impossible to overturn). There are currently manifestations of this suspicion in the form of websites for pilots on how to pass a medical examination (Pilot Medical Solutions, 2016; Aeromedical Consultancy, 2016; Flightphysical,com, 2016), online pilot forum threads providing advice on medical issues (Airline

Pilot Forums, 2016; Flyer, 2016; Pilots of America, 2016) and pilot unions taking positions and offering support to pilots in regards to medical issues (IFALPA, 2012; ALPA, 2016; European Cockpit Association, 2016).

The fraught relation between pilots and doctors goes back to the beginnings of aviation. Physiological aspects were used for selection of pilots already before aviation started to be used for military purposes a century ago, but psychological aspects were only started to be recognised as greater numbers of pilots had to be recruited for military aviation (Damos, 2007). There would have been reason for suspicion in regards to first tests that decided the future of candidate pilots, as one example such a test was referred to as a 'professional and mental examination' based upon 'the candidate's written answers to a series of questions covering his parentage, education, business experience, athletic attainments, responsibilities placed upon him by others, military training....' (Stratton *et al.*, 1920, p. 406). While this may have been the best possible attempt at the time, the method used was probably neither transparent nor explained to the candidate pilots and thus, as many methods at the time, would probably have raised suspicion among them.

In spite of good intentions, and due to the demands of war, there were more initiatives in regards to pilot mental health that supported a pilot perspective of suspicion on doctors and psychologists. During the RAF bombing campaign of WWII the term 'lack of moral fibre' (Jones, 2006) was used to blame, shame and punish 'weaklings and waverers' (Harris, 1940, p. 1) into continuing to fly in the face of high losses of aircraft and crew as well as 'rising psychiatric casualties' (Jones, 2006, p. 440). The pride that has always been a part of the profession was here used against pilots, and still today the threat of losing the associated professional and social status has a great impact on pilots, as seen often after unsuccessful training or checking events. Pilots have always carried the final and greatest burden of safety and other responsibilities of a flight, and thus confidence has been seen as an essential quality in them. If the confidence of a pilot is undermined, it may take a considerable amount of time and support for recovery of self-perceived ability, thus disgrace in front of fellow pilots still remains a severe stigma.

In consequence of the threat of losing the status as a professional pilot, the associated effect on ego and tradition of suspicion against doctors and psychologist, the relation between pilots and those in the field of mental health is still a difficult one. Even today it is common with discussions among pilots about which doctor to go to, and more importantly, which one not to go to (they go by different names, e.g. 'choppers'). Similar discussions can be found in regards to psychometric selection tests and interviews. This is also manifested in online discussions about what to say or not to say to the doctor at the next aeromedical examination or interview for an airline, with sleep apnoea being a recent topic of controversy (EAA, 2013). An example of the consequences of this fraught relation was reported as: 'crash scene investigation reports show drug use by pilots may have been a contributing factor in six out of 15 Oklahoma crashes between 2008 and 2010', with a former NTSB investigator adding 'What we're seeing is just the Oklahoma tip of the iceberg' (News9, 2013).

If there is any difference between the relation of pilots to medical doctors and to psychologists it is probably that the latter group is viewed with more suspicion than the former (Bor *et al.*, 2002). While an aeromedical examination is easy to understand for a pilot, and the criteria includes passing measurable parameters (as for blood pressure and values, heart function, vision, hearing etc.), the psychometric parameters are not as easy to understand to pilots. These psychometric tests include those aimed at intelligence and psychomotor skills as well as those aimed at social skills and personality. The fact that these tests are often shrouded in secrecy is what makes them the focus of discussions, online forums, guidebooks etc. for pilots in regards how to pass them, and this contributes to the suspicion towards all things related to psychology.

It should also be noted and understood that 'suspicion' today is a positively charged word in regards to safety. Bierly and Spender (1995, p. 644) observed 'collective bonds among suspicious individuals' in nuclear submarines, LaPorte (1996, p. 65) noted 'prideful wariness' in air traffic controllers and Rochlin (1993, p. 14) describes 'suspicion of quiet periods' in high-reliability organisations (HROs). In a highly dynamic and complex safety system such as aviation, where accidents are few and far between, complacency in regards to safety is always a potential threat. Thus pilots are continuously in their recurrent training encouraged to not take safety for granted, to check and check again, to challenge each other in the cockpit and others around them and to be attentive towards small, unusual or unexpected signals of deviation from any part of the system (machine, people or organisation); thus a part of being a competent pilot is to be suspicious. This desired suspicion may in other than operational circumstances come across as outright scepticism, but knowing the context clarifies the starting point from which trust needs to be generated with pilots to make the relation with them functional and productive.

The 'gatekeeper' role of medical doctors and psychologists in the selection and recruitment of pilots has been more emphasised than following up and supporting pilots; it has been about finding the best and excluding the rest. Once you have become a pilot the focus has been on piloting skills, with far more weight on the technical piloting skills than on other aspects of the person in the uniform. Even the focus of human factors has been on enhancing and reinforcing pilot skills rather than understanding the sources of these skills (i.e. 'calibrating the machine', yet another manifestation of the engineering paradigm). Human factors and crew resource management (CRM) training have focused on training workload management, decision-making, communication and cooperation by providing 'tools' in the form of acronyms, checklist-like guidance or proceduralised action sequences, rather than trying to understand the deviations by any individual pilot from the norms of ill-defined concepts such as 'airmanship', 'command ability' and 'flight discipline'.

The limited recognition of pilot mental health issues in the aviation industry has been highlighted by many in recent times, due to recent events (Morse & Bor, 2006). This in spite of some early aims to include them, such as when Grow and Armstrong (1941) in one of the first manuals for pilots emphasised various preventative measures to preserve the 'mental hygiene' of pilots. Certainly the roots of aviation as a new and pioneering field of human activity, with a considerable element of self-selection (or simply selection by survival) meant that mental health issues were not at the forefront in the transition to a modern pilot profession. However, as aviation has developed to a transport industry and the pilot to a regulated and regularly checked professional of this industry, the need to also look in-depth at the person behind the controls has increased. Considering that 'mental and emotional' issues represent the second and third most common reason for permanently losing a Class 1 medical certificate in the UK and Norway respectively (Dao, 2015), an increased integration of pilot mental health aspects into the framework for pilot performance is a reasonable and perhaps necessary step to take in the aviation industry.

Mental health is a field manifesting the full spectrum of human complexity in ways that clash with the more linear and mechanistic explanations and solutions provided by an engineering perspective in the aftermath of an incident (these are also often the desired explanations and solutions by many stakeholders after an accident). The often non-measurable, deeply qualitative approach relying on autonomous expert that is required when exploring and understanding human behaviour beyond the normal is not easy to translate and to correspond with an industry which has developed to be governed by regulations, procedures and multiple other forms of officially sanctioned guidance. As an example Anthony (2015) concludes that although intentional acts of harming others as part self-harm on a grand scale may hold elements of psychopathy, life-insurance fraud and leaving explanations behind, people can plan for such acts while at the same time planning for the future; 'Simply, it means that just because an individual has paid for a vacation holiday next month, it is not assured that he will not make a fatal decision today' (Anthony, 2015, p. 7). Thus the linear and mechanistic relations influencing the human factors view of pilot performance may often fall short of being able to bridge the gap to the more complex and multifaceted accounts provided by psychiatry.

## Human factors and pilot mental health

It would probably be reasonable for someone outside of the aviation industry to assume that the link between the fields of human factors and pilot mental health should be strong. There should be great overlap between these two fields and it could even be argued that pilot mental health should be a part of the field of human factors, as it is a field focused on pilot performance. In fact, the regulatory wording in ICAO documents does not mention human factors but uses the term 'human performance'. Given this, it could be expected to have pilot mental health integrated in human factors training for pilots (i.e. crew resource management training), since it affects 'human performance'. This is however not the case and as outlined previously this is not a new situation, but rather on where the roots go back in time.

In a story from 1759, Dr. Samuel Johnson tells a foreboding tale about aviation. The main character of the story meets a 'mechanist', i.e. an engineer, who aims to build an aircraft. In response the main character expresses concern with the physiological limitations of altitude: 'I am afraid that no man will be able to breathe in these regions of speculation and tranquillity. I have been told that respiration is difficult upon lofty mountains'. This is not recognised by the engineer working with him, whose main focus is on the mechanical aspects of his machine, and the engineer ends up failing and falling into the sea due to a lack of power to move the wings (Johnson, 1759).

In a follow-up to the different perspectives of those engineers concerned with human aspects of flight, Dr. John Fulton referred to Dr. Johnson's foresight in a lecture given at the University of London in 1947 (as referenced by Mitchell, 1992, p. 7):

> The most critical problem of aviation medicine, as we see it now, nearly two hundred years after Samuel Johnson's prescient pronouncements, is still to bring the engineer and the physiologist together in settling upon a design and other specifications essential to keep man, when in his machine, at the peak of his performance.

Even today the challenge of bringing the distinctly quantitative perspective of engineering and the more qualitative of mental health together is present, and especially in aviation. In fact, these conflicting perspectives can be found even within human factors, as represented by the duelling articles on situational awareness by Dekker & Hollnagel (2004), responded to by Parasuraman *et al.* (2008) and followed by a response from Dekker *et al.* (2010). These illustrate the continued confrontation between the perspectives on human performance as an entirely externally observable and controllable process or as an internal, inferred and interpreted process.

What we have here are two fields of science with definitions that are more inclusive than exclusive ('body and mind'), boundaries which are wide-ranging ('cross-disciplinary fields') and overlapping focus of study ('human behaviour'). Although often focused on the individual, modern psychiatry and medicine in general has moved to recognise a far wider spectrum of influences on their object of study, i.e. the patient. This has been paralleled by the gradually widening scope of human factors: from physiological to also psychological aspects of the individual, from individual to group (Foushee, 1984) and on to organisational and widely socio-technical systemic influences (e.g. design, culture, power) (Dekker, 2014).

This gradual widening of fields has led to the emergence of 'resilience engineering', an approach that rejects the engineered control of human behaviour as the only way to create safety in safety-critical human activities. Woods, one of the founders of this approach, describes its background almost as an 'awakening' among safety researchers:

Around 2000, I noticed a shift in the language and concepts that safety researchers were using to discuss how organisations succeed and fail. Many of the papers began to use words like resilience or robustness to describe organisations that were able to achieve ultra-high levels of safety despite high risks, difficult tasks, and constantly increasing pressures. Resilient organisations were proactive and adaptive, and this led to organisations that not only had high levels of safety but also were able to respond effectively to many types of changes in today's highly pressured business and operational settings.

(Woods, 2006, p. 1)

Resilience engineering recognises complexity of systems, as well as of humans, as an inherent property of modern socio-technical systems and one that leads to the emergence of shortfalls not foreseen in design, planning and preparation (Bergström *et al.*, 2011). It also recognises complexity as a potential resource for safety and not only as a problematic property that needs to be controlled. Rather than viewing the human operator as source of error and risk, the expertise of the operator is critical to provide flexible responses that can compensate for the shortfalls in the system. This approach offers a bridge to mental health issues, with its recognition of complexity, refocus on the human subject and interest in supporting and reinforcing the operator. Resilience engineering places pilot performance, and thus mental states of the pilot, at the centre of safety; and the field of mental health has at heart a full recognition of human complexity, adaptability and interaction with surrounding people and environment. Thus there is now, more than ever before, a distinctly defined overlap between the fields; an arena where the conversation can commence, and cooperation be developed.

## Way forward: integration and implementation

While human factors professionals are working in airlines or with other operators, such close proximity to day-to-day operations is rare for mental health professionals. Psychologists are common at airlines, but mostly in pilot selection, selection and recruitment in general, human resources, and organisational development. This remote relation to operations is problematic as not only the conditions of flying (e.g. environment, technology, work times) are unique for the pilot profession, but also the mandatory training and checking (to become a pilot and ongoing thereafter), professional culture (Dahlstrom & Heemstra, 2009) and many other work and life conditions. One of the foremost examples is the effect of living life by a pre-determined roster, planned long ahead and at times subjected to late changes. At the same time as pilots often enjoy talking about their profession, they can be reluctant to speak to non-pilots simply because of the efforts it may take to explain these conditions to 'operational outsiders'. Also, pilots are under constant external scrutiny (in the form of operational flight data monitoring, periodic medical examinations, and investigations of operational events) at the same time as the profession still has a high social status and sense of exclusivity. Taken together this can make pilots a bit 'tribal' in regards to who they consider worth (or worthy of) talking to, with a preference fellow pilots or other professionals from the operational setting.

In recent years the aviation industry has increasingly focused on identifying and training 'competencies', which are observed and assessed via 'behavioural markers'. Eight behavioural markers have been agreed on by the industry as representative for the competence of a pilot (ICAO, 2013; IATA, 2013). Three represent technical piloting skills, such as 'aircraft flight management, manual control', 'aircraft flight management, automation' and 'application of procedures'. The other five represent 'human factors', 'crew resource management' or 'resilience' skills: workload management, situation awareness, problem-solving and decision-making, communication, leadership and teamwork. In an in-flight situation these may be manifested and observed as below:

- management of workload, time pressures and stress for the individual pilot, fellow pilots, cabin crew and for the overall operation;
- monitoring of presented information, analysis of this information together with procedures and guidance, synthesising into awareness of the situation;
- conditioned aircraft handling in reaction to alarms, short-term decision-making and long-term thorough and methodical trouble-shooting and problem-solving;
- communication with other pilots, cabin crew members, passengers, operational and technical staff, and others involved in the operation;
- leadership and teamwork in taking command and coordinating situations such as passenger behaviour, medical emergencies and in-flight technical problems.

Although there are standard operational procedures (SOPs) available for most of the possible events requiring the competencies above, they require the adaptability and flexibility, i.e. resilience, mentioned previously. The behavioural markers for the competencies and associated narratives does not only provide information about pilot performance, but can possibly also offer information about the mental state and cognitive capabilities of a pilot, and by inference indications in regards to mental health (Voge, 1989). Lack of performance in general in these competencies or shortcomings in specific scenarios may be no more than indications of training needs, but when not remedied by training they may point to underlying issues, e.g. effects of life stress, saturation of attention, unstructured or too rigid decision processes, absence of empathy, lack of confidence, or over-confidence. Although rarely so, these issues may in turn be linked to mental health aspects, especially if they are manifested distinctly and repeatedly (Raymond & Moser, 1995).

To dare to take the step (or make the leap) from assessments of pilot performance to indications of relevance to mental health aspects there is a great need for more shared knowledge between human factors and mental health professionals. Human factors professionals need to learn at least some fundamental knowledge in the field of mental health. Mental health professionals need to learn about pilot performance in the operational environment. Such knowledge would not make either group competent to carry out the assessments of the other in regards to pilot performance of mental health, but it could create a shared platform for conversations between two professional groups with the performance and well-being of pilots as the focus of their professions.

Knowledge about operational and other conditions for pilot performance would not only facilitate relations between human factors and mental health professionals, it would also generate trust and facilitate contacts between pilots and mental health professionals.

At Emirates, different parts of the organisation are available to provide different approaches in support of pilot performance, and support pilot mental health.

Involved in this are AMEs, psychologists, human factors experts as well as others who work closely with the pilots. Information regarding pilot performance or behaviour can come from pilots contacting any of those who provide support, from operational or training events or from different types of reports, including from the confidential reporting system. Regular follow-up of health and general well-being is conducted by AMEs who are permanently employed by Emirates. They perform the annual medical examinations of Emirates pilots and refer pilots for medical treatment beyond that which is available at the company clinics. This brings continuity and coherence to assessments of pilot health issues as a potential source for pilot performance issues. However, in most cases pilot performance issues manifest themselves in training or operations without a link to any underlying health issues and may then be addressed to the human factors office or psychologists at Emirates.

The focus of human factors office is pilot performance in the strict operational perspective. If a pilot is not reaching performance standards in a training session or an upgrade interview, or has trouble in line flying, the chief pilot or training manager can refer the pilot for a human factors session. This is a coaching session where the human factors specialist (HFS) and pilot explore how to improve performance, and where guidance and tools from a human factors perspective are provided to the pilot. There is a benefit here in that the HFS continuously works close to the operation, with pilots, and essentially 'lives with the tribe' and thus understands the conditions for pilot performance in day-to-day operations. (Also, given the previously described traditional relations, not being a psychologist or a doctor facilitates the coaching role of the HFS.) Due to simulator recovery training sessions often being planned within a short time span after an event related to pilot performance, the HF sessions are normally limited to one or a few, with the aim of providing clear directions to the pilot on how to improve performance.

The reasons for not achieving performance standards or other unsuccessful behaviour can of course go deeper than being directly linked only to operational features of pilot performance. Underlying aspects such as stress tolerance and coping, information processing and judgement, lack of confidence and assertiveness, uncooperative behaviours etc. may require the full professional expertise of a psychologist also trained in coaching to be resolved. For this, there are psychologists available for this type of coaching. They normally provide a series of sessions to explore, support and develop the productive perceptions, cognitive controls and constructive behaviours needed to recover or improve successful pilot performance.

Available as a next step, or directly when required, are also clinical psychologists (available not only for pilots, but also for other employees). If performance issues cannot be resolved by the coaching provided in a human factors session, or by a series of sessions with a psychologist, and observations or information from the sessions indicates that further exploration of potential underlying aspects is prudent, then one or more sessions with a clinical psychologist can be the next step. The aim of these sessions is no different to the ones outlined previously; the focus is still on pilot performance and well-being. However, the focus and scope is likely to be wider and deeper, and can include psychometric testing beyond what is used in pilot selection. Beyond this, further support structures are available, but in essence this outlines the support structures available to cover everything but rare and exceptional situations.

Communication and coordination in regards to different options in support for pilots and their performance is a challenge in a large organisation. At Emirates there have been meetings between the different groups of professionals involved in support of pilot performance to create understanding, share information and coordinate the support. Also, a 'referral' structure is being developed to formalise the processes that gradually have emerged to handle coordination of different types of situations. As an example a pilot may in a human factors session be referred to a psychologist for further coaching, or a pilot starting with coaching by a psychologist may have a human factors session before returning to line operations in order to operationalise the skills developed in the sessions with the psychologist.

The cooperation described here is far from developed to its full potential, but represents an evolving partnership between human factors and psychology. This originated from work on shared projects of presenting information to upgrade candidates, development of team building and training events, and sharing of literature in respective fields. Initially the projects emerged from individual initiatives rather than supporting organisational structures, but gradually human factors and psychology have come to be seen by the organisation not as two separate parts, but as overlapping and complementary resources. If there is a learning point to pass on from this experience, it is for airlines and other operators to initiate, facilitate and support this type of cooperation – until there is full awareness in the organisation for how both human factors and psychology can support pilot performance and mental health. When both are seen as organisational resources available for the benefit of pilots, then further integration can follow.

The challenge in regards to pilot performance is the same for the pilot, the human factors and mental health professionals and everyone engaged in operations – ensuring the best possible conditions for pilot performance and providing support where there may be challenges in regards to pilot performance. Linked to this there is an industry need for knowledge and information sharing to go beyond the (often protected) professional boundaries of those involved in supporting pilot performance. Although well-intended attempts to increase communication and coordination, such as the one described here for Emirates, may go a long way to improve the situation, a framework from authorities and industry organisations is required that recognises this need and supports such initiatives.

# References

Aeromedical Consultancy (2016). How to pass your next medical. Retrieved 30 March 2016 from: http://dgcamedical.in/Passmedical.htm

Airline Pilot Forums (2016). Forum thread: 'Can I pass the FAA medical exam'. Retrieved 2 April 2016 from: http://www.airlinepilotforums.com/archive/index.php/t-87980.html

ALPA (2016). Aviation Medicine Advisory Service (AMAS). Retrieved 1 April 2016 from: https://www.aviationmedicine.com/consult-an-amas-physician/air-line-pilots-association-international-alpa/

Anthony, T. (2015). Human factors in extremis: The rogue pilot phenomenon. Paper for the 2015 ISASI Annual Seminar, 24–27 August, Augsburg, Germany. Retrieved 28 December 2015 from: http://www.isasi.org/Documents/library/technical-papers/2015/Human%20Factors%20in%20Extremis%206.26.2015.pdf

Batteau, A.W. (2001). The anthropology of aviation and flight safety. *Human Organization*, 60(3), 201–211.

Bergström, J., Henriqson, E. & Dahlström, N. (2011). From crew resource management to operational resilience. Paper presented at the 4th Resilience Engineering Symposium, June 8–10, Sophia Antipolis, France. Retrieved 2 January 2016 from: http://lup.lub.lu.se/luur/download?func=downloadFile&recordOId=1976598&fileOId=1976600

Bierly, P.E. & Spender, J.-C. (1995). Culture and high reliability organizations: The case of the nuclear submarine. *Journal of Management*, 21, 639–656.

Bor, R., Field, G. & Scragg, P. (2002). The mental health of pilots: An overview. *Counselling Psychology Quarterly*, 15(3), 239–256.

Chapanis, A., Garner, W.R. & Morgan, C.T. (1949). *Applied experimental psychology*. New York: Wiley.

Dahlstrom, N. & Heemstra, L.R. (2009). Beyond multi-culture: When increasing diversity dissolves differences. In S. Strohschneider & R. Heiman (eds.) *Kultur und Sicheres Handeln*. Frankfurt: Verlag für Polizeiwissenschaft.

Damos, D.L. (2007). Foundations of Military Pilot Selection Systems: World War I. Technical Report 1210. Arlington, VA: Rotary-Wing Aviation Research Unit, U.S. Army Research Institute for the Behavioral and Social Sciences.

Dao, T. (2015). Can we afford to ignore mental illness in aviation? Presentation at 7th Global Humanitarian Aviation Conference, 7–9 October, Geneva, Switzerland. Retrieved 2 January 2016 from: http://annualghac.com/assets/pdf/7ghac/Day1PDF/3DRTRANG.pdf

Dekker, S.W.A. (2014). *Safety differently – human factors for a new era*. Boca Raton, FL: CRC Press.

Dekker, S.W.A. & Hollnagel, E. (2004). Human factors and folk models. *Cognition, Technology & Work*, 6, 79–86.

Dekker, S.W.A., Nyce, J.M., van Winsen, R. & Henriqson, E. (2010). Epistemological self-confidence in human factors. *Journal of Cognitive Engineering and Decision Making*, 4(1), 27–38.

EAA (Experimental Aircraft Association) (2013). FAA sleep apnea policy would set a dangerous precedent. Retrieved 29 December 2015 from: http://www.eaa.org/en/eaa/eaa-news-and-aviation-news/advocacy/2013-11-19-faa-sleep-apnea-policy-would-set-a-dangerous-precedent

European Cockpit Association (2016). Aircrew medical fitness. Retrieved 29 March 2016 from: https://www.eurocockpit.be/pages/aircrew-medical-fitness

Fitts, P.M. & Jones, R.E. (1947). *Psychological aspects of instrument display. Analysis of 270 'pilot-error' experiences in reading and interpreting aircraft instruments.* Report No. TSEAA-694-12A. Dayton, OH: Aero Medical Laboratory, Air Materiel Command, U.S. Air Force.

Flightphysical.com (2016). Hints for your FAA medical examination and keeping your pilot medical certificate. Retrieved 28 March 2016 from: http://flightphysical.com/pilot/tips/Exam-Outcomes.htm

Flyer.co.uk (2016). Forum thread: 'Any AMEs here? I'm worried I won't pass my medical...'. Retrieved 2016-04-09: http://forums.flyer.co.uk/viewtopic.php?t=89411

Foushee, H.C. (1984). Dyads and triads at 35,000 feet. *American Psychologist*, 39(8), 885–893.

Grow, M.C. & Armstrong, H.G. (1941). *Fit to fly: A medical handbook for fliers.* New York, NY: Appleton-Century.

Harris, A.T. (1940). Letter from Air Vice-Marshal Harris, 10 October 1940. AIR2/8591, TNA.

Health and Safety Executive (2015). Introduction to human factors. Retrieved 29 December 2015 from: http://www.hse.gov.uk/humanfactors/introduction.htm

IATA (2013). Evidence-based training implementation guide. Montreal, Canada: International Air Transport Association.

ICAO (2013). Manual of evidence-based training. Doc 9995 AN/497. Montreal, Canada: International Civil Aviation Organisation.

IFALPA (2012). Medical review and appeals procedure. Retrieved 2 April 2016 from: http://www.ifalpa.org/store/13POS05%20-%20Medical%20review%20and%20appeals%20procedure.pdf

Johnson, S. (1759). *Rasselas, Prince of Abyssinia.* Retrieved 27 December 2015 from: http://www.gutenberg.org/ebooks/652

Jones, E. (2006). 'LMF': The use of psychiatric stigma in the Royal Air Force during the Second World War. *The Journal of Military History*, 70 (April), 439–458.

LaPorte, T.R. (1996). High reliability organizations: Unlikely, demanding and at risk. *Journal of Contingencies and Crisis Management*, 4, 60–71.

Mitchell, R.E. (1992). Aviation medicine research: A historical review. Fourth Lecture in the Ashton Graybiel Lecture Series. Compiled by R.E. Gadolin, NAMRL Special Report 92–3. Pensacola, FL: Naval Aerospace Medical Research Laboratory.

Morse, J.S. & Bor, R. (2006). Psychiatric disorders and syndromes among pilots. In R. Bor & T. Hubbard (eds), *Aviation mental health: Psychological implications for air transportation.* Aldershot: Ashgate.

News9 (2013). Pilots hide prescription drug use, create deadly trend. Retrieved 9 January 2016 from: http://www.news9.com/story/22848051/pilots-hide-prescription-drug-use-create-deadly-trend

Parasuraman, R., Sheridan, T.B. & Wickens, C.D. (2008). Situation awareness, mental workload, and trust in automation: Viable empirically supported cognitive engineering constructs. *Journal of Cognitive Engineering and Decision Making*, 2(2), 140–160.

Pilot Medical Solutions (2016). How to pass your next FAA medical. Retrieved 29 March 2016 from: https://www.leftseat.com/pass.htm

Pilots of America (2016). Forum thread: 'How does the FAA research people's medical history'. Retrieved 1 April 2016 from: http://www.pilotsofamerica.com/community/threads/how-does-the-faa-research-peoples-medical-history.47067/

Raymond, M.W. & Moser, R. (1995). Aviators at risk. *Aviation, Space & Environmental Medicine*, 66(1), 35–39.

Rochlin, G.I. (1993). Defining 'high reliability' organizations in practice: A taxonomic prologue. In K.H. Roberts (ed.), *New challenges to understanding organizations* (pp. 11–32). New York: Macmillan.

Roscoe, S.N. (1997). *The adolescence of engineering psychology*. Human Factors History Monograph Series 1. Santa Monica, CA: Human Factors and Ergonomics Society.

Stratton, G.M., McComas, H.C., Coover, J.E. & Bagby, E. (1920). Psychological tests for selecting aviators. *Journal of Experimental Psychology*, 3(6), 405–423.

Voge V.M. (1989). Failing aviator syndrome: A case history. *Aviation, Space & Environmental Medicine*, 60(7 Pt 2), A89–91.

Woods, D.D. (2006). Resilience engineering: Redefining the culture of safety and risk management. *Human Factors and Ergonomics Society Bulletin*, 49(12), 1–3.

# 15 Promoting mental health and well-being in aviation

*Ben Campion*

It is probably obvious that the promotion of positive mental health and well-being is a 'good thing'. Government agendas repeatedly endorse and promote positive mental health and well-being agenda. Examples such as the UK Health & Safety Executive[1] and US government[2] 'National Prevention Strategy' papers reflect a trend that crosses international boundaries. In a safety-critical industry such as aviation, promoting good mental health has become a current focus in the aftermath of recent incidents where pilots with psychological issues attracted media attention. Although such incidents are rare, there is now a window of opportunity to examine and implement robust mechanisms for supporting good mental health and well-being among pilots. How this might be done is the subject of this chapter.

Aviation encompasses many groups: pilots recreational and commercial, airlines, manufacturers, service providers and service users. The aviation industry necessarily makes a 'costs versus benefits' analysis prior to investment. The promotion of mental health and well-being in aviation needs to be considered on a group-by-group basis, to examine what considerations would be reasonable to be made by that group. The primary focus of this chapter is on pilots although we will consider possibilities for other groups.

The US National Prevention Strategy, 'Mental and Emotional Well Being'[3] is consistent with UK HSE policy, linked with CAA/EASA and FAA. It asks the questions:

- What can businesses and employers do?
- What can community, non-profit, and faith-based organisations do?
- What the federal government will do? ...

I shall take this approach in this chapter on aviation psychology;

- What can business (the aviation industry) do to promote mental health and well-being?
- What can the aviation community – and the individual – do to promote mental health and well-being?
- What do aviation authorities do to promote mental health and well-being?

## Aviation industry role in promoting mental health and well-being

As a number of authors, such as Kalkman, have demonstrated, there is a strong evidence base linking air accidents to poor mental health amongst pilots.[4] There have been a number of murder-suicides that have been attributed to pilot mental ill health: the March 2015 GermaWings crash[5] an exemplar; an event causing 264 deaths. Other chapters of this book explore the issues of screening, medical assessment, and psychological pathology. Bor[6] showed the potential benefit to employers of investment in employee well-being with links to improved productivity; indeed Hamar *et al.* demonstrated that schemes including pilots and other groups could potentially be cost neutral.[7] Industry gathers satisfaction ratings that repeatedly demonise airlines that don't recognise the well-being of their (paying) customers.

The US National Prevention Strategy recommends 'business' to:

- implement organisational changes to reduce employee stress (e.g., develop clearly defined roles and responsibilities) and provide reasonable accommodations (e.g., flexible work schedules, assistive technology, adapted work stations);
- ensure that mental health services are included as a benefit on health plans and encourage employees to use these services as needed;
- provide education, outreach, and training to address mental health parity in employment-based health insurance coverage and group health plans.

This mirrors guidance from other national governments with a 'paid for' healthcare system. A promising example for the aviation industry to further develop a healthy psychosocial working environment is the 'Management standards for work-related stress' developed by the United Kingdom Health and Safety Executive.[8] The management standards cover six key areas of work design that, if not adequately managed, are associated with poor health and well-being, lower productivity and increased sickness absence: demands, control, support, relationships, role and change.

The UK standards require companies to conduct risk assessments and create action plans to improve conditions. The threat of litigation under the UK Health and Safety at Work legislation is also an incentive for employers to start addressing the issue of work-related stress.

There are a reasonable range of actions that industry can take to promote mental health and well-being – both in their workforce and for their customers (the passenger) – beyond their statutory responsibility as an employer. These are reviewed below.

Fatigue is the subject of another chapter, and working hours in safety-critical aviation roles such as aircrew, engineers and ATC are strictly regulated. It is, however, important to consider the link between fatigue and mental health. While individual experience will vary, the combination of irregular shifts, restricted rest opportunities and long or unsociable hours is not generally viewed as promoting well-being. A key factor not always addressed is transit to and from place of work, which should be considered alongside the shift pattern of employees. Fell presents strong evidence from wider industry that flexible working hours for the workforce is seen as beneficial by employees.[9] The costs to the employer are dependent on role and are particularly complex in the regulatory and commercial environment of aviation. Any strategies related to this will be carefully scrutinised/costed before adoption, but are likely to pay dividends in terms of attendance and safety where they are possible.

While not all communication and IT technology impacts positively on mental health or well-being (consider your frustration with automated 'help lines'!) there is considerable opportunity to 'leverage' technology to promote mental health and well-being, which may include:

1   increased use of videoconferencing
    o   to reduce travel associated with 'face to face' meetings;
    o   to support counselling and therapy provision;
    o   to support management of personnel – particularly when 'down route'.
2   use of 'wearables' to monitor staff fatigue;
3   electronic flight bags to reduce carried luggage/manuals;
4   cockpit 'alertness' systems to reduce impact of boredom/underload;
5   remote working IT systems.

Crew resource management (CRM) refers to the comfort of the workstation environment, quality of food, fatigue management systems, consideration of overnight facilities and travel to/from airport of departure. All of these CRM factors can impact on the well-being – and thus mental health of crew. CRM systems aim to reduce crew physiological stress – on the flight deck and other workstation areas – which can be assumed to reduce both the pilot's stress and reduce risk.

Issues such as workload, work patterns and the working environment also need to be considered for the ground handling and support staff in the aviation industry; cabin crew and engineers are equivalently regulated to pilots now. The 'champion' against excess demands on the workforce has traditionally been a strong workforce union; the balance between union and employer remains contentious. Whilst the attention is focused on the professional aviator, the entire workforce must be mentally healthy to minimise risk.

The UK HSE standard is that:

•   the organisation provides employees with adequate and achievable demands in relation to the agreed hours of work;
•   people's skills and abilities are matched to the job demands;
•   jobs are designed to be within the capabilities of employees; and
•   employees concerns about their work environment are addressed.

How much control and influence an employee has in the way they do their work is an important factor influencing mental well-being. The aviation industry negotiates with unions to balance the needs of the employee with the commercial reality of a global industry. UK HSE has a legally enforceable requirement for the organisation to support development of skills, however it is accepted that implementing this in the aviation industry would be particularly complex. Enlightened employers would see the benefits to employee mental health and well-being were they to support skill training both directly valued to the aviation industry and those skills valued more to individual:

The UK HSE 'control' standard is that:

- where possible, employees have control over their pace of work;
- employees are encouraged to use their skills and initiative to do their work;
- where possible, employees are encouraged to develop new skills to help them undertake new and challenging pieces of work;
- the organisation encourages employees to develop their skills;
- employees have a say over when breaks can be taken; and
- employees are consulted over their work patterns.

Self-funding is becoming increasingly common for new airline pilots: and the costs can be prohibitive, further exacerbating the pressures felt by those in the industry not to disclose mental health issues[10] and risk potential grounding/loss of income. The aviation industry is a technically challenging one; training for most roles – flying and ground support – is extensive. There is a responsibility on the aviation training industry to consider individuals not merely on their technical competence (or their ability to fund the training), but also on their temperamental suitability to role. Consideration of training in mental health issues, alongside the advice in previous chapters surrounding the complex issue of assessment and monitoring of trainee pilots, could mitigate some of the culture of keeping a 'stiff upper lip' and avoiding emotionally difficult conversations.

Employers will consider the cost–benefit of providing formal stress management training. While individuals may groan when faced with 'mandatory training', raising awareness of factors that can elevate stress in the individual and stress management training can be useful in promoting positive mental health. Shultz & Shultz[11] and others have shown that stress management training programmes can reduce the level of physiological arousal associated with high stress. Participants who master behavioural and cognitive stress-relief techniques report less tension, fewer sleep disturbances, and an improved ability to cope with workplace stressors. Most airlines would claim to do this already as part of CRM training, however the higher standards proposed for career-long stress management policy that mandates a programme of education and support, coupled with embedded welfare support would be a reasonable 'minimum' for an organisation to provide, and would probably prove cost neutral.

The evidence in support of extensive pastoral, social, community, counselling, medical and mental health service support, is well established by Plsek[12] and others; indeed such support is mandated by many nations' industrial regulation. The extent to which this is provided will depend on how enlightened the organisation is. The key to provision of support services is to remember that support services may not be used, but not providing them risks causing public outcry.

The UK HSE 'support' standard is that:

- the organisation has policies and procedures to adequately support employees;
- systems are in place to enable and encourage managers to support their staff;
- systems are in place to enable and encourage employees to support their colleagues;
- employees know what support is available and how and when to access it;
- employees know how to access the required resources to do their job; and
- employees receive regular and constructive feedback.

Positive relationships among staff reflect and influence mental health and well-being. In military aviation there is an ethos of the 'team'. Thus, flying 'squadrons' operate, socialise, work and often live together, which fosters a 'family' atmosphere. This close-knit military 'family' offers early warning of deteriorating mental health and endorses peer and management support. There has been a number of research projects done – particularly by The Health Foundation in 2015 – demonstrating that the unit cohesion correlates strongly with improved safety outcome in such close-knit military community.[13] This is, however, not easy to replicate in a civilian aviation community; recreational pilots in local aviation clubs may have strong relationships which are mutually supportive and may also provide early warning of a mental ill-health. Industry aviators operate varied employment schedules; it is not unusual in large airline companies for pilots to meet their fellow co-pilot the first time on the day of their flight, and never work together again. The model discussed in 'aircrew scheduling'[14] and used by several airlines whereby senior pilots are paired for one to three months with more junior pilots may partly mitigate such risks. Clear guidance on the benefits as to what individuals could do to compensate outside of work – nurturing social and intimate relationships, along with encouraging extracurricular activities – would.

The UK HSE 'relationships' standard is that:

- the organisation promotes positive behaviours at work to avoid conflict and ensure fairness;
- employees share information relevant to their work;
- the organisation has agreed policies and procedures to prevent or resolve unacceptable behaviour;

- systems are in place to enable and encourage managers to deal with unacceptable behaviour; and
- systems are in place to enable and encourage employees to report unacceptable behaviour.

It is the responsibility of the employer to ensure that employees understand their role within the organisation and whether they have conflicting roles. Dame Carol Black's review of the health of Britain's working-age population, *Working for a healthier tomorrow*,[15] highlighted that health and well-being is not just a medical issue. The nature and characteristics of the jobs that employees do are vitally important in terms of satisfaction, reward and control. The role of the line manager is also key. Good line management can lead to good health, well-being and improved performance. Line managers also have a role in identifying and supporting people with health conditions to help them to carry on with their responsibilities, or adjust responsibilities where necessary.

The UK HSE 'role' standard is that:

- the organisation ensures that, as far as possible, the different requirements it places upon employees are compatible;
- the organisation provides information to enable employees to understand their role and responsibilities;
- the organisation ensures that, as far as possible, the requirements it places upon employees are clear; and
- systems are in place to enable employees to raise concerns about any uncertainties or conflicts they have in their role and responsibilities.

Again, aviation adds additional complexity because aircrew tend to transit briefly though places where they might encounter managers on their way to operate, often outside traditional management working hours. Face-to-face contact is challenging, building solid professional relationships between management and crew often almost impossible. Considerable effort is required by the aviation industry human resource managers to address this issue.

How organisational change (large and small) is managed and communicated in the organisation will have a significant bearing on how employees engage with the change process – and how they adapt to it. A whole industry of 'change gurus' exist to give advice to industry. The key message is that management must engage with the workforce in organisational change.

The UK HSE 'change' standard is that:

- the organisation provides employees with timely information to enable them to understand the reasons for proposed changes;
- the organisation ensures adequate employee consultation on changes and provides opportunities for employees to influence proposals;
- employees are aware of the probable impact of any changes to their jobs – if necessary, employees are given training to support any changes in their jobs;

- employees are aware of timetables for changes; and
- employees have access to relevant support during changes.

The aviation industry may provide occupational health services, dependent on the national healthcare provision. The causes of premature death are dominated by 'diseases of lifestyle', where smoking, unhealthy diet, excess alcohol consumption and sedentary lifestyles are contributory factors.[16] Employers have significant scope to facilitate an employee's early return from sickness absence. Early, regular and sensitive contact with employees during sickness absences can be a key factor in enabling an early return, yet as many as 40 per cent of organisations have no sickness absence management policy at all.[17] Provision of an occupational health service is a cost effective system of sickness management that enlightened organisations will provide.

Whilst this book focuses on tackling poor mental health – which we know could reduce our overall disease burden by nearly a quarter[18] – living with medical conditions that cause pain also affect individuals' mental health. The UK Department of Health cites musculoskeletal conditions, circulatory diseases and mental health disorders as accounting for over 70 peer cent of the burden of longstanding ill health in the UK.[19] A wider emphasis on supporting general health – through such things as provision of sporting and health facilities, gym membership, private healthcare provision – is a strong factor to be considered in any cost–benefit analysis, and is a key recommendation in the US, UK and EU.[20]

Sharing information – particularly medical and social problems that may be early warning of mental health problems – is highly dependent on national culture and medico-legal issues. It could be considered that the aviation industry should have a low threshold for disclosure, particularly when considered alongside the stigma/reluctance of professional aviators to acknowledge medical and social problems for fear of 'grounding'. Developing a relationship between clinical staff and aviators may relieve some of the reluctance to ask for help. US Air Force flying squadrons have an embedded medical officer for just this reason. Such resource-intensive – and costly – approaches are beyond the resources of most organisations. Other (cheaper) approaches can be considered by increased liaison with local clinical staff, providing healthcare plans, and resourcing health promotion campaigns using 'friendly' medical practices. Replacing the paper-based sick note with an electronic fit note may also increase 'help seeking' behaviour in the workforce, by switching the focus to what people can do instead of what they cannot, and potentially improving communications between employers and GPs.

## Aviation community role in promoting mental health and well-being

Individuals have a fundamental personal responsibility for maintaining their own health. At work, however, this becomes a shared responsibility. Dame Carol Black's review of the health of Britain's working age population[21] had a strong concluding statement:

> In addition to their existing legal duties, employers must work with their employees to change the nature of the modern workplace and ensure the health and productivity of their workforce. Trades unions must seize the opportunity to champion health and well-being in the workplace.[22]

This resonates with US National Prevention Strategy, whose guidance for 'community, non-profit and faith-based organisations' states:

- provide space and organised activities (e.g., opportunities for volunteering) that encourage social participation and inclusion for all people, including older people and persons with disabilities;
- train key community members (e.g., adults who work with the elderly, youth, and armed services personnel) to identify the signs of depression and suicide and refer people to resources.

How the wider aviation community can develop this guidance into effective action to promote mental health and well-being can be considered from both an individual and community viewpoint. Supporting one's peers, inclusivity agendas, supporting volunteering, aircrew selection and medical awareness all have a role to play, while promoting personal resilience is a fundamental feature in any health promotion agenda.

A chapter in this book on peer support models emphasises the benefit to employers of a model such as trauma risk management (TRiM). As such models are not a medical process – or therapy (although that remains debatable) – models designed to identify early those at risk after traumatic incidents and signpost them towards help have been well-documented to reduce stigma, raise psychological awareness and increase help-seeking behaviour.[23] Industry may see cost-neutral benefit from investment in other peer-support models, such as mental health first aid.[24]

Aviation awareness training for clinicians who are not approved aviation medical examiners is rare. It is rarer still for the wider mental health professional (MHP is the NATO-accepted term[25] for all psychiatrists, psychologists, mental health social workers, mental health nurses or specialist therapy personnel involved in delivering mental healthcare community to have specific aviation awareness training. An example of an on-line training package, designed for UK MoD to provide awareness of aviation medicine knowledge and understanding to treat aircrew, has been made mandatory for UK military MHP and strongly encouraged for GPs.[26] Efficacy studies are ongoing, but early indications report that stigma reduces and help-seeking behaviour increases in the military aviators it supports.[27]

The unwillingness of pilots to seek help early enough, in case they find themselves 'grounded' is a significant risk to passenger safety.[28] Issues of confidentiality were cited following the GermanWings incident.[29] National variations do occur, but the key point here is that any healthcare professional can recommend that aircrew are 'unfit to fly' – and that aircrew then has a responsibility to inform their employer. A useful analogy for health professional education is that an individual may be fit to run marathons, but not to fly.

Individuals who apply to become a commercial pilot rarely do so because they aim to be a passive systems monitor of a large machine. The military selection process requires potential pilots to be 'soldiers first, pilots second', which mitigate some of the risks associated with self-selection, but introduces other problems (adventurous, active types join the military; obsessional sedentary types may be better suited as commercial pilots). The short nature of military careers served the airline industry well; a 2003 paper found that 68 per cent of commercial pilots hired in the US were ex-military.[30] The significant costs associated with training – mostly met by the individual – will have a significant impact on initial selection – 'money talks' – placing pressures on the training industry to accept any and all who are willing to pay. Increased effort to assess temperament would be a cost-effective approach in the selection process. We discuss this further in another chapter.

The US National Prevention Strategy champions 'volunteering', as does the EU pact on health and well-being.[31] Altruistic activity – particularly where skill development may occur – has been reported by many authors to promote 'goodness' and to improve human 'quality of life'.[32]

Resilience is defined as 'the capacity to recover quickly from difficulties; toughness' by the Oxford English Dictionary; there are governmental, academic and popularist guidance ad nauseum on 'building personal resilience'. With an 'aviation psychology' focus, it is best to consider the simple aspects of physical, emotional and mental dimensions that promote our personal resilience:

1  *Physical:* strength, endurance and vitality.
2  *Emotional:* emotional flexibility, positive relationships, positive feelings, belief (in self, in others, in role, in life).
3  *Mental:* mental flexibility, attention span, understanding, optimistic world view.

Which can be summed up in the Buddhist 'mindfulness' philosophy... 'be happy & Be useful'.

And finally... time. Or, more accurately, 'time off'. 'One of the greatest labour-saving devices of today is tomorrow', is an infamous miss-quote of Benjamin Franklin's 'never put off until tomorrow what you can do today'. Modern life, alas, follows the mantra 'do more with less', which must inevitably result in the individual having less time for themselves. The key to mental health and well-being is to get balance in one's life. Balancing limited time is a skill most of us do not learn until we retire.

## Aviation authority role in promoting mental health and well-being

Following the March 2015 GermanWings murder-suicide, much has been done by the international and civilian aviation authorities to mitigate risk of such events reoccurring,[33] however it is well documented that those wishing to kill themselves, will.[34] As we describe above, the cost–benefit analysis of industry will be based on individual corporate strategy. There is an implicit role for the aviation authorities to stipulate certain minimum standards to which industry must comply – but which 'industry' may not have found 'cost effective'. Solving one problem (keeping terrorists out of the flight deck) has created another (locking out people we want in there). The aviation industry needs to compromise in almost every decision it makes and sometimes well-being may give way to safety.

The International Aviation Authority provides overarching guidance, which national aviation authorities impose as a regulatory framework that includes health and well-being, as well as medical regulatory framework for aviators.

National governments also impose regulatory controls on their public. The US government pledges to:

- support programmes to ensure that employees have the tools and resources needed to balance work and personal life and provide support and training to help them recognise co-workers in distress and respond accordingly;
- provide easy-to-use information about mental and emotional well-being for consumers, especially groups that experience unique stressors (e.g., US armed forces, firefighters, police officers, and other emergency response workers).

### Medical regulatory control

Individual pilots source specialist aviation medical examiners for routine medicals as mandated by their national aviation authority. It should be noted that annual pilot medicals have International Civil Aviation Organisation recommendations that are adopted by civil aviation authorities around the globe that include mental health assessments.[35] That said, the level of expertise and experience in mental health issues varies widely amongst the AME fraternity. The annual aircrew medical should be seen as an opportunity to discuss and promote mental health.

*Medical awareness*

Outcome measures repeatedly show that, once a person asks for help, they return to full employment in the vast majority of cases.[36] Professional aviators seem to understand and accept policy about such things as earache (leading to temporary grounding); approaching a clinician for mental health problems such as stress, anxiety or reactive depression would be less likely for aviators to be grounded and have a significant chance of effective treatment, if such is asked for. Fear of grounding from aircrew remains the greatest risk to flight safety, with some not asking for help until it is too late.

*Tackling stigma*

A recent UK government report highlighted that

> tackling stigma around ill-health and disability will be key to enabling more people with health conditions find work and stay in work. This is particularly true for those with mental ill-health, as many organisations often fail to recognise the full value of the contribution they can make.[37]

## Conclusion

By offering mental health and well-being promotion strategies, the stigma towards mental health is reduced and help-seeking behaviour is increased.

The case for promoting mental health and well-being in aviation is woven throughout the literature, both in cost and psychosocial benefits to the aviation industry. It is now the job of industry, the aviation community and the individual to take a positive role in 'making it so'.

## Notes

1  United Kingdom Health and Safety Executive. 'Management standards for work-related stress'. www.hse.gov.uk/stress/standards, accessed 3 November 2015.
2  The US National Prevention Strategy, (May 2015) 'Mental and emotional well being' www.surgeongeneral.gov/priorities/prevention/strategy/mental-emotional-well-being.pdf
3  *Ibid.*
4  Kalkman, C.J. (2011) 'Automation and automation surprises: Lessons from aviation: Should healthcare brace itself?', *Journal of Clinical Monitoring and Computing*, 25(1): 20–22.
5  BEA (2015) Preliminary Report D-AIPX, released 24 March 2015. www.bea.aero/uploads/tx_elydbrapports/d-px150324.en.pdf
6  Bor, R., Field, G. & Scragg, P. (2002) 'The mental health of pilots: An overview'; *Counselling Psychology Quarterly*, 15(3): 239–256.
7  Hamar, B., Coberley, C., Pope, J.E., Rula, E.Y. (2015) 'Well-being improvement in a midsize employer: Changes in well-being, productivity, health risk, and perceived employer support after implementation of a well-being improvement strategy', *Journal of Occupational and Environmental Medicine*, 57(4): 367–373.

8   United Kingdom Health and Safety Executive. 'Management standards for work-related stress'. www.hse.gov.uk/stress/standards. Accessed 3 November 2015.

9   Fell, S.S. (2015) 'Top 10 benefits of flexible work policies for companies'. www.huffingtonpost.com/sara-sutton-fell/top-10-benefits-of-flexib_b_4158603.html

10  Le Mignot, S. (2015) 'Pilots reluctant to disclose mental illness'. http://chicago.cbslocal.com/2015/03/27/experts-pilots-reluctant-to-disclose-mental-illness. Accessed 12 Novenber 2015.

11  Schultz, D.P. & Schultz, S.E. (2010) *Psychology and work today*. New York: Prentice Hall.

12  Plsek, P.E. & Greenhalgh, T. (2001) 'Complexity science: The challenge of complexity in health care', *BMJ* 323(7313): 625–628.

13  The Health Foundation (2015) 'Patient safety resource centre – Teamwork and communication'. http://patientsafety.health.org.uk/area-of-care/safety-management/teamwork-and-communication. Accessed 12 November 2015.

14  Wikipedia (n.d.) 'Aircrew scheduling'. https://en.wikipedia.org/wiki/Crew_scheduling. Accessed 12 November 2015.

15  Black, C. (2008) *Working for a healthier tomorrow: Dame Carol Black's review of the health of Britain's working-age population*. www.gov.uk/government/uploads/system/uploads/attachment_data/file/209782/hwwb-working-for-a-healthier-tomorrow.pdf

16  Health and Safety Executive (2010) *Health and Safety Statistics 2009/10*. www.hse.gov.uk

17  Department of Health analysis, *Health Survey England 2006* data.

18  *Ibid*.

19  *Ibid*.

20  European Union (2008) *European Pact for Mental Health and Well-being*. http://ec.europa.eu/health/mental_health/docs/mhpact_en.pdf. Accessed 12 November 2015.

21  Black, C. (2008) *Working for a healthier tomorrow*.

22  *Ibid*.

23  Creamer, M.C., Varker, T., Bisson, J., Darte, K., Greenberg, N., Lau, W., Moreton, G., O'Donnell, M., Richardson, D., Ruzek, J., Watson, P., & Forbes, D. (2012) 'Guidelines for peer support in high risk organizations: An international consensus study using the Delphi method', *Journal of Traumatic Stress*, 25: 134–141.

24  See http://mhfaengland.org

25  NATO technical terminology (2012) 'Mental health professional – MHP 2012-0208'. https://nso.nato.int/ttftracker

26  Rollo, J. & Campion. B.H. (2015) 'MHP Aviation Awareness Training', ICASM 2015 paper and presentation.

27  *Ibid*.

28  Cox, B. (2005) 'The stigma of mayday', *Plane & Pilot*. www.planeandpilotmag.com/proficiency/pilot-skills/the-stigma-of-mayday. Accessed 1 November 2015.

29  Reuters (2015) 'GermanWings crash triggers debate on confidentiality taboo'. www.reuters.com/article/2015/03/31/us-france-crash-germany-confidentiality-idUSKBN0MR2CT20150331 Accessed 1 November 2015.

30  According to a database of statistics compiled by AIR, Inc. www.jet-jobs.com

31  European Union (2008) *European Pact for Mental Health and Well-being*. http://ec.europa.eu/health/mental_health/docs/mhpact_en.pdf. Accessed 12 November 2015.

32  For example Corporation for National and Community Service (n,d,) 'Benefits of volunteering'. www.nationalservice.gov/serve-your-community/benefits-volunteering. Accessed 1 November 2015.

33  EASA (2015) '2015-04 Authorised persons in the flight crew compartment'. Issued 27 Mar 2015.

34 Paulozzi, L.J., Mercy, J., Frazier, L. Jr., Annest, J.L. (2004) 'CDC's national violent death reporting system: Background and methodology', *Injury Prevention*, 10(1): 47–52.

35 ICAO (2013) 'Mental health/depression in aviation'. www.icao.int/EURNAT Accessed 1 November 2015.

36 Thornicroft, G. & Tansella, M. (eds) (2010) *Mental Health Outcome Measures*. (third edition) London: RCPsych Publications.

37 Black, C. (2008) *Working for a healthier tomorrow.*

# 16 Stigma associated with mental illness among aircrew

*Todd Hubbard*

So what is the pilot thinking about as she or he flies the aircraft or monitors the instruments on your commercial flight? Is she wondering if you're having a good flight experience? Is he ensuring that your ride is as smooth as possible? Will the flight crew get you to your destination on time? Or are the minds of your flight crew plagued by personal problems: worrying about better trip bids that allow time to enjoy life, wondering if the present partner will understand why crazy flight schedules aren't the pilot's fault, or anticipating pay cuts because of the economy. As one retired commercial pilot said,

> I left the airline because of all the crap I had to put up with. I'm making less now than when I made Captain five years ago, and I doubt that will change. I already had to give up my pension, after the economy tanked in 2008, because management said it was either losing pensions or being furloughed. The union caved in and accepted management's offer. When I fly my monthly schedule, the First Officers I'm crewed with don't have a clue about what they are supposed to be doing. I have to babysit them on every flight. They know how to fly the airplane, but they don't know what it takes to get from point A to point B. I got so disgusted that I left the airline and went to work for the government.

Despite this person's candid remarks, is it safe to say that there aren't any commercial pilots flying under the U.S. Code of Federal Aviation Regulations who are wantonly dangerous or knowingly unsafe? The statistics appear to fall on the side of the notion that commercial flight is an extremely safe mode of travel. Sidney Dekker, in *Ten Question About Human Error*, tells us that there is a 1 in $10^7$ chance that you or I would be involved in an aircraft accident where there is major loss of life or property. That there is any chance of loss of life or property certainly invites a discussion on the safety of flight, but compared to other modes of transportation, commercial flight—whether flying with regional or major airlines—is a very safe mode. Problems with flight safety are often connected to general aviation experiences, not commercial flight experiences. Therefore, the flying public can expect a safe, efficient flight experience.

And if something unforeseen should happen, passengers expect their pilots and cabin crew to see to their safety even in disastrous circumstances. For example, a British Airways captain, commanding a Boeing 777, decided to forgo his last two flights before retirement because of the fire that consumed his aircraft while on the ground at Las Vegas, Nevada. Everyone evacuated successfully, due to his fast reaction and command to evacuate; but according to the captain, why tempt fate? And the avoidance of unnecessary risk or tempting fate runs deep among pilots.

But not all pilots are about to retire. Most commercial pilots have a long way to go to realize retirement. So what does it take for commercial pilots to stay focused when flying in complex airspace, in all kinds of weather, with varying challenges caused by the types of aircraft being flown and the sometimes troublesome instructions of air traffic controllers? Mental self-management and ongoing training and evaluation are the answers. So there are then both intrinsic and extrinsic factors to proper focus. Mental self-management is an intrinsic factor, while ongoing training and evaluation are essentially extrinsic factors, with some intrinsic requirements for the person being trained or evaluated.

Pilots are not generally trained to any depth in psychology and mental health, and airlines put a significant amount of effort into recruiting those with the aptitude to maintain a safe system. Pilots are expected to be resilient. This is one set of contributing factors to the significant and, I would argue, above average level of stigma attached to mental health issues among aircrew.

There is an additional safety management layer overseeing commercial pilots. Every six months, depending on age, each commercial pilot must undergo a physical. In the United States, the Federal Aviation Administration has given aviation medical examiners (AMEs) specific guidance on how to conduct periodic exams, which if passed would lead to a medical certificate. To start the process, pilots will go to the FAA MedXPress website and fill out the applicant history (items 1–20) on FAA Form 8500-8. Once the form is filled out, the pilot can schedule her or his exam. The AME will check height and weight; statement of demonstrated ability; head, face, neck, and scalp; nose; sinuses; mouth and throat; ear; ear drums; eyes; pupils; ocular motility; lungs and chest; heart; vascular system; abdomen and viscera; anus; skin; G-U system; upper and lower extremities; spine and other musculoskeletal; identifying body marks, scars, tattoos; lymphatics; neurologic; psychiatric conditions; general systemic; hearing; distant vision; near and intermediate vision; color vision; field of vision; heterophoria; blood pressure; pulse; urine test; and ECG. Compared to physicals given by family doctors, an AME appears to go a little further. And as a member of the flying public—knowing that the pilots up front on the flight deck undergo such physical exams—that makes me feel a bit safer, and I'm sure you as well.

In the middle of the physical exam items there is item 47, "psychiatric conditions." One's choices are either "normal," or "abnormal." This appears to be the only opportunity for a pilot to have a discussion about psychiatric issues, but it is highly doubtful that that discussion will ever occur. It is easier to tick the box "normal," than to begin confessing problems with depression or anxiety, or some other mental health issue. It is much easier to have that discussion with a psychiatrist, not the AME, who might not know what you do for a living. But no matter how effective the medical exam might or might not be, it is clear that the subject of mental health should have come up. However, concerns over stigma and the desire to remain employed are two very powerful motivators, and two very good reasons to avoid detection. It's a global concern.

The regulatory agencies in the U.S. have surely perpetuated, albeit not intentionally, a culture of dishonesty in pilots. Medical profile questionnaires ask applicants to tick off the boxes of maladies ever experienced, as opposed to once experienced but now am fine. One would think this to be a straightforward approach, but there are hidden landmines in the mix. Asthma is one such landmine. Children experiencing seasonal asthma, related to bronchitis, do meet the requirement for an "ever experienced" malady. But if the "asthma" box is ticked, does this suggest asthma for life? To avoid the discussion altogether, proctors of persons filling out the questionnaire are known to coach applicants on what boxes to tick and what not to tick. Leave "asthma" blank, they say, and also leave blank anything related to mental health or mental condition.

Confessing too much on a physical exam questionnaire can be risky, and can unnecessarily disqualify one for jobs sought, because society has learned how to discriminate against persons who exhibit stigmatized mental and physical weaknesses. This is not a new phenomenon, but an ancient one. Survival of the fittest is a long-term deselection of the weak. Stigmas are generally accepted disqualifiers. From society's perspective, a person with a stigma is not expected to be nearly as effective as the person without the stigma. Put plainly, a person with post-traumatic stress disorder (PTSD) is not expected to be effective or dependable in society, because of societal fear and foreboding over what is thought to be deficient in persons with PTSD. Perhaps not surprisingly, pilots who have lasted the longest in their career have sidestepped these disqualifiers by participating in the practice of *omertà*, a code of silence.

We naturally think that pilots are different, somehow more mentally tough, because of their training and the selection process. And there is some truth to that notion. Through all the certifications and ratings, a pilot becomes more prepared for and skilled at recovering from disadvantageous flight episodes. Flying by instruments, without any outside picture of where the ground is until touchdown, produces confidence in one's piloting skills. Operating an aircraft with accuracy, while being physically exhausted, produces confidence in one's ability to stay focused while fatigued. But pilots are not always good judges of their abilities. Many sleep deprivation and workload studies claim that stress and fatigue can produce effects similar to those of a person under the influence of alcohol. Both of these common mental and physical states, when taken beyond the limits of the pilot will deny that pilot of proper phasic and tonic alertness. A pilot will literally lose the ability to anticipate the next action and will lose time awareness. Airlines try to manage these challenges through crew resource management training. Pilots are then expected to be aware of the debilitating effects of stress and fatigue: depending more on the other pilot on the flight deck to watch for lapses in judgment or to trap errors of commission and omission.

It has been established then that passengers fly at a reduced risk, because of training and layers of system safety. But are passengers ever risk free? Does pilot training and the fact that there are normally two pilots on the flight deck prevent mishaps? For the airplane passenger, as you would hope, pilots' ongoing training makes your threat less. But mental health statistics—the reflection of persons presenting with symptoms related to mental disorders—might suggest that our trust in pilots, at least in part, is slightly misplaced unless we do a more thorough job of finding mental health weaknesses through the medical certificating process. Sickel, Seacat, and Nabors, in their 2014 published paper on "Mental Health Stigma Update: A Review of Consequences," found evidence suggesting that 46.6 percent of all adults in America will experience a mental disorder in their lifetime. A person would be quite daft to think that commercial pilots are on the better side of those statistics.

In a published 2007 study, titled "Medical Histories of 61 Aviation Accident Pilots with Postmortem SSRI Antidepressant Residues," Sen, Akin, Canfield, and Chaturvedi examined the U.S. National Transportation and Safety Board's histories of 61 civil aviation pilots who had died while operating aircraft between 1990 and 2001. They found that 59 of the pilots had medical records in the FAA's database. Seven of the 59 pilots reported disqualifying psychological conditions on their medical examinations. Three of the seven said they were taking medications with SSRIs. Six of the seven said they were no longer using SSRIs, so were reissued medical certificates on subsequent examinations. But 52 pilots never reported the use of SSRIs or the presence of a potentially disqualifying psychological condition, and yet they had SSRI residue in their blood. The list did not include pilots operating under Part 121 or 135: those parts normally associated with air carriers and commercial aviation.

We are left with the difficult question: Why would pilots be taking medications for depression and not reporting their use to FAA authorities? If you spent over $250,000 and participated in over four years of training to achieve a highly prized spot as a commercial airline pilot, would you be happy to leave your dreams and hard work just because you had some trouble with depression? If taking medication would eliminate the threat of depression, wouldn't you take the medication, if you thought it was a better way forward than fighting depression unaided? If you're honest, you might agree that mitigating the risk is a better choice than operating as a pilot without the pharmacological assistance. To some extent, the FAA agrees, but only to some extent.

In a press release on April 2, 2010, the FAA made public their decision to allow the use of fluoxetine (Prozac), sertraline (Zoloft), citalopram (Celexa), and escitalopram (Lexapro). For those pilots already taking one of these antidepressants, the FAA opened a six-month amnesty window, where pilots could confess their use without any worry of repercussions from civil enforcement agencies. Active behind this decision was the more than 40 years of work of specially trained psychiatrists and aviation medical examiners participating in the Human Intervention and Motivation Study (HIMS) program. The program's initial focus was rehabilitation of pilots who needed help with alcohol and drug issues.

Participants in the HIMS program helped to lessen the stigma associated with those suffering from depression. Nevertheless, it did not remove it altogether. For their service to public safety, we should be grateful. What the general public might be more willing to accept these days is that those depressed aren't always irresponsible, they aren't automatically suicidal, and they are not always withdrawn and morose. If disclosure of problems with depression will help pilots get proper relief through acceptable medications, then who would wish otherwise? Open and honest dealings with mental health issues are the better way. Forcing pilots to hide their problems will cause a disadvantage to both pilot and flying passenger. The GermanWings Flight 9525 incident might be a poignant example of such a disadvantage. One must wonder, will this incident reverse any good ground gained by cultural opening to pilot mental health issues?

Shall we be empathetic? Can we afford to be sensitive to the plight of professional pilots whose apparent weaknesses might affect safety? What is life like for a pilot who suffers from some debilitating weakness caused by an interruption within the central nervous system, the result of altered brain chemistry? At first there is only confusion: perhaps changes in mood, or unqualified feelings of terror, or a sudden loss of motivation. Unlike physical wounds, which are immediate signals that something isn't right in one's health, psychological "wounds" may not manifest or present as a particular disorder. Diagnosing psychological maladies is not the result of a definitive and immediate discovery. It is more of a long-term analysis with an apparent discovery. To the flying public, this is not the best news.

A pilot maintains a state of calm, even when external circumstances would dictate otherwise. When internal pressures continue to build, a pilot redoubles her or his efforts to maintain psychological equilibrium. Although some disregard the existence of compartmentalization as a means to disconnect non-operational events of life from the thoughts necessary to safely operate an aircraft, most pilots would agree that this separation is necessary. Arguments with significant others, bad news about the health of loved ones, financial problems, or trouble with children could distract a pilot, if she or he allowed. But commercial pilots have learned how to keep their private life separate from their professional life. But when the distraction is inside the pilot's mind, compartmentalization is tougher to achieve. Troubling thoughts can be intrusive: demanding greater concentration to keep them from interfering with operational thinking. When the intrusive thoughts are more pronounced, a pilot starts to doubt his or her ability to keep bad thoughts out.

In an unforgiving system, where the public expects that pilots with psychological issues should be relieved of their jobs, pilots will be reluctant to seek professional help, because they think that psychologists are working for the flying public and not for them. What commercial pilots have had to endure is similar to what U.S. military pilots endured for decades before PTSD became an acceptable and treatable battlefield diagnosis after U.S.-led coalition forces invaded Afghanistan and Iraq.

What follows is a personal account, a story where the reader is spectator to an unfortunate event and what happens thereafter. As a Cold War military pilot, a peacetime ejection from my single cockpit jet was left unhandled by psychiatrists and psychologists, because U.S. Air Force policy prohibited post-accident interviews. Moreover, I would be dismissed as a military pilot, if I confessed to having problems with my thoughts, following the accident. So for four years, I dealt with my thoughts and fears by myself. I flew secret missions and combat missions as ordered. Nobody cared how I felt, except my wife. To avoid mental health stigma, I chose a more acceptable path.

My first attempt at self-help was alcohol. Although I was a man of spiritual faith and often given to prayer as a means to cope with life, God seemed distant as I worked through my feelings after the accident. My injuries were extensive enough to keep me from flying for two months. After my hurried convalescence I was sent to Korea to fly operational reconnaissance missions. I carried out my duties responsibly. In-between missions I tried to fill my thoughts with anything other than difficult thoughts. Even the restrictive nature of keeping a code—staying true to my faith, following God—was too difficult to think about. I relaxed with the aid of alcohol and surrounded myself with party-goers.

During my first week in the hospital I was interrogated three times: the first just after some emergency-room stitching; the second in a medicated haze on pain meds; and the third after being fitted with a back brace. The result was always the same: the accident was not my fault. One would think that being exonerated of any fault for the accident would be cheering news, but squadron pilot opinions were largely negative. Squadron pilots, as a group, visited once while in the hospital, and then nobody wanted to have much to do with me. This became more evident in the next eight months, as I dealt with other pilots from my outfit, outside the mission.

It's difficult enough to endure psychological stress, but when those closest to you in your profession choose to stay away from you, you feel alone and without value. During a party, while celebrating New Year's in Korea, a pilot from my unit said, "I'll never forgive you for destroying the airplane. You should have ridden the plane into the ground." At another operational location, after an unsuccessful attempt to land on one runway due to crosswinds, but a successful landing on a different runway, the commander imposed a ban on any communication toward me, unless safety would be compromised. I am still unsure why, but it appeared to me that those negative opinions associated with the accident may have contributed to the sanction. At the end of the tour, the commander said, "Congratulations, you did a good job. Not just anyone could have gone through what we put you through." I just looked at him in disbelief, but with a smile to disguise my amazement.

People create their own truth, despite alternative evidence leading to another conclusion. In high-risk professions—like firefighting or law enforcement or, in my case, high-altitude reconnaissance—members of these groups form tight bonds, where each member depends on others in the group to protect them from harm. However, when a member is under investigation, even if just routine—like administrative leave for law enforcement officers who discharge their weapons—entry back into the group is sometimes difficult. Being singled out can separate one from the protective circle of group members. There is a perceived "something wrong" with the person being singled out, even if there is no apparent wrong behavior. Welcoming the outsider back into the group can only be done over time, as each member decides to accept or reject the perceived offender, the jinx. Being exonerated doesn't guarantee a speedy reentry.

Hoping that a change in station would help, I chose to move overseas: performing the same types of missions, but with a different group of pilots. My family also benefited, because I could stay home, rather than fly from forward operating locations, months at a time. I found the new group more accepting. But then things changed. I was unable to complete a secret mission, because of an aircraft malfunction just before executing the purpose of my mission. The object of the mission involved the saving of lives of those on the ground. By having to turn around and go back to base, I felt that I was responsible for the deaths of those I was trying to save. I was unprepared for my reaction.

On a Saturday morning I launched in my jet to a high altitude over Europe. I was to be on station for the day: at least nine hours. Toward the end of my mission I was advised that there were no suitable landing sites in the entire United Kingdom. The only suitable landing site was Ramstein Air Base, Germany. So I headed to Ramstein at my off station time. Landing was uneventful. Lucky for me, a C-130 was going to fly to Mildenhall Air Base, England, later that evening, when the weather permitted. Flying my jet back to base was out of the question. So I found a seat in the back of the C-130, next to others needing to get back to England. Sitting next to me was a psychiatrist from a base in England. He was debriefing two F-15 pilots who had collided in flight, both ejecting safely. I wondered why they got a visit from a psychiatrist when I wasn't accorded the same care. The psychiatrist kept saying that he did a lot of work off the record, because his main goal was to prepare crewmembers to return to flight. I shared my story with him, and he told me to look him up if I wanted to talk one on one, and off the record.

In the weeks that followed, my mind went to a very dark place. I couldn't shake the thought of being responsible for the deaths of others. I kept flying. I didn't act any differently to others, but I was concerned about how my thoughts were intruding in my everyday activities. Finally, I arrived at a thought that was the darkest of all. Although I was not contemplating suicide in any way, I could see why others might feel as if suicide was the best alternative to the pain of life. That realization scared me. I felt that I had ventured deep into the dark area of my life's operating envelope. Pilots study operating envelopes of aircraft, to make sure they don't exceed a limit and damage or destroy the airplane. Those limits include excessive speed, minimum speed, and excessive G limits at certain altitudes and angles of attack. I figured that people have operating envelopes as well. Those limits include physical fatigue and stress, psychological fatigue and stress, and abilities to mitigate risks caused by either instigator. I had journeyed deep into the danger zone of psychological stress, and felt that coping strategies weren't quite enough. So I called the psychiatrist from the C-130 flight and booked an "off the record" appointment.

On the day of the appointment I had to be excused from a unit war-fighting exercise. I didn't reveal the reason for the official "doctor appointment" excuse. My session went well with the chief psychiatrist at RAF Upper Heyford. He reassured me that stresses imposed by the unit, beyond my flying duties, were excessive and that changing my work details would cause immediate, positive changes. He urged me to approach my commander and ask for changes. I returned to my unit immediately after the appointment. But before I could ask for changes, I was summoned by my commander's boss, the Director of Operations. We'll call him Colonel D. I reported to his office as ordered and he let me sit. He started the conversation with, "Todd, I found out that you went to Upper Heyford to visit the base psychiatrist. Is that correct? "I responded, "Yes sir." He continued. He told me that several weeks before, lab tests designed to determine if his cancer had returned had come back positive. He would have to endure chemo or radiation treatments. He had survived skin cancer years before and returned to flying. Now he was to undergo treatment again. He said, "Todd, what do you want to do? You have six months before you go to Ramstein as a NATO staff officer." I said, "I'd like to only fly for the next six months." He said, "Okay, that's what will happen. I'll make sure everyone knows. There won't be any repercussions. This won't affect your career or your next assignment. You know, there is nothing more important than your family. You have to take care of you, so you can take care of them."

That the base psychiatrist lied about "off the record" counseling, only confirmed in my mind that some mental health professionals are the pilot's worst enemy. I was suckered in and then exposed. Not only did my unit know where I went, they also knew why I was there. I'm sure the entire discussion between me and the psychiatrist was made known. Had I not had a Colonel D in my corner, things could have gone much differently. But thank God, things went better than expected. And despite the double cross, my short visit with the shrink did have a good effect. I was able to fly enough to accumulate over 1000 hours of flight time in the reconnaissance jet I flew, which then set me up for better assignments in the future. Additionally, I had distanced myself from the dark zone of despair in my mind. My thoughts were free to roam in the middle of my cognitive sweet spot. I was happy and motivated. I looked forward to another several years in Europe.

My Upper Heyford visit did not eliminate the deep-seated fear I had. It only lessened its effect. I still had trouble with nightmares. Thinking of emergency situations only ended in disaster, rather than a promising outcome. But to my surprise, the effects of disastrous outcomes only tormented my mind when outside the airplane. Once I began concentrating on the act of flying, the fears and negative thinking disappeared. I did suffer from a heightened startle reflex, because when warning horns sounded in the cockpit, I jumped. But these episodes were short-lived and very manageable, even though repeated every time I flew. From 1984, the year of the accident, until 2004, I became part of the 30 percent of passengers who have a fear of flying. Because I wasn't at the controls of commercial flights, but flew as a passenger, I had no way of assuring a safe, uneventful flight. So I resigned myself to whatever end I couldn't control.

This resignation was the way I coped when I piloted aircraft. Perhaps my resignation was somehow related to my sense-making of flight accidents. Until having to eject, I naturally thought that every aircraft I piloted would perform as advertised and that all would be well throughout all phases of flight. Once I was made to concede that not all flights would end well, I had no other expectation than the possibility of a deadly end. So I quelled my fears by realizing that everybody will die at some point, and that any flight might be my last. This thought process helped me to move from crippling fear to managed fear.

After several years in a non-flying billet, having completed my tour of duty in NATO, I returned to flying in the same type of aircraft from which I ejected. In fact, out of all the staff officers working for Strategic Air Command that year, only six were allowed to return to flying duties. I was one of the six. My tour at Ramstein ensured a bright future in my career field. I was in line to command my own operational squadron. Upon my return to the States, I volunteered for command in Saudi Arabia as a provisional squadron commander, and did exceptionally well in that posting. Everything seemed to be going my way. I even flew combat missions, and was nearly shot down. I seemed to take things in stride while commanding my unit in southwest Asia. But upon resuming my flight duties after my stint in "the Kingdom," my nightmares became "daymares." While walking to and from the ops squadron, my mind would create a nightmarish fantasy of things gone wrong on a flight. I died in every fabricated episode. My body would shudder and then perspiration would form on my skin, causing a rivulet of sweat to course down the center of my back. I'd suddenly become aware that my shaking and sweating body might be observed by passersby as unusual, so I quickly regained composure, filling my mind with happier thoughts.

My destiny was not to command an ops squadron, but rather a support squadron of considerable size. My flight duties were at an end. The nightmares and daymares disappeared, but my fear of flying did not. I coped to the best of my ability. After another tour as a non-flying squadron commander in Saudi Arabia, I retired from the U.S. Air Force and began to settle into civilian life. I wanted to do something entirely cerebral. So I poured all my efforts into a doctorate, which I achieved in two years, seven months.

However, I found acclimation to civilian ways of doing things quite unsettling. I had been a driven person for nearly 21 years in service to my country. I had become a weapon of the state, and no longer myself. Now I was free to find what was lost of the person so vastly adjusted to military form and function. Everyone around me seemed to aimlessly go through life, without a plan or vision for their lives. And what was most aggravating was their total abandonment to aimless drifting. My studies helped to occupy my mind, distracting me from "them," but then I started noticing things running amuck in my feelings and behavior. For example, while driving to work one day I started weeping intensely; so much so that I had to pull to the side of the road. There was no apparent reason for the episode, it just happened. And as soon as it had occurred, it vanished without a trace of attached feeling to whatever had just happened. On another occasion, I was carrying on a conversation with my supervisor, when his boss came into the room and interrupted with nothing needing immediate action. I thought to myself, "Am I so unimportant that you think you can barge in and ignore that fact that we were talking business?" Without saying another word I spun round on my heels and headed back to my cubicle. En route, I slugged the wall with my fist. Every bit of effort behind that slug was an imagined connection with the interrupting boss. As I arrived at my desk, my first order of business was to call human resources and schedule a meeting. I knew I needed someone to look inside my head, to find out why these things were happening.

I talked to several psychologists and counselors over the next year. One psychologist said, "Nobody would want to be like you. I sure wouldn't." He wrinkled up his nose at me and sneered as he said those words. During an annual physical, after the doctor asked how I was doing, I started sharing how I felt. He cut me off and said that psychological issues were dealt with on the second floor. I could feel anger welling up inside me and the desire to punch his lights out; but instead, I hung my head and said nothing for the remainder of the exam. My diagnosis so far was PTSD. The clinicians explained that the behavior and thoughts I presented were most likely a reaction to my near-death ejection experience, and the unresolved issues emanating from that time.

I had chosen not to pursue a flying career, though having the experience and flight time to get a job with a major air carrier. Many of my Air Force buddies were flying for the majors. But every time I thought about flying for a career, I realized that the demons of the past were not far away. I couldn't imagine trying to fly. And then, with a few strokes of a pen, it was no longer possible for me to fly as a commercial pilot. PTSD had ravaged my mind and emotions, resulting in excursions in mood. An initial upset in my normal mood created ever-increasing swells, with depression in the trough, and mania at the crest. The cycle intervals became more frequent and more intense. A friend suggested I see another clinician. So I did reluctantly. I judged my counselors by how frank they could be, without attacking me. During my first session with the new clinical psychologist, she was the first to drop the F bomb expletive. My shoulders relaxed and my mind was relieved. Our sessions were going to get real. That relationship has lasted over 13 years, because it has taken that long to adjust to a new normal.

After several sessions, Dr. M diverted from a PTSD-only diagnosis to an additional bipolar disorder diagnosis. I had no idea what that meant. Over time this diagnosis became more and more evident to those caring for me. But after some years of regular sessions with Dr. M and less frequent visits with psychiatrist Dr. J, Dr. M wrote a letter to Dr. J, suggesting that it might be time for pharmacological assistance to combat mood issues and what I would call mental turbulence. I ruminated often when trying to sleep at night, which left me tired and less capable of using coping strategies the next day. Dr. M suggested that I involve my faith system in the mix, so I worked hard to balance therapy, faith, and medication. Auditory and visual hallucinations began to intrude in my waking life. And it was then that I understood why bipolar disorder is a disqualifying mental health issue: preventing private, instrument, and commercial pilots from gaining a medical certificate. Auditory hallucinations can be explained away as a misunderstanding of sounds nearby, but visual hallucinations are more troublesome to explain. And if they should occur during flight, there might be a disturbing interruption in aircraft control duties.

In the 2001 film *A Beautiful Mind*, the actor Russell Crowe played the part of John Nash, an asocial mathematician and Nobel Prize winner. In the film the viewer saw what truly didn't exist in real life. Windows and walls were covered in equations, and Russell Crowe's character behaved as if they were actually there. But there was nothing there. John Nash suffered from paranoid schizophrenia. Unrealistic or false beliefs were accompanied by perceptions or experiences of a reality that actually didn't exist. John Nash had to decide what was real and what was not real. I've had a similar experience, although from an entirely different diagnosis.

Bipolar disorder produces a cascading array of perceptions in the brain chemistry of one's central nervous system. Only one perception is the best perception. Only one perception elicits an accurate response to a stimulus or a cohesive group of stimuli. It's similar to receiving a dozen channels of cable on one's television at once, with discrete differences between each channel, allowing for different perceptions. Another illustration is raindrops on a still pool of water. As the concentric waves emanate from the droplet center and collide with other concentric waves from other drops, the intersections illustrate possible interactions of perceptions. Other perceptions might be close, but choosing the wrong perception can get one in trouble in social situations. Continued wrong guessing can result in failures in relationships and career. When visual hallucinations are added to a buffet of possible perceptions, chaos ensues. I was fortunate. I am a high-functioning bipolar. Analytical skills, honed over the course of 20 years of military aviation, helped me differentiate among choices. I kept my cool and chose to believe what was possible, even though the visual hallucination remained. In time, the hallucinations disappeared.

As I conclude my thoughts, I'd like to point out some things about my story that might help the reader understand the progression of events from no apparent mental health issues to debilitating mental health disorders, and the battle against stigma. In the classroom, I tell my undergraduates, who are studying to become commercial pilots, that depression and anxiety are not to be dismissed as unimportant. Perhaps the messages I instill in these young minds will change how pilots, managers, and regulators view mental health issues. In addition, I tell them that there is a huge difference between transient effects of depression and permanent effects of depression, and that the change from transient to permanent isn't always measured in months or years, but in a few seconds when one's brain chemistry is changed.

In my story, my life as a pilot was going well until I ejected from my military jet. I believe this to be true of many pilots. It scared me for some time after the event. But I was convinced that pilots with a stronger ability to cope would not have been so scared. I wasn't encouraged to talk to mental health professionals, and was warned that my flying days would end if I tried to get therapy. This might also be the way the older pilots think. Many of the older guys and gals had a military background, and the restrictions present then, might spill over into their civilian career. However, it is more likely that commercial pilots are welcomed to share how they feel, without any repercussions. And I doubt they're treated like I was by my flight doc. At the end of the first week in the hospital, the chief flight surgeon of the base asked me, "Are you going to return to flying after you recover?" I told him I didn't know yet. He said, "If you don't tell me that you're returning to flying duties right now, I'll put FEAR OF FLYING in your record." I told him I needed more time, and that trying to make a decision while still in the hospital and facing potentially years of recovery time was premature. So I used the only legal drug available. I used and abused alcohol. This I know I have in common with many pilots from times past. Drinking alcohol is a tradition among those pilots: usually more celebratory than cathartic. Sometimes alcohol "therapy" becomes a dependency, and we occasionally read about commercial pilots who attempt to fly under the influence. I made poor choices outside of my flying duties. I didn't let the torment I was feeling to intrude during my missions, but that torment was ever-present between flights. I don't know how commercial pilots would be affected by intrusive thoughts, as the result of an aircraft accident.

There remained the issue of disenfranchisement from the rest of the squadron pilots. Murmurs among some of the more senior pilots of the group seemed to put an idea in the minds of other pilots that something must be wrong with me, since I allowed a jet to be destroyed. This exacerbated the effect of stigma, unrelated to mental health issues. But I wasn't the only pilot in our squadron to eject that year. Two months before I ejected, another squadron pilot had to eject for similar reasons, but he wasn't injured. Everybody liked him, so no one thought poorly of him after the ejection. Two months later I ejected and two months after my ejection a third jet broke apart and that pilot ejected safely. The other two pilots ejected overseas. I ejected at the home base. There were fewer pilots at the forward operating location than at the home base, so squadron opinions were more intensified—due to numbers—at the home base, than at the forward base. Also, there seemed to be a greater team sense at the forward operating location than at home. Life and work at the home base was different. For example, at the home base, minor flying problems among less experienced pilots became sensationalized to the extent that those "without sin" found it easy to "cast the first stone." And once the stones began to be hurled, no one questioned whether they should be thrown in the first place. Minor problems were stigmatized.

Of the three of us who ejected from a U-2 that year, there were no career commonalities among us, other than we were all driven pilots with previous experience in other aircraft. There were few similarities in lifestyle. We all made time for exercise, and stayed in great shape. Two of us were married; one divorced, but living with his girlfriend. The first U-2 pilot to eject in 1984 had already been deployed to Korea and was on his second tour. I had yet to deploy and the third pilot was on his first operational deployment to Korea. Of the three, I was most likely more "religious" than the others: at least I was more demonstrative with my faith. I've wondered since the accident if being so closely tied to my faith system really helped me. At first, I'd say it didn't. My wife told me she felt a special presence of God after the accident. She held on to that faith, while I temporarily journeyed away from that faith. It would be nearly a year before I felt comfortable in my trust in God.

Perhaps my spiritual numbness can be summed up best in an encounter with my five years old son, at about a year after the ejection. One evening, my wife told me that my youngest son was having trouble with his bedtime prayers and wondered if I might help him. So I went to his bedside and asked him why he was having trouble praying. He said he couldn't think of anything to pray about. I told him, "Well, I'm flying tomorrow. Ask God to protect me." His response was priceless. He said, "Well it didn't work before." He saw God, perhaps as I had, quite distant and disinterested in the affairs of our family. He guessed that prayer was useless, since it was no guarantee for flight safety. And he was right. But I still wanted him to see that having faith was an important part of life.

Of the eight years I worked as a contractor with the FAA, I've watched how the administration deals with air traffic controllers who are having problems with PTSD: the result of tragic episodes while they were controlling traffic, especially where deaths were concerned. Some found jobs connected with training, but were not allowed to directly train ATC students in the art of controlling. I once engaged one of the persons who had found a job in training in a conversation about her feelings regarding her separation from the facility where she once controlled air traffic. During her telling of her story, she said that a commercial aircraft crashed while she was controlling traffic, even though she had no direct control of the ill-fated jet and its passengers. She reported for duty on her next shift, but she found that she was suffering from anxiety. Intrusive thoughts kept plaguing her mind. Her fellow controllers felt she shouldn't be controlling traffic anymore, so she was reassigned away from that facility. Before the tragic episode she was one of the better controllers at her facility. But then she noticed that her fellow controllers had a different opinion of her abilities after the fatal crash. She began having nightmares and at the time of our conversation, she appeared very nervous and was physically shaking. Although this story is not about pilots, it is indeed about the same intentional ostracism.

I help train FAA inspectors, and during my training sessions, I sometimes field questions about mental health issues. These particular inspectors are pilots, many of them with thousands of hours of flying time with commercial airline companies. We discuss the difference between a chemically induced depression and episodic depression during a block on risk management. Over the years I've had several inspectors take me aside during breaks to share their stories of depression and anxiety. Often there are tears of pain in their eyes. They practice discretion when telling their stories, and often speak in hushed tones, trying not to attract the attention of others. They know that if others learned of their back story, they might become the victim of ridicule from those not claiming to have a weakness. Not everyone in the class is welcoming of discussions about mental health or stories about depression and anxiety. Some of the inspectors complain on their critiques that too much time was spent talking about mental health, and they single me out as an example. The ugly head of stigma seems to follow me.

My guess is that far too many people are very uncomfortable with the subject, and would sooner ignore the issues altogether. But what is worse than the effect of an end-of-course critique is what happens in real life when those uncomfortable with discussing mental health issues take it upon themselves to separate and castigate those suffering from one of the byproducts of an aviation career: episodes of depression and anxiety sometimes accompanied by alcoholism. It is an easy thing to ignore those who are marginalized. We say there are plenty of pilots wanting in, so why not exclude those declared not fit? But rather than wait for a determination by aviation medical examiners, pilots take it upon themselves to ruin others' reputations with mean-spirited gossip. What is undiscovered by the tormentors is that there exists a chance that they too might fall prey to the ravages of a brain chemistry gone afoul and experience for themselves the same alienation.

Regardless of the stigma assigned to me after the accident, or the stigma of mental health issues because I trusted a clinician while in the Air Force, the best advice I can give those who suffer unfairly, is to press ahead. Keep moving forward in whatever you do. Don't stop to feel sorry for yourself. Find a good clinician who really cares about you, and unburden your mind to him or her. In all things, learn how to live well.

# References

Dekker, S. W. A. (2005) *Ten questions about human error: A new view of human factors and system safety*. Mahwah, New Jersey: Lawrence Erlbaum Associates.

Sen, A., Akin, A., Canfield, D. V. and Chaturvedi, A. K. (2007) Medical histories of 61 aviation accident pilots with postmortem SSRI antidepressant residues. *Aviation Space Environmental Medicine* 78(11): 1055–1059.

Sickel, A. E., Seacat, J. D. and Nabors, N. A. (2014). Mental health stigma update: A review of consequences. *Advances in Mental Health* 12(3): 202–215.

# 17 Psychosocial stressors associated with being a pilot

*Cristina Albuquerque and Maria Fonseca*

## Introduction

Aviation is a high-performance industry that frequently exposes professionals to high levels of stress due to very specific job characteristics, demands and pressures. Pilots are generally considered one of the most reliable and psychologically stable occupational group. Despite the fact that they are carefully selected and thoroughly trained prior to certification, they are not immune to the effects of stressors, and psychological problems can emerge among persons who pursue this occupation.

CareerCast (2016) evaluated 200 jobs in terms of 11 stress factors: travel required; growth potential; deadlines; working in the public eye; competition in the field; physical demands; environmental conditions; hazards encountered on a regular basis; own life at risk; life of others at risk; and meeting or interacting with the public at large.

Results of this study showed that being a pilot was ranked as the third most stressful job in 2016 (behind fire fighters and enlisted military personnel).

*Stress* generally results from the complex interactions between a large system of interrelated variables and occurs when the demands of a situation are perceived by the individual as threatening and as exceeding their personal ability to cope with it in a successful way.

Based on the Lazarus and Folkman transactional model of stress (Lazarus & Folkman, 1984), it can be said that a pilot's reaction to a stressor is dependent on the interaction between the capabilities of the person involved and the external situation being faced. The first thing that a person automatically does when faced with a stressful event is a *primary appraisal* of the situation to determine the level of danger, the potential risks, loss or discomfort and the amount of effort that will have to be exerted to handle the situation. If no threat is perceived, no stress is felt.

If a threat is perceived, the pilot goes through a *secondary appraisal* process in which he or she examines his or her perceived available resources to cope with the problem. How a person appraises the situation is a function of past experience and perceived ability to cope with the stressor. A person selects the "best solution", which is usually the least dangerous, most likely to succeed and the one for which the person has the most appropriate skills. If a person perceives that he or she can cope with the stress, *positive stress* (or eustress) is experienced. A perceived inability to fully cope with the situation leads to *negative stress* (or distress).

In this chapter the term *stressor* will be used to describe any element, which alone or in conjunction/interaction with other elements, causes a pilot to experience *negative stress* (a short- or long-term reaction that causes anxiety or concern, decreases performance and can lead to mental and physical problems). It must be emphasized that stressors are not always limited to situations where some external situation is creating a problem. Internal events such as feelings and thoughts can also trigger negative stress.

Because people process and interpret information differently, each pilot can react in a different personal way when exposed to specific stressful circumstances.

The duration of a stressful event or situation defines whether the stress is acute or chronic and the effects of these two types of stress can be very different.

*Acute stress* is caused by *stressors* that generally arise from an immediate threat such as fire on board, engine failure, landing gear malfunction, shortage of fuel, pilot incapacitation, bird strike, bomb threat or hijacking. Usually, the pilot has the technical and psychological resources to cope with the stressful situation and his natural capacity to recover equilibrium is not put in jeopardy. However, if levels of acute stress are extremely high, the event can lead to a state of physical and emotional exhaustion and the capacity to recover may be compromised. In extreme cases, post-traumatic stress is a psychiatric disorder that can develop.

*Chronic stress* is caused by a constant stream of demands, risks, pressures and threats that go on for significantly long periods of time and are mostly related with relationship difficulties, financial worries, health concerns, bereavement issues and work-related problems. These stressors slowly drain mental and physical resources and create a sense of hopelessness or inability to cope. Eventually, too much stress over a long period of time can lead to burnout – a state of complete mental, physical, and emotional exhaustion. If prolonged, it can have serious health implications such as the onset of a stroke, heart disease or even heart attack (Bosma *et al.*, 1998). Chronic stress can become so routine and familiar that you lose awareness of its presence, yet it still carries its harmful effects.

Prolonged and cumulative stress may affect cognition – the process of perception, attention, memory, knowledge, problem-solving and decision-making – just as it affects emotions and behaviour. This is a serious issue for pilots, because problems with judgment, attention or concentration present a great risk for flight safety.

Pilots are exposed to three main categories of stressors: a) physical/physiologic stressors, b) job-related stressors and c) personal stressors.

## Physical/physiological stressors

Physical/physiological stressors are brought on by specific work conditions such as workload, sitting for long hours in the cockpit, confined to a small workspace, exposed to physical conditions like altitude effects, high noise levels, vibration, acceleration, cramped legs, turbulence, uncomfortable temperature, poor air quality, insufficient lighting conditions, lack of humidity, harsh weather conditions, etc.. While some of these negative elements are unavoidable because they're simply part of the aeronautic milieu, many others are permanently in the scope of a cutting-edge technology where aviation experts (aeronautical engineers, ergonomists and human factor specialists) work together in order to introduce improvements to meet pilots' best working conditions.

## Job-related stressors

Job-related stressors represent any occupational/organizational condition which needs adaptive responses from the individual. The most often quoted stressors in the specialty literature *(*Colligan *et al.*, 2006) are: ambiguity and role conflict, work overload, danger of accidents and rhythm of work and any situational constraints imposed to the individual by the employer. Concerning the pilot's profession, job-related stressors include several demanding conditions and pressures such as intense workload, precarious job conditions, irregular working hours, exposure to critical incidents, increased automation, roster instability, etc.

## Personal stressors

Personal stressors refer to life-events occurring outside of the workplace that can affect an individual's performance at work (e.g. divorce, grief, illnesses, financial problems, social isolation, etc.). Many pilots believe that they can separate their private and working lives and keep one from affecting the other. However, this is not always possible. Preoccupation with personal problems consumes mental resources and distracts a person from the task at hand. If personal stressors are not adequately dealt with, they can contribute to the development of mental health problems such as depression, anxiety or other psychological disorders.

A literature review performed by NASA (Young, 2008) found a substantial body of research demonstrating that

> a sizeable percentage of pilots (military and civilian) experience noteworthy stress symptoms when faced with difficult life circumstances ... with regard to mechanisms by which life-stress may impair performance, some evidence suggests that life-stress may negatively influence underlying cognitive processes such as information processing, working memory, problem solving and decision-making. To the degree that these important processes are affected, one might expect an associated decrement in performance. Additionally, there is evidence suggesting that life-stress disrupts sleep

and leads to increased levels of fatigue, which in turn impairs cognitive and social performance (e.g., decreased response accuracy, narrowing of attention, social withdrawal).

(Young, 2008, p. 20)

Since stress in the workplace can come from a variety of sources besides physical stimuli such as various *psychosocial factors* (*job-related* and *personal stressors*), this chapter will mainly focus on some of the most impacting psychosocial stressors faced by pilots. The stressors are selected based on a review of the most relevant research available but also relying on our professional experience as clinical psychologists working in both civil and military aviation settings.

The aim of this chapter is to illustrate some of the potential stressors that pilots are exposed to. Without claiming to be exhaustive, the idea is to raise awareness on a relevant subject that has been overlooked by most of the professionals involved in the aviation community (pilots, aeromedical examiners, mental health professionals, operators, employers and regulators).

As commercial pilots normally do not face the same kind of stressful events that military aviators expect to encounter, the specific psychosocial challenges experienced by civil and military pilots will be addressed separately.

## Psychosocial stressors in military pilots

Military pilots are a very specific professional group. Due to the careful fostering of certain attributes in the selection and in the training phase, we can say that they are a group with a lower propensity to psychological difficulties.

Candidates entering the Air Force Academy have the physical, behavioural, emotional and academic qualifications that allowed them to accomplish the pilot apprenticeship. They are a highly screened, selected and trained group.

Despite the initial selection, there is still a screening that is performed in the early years at the academy. This process basically divides cadets in two groups, with one group comprising those who are unable to mobilize sufficient coping resources to live up to the academy's requirements, and the other including those cadets that can swiftly develop enough internal resilience to deal with multiple stressors. This includes: the family and social uprooting, the stressors inherent to internship at academy (which includes experiential variables, relational and internalization of specific social norms), and the level of training required by the military component, academic component as well as the aeronautical component.

The aeronautic component usually present stressors related to physiological adaptability, with the perception of high cognitive workload and the reconciliation between academic and flight responsibilities (i.e. preparation of missions, flight knowledge, etc.).

Alongside the development of a whole range of personal, interpersonal, cognitive and emotional skills, the academy also starts the whole process of psychological desensitization towards general stressors, usually present in operational realities. The ambiguity and the need to tolerate the unknown are part of this process.

The pilot apprenticeship usually happens after a number of years of academic training in the Air Force Academy where there is an organizational acculturation performed by the cadet before the apprenticeship. In this sense, there is a reduction of organizational stressors, concerning the whole relational and experiential dynamics specific to these military. However, there is also a significant increase of flight-associated stressors. In addition to the physiological issues and reconciliation with times for study and preparation of missions, there is a demanding and rigid aeronautical course syllabus. Although the syllabus may have some variability from country to country, it is generally demanding and requires constant effort from the cadet to follow the pace of progress.

All this initial organizational process, aiming to select and train a military pilot, results in a professional group with its own characteristics. Good skills in leadership, communication, organization, planning, decision-making, analytical thinking, high self-confidence, motivation for recognition and approval, task orientation, skills and ability in teamwork, tend to be free from intrapsychic conflict, as well as no propensity for emotional introspection, while motivation, competitive nature and energy are some of the displayed characteristics (Marsh *et al.*, 2010).

### Psychosocial stressors in military aeronautics

Military aviation is, indubitably, a high-risk environment, presenting multiple potential stressors. The aeronautical military context presents, nowadays, very significant adaptive levels of demand. This growing demand is linked to a multiplicity of factors as diverse as the national finances and the type of modern military air operations, to the progressive and unstoppable technological advancements.

Because flying is not an innate human competence, pilots have to face several challenges/stressors in terms of their physiological adaptability. Examples of inherent stressors are, among others, noise, acceleration, difficulties in communication, temperature, vibration, hypoxia, motion sickness, and decompression sickness.

Moreover, the functions of a pilot comprise a series of complex tasks that occur in a dynamic and diverse environment, predisposing to the development of stressors. We may say that it is a profession where there are often stressors associated with the workload.

The complexity of the flight tasks arise often associated with high peaks of work, which can create work overload. This is an extremely important concept, not only because it is a significant stressor but also, if it persists continuously, there is a clear potential to generate fatigue. Stress and fatigue present a close relationship, i.e. the continued stress generates fatigue, and fatigue multiplies stress. Both compromise performance since both impact on cognitive resources involved while processing information, whether in perception, attention, memory, recall, and/or language, and also in executive cognitive processes, such as planning, situational awareness, judgment and decision making (Stetz *et al.*, 2007).

In the military environment there are a number of contributing factors to increased workload. Examples are night flights, landings and multiple take-offs, differences in time zones, which can be aggravated by emergencies, in-flight malfunctions, weather difficulties, and many others.

Adding to this are life stressors, mostly related with the military environment that undoubtedly increment the diversity of stressors, which a military pilot has to deal with. Among these we find frequent moves, qualifications and promotion courses, social expectations, career-enhancing additional duties, military disciplinary actions, flying operational missions, involuntary assignments, following orders and deference to those of higher rank.

The operational environment is very demanding, even if does not occur in an actual combat scenario. Stressors inherent to the operational environment include the amount and speed of information, diversity of tasks, challenging roles and responsibilities (sometimes unclear, changing and competing), and the imperative for rapid and accurate decision-making processes. There are additional stressors, which multiply the effect of those previously mentioned, such as exposure to real danger, serious injury, emergencies and traumatic loss. Some missions, such as search and rescue, have the potential to combine it all, since the aircrew have to deal with multiple stressors, very high workload, permanent evaluation of data, many times with significant adverse weather conditions, high probability of life-threatening situations, and a critical and very demanding multiple decision-making processes.

### Military aeronautics and psychosocial stressors in operational missions

The operational context, whether humanitarian, peacekeeping, combat or a combination of all three, is rich in traumatic events; these events can compromise the aircrew mental health and emotional homeostasis. There is a well-known correlation between operational combat experiences and a multitude of negative psychosocial, mental, health and occupational effects.

Grinker and Spiegel (cited by Joseph, 2007) described the aetiology of combat stress disorders in the aircrew into four categories: a) threat of injury or death, b) threat of injury or death of friends, c) requirement to engage in destructive activity, and d) adverse effect of combat-related stressors on the motivation to fly and fight.

Stress is inherent to the military context and the environments where the military operate normally, but there are some particularities associated with high-stress events. They are a more extreme type of stressor and are associated with situations that are threatening, overwhelming, unexpected, uncertain and ambiguous. In military positions, some of these extreme events can occur in daily life, but they are more common when military are deployed to operational missions. A systematic way to approach the demands associated with a deployment is to divide them into two groups: the daily difficulties of deployed life and the stressors/dangers experienced from operational missions.

### Daily difficulties of deployed life

Operational deployments are a requirement for military personnel, aircrews included. We can say that deployments begin psychologically much earlier than the day on which the military is deployed. This is justified, not only because there is a whole preparation at various levels, but also because psychologically there has to be a mobilization of resources, in order to address the stressors inherent to family separation and also to stressors of anticipation associated with the deployment/mission.

The preparation phase, usually called pre-deployment, can be considered a precursor of what is to come, because it implies field training and preparation, frequently away from home. The aim is to create a sense of cohesion between all unit members, but also to create a sense of increasing emotional distance from family. The stressors in this phase have to do with accepting the warning order for deployment, anticipating family separation (sometimes developing increased tension in the family members), getting matters in order, and succeeding in military preparation for deployment. This phase is characterized by different and sometimes opposing emotions, such as irritability, excitement, anxiety, sadness and fear of the unknown.

Although pre-deployment training aims to prepare both military and families, deployment stressors are always challenging. Deployments usually take place in remote places with difficult and extreme climate, and even if there is an effort to minimize some of these extreme living conditions, there are a variety of stressors that cannot be supressed. Part of the daily hassles in a deployment have to do with working with inadequate living conditions, very difficult climates, long duty hours and inadequate rest, sleep deprivation, high workload, perceived threat from conventional, biological or chemical weapons, difficulties with other military, domestic and personal problems. These stressors are cumulative and result frequently in fatigue, acute sleep deprivation and sometimes in depression.

These extreme living conditions have a negative impact in all military personnel, but they are of great concern in aircrew, particularly in military pilots, because some of these stressors affect key competencies for the flight. To give one example, a study revealed that acute sleep deprivation degrades visual perception, simple motor and complex motor performance (Joseph, 2007).

Paul T. Bartone (2012), supported by extensive work with the US military deployments, from 1993 through 1996, identified the five primary dimensions of psychological stress in modern military operations:

- *Isolation*, since deployments frequently occur in remote places, with different language and culture, where there is a familiar and social uprooting.

- *Ambiguity*, that includes difficulties in clarifying information about the mission, rules of engagement, command/leadership structure, role, norms and standard behaviour.
- *Powerlessness*, a diverse concept related to movement restrictions, indeterminate deployment length, inability to influence what is happening at home.
- *Boredom* (alienation) that has to do with long periods of repetitive work, absence of meaningful work, few options for entertainment, difficulties in understanding the mission and assign it a worthiness.
- *Danger* (threat), concerning the real risk of serious injury or death, accidents, including friendly fire, weapons (chemical, biological, or nuclear materials).

Taking into account the characteristics of actual deployments, Bartone introduced one more dimension: *workload* or *"operations tempo"* (Castro *et al.*, 2000). This dimension is a fair description of the frequency, length and rapid pace of deployments today, but also of the pre-deployment activities, and still of all the work of the retraction phase.

Experiencing deployment for a significant period can change military personnel as individuals, in what their priorities are, what is important to them and also in the way they see themselves and the world.

### Stressors from operational missions

Operational missions can expose aircrew to extreme stressors. Potentially traumatic events are easy to recognize as significant stressors, and can have a devastating effect on individuals and units. Operational stressors are likely to vary by operation, mission and branch of service.

Performance in operational environments is critical, particularly when the aircrew is operating high performance aircraft in tactical missions, such as air defence, air support missions and ground attack. The level of complexity in operational missions, brought by all the technological advances, has the potential to increase even more the aircrew stress.

The actual air combat context includes missions for fighter, transport and helicopter crews. For fighter squadrons there are ground-attack missions, coordination of strike areas with forward air controllers, reconnaissance pilots image areas for assessing damage and planning further missions, and others where the need for low flying can be fatal. Transport crew will move troops, airlift supplies and equipment. In this type of mission one of the significant stress factors will be the size and low velocity of the aircraft, mainly because part of their activities occurs in locations familiar to the enemy. Another stressor has to do with the number of landings and take-offs that are usually significant in combat missions, multiplying the vulnerability to enemy fire, and placing the crew in a state of permanent stimulation. Helicopter squadrons are in charge of special missions, deploying, evacuating and rescuing wounded or causalities sometimes under fire, and at least in conditions far from ideal to operate (Joseph, 2007).

Tactical aircrews deal with a whole series of dangers such as enemy air defence fighters, small arms fire, and anti-aircraft artillery, among others.

In this dangerous and adverse environment which includes a multitude of factors, from cognitive impairment caused by fatigue, unexpected attack and the stress of uncertainty, to the operating conditions that interfere with visibility, is not excluded the possibility of friendly fire. Another stress that adds to the strain is the possibility of chemical or biological attack and the consequent use of a protection suit, which is in itself a stress generator.

## The way military pilots feel stressors

The effects of stressors on performance are complex and diverse. As stated by Farmer and McIntyre (2000), who published a review of 300 studies on aircrew stress, no agreement was found and there was a clear and significant variation in the effects of some stressors.

For military pilots it is well known that stress is an insidious threat to aviation safety because of the impairments it produces in cognitive performance, transforming the flight situation in an error-prone environment.

The need for the most favourable cognition during operations in critical environments is a certainty for military pilots and military leaders. One military training goal is to increase the ability for better cognitive effectiveness under stress. Concepts like psychological fitness and stress inoculation seek through repeated practise of skills, increased level of challenge, with meaningful feedback and successive approaches with realistic training, to create a progressive sense of control and mastery in extreme and unstructured situations.

Some studies (Khodabakhsh & Kolivand, 2007; Ribeiro & Surrador, 2006) revealed that life and organizational stressors are those that are felt most significantly by military pilots. According to Ribeiro and Surrador (2006: 160–161) the dimensions of personal life relate to dimensions as "repercussions of work in personal life, involvement of work in the personal and family sphere, and work demands with interference with spouses and children", while the most significant organizational dimensions were "relationship with the direct leadership, have no control over the time, and career development". In the other study (Khodabakhsh & Kolivand, 2007: 161–162) the dimensions that scored higher were "life stress and organizational stress. Life stressors such as relationship with the wife, communication with children, familial interaction, family and friends, financial problems, and marital conflicts" scored significantly and had the highest correlation with job satisfaction. These findings may suggest that although much is done to optimize professional, technical, military and operational skills in military pilots, it has been not sufficiently considered the need to develop skills of compatibility and management of social and family life.

As military aviation is incompatible with psychological or physical problems, there is the possibility of pilots intentionally concealing symptoms. An alternative to this is to seek help as a civilian which means without informing the organization. Milder symptoms may not be perceived because of the defence mechanisms usually presented by pilots, such as denial and repression. Fear of compromising the personal image in the organization, of damaging the career and also the financial aspects of flight supplements, are the usual arguments that justify the omission of reporting. Since military aeronautics environment is stressful by nature, it is imperative to assess the origins and the level of stress experienced by military pilots with the aim of developing organizational strategies to reduce it, knowing the likelihood of having pilots continuing to fly despite their psychological difficulties.

Currently the global financial crisis has had a concrete impact on armed forces. One example is the rotation frequency and duration of the deployments. Tendentiously, rotations of troops deployed occur less frequently, increasing the time the military stay deployed, maximizing human resources but minimizing financial costs. On the other hand, in national terms the trend is a reduction in flying hours, leading pilots to remain in flight squadrons without flying. This is an obvious stressor for pilots and it is essential to take this time with activities that allow levels of educational, emotional, physical, personal, social and professional development.

## Psychosocial stressors in commercial pilots

Becoming a professional airline pilot is a coveted and prestigious position. However, it is also one that requires fortitude and a tough mentality, due to the increasing levels of stressors that pilots are exposed to on a regular basis. There are several sources of stress for a typical pilot, not least of which is the number of lives which are in their care with every flight. Dealing with these factors is a large part of flight training, but under certain circumstances, especially when other stressors are involved, they can be difficult to cope with.

The first sociological study about the commercial pilot's work and home life has been published by Simon Bennett of the University of Leicester's Civil Safety and Security Unit (CSSU). Funded by a grant from the British Air Line Pilots' Association (BALPA), the aim of the study was to gain a fuller understanding of the pilot's lifestyle and analyse its relation with fatigue, stress and several other factors. The intention of this investigation was to use the data to inform EASA's deliberations on a new Europe-wide flight-time limitation (FTL) scheme. Three research instruments were used: sleep diaries (kept by volunteers for three weeks), an online questionnaire (containing 54 questions about pilot's lifestyle) and extensive interviews (which were tape-recorded, then transcribed verbatim). The study began in mid-2010 and ended in 2011 and was notable for its scale: 130 sleep diaries and 433 questionnaires were received (76 per cent of which came from British Airways pilots). All three instruments generated quantitative and qualitative data concerning fatigue, stress, organizational culture, job satisfaction, motivation, indebtedness, commuting, industrial relations, medical and psychological support and the work–life balance (Bennett, 2011).

The following description of psychosocial stressors is partially based on some of the findings of this ground-breaking report on the lifestyle of commercial pilots.

### Erosion of the pilot profession

Decades ago a pilots' career was considered prestigious, promising and full of benefits. In the initial 'honeymoon' period, the opportunity to travel, to see the world and to meet a wealth of differing peoples and cultures contributed to the perceived 'glamour' of the profession. The opportunity to escape the routine of many ground-based jobs added to this attraction.

However, worldwide recession, soaring fuel prices and high competition between airlines have intensified the pressure for cutting measures, and the pilots profession has felt the collateral effects of this situation.

"Escalating training costs and downward pressure on salaries are impacting the financial position of some pilots" (Bennett, 2011). Most aspiring pilots now bear the full costs of training and of course the resulting indebtedness impacts their personal quality of life. Frequently, pilots on low incomes cannot afford to live close to major airports, neither can they afford pay for temporary accommodation. Obliged to 'follow the work', pilots can find themselves commuting long distances. According to a BALPA study, over 30 per cent of respondents took between 60 and 120 minutes to commute. One solution to flight crew dislocation would be for airlines to provide accommodation. However, over 83 per cent confirmed that their airline would not subsidise hotel accommodation for fatigued crew returning to base.

Currently, pilot morale is not as high as it used to be and the BALPA study clearly reflects how pilots perceive this new reality: nearly 35 per cent of respondents said the profession had not met their expectation and only 19 per cent said they would recommend a career in aviation to their offspring.

### Irregular working hours

Very few pilots are able to keep a steady working schedule and are subject to extended periods of wakefulness on duty days. They are expected to fly all times of the week, both day and night and in all kind of weather conditions. This irregular schedule has been shown to cause both mental and physical problems. In addition to the strain caused by irregular working hours, pilots also need to contend with regular jet lag.

International Civil Aviation Organization defines fatigue as "a physiological state of reduced mental or physical performance capability resulting from sleep loss or extended wakefulness, circadian phase, or workload" (ICAO, 2013: 2). Fatigue is particularly prevalent among pilots because of "unpredictable work hours, long duty periods, circadian disruption and insufficient sleep". These factors can occur together to produce a combination of sleep deprivation, circadian rhythm effects, and "time-on task" fatigue. The phenomenon places great risk on the crew and passengers of an airplane because it significantly increases the chance of pilot error (Caldwell *et al.*, 2009).

BALPA research showed that both long- and short-haul pilots ($N$ =433) accumulate sleep-deficit. Over 86 per cent of the respondents said they had flown a sector when knowingly fatigued and had experienced a period of continuous wakefulness exceeding 18 hours on a duty day. It was documented that the sleep deficit problem can start at home. Over 84 per cent of respondents said they had failed to get adequate rest at home because of telephone calls (23 per cent), extraneous noise (23 per cent), household noise (24 per cent), work-related stress (27 per cent), household duties (43 per cent) and family-related stress (53 per cent).

### Roster instability

Whereas pilots are responsible for the safety of their passengers, aircraft and crew, they often have little or no control over their rosters. These are generally designed and controlled by back-office staff who sometimes are pressured to meet operational requirements – certainly within established safety limits – and, therefore, sometimes compromise pilots' best needs. Pilots plan their sleep and their personal lives according to a current roster. However, rosters are frequently changed at short notice and this can undermine work–life balance. Pilots may find themselves short of sleep and may feel thwarted because they have to suddenly change previous plans for rest and recreation. The BALPA study showed that nearly 80 per cent of pilots said they had felt unduly stressed at home, and over 73 per cent of respondents said they had felt unduly stressed at work.

A study conducted by Bennet (2003) about flight crew fatigue and stress in low-cost commercial operations, showed that rostering was seen as a contributing factor for fatigue and psychological stress by most interviewees.

### Poor job conditions

Current precariousness of job conditions is another issue to consider as a source of stress for pilots. The global financial recession has had a negative impact in all industries and aviation is no exception. In the last decade airlines have been forced to become extremely competitive in order to survive. The industry has grown exponentially, due in part to rising individual prosperity in emerging economies and the boom of the budget airline.

Liberalization and the growth of the low-cost sector have transformed international aviation into a very competitive market. The low-cost business model is uncompromising: costs are pared down and resources used to maximum effect. By stripping commercial flying of all adornment (in-flight meals, in-flight entertainment, passenger service departments, allocated seats, use of tertiary airports etc.), low-cost carriers are able to provide cheap air travel. This continuous pressure to reduce costs has led to increased focusing on reducing payrolls and conditions of employment. Nowadays, some pilots have to bear the brunt of training costs, need to cope with unpredictable employment conditions and are exposed to an increase in hours flown and faster turnarounds.

The so called 'pay-to-fly' phenomenon (described in *Atypical Employment in Aviation*" a study undertaken by Ghent University with the financial support of European Commission (Jorens *et al.*, 2015)) is an atypical employment form practised by some airlines who require the pilot to pay for his/her 'line-training' on board of revenue-earning flights, instead of earning a salary. The pilot flies an aircraft on a regular revenue-earning flight – as any other qualified crewmember – but instead of receiving a salary he/she pays the airline for the flight hours. Usually, these flight hours are part of the 'type rating' – a standard in-house training course on a specific type of aircraft – which is part of every pilot's professional career.

The possibility that the low-cost paradigm of economic efficiency may have implications for the physical and mental health of pilots has prompted concern amongst both flight crew, unions and regulatory agencies.

Bennett (2003) interviewed a group of pilots and first officers employed by a UK-registered low-cost carrier. Despite the small sample size and the subjectiveness of the data, this research highlights several stress-related themes. Most pilots stated they felt stressed and fatigued. Symptoms included poor short-term memory, slowed reactions, reduced motivational drive, decreased work efficiency and greater risk-taking. Perceived symptoms of stress and fatigue were attributed to the requirements of the low-cost business model: commercial pressures, bureaucratic problems, rostering, aircraft changes and 25-minute turnarounds, eating and accommodation arrangements, and low salaries.

A study of commercial pilots working for airlines with a history of corporate instability reported significantly more stress and depression symptoms and a greater accumulation of symptoms than did the pilots employed by stable airlines (Little *et al.*,1990).

Precarious working conditions create pressures and difficult challenges for pilots who tend to feel pressured and undervalued by employers. This necessarily has implications for job motivation, satisfaction and general well-being. Feelings of demoralization, low self-esteem, deception, anxiety or even depression may arise.

*Flight deck automation*

Flight deck automation has become another potential stress factor for pilots. The necessity for direct human control of the flying operation has progressively been removed and replaced by automation through a mix of economic, environmental and social incentives. Through automation, the tendency to commit error on well-established procedural routines is dramatically reduced. Fuel, which is the leading player in the financial welfare of the global airline industry, is optimally managed and crew-training time is reduced. However, sustainable maintenance of these desirable automation-driven benefits requires the consideration of human factor issues that are detrimental to safe aircraft operations.

There is no doubt that automation has made pilots' lives easier, reducing some workload and relieving them from repetitive or non-rewarding tasks for which humans are less suited. However, it changes the pilots' active involvement in operating the aircraft into a monitoring role, which humans are particularly poor at doing effectively or for long periods (Casner, 2006). In other words, pilots used to fly by brawn and brain. Now they do it by computer, with the brawn and brain as a backup.

One of the likely by-products of a highly automated cockpit is an increase in boredom and monotony among pilots as a result of the anticipated reduction in task demands. Boredom and monotony are generally considered to be negative factors that can have adverse effects on morale, performance, and quality of work (Eastwood *et al.*, 2012; Thackray,1980).

Another issue introduced by cockpit automation is a weakening of the hierarchy between captain and co-pilot (Chialastri, 2012). The captain is indeed the person with the greatest responsibility for the flight and this implies a hierarchical order to establish who has the final word on board. This hierarchical order is also accompanied by functional task sharing, whereby on every flight there is a pilot flying and a pilot not flying (or monitoring pilot). Airplanes with a high level of automation require task sharing, in which the pilot flying has a great degree of autonomy in programming the flight management system. Above all, the pilot flying also determines the timing of the collaboration offered by the pilot not flying, even in an emergency situation. In fact, since the crew must act in a procedural way in fulfilling the demands of the automation system, both pilots must cooperate in a more horizontal way, weakening the traditional hierarchical position of commanders.

In summary, as piloting becomes increasingly automated, the various implications of this trend should be considered. Although automation has improved the overall safety level in aviation, problems that emerge from a new way of operating must be adequately addressed.

### Increased security measures

Increased security measures and the threat of terrorism in aviation are aspects that can add to the psychological strain for pilots. The tragedy of Germanwings flight 4U9525 triggered a number of initiatives and interim measures within the aviation industry. Among other measures, *the European Aviation Safety Agency (2015) recommended airlines to have two people in the cockpit at all times.* This means that when there are only two pilots on the flight deck, and if one of them has to leave for physiological needs or any other operational reason, another member of the crew (generally from the cabin crew) must be present on the flight deck with the remaining pilot. The "two crewmember rule" has also been mandatory for all US passenger airlines since 9/11. The Eurocockpit Association (2016) believes that the "minimum occupancy" concept will not prove effective against the reoccurrence of the Germanwings situation, and does not support its continuation and/or implementation. Moreover, ECA says, "inferring that flight crews require monitoring when they are on their own in the flight deck risks reducing passenger confidence in the pilots, whose daily task and responsibility is to fly them safely to their destination".

Fortunately, tragic accidents such as Germanwings are extremely rare. However, the subsequent negative perceptions held by passengers (such as questioning of credibility, image and trustworthiness of pilots) can be long-lasting and this suspiciousness certainly undermines pilots' professional self-esteem. Feeling that many people getting on airplanes were fearful and "wondering if their pilots were potential mass-murderers", was many times felt as offensive and frustrating for pilots. Following this accident, it was touching to see how many pilots (equally affected by an event that killed innocent passengers and who were still dealing with grief from losing their colleagues) showed up in communication forums in an attempt to re-establish the trust and confidence of the public. In an attempt to regain passengers' confidence and mitigate unfounded fears, many pilots began to come out of the cockpit to welcome passengers during boarding, deliberately exposing themselves to passengers' appraisal and calming them down.

The threat of terrorism and increased security measures can represent another source of stress for pilots. Airports are a potential target for terrorism and other forms of crimes because of the number of people located in a particular location. The high concentration of people on large airliners, the potential high death rate with attacks on aircraft, and the ability to use a hijacked airplane as a lethal weapon makes them an appealing target for terrorists.

Since the 9/11 terrorist attacks, airport security measures have been tightened all over the world aiming to protect passengers, staff, airliners and airports from crime and other threats. Although security measures are welcome and necessary, they generate a climate of suspicion that can be uncomfortable and stressful for many of us when flying as regular passengers. This stressful effect is understandably heightened within aircrews that have to go through the whole process several times during a working day.

In the BALPA study over 95 per cent of respondents considered that current security measures were "excessive" and that they added to the stress level of flight crew. As an example, we report the case of a pilot that had a "humiliating and distressing" experience with a security agent when he refused to let him palpate his feet, a procedure he considered invasive. The pilot became so angry and disturbed that he refused to make the flight.

### Critical incidents

Exposure to potential critical incidents is an additional aspect of pilots profession. Although pilots are typically self-confident and generally very well-prepared and trained to anticipate and cope with almost all kind of stressful situations, they are not immune to the effect of traumatic events. While flying, they can face incredibly demanding situations like systems failures, in-flight medical emergencies, hijackings, terroristic threats, emergency landings, wind shear, accidents, critical air mishaps, etc. When these situations get out of hand due to its extraordinary dynamics and prove to be a challenge to established coping mechanisms, they have the potential to psychologically affect crewmembers and may produce functional impairment.

A critical (or traumatic) incident is any event that has the potential to evoke a reaction of intense fear or helplessness and that undermines the person's sense of safety, security or competence. Critical incident stress occurs when the event overwhelms the individual's ability to cope effectively in the face of such a perceived challenge or threat. It can be said that critical incident stress reaction is a normal reaction to an abnormal event.

For instance, in-flight medical emergencies (IFMEs) can represent a critical incident for pilots since a "bad decision" might have an unfavourable outcome, including the death of a passenger (or of a colleague). If this should happen, pilots can be at risk for long-lasting feelings of personal guilt and view themselves as having failed even if there is no reasonable cause for it.

IFMEs are increasing due to the steadily rising number of air travellers, the aging of passengers, and the increasing mobility of people with acute and chronic illnesses. Although relatively infrequent, IFMEs generally represent an extra challenge to a pilot's regular duties. Based on the information provided, the captain has the responsibility to quickly decide to either continue the flight to the planned destination or to divert. Irrespective of the continue/divert decision, when first informed that there is a passenger with a critical medical issue, there are numerous operational factors to be considered when planning and executing a diversion: Is the aircraft below maximum landing weight? Will fuel dumping or an overweight landing be required? Is the planned diversion suitable in terms of runway length, approach capability and parking? Is the weather at the diversion aerodrome suitable? Does the diversion airfield have the required ground support equipment inclusive of steps, baggage handling capability, towing capability etc. for the aircraft type? Is fuel available? Will the diversion result in the inability of the crew to continue to planned destination? Commercial questions also arise: Is it possible to divert to an airfield that is normally serviced by the company? Which diversion choice will cause the least schedule disruption? Are replacement crewmembers available at the planned diversion, if necessary?

The pilot's reaction to a critical incident is dependent on the interaction between the capabilities of the person involved and the external situation being faced. Factors include: the pilot's physiological state at the time (health, fatigue, lack of sleep, etc.); intensity, duration and predictability of the critical incident (the less predictable the more stressful it becomes); the pilot's personal evaluation of the stressor; and willingness of other crewmembers to give support (both social and practical).

If the elevated state of arousal caused by a critical incident is not properly addressed, it may lead to several psychological disorders including acute stress disorder, post-traumatic stress disorder, panic attacks, depression, alcohol or substance abuse.

Critical incident stress management (CISM) is a preventive systematic approach led by trained peer support groups and mental health professionals aimed to mitigate the psychological impact of the event, facilitate normal recovery processes and restoration to normal life (Mitchell & Resnik, 1981).

Several programmes exist within airlines to provide assistance to pilots, in case of personal, emotional or mental difficulties. These programmes offer referral service, peer support and advice in a "safe zone", in conditions of absolute confidentiality, while maintaining the high level of safety for the airline (Mayday Foundation and ALPA's Critical Incident Response Programme are two good examples of such programmes).

### Home/family factors

Irregular duty periods and missing out on activities at home can spur a significant and detrimental cycle of stress that disrupts family balance. Most pilots will be flying several multi-day trips per month where they will be gone for several nights at a time, sometimes up to a week or more for larger international-type aircraft. Pilots frequently miss many events – from birthdays, to public holidays, and even vacations.

Emotional stress associated with family separation for nearly one third of the working life can be particularly disturbing when children are growing up and the spouse needs support.

Physiological and psychological effects of rotating shift work are fairly well known (tiredness, fatigue, sleep deficit, sometimes exhaustion) and many times pilots end a duty cycle feeling too exhausted to participate in family functions. This can undermine marriage and probably explains why pilots tend to have a higher-than-average divorce rate.

The term "intermittent husband syndrome" (IHS) was introduced by Morrice and colleagues (1985: 482) to describe how wives react and feel when their husbands are regularly away from home for extended periods of time. They considered that "swiftly recurring partings and reunions were related to depression in the wife and behavioral problems in the children". A wife with IHS would become

> depressed during the latter part of the husband's absence, or shortly after his return, experiencing feelings of desertion, anger, sadness and recrimination towards the husband, leading to disruptive behavior between the couple and an increase in physical and emotional symptoms in the wife.

However, reactions of women who lived with intermittent husbands were not always the same: while some became depressed when husbands were absent but improved on their return home, others felt better when they were away.

Different lengths of time apart will affect people in different ways depending on the couple's capability to adjust to the new circumstances. The "intermittent husband" who goes away and returns at frequent intervals, seems to be the most disruptive pattern because readjusting to life back at home has no time to occur (Rigg & Cosgrove, 1994).

Sloan and Cooper (1986) described the sources of stress on aircrew wives and identified five main groups: domestic role overload; fear of husband's job loss; threats to the marriage; distance from husband's career; and finally, the job impact on the family's social life.

In a study conducted by Fiedler and Cols (2000) about the relationship between domestic situations and perceived effectiveness on duty, a group of U.S. Coast Guard helicopter pilots ranked six family-related factors highest among 53 potential sources of stress. The factors included backlogs of tasks, arguments, lack of money, child-related issues, use of time at home, and the overall degree to which home life matches expectations. Pilots perceived their flying performance as degraded during periods of high stress at home. When family problems carry over into the cockpit, they negatively affect several aspects of performance, including situational awareness, landing accuracy and smoothness, ability to divide attention, and the perceived degree of general airmanship. The responses also indicated that the presence of a stable marital status was the greatest moderator of home-based stress ("stability with a spouse" and "smooth and stable home life" were cited as the most important factors to keep job efficiency by all pilots surveyed). Having a spouse with some knowledge of flying also was perceived as contributing to better flying performance (Fiedler *et al.*, 2000).

A similar survey of British commercial pilots (Cooper & Sloan, 1985) found that work/family factors significantly influenced both job performance and the ability to cope with stress, and that the most important aid in coping with stress was stability in relationships and in home life. The study noted that the primary effect of home stress on work is in the mental or cognitive consequences: recurring thoughts during periods of low workload, decreased concentration and a tendency not to listen. In other words, demands at home can lead to preoccupied workers, a perilous condition in a safety-sensitive business.

The role of the pilot's spouse in the stress management equation was emphasized by Karlins *et al.* (1989: 1114), who suggest that the spouse represents a major social support system for the aviator and a significant factor in the pilot's ability to deal effectively with psychosocial stress. The authors recommended that

> airlines should develop programs that: a) recognize the spouses for their contribution to safe aircraft operation (by helping the aviator cope with stress more effectively); and b) make both husband and wife more aware of the special needs, concerns, and challenges that each partner faces in an airline marriage. These programs, would enable aviators and their spouses the opportunity to become more aware of their dual role and contributions

to effective stress management which, in turn, could enhance flight deck performance.

For countering the contamination of problems from work to home and vice-versa, pilots have developed a natural protective mechanism described by Searle (2012) as the phenomenon of "psychological detachment" (the ability to not think about work at home and to keep personal issues/feelings/thoughts outside the cockpit). When work interferes with family responsibilities and family problems are known to negatively affect several aspects of performance, the capacity for psychological detachment (or compartmentalization) seems to be an effective coping strategy to diminish the effects of conflict and for relieving pilots' psychological strain.

### Social isolation

Having a network of supportive relationships contributes to psychological well-being. Numerous studies indicate social support is essential for maintaining physical and psychological health. The harmful consequences of poor social support and the protective effects of good social support in mental illness have been well documented. Social support moderates genetic and environmental vulnerabilities and converts resilience to stress (Ozbay *et al.*, 2007)

Apart from the well-known physical constraints of around-the-clock jobs (e.g. fatigue, sleep debt and tiredness) and the already-mentioned effects on family dynamics and routines, pilots' work schedules can also produce negative consequences on social life.

Social relationships are difficult to maintain when dealing with extended absences or irregular duty periods. Many people who work rotating shifts reduce their social activities because flight schedules do not allow consistent involvement. A commitment to this kind of lifestyle produces a consequential lack of investment in home life and often results in difficulties with establishing and maintaining personal relationships.

Sporting activities, encounters with friends, parties and most of recreational activities usually occur in the evenings, on weekends or on holidays when a flight crewmember might be on duty. As time goes by, friends or relatives with no exposure to the same lifestyle learn to not count on the presence of the pilot, assuming he will not be available to show up and, gradually, may exclude him from social activities.

If these resulting social constraints are not compensated with proper coping strategies, a sense of deep loneliness can arise, accompanied by feelings of insecurity, non-belonging and unworthiness leaving the pilot more vulnerable to emotional stress.

# Conclusion

Despite the fact that pilots are generally considered to be at less risk for mental health disorders and are better equipped to cope with stress, they are normal human beings who also have personal limits and emotions.

Given their high professional responsibility, pilots are a unique occupational group that is systematically subject to technical, physical and psychological screenings in order to prove their "fitness to fly". However, there is nothing to prevent them from feeling emotional instability when going through some of the psychosocial stressors as described above.

The pilot's overall reaction to one or more stressors is cumulative through time and is dependent on the interaction between several variables: a) pilot's physiological state and personal circumstances at the time (health, fatigue, lack of sleep, emotional stability, etc.); b) the intensity, duration and predictability of the stressor itself (the less predictable the more stressful); c) personal evaluation of the stressor and perceived resources to cope with it (mediated by variables such as technical preparation, personality, self-confidence, self-esteem); and d) confidence in the other crewmembers' abilities to give support (both technical and social).

Stress is a subject that is often ignored on both a personal and professional level. People may feel ashamed, see it as a personal sign of weakness, or worry about repercussions in their workplace. This may be especially true within the aviation industry. However, stress has the potential to develop serious mental health issues and can ultimately compromise flight safety if unrecognized or underestimated.

Evans & Radcliffe (2012) analysed all medical incapacitations occurring among UK commercial pilots, in-flight and off-duty, in 2004. Mental health problems ranked as one of the most common reasons for medical incapacitation (10 per cent), after musculoskeletal disorders (18 per cent) and cardiovascular illness (14 per cent). These findings highlighted the medical risks that require most attention and confirmed the need to monitor and be more aware of the mental health of pilots.

Recognizing sources of stress and reducing them is an important duty of aviation industry. Over the years, military and civil aviation organizations have developed stress management mechanisms which have proved to be highly efficient. The conventional flying training, the SOPs (standard operation procedures), CRM (crew resource management) and LOFT (line-oriented flight training) are some of the effective tools meant to help a pilot have a grip of the situation, including stressful ones.

Although extremely valuable, these tools are mainly focused in technical aspects of the profession and usually don't cover the wide range of psychosocial stressors (job-related and personal circumstances) that pilots encounter throughout their careers.

For countering the effects of psychosocial stressors on pilots' mental health and mitigate its impact on flight safety, more proactive and preventive measures are needed.

# References

Adler, A.B., Bliese, P.D., McGurk, D., Salvi, A., & Eckford, R. (2008). Remaining resilient after combat: Emotional disclosure in US Soldiers. Paper presented at the International Military Testing Association Conference, 23 September–3 October, Amsterdam.

Bartone, P.T. (2012). Social and organizational influences on psychological hardiness: How leaders can increase stress resilience. *Security Informatics,* 1(21). http://security-informatics.springeropen.com/articles/10.1186/2190-8532-1-21

Benight, C.C., & Bandura, A. (2004). Social cognitive theory of posttraumatic recovery: The role of perceived self-efficacy. *Behaviour Research and Therapy,* 42, 1129–1148.

Bennet, S. (2003). Flight crew stress and fatigue in low-cost commercial air operations: An appraisal. *International Journal of Risk Assessment and Management,* 4(2/3), 207–231.

Bennett, S. (2011). *The pilot life-style: A sociological study of the commercial pilot's work and home life.* Leicester: University of Leicester Institute of Lifelong Learning.

Bolton, E.E., Tankersley, A.P., Eisen, E.M., & Litz, B.T. (2015). Adaptation to traumatic stress: Resilient traits, resources, and trajectories of outcomes. *Current Psychiatry Reviews,* 11, 150–159.

Bosma, H., Peter, R., Siegrist, J., & Marmot, M. (1998). Two alternative job stress models and the risk of coronary heart disease. *American Journal of Public Health,* 88, 68–74.

Caldwell, J.A., Mallis, M.M., & Caldwell, J.L.. (2009). Fatigue countermeasures in aviation. *Aviation, Space, and Environmental Medicine,* 80, 29–59.

CareerCast (2016). The most stressful jobs of 2016. Retrieved from http://www.careercast.com/jobs-rated/most-stressful-jobs-2016 (accessed 30 November 2015).

Casner, S. (2006). *Cockpit automation: For general aviators and future airline.* Ames, Iowa: Aviation Supplies and Academics.

Castro, C.A., Huffman, D.C., Bienvenu, R.V., & Adler, A.B. (2000). Working in the zone: Maintaining optimal readiness in U.S Soldiers. Presented in 36th IAMPS, Split, Croatia, 11–15 September.

Chialastri, A. (2012). Automation. In F. Kongoli (ed.), *Automation in aviation* (pp.79–102). Rijeka, Croatia: In Tech.

Colligan, T., Colligan, M., & Higgins, M. (2006). Workplace stress-etiology and consequences. *Journal of Workplace Behavioral Health,* 21, 89–97.

Cooper, C., & Sloan, S. (1985). Occupational and psychosocial stress among commercial aviation pilots. *Journal of Occupational and Environmental Medicine,* 27, 570–575.

Eastwood, J., Frischen, A., Fenske, M., & Smilek, D. (2012). The unengaged mind: Defining boredom in terms of attention. *Perspectives on Psychological Science,* 7, 482 –495.

Eurocockpit Association. (2016). Minimum occupancy of the flight deck. ECA position paper. Retrieved from: https://www.eurocockpit.be/stories/20160216/minimum-occupancy-of-the-flight-feck-eca-position-paper (accessed 12 March 2016).

European Aviation Safety Agency. (2015). Task force on measures following the accident of Germanwings flight: final report. Retrieved from http://ec.europa.eu/transport/modes/air/news/doc/2015-07-17-germanwings-report/germanwings-task-force-final-report.pdf

Evans, S., & Radcliffe, S. (2012). The annual inacapacitation rate of commercial pilots. *Aviation, Space, and Environmental Medicine,* 83, 42–49.

Farmer, E.W., & McIntyre, H.M. (2000). Crew resource management. In J. Ernsting, A. Nicholson, & D.J. Rainford (eds), *Aviation medicine* (third edition) (pp 609–610). London: Butterworth-Heinemann.

Fiedler, E.R., Rocco, P.D., Schroeder, D.J., & Nguyen, K.T. (2000). The relationship between aviators' home-based stress to work stress and self-perceived performance. Oklahoma: Civil Aeromedical Institute, Federal Aviation Administration.

ICAO. (2013). International Standards and Recommended Practices: Operation of Aircraft. Retrieved from http://www.icao.int/safety/fatiguemanagement/frms%20 tools/amendment%2037%20for%20frms%20sarps%20(en).pdf (accessed 27 February 2016).

Jorens, Y., Gillis, D., Valcke, L., & Coninck, J., (2015). *Atypical employment in aviation: Final report.* Brussels: Ghent University, European Commission.

Joseph, C. (2007). An overview of psychological factors and interventions in air combat operations. *Indian Journal of Aerospace Medicine*, 51, 1–16.

Karlins, M., Koh, F., & McCully, L. (1989). The spousal factor in pilot stress. *Aviation, Space, and Environmental Medicine*, 60, 1112–1115.

Khodabakhsh, A., & Kolivand, A. (2007). Stress and job satisfaction among air force military pilots. *Journal of Social Sciences*, 3, 159–163.

Lazarus, R.S., & Folkman, S. (1984). *Stress, appraisal and coping.* New York: Springer Publishing Company.

Little, L., Gaffney, I., Rosen, K., & Bender, M. (1990). Corporate instability is related to airline pilots' stress symptoms. *Aviation, Space, and Environmental Medicine*, 61, 977–982.

Marsh, R.W., Sowin, T.W., & Thompson, W.T. (2010). Panic disorder in military aviators: a retrospective study of prevalence. *Aviation, Space, and Environmental Medicine*, 81, 589–592.

Mitchell, J.T., & Resnik, H.L.P. (1981). *Emergency response to crisis: A crisis intervention guidebook for emergency service personnel.* Phoenix, AZ: Prentice-Hall.

Morrice, J., Taylor, R., Clark, D., McCann, K. (1985). Oil wives and intermittent husbands. *British Journal of Psychiatry*, 147, 479–483.

Ozbay, F., Johnson, D., Dimoulas, E., Morgan, C., Charney, D., & Southwick, S.(2007). Social support and resilience to stress: From neurobiology to clinical practice, *Psychiatry*, 4, 35–40.

Parasuraman, R., & Hancock, P.A. (2008). Mitigating the adverse effects of workload, stress, and fatigue with adaptive automation. In P.A. Hancock, & J.L. Szalma (eds.), *Performance under stress* (pp. 45–58). Farnham: Ashgate.

Ribeiro, R.B., & Surrador, A.A. (2006). Stress in military and aeronautical context: Identification of the most frequent stressors and indication of organizational and personal strategies for well-being improvement. In A.L. Silva, & A.M. Pinto (eds.), *Stress e bem-estar: Modelos e domínios de aplicação [Stress and well-being: Models and application domains]* (pp. 151–165). Manuais Universitários, Climepsi Editores.

Rigg, R., & Cosgrove, M. (1994). Aircrew wives and the intermittent husband syndrome. *Aviation, Space and Environmental Medicine*, 65, 654–660.

Searle, B. (2012). Detachment from work in airport hotels: Issues for pilot recovery. *Aviation Psychology and Applied Human Factors*, 2, 20–24.

Sloan, C.L., & Cooper, S.J. (1986). *Pilots under stress.* London: Routledge.

Stetz, M.C., Thomas, M.L., Russo, M.B., Stetz, T.A., Wildzunas, R.M., McDonald, J.J., Wiederhold, B.K., & Romano, Jr. J.A. (2007). Stress, mental health, and cognition: A brief review of relationships and countermeasures. *Aviation, Space, and Environmental Medicine*, 78, 252–256.

Thackray, R. (1980). *Boredom and monotony as a consequence of automation: A consideration of the evidence relating boredom and monotony to stress.* Oklahoma City, OK: Civil Aeromedical Institute, FAA.

Young, J. (2008). *The effects of life-stress on pilot performance*, Moffett Field, CA: National Aeronautics and Space Administration, Ames Research Center.

# 18 Promoting good psychological health amongst pilots

## Coping strategies for identifying and managing stress to reduce the risk of mental health problems and improve performance at work

### Carina Eriksen and Robert Bor

Psychological problems within the pilot population are an insidious threat to safety because of impairments to task performance. The FAA (US Federal Aviation Administration) guide for AME's (aviation medical examiners) includes specific requirements with regard to the psychiatric assessment and medical exclusions for mental health problems and these are very similar to the criteria stipulated by most other regulatory authorities worldwide. Severe psychological disturbance among pilots is rare but just as in other occupational groups, they may, however, suffer from a range of psychological difficulties which may be mild to moderate in severity and in most cases be transient and treatable (Bor and Hubbard, 2006; Bor et al., 2002; Elliot, 2013). As is the case with many mental health conditions, shame associated with social stigma and failure to access timely and appropriate treatment may increase the severity and duration of symptoms, thereby potentially leading to more serious and possibly intractable psychiatric problems. The prevention of mental health problems and reduction of stigma in the workplace associated with mental illness must be a priority in aviation. EASA made this the sixth and final recommendation of their action plan for carriers following the Germanwings pilot suicide crash in 2015.

Psychiatric disorders are not uncommon among the general population but are frequently under-recognised (Reid, 2016). Pilots are generally considered to be at less risk for psychiatric disorders and better equipped to cope with stress. This may be due to the crew selection process which consists of a number of psychological and skills-based assessments. Psychological testing is effective in the beginning before a pilot starts training to select the right person for the job. It may help to rule out those with a history of or who display overt signs of psychological disturbance, or who conceal significant psychological problems. But psychological tests may be less effective in predicting life events and how people cope with them. Despite the stereotypic image as 'the right stuff', pilots are of course human and therefore prone to all of life's vicissitudes and to the ailments that may lie dormant within one's brain chemistry.

Pilots are in many ways a unique occupational group. They work shifts, have no office, and are required to undertake multiple duties at 35,000 feet as well as being subject to frequent absence from home and frequent travel across time zones. It has been suggested that people who fly for a living may also have health concerns above and beyond those who work on the ground (Brown *et al.*, 2001; Eriksen, 2009). Most health concerns specific to the flying profession are thought to be environmental, arising from the unique conditions inside the airplane. This includes air quality, potable water quality, pressure changes, reduced oxygen in the air at altitude, and exposure to cosmic radiation, vibration and noise. Since most flying jobs entail irregular and frequently changing schedules, long work hours, frequent absence from home and frequent travel across time zones, considerable disruption to biological rhythm can result (Waterhouse *et al.*, 2006).This can cause sleep problems, fatigue, as well as disruptions to normal patterns of eating and other bodily functions. Aircrew are also required to spend long periods away from partners, family, and friends at home. When this is compounded by irregular patterns of work and difficulties with planning ahead, there is a consequential lack of investment in personal living (Eriksen, 2009).

## Common psychological disorders amongst pilots

Some of the more common psychological problems amongst pilots include adjustment disorder, mood disorder (Jones and Ireland, 2004), anxiety and occupational stress (Cooper and Sloan, 1985; Girodo, 1988; Steptoe and Bostock, 2011), relationship problems (Raschmann, Patterson, and Schofield, 1990), sexual dysfunction (Grossman *et al.*, 2004), and alcohol and drug misuse (Harris, 2002; Kraus and Li, 1990).

Whilst it is beyond this chapter to give a detailed outline of each specific disorder, all of these problems and symptoms have apprehension and impaired function in common. The presentation of anxiety disorders involves a complex interplay of biological, genetic and stress factors. Although each type of anxiety may carry its own set of physical, cognitive and emotional impairments, there are some general symptoms often described by the sufferer including: increased worry, catastrophic interpretations of the feared event(s) or stimuli, a racing mind, irritability, restlessness, increased heart palpitations, hyperventilation, sweating, tingling sensations, nausea, dizziness, chest pains and avoidance of the feared event(s) or stimuli. A study investigating anxiety and depression amongst pilots in the UK and Europe found that almost 40 per cent of the participating pilots had possible anxiety disorders (Steptoe and Bostock, 2011). Pilots who suffer from anxiety are most likely to experience physical symptoms. They may even present to a physician thinking that they are suffering from physical ill health.

Many psychological disorders are treatable and pilots can return to work, but they may not always present to psychologists and psychiatrists for treatment (Bor and Hubbard, 2006; Elliot, 2013). This may be due to a fear of jeopardising their medical licence and therefore their career by a visit to a doctor or specialist psychiatrist, psychologist, psychotherapist or clinical social worker. Mental disorders that automatically deny medical certification include psychosis, affective disorders (major depression), personality disorders, substance abuse or dependence, neurosis, self-destructive acts, disturbance or loss of consciousness, transient loss of control of the central nervous system, epilepsy or convulsive disorders and a progressive disease of the nervous system. Many other psychological problems, such as but not limited to, mild to moderate reactive depression, adjustment disorders, anxiety, obsessive compulsive disorder, sleep problems, relationship problems, among many others, are treatable and pilots can usually return to work once symptoms have abated and a period of monitoring has passed where the pilot has been free of their conditions.

## Mental health stigma

Pilots may not always present to psychologists and psychiatrists for treatment. This may be due to a fear of losing their licence and career by seeking professional support or there may be a stigma associated with psychological problems. Stigma and fear can amplify some symptoms and create additional stress that would be avoidable. Furthermore, the pressure of loss of licence may lead some pilots to seek help outside of the aviation specialist field. They may consult whilst abroad or see a specialist privately so as to avoid the record of their visit and possible medical certification problems. This could lead to incorrect or misguided treatment, especially if there is no communication between the external professionals and the pilot's AME (Reid, 2016).

In a recent investigation by the Bureau d'Enquêtes et d'Analyses, following the Germanwing incident March 2015, it was recommended that airlines should consider setting up a peer-support programme to help pilots deal with psychological problems. Furthermore, the report suggests that airline companies may need to work actively on reducing the fear of loss of licence amongst pilots by, for example, offering alternative work on the ground to counterbalance financial loss or loss of daily structure when a licence has been revoked. This may of course offer its own challenges, especially if a pilot has a long commute to work or the work–life balance is built or organised so that it fits with their flying schedule.

Stigma may also prevent airline pilots from pursuing treatment for psychological problems because it may not be seen as the 'norm' within the work culture. Pilots have a reputation for being high achievers, competent, dutiful, disciplined, assertive, confident and calm in challenging situations (Butcher, 2002). Stigma may lead some pilots to perceive mental illness as a weakness, which conflicts with typical pilot traits. Pilots, as may also be the case for many other professionals, may not know the symptoms of mental illness or treatment options. It is therefore important for the airline company to encourage de-stigmatisation and promote a positive mental health awareness at work. This is hopefully changing with recent trends in the industry where some airlines are actively working on helping pilots identify and manage psychological stress by linking in with psychological services and setting up peer-support programmes at work.

## Personal relationship difficulties

Relationship difficulties can cause stress and emotional upset. This can have a negative impact on performance including concentration, ability to think clearly and making sound decisions. There are relatively few studies demonstrating the link between relational problems and pilot performance. Further investigations may be needed to assess the degree to which flight-deck duties are negatively affected by couple or family discord. Another issue to consider is whether lack of support from a spouse, friends or family could potentially reduce a pilot's ability to cope with the many stressful aspects of their jobs.

Where there is a link between relationship problems and sudden changes in a pilot's behaviour, it is important that pilots do not undertake further flying duties until their normal level of functioning has been restored. This may occur when, for example, a confident and experienced captain who is usually able to make decisions becomes overly hesitant and anxious whilst operating on a flight. Jones and colleagues (1997) suggest that family issues could have a negative impact on pilot performance and they argue that such family issues must be addressed and resolved before allowing the pilot to resume flying. Other studies have found a link between interpersonal problems, financial difficulties and career strains with aircraft mishaps (Little *et al.*, 1990). Moreover, Raschmann and colleagues (1990) studied the psychosocial lives of pilots and observed that pilots who suffered marital distress reported a reduced ability to concentrate effectively on their piloting duties and responsibilities.

Whereas some studies demonstrate the importance of relationship support in predicting pilot performance (Levy *et al.*, 1984; Rigg and Cosgrove, 1994), it may equally be that individual competency leads to a happier domestic life. In a study on spousal support, Karlins and colleagues (1989) recognised that a stable and happy relationship with a partner could strengthen pilots' existing coping mechanisms to deal with work stress. On the other hand, disruption to personal relationships was thought to weaken pilots' ability to manage the more stressful aspects of their jobs. This indicates that spousal relationship can buffer the effects of work stress and they may therefore play an important role in reducing the likelihood of unsafe acts in flight (Morse and Bor, 2006; Eriksen, 2009). The same may be true for other kinds of supportive relationships including friends, family and colleagues. Sloan and Cooper (1986) studied the coping strategies of commercial airline pilots and found a close association between mental health problems and fatigue, lack of social support and lack of work autonomy.

## Stress in commercial aviation

According to research carried out by the Health and Safety Executive, one in five people suffer from workplace stress, and the Health and Safety Commission report that cases of work-related stress has doubled over the past decade. Workplace stress, according to a survey carried out by the Mental Health

Foundation, is the highest reported cause of stress (28 per cent), even over money worries (26 per cent).

It is important to understand and consider how stress affects pilots at work and beyond, specifically with a view to developing methods by which a pilot can alleviate stress and mental health problems. The aim is to reduce the impact of stress on pilots' psychological well-being, work performance and relationships, and also enable them to cope better with life stressors when they do occur. Mental health awareness, building resilience and the prevention of mental health problems is now a priority within aviation, although it is left to each organisation and carrier to develop their own strategies for this.

Drawing on the existing literature in commercial aviation there appears to be four major work-related stressors that could have a negative impact on pilot well-being. First, shift work and frequent travels through differing time zones may cause symptoms of fatigue and excessive tiredness, even for the more resilient pilot (Caldwell, 2012). Second, the experience of irregular patterns of work could make it difficult for crew to balance their work with life outside of work (Eriksen, 2009). Third, the variable work schedule and relatively lengthy time away from home may come at a price in terms of stable social and personal relationships (Rigg and Cosgrove, 1994; Young, 2008). Fourth, the pressures of the job itself including the realisation of having responsibility for the lives of hundreds of passengers, and frequent competency checks where if a minimum level is not achieved then their job could be in question (Baltic Aviation Academy, 2013).

Irrespective of the specific effects of workplace stress on particular individuals, there are several areas in which stress can have a known generally negative effect on well-being. This is why some organisations have, in recent years, made stress management and stress reduction an important part of employee training. It is well known that stress can lead to high levels of absenteeism, which is not only detrimental to the individual but obviously also has logistic, financial and morale-related consequences for the organisation where they work.

Stress at work can also lead to conflict between individuals working in teams, which often reduces the capacity of the team to function effectively. This has been well documented in Chapter 19 where the authors illustrate the importance of healthy dynamics between operating pilots to ensure the safety of the operation. In addition, there are likely to be higher levels of staff turnover in organisations where stress levels are high amongst employees – staff may be inclined to leave for another organisation where there is a less stressful environment. This obviously is a serious loss to any organisation, given that employees are a costly asset, and there is a looming worldwide shortage of pilots, but there may also be other considerations such as expensively trained and knowledgeable staff leaving to join a competitor organisation. Legal wrangles, which are costly, time-consuming, and emotionally draining may also result in organisations where employees are under continual stress.

Physical health problems can result from prolonged stress. There is evidence that stress of this type can impair immunity, making people more susceptible to infections, and can lead to other problems ranging from skin disorders to reduced cardiac functioning (Bor *et al.*, 2014).

Stress can also impair task performance. It is increasingly recognised that a stressed worker is more prone to making mistakes and causing accidents – which is obviously particularly of concern in the cockpit where safe working is critical. In the light of this, several studies have examined whether there are particular stressors that are more likely than others to precipitate an aircraft accident. A study of flight-related mishaps in the US Navy in the early 1980s showed that various situational factors including disputes with loved ones, authority or peers, significantly predisposed aircrew to involvement in accidents where human error was a contributing factor (Alkov *et al.*, 1985). The authors concluded that many of the errors committed by flight crew were symptoms of inadequate stress coping behaviours. Young (2008) has suggested that whilst the relationship between life stress and pilot performance does not offer conclusive answers, the literature suggests that life stress can impair performance, and it points to possible mechanisms. Life stress can, for example, negatively influence underlying cognitive processes such as decision-making, problems-solving and information-processing (Young 2008; Kirschner *et al.*, 2014). According to Young (2008), life stress can also disrupt sleep and lead to increased fatigue, which in turn impairs social and cognitive performance.

Stress can also have a negative impact on relationships. Pilots can find their ability to tolerate problems impaired, and their frustration threshold lowered. Feelings of anger, anxiety, resentment and low mood can stem from stress which has been generated in the workplace and over which they feel they have no control and which they are unable to handle. Sexual functioning can also be adversely affected by stress, which in turn can make partner relationships feel stressed and, in a vicious cycle, increase the stress in the relationship (Bor *et al.*, 2014).

## Promoting psychological well-being: coping with stress

Most pilots who experience stress at work can identify a combination of factors they believe have caused or contributed to their stress. Some factors may be unique to them or to their particular workplace, reflecting the specific circumstances of a job, role or organisation, while others may apply more generally across a range of settings and affect people at different levels of responsibility. Broadly, pilots may experience stress from several sources:

### Working conditions

Working conditions such as shift work or particular shift patterns, long hours, the need for constant alertness, repetitive physical work, etc. can be the source of stress in the workplace. For example, noisy hotels near airports may lead to further sleep disruptions thereby causing greater risks of pilot fatigue.

### Demands of the job

Demands at work may exceed either original expectations of the job, or the personal resources to cope with the demands may be beyond an individual, distasteful, or may have palled or become wearisome over time. A pilot may, for example, feel increasing despair about his work if the rostering system allocated 'heavy duty' trips with limited time at home over lengthy periods of time.

### Support in the role

For many pilots their performance in the workplace is enhanced, or at the least maintained, if they feel supported in their role by colleagues and managers. Support is an important source of validation; without this, pilots may question their value and worth to the organisation, or even self-worth. Simulator and check rides may be a source of stress for some pilots, and the degree to which they cope (or not) can often be affected by the perceived support given by the training pilot on the day.

### Relationships with colleagues

Most jobs involve some level of interaction with colleagues and difficult feelings arise where there is a perception or experience of bullying, exclusion, or denigration by a colleague. Crew relationships are so central to safe operations that part of the pilot's training covers crew interactions, communication and safety in the form of crew resource management courses. Interaction can also be soured by colleagues and managers not having time to spend in helpful interaction because they are overworked and stressed, leading to people feeling alone and unsupported in their roles.

### Culture

Stress in the workplace may be temporary, episodic, or relate to specific staff or circumstances. However, there are certain jobs or roles which are inherently stressful. A brain surgeon working in a multidisciplinary team undertaking highly specialist, sensitive, and potentially life-saving work has an inherently stressful job, as does a fighter pilot operating under combat conditions, or a commercial pilot descending towards a busy airport, in turbulent conditions, with low fuel reserves and under pressure to turn around the aircraft for their next sector.

### Stress at home

Whilst not directly related to the work setting, as has been illustrated earlier in the chapter, stress is cumulative, and therefore experiencing high levels of stress in the home environment can make dealing with challenges in the workplace more difficult, and work stress can have a negative impact on personal relationships. A pilot may, for example, sit in a hotel room away from his family fearing that his marriage is breaking down following a string of rows with his wife shortly before departing on a long-haul flight.

★ ★ ★

What can pilots do to overcome stress at work?

1   Evaluate the causes and specific triggers of the stress: is the stress something the individual has some control over or are parts of the stress amenable to change?
2   Establish to what extent a pilot's expectations, thoughts and perceptions of their job and their role at work is part of their stress. Is the dissonance between what they thought being a pilot was going to entail and the day-to-day realities of working irregular hours often in a confined environment the root of the problem? Has their situation changed; for example, has the pilot been based at a different airport leading to longer commutes and absences from home? Does the pilot consider that they should be at a more senior level in their job (for example, have achieved their command within an expected time limitation) and feel that they have failed or that the company has denied them of the promotion which should have been theirs?
3   Ask questions about their work–life balance and beliefs about how their life should be: do they see things out of proportion at work because the lifestyle at work is the centre of their life? Do they feel that everything which happens at work reflects on them personally and are their responses or reactions proportionate to the challenges they face?
4   Do they have fears about losing their job (or retiring)? And if so, are these realistic? If they were to lose – or give up, or change – their job, what would really be the effect on the pilot, their family, their social standing?
5   Is the pilot getting the support he or she needs at work? Do their colleagues, their boss, senior managers and their family know what they do in their work role and what it is about that role which causes the individual pilot stress? Has the pilot undergone an appraisal at work? Have they drawn up workable plans and strategies and put them in front of the right people at work? Has the pilot been able to share with his or her family in what ways they need their practical or emotional support when they are experiencing stress at work?

## General tips and hints for avoiding and preventing stress

It may be helpful for those working with pilots to encourage individual strategies for managing stress to prevent the onset of mental health difficulties. There is a wealth of effective books on how to identify and manage stress including *Overcoming Stress* (Brosan and Todd, 2009) or *Overcoming Stress* (Bor, Eriksen and Chaudry, 2014) to name a couple. The strategies below could be used in conjunction with self-help materials.

1   People may find it helpful to take regular breaks from what they are doing. This helps to stimulate a person to refocus on the task in hand, and, by stepping away and changing body position and environment for a short while, they will be physically refreshed. Depending on the number of pilots operating on a given aircraft, rest will be allocated on a rotational basis ensuring the minimum complement needed for that stage of the flight. Controlled rest in the seat to avoid fatigue can also be agreed upon between operating pilots at times of suitable low work load. This is often arranged and planned at an early point in the cruise phase.

2   Eat as healthily as possible. How, what and when we eat has a direct effect on our mood, our energy levels, and our short- and long-term well-being. It goes without saying that unhealthy snacking causes fluctuations in blood sugar levels which stress the body and can also mimic mood fluctuations.

3   Reduce alcohol consumption as this improves mental well-being and alertness, but alcohol used as a measure to reduce stress and anxiety is contraindicated as it is a central nervous system depressant and, whilst often desirable and beneficial in helping initial relaxation, ultimately can have a negative impact on sleep, mood, concentration, and also sexual performance. The federal regulation prohibits any individual from acting or attempting to act as flight crew within eight hours of having alcohol or while having a blood alcohol concentration (BAC) of 40mg or greater. Kraus and Li (2006) studied the frequency of reported incidents of alcohol abuse amongst pilots in US-based newspapers and found a significant increase of alcohol violation by pilots since 2001.

4   Sleep is important for restoring and maintaining good mental health, and without deep and uninterrupted sleep, stress can escalate or can seem never to abate. There is a short section on sleep management later which may be helpful for pilots to consider.

5   Regular exercise is an effective countermeasure to stress. The effect of any exercise which is mildly aerobic (at the very least something like climbing a long flight of stairs or a power walk) helps at a chemical level to release endorphins into the bloodstream and the brain, which gives a sense of natural well-being – and even a small 'high'. Aerobic exercise also suppresses the secretion of cortisol, a hormone particularly associated with stress. This type of exercise can also help to counteract the negative effects of having a sedentary job, and in maintaining a healthy weight which, again, will help to lower stress levels.

6   Having hobbies and interests outside work – and which are very different from what people do in their job – can sustain and replenish the individual pilot. Hobbies and outside interests help to widen social contacts outside the workplace and sharpen their focus through new skills acquisition. Hobbies can also be a welcome distraction from workplace problems and issues.

7   Set aside time for companionship and personal relationships. This entails scheduling time with friends and family and seeing this as being equally important as time spent engaged in work activities. Enjoying time with family and other significant others is psychologically beneficial and helps to develop and reveal other aspects of our personalities.

8   At work, establish boundaries to serve as proper limits to the amount of work with which a person can reasonably be asked to cope. This can be achieved by ensuring that annual leave is booked on a regular basis or avoiding working overtime if a pilot is feeling excessively tired. If pilots are in a position to bid for or request work trips it may be worth planning ahead to help promote a positive work–life balance.

9   Delegating to others is an important part of managing stress in daily life and at work. A reluctance to delegate can stem from an over-controlling and distrustful personality, a fear that other people will encroach on their job or work, and/or undermine the person in some way so that they feel less worthwhile or even feel redundant.

10   Learn to voice feelings of stress and distress to others. It is not sensible or healthy to 'carry on regardless' or to assume that other people will understand and realise what a person is experiencing without telling them. Without communicating individual stress to others, clearly and as positively as possible, people cannot expect others to understand their experience of stress and provide them with help in alleviating it.

11   Keep a focus on the task at hand and try not to be distracted by others which come one's way in the meantime. If necessary and helpful, people may wish to make lists of what they need to accomplish and assign priorities to the various tasks. Stress increases when people are overwhelmed by information or conflicting demands, leading to poor performance and therefore lower levels of achievement and satisfaction. It is better to do one thing completely and well rather than trying to do several things and achieving only minor levels of success with each.

12   Where possible, pilots may wish to manage time better by creating free space in their day rather than cramming every hour with tasks. This may be especially relevant when returning from duty abroad and there is a conflict between getting some sleep or spend time with family, friends or attend to domestic chores.

## Sleep management

Disrupted sleep is often one of the first signs that a person is feeling stressed, and can in turn exacerbate stress, so it is important that pilots deal with sleep issues as soon as they arise, before a negative pattern develops. This can of course be a challenge for pilots as their work often requires them to work irregular shift work which includes operating during the night-time and dealing with frequent transitions to other time zones.

1   Be consistent with sleep routine – whenever possible, try to keep a regular routine of going to bed at around the same time every night and getting up around the same time in the morning.

2   Consistency helps the body to learn when to slow down for sleep and when to wake up in the morning. Of course it is not always easy to have a regular pattern of going to bed and getting up at the same time each day, but make a regular pattern the base and try not to disrupt it too often when not working a night shift or travelling to countries with a large time difference from base. The aim of keeping a consistent sleep pattern during periods of stress is to minimise the risk of sleep deprivation and/or becoming excessively nocturnal.

3   Engage in non-stimulating activities before bedtime – try to wind down a couple of hours before going to bed. Listen to relaxing music, read something light, or practise yoga, meditation, relaxation techniques, or have a massage, for example. This will help the body and mind to feel relaxed and ready for sleep. Watching television, for example, is unhelpful in terms of preparing for sleep as over-bright light such as that of a television (or computer) screen wakes up the body rather than relaxes it because our bodies are programmed to respond to light (wakefulness) and dark (sleep).

4   Avoid eating before bedtime – try not to eat for two hours (at least) before going to bed. If the body is digesting, it is doing some very hard work and will not be able to prepare for sleep (for example by lowering the core body temperature).

5   Reduce environmental disruptions – is the temperature, light or noise levels in the bedroom helping or hindering sleep? If, for example, the room is too noisy try to reduce or remove the source of the noise, or consider using earplugs; if waking up too early because the room is too light in the morning, invest in blackout blinds or curtain linings.

6   Do not use the bedroom as an entertainment centre – if watching television, browsing the internet for long periods of time, texting friends or business associates etc. whilst lying in bed, can cause the mind to associate bed with activity rather than sleep. Also, electrical humming, standby lights etc. from electronic equipment can impinge on the brain and disrupt relaxation and sleep.

7   Deal with worry or an active mind at night – if pilots cannot fall asleep within the first fifteen minutes after turning the light off, try getting up and doing something non-stimulating for a short while before going back to bed and trying to fall asleep again. A person may have to repeat this strategy a couple of times before they fall asleep, and they may need to repeat this strategy for several nights before it works for them. Research has shown that people are more prone to worry or engage in problem-solving or circular thinking during the first fifteen minutes of trying to fall asleep. It is therefore important to try to distract the mind from worry during this period.

## Managing emotions

There are a number of studies which suggest that writing feelings down can be emotionally beneficial. Psychologists have discovered that, for some people going through a particularly stressful period of their lives, writing a diary, or journal, helps to reduce their stress levels and lifts their mood.

More recently, neuroscience has provided us with a greater understanding of the brain's activity in relation to our emotions and writing things down. Research has demonstrated that, during the process of documenting feelings on paper, the activity in the amygdala (which is a part of the brain responsible for regulating our emotional responses, especially fear, anger and pleasure) decreases significantly. The research also showed that the activity in the ventrolateral prefrontal cortex (the part of the brain involved in suppressing emotional responses related to negative stimuli) was significantly increased. This research suggests that the brain works to regulate the difficult emotions that are expressed during the process of writing.

Keeping a journal, or diary, can be a powerful tool in a number of ways. It can serve as a means for expressing worrying thoughts and associated feelings. Recording those uncomfortable feelings on paper offers people a form of release by providing an emotional outlet. It helps a person to avoid the pitfalls of bottling up difficult emotions which can then become too overwhelming to manage.

Setting a definite time during the day to write in the diary is best, because a person then know they have a special space in which they can release the anger, frustration or fear that they might be feeling. They will then know that they can do this without letting those feelings spill over into other parts of the day and get in the way of work and relationships.

Writing can also give a person the opportunity to identify the triggers and the negative thinking which are associated with their emotions, and allow them to see how they behave in response. It offers a chance to step back and gain some perspective, and even to challenge negative thinking. It may also show patterns and themes emerging over a period of time, when people look back through their diary, enabling them ultimately to make sense of their feelings.

### Physical exercise

Another way to become more relaxed is to engage in regular exercise. Exercise helps the body to relieve tension caused by stress. Exercise does not have to be over-strenuous or 'military' in style – it can include going for a brisk walk, walking up a set of stairs as opposed to taking the lift or escalator. If people enjoy more strenuous exercise, then going to the gym, for example, might be fun and rewarding for them – but if not, then taking up a social hobby which involves vigorous exercise (such as dancing, tennis or swimming) is another option.

Positive effects of regular exercise are:

- It has a positive effect on the mood. Exercise stimulates various chemicals in our bodies, such as endorphins, which leaves people feeling happier and more relaxed.
- It stimulates blood flow, oxygen and nutrient use in the body and helps the entire cardiovascular system work more efficiently.
- It can help people fall asleep faster and deepen their sleep.
- It has a positive effect on health, weight and energy levels.

Pilots can start exercising by setting themselves small goals such as walking instead of driving whenever possible, signing up for a gym or for dance classes or suchlike, or digging their bicycle out of the garage and trying it out again.

### Mindfulness practice

Mindfulness-based stress reduction was originally a religious practice which evolved from the ancient Buddhist practice of meditation. It is about using sensory stimuli to focus on being fully 'in the moment' with the use of enriched awareness. At the heart of the practice is a philosophy promoting being in a way that is non-judgmental and accepting.

Often internal dialogue can be anxiety provoking. People tend to fast-forward into the future with worrying thoughts, delving around in uncertainty and trying to find answers that are not necessarily there. People are also prone to rewinding the past, ruminating over situations and events we tell themselves they could have handled better, that should have been avoidable. This type of negative thinking about both past and future can be detrimental and contribute to feelings of being stressed. When people continually focus their attention on past and future they run the risk of missing life in the present.

Mindfulness helps people to take control of the ruminations that contribute to stress by allowing them to focus attention elsewhere for a short period of time, to take a temporary breather from the racing negative thoughts and internal critical commentary that often seeps into a person's conscious awareness. Instead, the mediations involve heightened awareness of bodily sensations and the physical environment, which helps to anchor people in the here and now. It enables people to achieve an observant and non-critical attitude which helps to dispel the internal dialogue. There are a number of electronic mindfulness applications available online.

### Yoga

Yoga is an ancient Eastern practice which aims to relax and strengthen both body and mind through the use of breathing control, meditation, and placing and holding the body in different postures (or 'asanas'). There are a number of different yoga practices, including Hatha, Ashtanga, Bikram, Anusara, Vinyasa and Kundalini, to name but a few of the most popular ones adopted in the West. The different types of yoga all include a concentration on posture, but each also has its own particular emphasis or difference such as pace, intensity, use of breathing, level of physical demand, or the importance placed on physical alignment and the use of chanting.

### Breathing techniques

Deep breathing relaxes the body and makes it virtually impossible for the mind to remain anxious and tensed. The physical benefits of deep breathing have an immediate impact on energy levels and people's ability to deal with stress (see Bor *et al.*, 2014 for further details).

### Progressive muscular relaxation

This exercise will help to make a distinction between tensed and relaxed muscles. This will help people to identify when they are tense so that they can relax your muscles and relieve the tension. Muscular tension can occur automatically as a reaction to uncomfortable thoughts and stress. People are not always conscious of physical tension, and as a result it is not uncommon for people to experience prolonged periods of muscular strain. This exercise will increase people's awareness of bodily tension and can therefore act as a cue for when it should be used to help let go of unnecessary muscular strain (see Bor *et al.*, 2014 for further details).

## Conclusion

Early identification of disruptive health threats can help pilots to deal with arising issues before they affect psychological well-being. Occupational stress is increasingly recognised as a factor in health and safety. Following an incident that took place on 27 March 2012, where a pilot of a major commercial airline experienced a serious disturbance in his mental health, the Aerospace Medical Association formed an ad hoc working group on pilot mental health. The group recommended greater attention to be given to mental health issues by aero-medical examiners, especially to the more common and detectable mental health conditions and life stressors that can affect pilots and flight performance. This could be achieved by increased education and global recognition of the importance of mental health in aviation safety (Aerospace Medical Association Ad Hoc Working Group on Pilot Mental Health, 2012).

Trying to adjust the way in which people go about managing change is important. This helps directly with coping with stress. If a person is more likely to use crisis management or deal with problems spasmodically, they may wish to try to approach problems differently, setting specific and broader goals for stress-countering strategies. Be proactive rather than reactive to stress. Make it part of an action plan to review and adapt as new stresses are encountered. In this way people will feel more in control of stress rather than stress overwhelming them.

# References

Alkov, R., Borowsky, M., & Gaynor, L. (1985). Pilot error as a symptom of inadequate stress coping. *Aviation, Space and Environmental Medicine*, 56, 244–247.

American Psychiatric Association (2013). *Diagnostic and Statistical Manual of Mental Disorders.* (fifth edition.) Washington DC: APA.

Baltic Aviation Academy (2013). The importance of coping with stress that pilots are exposed to on a daily basis. Accessed at http://www.balticaa.com/the-importance-of-coping-with-stress-that-pilots-are-exposed-to-on-a-daily-basis-2/ (16 April 2016).

Bor, R., & Hubbard, T. (2006). *Aviation Mental Health: Psychological Implications for Air Travel.* Ashgate: UK.

Bor, R., Eriksen, C., & Oakes, M. (2009). *Overcome your Fear of Flying.* London: Sheldon Publishing.

Bor, R., Eriksen, C., & Chaudry, S. (2014). *Overcoming Stress.* London: Sheldon Publishing.

Bor, R., Field, G., & Scragg, P. (2002). The mental health of pilots: an overview. *Counselling Psychology Quarterly*, 15(3), 239–256.

Brosan, T., & Todd, G. (2009) *Overcoming Stress.* London: Robinson Publishing.

Brown, T., Rushton, l., Schucher, L., Stevens, J., & Warren., F. (2001). A Consultation on the Possible Effects on Health, Comfort and Safety of Aircraft Cabin Environments. Leicester: Institute for Environment and Health.

Butcher, J. (2002). Assessing pilots with 'the wrong stuff': a call for research on emotional health factors in commercial aviators. *International Journal of Selection and Assessment*, 10(1/2), 168–184.

Caldwell, J.A. (2012). Crew schedules, sleep deprivation, and aviation performance. *Current Directions in Psychological Science*, 21(2), 85.

Cooper, C., & Sloan, S. (1985). Occupational and psychological stress among commercial airline pilots. *Journal of Occupational Medicine,* 27, 570–576.

Elliot, R. (2013). Aviation mental health and the psychological examination. In G. Kay and C. Kennedy (eds.), *Aeromedical Psychology.* Farnham: Ashgate.

Eriksen, C. (2009). *Managing Work and Relationships at 35,000 Feet.* London: Karnac Publishing.

Girodo, M. (1988). The psychological health and stress of pilots in a labor dispute. *Aviation, Space and Environmental Medicine*, 59(6), 505–510.

Grossman, A., Barenboim, E., Azaria, B., Sherer, Y., & Goldstein, L. (2004). Oral drug therapy for erectile dysfunction: an overview and aeromedical implications. *Aviation, Space and Environmental Medicine*, 75(11), 997–1000.

Harris, D. (2002). Drinking and flying: causes, effects and the development of effective countermeasures. *Human Factors in Aerospace Safety*, 2(4), 297–317.

Jones, D., & Ireland, R. (2004). Aeromedical regulations of aviators using selective seretonin reuptake inhibitors for depressive disorder. *Aviation, Space and Environmental Medicine*, 75(5), 461-470.

Jones, D., Katchen, M., Patterson, J., & Rea, M. (1997). In R. DeHart (ed), *Fundamentals of Aerospace Medicine.* Baltimore, MD: Williams and Wilkins, pp. 593–642.

Karlins, M., Koss, F., & McCully, L. (1989). The spousal factor in pilot stress. *Aviation, Space and Environmental Medicine,* 60, 1112–1115.

Kirschner, J., Young, J., and Fanjov., R. (2014). Stress and coping as a function of experience level in collegiate flight students. *Journal of Aviation Technology and Engineering*, 3(2), 14–19.

Kraus, C., & Li, G. (2006). Pilot alcohol violations reported in U.S. newspapers 1990–2006. *Aviation, Space & Environmental Medicine*, 77, 1288-1290.

Levy, D.E., Faulkner, G.L., & Dixon, R. (1984). Work and family interaction: the dual career family of the flight attendant. *Journal of Social Relations*, 11, 67–88.

Lewis, R., Forster, E., Whinnery, J., & Webster, N. (2014). *Aircraft-assisted Pilot Suicides in the United States, 2003–2012.* Oklahoma City, OK: Civil Aerospace Medical Institute, Federal Aviation Administration.

Little, L., Gaffney, I., Rosen, K., & Bender, M. (1990). Corporate instability is related to airline pilots' stress symptoms. *Aviation, Space and Environmental Medicine*, 61, 977–982.

Morse, J., & Bor., R. (2006). Psychiatric disorders and syndromes among pilots. In R. Bor & T. Hubbard (eds), *Aviation Mental Health* (pp. 107–125). Aldershot: Ashgate Publishing.

Oakes, M., Bor, R., & Eriksen, C. (2012). *Coping Successfully with Shyness and Social Anxiety.* London: Sheldon Publishing.

Raschmann, J., Patterson, J., & Schofield, G. (1990). A retrospective study of marital discord in pilots: the USAFSAM experience. *Aviation, Space and Environmental Medicine*, 61, 1145–1148.

Reid, G. (2016). Aviation psychiatry. In D. Gradwell and D. Rainford (eds.), *Aviation and Space Medicine* (fifth edition). Boca Raton, FL: CRC Press.

Rigg, R.C., & Cosgrove, M.P. (1994). Aircrew wives and the intermittent husband syndrome. *Aviation, Space, and Environmental Medicine*, 65, 654–660.

Sloan, C.L., & Cooper, S.J. (1986). *Pilots Under Stress.* London: Routledge.

Waterhouse, J., Edwards, B., Atkinson, G., Reilly, T., Spencer, M., & Elsey, A. (2006). Occupational factors in pilot mental health: sleep loss, jet lag and shift work. In R. Bor & T. Hubbard (eds.), *Aviation Mental Health* (pp. 69–82). Aldershot: Ashgate Publishing.

Young, J. (2008). *The Effect of Life Stress on Pilot Performance.* Accessed at http://humansystems. arc.nasa.gov/flightcognition/Publications/Young_TM2008_215375_final.pdf. (16 April 2016).

# 19 Behavioural dynamics on the flight deck and implications for mental health

*Martin Casey and Benjamin Lawler*

## Background

Each working day a pilot can expect to be teamed up with a different set of individuals, many of whom they will never have met. Each person in the team has a specific role and rank, and these roles are an important factor in the development of the relationship between the team members. In the context of the pilot work force, the dynamic refers to the relationships formed through these interactions on a given workday.

Within the airline industry the normal working schedule for a pilot is not Monday to Friday, or nine to five. The office team does not comprise the same people every day, and the office moves both time zones and location. Although airline dependent, all pilots expect to work varying hours. Typically they will receive their working roster one or two weeks before the start of each month, defining what they can expect to do for the month that follows. This can comprise a mixture of early starts and late finishes, and often working over weekends or public holidays.

Again dependent upon the airline, some pilots will fly a mixture of short-haul and long-haul routes, and others will be assigned to just one or the other. A short-haul pilot can expect to fly a number of sectors or individual flights each day, possibly finishing and starting at their home base, whereas a long-haul pilot will usually fly just one sector (due to the flight's duration) and then spend a period of time, usually twenty-four hours or more, at destination.

Pilots are normally assigned to fly a particular type of aircraft. To enable a pilot to obtain a type rating he or she will have to undergo an intensive course focused solely on the specifics of that aircraft type. Often variants are included within a type rating, or similar aircraft may be grouped together. These groupings are decided between the airline manufacturers and the aviation authorities, with safety being the prime concern. A pilot may be qualified to fly the Airbus A318, A319, A320 and A321 but the same pilot could not fly any Boeing aircraft without significant re-training. Equally the 777 and 787 are considered similar enough to be operated under the same rating, but a pilot with that rating could not fly an Airbus aircraft or another Boeing aircraft such as the 747.

Modern airliners are multi-crew aircraft, meaning that to be safely and successfully operated they require a minimum of two pilots. In order for two pilots who have never previously met to operate in a safe manner, a predesignated set of operating procedures are put in place. These procedures are often referred to as 'standard operating procedures'. In essence they clearly lay down who is expected to do what and when. To effectively and efficiently divide the tasks between the pilots, specific roles are needed. One pilot is defined as the Pilot Flying and one is defined as the Pilot Monitoring. Through these roles the huge number of tasks required to be completed throughout the working day can be efficiently handled. Generally the pilot flying will be responsible for flying, or handling the aircraft, and the pilot monitoring will carry out the secondary tasks, such as operating the radios, moving levers and coordinating other functions.

The flight-deck crew will comprise a minimum of two pilots, one holding the role of captain and the other being the co-pilot, or first officer. The captain has overall responsibility for the aircraft, all aspects of safety, security and overall customer experience conducted on board the aircraft. He or she is held accountable not only by the airline, but is also under the jurisdiction of the aviation authority. The first officer is the nominated deputy for this role. If the duration of the flight or other circumstance dictates, there may also be additional pilots of either rank on the flight deck. A senior cabin crew member will, on behalf of the captain, be responsible for both normal and emergency procedures within the cabin.

## The flight deck dynamic

The dynamic that develops between pilots of commercial aircraft each time they fly is dependent upon an enormous number of variables. In this chapter we will look at some of the factors that affect how this dynamic is developed, and how different issues may manifest themselves to the pilot's colleagues on the day. Some aspects are organisational, such as the size of the specific fleet a pilot operates on within the company or the system used by the airline to allocate trips to its pilots, whereas others will be individual, such as personal preferences, professional standards, personality traits or social skills. Other factors may be psychological including a person's ability to manage stress, fatigue and interpersonal relationships.

The dynamic begins, as with most relationships, at the point of first contact. This will usually be at or shortly before the start of the briefing for a flight. In a small airline, or perhaps a small fleet within a larger airline, it is likely that the pilots will have worked together previously, or at least be aware of each other through reputation. This of course can put them at an immediate advantage as they could already have developed a relationship in the past, although very occasionally this will not be a positive influence. In a larger fleet, however, this is rarely the case, and often pilots are reporting for duty with individuals with whom they have never met. This means that they are trying to develop the dynamic from the first point of meeting, however this environment is not necessarily ideal to achieve this.

From the moment that a pilot reports for work with their colleague, they are immediately involved in a very task-based environment. Often time is limited prior to the departure of the aircraft and the pilots must initially gather and process a large amount of information in order to quickly raise their situational awareness prior to the flight. Some of this information must then be shared with the cabin crew before the journey to the aircraft begins. This in itself can introduce stressors into the duty, such as security delays, or perhaps the aircraft not being ready. Once on board, the preparation for the flight means that the workload remains quite high, with numerous agencies to communicate with which include air traffic controllers, the onboard crew, engineers and dispatch coordinators. There is also a very regimented set-up procedure for the aircraft.

**Briefing Room**

Task-focused
information process

Short time for greeting
and familiarisation

*Figure 19.1* Building the relationship

Due to the task-focused nature of this part of the process, a simple brief introduction is commonplace. The first interaction, frequently led by the captain, is to specify the roles that each crew member can expect and specific tasks are assigned to each crew member. A large amount of information has to be produced and processed during the briefing and the delivery and processing of this information is the first point of assessment of peers within the group.

Generally the pilot assigned with the task of flying the aircraft for that sector will be the one who leads the briefing. Within these first brief exchanges each member of the crew is assessing each other and forming their opinion based on first impressions.

- Although standard operating procedures define what must be discussed, each pilot will have their own style and manner which starts to become apparent very quickly in these initial task-oriented exchanges.
- Each pilot is assessing the other, their approach, style, knowledge base, experience level, tone and professionalism.
- Each is making an internal assessment of how the day will go.
- They must then decide how they should act in accordance with the team; where and how they fit in and how to work most effectively with their colleague.
- Flight crew and cabin crew initial exchanges and combined briefings may occur at this point in time, again although brief, expectation and tone is set at this early stage.

**Transfer to Aircraft and Security Check**

Time to become acquainted

Often where dynamic is decided

*Figure 19.2* Transfer to aircraft

After the initial briefing the next challenge is for the crew to transfer to the aircraft side. This passage is airport and company specific, however all crew must pass through a security check. For some, this experience can be invasive and upsetting. In many countries aircrew and passengers alike are subjected to the same security checks, which contain strict rules and limits for what can be taken through security. While all crew are very aware that security checks are designed to keep everyone safe, encountering abrupt staff, being reprimanded for forgetting to remove electronic devices for screening or feeling that a search has been invasive can be stressful. The abrupt nature of some of the security team, and the blanket approach has been known to cause friction and distress for the aircraft crew.

> That guy at security was so unreasonable, I can't stop thinking about it. I'm really annoyed.
>
> I'm the pilot, if I wanted to hijack the aircraft I wouldn't need a pair of scissors to do so!
>
> The toughest part of our job is getting past those security checks. I hate them!

This experience, if negative, can linger and change the mood of an individual to the extent that it proves a distraction from the main task of setting up and flying the aircraft. Of course security checks are an unavoidable factor of everyday life for aircrew, but for some these experiences can affect an individual's state of mind, and any change affecting the individual will in turn have an impact on the group.

The period of time during transfer can be very influential to the dynamic of the team as this stage of the process is much less formalised. Conversations between crew are varied; common ground can usually be found in discussing company-related material, such as rostering or SOP changes, however some will tend towards discussions of a more personal nature. Each individual's interpersonal skills become evident at this stage, and each crew member indicates consciously or otherwise to their peers on what level they wish the relationship to continue. Occasionally, the individuals in the crew will have quite differing interests and styles, however this doesn't necessarily upset the dynamic; it's quite possible to have an effective and even enjoyable day at work and not even know, for example, if your colleague is married!

The number of crew within the team also plays a significant role in the dynamic being created at this stage. For example, within a crew of three or four pilots, group dynamics can result in the team splitting into significant subgroups, or isolating individuals within the group. This can have a marked effect upon how valued each member feels.

Pilots may share personal information about home life, or outside stressors as each pilot is carrying out a peer assessment. At this stage any information that is offered, if significant enough, could cause concern or doubt amongst the crew about an individual's ability to focus upon the primary task.

**Aircraft Preparation**

Task-focused and time-focused.

Establishment of expectation and work style

*Figure 19.3* Aircraft preparation

Once onboard the aircraft and inside the flight deck the pilots have finally arrived at their office, a familiar and secure environment for most. Their roles and tasks are clearly defined at this stage and many airlines specify a detailed and sometimes challenging timeline for completion. This results in the development of a task-focused, time-pressured environment.

Generally, this is also the point at which other staff need to interact with the pilots: dispatchers will deliver load details and may have questions relating to aircraft loading or potential delays. The pilots may need to liaise with engineers, fuellers or de-icing crews, and the cabin crew may need help or information. Although the pilots may not directly communicate with all teams in each department, they are responsible for driving forward the operation and ensuring its timely completion. Interpersonal skills are particularly important during this phase to get everybody working towards the same goal. Sometimes these interactions may require a response from the captain, who may be outside doing the external aircraft checks. For the first officer, making a decision on behalf of a senior colleague you barely know can be challenging! Pilot interactions at this stage are subject to significant levels of time pressure and demands from outside the group.

From now on, each pilot is responsible for his or her own duties but also to ensure the others within the crew have completed theirs. Peer assessment of each other's working style, ability and aptitude now becomes evident. If a pilot is distracted or making errors at this stage his or her peers may begin to question why this may be. Personal information gathered previously, whether technical or non-technical, can assist in this judgement. A technical level assessment may come from each pilot's previous experience level and the amount of time he or she has spent on that aircraft type. Non-technical factors could include previous roster duties, home-life stressors or external stressors experienced on that day.

When a problem with any particular part of the operation occurs, the pilots must remain fluid and flexible, whilst still working within a safety-based rule set. It is during these more pressured situations that differences in operating styles between pilots can sometimes become apparent. For example, an abruptness or lack of patience demonstrated by one of the flight crew towards a member of another working group can be an indicator or precursor to a poor behavioural dynamic. This attitude or behaviour is often not commented on directly, but can lead to a subgroup forming within a multi-crew pilot environment. The other pilots within the flight deck may be reticent to comment upon the incidents like this as they are acutely aware that they must work in close proximity to the individual concerned for a significant period of time going forward.

All of these factors combine to make it very difficult to make an accurate assessment of your colleagues' state of mind. Of course with more experience, pilots become better at assessing what type of person they are working with, but different people will look for different triggers to indicate different qualities. For example, some will feel more at ease when their colleague demonstrates a high level of knowledge or professionalism, whereas others will feel more comfortable with someone who can demonstrate a good level of sociability which puts them at ease. It is well-known outside aviation that there are some personality types that work well together and others that do not, and this is no different in the flight deck. The only differing aspect is that if two pilots do not work well together, the results can be fatal.

It is an industry-wide procedure that a thorough briefing occurs between the pilots prior to departure. The style of a briefing in the flight deck can differ considerably from briefings in other environments. Rather than one person sharing information with the other, the information flow should, in an ideal world, be a two-way process. Of course there are times when the information flow is more one-way than others, for example an experienced captain briefing an inexperienced first officer, or perhaps a first officer who is more familiar with a particular airfield than the captain. An example briefing may contain the following:

- Checking elements of aircraft set-up, including important data entry;
- what we plan to do;
- how we plan to do it;
- what we will do if something unexpected happens;
- how to manage emergency situations.

During the discussion and briefing, pilots often check understanding and comprehension between all members of the flight crew team. The pre-departure briefing stage can feel intimidating to some depending upon the dynamic between the pilots within the team. Until this point much of the peer assessment which has occurred has been at an interpersonal level, however during the briefing the assessment becomes more weighted towards the level of a pilot's technical and procedural knowledge. Ideally, these briefings are open and interactive; the primary aim being to share information and check each other's understanding of what lies ahead. Different personalities bring different qualities to briefings, but occasionally the effects can be negative. An example would be that of a simple check of understanding being misinterpreted as having your technical knowledge tested. Setting the tone during this pre-departure brief very often defines the type of day that will follow.

Over time each pilot develops a particular work persona and attributes. Each persona can differ greatly. Some pilots come across as relaxed and laid back, possibly even over-confident. Others may appear super-engaged and obsessed with every detail. Some could appear distracted and vacant, whilst others may came across as abrupt, short and uninterested. It is difficult for colleagues who have not worked together on previous occasions to assess whether these behaviours differ from their norm.

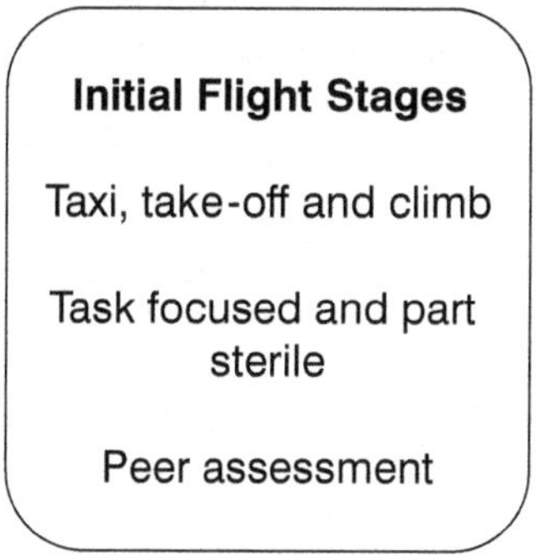

**Initial Flight Stages**

Taxi, take-off and climb

Task focused and part
sterile

Peer assessment

*Figure 19.4* Initial flight

During the initial stages of taxi, a well-functioning crew are very much focused on the task of safely and correctly manoeuvring the aircraft to the runway hold point. Taxi routes can be unfamiliar and complicated, with different designators and local rules to be followed and observed. Due to the volume of civilian aircraft traffic movements, airfields can be extremely busy environments leading in turn to busy radio frequencies.

Pilots strive to build upon their situational awareness and are using information observed visually and audibly to create a picture of what is going on around them.

At this stage a crew will be trying to avoid distraction from these tasks, and therefore the working environment may be somewhat sterile. Often little conversation other than that of an operational nature occurs. Some airlines insist upon a sterile cockpit environment at this stage. If, however, a pilot is constantly missing radio calls or seems distracted from their assigned tasks at this point, other colleagues on the flight deck may again start to question why. These errors can be attributed to differing levels of professionalism, experience, fatigue levels or other stressors, but all begin to build a picture of an operator's capacity to carry out his or her role on that day.

During the take-off and the initial climb a similar task-based operation continues. Each pilot is responsible for monitoring the other, and ensuring safe aircraft operation. It is here where standard operating procedures are vitally important. It is expected that each airline's pilots will work within this framework of actions, calls, challenges and responses. If a pilot appears purposely or otherwise outside of these procedures or boundaries, then his peers are expected to challenge him.

The flight deck dynamic can be put under strain through this procedure. As previously discussed there are many different personality types within the work force with very differing ideals and standards. The style, reasoning or timing for such a challenge very much depends on the personality of each individual.

He's a point scorer; he will pick you up on every little irrelevant detail.

If I do something non-standard please tell me. We are all here to get the job done safely and without any unnecessary paperwork!

In some scenarios where there are more than two pilots operating, the role of the third pilot must be a considered one. It is very much the job of the two pilots flying to use him as a resource and engage him in the operation, however he or she should not be overbearing or distracting.

Wow, I thought the guy on the observer seat (third pilot) was going to lean forward and press the buttons for me at one point. I found that more of a distraction than a help.

Great spot buddy! I'm glad you're here today keeping an eye on us guys at the front.

During these phases of flight where workload is high, peer assessment and appraisal are an inevitable part of the operation. A poor performance standard requiring peer intervention is seldom witnessed, but intervention is occasionally necessary. Interventions can be awkward, especially if they are opposing to the structure of command, but they can also be the last line of defence in safety-critical situations, so are absolutely necessary. If an intervention occurs, a debrief or discussion as to why it happened and how it occurred will usually take place afterwards at a suitable time of low workload. This may well not occur until the aircraft reaches cruise, as managing distraction is an important safety skill integral to the pilot role. Any internal or external factors affecting the pilot may be brought to light during this discussion between peers, however the dynamic experienced prior to this point could well affect the content of information that is shared.

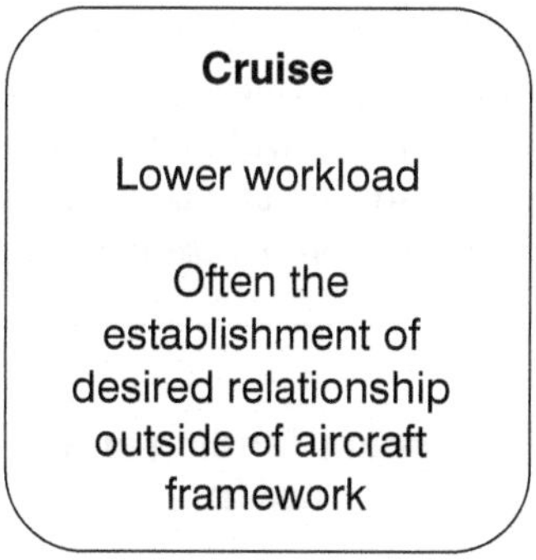

**Cruise**

Lower workload

Often the establishment of desired relationship outside of aircraft framework

*Figure 19.5* Cruise

The workload for most pilots reduces somewhat in the cruise. Due to modern systems and higher levels of automation, at this stage the job becomes one of monitoring systems and planning for eventualities. Pilots strive to stay ahead of the aircraft and maintain a high level of situational awareness. During the cruise phase, dependent upon the length of the flight, there is usually time for pilots to get to know one another better on a personal level.

The focus of the dynamic now shifts from task to personal. Some pilots have little or no interest in forming a relationship on this level whereas others are very keen to do so. Events that may have occurred previously can have a bearing upon what happens at this point in the flight. This part of the behavioural dynamic is probably the most personal of all as there is no prescribed necessity for any conversation to occur outside of the boundaries of the aircraft operation.

Within the flight deck community there is a large socio-cultural demographic. Differing age, gender, culture, race, religion and other social sub groups play an influential part in the interpersonal relationships which are formed between pilots within the operating team.

At times of low workload some pilots like to activate and stimulate their minds by engaging in crosswords, number puzzles or reading newspapers, others like to sit and chat with their colleagues. Another sub group of pilots are reluctant to do anything which distracts them from the primary task of aircraft and systems monitoring. A comfortable balance is usually found between the members of the group.

If the members of the team are new to each other then they will not know whether these behavioural patterns are normal for the individual or whether they are being influenced by external stressors.

- Topics discussed often include plans for the trip ahead, home life, hobbies and interests;
- an understanding and closeness can sometimes be created very quickly within the working group.;

- an individual may 'open up' and wish to share personal information about his or her current state of affairs;
- some pilots like to 'vent steam' to an understanding co-worker at a suitable time – a captive audience;
- usually many of the comments made are of a light hearted manner;
- peer support becomes evident within the group dynamic – a unique understanding of the pressures and challenges experienced by peers can lead to a strong feeling of support, empathy and understanding.

> **Descent, landing and taxi in**
>
> Task focused
>
> Relationship firmly established

*Figure 19.6* Descent and landing

Approaching the top of descent the workload increases once again for the operating pilots. Another briefing between the crew prior to descent is normal and the focus is very much back on the primary tasks. By this stage a much clearer picture of each individual's operating style and experience level has been developed and this can vary the content of that discussed. Peer assessment, appraisal and support is still very much evident with all working towards a safe and efficient conclusion to the day's work.

Further personal discussion will usually be kept to minimum during these final phases. If necessary, time can be made after the aircraft has arrived at its final parking place and all procedural work has been completed.

If the dynamic between the pilots has been positive up to this point then a relaxed, calm environment may well be witnessed during these stages.

> She's such a fantastic captain, she has a wealth of experience and brings out the very best in all the people around her. I learn so much when I work with her.

The opposite may also be true, a fractious or difficult relationship between work colleagues leading to this point can create a challenging or complicated work dynamic.

> He makes me feel so uncomfortable. I feel like every decision I make is being scrutinised. I lose all confidence in my ability to operate the aircraft in his presence.

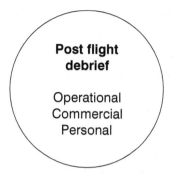

*Figure 19.7* Post flight

After the aircraft has been shut down, some airlines now mandate that their pilots carry out a post-flight debrief in order that they can learn from every flight. The pilot workforce is known to be highly self-critical, and this can lead to the debrief becoming focused on the negatives from the flight rather than looking to learn from the positives. A threat within this approach is that if the flight has gone very well, the pilots may feel that there is nothing to debrief. If this is the case they may miss an opportunity to learn from what they, or their colleagues do well. Equally from a mental health perspective, to have your faults regularly pointed out to you can be very disheartening when not accompanied by positives. The debrief will of course be influenced by the dynamic that has developed throughout the flight, but ideally should be conducted on a completely level playing field for all pilots to get the most benefit from it. If the focus of the debrief is the performance of the crew as a whole, rather than the performance of the individuals, this should lead to better results.

## More than two pilots

Often due to the length of the sectors involved in long-haul flying the cockpit crew can comprise more than just two pilots. An additional pilot may also be present on flights to facilitate training, to observe, or for other operational reasons. When a third pilot, or at times a fourth pilot, is involved the group dynamic can change considerably. To enable the most effective outcomes, all members must be engaged and valued within the group. The varied backgrounds, previous experience and previous aircraft types can lead to very differing behavioural dynamic combinations.

As we discussed earlier in the chapter, the first point of meeting is usually the briefing room. With any group greater than two, two will usually meet first with a third approaching at a later time. Misconceptions can occur at this stage due to wrong assumptions made by some, or all of the group. Commonly for a newcomer to the group, there can be a feeling of exclusion from the more senior, or familiar members. This can lead to a belief of need to prove oneself worthy to be a member.

> Sorry old boy, Rick and I go way back. We were on the same squadron together in the Air Force.

> Those were the days, a group of proper pilots doing real flying, not like today.

Two of the group members may well have previous experience together, and may purposely or otherwise make reference to these previous experiences without clear explanation or reference; this can make the newcomer feel excluded. There may also be patterns of communication previously established which are not familiar to the newcomer.

> Morning Steve. Rich and I have flown together many times before, we had a great time in Vancouver last week. Same rules as before Rich?

> Are you new on the fleet? Neither of us old boys have seen you before.

These factors need to be managed carefully. An extra effort to include rather than exclude the new team member should be made by the familiar members to ensure an effective and positive dynamic.

## Environmental factors

There are of course many environmental factors that can affect both the behavioural dynamic on the flight deck, and the mental health of the crew concerned. These range from industrial issues, such as rostering and pay, through to the working environment on and off the aircraft.

One of the most influential factors is that of rostering. The majority of pilots really enjoy their job; it is often something that they have strived towards for many years, and many feel privileged to hold their positions. Having said that, despite it being an inevitable part of the job, the impact of a pilot's roster can be a hugely negative influence (or indeed a positive one).

When the roster is first published most crew look to see who they are working with. This creates an expectation of how the trip may pan out on a personal level. There can be a pre-conceived opinion that each colleague has of each other, either formed in first person through previous experience or through word of mouth. There is often an unspoken idea of how things are going to be, or how people are going to behave and react due to this expectation. This may in turn cause the others in the group to react in a different manner to a situation than they would normally.

There are many different ways in which pilots' rosters are produced and these vary enormously from company to company. Some pilots are simply allocated their work each month and the only consideration made by their employer is ensuring that all of the flights are covered. Some work a regular pattern of days, for example a rolling 'six days on, three days off', and others have preference systems of varying degrees of complexity based on seniority (how long you have worked for the company). From a work–life balance perspective some of these systems are better than others, but even the most advanced systems cannot satisfy the whole workforce. This is simply because most airlines are 24/7 operators, and they will always require people to work over weekends and public holidays.

The impact on the individual of regularly being absent for events at home, such as children's birthdays, should not be underestimated and can build cumulatively over time. Unfortunately this is very difficult to address, as the flights concerned will always need pilots to fly them. For those that do have the ability to 'bid' for their work, an additional stressor is having to continually plan a month or two in advance and having to be realistic about what is achievable. Of course this is the lesser of two evils, but can still have a negative effect. It is the nature of any shift work that it may lead to tension with family members or friends if the pilot concerned is seen to 'never be around' for important events.

The industrial environment can also have a significant effect. It should be noted that pilots as a group are a very remote workforce. Although their day-to-day work brings them into contact with many frontline staff (cabin crew, engineers etc.), they interact with very few support staff and managers, and as such some can feel quite detached from the company that they work for.

The airline industry is notoriously fragile. This is partly due to the fact that operating aircraft is enormously expensive (hence the operating margins are very low) and partly due to the fact that the industry is very sensitive to current affairs. An example of this is that in the event of a financial downturn, not only are the airlines themselves affected financially, but many of their customers will stop flying, or change the class of travel in which they fly in an effort to save money. This is also true of terrorist attacks or the outbreak of war; all of these events result in a reduction in passenger numbers, which in turn results in a reduction in profit.

As a result, as within all companies, there is a constant pressure to reduce costs. This is in itself an entirely reasonable notion, but some pilots will feel that their terms and conditions are on a constant downward trajectory. This can lead to a very negative dynamic on the flight deck, either due to disagreement on the industrial issues between the pilots, or due to both pilots reinforcing each other's negative feelings.

It's not the job it used to be!

This company just takes, takes, takes; they don't realise the damage they are doing to pilot morale.

Tied in with industrial factors are the hotels that the pilots stay in when 'downroute'. Again, these will vary dramatically from company to company, but the quality of the hotel can have a big impact on the pilot. First, and most obviously, lack of quality sleep can be hugely detrimental to mental health (not to mention flight safety), so the hotel rooms need to be quiet with the ability to block out any natural light. Making the room dark is particularly important for long-haul crews who often find themselves sleeping during the day due to not being acclimatised to the local time zone. Another aspect that is rarely considered is how the location of the hotel can affect the pilot's state of mind. The time spent away from home is of course intended for resting between duties, but this recuperation can take many forms. Whether it is meeting with other crew members for a meal or a drink, doing some exercise or going to the cinema, people relax in many different ways. In some instances the location of a hotel can restrict these forms of relaxation (for example an airport hotel located by a motorway) and the crew can feel isolated or trapped. Should the pilots not have 'gelled' well initially, this can lead to quite a lonely existence for them, particularly if they are away for several days, or have similar experiences on consecutive trips.

> What a great hotel, it's got a fantastic gym, it's in a really nice area of town and the staff always make us feel welcome. It's like a second home to me.

> Every night in that place is like a prison sentence. There's nothing to do, the food is terrible and I can't sleep because of the noise from the freeway. I just watch the clock and count down the minutes until the wake-up call.

Another occupational stressor, which is simply due to the high level of regulation required in a safety-critical industry such as the airline industry, is that of regular competency checks. As a rule, pilots are assessed in their ability to operate the aircraft in various emergency situations in a simulator for two days every six months. This is then supplemented with an annual 'line check' which is where a trainer will accompany a crew on a normal trip to see how they operate in the real world. Following these training and checking events, there will be a debrief where the trainer will explain their observations of what the crew did well, and also what they could improve on. Much of the time in the simulator is spent on training rather than checking, but there is a perception amongst the majority of pilots that their licence is 'on the line' for the duration of the simulator time, and this causes many anxiety. Many pilots are naturally self-critical and set themselves high standards to meet, and it is quite common for the pilots under check to only remember the negative debrief points at the expense of the positive ones. The combination of these factors can leave some pilots feeling like they are perpetually under the spotlight, and jumping from one check to the next under constant pressure. Many pilots describe the 'sim checks' to be the most disliked and worrying aspect of their job profile.

34 years in the job. I only have two sim checks left to retirement. I'm counting them down.

I hate the sim check. Even after 15 years on the aircraft, I'm physically sick in the washroom just before I enter the sim.

As soon as a simulator duty appears on my roster my wife says my mood changes. I become short-tempered and tetchy.

The pressure is immense. I tell myself it's always ok, but the reality is if I mess up badly I could lose my job. Who pays the mortgage then?

Each individual deals with the pressures of being under check differently. Most find strategies which suit them, and help them to cope with the necessity of continuous checking and training in the role.

Some pilots perform much better under scrutiny than others. Differing performance levels will always be evident, but the majority are within the acceptable high standards required. Occasionally however, performance levels do not meet that which is required by the organisation or the aviation authority. At this point a reference may be made to the detailed records of an individual's past performances. A significant drop in performance from the normal can often indicate outside stressors playing a factor. It is often the case when quizzed about possible reasons for poor performance that an individual will 'open up' to the trainer or examiner about external factors.

During the annual line check it is hoped that no emergency scenarios occur and it will just be an easy day out, however the fact that the third, or fourth crew member is a trainer can exacerbate some of the multi-crew dynamic issues mentioned earlier and also add to the perceived pressure of the training environment. In this case (as in all cases of training or checking), it is incumbent upon the trainer to set the correct tone and an appropriate environment for learning.

Finally, as with any occupation, there are stressors that come with actually doing the job. The cabin environment of a modern commercial aircraft varies from type to type, but it is always at a lower pressure than sea level (i.e. contains less oxygen) and it tends to be very dry due to the lack of moisture in the air at altitude. Both of these factors can have a fatiguing effect. Other day-to-day stressors may be delays, dealing with bad weather or managing customer issues.

Having already mentioned rostering and hotels it seems appropriate to discuss fatigue. Fatigue is an ever-present threat to airline pilots. Due to the safety implications of fatigue, there are strict rules that govern how pilots are rostered in an effort to avoid them becoming 'fatigued'. What these rules do not account for is the situation where the pilot is affected by lack of sleep, but not to the point where it becomes detrimental to the immediate safety of the aircraft. The rules are an excellent mitigation tool, but if we are to have pilots flying through the night then they are going to be affected by sleep debt, and this in turn can impact mental health.

## How a mental health issue may manifest itself

One of best indicators of a mental health issue developing is change in behaviour. As previously mentioned, many pilots do not know their colleagues well, and may regularly find themselves flying with someone with whom they have never flown before. As a result, spotting a behavioural change can be enormously difficult. Someone who has become withdrawn for example, may be misinterpreted as someone who is rude or disinterested. Equally someone who appears to be distracted and is missing important information may just be viewed as a less competent operator.

A good question to ask may be whether it is possible to assess whether someone's behaviour or mood is differing from their established norm on first encounters? Many pilots have conscious or subconscious personas within the flight deck which differ greatly dependent upon their personality types. This makes it difficult to assess if the persona proffered on the day is differing from the norm and if so, why. A colleague would struggle to know if the outside stressors of life are a contributing factor to differing performance or behaviour.

But does a performance degradation necessarily indicate outside stressors? On a regular basis a pilot is expected to perform complex tasks when subjected to time zone changes, reduced quality or quantity of sleep and with possible distractions. It is therefore a great challenge for a peer to recognise whether performance decrements are due to outside stressors, or the normal stressors associated with the job.

One may wish to consider at what point information offered during an informal chat becomes serious enough to question a peer's ability to perform his task. This can quickly become a very delicate situation. Within the community, trust plays a vital role between peers. If information shared willingly is seen to be used against an individual, even with good intentions, then animosity may rise.

## Peer support

The role of a pilot is seen as a very glamorous one: staying in beautiful parts of the world in high-standard hotels within a group who have both disposable time and income to enjoy their surroundings.

Often the reality can be somewhat different, and many can find themselves alone in a place they don't desire to be, without the very people they wish to be with. It is here where peer support becomes so important.

Within the flight deck informal support is available and sometimes offered in the form of positive personalities and flight deck dynamics which may have a positive impact on performance. There is also the manner in which a pilot feeds back to another when he or she feels that another pilot's operational standards or decisions are dubious (and how the other pilot is able to receive such feedback). This however must be considered within the context of the seniority gradient, pilot in command to second in command and vice versa.

Due to widespread availability of the Internet, communication is much easier anywhere around the world than previously. This can make faraway places feel closer to home, contact with loved ones and close friends is nearly always available. Through the medium of the Internet, crews share information with each other about places to go, good restaurants and local companies that offer discounted activity packages. There are also discussion threads about new procedures and discussions available for clarification purposes. Contact with technical experts or pilot managers is also more readily available.

Downroute, people will often arrange to spend time together socialising, meeting for a lazy breakfast or in the evenings, for dinner and drinks. During these times matters of a personal nature are likely to be discussed, and if a crew member feels comfortable in the environment, he or she may share with his colleagues any concerns or issues he or she is experiencing.

Due to the transient nature of the job and the work force, it is not unusual for members of a group to share very personal information quite early on in the relationship, and much earlier than would normally be expected.

## Support options

To an extent, some of the mental health issues experienced by pilots can be addressed by appropriate training. Some training in self-management may help those find themselves adversely affected by the frustrations of the job. An example of where this might be appropriate is the security check situation mentioned earlier in this chapter. Creating an understanding of why pilots are subject to the same security screening as passengers (primarily so that pilots are not seen as a weak link in the security process) may help reduce some of the frustration. Equally, training in what to look for in your colleagues and how to address any concerns that you may have could potentially trap any developing mental health problem early enough to avoid the need for significant intervention. Of course this method would require a very overt support structure to be in place, and possibly a programme of education to demystify mental health issues and remove any stigma that may be associated with them.

One of the most important factors to any programme of support is that it must be seen to have a positive outcome. Of course that is always the aim of any intervention, but the perception developed by the pilot community is hugely important, and what may been by the psychologist/psychiatrist and the pilot concerned as a positive outcome, may not appear that way to the pilot workforce as a whole. Should any form of treatment or assessment be seen to directly result in a pilot losing his job or his licence, then other pilots will not admit to having issues, nor will they seek treatment.

Many airlines recognise that mental health issues affect a large proportion of people at some stage in their lives, and as such already offer access to professional counselling services for their pilots and their families. Some pilot unions will offer support services, for example the British Airline Pilots Association (BALPA) offer a service called the Pilots Advisory Group. These are groups of pilots from varying (flying) backgrounds who make themselves available to chat to BALPA members in confidence about any personal or professional issue that may be affecting them. There are also publicly available services such as (in the United Kingdom) the Samaritans, who are a national group of volunteers who operate a free counselling service over the telephone.

It has become practice in some airlines for the pilots to meet with a psychologist every couple of years. This is an opportunity to chat with someone about the issues at work, but it also involves a discussion about their particular personality type and how they can best address their weaknesses. The primary focus is of course to make them more effective in their role, but it could be extended to cover mental health too.

## Summary

As discussed in this chapter, the working environment of the modern commercial pilot is quite unique in many ways. It also varies greatly from one airline to another and, in the case of large airlines, from one fleet to another. As with all occupations, there are many stressors of differing magnitudes and frequencies that affect pilots, and although they work in very close-knit teams from day to day, it can become quite a lonely position.

Modern flight safety training fully embraces the concept of crew resource management (CRM). CRM is a very broad subject, but essentially covers the human aspect of operating aircraft, from how pilots interact with the aircraft and each other, to human physiological responses to stress or sleep deprivation.

Some of the techniques discussed in CRM training can help pilots to manage or identify mild mental health issues; in fact mental health could be described as a CRM issue. One aspect of CRM is having an understanding when you or your colleague are not operating to the best of your ability. As discussed earlier, this can be difficult to establish in someone that you have just met, but many airlines use scales of intervention which can be useful. These scales are designed to assist in the technical operating of the aircraft, but they could also be applied to intervening in a developing mental health issue. One such scale comes from some research done by Dr Robert O. Besco and is entitled, 'To Intervene, or not to Intervene? The Co-Pilot's Catch 22.'

The scale can be remembered by the simple acronym, PACE:

- PROBE: Probing for a better understanding.
- ALERT: Alerting the individual to anomalies.
- CHALLENGE: Challenging the suitability of the present strategy.
- EMERGENCY WARNING: Warning of critical or immediate dangers.

Of course this would need to be approached very carefully, but it must not be forgotten that the flight deck is a safety-critical environment and the earlier a mental health issue is resolved, the better (for both the individual, and the operation as a whole).

CRM training in itself however is not enough, and the real area where progress could be made is in the recognition of a developing mental health issue both within the pilots themselves, and also in their colleagues.

# 20 Peer-to-peer support and development programmes for pilots

## Time for a holistic approach

*Gerhard Fahnenbruck and Gunnar Steinhardt*

### Introduction

Imagine you are a pilot talking to your aeromedical examiner (AME) during routine medical examination. You know that if any significant medical and/or psychological problem arises the AME will withdraw your medical or will report to the Civil Aviation Authority to take the same action. How willing will you be to openly talk to him or her about any problem you might have? If you have an obvious medical problem you will have to disclose your symptoms because your AME will probably discover the medical condition anyway. However, if you have problems that could be hidden from a medical examination then you have a choice as to whether you disclose or not. Not disclosing problems may help you keep your medical certification for the moment. However, speaking openly may provide an opportunity for you to get support but involves the risk that your medical is withdrawn. AMEs try to keep pilots 'in the air' but the pilot's risk to their medical certification remains. Where the threat to your licence exists, some pilots may decide not to disclose emotional concerns to their AME and try to find different resources to help them, if indeed they do seek any at all. That pilot's behaviour is independent of the AME's ability to treat confidential information confidentially and is also independent of the AME's willingness to keep the pilot flying as long as possible. It is just natural self-protective behaviour among pilots and a system with inherent structural weakness.

This chapter highlights the importance of peer-to-peer systems and opens up a new perspective on pilot support by integrating pilot development programmes into airline operations. The first section of this chapter discusses a peer-to-peer system and the second section presents pilot support and development programmes within airline operations. Both pilot-supporting programmes can be successfully implemented independently of one another. Nevertheless, a combined approach offers an added value to the pilot community and consequently to the operator.

# Stiftung Mayday

*Figure 20.1* Stiftung Mayday

## Stiftung Mayday: a prototype for a 'safe haven' concept for pilots in need of emotional support

Pilots have different resources available depending on the country, the pilot's insurance situation and the operator the pilot is working for. Some operators have internal structures available or offer external employee assistance programmes (EAPs); some unions offer a similar assistance to their members. Sometimes non-governmental organisations like Stiftung Mayday in Germany are available to support pilots in need. Health insurance companies are usually willing to support their customers, preventing illnesses instead of curing them.

But there is a problem similar to the structural problem with AMEs (see above) with health insurances and also with EAPs in conjunction with aviation: The systems are at least partly non-compatible. Within the mental health ethics, a medical doctor or psychologist is allowed to treat a patient only if he or she is diagnosed properly. This makes sense from the practitioner's perspective: If the problem is *not* known (diagnosed) properly a treatment could be anything between appropriate to non-effective or even harmful. Therefore, a proper diagnosis is needed to increase the probability of an appropriate and effective treatment. However, a correct or accurate diagnosis very often ends up in a withdrawal of the pilot's medical. That medical has to be withdrawn because the aviation law requires it. The AME does not have a chance to act differently. Instead of thinking in terms of: 'What can be done to support the pilot to carry out his or her job professionally?', the legal framework requires the AME to determine under which conditions to withdraw the pilot's medical certificate to make sure that the aviation system remains safe. Thus, legal considerations force the AME to precautionary withdrawals of medical certificates to improve safety. This is easy to understand from the AME's perspective. Nonetheless, it is equally easy to understand that the pilot's natural reaction is to protect his or her career by hiding at least the temporary critical conditions. This understandably defensive behaviour worsens the situation and in the long run ends up in even more restrictive legal requirements.

As a consequence of this dilemma, pilots have developed their own support structures independent from the operator's and regulator's and any kind of screening or assessment to make support available to pilots to help them to overcome temporary conditions or in rare cases to help them to leave the job safely. Stiftung Mayday is one of these organisations and is described here as a well-functioning prototype for this kind of organisation.

### History of Stiftung Mayday

Stiftung Mayday is a German non-governmental organisation founded after an aircraft accident at the ILA Berlin Air show 1994. A Russian pilot crashed, leaving behind a wife, two children and his mother. Money spontaneously collected was used by Stiftung Mayday to care for this family for a number of years.

The purpose of Stiftung Mayday in general is twofold: It takes care of licence holders, former licence holders and their next of kin in need. Stiftung Mayday provides care to crew member (including flight attendants of passenger aircraft, rescue personnel in helicopters or load master on freight flights) after aviation-related critical incidents or accidents.

The focus of Stiftung Mayday is Germany but the by-laws allow it to take on international cases as well. In practice, about one to two per cent of its cases are international. If Stiftung Mayday is approached by a person outside Germany, then the person in need is referred to a local organisation within its international network.

Statistics on the work of Stiftung Mayday are available from 1998. They show the increasing demand on support and high client satisfaction with Stiftung Mayday and its work. Instead of approaching people who have been involved in an incident, Stiftung Mayday has informed almost all flying personnel in Germany that Stiftung Mayday exists and that they should contact Stiftung Mayday if they feel in need. The contact is always voluntary. Stiftung Mayday does not approach anyone on behalf of someone else.

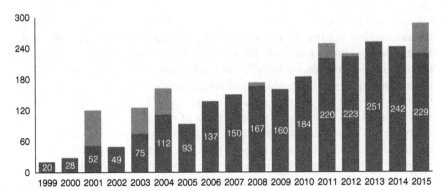

*Figure 20.2* Number of incidents

In Figure 20.2 the dark grey columns are 'regular' cases whereas the ligher ones are terror attacks, natural disasters, wars and other situations outside the ordinary work of Stiftung Mayday.

The reasons why pilots or flying personnel request support are very different. They range from critical incidents via fear of flying to very personal problems around health issues, family problems or problems with the employer.

Concerning critical incidents and in the direct aftermath of these incidents, Stiftung Mayday strictly follows the standards set by the International Critical Incident Stress Foundation (ICISF). This organisation has developed standards for operational personnel such as rescue workers, police, military personnel and also aviation personnel. Stiftung Mayday conducts regular refresher courses at least every second year to keep its personnel trained.

Beyond critical incidents, Stiftung Mayday has specially trained personnel to assist with psychological, psychiatric or any medical problem, but flight licence holders may also approach Stiftung Mayday with any kind of legal, financial or insurance problems. When Stiftung Mayday cannot provide direct help, advice is given on whom to contact. In total, 50 per cent of all cases are in this category, either because the incident is too long ago so that the tools available from ICISF are no longer applicable or because the support needed is not to do with a critical incident as defined by ICISF.

In terms of numbers of people assisted, Stiftung Mayday provides assistance to approximately 250 cases per year. Since several people may be involved in a single event this means Stiftung Mayday is reaching about 600 to 800 licence holders or flying personnel per year.

In about 90 per cent of all cases, the people in need recover quickly (within a few days) with no further action required. Almost 10 per cent of cases are somehow more complex and very often safety critical. The reasons are very diverse and range from sleeplessness, psychological, psychiatric or medical conditions to any kind of critical life events like a marriage or a birth of a child on the positive side, to the death of a close relative to divorces, financial or legal problems on the other side. Eighty per cent of these usually need someone to coach them through the situation and sometimes some short-term support

**81% aviation-related incidents** (84%, 81%, 81%, 84%, 87%)

    10% medical problems on board (13%, 21%, 17%, 15%, 14%)
    9% death on board (15%, 9%, 17%, 17%, 11%)
    7% total loss (7%, 5%, 4%, 3%, 3%)
    6% smoke, fume and/or fire (10%, 10%, 9%, 7%, 6%)
    6% unruly pax (5%, 7%, 6%, 5%, 5%)
    5% turbulence (6%, 6%, 6%, 4%, 5%)
    5% fear of flight (5%, 3%, 3%, 3%, 3%)
    3% technical failures (7%, 8%, 7%, 5%, 6%)
    ...

**19% private problems**, very often licence-threatening and/or related to the death of a next-of kin (16%, 19%, 19%, 16%, 13%)

*Figure 20.3* 2015 at Stiftung Mayday (2014, 2013, 2012, 2011, 2010)

from the employer, mostly in terms of a specific rostering for a couple of weeks or month. With this support they usually recover quickly.

Twenty percent of the complex cases, which amounts to two per cent of overall cases (for Stiftung Mayday this is about 12 to 16 people per year), are really safety critical and are unable to fly for some time. They need proper treatment either by a practitioner or as an inpatient in a clinic. Eighty percent of these recover with treatment and on average within six months. The remaining 20 per cent need to leave their job and/or the industry. Stiftung Mayday usually accompanies these people through this process. This very often takes a lot of effort and a high frequency of appointments between Stiftung Mayday and the pilot in need in the beginning of the process. The frequency of appointments usually decreases over time, but overall the process can easily take a few years.

So, putting things into perspective, a 'safe haven' metaphor is basically a preventive concept offering tools to give licence holders and other flying personnel the opportunity to receive support before situations or people become safety critical and before licences are endangered. Only about 15 out of about 700 people contacting Stiftung Mayday are to be categorised as safety critical. That is only about two per cent of all pilots asking for support.

The process for contacting Stiftung Mayday is shown in Figure 20.4.

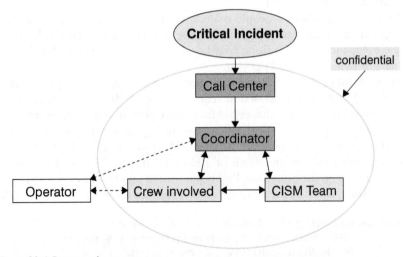

*Figure 20.4* Intervention process

Anyone can contact Stiftung Mayday after an incident or when in need for any other reason. This call is taken by a 24/7 hotline registering the name and call back number of the caller and, if given by the caller, a headline or topic why this person is calling. With that information, all coordinators are contacted through an automated text messaging system. As soon as one coordinator takes over the case, the others are informed that the case has been taken care of. With the information given, the coordinator either contacts the caller him- or herself or asks a so-called peer – a properly trained person with the same professional background as the caller – to call the caller back. Pilots are taken care of by trained pilots, flight attendants are taken care of by trained flight attendants etc. Depending on the situation and the support needed, different tools are used and different protocols are followed. The programme Stiftung Mayday follows has been ISO certified to make sure that the necessary quality standards are met.

All information is kept strictly confidential from the very first call on. The one who controls the flow of information is the caller, and not anyone else. Information to the operator or the authority is only given with prior permission of the caller. The only legal limitation to this is the risk of suicide or homicide by a pilot, which has to be reported. This has never happened during the 21 years that Stiftung Mayday has existed.

The preventive tools available to Stiftung Mayday are:

• pre incident education;
• ICISF-trained peers and an infrastructure able to react quickly, efficiently and professionally;
• a well-trained team of specialists being able to coach pilots through critical life events, and also psychologists, psychiatrists and other mental health professionals trained to work with aviation personnel.

The pre-incident education (especially in all German airlines) takes place during initial training, CRM training, in the simulator, during upgrade and many other occasions while conducting practical exercises. Pre-incident education also means that most managers within airlines are trained in how Stiftung Mayday operates to support their personnel. Pre-incident education is also conducted through regulations and background information in the airlines' operating manuals. Thus, Stiftung Mayday has become a normal procedure for abnormal situations.

Pre-incident education in general aviation is somewhat more complicated because the field is very diverse. There are sky divers, glider pilots, private pilots, test pilots and others. Additionally there are many flying clubs, associations, independent pilots so that it is almost impossible to get the necessary information across to everyone. Stiftung Mayday trains flight instructors, appears at air shows and fairs, and writes articles for bulletins. Everything that can possibly be done to make sure that pilots and their next of kin know that Stiftung Mayday is available is done.

All this effort is necessary to be able to support people in need. If people know in advance about the support, they accept it much more easily and quickly if it is needed. The more quickly support is available, the more efficient it is.

When talking about critical incidents it is very important to have a properly trained team available in as many places as possible. Most of the teams in aviation world-wide agree to follow the standards set by the International Critical Incident Stress Foundation (ICISF). That allows work in international teams if necessary. It also allows supporting pilots initially through a foreign team when abroad and continues without a break when returning home. Stiftung Mayday has about 250 team members actively trained according to this standard.

Stiftung Mayday also keeps about 30 coaches and mental health professionals (MHPs) trained and familiar with the aviation environment and its inherent problems. All MHPs know the risk of specific diagnoses for licence holders so that they know what to avoid not to do harm to the pilots' careers.

For the few cases where preventive measures and psychological first aid is not sufficient, Stiftung Mayday has a team available consisting of private doctors, psychologists or other specialists including clinics trained to deal with pilots. Because of the very small number of cases the industry is dealing with, Stiftung Mayday needs to fall back on existing entities but keeps them trained anyway.

The whole team of Stiftung Mayday presently (2016) consists of the team members shown in Figure 20.5.

- 203 Peers
- 22 Coordinators
- 26 Mental Health Professionals
- 1 Clinical Director, 2 deputies

- Organisation- /Airline- representatives

*Figure 20.5* The Stiftung Mayday team in 2016

*Figure 20.6* The international network

All team members receive regular training at least every second year. Anyone who does not participate in the necessary training leaves the team automatically. The minimum training follows the ICISF standard plus refresher training, but there are team members who receive extra training as coaches, trainers or for special tasks like the Home Escort Team whose members, for example, accompany bodies home after death.

The worldwide teams Stiftung Mayday is working with are fully independent but follow similar standards at least after critical incidents or accidents. The independence is important to make sure that they can adapt to local needs and differences and to be flexible enough in case it's needed. But even if independent, all the teams are working in close collaboration. They meet at least once a year to stay in contact and are updated.

The costs involved in running the team working for the airlines in Germany are as shown in Figure 20.7.

| Costs | 482.500 € |
|---|---|
| Fix | 145.000 € |
| Training | 100.500 € |
| Personnel in training | 147.000 € |
| Supervision | 90.000 € |
| **Savings** | **2.646.000 €** |
| Short term sick leave | 846.000 € |
| Long term sick leave | 1.800.000 € |
| **Balance** | **2.163.500 €** |

*Figure 20.7* Simplified cost structure

*Figure 20.8* Dr. Otto Schily hands over as patron to Dr. Thomas Enders in 2015

Because Stiftung Mayday saves so much money for all operators involved it has never been a financial problem to run the organisation.

The non-airline part of Stiftung Mayday basically depends on donations. As most of the work is done by volunteers, Stiftung Mayday most of the time talks about friend-raising instead of fund-raising. It is much more important to have the right people at the right place to support instead of having only money available. It also helps to have the right patron for the team. In the case of Stiftung Mayday it used to be the former Minister of the Interior, Dr. Otto Schily and since 2015 it is the CEO of Airbus, Dr. Thomas Enders. Both are very quietly supportive in the background.

### Programme requirements

Because authorities are beginning to recommend peer support systems (PSPs) to be implemented after the tragic Germanwings 4U9525 accident, Stiftung Mayday has developed requirements for functioning PSPs.

There are basically three different PSPs:

1   Substance abuse programmes
2   Critical incident response programmes
3   PSPs focusing on pilots' wellbeing including everyday problems (domestic problems, training issues, etc.).

All the systems share a common requirements, but there are additional requirements specific for each programme.

The programmes are run by voluntary peers (colleagues with the same professional background, but also trained in the area of psychological first aid). The number of peers required for PSPs should be in total approximately one per cent of the employees served by the programmes. However, the number required for substance abuse programmes or purely critical incident stress programmes is fewer than that.

Mental health professionals (psychologists, psychiatrists or other specialists in the field) should be responsible for the oversight of the programme, the training of the peers and in cases where a person needs referring to a specialist.

Programmes can be established by the operator itself, by the union or by a fully independent agency:

• If the programme is run by the operator, the people running it need a written statement that they are independent internally and that they don't have to report details of a single case to anyone. Persons running these programmes need to have trust of the management and the employees.
• If the programme is run by the union it needs similar safeguards. People running the programme ideally are only working for the programme and are not involved in any of the union's responsibilities or tasks.
• For independent programmes, trust building is somehow easier because the organisations are independent without an obligation to report. Independent

organisations also have the advantage that small airlines can, by using independent organisations, 'outsource' the PSP.

Annual statistics, without names or details of cases, protecting individuals' data, need to be made available to the operator, the authorities, and interested internal staff.

Making use of the PSPs should be open to 'self-reporting' as the preferred option, but reporting by colleagues to the peers of concerns about another colleague should be an option as well. In that case, internal procedures need to be established to protect the reported pilot against misuse of the system.

Confidentiality is the key element for PSPs. However, there are cases when the confidentiality must be breached, and these should be clearly defined: 'Breaching confidentiality is only possible in case of clearly evident risk to public safety' is the term already used by the Aerospace Medical Association, the Human Intervention Motivation Study and other programmes, and is anyway a legal requirement in most countries.

Programmes need to be fully independent from any kind of management influence and fully independent from regulatory structures.

Funding of these programmes need to be assured by operators.

There are specific training requirements for PSPs to be established for different groups within the system:

- Peers
  - need initial training including PSP structure, psychological first aid, national health care system, where to refer etc.;
  - need recurring training;
  - should have access themselves to debriefing if needed.
- Management
  - The company's management needs basic psychological knowledge as well and being very aware that trying to manage such a system on a case basis would destroy the system immediately. The company's management also needs to know that confidential information will not be made available to them and that it is absolutely necessary to respect this.
- Employees
  - need training on what PSP is and how it works;
  - the fact that reporting a fellow pilot to the system offers a support network to that pilot and is definitely not a punishment; rather it is professional support.
- AMEs
  - need training about PSPs;
  - need further training in principles of psychological evaluation and diagnostics.
- Health care professionals included in the PSP programmes
  - need training on regulations in aviation;
  - need training on pilots certification criteria and loss of medical certificates.

There are numerous well-established substance abuse programmes available in the aviation industry. These programmes fulfil the following requirements which also need to be fulfilled by new programmes:

- it needs to have an agreement between the operator, aviation authority and pilot unions;
- it needs to have substance abuse experts (doctors) as well as the possibility of in-patient rehabilitation;
- after rehabilitation, participants need intensive visits to doctor and peers;
- it maybe needs some random testing during two years period of sobriety (as required by regulations);
- will allow early return to flying.

## Pilot support and development programmes

Peer support systems are essential in assisting pilots to overcome critical temporary conditions or if needed to guarantee a proper referral to a specialist. The first part of this chapter described the full scope and effectiveness of those systems.

The second part of this chapter aims to highlight the potential of pilot support and development programmes within the operational environment. The overall goal of these programmes is to focus on personal development and growth throughout a pilot's career from the position as co-pilot progressing to commander, and even beyond when taking over additional functions such as an instructor or other management positions. These programmes are considered as fundamental as the effective implementation of peer support systems.

The implementation of pilot support and development programmes requires an investment of time and money, e.g. additional ground duty time and management capacity. However, the same positive effects on crew members (but also in monetary terms, as outlined in the first part of this chapter – e.g. reduction of crew absenteeism) can be expected from successful implemented pilot support and development programmes.

At this stage, it is important to distinguish the above-mentioned programmes from already existing and mandatory training for pilots within the EASA regulatory framework. The common training schedule of pilots in terms of human factors-related topics is clearly regulated by the authorities and well-established within the airline community. Crew resource management (CRM) training elements are well defined and role-specific aspects (e.g. CRM initial training, recurring training, command training) are thoroughly reflected. Overall the objective of CRM can be defined '[…] to manage all the resources available to them [pilots] in the cockpit including other crew members, procedures, the machine interface, and themselves' (CAA, 2014). The process of further development of CRM training programmes will be enhanced by new guidance material and applicable means of compliance based on the EASA RMT.0411 (EASA, 2015a). New training elements like 'resilience development' amongst others are introduced. This can – alongside already existing training elements –

be considered as an opportunity to support pilots' individual development and growth in his or her professional competencies.

Due to the nature of the CRM training, the opportunity to support crews in difficult or critical psycho-social situations is limited. Usually CRM is trained in groups only for a few hours or days per year and provides fundamental knowledge to deal with individual issues or problematic circumstances. CRM training does not exclusively focus on personal development of pilots based on individual needs at their specific level of experience.

Both approaches, peer support systems and pilot development programmes, do not compete with the concept of CRM as they build on the CRM concepts learnt during training in the classroom or simulator.

It is of utmost importance to note that the suggested programmes should be seen as a fundamental extension to supplement existing trainings or schemes in place within the operational environment.

The following part of this chapter outlines pilot support and development programmes as a generic approach for a medium-size operator. Well-established airlines worldwide have developed programmes – beyond the required mandatory trainings – to support and promote their pilot staff according to their identified areas or potential risks within the system. Most of these programmes had been developed due to incidents, accidents or other occurrences to react and mitigate consequences. The enhancement of crew members' resilience from the very beginning by applying a proactive approach does not appear to be desirable as the future return of investment is unrecognised.

Pilot development programmes offer an approach to focus on the needs and requirements of pilots at certain stages of their career with the aim to promote a healthy growth and personal development. All this from the beginning of a pilot's career.

Overall there will be four cornerstones presented and summarised by a SWOT analysis (strengths, weaknesses, opportunities, threats) to emphasise the enablers and barriers of the entire approach.

The four cornerstones are presented in Figure 20.9 overleaf.

### *Pilot initial guidance and support*

The first cornerstone encompasses the initial guidance of pilots when joining an operator. This contact should preferably be initiated by a human factors expert with expertise in aviation psychology and well-informed about the specific operational environment of the operator. The content of the appointment between the individual pilot and the human factors expert should be kept strictly confidential. The aim is to build a trusting relationship which allows an open and honest exchange in order to guarantee an effective and successful guidance.

During the initial phase, the pilot's need for reassurance and gaining self-confidence is the main point of interest. It is often forgotten that some of these pilots are not sure how to judge their own initial performance within their new

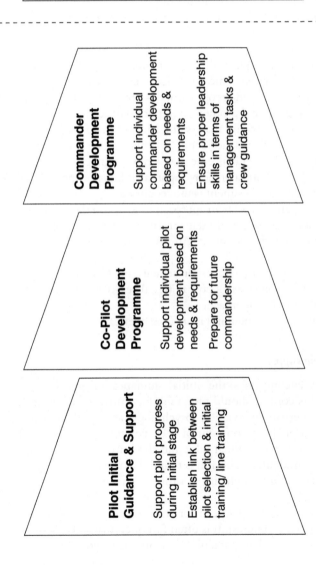

**Pilot Initial Guidance & Support**

Support pilot progress during initial stage

Establish link between pilot selection & initial training/ line training

**Co-Pilot Development Programme**

Support individual pilot development based on needs & requirements

Prepare for future commandership

**Commander Development Programme**

Support individual commander development based on needs & requirements

Ensure proper leadership skills in terms of management tasks & crew guidance

**Pilot Peer to Peer Support**

Psycho-social support of crew members in critical situations, incidents and accidents

Everyday Support

Supporting Pilot's Individual Development throughout Career →

*Figure 20.9* Generic approach for pilot support – a development programme

operational context. They are simply lacking reference points and this should be considered as a normal phase of adaptation.

Before conducting this appointment the human factors expert should be well prepared. An in-depth review on the selection results is suggested. Any available training files representing the overall performance should be reviewed. Instructors who have been directly involved with the pilot might also provide additional insight. It is recommended that instructors from various phases of training should be contacted in order to minimise the effects and influence of subjectivity. The individual pilot can also prepare for this appointment by reflecting on his or her own performance and development.

The meeting itself allows the linking of selection results with the documented progress and actual performance of the pilot. Often the positive selection results are fed back to the candidate directly after the selection process. Usually only limited information is processed or kept in mind due to the stressful situation directly after receiving the positive result.

During the appointment within this programme, sometimes months later, it might be beneficial to again provide insight into the selection results with proper explanation emphasising on the identified strengths and also addressing the areas recognised for further development. A positive approach towards the pilot should be paramount.

The feedback collected from instructors involved should be openly discussed. Preferably the pilot should be asked first to provide a personal and subjective opinion concerning his or her performance and how they have progressed.

An open discussion and exchange should positively emphasise the current level of performance and development without neglecting deficiencies and their proper treatment. The aim is to support growth and enhance personal resilience. Giving compliments is most probably one of the strongest tools in encouraging further progress.

Opportunities for additional support can be agreed and coordinated.

In order not to disturb the pilot during the very early stage of training, it is recommended to schedule the appointment during the line training and not before.

This meeting establishes a trusting relationship between the pilot and human factors expert and at the same time lowers the barrier for the pilot to contact the expert in case of difficult or critical psycho-social situations that might arise at a future point in time.

From an organisational point of view the cornerstone of 'initial guidance and support' may provide essential data that can be used to validate the selection process and may help to identify strengths as well as potential improvements within the system. It is essential that the processed data must be made anonymous beforehand and the confidentiality must be guaranteed.

### Co-pilot development programme

This cornerstone focuses on the personal development of first officers. As already stated earlier, basic CRM training provides a solid base on which this programme may be built. To further describe a reasonable concept for this programme, a timeframe of ten years before promotion to commander is assumed. Concept adaptations might be necessary according to differences in span of time.

The goal of this programme is to enhance the individual co-pilot's development. During a timeline of ten years, co-pilots develop specific needs and they face different requirements. In order to initiate necessary change and support personal growth, a three-step programme is recommended.

The first step of this programme should be implemented two to three years after joining the organisation. At this stage co-pilots usually have gained basic experience in terms of corporate culture, atmosphere, operational environment; and last but not least, increased their operational skills and self-confidence in performing as expected by themselves and by the operator.

In order to allow a valuable exchange amongst co-pilots having the same level of experience and at the same time enhance personal development of each individual co-pilot, a course lasting one or two days should be scheduled. The idea is to create a peer-centred approach. This approach may initiate an open exchange on beneficial as well as on critical experiences and may create an atmosphere where advice by peers might be considered more easily. Human factors considerations according to the level of experience and training concepts can be designed based on the specific needs for those course participants.

In general, most of those co-pilots will have less contact with the operational management at this stage. An open dialogue can offer the opportunity to the management to encourage these co-pilots – and lower the barrier – to contact them when needed.

The same is true with respect to the safety management. A direct relationship should be established to encourage proper application of reporting systems and other safety tools. Analysis of safety data concerning the performance of co-pilots reflecting their specific level of experience compared to other groups (e.g. co-pilots with higher seniority) may foster new insights. Interesting questions may be: Is there anything that they do better than others? Do they make more mistakes or different mistakes than others?

To sum up, the approach to involve management may also be extended to other areas and departments.

The first step of the programme should preferably be led by the human factors expert who has already established a trusting relationship with the co-pilots during the first 'initial guidance and support' phase. The trusting relationship may now be deepened and any possible need for support (e.g. psycho-social support or coaching) might more likely be identified and easier to offer.

During the entire programme experienced CRM trainers who are also active as pilots within the same operational environment as the course participants should accompany the human factors expert.

The second step of this programme should take place after five to six years.

At this time the co-pilots usually have developed a stable and consistent levels of performance. They are well-established within the pilot community and gained valuable experience. In general, the same course setup and duration should be applied as laid out in the step above. The course concept – again a peer-centred approach – should allow the sharing of beneficial as well as critical experiences. The course concept and the focused human factors themes should be adapted to level of proficiency.

The involvement of management should be continued and deepened. Again an open exchange with flight operations management and safety management can be considered crucial. Additional insights into less focused departments in the past may stimulate curiosity and help capture participants' attention.

It can be assumed that at this point in time the co-pilots' motivation might be lower than compared to the beginning of their career as they now reach the middle of their co-pilot career and the time to promotion seems quite far away. Therefore, in order to enhance personal growth, an emphasis on the development of future left-hand seat competencies should be initiated. The insight in related human factors principles should be kept on a basic level. Here it is important to be careful not to overdo this topic as there might be a risk of raising unnecessary expectations. Nevertheless to create the mind set to think ahead might be beneficial.

The third step of this programme should take place after eight to nine years.

At this level of experience the focus should be on expanding existing skills for the future role of commander and as well on the relevance of changing perspective from the right-hand to the left-hand seat. The whole scope of the commander's role concept should be thoroughly revealed. The implementation of simulator sessions may be considered as a supporting method to close the gap between theory and practice. The direct exposure and a closed feedback loop by fellow pilots and instructors may underpin the subsequent development and identification with the future role as commander. As noted earlier the estimated time to promotion at this point would still be one to two years. The individual strengths as well as the (pre)identified development areas can be further processed within a reasonable timeframe to further change and develop the required appropriate skill sets.

At this final step, the flight operations management is asked to highlight their expectations towards the future commanders whilst discussing openly possible challenges as well as strategies to cope with upcoming demanding situations. Again, the peer-centred approach may also be helpful to share concerns as well as curious expectations about the upcoming challenge.

All three steps of this programme should be conducted by a human factors specialist accompanied by an experienced CRM trainer with the same professional background as the participants of this development scheme. It is recommended that the course design features preparatory and accompanying measures as well as a follow-up process at each step of this programme to support the effective implementation and to guarantee valuable individual development.

At the final stage of this three-step programme, the question as to whether co-pilots are ready for promotion should be answered clearly. Actually this question should be best answered by the co-pilots themselves. The guidance by the trainer team, as well as the generated self-initiative to develop towards future left-hand seat, and the feedback given by peers and instructors during the whole process should be seen as a well-balanced approach to promotion.

The alternative approach 'upgrade assessment' commonly used in the industry shortly before the planned promotion to commander seems less effective and is more prone to generate fear and – when failed – lasting frustration amongst the co-pilot community. The latter is especially true when all recurrent checks had been passed beforehand successfully.

### Commander development programme

The third cornerstone aims to support the commanders in their individual development and to foster already achieved personal as well as interpersonal competencies during their pilot career. The same framework and course principles laid out in the co-pilot development programme should be applied. The same is true for the basic principles of a trusting relationship with the course leaders and open atmosphere within the group of participants.

The peer-centred one to two day course design as well the suggested three-step programme might be as advantageous as it is for the co-pilots, especially when these commanders have already experienced this integrated approach in the first part of their career. It is very often forgotten that the time frame of serving as commander is usually longer than the time span as a co-pilot, quite often twice as long or even longer.

The specific individual needs on one side and the operator's demands and requirements towards the commanders on the other side are subject to change during this time span. Whilst the aircraft types stay unchanged over long periods of time, the operational environment and the expectations from the operator towards the commander in regard of how to adapt or to fulfil the commander role and its required competencies may change drastically over time.

The first step of this programme should be implemented one to two years after promotion to commander. Having received a co-pilot development programme and having developed the necessary skills, knowledge and attitudes, it is now time to review the first experiences gained in the left-hand seat. The opportunity to initiate exchange between fellow commanders with the same level of experience may allow for them to talk about experiences – e.g. successfully applied strategies or strategies applied with good intentions but inappropriately realised.

It is widely known that the shift from the right to left seat may in some situations be straightforward even though the upgrade can be very intense and demanding, whereas to develop a healthy sense of identity and self-confidence within the new role takes time. Based on this predictable process the course outline should strengthen and enhance the self-esteem of these pilots. The proposed human factors principles should focus on these aspects and may as well emphasise on how to make best use on all available resources within the crew or elsewhere.

At this stage, an additional need for coaching or additional advice may be identified – by the course lecturers or the affected pilots themselves. Again the course concept should aim to lower the barrier for pilots to request additional advice.

The contact to flight operations management and safety management should be continued to re-emphasise the beneficial and trusting relationship with their new commanders by providing effective guidance and helpful recommendations.

The second step of this programme should take place after five to six years after performing as commander. At this time the pilots have generally reached stable and consistent performance levels. They have gained experience in operating the aircraft efficiently in various demanding situations. All these valuable experiences might be constructively exchanged during the already suggested peer-centred approach.

The pilots have settled down and are well balanced in their new position as commander and are able to lead the crew effectively by applying the achieved competencies and appropriate hierarchy grading. At this stage, realised favourable as well as reoccurring unfavourable behaviour patterns might be worth reflecting on. The course design should suggest human factors principles that help each individual pilot to mirror positive behaviour patterns and support to adapt, change and discover new strategies to lead a crew effectively.

At this level of experience a wish to expand further competencies towards an additional function as instructor or management position might be developed. The motivation to aim for additional expertise and qualifications should be noticed and where appropriate supported. To enhance the insight into flight operations and all related segments within the operator, the exchange with various departments might be well perceived by the pilots. Generating an exchange ranging from ground operations, sales and other departments would strengthen the identification with the company. Further open discussions with management – especially upper management – could be equally beneficial for both sides.

The third step of this programme should take place nine to ten years after serving as commander. Generally the course concept should be designed in the same line as the second step of this programme. Even at this high level of expertise the demand for continuous development might be openly raised by the pilots themselves or the necessity for changing behaviour patterns might be identified – especially those routine patterns which were beneficial in the past may become less effective or even counterproductive. After such a period of time within the airline in the left seat, very often new operational requirements or changing operational environment call for flexible and adaptive capacity. The applied human factors topics should focus on change management principles and emphasise strategies on how to adapt to environmental changes and present or upcoming operational challenges. This should be done without disregarding former successful – but may be outdated – strategies that have been applied. The application of resilience engineering principles may be recognised as a valuable approach.

With the background of highest level of experience and developed expertise the exchange between these commanders and (upper) management may be given particular attention. As subject matter experts these pilots may provide essential information for improving operations or may as well raise valuable questions which have not been considered before. The last step of this programme may be repeated according to the remaining command time span.

All three steps of the commander development programme should be designed similar to the previously presented co-pilot development scheme. The same principles in terms of course instructor expertise should be applied as well as building a professional and confiding atmosphere. Besides the human factors specialist an experienced CRM instructor holding a position as commander should be part of the instructor team. This would facilitate a practical integration and transfer of human factors principles into the course concept.

To enhance the effective and successful implementation of the course concept, accompanying measures and a follow-up programme should be considered.

One essential asset of the overall approach might not be obvious in the first place. Quite often a gap between the pilot community and management results in grave consequences for the pilots (e.g. frustration, anger if not taken seriously) as well as for commercial success (e.g. loss of money due to industrial action). This programme does not intend to avoid these consequences from happening but due to a continuous open exchange and respectful interaction with management, potential conflicts could be identified or mitigated at an early stage.

### Pilot peer-to-peer programme

The fourth cornerstone of this scheme differs from the above-mentioned programmes because of its offer of ongoing support right from the beginning and throughout the pilot's career.

The aim is to provide psycho-social support to pilots by fellow pilots who are carefully selected and trained to provide this challenging assistance. The pilot peer-to-peer programme will not be discussed in detail. The basic principles, a proper design and implementation of such a support is clearly outlined in the first part of this chapter. However at this point it may be added that the possibility to integrate a pilot peer-to-peer programme within an airline operator could be beneficial. The opportunity for concerned pilots to contact fellow pilots who they know personally and who work in the same environment can be seen as an asset. It should also be considered that the possibility for peers to actively contact fellow pilots in need may be considered as an advantage.

As an important prerequisite for proper implementation, the responsibility for oversight of the programme must be led by a competent human factors specialist, preferably by an aviation psychologist with the appropriate background. This person should also be responsible for the training of the peers and should be able to suggest professional advice in case a pilot in need requests referral to a specialist.

As confidentiality is the key element for a peer-to-peer programme it must be fully independent from any kind of management influence. A corresponding company policy covering the whole content of the programme and the guaranteed assurance of confidentiality should be signed by the operator and pilot unions.

## Summary

The following summary on peer-to-peer support and development programmes for pilots will be presented by a SWOT analysis (strengths, weaknesses, opportunities, threats) to emphasise the enablers and barriers of the entire approach.

The strengths of the programmes are presented below and in Figure 20.10.

- Enhance pilot competencies by individualised development programmes
- Enhance safety through psycho-social support (peer to peer)
- Identifying need for 'coaching' support
- Reduce crew absenteeism
- Encourage desirable pilot development as well as identify 'critical' trends
- Bridge the gap between management and pilot community
- F/O ready for captaincy when required
- Cpt. ready for management tasks & crew guidance

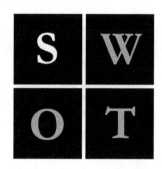

*Figure 20.10* Summary of strengths for pilot support and development programmes

The approach of guiding and supporting pilots throughout their career allows a healthy growth of each individual pilot all the way through his or her career. The offer to contact peers when needed and being sure that any support will be treated confidentially means a substantial asset to the system.

Each of these supporting systems – peer-to-peer support and pilot development programmes – can be implemented independently, whilst an integration of both systems into an airline operator as a 'holistic approach' could even enhance the gain and effectiveness for both parties – the pilot community and the operator. On one hand the personal development will be encouraged, psycho-social support will be guaranteed and on the other hand a return of investment is obvious. Less crew absenteeism has already been discussed in the first part of this chapter. The positive impact on the crew community when recognising that there is professional support when needed and the continuous offer for personal development throughout the career enables a high identification with the company and enables as well the willingness to 'go the extra mile' when the company is in need.

The continuous individual guidance of pilots and close feedback loop enables a smooth transfer of changing the role from co-pilot to commander and by this avoiding tremendous costs for unnecessary – often overstraining and frustrating – training.

The opportunity for an open exchange with the pilot community would allow the management to receive valuable suggestions and questions on operational matters.The greatest contribution in terms of return of investment would be enabled by an open and trusting atmosphere where also critical issues can be addressed. This would allow conflicts to be handled at an early stage and where mitigating strategies can be applied successfully (e.g. in order to avoid cost intensive industrial actions).

The weaknesses of the entire programmes are presented below and in Figure 20.11.

- Investment needed
- Implementation of process is time consuming
- Difficult to prove effectiveness of development schemes/peer support programmes

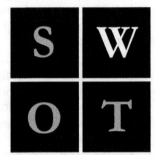

*Figure 20.11* Summary of weaknesses for pilot support and development programmes

Besides highlighting the assets of the holistic approach the system must be reflected critically as well.

An investment in terms of time and money has to be accepted. The programmes have to be developed and realised by a human factors expert or aviation psychologist. Additional ground duty time for pilots and involved instructors has to be calculated as well.

It is difficult to prove the overall programme effectiveness due to its estimated time spans of ten years or even more. To achieve proper results on the programmes' value and efficiency, the tools to analyse the system have to be customised to the different programme parts and time frames.

The opportunities of the entire programmes are listed below and in Figure 20.12.

The EASA recommendations on peer support systems will result in new regulatory requirements. The early anticipation of these recommendations and upcoming regulatory changes will allow a flexible and effective realisation of such programmes (EASA 2015b, 2016a, 2016b).

- Anticipating EASA recommendations
- Positive influence on company (safety) culture and atmosphere
- Support trustful relationship between management & pilot community
- Integration into SMS without compromising confidentiality

*Figure 20.12* Summary of opportunities for pilot support and development programmes

A successful implementation of the suggested programmes would positively influence the company culture and atmosphere and may therefore ensure or even enhance the companies' safety culture.

The main barriers to successful realisation of peer-to-peer and development programmes for pilots can be summarised by few but significant influences as listed in  Figure 20.13.

- Low acceptance by crew community
- Poor concepts/weak realisation of programmes
- No clear commitment by management
- No clear or weak guidance by regulator

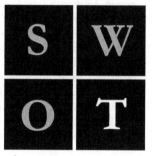

*Figure 20.13* Summary of threats for pilot support and development programmes

An unambiguous expression of continued strong commitment by management is an absolute prerequisite for the long-term success of the programmes.

The willingness by the pilot community to open up to a new approach needs to be supported by convincing strategies of change management.

The expertise of the assigned personnel to design and realise these demanding programmes has to fit to the comprehensive tasks and responsibilities.

A well-developed framework by the regulator accompanied by significant guidance material will facilitate an effective implementation.

To conclude this summary, it should be noted that the evidence of already successful implemented peer support systems (e.g. Stiftung Mayday) for more than two decades may create a good basis to aim for a holistic approach. The integrated implementation of pilot support and development programmes enables positives for both parties – the pilot community and the operator.

## Relevant readings

Everly, G.S. & Mitchell, J.T. (1997). *Critical Incident Stress Management (CISM): A New Era and Standard of Care in Crisis Intervention*. Ellicott City, MD: Chevron.

Everly, G.S. & Mitchell, J.T. (2008). *Integrative Crisis Intervention and Disaster Mental Health*. Ellicott City, MD: Chevron.

Mitchell, J.T. (1983). When disaster strikes… The critical incident stress debriefing. *Journal of Emergency Medical Services*, 13(11), 49–52.

Mitchell, J.T. & Everly, G.S. (1995). *Critical Incident Stress Debriefing, An Operations Manual for the Prevention of Traumatic Stress Among Emergency Services and Disaster Workers*. Ellicott City, MD: Chevron.

## References

CAA (Civil Aviation Authority). (2014). *Flightcrew Human Factors Handbook*, CAP 737. London: CAA.

European Aviation Safety Agency. (2015a). Crew Resource Management (CRM) Training, RMT.0411. Retrieved from https://www.easa.europa.eu/document-library/rulemaking-subjects/crew-resource-management-crm-training (accessed 6 October 2016).

European Aviation Safety Agency. (2015b). *Task Force on Measures Following the Accident of Germanwings Flight 9525 Final Report*. Retrieved from http://ec.europa.eu/transport/modes/air/news/2015-10-20-easa-action-plan_en.htm (accessed 6 October 2016).

European Aviation Safety Agency. (2016a). Pilot Support and Reporting System, Recommendation #6 'Germanwings Task Force'. Preliminary concept paper. Retrieved from: https://www.easa.europa.eu/newsroom-and-events/events/aircrew-medical-fitness-workshop (accessed 6 October 2016).

European Aviation Safety Agency. (2016b). Aircrew Medical Fitness, Rulemaking Task RMT.0700. Retrieved from: https://www.easa.europa.eu/newsroom-and-events/news/aircrew-medical-fitness-rulemaking-task-rmt0700 (accessed 6 October 2016).

# 21 Peer support programme for pilots

*Sean Gibbs*

This chapter examines the topic of peer support. We examine why pilots in particular need this support, and how it can be implemented. We also assess the elements that make up an effective peer support programme (PSP) and outline the main features of a PSP that is about to be rolled out in the UK.

## Why the need for peer support?

> Pilots, like other professionals, are susceptible to the effects of stress or negative personal situations and may sometimes be hesitant to seek help and support for a number of reasons. The obvious stressors include the work environment, psychosocial hazards such as fatigue and workplace or private problems, time pressure and stress sources all adults must deal with. This combination of factors may lead to temporary mental health issues or, if not recognised and treated, possible permanent issues.
>
> (EASA, 2015: 15)

Peer support may be defined as 'offering and receiving help, based on shared understanding, respect and mutual empowerment, between people in similar situations' (Mead *et al.*, 2001). Peers help peers by providing knowledge and experience, both emotional and practical, in order to support each other and a peer is in a position to offer this support by virtue of their relevant and shared experience. Relationships between peers are built around a mutual understanding and trust, not on the basis of power differentials. An effective peer support structure provides a mechanism whereby employees can seek help either for themselves or for their colleagues without having to approach management.

By their very nature, welfare issues tend to be highly personal and sensitive. Employees often feel uncomfortable raising such issues with managers, who rarely have the time, training or skills to be able to deal with them properly. Trained peers who are easily accessible, understand the work culture and are able to offer confidential support in a variety of circumstances, providing a vital additional (or alternative) avenue for employees to get help, crucially in what is perceived as a 'safe' way. Peer supporters are normally highly valued by colleagues because most are more comfortable discussing issues and feelings with somebody who can relate directly to their situation, rather than someone in authority.

Employees working alongside each other are best placed to notice subtle changes in a colleague's behaviour or demeanour. At the same time, it is often difficult for an employee to approach management if they notice such changes in a fellow employee. For example, if an employee is concerned that their colleague is misusing alcohol or drugs, the fear of betraying a colleague by raising concerns with management tends to prevent issues being raised, thus allowing those issues to continue and deepen. The irony is that by allowing the issues to continue, there is a greater likelihood of resulting employment problems, such as disciplinary action, absenteeism or poor performance.

An effective PSP should address psychological issues before they have deepened into seriously problematic behavioural patterns. Arguably, early intervention and support in a highly confidential structure is far more likely to lead to a successful resolution of an employee's issues than a system that relies on management detecting emotional and relationship problems. Early intervention and support is likely to be beneficial in any workplace environment, but in the case of pilots, cabin crew and engineers – those professions directly associated with flight safety – the implications are crucial.

## The wider benefits of peer support

Despite the relatively limited research into the effectiveness of peer support, the studies that have been published paint a positive picture of the benefits. A literature review of peer support commissioned by Together and the University of Nottingham (Repper and Carter, 2010) found that support provided by peer workers can promote hope and belief, empowerment and increased self-esteem, self-efficacy and self-management of difficulties, as well as providing greater social inclusion and engagement. Repper and Carter also found that employment as a peer support worker almost universally brings benefits for the peer support workers themselves.

Recently, there has been an increasing realisation of the value of peer support in the UK's National Health Service, particularly within the mental health sector. Peer support is mentioned in the mental health outcomes strategy 'No health without mental health' (Department of Health, 2011) as one way in which local voluntary groups can support 'people to manage their own mental health better in the community'. In addition, the Department of Health, in the related implementation framework, recommends peer support as one of the roles of mental health organisations in supporting delivery of the strategy (Department of Health, 2011).

A successful workplace PSP should be a powerful tool for safeguarding mental health in the workplace, and is likely to have a positive impact on peers, peer supporters and the workplace culture. Peer support can improve employee engagement, and enable the peer to feel valued and appreciated. It can also provide a positive impact on the organisation's financial bottom-line by reducing sickness and providing a greater understanding of the issues that affect crews and the demands placed on them. Another key benefit is to enable a greater sense of normalisation around mental health issues, rather than stigma and isolation.

EASA (2015: 16) provides a neat summary of the wider benefits of PSP:

> Peer support structures provide individuals a place to turn to in order to share their issues with trusted peers in as close to a non-threatening environment as possible, with the knowledge that fellow pilots are likely to help rather than immediately seek to penalise a colleague. The structures also enable organisations to more easily approach individuals that display behavioural or other issues via their peers. As a last resort, reporting systems may be used in case of identified unresolved perceived safety issues. A well-organised support system may prevent mental or personal issues from becoming a greater liability to both the individual's career and the organisation's safety performance.

## Brief history of peer support in the airline industry

In the USA in the 1970s, a medical research project called HIMS (Human Intervention Motivation Study) was spearheaded by the Air Line Pilots Association (ALPA), a labour union, and funded by the National Institute for Alcohol Abuse and Alcoholism (NIAAA), a federal agency. The research project was designed to test a programme for dealing with the presence of alcoholism in the airline pilot population. The justifications given for developing a pilot-specific model were that the commercial aviation environment does not lend itself to a traditional on-the-job supervisory programme, and that a recovering pilot's ability to function effectively is best observed by fellow pilots.

Accordingly, a peer identification and referral system was established to underpin a pilot-centred, confidential and participatory programme. Given the sensitive nature of a pilot's responsibilities and the interrelationship between medical and technical performance standards, it was apparent that involvement of the airline, the Federal Aviation Administration, and peer pilots was essential to the success of the programme. Since its inception, over 4,500 professional pilots have been successfully rehabilitated and returned to their careers.

Peer support has also been an integral part of some US airlines' response to critical incidents for many decades. In the early 1980s, a few airlines started to initiate crisis intervention programmes and sent key airline personnel for crisis intervention and stress management training. ALPA became involved in developing crisis support programmes for its members in the early 1990s. Captains Alan Campbell, Robert Sumwalt and Mimi Tompkins researched and developed the original concept of a Critical Incident Response Program (CIRP) on behalf of ALPA.

The purpose of CIRPs was to mitigate the psychological impact of an incident or accident and aid in the normal recovery from these events before harmful stress reactions affect job performance, careers, families, and health. The CIRP provides pre-incident education and post-incident or accident crisis intervention services to ALPA members involved in critical incidents and accidents. Peer support volunteers (PSVs), who are line pilots, are trained and certified to provide support in critical incident stress management. ALPA formally implemented this programme in 1994 to improve flight safety by assisting crew members, accident investigators, and their families following a critical incident or accident (ALPA, 2012).

With these programmes, ALPA took a lead role in reducing the stigma and negativity surrounding the issues of pilots' mental health. Peer support was, and still is, a vital and well-recognised part of an overall support package for crew. The HIMS study demonstrated that intervention that includes peer support can be instrumental in helping to return pilots to work. With CIRPs, what began as a response to a critical incident developed into a service that offers pilot-to-pilot peer support for meeting a pilot's unique needs. These include stress related to job security, financial pressures, demotion from left to right seat, relocation to new bases, increased security, annual simulator checks and commuting. Recently, ALPA added family support and a new grief programme in response to 9/11.

In the UK in 1983, the British Airways (BA) director, Nick Georgeoduous, became aware of the lack of support for cabin crew in BA after the suicide of two crew members. In 1985, Gerard Egan was invited to work with a core group of counsellors. BA's human resources team began a training programme for its cabin crew members which, over the years, evolved into 'Crew Care'. The service, initially run by cabin crew members, focused on providing counselling to other cabin crew. After some years, the counselling provision was put out to tender and the Independent Counselling and Advisory Service (ICAS) won the contract for the entire BA workforce.

Crew Care survived, and today offers effective and immediate crisis counselling for cabin crew as its main focus. This takes the form of a single session with a trained counsellor. The main success of the service is the integration of cabin crew into the crisis counsellor role. Feedback from service users indicates a preference for cabin crew to talk to other cabin crew, reinforcing 'the shared experience' as being integral to the support role. In this unique community, the value of shared experience is magnified. As Coles (2003: 17–18) observes:

> Crew Care... seems to contain most of the elements required for the establishment of an internal counselling system. An initial human crisis, an awareness of contemporary therapeutic practices and human resources practice and a willingness within the leadership of the organisation to assist the workforce and working community.

Within the UK, Crew Care has gone some way to making this support more generally accessible to BA cabin crew, to help cope with major incidents and the everyday stresses of a highly demanding job. The success of Crew Care is probably due to the fact that it evolved from a genuine need from within the flying community but it is interesting to observe that this service is offered only to cabin crew and not to pilots. At the time it was cabin crew who asked for this service and who embraced the idea that it was 'OK' to ask for help. But what of the pilot community, was their need for this support not just as great? The answer of course is 'yes', but by their very nature pilots tend to be solution focused and have a 'can do' mentality. A problem in the flight deck be it technical or some other safety-related issue has to be dealt with methodically, and check lists and standard operating procedures are there to guide them. Whilst they would be happy to seek help and advice from their flight operations department or maintenance department when in the flight deck, in their personal lives when it comes to issues surrounding their mental health most would be far more reluctant.

As we will see, BALPA in conjunction with a major UK airline have begun to address this lack of pilot support with a new Welfare Intervention Programme (WIP) specifically designed for its pilot community.

In Germany in 1994, Stiftung Mayday set up a non-governmental organisation in response to an aircraft accident at the ILA Berlin Airshow. Its primary function was two-fold: first, to care for all flight crew after aviation-related critical incidents or accidents and second, to provide support to licence holders and their next of kin in times of need. How the programme operates and the way in which it is structured is dealt with in Chapter 20. However it is interesting to note that whilst many of the core structures and defined requirements for a functioning PSP laid out under the German system are echoed in this chapter, there are some interesting differences to that of the proposed BALPA WIP.

The main difference is that the German approach is an industry-wide service mainly concentrated on operators in Germany but occasionally dealing with international cases also; whilst the proposed BALPA approach, as we shall see later in this chapter, is airline-specific. Undoubtedly both approaches will have merit. The German approach will have the benefit, amongst others, of keeping operating costs down and therefore enabling smaller airlines to benefit from the service, some of whom would not be able to implement a programme of their own. However there is no doubt that, for the larger airlines, having control over their own programme will allow them to tailor their programme to suit their requirements. It remains to be seen how this approach will stand up against the more-established German approach.

## Pilot welfare and management

Airline pilots and cabin crew find themselves under growing pressures at work. Commercial pressures are leading to longer multi-sector days and shorter turn-arounds. Report times are getting earlier and finish times later, and crews are often expected to move from early duties to late duties from one block of work to the next, thereby disrupting sleep patterns and leading to fatigue.

According to the British Air Line Pilots' Association (BALPA, 2014), fatigue is becoming an ever-increasing threat to aviation safety and pilots' mental health. A recent ComRes poll of pilots commissioned by BALPA found that 47 per cent of respondents reported fatigue as the single biggest threat to aviation safety and that 88 per cent have had their abilities compromised by fatigue in the previous six months (BALPA, 2014). The principal characteristics of fatigue are that it mostly acts covertly and increases the risk of nearly all types of error.

> Although fatigue has been the focus of a substantial amount of research, it generally remains an elusive concept to grasp. However, one of the most consistent findings in research on fatigue has been the strong relationship it has with common psychiatric symptoms, and depression in particular.
>
> (Leone, 2010: 86)

Very few airlines offer regular appraisals or one-to-one supervision, other than perhaps in the flight simulator. However the simulator is very much a training environment where skills are being tested and practised, and not a forum for raising personal concerns. Simulator trainers are not trained to evaluate or indeed support other pilots in this way.

At present, in many organisations, a pilot manager usually only becomes aware of a colleague's personal problems if that person has the resources to ask for help or their behaviour or performance has significantly deteriorated. At that point, performance management protocols are followed and disciplinary measures taken. This, however, does not always address the underlying causes of the problem. Such formal actions may not always be necessary if the issues are highlighted and addressed earlier.

Unfortunately, managers are often the last to know that a member of their team is in crisis. In addition, as already mentioned, pilots, by their nature, find it hard to ask for help and many would rather hide problems than share them with a colleague. They may be willing to discuss a physical problem such as a broken wrist, but are far less likely to discuss or disclose a situation that involves their mental health. They are more likely to be embarrassed, fearing negative reactions and repercussions, believing mental illness to be a sign of weakness. A vicious circle may develop between the need for help and the fear of losing their medical certificate which then contributes further to their stress. On the other side of the desk, many managers are for more comfortable dealing with colleagues who have a broken wrist, and far less comfortable, or able to deal, with those who are suffering from depression, panic attacks, addiction and other mental health issues.

In promoting peer support, EASA (2015: 16) points out that the cockpit of an aircraft creates a natural environment to promote pilot relationships with peers:

> Pilots work as part of a crew where they interact with other pilots as part of their daily duties. Most of this time is spent in the cockpit of an aircraft, by definition a closed space where close human interaction is present. The fact that the work is very proceduralised, with checklists, call outs and structured

decision-making, can allow for the recognition of issues. Pilot relationships with peers are easily formed and this often permits an understanding and insight that others in the organisation do not have access to. A number of organisations have been able to make use of this by setting up peer support groups, usually with the involvement of crew representation bodies or professional pilot associations.

Whilst this 'understanding and insight' might be valid for the majority of crews it could also be argued that the cockpit environment is so proceduralised that the task-focused nature of the job can allow for personal issues to remain hidden behind standard operating procedures and checklists. Also pilots can suffer from a lack of engagement and isolation. Due to the nature of the job, in which crews tends to fly with different colleagues every day, it can be a solitary existence and hard to build up lasting and meaningful relationships within the work environment on a day-to-day basis. This is compounded by shift work and roster patterns, which can also hinder relationships with peers outside of the work environment. Consequently, it can be quite easy for a pilot to hide a mental health issue if it has not reached the stage where the pilot's immediate performance is affected on the flight deck.

So we have seen that the combination of commercial pressures, longer working hours, a solitary lifestyle, together with a sometimes less than adequate man-management support structure and a reluctance on the part of pilots to ask for help can, at times, lead to temporary mental health issues that, if left unmonitored, can become permanent.

## Recent drivers for peer support programmes

In the UK, the Railways and Transportation Safety Act 2003 deemed that safety-critical workers, including pilots, who are found to have residual drugs or alcohol in their systems whilst at work are liable to prosecution. Offenders can be subject to a fine of up to £5,000 and six months in prison. Termination of employment almost always follows. A failure to stop all drug or alcohol misuse could have serious consequences for safety and any airline seen to be negligent would attract negative publicity. It is clear, therefore, that in the aviation industry, the stakes have risen dramatically for failing to address drugs and alcohol misuse.

The Germanwings (Flight 9525) incident in March 2015 tragically added mental health to the list of welfare issues that can have major consequences if not addressed. Flight safety should benefit if PSPs can identify individuals who are suffering with psychological and emotional problems. Widening the net to identify those who have problems much earlier than at present, and making it as straightforward as possible to report concerns and get them addressed swiftly, can only have a significantly beneficial impact on flight safety. For these reasons, as we have seen, the European Aviation Safety Agency (EASA) is taking a keen interest in the subject. In its final report in response to the Germanwings incident, EASA made a number of recommendations.

Recommendation 6: The Task Force recommends the implementation of pilot support and reporting systems, linked to the employer Safety Management System within the framework of a non-punitive work environment and without compromising Just Culture principles.

## The essential features of a peer support programme

In this section we will examine how a pilot support and reporting system might be structured in the form of a peer support programme and look at the key elements that need to be considered in setting up such a programme.

Ideally, a PSP should contain the following key elements:

1   a clear framework within the corporate structure;
2   an easy method of raising concerns;
3   use of an independent healthcare provider;
4   use of a team of peer supporters;
5   a monitoring group;
6   close cooperation between operator and pilot association;
7   a mixture of proactive and reactive support for pilots;
8   the highest degree of confidentiality;
9   active promotion of the programme by both the airline and the pilot association.

### Framework within the corporate structure

Operation of a PSP would need to be part of company policy, supported at board level, and with top-level management endorsement and engagement from the outset. The PSP would fall under the remit of one of the directors (typically the HR director). The programme would need to be integrated into the company quality and management system, typically within the safety management system, and terms of reference would be needed for a PSP steering committee or monitoring group. The airline would own the programme, and employees acting under the programme (e.g. peer supporters) would do so in their capacity as airline employees.

### An easy method of raising concerns

It is important to establish how the programme is accessed by pilots. Due to the nature of the job and the transient life of crew, the main means of reporting concerns and communication would be by telephone. Modern technologies, such as video calls or mobile device apps could also be used for reporting purposes, though it remains to be seen whether employees would feel comfortable reporting concerns about a colleague's behaviour via an app. A single telephone number would be published, administered by the independent healthcare provider (see below). All contact would be logged and details of the reporter taken. Anonymous reports should be rejected, as further contact will be required to acquire more details in order to make an effective intervention. Confidentiality, however, should be assured to the reporter that their name will never be revealed to anyone except the peer supporter, and certainly not to the pilot being reported.

Use of the telephone throughout the process is an interesting area. Whilst ideally, any intervention is best done face-to-face, the peculiar displaced nature of the pilot workforce means that this is practically very difficult. However, communication by telephone does offer some distinct advantages as the reporter may feel more able to divulge details of their concern over the phone rather than face-to-face. Telephone support offers easy access, convenience and flexibility, and also enables a 24-hour service to be delivered in a cost-effective manner.

### Use of an independent healthcare provider

How best to deal with medical information (i.e. welfare-related) that might have an impact on flight safety is a difficult issue. A balance must be struck between acting on every report, however trivial and malicious, and not acting on a single report and then that pilot having an incident. The former has the potential to discredit the whole programme, while the latter has serious legal implications. Experience has shown that for management to hold the reports leads them towards caution investigating them, which in turn leads to the reports drying up and the programme becoming ineffective. Equally, whilst the pilot associations are trusted to hold this information, it is legally almost impossible for them to be the data controller.

Using an independent healthcare organisation (IHO) – if the airline is large enough – or the company occupational health provider – if it is not – that has expertise in this area goes a long way to mitigating this problem. In practice, the IHO/occupational healthcare provider is best placed to make that careful assessment of the potential legal risks of confidentiality versus being in possession of information pertaining to flight safety yet not acting on it. The contract with the airline should be clear about legal responsibility for data control.

The use of an IHO provides a clear firewall between the programme and management, which is vital for creating trust in the programme among the workforce. The IHO effectively runs the PSP: logging and assessing the reports, determining if an intervention is required, activating a peer supporter to make that intervention, and acting as a final arbiter (in conjunction with the company doctor). If the intervention is unsuccessful then the IHO decides whether to remove the pilot from the roster and call them themselves. In addition, they manage and mentor the peer supporters and sit on the monitoring group which has oversight of the whole process (see below).

### Use of a team of peer supporters

The core element of any PSP is a team of peer supporters: recruited from the pilot community, varing in age and experience and who do not hold a managerial or union representative role. When activated by the IHO, their job is to either respond to the pilot who has asked for support or to investigate the reported individual by calling the reporters and finding out more about the concerns. Then, at the start of a block of days off for the reported pilot, they make the intervention call to ascertain if there is a problem or not. This may require multiple calls over some days to work through the shock/anger/rejection cycle, which the reported pilot is likely to exhibit.

If the reported pilot does agree that there is an issue, the peer supporter guides the pilot through the process of self-referring into existing company policies, where they will receive appropriate support. If the pilot does not co-operate with the peer supporter and the latter is not satisfied that a reasonable explanation for the reports has been given, they will refer the case back to the IHO.

Peer supporters will need to have a number of qualities, specifically empathy, compassion and excellent listening skills. Other qualities should include: good communication, non-judgemental attitude, easily approachable, respected, trusted by others and discreet. They should also have a thick skin to cope with the varied reactions of the reported pilot in the initial intervention call, and be able to spot the difference between a denial and a genuine explanation.

Training is critical and should be offered either off-site by a training organisation or in-house by the IHO. The training should include:

- mental health issues most relevant to pilots and early warning signs of identifying a colleague in distress;
- how to make the intervention call/advanced listening skills;
- the importance of confidentiality and when or how to refer a peer on to a mental health professional and/or company processes if the pilot cooperates;
- how to deal with special challenges, including critical incidents;
- resources available to support a pilot with issues;
- how to support and care for themselves.

Ongoing continuing professional development should be facilitated by the airline in the form of time off for a quarterly meeting organised and run by the IHO, where cases are shared and best practice identified. A lead peer supporter should be identified who will prepare a report for the monitoring group on trends, workload, areas which might require further training and so on. The responsibility placed on peer supporters is significant and they would need to be indemnified by the company to mitigate any concerns of being held liable if any mistakes were made. There should be a selection process run by the monitoring group and time given as part of their rostered duties for PSP work.

## Monitoring group

A monitoring group should be established to have oversight of the entire programme. It should be made up of the company doctor, representatives from the IHO, the pilot association (in the UK, BALPA) and flight ops. The committee would meet regularly to consider the anonymous data from the programme provided by the IHO, as well as the reports from the peer supporters, and review any emerging trends or issues. They will make recommendations as appropriate regarding the promotion of the wellbeing of pilots within flight ops, which would then be passed on to the company for consideration. They will also consider the workload and skill set of the peer supporters, and facilitate further recruitment and training as necessary.

## Close co-operation between operator and pilot association

It is interesting to note that EASA recommends that PSPs should be joint initiatives between the airline and the relevant pilot association. This is a recognition that the success or failure of a PSP within an airline will depend on the workforce's trust in the programme. Management-only initiatives in this area are often viewed with suspicion, and therefore it is vital that the pilot association is involved in the creation, promotion and monitoring of the PSP to ensure the maximum possible trust in the programme and the workforce's participation in it. Yet the pilot association can have no role in the day-to-day management of the programme, and in this regard it holds a similar function to Flight Ops management. The BALPA PSP (see below) has been created as a stand-alone programme within the airline concerned and has been branded and marketed as such by both BALPA and their Flight Ops Department. Both groups' only involvement is in the oversight role of the monitoring group, although if an individual member reported into the programme requests BALPA support, then that is freely available at that level.

## Reactive or proactive peer support

Reactive support is when a pilot or cabin crew member chooses to seek support from or 'reach out' to a peer supporter. Proactive support is when a colleague or peer supporter notices a change or deterioration in a colleague's performance or behaviour and provides early intervention. This is another key area to get right. If the PSP is to have a proactive component, then any perception by the crew that they are being monitored and their privacy invaded by the programme is to be avoided as it would clearly become counterproductive. Similarly, if support is offered and refused by the crew member, clear guidelines need to be established on a course of action to take, namely referral back to the IHO.

## Confidentiality

Stressing the confidentiality of the programme is key to ensuring trust. A peer needs to be seen as somebody who can be trusted and who has the interest of the pilot as his or her priority. If they are seen as potential punishers this could jeopardise the success of the programme. Whilst a peer supporter is not a clinical function, the nature of the relationship with the reported pilot means that they must respect confidentiality and only breach this trust if they feel the safety of the individual and/or passengers are at risk. This is in line with General Medical Council principles. There must be a clear path for peer supporters to follow when passing the reported pilot on to professional services. The role of the IHO in offering advice to peer supporters is crucial here. Pilots must feel comfortable and 'safe' discussing issues with their peer supporter.

However, EASA (2015: 16) advises that implementing a PSP is not without its problems:

> Peer support and reporting systems ... present significant implementation challenges. For these programmes to work, mutual trust between the flight crews and hierarchical structures of the operator is necessary. The crew needs to be assured that mental health issues will not be stigmatised, concerns raised will be handled confidentially and appropriately, and that the pilot will be well-supported with the primary aim to allow him/her to return to the flight deck. Organisations must foster the development of these systems by integrating them into the organisation's daily way of working. In any future environment where mental ill-health awareness is formalised, the bond of mutual trust and cooperation should not be compromised through an atmosphere of fear. The successful implementation of pilot support systems relies heavily on a supportive working environment. The risk of protection and confidentiality being perceived as inadequate is for pilots to deal with issues underground instead of using the peer support system.

At all times, maintaining the 'bubble' of confidentiality between the peer supporter and the reported pilot, subject to the conditions described above, is paramount to keeping the trust in the programme by the workforce and thus to its success. However, there is the issue of the responsibility resting on the peer supporter when to 'raise the flag' with a peer who is not cooperating with the intervention, whilst respecting confidentiality. In an effective PSP, if the peer supporter has concerns about the pilot they are helping, they will report the fact that they are concerned back to the IHO and recommend that the pilot is removed from the roster for further investigation. No details of the conversations the peer supporter had with the pilot should be passed back, as those are medically confidential. This is why the intervention should be made during a period of days off from the flying roster, namely to prevent the possibility, albeit a highly remote one, of an incident happening during the course of an intervention.

### *Promoting a PSP within the airline*

Communicating the programme to pilots is key, as is reducing the stigma of seeking help when needed. Active promotion of the benefits of the programme – by both flight ops and the pilot association – is vital, and the level of participation in the programme should be regularly assessed by the monitoring group. Further promotion should be initiated as appropriate. Pilots must be convinced that the programme is a method of getting help for either themselves or for a colleague, rather than 'shopping' them. A dialogue needs to be established that begins to break down the stigma associated with mental health issues, and if the airline has initiatives in areas such as wellbeing, there should be links between the various programmes to raise the general level of awareness of mental health issues amongst the workforce, with the emphasis that through the PSP there is a mechanism to seek help, either for oneself or for a colleague, in a 'safe' fashion.

To establish a successful PSP requires a gradual, participative approach to fostering the trust of employees. There needs to be a significant degree of employee participation from the start and certain factors need to be considered. At the onset, pilots and cabin crew need to be informed about the programme and invited to offer their input, opinions and concerns. This process should enhance the employee's perception that the airline is engaged and willing to help them. Also, it should set the foundation of trust and promote a climate in which employees feel safe to later apply to become a peer supporter themselves.

## BALPA: A model PSP

As previously mentioned, a new Welfare Intervention Programme (WIP) has been devised under the direction of the British Airline Pilots' Association (BALPA) and a major UK airline. The programme, the first of its kind in the UK, embodies the principles laid out above. It is in the early stages of implementation but the early indications are that there is a need for such a programme as a number of pilots have already been helped by the process.

The programme states that an independent healthcare organisation (IHO), specialising in the field, will be appointed by the airline and will run the WIP. Peer support advisors (PSAs) are being recruited and trained under the guidance of the IHO, selected by a panel consisting of the IHO, the chief pilot and a senior BALPA representative. The airline in question is large enough to have its own health services (BAHS), and a representative from HS sits on the monitoring group and also forms part of the medical panel that determines the course of action should an intervention be unsuccessful. HS has the ability to remove a pilot from the roster whilst maintaining medical confidentiality from the flight operations department, and can request that the pilot attends for interview and assessment. The monitoring group consists of two flight operations representatives, and one each from BALPA, HS and the IHO.

Under the BALPA Welfare Intervention Programme, there will be two clear and separate processes.

### The peer support process

Pilots seeking personal support will be able to make contact online or by telephone with the IHO. All contacts will be logged and recorded in a dedicated and confidential system to which management have no access. Details would then be passed onto a PSA, who would contact the individual. This is effectively self-referral into company support processes where the pilot is wary of approaching management directly.

### The peer intervention process

When a pilot reports another pilot with concerns regarding their mental health, they will again contact the IHO either online or by telephone. Again, these contacts will be logged and recorded. Under the WIP, a traffic light system will be used. Single uncorroborated reports (green) will be retained on the database, but no action will be taken unless the IHO deems that report serious enough to warrant intervention. Such an example would be the partner of a pilot reporting that the pilot has a long-standing alcohol problem and has tried and failed over the years to get them address it, and it is getting worse. Multiple green reports result in a change of status to amber, which requires an intervention. The decision of when to intervene will be made on a case-by-case basis by the IHO. Red reports are time-critical reports and will trigger an automatic intervention, albeit under a separate process outwith the WIP because it is operationally critical.

When an amber intervention is required, the IHO will contact a PSA, who will be assigned to take on the case and intervene as described above. Confidentiality is assured at all stages (with the provisos surrounding personal safety) and the pilot is urged to work with the PSA to resolve any issues they might have. The emphasis is that if they do so, then the pilot retains control of the agenda, in that they are self-referring and choosing to come off the roster rather than being removed from it. Note that in both cases, however, medical confidentiality is retained and all flight ops know is that HS has requested the pilot to be removed from the roster for medical reasons.

This BALPA Welfare Intervention Programme's main objective is to establish an independent and confidential programme to promote the mental wellbeing for this particular airline's air crew; it is hoped that if successful, other airlines will initiate similar programmes in the future.

## Summary

The available evidence indicates that PSPs can provide numerous benefits, not least in helping to reduce the stigma and negativity surrounding the issue of mental health. Such programmes can be a powerful tool for safeguarding mental health in the workplace and are likely to have a positive impact on peers, peer supporters and the workplace culture.

The success of programmes such as HIMS and CIRPs in the USA, and BA's Crew Care in the UK, demonstrate that interventions which include peer support are effective in helping to return pilots and cabin crew to work. Arguably, early intervention, and offering an initial point of reference for pilots concerned about either their own mental health or that of colleagues, are key to preventing mental health or personal issues from becoming a greater liability to both the individual's career and wellbeing, as well as to the organisation's safety performance.

BALPA, by recognising the value of investing in protecting pilots' mental health, have taken a lead role in the UK by introducing a WIP in conjunction with a major UK airline, that has at its core the values of peer-to-peer support. In the light of EASA's recommendations following the Germanwings incident, which call for the implementation of pilot support and reporting systems among other things, airlines will no doubt be looking closely at the success of BALPA's WIP. It is to be hoped that further research into the benefits of BALPA's investment in its WIP will convince other airlines to set up similar programmes across the industry.

## Acknowledgement

I would like to thank Captain Dave Fielding (BALPA) for his valued comments and suggestions, which proved so helpful in finalising the content of this chapter and also for his contribution in detailing the Welfare Intervention Programme devised by himself and BALPA, from which we have quoted with kind permission of BALPA.

## References

ALPA (Air Line Pilots Association) (2012). *Critical Incident Response Program Guide*. www. arwalpa.org/wp-content/uploads/2015/12/ALPA-CIRP-Guide-Faccess. Accessed 23 August 2016.

BALPA (British Air Line Pilots' Association) (2014). *The Safety Plan 2014–16*. Retrieved from www.balpa.org/My-Airline/Airlines/Balpa/Document-library/Flight-Safety/ BALPA-Safety-Plan-2014-07-14.aspx (accessed 18 April 2016).

Coles, A. (2003). *Counselling in the Workplace*. Maidenhead: Open University Press.

Department of Health (2011). *No Health Without Mental Health: A Cross-government Mental Health Outcomes Strategy for People of All Ages*. London: Department of Health.

EASA (European Aviation Safety Agency) (2015). *Task Force on Measures Following the Accident of Germanwings Flight 9525. Final Report*. Retrieved from http://ec.europa.eu/ transport/modes/air/news/doc/2015-07-17-germanwings-report/germanwings-task- force-final-report.pdf (accessed 5 September 2016).

Leone, S.S. (2010). A disabling combination: fatigue and depression. *The British Journal of Psychiatry*, 197(2), 86–87.

Mead, S, Hilton, D. & Curtis, L. (2001). Peer support: a theoretical perspective. *Psychiatric Rehabilitation Journal*, 25(2), 134–141.

Repper, J. & Carter, T. (2010). *Using Personal Experience to Support Others with Similar Difficulties: A Review of the Literature on Peer Support in Mental Health Services*. London: Together/University of Nottingham/NSUN.

# 22 Pilots' emotions in the cockpit

Vergard Nergård and Bengt Svendsen

How do pilots learn from experience through post-flight debriefing? As a case study of pilots flying air ambulances, this chapter examines the importance of learning from direct experience rather than from instruction, study, etc. In this chapter, we report on a study that we carried out which focused on how pilots 'work through' or 'emotionally process' their professional experiences. Our study examined how a pilot of an air ambulance processes difficult and conflicted emotions. We argue that the evolvement of good airmanship in general and in air ambulance operations, in particular, is intimately related to the ability to learn to cope with emotions.

An air ambulance is an aircraft used for emergency medical assistance in situations where a car ambulance cannot reach the scene easily or quickly enough. The aircraft are equipped with medical equipment that enables the crew to provide intensive treatment to a critically injured or ill patient. An air ambulance operation carries medical staff. Pilots who operate ambulance aircraft are part of the medical operation, and the medical staff is part of the flight crew. On the ground, pilots assist the onboard medical staff in boarding and offloading patients and relatives.

Air ambulance pilots are highly trained and well-experienced in operating their aircraft. The conditions they face are usually more challenging than regular non-emergency flights. Flight conditions are often extreme, and so pilots must simultaneously focus on operational tasks as well as demonstrating competence to others. Pilots must deal with emotions that are evoked through their close interaction with the patients and medical staff in the cabin.

Although operative debriefs have a formal structure and strong focus towards quality improvement and performance at work, we claim the debrief plays an active role helping pilots and crewmembers with their everyday social interaction and managing their feelings. We focused our study on a pilot's experiential learning as conceptualised by Bion (1962) and in particular we explore the following question: What is the role of the post-flight debriefing?

# How do pilots' deal with strong emotions?

Stress is a well-known phenomenon in aviation. To fly and operate an aircraft can be extremely stressful due to the workload, responsibilities and safety of passengers. Pilots experience stress in flights, on the ground during work-related activities, and during personal time (Bond & Flaxman, 2006). Nevertheless, there are few studies on the long-term effects of stress and emotional challenges on pilots. The reason may be that pilots are assumed to be well able to cope with their own mental health and wellbeing. In several studies, pilots score very low on the neuroticism scale, meaning they are not anxious and are calm (Ursano, 1980; Rose, 2001; Fitzgibbons, Davis & Schutte, 2004). Low neuroticism reflects a low dispositional tendency to experience negative emotions. Nevertheless, in situations that are clearly threatening, pilots also experience stress and anxiety. Pilots are so well trained that when a problem emerges (for example engine fire), they have learned through training and experience the correct procedure, so that they normally can do the right thing, despite arousal of anxiety. Most pilots are confident in their ability to handle a difficult situation, which is a critical trait for pilots to have, especially during an emergency.

Pilots must regulate their emotions because safe flight operations require high levels of rational thinking and unbiased processing of large amounts of data. Pilots and crewmembers must have the ability to maintain very high levels of situational awareness while operating and monitoring complex systems even with the autopilot engaged. The pilots and flight crew must create safety in every flight through their practice (Decker, 2006; Antonsen, Almklov & Fenstad, 2008). Pilots must manage the workload connected with the individual tasks in the flight operation. Alongside ideally being cooperative, communicative, assertively empathetic and emotionally stable, they must also be able to engage in interactions in a hierarchical environment. In sum, pilots must maintain a mental state in which their emotions do not negatively affect flight safety. In addition, they must create and, at all times, potentially reconsider their mental picture of the flight and its progress. Simultaneously, the crew must plan ahead to avoid or mitigate hazardous situations (Cannon-Bowers & Orasanu, 1993).

A pilot is expected to keep control over his or her emotions and not lose composure, and be even-tempered and stable. While this might be an unachievable ideal, there are limits to emotions a pilot can allow himself or herself to articulate towards other pilots, crewmembers and passengers during a flight. No one has explicitly instructed him or her on the importance of this emotional control, but it is an integral part of being a good pilot and found to be a key factor in good 'airmanship' (Nergård, 2014). The ideal of airmanship can be understood as a cultural 'dictionary' for professional conduct. According to these ideals, pilots are encouraged and expected to be self-aware, and critically reflect on and evaluate their own performance in order to seek continuous improvement. Such critical self-evaluation can be emotionally taxing. Nevertheless, pilots have little formal training in how to appropriately deal with and express emotion on the flight deck including how to deal appropriately with emotions (Nergård, 2014). The post operative debrief may serve an important role in the construction and dissemination of the professional ideals, and more importantly, holds the potential to provide a context where pilots can develop the emotional competence required to manage emotions effectively in the cockpit.

## Method

We present a pilot's story about a time where a patient died during the flight. We analyse the narrative from a psychoanalytical perspective and emphasise the continuous psychological work necessary for a pilot to accommodate in an air ambulance flight operation.

The story is the pilot's retrospective reconstruction of the flight. Using narratives is methodologically challenging, from both a validity and reliability point of view. Nevertheless, the story is interesting because it illustrates how the post-flight debriefings construct individual and collective emotional experiences. We present the case study in a narrative reconstructional form also because this illustrates the pilot's personal development. The purpose of the narrative is not to analyse the pilot as a person, but rather gain an understanding of the emotional coping processes among pilots (Fonagy *et al.*, 2002).

### The day the patient died in the cabin

The case is about a senior captain, 43 years old, 12,000 hours total flight hours, ten years' experience in the air ambulance service. He worked for a Scandinavian air ambulance operator.

> It started out as an ordinary ambulance flight around ten o'clock in the evening. The weather at the destination was below the minimum, so our coordination centre decided to take the patient by car or fly to another hospital. After a few minutes, the plan was again altered when they called back with a revised plan to fly the patient to another hospital.
>
> Just as we were to depart, the local emergency office called us up again and informed us that they had just received information about a second patient they wanted us to bring to the same hospital. Our flight nurse was negative about this second patient as she considered his medical condition to be too severe to be flown together with the first one. After some discussion and a little pressure, she accepted the idea of having two patients onboard this flight. When the second patient was delivered to us, the accompanying doctor perceived the patient's medical condition to be so poor that he decided to go along as a precaution.
>
> The take off was made about 90 minutes after our scramble.
>
> After we reached our cruising altitude, the flight nurse came into the cockpit with a part of her seat belt in her hand. It had broken off close to the fastening bolt. We immediately understood that we had no chance to

repair this in flight and realised we had a problem: Norwegian laws and regulations state that no airplane is to take off or land unless all persons aboard are securely fastened by seat belts. So there we were – in mid-air and de facto not allowed to land the aircraft.

A few minutes later there was another occurrence. The second patient died. His heart stopped, and the doctor and nurse were unable to restart it. Patients dying in the cabin is a rare occurrence, but sometimes the medical staff are unable to keep them alive long enough to reach our designated hospital. Since our first patient was awake and clear-minded, we tried to keep him unaware of the latest development. So our communication became a little 'off normal'. In order to solve the problem with the flight nurse lacking a seat belt, the nurse was secured by baggage ropes fastened to the floor. We reached our destination and made a normal landing.

After landing, we tried to convey to our coordination centre that we only needed one ambulance to transport the patients from the airfield to the local hospital, and not two. What we did not know was that neither the coordination centre nor the local hospital had been informed that we had two patients on board. They were, therefore, a bit puzzled by our message. On board, we had a short discussion to decide what to do with the dead body we had on our plane. The consensus was that we had to bring the body back with us. In order to do so according to regulations, the patient had to be brought to the receiving hospital and be declared dead before we could transport the body back to the hospital he had originally been transported from. We decided to go through with this, as we decided that this was the most practical thing to do, both from the operative point of view and in consideration of the patient's next of kin.

A short break was then called for, and we refuelled the aircraft. As this was late at night, there were no professional fuel loaders available. In our air ambulance operation, we fly twenty-four/seven, so it is common that if there are no professional fuel loaders available, we fuel the aircraft ourselves, which we have been thoroughly trained to do. That particular night, I ordered my co-pilot to go and get the fuel truck and to refuel the aircraft at the airfield's fuel facility. Near the completion of the fuelling, he had an unfortunate accident. Due to a technical malfunction with the fuelling system, the co-pilot got fuel spilled on his face and in both eyes. I instantly informed the doctor and nurse who took immediate action. They discussed how to best rinse his eyes and check for damage. The nurse was transported to the local hospital to obtain adequate medical equipment and chemicals to use for treating the co-pilot.

Clearly, due to the fuel accident, the co-pilot could not continue his function as a pilot on the return flight to our home base. Yet again that night, we had to take a mental step back and assess the situation: We had a body aboard, and we had a seat without a seat belt. Now we were well into the night, and we all were starting to feel tired. At the same time, we tried to keep our coordination centre informed about what we were doing.

To get our plane, the dead body and our co-pilot back to our home base, we scrambled a new co-pilot from our base at the site. My original co-pilot was now a patient, and we placed him on a second stretcher on board the aircraft, next to the corpse lying by the first patient. The flight nurse had to again be secured by baggage ropes fastened to the floor at the back of the cabin. We then performed a normal flight home.

After landing at around seven in the morning, we met for a short debriefing, though the debriefing we performed was nothing more than a short-term decision-making process and I took the initiative to postpone it. We were tired and perceived ourselves as being too fatigued to perform a thorough debriefing. Another decisive factor in our decision to postpone was that we were not in the right mood for it. We pointed out to ourselves that through the entire trip we had an ever so light-hearted atmosphere. We had smiled and laughed throughout the night. At no time was there a shortage of humorous and witty remarks as the series of surreal incidents was played out before us. Flying home, a hindsight atmosphere closed down around us. In a sense, the witty remarks stood in sharp contrast to the dead man lying on the stretcher. Instead of just performing an operational debriefing there and then and being done with it, we agreed to meet later that day for the debriefing. We went to bed and slept.

The next day the doctor, nurse, co-pilots and myself met for the debriefing. The entire trip from start to finish was discussed. Since there were few operational questions, the main discussion was on the mental and emotional issues, with the humorous atmosphere as an important starting point. We tried to make a common narrative on what we experienced during the whole operation. In this narrative, we also tried to identify what happened when, and who said what. Why, and how, did we end up as we did? Did we solve our problems in the right way? What could have been done differently? How did each of us react to the various problems we faced during the night? We took the time to write down our own separate view on the night and even invited the coordination centre to write their version as well. The debriefing was thorough; we spent hours letting everyone in the crew speak their mind and tell the others what their feelings were during the mission as the different occurrences took place. After everyone had their turn and expressed their feelings and thoughts, we discussed the similarities and differences in the emotional reactions within the crew.

As it all worked out, we agreed that we did the best we could at the time. All participated and contributed to solving problems, and all felt informed about our situation as it progressed. Hindsight could tell us what we should not have done, but we were all quite pleased with how we had reacted during the night. As we said in our individual reports, the light-hearted atmosphere could partly be explained by fatigue. But most of all, in retrospect, we explained the atmosphere as being the result of us trying to cope with all the problems we faced, with a common understanding that we needed cheering up as we worked a series of surreal events throughout the night. We agreed that ethically we could defend our humorous atmosphere because our alternative was to sink more and more into despair over the course of the night. If we had become overwhelmed by our feeling of despair, we could not have pulled through the mission. That was not an option, so we had to pull through. We, therefore, more or less had to create an atmosphere that allowed us to process the situations at hand and leave us with the capacity to deal with the experience. In the debriefing, we also discussed that the humorous atmosphere was the opposite of what we really felt, though we still had rather the same attitude during the debriefing.

In a follow-up interview, the pilot told us that the general rule in the operative pilot culture is that the individual must have a clear understanding as to what the pilot can allow him or herself to feel at any stage of the flight. For that reason, pilots must have an emotional distance to the feelings evoked in their personal life in order to prevent them from entering the professional atmosphere in the cockpit. Similarly, it is important to have a distance to the feelings evoked in the professional setting in order to prevent them from entering personal and social settings.

The captain elaborated on this operative standpoint by telling what happened in the cockpit when the flight nurse informed the pilots that one of the patients had died. The pilot explained that when the flight nurse entered the cockpit and informed him, he dealt with the information with a purely operational attitude:

> Since it had no operational implications, I disregarded the information at the time. We were descending towards our destination, and I had to focus my attention on flying the aircraft. I remember my immediate reaction and the inner dialogue in my head, saying to myself it was a pity that he had died, but he was old and very ill. After landing, I felt quite a bit of guilt for not being more emphatic. In the follow-up debriefing, we discussed the death further, and I expressed my feelings of guilt to the rest of the crew: no one should have to die in an aircraft. The decision to try to move him to another hospital should not have been made. He should have been allowed to die in familiar surroundings with his relatives near him. The crew agreed with me. Even the doctor and nurses agreed that the decision to move the patient from the local hospital to the university hospital was disastrous, also from a medical perspective regarding the analysis of the medical condition of the patient. At the same time, the medical staff, sharing my frustration, assured me that this patient would have died anyway. There was nothing else that could have been done to save him, even if he was on the ground in a hospital. That information helped me because there was nothing we could have done differently. If there had been something that we could have done that would have made a difference in the outcome, for instance, that we should have used less time than we did, then the feeling of guilt would not disappear. In the follow-up debriefing, the flight nurse also expressed that she felt guilty for not being more assertive towards the medical doctors

who had taken the decision to move the patient. We used a lot of time to share our feelings of guilt. But with the crew's help, our feeling of guilt evaporated in the common agreement that we had done the best we could in the situation. With each problem that we solved that night, we became a tighter crew. We were pleased that we had managed to operate in a safe manner and that we had succeeded in maintaining a good work atmosphere, despite all the problems we faced that night.

Another pilot flying in an air ambulance operation explained his attitude towards debriefings:

Flying air ambulances, I experience episodes that trigger my personal and deep emotions on a day-to-day basis. Meeting patients, barely hanging on to life, often reminds me of my own friends and families, and even of my feelings on life and death. As a young captain flying in an air ambulance operation, I remember a particular flight where I felt I had to use my mental capacity in order not to lose my composure. Before the flight, the medical staff operating as our cabin attendants briefed us that we were going to be flying a young child. Although the operative rule is that we as pilots are not to be informed of the medical conditions of the patients we transport because this information can potentially influence us in a negative way, I instantly understood this was not a normal transportation flight. It turned out that our passenger was a young boy with terminal cancer. The doctors had given up treating him. All hope was gone, and he was being sent home to die. I knew when the young boy boarded that this was going to be his last flight ever. He was also aware that he was going to die soon, but still he showed great courage about his situation. The young boy reminded me of my own children and how fragile happiness is. Seeing him affected me deeply, but I could not let it stand in the way of performing the flight safely. I remember this flight very well. Because when we reached our cruising altitude, I remember that I used time to reflect on how, we as pilots and crew, should approach the situation when we landed and offloaded the patient: How do I say goodbye to a patient leaving the aircraft that everyone, including the patient himself, knows is going to die within a short period of time? I remember thinking to myself that I could not use my standard phrase when we were finished offloading the patient. I could not wish him good luck and hope for a speedy recovery.

You cannot work in this business without getting emotionally involved with the patients we fly. If you never become emotionally involved, it is my impression that you are unfit to do this job. Debriefings are important to me because in these sessions we discuss emotional matters and issues. In a debriefing, you learn why and how emotions can surface and the best way to deal with them. In debriefing sessions, we sometimes discuss our own professional and personal feelings, which are often dealt with within an informal atmosphere. Even though the debriefing plays an important role in coping with emotions we experience during missions, it can never prevent you from taking home some of the emotions it evokes. For most pilots, it is difficult to deal with emotions that are evoked during flights. In the same way, it is also difficult for pilots to prevent emotions evoked in their personal life from entering their job.

In some debriefings, we allow ourselves to be quite intimate with one another and share our emotions with other crewmembers, either about what is happening in our personal lives or about what we experience during the flights. Sharing my emotions allows other crewmembers to understand and accept my reactions. But sometimes the sharing also helps in the way that other crewmembers make my emotions bearable to me. To me, a debriefing is not a question of the formal setting; it is more a question of togetherness within a crew.

## Learning from experience – a psychoanalytical perspective

In the following, we will concentrate on the role of post-flight debriefing as one of the most important institutional ways of learning and maintaining a professional attitude in aviation. The psychoanalyst Wilfred Bion (1897–1979) offers an approach to understanding how airmanship evolves and is maintained as a result of pilots learning from their experiences through post-flight debriefings (Bion, 1962). Contrary to Freud, Bion himself had extensive operative experience in working in groups. Bion was a soldier of both the world wars. Bion's line of thought represents a relevant approach to understanding individual learning and learning processes that take place within a group environment. Through his concept of 'workgroup mentality' (Bion, 1961, p. 173), he describes the disposition and dynamics that characterise the life of a group, to the extent that its members can manage their shared tensions, anxieties, and relationships, in order to function effectively; the outcome is a 'capacity for realistic hard work' (Bion, 1961, p. 157).

Wilfred Bion claimed that developing skills and competence in doing something is intimately related to the evolution evolvement of a specific awareness. For Bion, gaining a piece of particular knowledge is equal to learning from our emotional experiences. We learn to deal with emotions in the same way we learn a particular set of skills. Bion is well-known for his work on group dynamics. His theory of thinking is interesting for acquiring an understanding of the development of competence among aviation pilots.

Bion (1961) is concerned with two parallel developmental learning processes: a developmental process he refers to as 'K' and an anti-developmental process referred to as '–K'.

In both, emotions and skills are pieced together. Learning in a positive mode leads to progression in the learning process, but when skills and emotions are linked in a negative mode, it leads to regression. It is impossible to distinguish between emotion and reflection says Bion. The link of emotion to expression and expression to emotion is essential for thinking (Bion, 1962). Thinking is, in an emotional sense, a continuous transformation of turning the 'raw material' of feelings into emotional experiences, which irrevocably changes the thinker and his or her perception of inner and outer reality.

Bion perceived emotional development and learning a skill as parallel processes. Learning a skill and emotional development take place in the same way. Nevertheless, he also acknowledged how these processes were closely intertwined with one another. The crucial point in deciding whether a person engages in a positive developmental learning process or an opposite, anti-developmental, is itself emotional. The challenge is to cope with emotional uncertainties and mental pain until it is possible to link the situation to a conscious thought. If a person does not manage this uncertainty, the potential learning becomes denied by an emotional defence mechanism and becomes unavailable for conscious reflection. The potential 'thought-out action' will, therefore, be lost and will have the opposite effect, as an unconscious emotion in which the individual experiences a fear of feeling. Thus this process of anti-development results in a process of repetition and stagnation (Ramvi, 2007; Ramvi & Roland, 1998).

## The post-flight debrief

In contrast to many other professions, the aviation communities have formal procedures with the motive of developing pilots' competence. While operative debriefs have a strong focus work performance, we argue the debrief may play an active role helping pilots and crewmembers with their everyday social interaction and managing their feelings.

After every flight, pilots and crewmembers are in principle obliged by law to have a post-operative debriefing and to submit a retrospective report to the company (EU OPS 1.085b, EU OPS 1.037(a) (2), Appendix 1 to EU OPS 1.1045 Operations Manual contents, Annex 6 to the Convention in International Civil Aviation, Part I, paragraphs 3.2.3. and 3.2.4.).

In many aviation operations, all of the members of the flight crew have some sort of assembled gathering after every flight to ensure that none of the crewmembers has experienced anything unusual during the flight. An experienced captain explained post-flight debriefings in the following way:

> After each flight, the crew gathers in the crew office. We report to the company on the status of the crew and the aircraft. After doing so, we spend a few minutes evaluating the flight. Normally the operative debriefing is straightforward and amounts to declaring that everything went according to normal operations. Occasionally, we need time to work through specific events that occurred during the flight, either in the cockpit or in the cabin. The debriefing will then continue to its conclusion with no regard to time. Sometimes we submit a written report to our superiors because the nature of the event legally demands us to report it. In the majority of cases, we report

events that we as a crew have handled in a good manner as well as when we have handled a situation poorly. We hand in a written report because we feel the event had elements that other crews can learn from, helping them to be able to handle a situation similar to ours differently or better.

(Interview, 2010)

Primarily, the post-flight debriefings are an institutionalised instrument to improve safety as well as enhance the competence of an individual crewmember (Baker & Key Dismukes, 2002; Dismukes & Smith, 2000). In order to enhance individual competence, post-flight debriefings serve a dual function: a review of the technical operation of the flight and, potentially, the opportunity to review and process emotional experiences. In one interview, an experienced captain reflected on the importance of post-operative debriefings: 'In a debriefing you learn what and how emotions can surface and the best way to deal with them' (Interview, 2010).

The importance of debriefings is a topic under dispute (Everly & Mitchell, 2005). Nevertheless, Bartone (2006) characterises post-flight debriefings as an after action group event which when properly timed and conducted with a correct focus can have a great therapeutic value for many participants. From a psychoanalytic perspective, debriefs help pilots and crewmembers to place potentially traumatising events in a broader context of positive meaning. In this sense, debriefings will have positive individual as well as collective effects regarding hardiness and resilience (Stueland, 2006).

## Learning airmanship through experience – an analysis of the importance of debriefings

Within the aviation community, there is an overwhelming understanding of the importance of the individual learning from his or her own experience (Nergård *et al.*, 2011). Characterising a good airman, it is said that an individual must have: 'The attitude and eagerness to always want to learn more and have a well thought through understanding of what you have going on in your life', as stated by a chief pilot (Interview, 2006).

Through the post-operative debriefing, pilots learn from their experience. The debriefing is part of an everlasting learning process in which the pilot learns to act in a well-thought-out manner in Bion's terms, as opposed to conducting a flight operation on impulse or in a thinking avoidance mode (Nergård, 2014).

In order to learn from one's own experience, there is a common perception that a pilot must share his or her experience with others. In aviation, it is not only a question whether the individual learns from his or her own experience. It is also just as important to question how the crew as a group has learned from their experience. What is implicit in eventual differences? A modern flight operation consists of several coordinated actions, which demand several people working together. Consequently, we must look for similarities between individual and group learning.

Within pilot culture, the debriefing serves as an institutionalised alpha function in which individual emotional experiences are transformed into collective experiences (Bion, 1962; Benjamin, 1991). For outsiders to the aviation community, accident and occurrence reports generally do not have a significant emotional impact – the reports are strict narratives about the technical and operational aspects of what, how and why the accident or occurrence took place. The reports are also focused on the possible learning and safety enhancements. For aviation insiders, the reports may serve additional purposes. In debriefings, individual pilots can make use of existing reports, cultural narratives, in order to find a frame of reference for their own mistakes. Cultural narratives also facilitate the process of sharing emotional experiences among pilots. From a psychoanalytic perspective, the debrief is an active construction of a narrative with meaningful explanations as to what happened. The debrief process thus serves to formulate individuals' emotions and provide the individual with meaningful explanations for emotions experienced during the flight. By sharing one's experiences, other pilots' experiences can help the individual to bear his/her own experiences. Through narrating one's experiences, the individual offers an opportunity for other pilots and crewmembers to learn from the same experience as if they had been there. In that way individual experiences open the opposite opportunity – learning from others' experiences:

> When I read incident and accident reports, I try to imagine myself being in the same situation. I picture myself being in the same cockpit and try to imagine how I would react and deal with the matters at hand. When I read or hear people telling about other occurrences and accidents, I always question whether I would have done the same thing as the pilot and crew in question, or whether I would have reacted differently, knowing my level of skills and level of competence.
>
> (Personal interview, 2010)

In post-flight debriefings, pilots and crewmembers are able to 'let off steam' together with others. Debriefings are particularly important after difficult, frustrating, stressful and painful experiences.

Debriefings are sometimes a chance for crewmembers to exchange small stories over which they shake their heads and laugh, which was also the case in this situation. During the flight, the crew was laughing and trying to make the best out of the situation. By conducting a debriefing immediately after landing, the crew also fulfils legal requirements.

Why was it so important for the pilot and crew to perform a second debriefing? The crew could easily have conducted a short debriefing session in accordance with what was legally required and report the irregularities that occurred during the event (i.e. the lack of communication about the second patient, reporting to the technical department about the seat belt incident, etc.). Was the decision to perform a second debriefing a result of that it was the most convenient thing to do, given the fact that it was late at night, and the crew was fatigued? Or could the decision to perform a second debriefing be understood as prolonging the need to follow the unwritten rules of good airmanship and that the crew felt the need to take time in dealing with the raw material of experiences and emotions evoked during the flight?

A pilot must be able to contain his feelings, and we can claim that he possibly has an unconscious need to deal with them. In psychodynamic terms, the pilot must control his emotions during flight operations. He has to struggle with coping with his emotions in order to follow the operational rules and not lose his composure. In other words, he has to display feelings differently from what he has actually experienced. But the very act of being technically engaged and maintaining situational awareness acts as a barrier to difficult emotions and provides a less emotionally fraught focus. In the case study presented here, the crew was able to concentrate on flying safely and dealing with the broken seatbelt rather than the emotional impact of flying with a corpse.

Considering the analysis of this case study, we can say that the pilot acknowledged his feelings during the event. In the interview, he reported that during the flight he experienced feelings of helplessness, feelings of mortality, feelings of ignorance and a fear of being out of control. With his initiative to do a follow-up debriefing, the pilot had the possibility to take a psychological step back and relate to the experience in a more mature manner. According to Bion (1962), relating in a mature way requires working with thoughts about feelings. Through his own efforts and with the help of others in the crew, he could deal with the emotions he experienced through the course of events. Through other crewmembers' projective identification, the pilot was able to distinguish between what is to be learned from the experience and what were his individual emotions during the event. Because of airmanship ideals and through his day-to-day experience of flying patients, the pilot is in a constant emotional learning process, which changes him and the social environment of which he is part. In turn, this means that the next emotional experience will potentially be easier to understand and give him the possibility of acting differently and more in accordance with the ideals of airmanship.

The point we are trying to make here is was it only his efforts to follow the rules of professionalism that urged him to do the follow-up debriefing? During the event, he had to hold his emotions in check. Through the pilot and other crewmembers' ability to project and identify their emotions during the debriefing, the pilot was able to observe his emotions, compare them with those of the other crewmembers, and reflect on them. On an individual level, if he had not taken the initiative to the follow-up debrief, he would, from a theoretical point of view, risk the long-term probability of experiencing feelings of fear or anxiety as a result of not dealing with the emotions he experienced during the trip. In other words, there were at least two motivations: the fear of not being able to live up to the airmanship ideals and. even more so, potentially losing touch with his emotions (Lear, 2009).

In Bion's theory, the debriefing created an (emotional) experience and thereby a thought-through action, rather than acting as if possessing the knowledge and thereby running the long-term risk of losing control and not being able to keep his cool the next time a similar situation presents itself. To think and reflect about his emotions by putting them into words in the follow-up debrief makes it possible for him to take responsibility for them.

Tolerance or the ability to bear pain demands courage (Lear, 2009) as well as emotional support through others' projective identification (Greenberg & Mitchell, 1983). If these factors are not in place, omnipotence in relation to emotions may be used as a defence mechanism. The use of this defence mechanism would be challenging for individual thinking (–K) and have anti-development as a potential outcome.

The element of containment in the colleagues' way of sharing stories with each other creates a good condition for learning from experience. The post-flight debriefing offers a sense of conjunction between what the pilot feels and the relief of not having to simulate feelings. Bion (1961) described how certain types of groups learn from experience, and labelled these types of groups literally as the W-group (work group). The group who learns from experience is characterised by K activities. Within the group, there is a climate in which diversity in opinions is allowed and appreciated. This type of climate is development in itself, Bion claimed. Nevertheless, such a group climate is dependent on toleration for one another and the fact that different opinions can be put forward without giving one opinion moral priority over another.

In contrast, the group functioning in a manner contradictory to a learning group environment is characterised by –K activities. Bion described this type of group interaction as he labelled it. The interaction is based on the individual's basic assumptions (BA-group). All group members share an unspoken and unconscious agreement that a work task can be resolved without any effort, without thinking and learning. 'There is a hatred of having to learn by experience at all and lack of faith in the worth of such kind of learning' (Bion, 1961: 89). The group, therefore, acts 'as if' their basic assumptions are real.

While there is a good connection with reality at the W-group level, the BA-group is irrational and out of contact with reality. Even so, the team spirit and relationships at the BA-group level can thrive in a seductive way.

More than anything, the follow-up debriefing demonstrated a W-group mentality. By literally letting each other sleep on it, they met the following day again and performed a debriefing in which the idea was to inform each other of the difficult emotions the events evoked. The general idea was that the individually experienced painful emotions would evaporate through sharing them with the same people they shared the experience with. The emotions that emerged as a result of the flight did not become an individual matter. Crewmembers were not allowed to deal with the emotions alone or had to deal with them with others, i.e. family members and others, who would have a totally different starting point for projective identification simply because they were not there and did not see all the details and sense the atmosphere. The pilots and other crewmembers evolved and developed (K) as individuals and crew (W-group) because they talked together seriously and shared the individual worries, painful emotions and frustrations they experienced.

Learning from experience is about having the capability of containing one's feelings, taking responsibility for having them, passing them on, and not denying them.

To be able to learn from experience, pilots must be able to contain their own fear of feeling ignorant and helpless. Nevertheless, the pilot's main conclusion after telling his story is that the debriefing helped him to see and understand his own emotional reaction as this was important to him.

By being a good crewmember and making an effort to create a K environment, or a holding environment within the crew in Winnicott's term (1972), not only puts the pilot in a position that enables him to help other crewmembers to contain their emotions, but also constitutes conditions to contain his own emotions and his own learning from experience.

## Concluding remarks: the role of debriefing

In this chapter, we wanted to explore an actual incident in aviation. We have tried to relate Bion's concepts to a pilot's everyday life, particularly to a situation that involved strong emotions, as well as situations that require crewmembers to contain their feelings. The story about the special flight is, therefore, not only a story about a particular flight. The emotional challenges pilots are exposed to, require them to accept the potential pain of knowing (+K) and to be able to think about their own difficult feelings. This process of containing instead of having omnipotent control may present a great deal of anxiety, but according to Bion, this may be the beginning of learning from one's own experiences. The alternatives to Bion's line of thought are frequently used in aviation: alcohol, exercise, 'pulling yourself together', being task-focused and suppressing emotions.

The pilots' need to control their emotions and learning from experience have a double rationale. The pilot's story of the unusual flight highlights the many obstacles that appeared when he and his colleagues were exposed to events that evoked strong emotions. The operational situation enabled the crew to act as containers for emotions aroused during the flight both in themselves and in other crewmembers. They recognised each other, and the use of humour functioned as a common denial of their emotional experiences until they were able to sit down and deal with the strong emotions they were exposed to. The crew distanced themselves from a surreal situation by omnipotent relations to avoid pain. In order to learn from experience, the pilots and crew had to deal with them in the debriefing. The post-flight debriefing helped the crew to maintain relationships and deal with the individual pain and their fear of ignorance. In this sense, the post-operative debriefing has a therapeutic function that allowed room for reconciliation between the pilots' ideals and the meeting of reality. In regard to many other professions, it seems as if aviation does, ideally speaking, not leave it to the individual to process emotions and their vulnerability.

From a psychodynamic perspective, airmanship is knowing when to do what, when to contain and when to use defence mechanisms in order to deal with an operational situation that demands their full attention. Consequently, airmanship is not only about the knowledge of flying an aircraft, but it is also an emotional and relational skill (Eid *et al.*, 2008).

The post-operative debrief has a dual purpose. First, it helps the individual as well as the group create distance from the event, allowing participants to reach a shared understanding of what really took place. Second, this shared understanding enables coping with the emotions experienced during the event. Learning and coping are two sides of the same coin, enabling long term containment. Learning from experience points towards better coping with similar situations in the future.

The reflections in this chapter are in accordance with research on the effects of debriefing. When properly timed and conducted, with a focus on events rather than emotions and reactions, post-operative debriefings can have a great reconciliational and restorative value for many of the participants. This is by helping them to place potentially traumatising events in a broader context of positive meaning that will yield positive individual and collective effects regarding hardiness and resilience (Bartone, 2006; Eid *et al.*, 2005).

# References

Antonsen, S., Almklov, P., & Fenstad, J. 2008. Reducing the gap between procedures and practice – lessons from a successful safety intervention, *Safety Science Monitor*, 12(1): 1–16.

Baker, D.P., & Key Dismukes, R. 2002. A framework for understanding crew performance assessment issues, *The International Journal of Aviation Psychology*, 12(3): 205–222.

Bartone, P.T. 2006. Resilience under military operational stress: can leaders influence hardiness?, *Military Psychology*, 18(Suppl.): 131–148.

Benjamin, W. 1991. *Kunstverket i reproduksjonsalderen. Essay om kultur, litteratur og politikk.* Oslo: Gyldendal Norsk Forlag (in Norwegian).

Bion, W.R. 1961. *Experiences in Groups; and Other Papers.* London: Routledge.

Bion, W.R. 1962. *Learning from Experience.* Northvale, NJ: Jason Aronson.

Bond, F.W., & Flaxman P.E. 2006. The ability of psychological flexibility and job control to predict learning, job performance, and mental health, *Journal of Organizational Behavior Management*, 26(1–2): 113–130.

Cannon-Bowers, J.A., Salas, E., & Converse, S.A. 1993. Shared mental models in expert team decision making. In: N.J. Castellan, Jr. (ed.). *Current Issues in Individual and Group Decision Making*, (pp. 221–246).

Dekker, S. 2006. *The Field Guide to Understanding Human Error.* London: Ashgate Publishing.

Dismukes, K.R., & Smith G.M. (eds.). 2000. *Facilitation and Debriefing in Aviation Training and Operations.* Aldershot: Ashgate Publishing.

Eid, J., Johnsen, B.H., Saus, E-Re. 2005. Trauma narratives and emotional processing. *Scandinavian Journal of Psychology*, 46: 503–510.

Everly, G.S., & Mitchell, J.T. 2005. A primer on critical incident stress management (CISM) [online], accessed 21 November 2005 from http://www.icisf.org/about/cismprimer.pdf.

FAA. 2004. *Airplane Flying Handbook*. Washington DC: U.S. Government Printing Office. 15–7 to 15-8. FAA-8083-3A [online], accessed 1 March 2010 from http://www.faa. gov/library/manuals/aircraft/airplane_handbook/.

Fitzgibbons, A., Davis, D., & Schutte, P.C. 2004. *Pilot Personality Profile Using the NEO-PI-R*. Hampton, VA: National Aeronautics and Space Administration Langley Research Center.

Fonagy, P., Gergely, G., Jurist, E.T., & Target, M. 2002. *Affect Regulation, Mentalization, and the Development of the Self*. New York: Other Press.

Greenberg, J.R., & Mitchell, S. 1983. *Object Relations in Psychoanalytic Theory*. Cambridge, MA: Harvard University Press.

Lear, J. 2009. Technique and final cause in psychoanalysis: four ways of looking at one moment, *The International Journal of Psychoanalysis*, 90: 1299–1317.

Nergård, V. 2014. Airmanship – a qualitative approach, *Aviation*, 18(3): 147–156.

Nergård, V., Hatlevik, O.E., Martinussen, M., & Lervåg, A.O. 2011. An airman's personal attitude: pilots' point of view, *Aviation*, 15(4): 101–111.

Ramvi, E. 2007. Læring av erfaring? Et psykoanalytisk blikk på læreres læring. Forskerskolen i Livslang Læring; Institut for Psykologi og Uddannelsesforskning Roskilde Universitetscenter [online], accessed 20 May 2010 from http://rudar.ruc. dk/bitstream/1800/2998/3/Ellen%20Ramvi2(1.1).pdf (in Norwegian).

Ramvi, E., & Roland, P. 1998. *Containing Function*. (RF Report No. 1998/264). Stavanger: Rogalandsforskning.

Rose, G.R. 2001. Practical use of the pilot's personality profile. AVweb. Accessed 6 October 2016 from http://www.avweb.com/news/aeromed/181606-1.html.

Stueland, E. 2006. Mental oppfølging etter hendelser – en mangelvare i dagens Luftforsvar?, Hovedoppgave LKSK II/2 Modul VI Luftkrigsskolen 2006-MARS (in Norwegian).

Ursano, R.J. 1980. Stress and adaptation: the interaction of the pilot personality and disease, *Aviation Space and Environmental Medicine*, 51(11): 1245–1249.

Winnicott, D.W. 1972. *Holding and Interpretation. Fragment of an Analysis*. New York: Grove Press.

# Index